Whitfield's University

RHYMING DICTIONARY

Whitfield's University
RHYMING DICTIONARY

by Jane Shaw Whitfield

Edited by Frances Stillman

BARNES & NOBLE BOOKS
A DIVISION OF HARPER & ROW, PUBLISHERS
New York, Cambridge, Hagerstown,
Philadelphia, San Francisco, London,
Mexico City, São Paulo, Sydney

This work was originally published under the title *The Improved Rhyming Dictionary* by Thomas Y. Crowell, Publishers.

 For information address Harper & Row, Publishers, Inc., 10 East 53rd Street, New York, N.Y. 10022. Published simultaneously in Canada by Fitzhenry & Whiteside Limited, Toronto.

First BARNES & NOBLE BOOKS edition published 1981.

ISBN: 0-06-463538-4

85 10 9 8 7 6 5 4

Contents

Preface

RHYME is "the correspondence, in two or more words or verses, of terminal sounds beginning with an accented vowel, which, in modern English usage, must be preceded by different consonant sounds, or by a consonant in one case and none in the other." A rhyme is one of two or more words which correspond as described, and a list of rhymes is a group of such words. A rhyming dictionary, therefore, is a compendium of complete lists of rhymes, as exhaustive as it is possible to make it.

This rhyming dictionary is organized on the modern principle of giving the lists of rhymes according to the key vowel sound, and progresses from A– (ay, bay, etc.) through UZ'i-ness– (fuzziness, etc.).

The vowel sounds *A*, *E*, *I*, *O*, and *U* and their variations (see table of contents) are taken up in turn. Under each, the lists of rhymes are given in three sections: single or masculine rhymes, double or feminine rhymes, and triple rhymes. In each section, one proceeds in an orderly, alphabetical fashion, as, for example, from AB– (Abe, babe, etc.) through AZ– (daze, etc.), AB'i– (Abie, baby, etc.) through AZ'ing– (hazing, etc.). Due to phonetic considerations, the letter *c* is always alphabetized under *k* or *s*, its two possible sounds. The *ch* sound still stands third in alphabetical order.

In each entry, the list of rhymes is given according to number of syllables, for easier reference. One-syllable words come first, of course, then two, and so on, with each group being preceded by a figure showing the number of syllables. This will facilitate finding the right rhyme when, for example, the poet has only one accented syllable left to fill in to complete his line. Time will be saved and the rhyme more quickly found.

When the rhyme sound is preceded by one or more syllables, in longer words, the rhymes are arranged according to the consonant directly preceding the rhyme sound —or, in other words, alphabetized backwards. This is useful because multiple rhymes thus are listed together.

In modern poetry, very frequently a kind of offbeat rhyming is used to good effect, and it is for that reason that we have included many so-called "imperfect" rhymes. These are considered to be, for the purposes of this book, words which contain the rhyme sound, but in which the sound is not accented. Such imperfect rhymes are printed in italics. Another device of modern poetry is the use of consonance, as, for example, *late*, *let*, *light*, *lot*, *lute*. Such examples of consonance may be easily found simply by looking up the corresponding section under each vowel sound.

For the sake of writers of humorous and light verse, very numerous slang and colloquial expressions have been included for the first time in such a reference book. The inclusions of foreign-language expressions commonly used in English are unusually rich, and it is hoped that they may prove useful alike to poet and verse-writer.

The thesaurus-like arrangement of this dictionary makes it easier and quicker to use than the more old-fashioned, vertical-list kind of arrangement. Another advantage of this arrangement is its compactness, which makes the book far more portable than rhyming dictionaries containing much less material. Indeed, this is the most complete and inclusive, as well as the most usable, of modern rhyming dictionaries.

A Brief Guide to English Versification

IT IS easy to say what verse is: it is a written composition which uses a metrical pattern and frequently also the device of rhyme to heighten its effectiveness.

It is hard to say what poetry is. Real poetry, like beauty itself, is somehow beyond definition. Great poets have written it, but have not been able to define it.

This brief chapter on versification is about the tools of both poetry and verse—meter and rhyme.

Meter is the basic pattern of rhythm which is repeated throughout a verse. It is like the time, or repeated beat, of music.

Rhyme is the chiming of identical terminal sounds of words. It may occur regularly at the ends of lines, and within lines as well, as in many of the poems of Edgar Allan Poe. In English, rhyme is based on an accented vowel sound. This rhyme sound usually consists of accented vowel plus final consonant, and in that case is called a masculine, or one-syllable, rhyme. It may be composed of accented vowel (with or without consonant) followed by one or two unaccented syllables. A two-syllable rhyme is called a feminine rhyme, while a three-syllable rhyme has no special name.

In rhyming, there are only two rules. The rhyme sounds must be identical. And each rhyme used must vary from all the others in the consonant-sound which precedes the rhyme. Thus, vac*ation* and obl*ation* are acceptable rhymes, while va*cation* and extri*cation* are not, being mere repetitions of *-cation*, instead of rhymes on *-ation*.

One out of every two or three syllables is ordinarily accented in English. In prose, the accent is allowed to fall at random, but in verse the writer arranges his language so that the accent comes at regular intervals, and the thought breaks naturally into regular lines.

As far back as we know, rhythm has been employed to make things catchy and easy to remember. Rhyme seems to have come into use a little later, but served the same purpose. The early sagas and tales of the minstrels were carried by word of mouth, and employed these devices. In the history of the world's literature, poetry came long before prose.

There are four kinds of meter in English. These are used straight, or mixed, as the occasion and the verse demands.

One unit of meter is called a foot, or a metric foot.

ENGLISH METERS

1. Iambic meter, composed of units of two syllables with the accent on the second.
   One imabic foot is called an iamb. (Pronounced eye-am′-bik, eye′-amb)
   Example: "The sea | is calm | tonight. |
   The tide | is full, | the moon | lies fair | "—Matthew Arnold
2. Trochaic meter, composed of units of two syllables with the accent on the first.
   One trochaic foot is called a trochee. (Pronounced tro-kay′-ik, tro′-kee)

Example: "On the | shores of | Gitche | Gumee |
Of the | shining | Big Sea | Water, | "—Longfellow

3. Anapestic meter, composed of units of three syllables with the accent on the third. One anapestic foot is called an anapest. (Pronounced an-a-pest′-ik, an′-a-pest)

Example: "The Assyr|ian came down | like the wolf | on the fold | "—Byron

4. Dactyllic meter, composed of units of three syllables with the accent on the first. One dactyllic foot is called a dactyl. (Pronounced dak-till′-ik, dak′-till)

Example: "This is the | forest prim|eval. The | murmuring | pines and the | hemlocks
Bearded with | moss and in | garments of | green, indis|tinct in the | twilight"—Longfellow

A convenient way to remember the kinds of meter is to memorize a little rhyme, such as:

The iamb saunters through my book,
Trochees rush and tumble;
While the anapest runs like a hurrying brook,
Dactyls are stately and classical.

In addition, one more kind of meter must be noted—Spondaic meter, composed of units of two syllables, both being accented. One spondaic foot is called a spondee. (Pronounced spon-day′-ik, spon′-dee)

Example: "Stop′ thief′ | "

Spondaic meter is not, properly speaking, an English meter at all, as it is impossible in English to sustain for long a meter in which every syllable is accented. However, it may occasionally be substituted for a foot in some other meter, when the effect would be heightened by it.

Scansion or scanning of verse is the analysis of its meter, and is accomplished by marking each syllable according to whether it is accented or not. Then a mark is placed between each metric foot, and it may be determined what meter predominates. When a line is out of time with the rest, it is frequently said that "it does not scan."

In addition to the kind of meter of a poem, such as iambic, it is further described according to the number of metric feet (or accents) in each line. For example, a sonnet is written in iambic pentameter, which means in five-foot iambic lines. The kinds of lines are as follows:

one-foot	monometer (mo-nah′-meh-ter)
two-foot	dimeter (di′-meh-ter)
three-foot	trimeter (tri′-meh-ter)
four-foot	tetrameter (teh-tra′-meh-ter)
five-foot	pentameter (pen-ta′-meh-ter)
six-foot	hexameter (hex-a′-meh-ter)
seven-foot	heptameter (hep-ta′-meh-ter)
eight-foot	octometer (oct-ah′-meh-ter)

Iambic pentameter is said to be the most natural English line, and it is used in most long narrative, epic, or dramatic poems in English.

Hexameters are the lines of classical poetry in Greek and Latin, as well as French and certain other modern languages. In English, the hexameter is often called an Alexandrine, and is sometimes used to give greater weight to a poem which is mainly in pentameters. Alexandrines occur regularly in certain stanza forms, such as the Spenserian stanza.

The length of the line, in verse, generally follows a pattern. Either all are the same, or else the varying lengths recur in a regular fashion. Beginning verse-writers would do well to check their poems from this point of view. For example, if a poem is written in four-line stanzas, with lines alternating between three and four feet, it is not a good idea suddenly to insert a line of five feet somewhere, nor should one substitute a four-foot line for a three-foot line in the pattern.

THE STANZA

A stanza is a division within a poem, and is composed of a group of lines, sometimes only one line; it is set off by space between it and the next stanza.

A poem may be written in set stanzas that follow a regular pattern, or the poet may divide his stanzas according to the thought content, in which case the stanza division is entirely analogous to pargaraphing in prose. These two different ways of handling the stanza may be called formal stanzas and free stanzas.

Stanzas are named according to the number of lines they contain.

couplet	two lines
triplet or tercet	three lines
quatrain	four lines
cinquain	five lines
sestet	six lines
septet	seven lines
octave	eight lines

Beyond these, one refers simply to a nine-line stanza, and so on. The length of the lines in a stanza, and the ryhme scheme, if any, are a matter of choice for the poet. Infinite variety is possible, but there are a number of fixed stanza forms which have qualities of charm and malleability, which the beginning poet would do well to practice.

The quatrain is probably the most widely used stanza form, and may be rhymed in a number of ways. The loose ballad quatrain, with the first and third lines, and second and fourth lines rhyming, or with only the second and fourth lines rhymed, is a universal favorite. The lines may be of any length, but alternating four- and three-foot lines are perhaps the most used.

To indicate a rhyme scheme, one marks the first rhyme with the letter *a*, the second *b*, and so on. For example:

I never saw a purple cow, (*a*)
I never hope to see one, (*b*)
But I can tell you, anyhow, (*a*)
I'd rather see than be one. (*b*)
—Gelett Burgess

Thus, the rhyme scheme of the above quatrain is *a-b-a-b*.

A combination of triplets which can be very effective is called terza rima; it was originally an Italian form. This is composed of three-line stanzas with interlocking rhyme, ending with a couplet. It goes *a-b-a*, *b-c-b*, *c-d-c*, *d-d*—or it may go on much longer before the concluding couplet. Shelley's "Ode to the West Wind" is written in this form.

Another famous Italian stanza is the ottava rima. It contains eight lines and three rhymes, as, follows: *a-b-a-b-a-b-c-c*.

The Spenserian stanza contains nine lines, the first eight in iambic pentameter and the last line an Alexandrine. The rhyme scheme is an interlocking one, and goes: *a-b-a-b-b-c-b-c-c*.

POEMS IN FIXED FORMS

The Sonnet

The sonnet is the best-known and most widely practiced of all the fixed forms of poetry. It consists of fourteen lines in iambic pentameter, and has one of several rhyme schemes and thought divisions.

The Italian, or Petrarchan, sonnet, so called because it was first used by Petrarch, is the oldest of the sonnet forms. It is composed of an octave and a sestet, and it may be said in general that the octave states the case, while the sestet resolves it or in some way presents the main point which the poet has in mind. The rhyme scheme of this kind of sonnet is: *a-b-b-a*, *a-b-b-a*, *c-d-e*, *c-d-e*. Edna St. Vincent Millay wrote many beautiful sonnets in this form. Throughout English and American literature one finds it used, although the Shakespearean sonnet has been on the whole more popular. Here is a good example:

MILTON

I pace the sounding sea-beach and behold (*a*)
How the voluminous billows roll and run, (*b*)
Upheaving and subsiding, while the sun (*b*)
Shines through their sheeted emerald far unrolled (*a*)
And the ninth wave, slow gathering fold by fold (*a*)
All its loose-flowing garments into one, (*b*)
Plunges upon the shore, and floods the dun (*b*)
Pale reach of sands, and changes them to gold. (*a*)

So in majestic cadence rise and fall (*c*)
  The mighty undulations of thy song, (*d*)
  O sightless bard, England's maeonides! (*e*)
And ever and anon, high over all (*c*)
  Uplifted, a ninth wave superb and strong, (*d*)
  Floods all the soul with its melodious seas. (*e*)

—Henry Wadsworth Longfellow

There have been many variations on the Italian sonnet. Sometimes the break between the octave and the sestet does not mark any break in the thought. The break may come elsewhere, even in the middle of a line. The rhyme scheme may be varied. One may have *a-b-b-a*, *c-d-d-c*; *a-b-b-a*, *a-c-c-a*; or *a-b-b-a*, *c-b-b-c*, in the octave. The sestet may also be varied in many ways. Here is an example.

EVENING ON THE BEACH

It is a beauteous evening, calm and free; (*a*)
The holy time is quiet as a nun (*b*)
Breathless with adoration; the broad sun (*b*)
Is sinking down in its tranquillity; (*a*)
The gentleness of heaven is on the sea: (*a*)
Listen! the mighty Being is awake, (*c*)
And doth with his eternal motion make (*c*)
A sound like thunder—everlastingly. (*a*)
Dear child! dear girl! that walkest with me here, (*d*)
If thou appear untouched by solemn thought (*e*)
Thy nature is not therefore less divine: (*f*)
Thou liest in Abraham's bosom all the year, (*d*)
And worship'st at the Temple's inner shrine, (*f*)
God being with thee when we know it not. (*e*)

—William Wordsworth

The Shakespearean sonnet has probably been the most popular of all the fixed forms in English poetry. Like other sonnets, it has fourteen lines written in iambic pentameter. The rhyme scheme and divisions of thought are different from those of the Italian sonnet. It is composed of three quatrains and a final couplet, and the rhyme scheme goes: *a-b-a-b*, *c-d-c-d*, *e-f-e-f*, *g-g*.

As is readily seen, the rhyme scheme is easier to use because there are only two rhymes on each terminal sound throughout. The final couplet is usually the climax of the poem, stating the point in a memorable fashion.

The matter of indenting the lines of a sonnet is one of personal preference. They may be indented according to the rhyme scheme, or not indented at all.

Here is one of Shakespeare's sonnets:

SONNET 29

When, in disgrace with fortune and men's eyes, (*a*)
I all alone beweep my outcast state, (*b*)
And trouble deaf heaven with my bootless cries, (*a*)
And look upon myself, and curse my fate, (*b*)
Wishing me like to one more rich in hope, (*c*)
Featured like him, like him with friends possessed, (*d*)
Desiring this man's art and that man's scope, (*c*)
With what I most enjoy contented least; (*d*)
Yet in these thoughts myself almost despising, (*e*)
Haply I think one thee, and then my state, (*f*)
Like to the lark at break of day arising (*e*)
From sullen earth, sings hymns at heaven's gate; (*f*)
For thy sweet love remembered such wealth brings (*g*)
That then I scorn to change my state with kings. (*g*)

—William Shakespeare

The Triolet

This is an eight-line poem, in which the first line is repeated as the fourth line, and the first and second lines repeated as the seventh and eighth. These lines should be identical in sound, if not in meaning—that is, they may contain puns and various plays on words, if desired. However, a triolet in which the lines are repeated as a simple refrain can be very charming. The rhyme scheme—with (*R*) following the indication of lines which are repeated—is as follows: *a-b-a-a*(*R*)*-a-b-a*(*R*)*-b*(*R*). An example of a triolet which is not quite regular follows.

ROSE FEVER

Go, lovely rose!
I think you'll drive me mad.
Kerchoo! the mischief grows—
Blow, lovely nose!
I've nothing now but woes,
And all the joys I had
Go.—Lovely rose,
I think you'll drive me mad.

The Rondel

The rondel contains fourteen lines and two rhymes. The first and second lines form the refrain, and are repeated as the seventh and eighth, and thirteenth and fourteenth. The rhyme scheme is *a-b-b-a*, *a-b-a*(*R*)*-b*(*R*), *a-b-b-a-a*(*R*)*-b*(*R*).

A rondel of thirteen lines omits one of the last two lines, and goes exactly as above except for that omission.

The Rondelet

The rondelet, or little rondel, has seven lines, of which the first, third and seventh are the refrain, in iambic dimeter, while the other four lines are in iambic trimeter or tetrameter. The rhyme scheme is *a-b-a*(*R*)-*a-b-b-a*(*R*).

The Rondeau

The rondeau contains fifteen lines in iambic tetrameter or pentameter. The fourth and the fifteenth lines are the refrain, and are composed of the first part of the first line; this refrain does not rhyme. The rhyme scheme follows: *a-a-b-b-a*, *a-a-b-R*, *a-a-b-b-a-R*.

IN AFTER DAYS

In after days when grasses high (*a*)
O'ertop the stone where I shall lie, (*a*)
  Though ill or well the world adjust (*b*)
  My slender claim to honored dust, (*b*)
I shall not question or reply. (*a*)

I shall not see the morning sky; (*a*)
I shall not hear the night-wind's sigh; (*a*)
  I shall be mute, as all men must (*b*)
    In after days! (*R*)

But yet, now living, fain were I (*a*)
That some one then should testify, (*a*)
  Saying—"He held his pen in trust (*b*)
  To Art, not serving shame or lust." (*b*)
Will none?—Then let my memory die (*a*)
    In after days! (*R*)

–Austin Dobson

The Villanelle

The villanelle is a poem in three-line stanzas in which the same two rhyme sounds are used throughout. The first and third lines of the first stanza serve as refrains, returning in alternation as the last line of each following stanza. The last stanza is a quatrain and ends with both refrain lines. The most usual length of the villanelle is six stanzas, but it may be longer or shorter if the poet so desires. The rhyme scheme is: *a-b-a*, *a-b-a*(1), *a-b-a*(3), etc., *a-b-a*(1)-*a*(3).

The Ballade

The ballade is a lyric poem containing three stanzas and an Envoy, or fourth stanza, usually half the length of the others.

There are two main forms of the ballade, that using an eight-line stanza and four-line envoy, and that using a ten-line stanza and five-line envoy.

The last line of every stanza and of the envoy is a refrain.

The eight-line ballade, strictly speaking, should be written in iambic tetrameter, while the ten-line form should be written in iambic pentameter. However, these rules are not now observed so strictly as in the original French ballades of several centuries ago.

The rhyme scheme of the eight-line stanza ballade is as follows: *a-b-a-b-b-c-b-c*(*R*) for three stanzas, then *b-c-b-c*(*R*) for the envoy.

The ten-line stanza ballade goes: *a-b-a-b-b-c-c-d-c-d*(*R*) for three stanzas, then *c-c-d-c-d*(*R*) for the envoy.

A seven-line stanza was used by Chaucer, as follows:

BALLADE OF GOOD COUNSEL

by Geoffrey Chaucer

Flee from the crowd and dwell with truthfulness, (*a*)
  Suffice thee with thy goods, tho' they be small; (*b*)
To hoard brings hate, to climb brings giddiness, (*a*)
  The crowd has envy, and success blinds all; (*b*)
  Desire no more than to thy lot may fall, (*b*)
Work well thyself to counsel others clear, (*c*)
And Truth shall make thee free, there is no fear! (*cR*)

(modern version by Henry van Dyke)

The Limerick

The limerick is a light-verse form containing five lines, the first, second and fifth lines having three metric feet, and the third and fourth lines two metric feet. It is rhymed *a-a-b-b-a*, and as written by many famed practitioners the last line is a repetition or partial repetition of the first. It is usually written in mixed iambs and anapests.

The subject of a limerick is frequently a person, but it may be anything in this wide world, or out of it. A few examples follow.

There once was a man from Nantucket
Who kept all his cash in a bucket;
  But his daugher, named Nan,
  Ran away with a man,
And as for the bucket, Nantucket.

—Anonymous

An epicure, dining at Crewe,
Found quite a large mouse in his stew.
 Said the waiter, "Don't shout
 And wave it about,
Or the rest will be wanting one, too!"

—Anonymous

VERSE, BLANK VERSE, AND FREE VERSE

The expressions that head this paragraph often seem to cause confusion, and yet they are not really so difficult. Verse applies to any of the forms which have been described thus far. In fact, it may apply to anything which is written with the line-separations common to poetry. Blank verse is metrical verse which is unrhymed. Free verse is verse which is separated into lines, but has not any definable meter. It is usually cadenced, or rhythmical in a loose way. It is called "free" because it does not have any identifiable rules.

KINDS OF POETRY

Poetry and verse, like heaven, have many mansions.

There are certainly as many kinds of poetry as there are of prose, and probably more. Thus far, we have only considered the tools of writing verse, but before we close, it will be a good idea to mention briefly some of the kinds of verse which have been written in the past.

Poetry That Tells a Story

1. Epic poetry is storytelling on a vast and majestic scale. It tells not just the story of one person, but of nations and wars and great cataclysms, in which the supernatural often plays a part.

2. Narrative poetry, such as "Hiawatha" or "Evangeline," tells a long story, but is on a smaller scale than an epic. It has been very popular in the past. In recent years long narrative poems, novels in verse, have continued to appear, but have not found great popular favor.

3. The Ballad. This is short, lyrical storytelling, as old as time, and just as universal. The earliest known ballads are folk ballads, whose authors are unknown, such as "Sir Patrick Spens." "The Rime of the Ancient Mariner," by Coleridge, the "Ballad of Reading Gaol," by Oscar Wilde, the "Ballad of William Sycamore," by Stephen Vincent Benét, are some examples of ballads that might be read again by the student of verse-writing.

Poetry That Teaches a Lesson

This is so-called didactic or religious verse and may take the form of long philosophizing. On the other hand, some beautiful lyrics may fall in this category.

Poetry That Describes Something

This is called descriptive poetry, and has as its primary aim the painting of a picture. It may be quite long, or it may be in lyric form, but it usually strives to be objective.

Poetry to Be Acted Out

This is called dramatic poetry. It is found in Shakespeare's plays and in Browning's dramatic monologues, to name but a few examples.

Poetry That Expresses Feelings

This is usually called lyric poetry and comprises the greatest variety imaginable. There are many forms of lyric poetry—odes, or poems in praise of something or somebody; elegies, or poems lamenting the loss of something or somebody; epigrams, epitaphs, lullabies, or just plain lyrics, or songs.

Light or Humorous Verse

This kind of verse usually expresses feelings, too, but in such a light way that it deserves a separate category. Its object is to amuse the reader.

Occasional Verse

This may be either light or serious, and is written to suit some special occasion. It runs the gamut from Kipling's famous "Recessional" to greeting-card verse.

As usual when one talks about poetry, one has the cage without the bird. Yet one must start somewhere, if one wishes to write poetry or verse, and where else but in a discussion of technique can one learn how to go about it?

Aside from the special rules of writing verse, all the general precepts of good writing in general apply to the writing of poetry. Freshness of expression and of viewpoint are usually rewarded with success; clichés and worn-out, second-hand ideas with failure.

Above all, Socrates' old advice to "know thyself" applies to poets. "Fool, said my muse to me, look in thy heart and write!" remains as good advice as when Sir Philip Sidney wrote it.

KEY TO VERSIFICATION

Meters

NAME OF METER	ONE UNIT	NO. OF SYLLABLES	ACCENT ON	PATTERN	EXAMPLE
iambic	iamb	2	2nd	–ʹ	Marie
trochaic	trochee	2	1st	ʹ–	Dickens
anapestic	anapest	3	3rd	––ʹ	cigarette
dactyllic	dactyl	3	1st	ʹ––	Italy
spondaic	spondee	2	both	ʹʹ	stop! thief!

Lines, according to number of metric feet

monometer	one foot	pentameter	five feet
dimeter	two feet	hexameter	six feet
trimeter	three feet	heptameter	seven feet
tetrameter	four feet	octometer	eight feet

Stanzas

couplet	two lines	sestet	six lines
triplet or tercet	three lines	septet	seven lines
quatrain	four lines	octave	eight lines
cinquain	five lines		

Fixed Forms*

NAME	NO. OF LINES	METER	LENGTH OF LINE	RHYME SCHEME
sonnet	14	iambic	pentameter	*abba*, *abba*, *cde*, *cde* or *abab*, *cdcd*, *efef*, *gg*
triolet	8	any	any	*abaa*(*R*)*aba*(*R*)*b*(*R*)
rondel	14 or 13	any	any	*abba*, *aba*(*R*)*b*(*R*), *abbaa*(*R*)*b*(*R*) same, minus last line
rondelet	7	any	any	*aba*(*R*)*abba*(*R*)
rondeau	15 or 12	iambic	tetrameter or pentameter	*aabba*, *aabR*, *aabbaR* *abbaabR*, *abbaR*
villanelle	19 (or 12, 26, etc.)	any	any	*aba*, *aba*(1), *aba*(3), *aba*(1), *aba*(3), *aba*(1)*a*(3).
ballade	28 (8-line stanza) 35 (10-line stanza)	iambic (or other) iambic (or other)	tetrameter pentameter	*ababbcbc*(*R*) (3 times), *bcbc*(*R*) *ababbccbcb*(*R*) (3 times), *ccdcd*(*R*)
limerick	5	mixed	trimeter and dimeter	*aabba*

*Note: This chart is not exhaustive. While these are the main fixed forms, others exist, as well as variations of the ones given.

How to Use This Rhyming Dictionary

1. Look for rhymes under the vowel sound of the rhyme you want. For example, if you want a rhyme for "hat," look under short *A*; for "table," look under long *A*.

2. The vowel sounds are given in alphabetical order. In case you are looking for a vowel sound which puzzles you, consult the table of contents.

3. The page head at the top of each page will tell you which rhyme sound you have before you. Within the vowel sound, there are always three sections: one-, two-, and three-syllable rhymes. Within each section, the entries are arranged alphabetically, except that the letter *c* is put with *k* or *s* according to which of its two pronunciations is used.

4. Note that within each entry the words are arranged in numbered groups, according to the number of syllables. Thus, if you need a one-syllable word to finish your line, you need look no further than the words following the numeral 1. If you need three syllables, look at the words which come after the number 3. You might also take a one- or two-syllable word for the rhyme and qualify it with an adjective, thus making up your three syllables.

5. In a few cases where regional pronunciations vary, words have been included which may not seem to be rhymes according to your pronunciation. This may be true in a few words ending in *r* in particular, for this is a sound which often modifies the pronunciation of the preceding vowel. If this is the case, do not use the word which does not rhyme for you. Remember, it rhymes for some people, and that is why it is there.

6. Cross references to entries containing additional rhymes are usually to another entry in the same section. In this case, the indication "above" or "below" is given. Otherwise, the reference is to another section and will be found by turning to the appropriate vowel sound and one-, two-, or three-syllable rhyme section.

ABBREVIATIONS USED IN THIS BOOK

Ar.	Arabic	exc.	except	loc.	local
Aram.	Aramic	F.	French	M.L.	Medieval Latin
arch.	archaic	G.	German	N.	north
coll.	colloquial	Gr.	Greek	N.L.	New Latin
D.	Dutch	Heb.	Hebrew	obs.	obsolete
dial.	dialect	Hind.	Hindustani	Pg.	Portuguese
e.g.	*exempli gratia* [L.], for example	Ir.	Ireland	Pol.	Polish
		It.	Italian	Sp.	Spanish
Eng.	England	Jap.	Japanese	Scot.	Scotland
etc.	et cetera	L.	Latin	Tag.	Tagalog

Note: "loc.," "slang," and "dial." are assumed to refer to the United States unless otherwise indicated.

A (ay)

1.

SINGLE (MASCULINE) RHYMES IN A (ay)

Primary or Secondary Accent Falls on Last Syllable; Imperfect Rhymes Are in Italics.

A– **1.** a, A, ay, aye, eh **2.** Coué, roué [F.] **3.** mariée [F.], à pied [F.] **4.** couturier [F.], roturier [F.], habitué [F.].

BA– **1.** bay, bey **2.** abbé [F.], *ambay*, embay, Bombay, *bomb bay*, obey **3.** disembay, disobey, Baffin Bay, dapple bay.

DA– **1.** day, dey **2.** today, *heyday*, *playday*, *Mayday*, *payday*, idée [F.], *midday*, *Friday*, *weekday*, undé, *Monday*, *Sunday*, *noonday*, *doomsday*, *Tuesday*, Lord's Day, *Thursday*, *birthday* **3.** workaday, wedding day, working day, holiday, every day, quarter day, Easter Day, yesterday, Saturday, Wednesday, market day, judgment day, Christmas Day **4.** alackaday.

FA– **1.** fay, fey, fe [Sp.] **2.** café, parfait, au fait [F.] **3.** Santa Fe, coryphée, rechauffé [F.], pousse-café [F.].

GA– **1.** gay, gai [F.] **2.** *nosegay*, *margay*, *morgay* **3.** distingué [F.].

HA– **1.** hay, hey **2.** ahey.

JA– **1.** j, J, jay **3.** popinjay.

KA– **1.** k, K, Kay, kay, cay, quai [F.] **2.** decay, piqué, okay, bouquet, roquet, croquet, tokay, parquet, *Biscay*, risqué [F.] **3.** appliqué [F.], sobriquet [F.] **4.** communiqué [F.].

LA– **1.** lay, lei, blé [F.], clay, Clay, flay, play, splay, slay, sley, sleigh **2.** allay, Malay, ailé, waylay, Calais, chalet, belay, delay, relay, inlay, *parlay*, parler [F.], soleil [F.], mislay, *outlay*, coulé [F.], soufflé [F.], *morglay*, fair play, *byplay*, display, misplay, *horseplay*, *bobsleigh* **3.** Mandalay, roundelay, virelay, De Molay, reveille, Chevrolet, underlay, interlay, overlay, rissolé [F.], photoplay, Passion Play etc., underplay, overplay, interplay, pourparler [F.] **4.** cabriolet, café-au-lait [F.], au pis aller [F.], coup de soleil [F.], cantabile.

MA– **1.** Mae, May **2.** lamé [F.], semé [F.], *gourmet*, dismay **3.** entremets, consommé, resumé.

NA– **1.** nay, né, née [both F.], neigh **2.** ainé [F.], Chiné [F.], donnée [F.], tourné [F.] **3.** Hogmanay, matinee, satiné [F.], Ciboney, dragonné [F.], raisonné [F.], dejeuner [F.], cloisonné **4.** estaminet [F.].

PA– **1.** pay, spay **2.** frappé, epée [F.], repay, prepay, Gaspé, coupé, toupet **3.** canapé [F.], overpay.

RA– **1.** ray, re, rey [Sp.], bray, brae, scray, dray, fray, gray, gré [F.], grey, pray, pré [F.], prey, spray, tray, trey, stray **2.** array, bewray, *chambray*, padre, André, *Deirdre*, affray, defray, beret, *stingray*, doré [F.], *foray*, *moray*, moiré, soiree, repray, bespray, respray, betray, entrée, portray, astray, estray, distrait, outré [F.], hurray, curé [F.], purée **3.** disarray, liseré, autospray, emigree, émigré [F.], dapple gray, iron-gray, silver gray, Honoré, Monterrey **4.** jeunesse dorée [F.].

SA– **1.** say, se **2.** assay, glacé [F.], *naysay*, passé, chassé, essay, essai [F.], blessé

[F.], presay, missay, lycée [F.], plissé [F.], gainsay, pensée [F.], unsay, *hearsay*, foresay, *soothsay* **3.** fiancé, fiancée, déclassé [F.], divorcé [F.], divorcée [F.], repoussé [F.], retroussé [F.]; *see* also **ZA-** blasé etc. below.

SHA- **1.** shay, chez [F.] **2.** cachet, sachet, sashay, cliché, broché, crochet, cherchez [F.], touché [F.] **3.** attaché, ricochet, recherché **4.** papier mâché [F.], à bon marché [F.].

TA- **1.** tay, the [F.], stay **2.** paté [F.], été [F.], astay, *bobstay, backstay, jackstay, mainstay, forestay,* outstay, santé [F.], bonté [F.] **3.** comité [F.], overstay, liberté [F.], velouté [F.] **4.** légèreté, égalité, fraternité, éternité, déporté [all F.].

THA- **1.** they **2.** Cathay.

VA- **2.** pavé [F.], nevé [F.], inveigh, convey, corvée [F.], kurvey, purvey, survey **3.** reconvey, repurvey, resurvey, énervé [F.].

WA- **1.** way, wey, Wei, weigh, qua, quey, sway, tway, whey **2.** away, aweigh, *subway, hatchway, archway, headway, roadway, Broadway,* midway, *guideway, leeway,* reweigh, *seaway,* halfway, *gangway, cogway, byway, highway, walkway, railway, hallway, tramway, someway, runway, slipway, fairway, stairway, doorway, crossway, straightway, outway,* outweigh, *pathway, causeway* **3.** breakaway, Rockaway, stowaway, wellaway, runaway, straightaway, getaway, caraway, castaway, cutaway, milky way, entryway, everyway, passageway, cableway, Galloway, underweigh, waterway, overweigh.

YA- **1.** yea **2.** denier [F.], foyer, croupier [F.], dossier [F.], métier, soigné [F.] **3.** ennuyé, escalier, chevalier [all F.].

ZA- **2.** blasé, visé **3.** exposé **4.** Champs Élysées.

ZHA- **2.** congé [F.], Roget **3.** dégagé [F.], agrégé, protégé, protégée, négligée.

AB- **1.** Abe, babe **3.** cosmolabe, astrolabe.

ACH- **1.** h, H, aitch.

AD- **1.** ade, aid, aide, bade, bayed, fade, hade, jade, cade, lade, laid, blade, flayed, glade, played, sleighed, slade, made, maid, neighed, paid, spade, spayed, raid, braid, brayed, grayed, grade, prayed, preyed, sprayed, trade, strayed, shade, staid, stayed, wade, weighed, suéde, wheyed **2.** obeyed, gambade, forbade, brigade, baccade, decayed, alcaide, falcade, cockade, blockade, brocade, stockade, arcade, cascade, allayed, delayed, relayed, relade, relaid, inlaid, unlade, unlaid, parleyed, old-maid, handmade, *handmaid,* remade, self-made, *milkmaid,* homemade, pomade, unmade, *mermaid, bridesmaid,* dismayed, *nursemaid, housemaid,* grenade, apaid, repaid, prepaid, unpaid, postpaid, respade, croupade, parade, charade, abrade, un braid, upbraid, afraid, aggrade, degrade, regrade, tirade, retrade, glacéed, passade, chasséd, glissade, torsade, crusade, *sunshade,* crocheted, *nightshade,* sautéed, unstaid, evade, invade, pervade, conveyed, purveyed, surveyed, reweighed, persuade **3.** orangeade, renegade, lemonade, citronade, gingerade, appliquéd, barricade, cavalcade, ambuscade, escalade, defilade, enfilade, fusillade, accolade, everglade, readymade, dairymaid, undismayed, esplanade, promenade, serenade, marinade, pasquinade, dragonnade, gasconade, colonnade, cannonade, carronade, escapade, gallopade, overpaid, disarrayed, masquerade, unafraid, centigrade, retrograde, balustrade, palisade, overweighed **4.** harlequinade, fanfaronade, rodomontade.

AF- **1.** chafe, kef, strafe, safe, waif **2.** enchafe, vouchsafe, unsafe.

AFD- **1.** chafed, strafed **2.** vouchsafed.

AG- **1.** Hague, plague, Prague, vague **2.** fainaigue.

AJ- **1.** age, gage, gauge, cage, mage, page, rage, sage, stage, wage, swage **2.** engage, encage, *nonage*, repage, rampage, enrage, outrage, presage, Osage, backstage, *forestage*, upstage, assuage **3.** overage, disengage.

AJD– **1.** aged, gauged, caged, paged, raged, staged, waged **2.** engaged, encaged, repaged, rampaged, enraged, outraged, upstaged, assuaged **3.** disengaged.

AK– **1.** ache, bake, fake, hake, haik, jake, cake, lake, flake, slake, make, snake, spake, rake, brake, break, drake, crake, traik, strake, sake, take, stake, steak, wake, quake **2.** *headache*, *backache*, *earache*, *heartache*, *toothache*, *clambake*, *friedcake*, *hoecake*, *nocake*, *shortcake*, *nutcake*, *fruitcake*, remake, opaque, *daybreak*, *heartbreak*, *outbreak*, *sheldrake*, *mandrake*, *muckrake*, *namesake*, *keepsake*, forsake, betake, retake, *intake*, *uptake*, partake, *grubstake*, *beefsteak*, mistake, *sweepstake*, awake, rewake, *earthquake* **3.** johnnycake, griddlecake, havercake, rattlesnake, undertake, overtake.

AKS– aches, etc., *see* **AK–** ache etc. above, plus "s" or " 's."

AKT– **1.** ached, baked, faked, caked, flaked, slaked, snaked, raked, braked, traiked, staked, quaked **2.** *grubstaked*, rewaked.

AL– **1.** ail, ale, bale, bail, Bel, dale, fail, gale, Gael, hale, hail, gaol, jail, kale, scale, flail, mail, male, nail, snail, pail, pale, spale, rail, brail, Braille, frail, grail, Graal, trail, sale, sail, shale, tale, tail, tael, stale, vale, vail, veil, wail, wale, quail, squail, whale, Yale **2.** *Clydesdale*, regale, inhale, exhale, percale, hallel, remail, *blackmail*, *hangnail*, canaille, *hobnail*, tenaille, *agnail*, *thumbnail*, empale, impale, *handrail*, *landrail*, *pedrail*, *guardrail*, derail, *taffrail*, *cograil*, engrail, assail, *resale*, *wholesale*, grisaille, *staysail*, *headsail*, resail, *lugsail*, *skysail*, *trysail*, *mainsail*, *topsail*, *foresail*, *spritsail*, outsail, *telltale*, *bobtail*, *broadtail*, detail, retail, entail, *pigtail*, *bangtail*, *cocktail*, *forktail*, *bucktail*, *fantail*, *pintail*, *horntail*, *thorntail*, *sheartail*, curtail, *cattail*, *sprittail*, *boattail*, *coattail*, *foxtail*, *shavetail*, *dovetail*, avail, travail, prevail, enveil, bewail, *narwhale* **3.** Abigail, farthingale, nightingale, martingale, fingernail, monorail, tattletale, fairy tale, draggletail, disentail, swallowtail, scissortail, paravail, intervale.

ALD– **1.** ailed, aled, baled, bailed, failed, galed, haled, gaoled, jailed, scaled, flailed, mailed, nailed, snailed, paled, railed, trailed, sailed, tailed, veiled, wailed, waled, quailed, whaled **2.** regaled, inhaled, exhaled, remailed, *blackmailed*, *hobnailed*, empaled, impaled, derailed, assailed, resailed, outsailed, *bobtailed*, *broadtailed*, detailed, retailed, entailed, *pigtailed*, *bangtailed*, *cocktailed*, curtailed, availed, travailed, prevailed, envailed, unveiled, bewailed **3.** unregaled, farthingaled, draggletailed, disentailed, swallowtailed.

ALZ– ails etc., *see* **AL–** ail etc. above, plus "s" or " 's"; **1.** Wales **2.** Marseilles.

AM– **1.** aim, dame, fame, game, hame, came, lame, blame, flame, claim, maim, name, frame, crême, same, Sejm [Pol.], shame, tame **2.** defame, became, aflame, inflame, acclaim, declaim, reclaim, proclaim, disclaim, exclaim, *quitclaim*, rename, *byname*, *nickname*, *forename*, *surname*, misname, *doorframe*, *selfsame* **3.** overcame, counterclaim.

AMD– **1.** aimed, famed, gamed, lamed, blamed, flamed, claimed, maimed, named, framed, shamed, tamed **2.** defamed, inflamed, acclaimed, declaimed, reclaimed, proclaimed, disclaimed, exclaimed, renamed, *nicknamed*, misnamed, ashamed **3.** undefamed, counterclaimed.

AMZ– aims etc., *see* **AM–** aim etc. above, plus "s" or " 's"; **1.** James **2.** St. James.

AN– **1.** bane, chain, Dane, deign, feign, fane, fain, gain, gaine, Jane, cane, Cain, skein, lane, lain, laine, blain, plane, plain, slain, Maine, main, mane, pain, pane, Paine, Spain, rein, reign, rain, brain, drain, grain, crane, sprain, train, strain, sane, sain, tain, stain, thane, vane, vain, vein, wane, swain, twain, zain **2.** urbane, *herbbane*, *fleabane*, *wolfsbane*, rechain, enchain, unchain, *mundane*, ordain, disdain, profane, regain, chicane, again, Elaine, delaine, *chilblain*, *seaplane*, *biplane*, *triplane*, *volplane*, *airplane*, Champlain, explain, amain, demesne, remain, domain, romaine, ptomaine, germane, humane, chow mein, inane, cocaine, Cockaigne, campaign, champagne, champaign, arraign, Karen, terrane, terrain, *checkrein*, unrein, forane, moraine, *subdrain*, refrain, migraine, engrain, ingrain, *grosgrain*, *crossgrain*, detrain, entrain, restrain, distrain, constrain, insane, attain, obtain, detain, retain, maintain, contain, pertain, abstain, *bloodstain*, *tearstain*, distain, dustain, *cordwain*, *coxswain*, *boatswain*, sixain **3.** inurbane, hurricane, sugar cane, reordain, preordain, foreordain, aquaplane, multiplane, monoplane, aeroplane, hydroplane, gyroplane, Charlemagne, inhumane, windowpane, counterpane, scatterbrain, featherbrain, subterrane, suzerain, overstrain, chevrotain, ascertain, appertain, entertain, quatorzain **4.** demimondaine, legerdemain, elecampane, mediterrane.

ĀND– **1.** chained, deigned, feigned, gained, caned, planed, pained, rained, reigned, brained, drained, grained, craned, sprained, trained, strained, stained, veined, waned **2.** enchained, unchained, rechained, ordained, disdained, unfeigned, profaned, regained, arraigned, explained, remained, campaigned, unreined, engrained, ingrained, detrained, entrained, restrained, distrained, constrained, attained, detained, retained, maintained, contained, pertained, abstained, *bloodstained* **3.** preordained, foreordained, featherbrained, scatterbrained, overstrained, ascertained, entertained.

ĀNJ– **1.** change, mange, range, grange, strange **2.** exchange, shortchange, arrange, derange, estrange **3.** rearrange, prearrange, disarrange, interchange.

ĀNT– **1.** faint, feint, plaint, paint, saint, taint, quaint **2.** complaint, bepaint, repaint, Geraint, restraint, distraint, constraint, ensaint, attaint, acquaint.

ĀNTS– faints etc., *see* **ĀNT–** faint etc. above, plus "s" or " 's."

ĀNZ– banes etc., *see* **ĀN–** bane etc. above, plus "s" or " 's."

ĀP– **1.** ape, chape, gape, jape, cape, scape, nape, rape, drape, grape, crape, crepe, scrape, shape, tape **2.** agape, *landscape*, escape, *seascape*, *skyscape*, bedrape, reshape, misshape, transhape, *shipshape*, red-tape.

ĀPS– apes etc., *see* **ĀP–** ape etc. above, plus "s" or " 's"; **1.** traipse **3.** jackanapes.

ĀPT– **1.** aped, gaped, shaped, raped, draped, scraped, taped **2.** escaped, bedraped, reshaped, red-taped, untaped.

ĀR– **1.** air, Eir, heir, eyre, e'er, bear, bare, chair, dare, fair, fare, faire [F.], hair, hare, care, scare, lair, blare, flare, flair, glare, glair, Clare, mare, mer [F.], mère [F.], n'er, snare, pair, pare, pear, père [F.], spare, rare, frère [F.], prayer, share, tear, tare, terre [F.], stair, stare, there, their, vair, ware, wear, swear, square, where, yare **2.** Pierre, coheir, whene'er, where'er, howe'er, *threadbare*, *cudbear*, *bugbear*, *forebear*, forbear, misbear, *armchair*, bedare, outdare, affair, *Mayfair*, *fieldfare*, *welfare*, *warfare*, *horsehair*, *mohair*, eclair, declare, *nightmare*, grand'mère [F.], belle-mère [F.], ensnare, repair, prepare, impair, compare, grand-père [F.], beau-père [F.], despair, *confrere*, *corsair*, *plowshare*, Voltaire, parterre, outstare, trouvère [F.], aware, *hardware*, beware, *tinware*, *glassware*, *footwear*, outwear, resquare, unsquare, hiver [F.], *somewhere*, *nowhere*, *elsewhere*, première [F.], portière [F.] **3.** overbear, Camembert, rocking-chair, thoroughfare, maidenhair, mal de mer [F.], jardinière [F.], doctrinaire, debonair, billionaire, millionaire, questionnaire, disrepair, proletaire, solitaire, countervair, Delaware, unaware, earthenware, ironware, underwear, silverware, otherwhere, anywhere, everywhere, wheresoe'er, savoir faire [F.], laissez-faire [F.], vivandière [F.], fonctionnaire [F.] **4.** commissionnaire [F.], concessionnaire [F.], Finistère, Finisterre.

ARD– **1.** aired, bared, dared, fared, hared, cared, scared, laird, blared, flared, glared, shared, snared, spared, rared, stared, squared **2.** gray-haired, fair-haired etc., declared, ensnared, repaired, prepared, impaired, compared, outstared **3.** undeclared, curly-haired, golden-haired, Titian-haired, raven-haired.

ARN– **1.** bairn, cairn, tairn.

ARS– **1.** scarce, Perse [F.] **2.** commerce [F.].

ARZ– airs etc., *see* AR– air etc. above, plus "s" or "'s."

AS– **1.** ace, base, bass, chase, dace, dais, face, case, lace, place, plaice, mace, pace, space, race, brace, grace, trace, Thrace, vase **2.** abase, debase, surbase, enchase, vendace, efface, deface, reface, *boldface*, *frogface*, *blackface*, *paleface*, *catface*, outface, *cardcase*, *bookcase*, encase, *showcase*, *staircase*, *notecase*, *suitcase*, ukase, *bridelace*, anlace, enlace, *shoelace*, replace, *fireplace*, displace, misplace, *birthplace*, grimace, apace, *footpace*, outpace, erase, *tailrace*, *millrace*, embrace, *scapegrace*, disgrace, retrace, Alsace, *ambsace* **3.** contrabass, octobass, steeplechase, Boniface, platterface, baby face, angel face etc., interlace, populace, hiding place, resting place, commonplace, interspace, chariot race.

AST– **1.** baste, based, faced, haste, cased, chaste, chased, laced, placed, paste, paced, spaced, raced, braced, graced, traced, taste, waste, waist **2.** abased, lambaste, unchaste, bald-faced, bold-faced, shamefaced, two-faced etc., posthaste, encased **3.** baby-faced, dirty-faced, angel-faced, double-faced, freckle-faced, interlaced, aftertaste.

AT– **1.** eight, ate, ait, bate, bait, date, fate, fête, gate, gait, hate, Kate, skate, late, plate, plait, slate, mate, pate, rate, freight, grate, great, crate, prate, trait, strait, straight, sate, state, weight, wait **2.** create, abate, debate, rebate, *crowbait*, *whitebait*, redate, predate, sedate, misdate, postdate, outdate, *floodgate*, *negate*, *seagate*, *Vulgate*, *placate*, *oblate*, sublate, elate, belate, delate, relate, deflate, inflate, conflate, sufflate, collate, breastplate, translate, playmate, cremate, checkmate, stalemate, *comate*, *shipmate*, *helpmate*, *classmate*, *messmate*, mismate, *tentmate*, enate, innate, ornate, berate, prorate, cut-rate, estate, restate, instate, misstate, await, lightweight **3.** recreate, procreate, discreate, celibate, approbate, reprobate, incubate, depredate, antedate, candidate, validate, lapidate, cuspidate, liquidate, inundate, afterdate, decaudate, denudate, nucleate, permeate, roseate, nauseate, propagate, divagate, ablegate, delegate, relegate, abnegate, segregate, aggregate, congregate, crash the gate, get the gate [both slang], obligate, profligate, fumigate, irrigate, litigate, mitigate, castigate, instigate, navigate, abrogate, subrogate, subjugate, conjugate, corrugate, fasciate, gladiate, radiate, mediate, foliate, opiate, expiate, seriate, floriate, satiate, vitiate, tertiate, aviate, obviate, deviate, desiccate, exsiccate, deprecate, imprecate, abdicate, dedicate, mendicate, judicate, delicate, triplicate, implicate, complicate, supplicate, duplicate, explicate, formicate, tunicate, fabricate, imbricate, fimbricate, lubricate, rubricate, intricate, extricate, vesicate, corticate, masticate, rusticate, relocate, allocate, collocate, dislocate, embrocate, advocate, demarcate, altercate, bifurcate, confiscate, expiscate, obfuscate, infuscate, coruscate, educate, correlate, sibilate, jubilate, depilate, pupilate, mutilate, ventilate, cancellate, flagellate, lamellate, crenellate, immolate, desolate, isolate, contemplate, copperplate, silver plate, legislate, mistranslate, ambulate, tubulate, peculate, speculate, calculate, flocculate, circulate, osculate, adulate, pendulate, undulate, nodulate, regulate, angulate, ungulate, stellulate, ululate, emulate, simulate, stimulate, formulate, cumulate, granulate, crenulate, lunulate, stipulate, populate, copulate, spherulate, insulate, consulate, decimate, animate, ultimate, intimate, optimate, estimate, consummate, dichromate, conformate, explanate, sultanate, hyphenate, alienate, arsenate, catenate, septenate, juvenate, impregnate, obsignate, designate, turbinate, vaccinate, fascinate, ordinate, marginate, machinate, echinate, declinate, pollinate, geminate, fulminate, dominate, marinate, patinate, pectinate, destinate, glutinate, bipinnate, carbonate, functionate, coronate, assonate, detonate, intonate, hibernate, quaternate, inornate, fortunate, adipate, dissipate, exculpate, syncopate, extirpate, saccharate, separate, disparate, celebrate, cerebrate, calibrate, obsecrate, desecrate, consecrate, execrate, dehydrate, liberate, lacerate, macerate, ulcerate, federate, moderate, tolerate, numerate, generate, operate, asperate, desperate, literate, integrate, emigrate, immigrate, transmigrate, aspirate, decorate, perforate, biforate, camphorate, pignorate, corporate, perorate, doctorate, overrate, penetrate, impetrate, perpetrate, arbitrate, infiltrate, concentrate, orchestrate, fenestrate, sequestrate, magistrate, registrate, capistrate, demonstrate, remonstrate, illustrate, accurate, obdurate, figurate, fulgurate, sulphurate, tellurate, suppurate, purpurate, saturate, inspissate, tête-à-tête [F.], delectate, eructate, acetate, vegetate, oscitate, meditate, agitate, digitate, cogitate, gurgitate, militate, imitate, limitate, sanitate, capitate, crepitate, palpitate, irritate, hesitate, nictitate, quantitate, gravitate, levitate, occultate, edentate, segmentate, potentate, annotate, connotate, decurtate, devastate, *intestate*, reinstate, apostate, understate, interstate, overstate, degustate, acutate, permutate, amputate, vacuate, graduate, valuate, tenuate, sinuate, adequate, antiquate, actuate, punctuate, fluctuate, fructuate, situate, excavate, aggravate, depravate, elevate, salivate, derivate, titivate, cultivate, motivate, captivate, estivate, renovate, innovate, enervate, recurvate, hundredweight, pennyweight, heavyweight, bantamweight, underweight, featherweight, paperweight, welterweight, overweight **4.** elucidate, invalidate, consolidate, intimidate, accommodate, enucleate, delineate, extravagate, variegate, depreciate, appreciate, officiate, associate, dissociate, eradiate, irradiate, repudiate, collegiate, trifoliate, calumniate, ammoniate, pogoniate, marsupiate, inebriate, excoriate, depatriate, negotiate, exuviate, asphyxiate, hypothecate, syllabicate, irradicate, rededicate, revindicate, adjudicate, indelicate, multiplicate, authenticate, decorticate, domesticate, sophisticate, prognosticate, intoxicate, reciprocate, equivocate, annihilate, assimilate, nucleolate, alveolate, inviolate, interpolate, disconsolate, apostolate, capitulate, expostulate, salicylate, amalgamate, legitimate, penultimate, permanganate, hydrogenate, concatenate, rejuvenate, predesignate, vaticinate, hallucinate, inordinate, immarginate, ingeminate, inseminate, disseminate, peregrinate, indoctrinate, procrastinate, predestinate, conglutinate, exsanguinate, bicarbonate, impersonate, subalternate, emancipate, invertebrate, deliberate, reverberate, protuberate, incarcerate, eviscerate, confederate, preponderate, vociferate, exaggerate, refrigerate, accelerate, conglomerate, exonerate, remunerate, cooperate, exasperate, recuperate, commiserate, reiterate, adulterate, presbyterate, asseverate, redecorate, imperforate, invigorate, ameliorate, commemorate, evaporate, incorporate, recalcitrate, extravasate, improvisate, tergiversate, capacitate, felicitate, resuscitate, premeditate, tridigitate, inadequate, effectuate, perpetuate, accentuate, eventuate, insalivate, recaptivate **5.** baccalaureate, circumnavigate, supererogate, intermediate, unifoliate, circumstantiate, differentiate, renegotiate, quadrifoliate, excommunicate, recapitulate, insubordinate, unaffectionate, disproportionate, incompassionate, deteriorate, incommensurate, incapacitate, individuate, superannuate.

ATH– **1.** faith, wraith, staith **2.** unfaith, misfaith.

ATH– **1.** bathe, scathe, lathe, snathe, spathe, rathe, swathe **2.** unswathe.

ATHD– **1.** bathed, scathed, lathed, swathed.

ATS– eights etc., *see* **AT–** eight etc. above, plus "s" or "'s."

AV– **1.** Dave, gave, cave, lave, glaive, slave, nave, knave, pave, rave, brave, grave, crave, trave, save, shave, stave, wave, waive, suave **2.** forgave, behave, portglaive, enslave, repave, engrave, ingrave, deprave **3.** misbehave, autoclave, antenave, architrave.

AVD– **1.** caved, laved, slaved, paved, raved, braved, craved, saved, shaved, staved, waved, waived **2.** behaved, enslaved, repaved, unpaved, engraved, depraved **3.** misbehaved, unenslaved, unengraved.

AVZ– Dave's etc., *see* **AV–** Dave etc. above, plus "s" or "'s."

AZ– ayes etc., *see* **A–** ay etc. through ZHA– congé etc. above, plus "s" or "'s" (except for French plurals, where the "s" is not pronounced); **1.** baize, daze, faze, phase, gaze, haze, Hayes, laze, blaze, glaze, maze, maize, raze, raise, braise, braze, phrase, graze, craze, praise, chaise, vase **2.** bedaze, malaise, ablaze, emblaze, amaze, bemaze, *mizmaze*, rephrase, upraise, appraise, bepraise, *sideways* **3.** nowadays, Marseillaise, hollandaise, mayonnaise, lyonnaise, polonaise, paraphrase, metaphrase, reappraise, underpraise, overpraise.

AZD– **1.** dazed, fazed, gazed, hazed, lazed, blazed, glazed, raised, razed, braised, phrased, grazed, crazed, praised **2.** bedazed, emblazed, unglazed, amazed, bemazed, unraised, upraised, rephrased, unphrased, appraised, unpraised, dispraised **3.** paraphrased, reappraised, underpraised, overpraised.

AZH– **1.** beige, greige.

A (ay)

2.

DOUBLE (FEMININE) RHYMES IN A (may'hem)

Primary or Secondary Accent Falls on Next to Last Syllable; Imperfect Rhymes Are in Italics.

A'a- **2.** haya, Maia, Freya **3.** Isaiah **4.** Himalaya.

A'ad- **1.** naiad, sayid.

A'al- **1.** Baal. **2.** Ethbaal. **3.** defrayal, betrayal, portrayal, conveyal, purveyal, surveyal.

A'am- **2.** faham, mayhem, graham, play 'em.

A'an- **3.** Biscayan, Malayan **4.** Paraguayan, Uruguayan.

A'ans- **3.** abeyance, conveyance, purveyance, surveyance.

A'ant- **2.** mayn't **3.** abeyant.

AB'an- **2.** Laban, Leben [G.], geben [G.].

AB'er- **2.** Gheber, Ghabre, caber, labor, neighbor, saber, sabre, tabor **3.** belabor.

AB'erz- Ghebers etc., *see* AB'er- Gheber etc. above; **2.** jabers **3.** bejabers.

AB'e- **2.** baby, gaby, maybe **3.** *crybaby.*

AB'ez- **2.** babies, gabies, Jabes, scabies rabies, maybes **3.** *crybabies.*

AB'l- **2.** Abel, able, Babel, fable, gable, cable, label, labile, Mabel, sable, table, stable **3.** enable, unable, disable, retable, *timetable*, *turntable*, unstable **4.** fibble-fable [dial.].

AB'ld- **2.** fabled, gabled, cabled, labeled, sabled, tabled, stabled **3.** enabled, disabled, besabled, retabled.

AB'ler- **2.** abler, fabler, cabler, labeler, sabler, tabler, stabler **3.** enabler, disabler, retabler, unstabler.

AB'lest- **2.** ablest, stablest **3.** unstablest.

AB'ling- **2.** cabling, labelling, tabling, stabling **3.** enabling, disabling, retabling.

AB'lz- Abels etc., *see* **AB'l-** Abel etc. above, plus "s" or "'s."

AB'rum- **2.** Abram, labrum, flabrum **4.** candelabrum.

AD'a- **2.** Ada, Veda **3.** cicada, armada, Pinctada **5.** Digitigrada.

A'da- **2.** heyday, Mayday, payday, playday.

AD'ans- **2.** aidance, cadence **3.** decadence.

AD'ant- **2.** aidant, cadent **3.** decadent, abradent.

AD'ed- **2.** aided, faded, jaded, bladed, gladed, spaded, raided, braided, graded, traded, shaded, waded **3.** unaided, unfaded, cockaded, blockaded, brocaded, cascaded, paraded, unbraided, upbraided, degraded, crusaded, evaded, invaded, pervaded, dissuaded, persuaded. **4.** barricaded, ambuscaded, enfiladed, double-bladed, accoladed, promenaded, serenaded, colonnaded, cannonaded, masqueraded, retrograded, unpersuaded.

AD'en- **2.** Aden, Haydn, laden, maiden **3.** menhaden, snow maiden **4.** overladen, heavy-laden.

AD'ens- **2.** cadence **3.** decadence.

AD'er- **2.** aider, fader, spader, raider, braider, grader, trader, Seder, staider, wader **3.** unbraider, upbraider, crusader, invader, dissuader, persuader 4. barricader, promenader, serenader, masquerader.

ĀD′est– 2. staidest.

ĀD′ez– 2. Hades, Cadiz, ladies.

ĀD′i– 2. fady, shady, jady, cadi, lady, glady, maidy, Brady, 'fraidy, Grady, Sadie, vade 3. O'Grady, milady, *forelady.*

ĀD′ing– 2. aiding, fading, lading, spading, raiding, braiding, grading, trading, shading, wading 3. blockading, cascading, unfading, parading, unbraiding, upbraiding, degrading, crusading, evading, invading, pervading, dissuading, persuading 4. barricading, ambuscading, serenading, cannonading, masquerading.

ĀD′ish– 2. jadish, staidish 3. oldmaidish, *mermaidish.*

ĀD′l– 2. ladle, gradal, cradle, tradal 3. encradle.

ĀD′less– 2. aidless, fadeless, bladeless, spadeless, braidless, gradeless, tradeless, shadeless 3. paradeless, cockadeless, crusadeless.

ĀD′li– 2. staidly 3. dismayedly.

ĀD′ling– 2. ladling, maidling, cradling 3. encradling.

ĀD′ness– 2. frayedness, staidness 3. afraidness, unstaidness.

ĀD′o– 2. dado, credo 3. gambado, fumado, tornado, strappado 4. bastinado, carbonado, desperado, camisado.

ĀD′os– 3. Barbados, intrados, extrados.

ĀD′oz– dados etc., *see* **ĀD′o–** dado etc. above, plus "s" or "'s."

ĀD′us– 2. cladus, gradus, made us etc. 3. dismayed us etc.

Ā′er– 2. feyer, gayer, layer, flayer, player, slayer, mayor, payer, brayer, grayer, prayer, preyer, sprayer, strayer, stayer, weigher 3. obeyer, waylayer, delayer, bricklayer, parleyer, outlayer, displayer, mormaor, taxpayer, forayer, hoorayer, defrayer, betrayer, portrayer, assayer, essayer, gainsayer, soothsayer, inveigher, conveyer, purveyor, surveyor.

Ā′est– 2. feyest, gayest, grayest, greyest 3. assayist, *essayist*; *see* also **Ā′ist–** Ptolemaist etc. below.

ĀF′er– 2. chafer, safer, strafer, wafer 3. cockchafer, vouchsafer.

ĀF′ing– 2. chafing, strafing 3. enchafing, vouchsafing.

ĀG′a– 2. saga 3. omega 4. rutabaga, Onondaga.

ĀG′er– 2. plaguer, vaguer, jager.

ĀG′in– 2. Fagin, plaguin', regen [G.] 4. Copenhagen.

ĀG′l– 2. plagal, paigle, vagal 3. finagle.

ĀG′o– 2. Dago, sago 3. Sebago, lumbago, plumbago, Diego, galago, imago, farrago, suffrago 4. Solidago, San Diego, Archimago, galapago 6. Tierra del Fuego.

ĀG′rans– 2. flagrance, fragrance, vagrance.

ĀG′rant– 2. flagrant, fragrant, vagrant 3. infragrant, unfragrant.

ĀG′us– 2. Magus, pagus, plague us, tragus, vagus 3. choragus 4. archimagus.

Ā′i– 2. Dei [L.], clayey, Mayey, wheyey 4. Agnus Dei [L.].

Ā′ij– 2. drayage, weighage.

Ā′ik– 2. laic 3. Chaldaic, Judaic, trochaic, archaic, Romaic, Spondaic, Hebraic, Passaic, mosaic, prosaic, altaic, deltaic, voltaic, stanzaic 4. Aramaic, Ptolemaic, stenopaic, algebraic, tesseraic, Pharisaic.

Ā′ing– 2. baying, laying, slaying, sleighing, Maying, neighing, fraying, graying, preying, praying, straying, saying, weighing 3. obeying, decaying, croqueting, waylaying, parleying, displaying, a-Maying, dismaying, foraying, defraying, portraying, assaying, essaying, gainsaying, crocheting, conveying, surveying, reweighing 4. disobeying, appliquéing, overpaying, disarraying, overstaying.

A'is– 2. dais, Lais, nais.

A'ish– 2. bayish, gayish, clayish, grayish, wheyish.

A'ist– 4. Ptolemaist, algebraist, Pharisaist; *see* also **A'est–** gayest etc. above.

AJ'ed– 2. aged 3. coaged.

AJ'ent– 2. agent 3. reagent.

AJ'er– 2. ager, gager, gauger, major, pager, sager, stager, wager, swager 3. drum major, presager, assuager 4. trumpet major.

AJ'est– 2. sagest.

AJ'ez– 2. ages, gages, gauges, cages, pages, rages, sages, stages, wages, swages 3. engages, encages, impages, compages, outrages, presages 4. disengages.

AJ'i– 2. cagey, Meiji, sagy, stagy.

AJ'ing– 2. aging, gauging, caging, paging, raging, staging, waging 3. engaging, enraging, presaging, assuaging 4. disengaging.

AJ'less– 2. ageless, gageless, gaugeless, cageless, pageless, stageless, wageless.

AJ'li– 2. sagely.

AJ'ment– 3. engagement, enragement, presagement, assuagement 4. pre-engagement, disengagement.

AJ'us– 2. age us etc. 3. ambagious, rampageous, outrageous, courageous, umbrageous, contagious, enrage us etc. 4. advantageous, noncontagious 5. disadvantageous.

AK'a– 2. Cheka, raca, weka, cueca 3. Macaca, Jamaica, Kapeika, bareca 4. abhiseka.

AK'at– 2. placate, pacate, vacate.

AK'en– 2. Aiken, bacon, Macon, shaken, taken, waken 3. Jamaican, forsaken, unshaken, wind-shaken, untaken, mistaken, awaken, rewaken 4. Godforsaken, unforsaken, undertaken, overtaken, reawaken.

AK'er– 2. acher, acre, baker, faker, fakir, laker, maker, nacre, raker, breaker, shaker, Shaker, taker, staker, waker, Quaker 3. *wiseacre, matchmaker, watchmaker, bookmaker, peacemaker, dressmaker, lawmaker, shoemaker, strikebreaker, heartbreaker, lawbreaker*, forsaker, *salt-shaker*, partaker, mistaker, painstaker 4. simulacre, mischiefmaker, Sabbathbreaker, pepper-shaker, undertaker.

AK'erd– 2. acred, nacred 3. wiseacred.

AK'erz– achers etc., *see* **AK'er–** acher etc. above, plus "s" or "'s."

AK'i– 2. achy, faky, caky, laky, slaky, snaky, braky, traiky, shaky, quaky 3. headachy.

AK'ij– 2. flakage, brakeage, breakage.

AK'ing– 2. aching, baking, faking, caking, slaking, raking, braking, breaking, shaking, waking, quaking 3. *watchmaking, bookmaking, dressmaking, heartbreaking*, forsaking, partaking, mistaking, *painstaking* 4. merrymaking, unforsaking, unpartaking, undertaking.

AK'ish– 2. achish, snakish, rakish.

AK'less– 2. acheless, fakeless, cakeless, lakeless, slakeless, snakeless, rakeless, breakless, shakeless, takeless, stakeless, steakless, wakeless, quakeless 3. mistakeless.

AK'man– 2. cakeman, brakeman, steakman.

AK'o– 2. Draco, Waco 3. macaco.

AK'red– 2. sacred.

AK'rum– 2. sacrum 3. synsacrum 4. simulacrum.

AL'a– 2. ala, chela, gala, mala 3. kamala, canela [Sp.], panela, osela.

AL'aks– 2. Galax, malax, Spalax.

AL'anks– 2. phalanx, Caranx.

AL'ek– 2. alec.

AL'ens– 2. valence 3. trivalence, covalence 4. univalence, equivalence.

AL'ent– 2. valent 3. inhalant, exhalant, transcalant, assailant, bivalent, trivalent, surveillant **4.** ambivalent, *equivalent*, polyvalent.

AL′er– **2.** alar, baler, bailer, bailor, haler, jailer, jailor, gaoler, scalar, scaler, malar, mailer, nailer, paler, frailer, trailer, sailer, sailor, talar, tailer, tailor, Taylor, staler, wailer, squalor, whaler **3.** regaler, inhaler, exhaler, assailer, *wholesaler*, *retailer*.

AL′erz– alars etc., *see* **AL′er–** alar etc. above, plus "s" or "'s."

A′less– **2.** dayless, payless, playless, rayless, prayless, preyless, wayless, swayless.

AL′est– **2.** halest, palest, frailest, stalest; and verbs ending in **AL** plus -est.

AL′ful– **2.** baleful, pailful, wailful.

AL′i– **2.** aly, bailie, Bailey, daily, gaily, scaly, snaily, grayly, traily, taily, waily **3.** shillalah **4.** apercaillie, ukelele, counterpaly; *see* also **AL′li–** palely etc. below.

AL′if– **2.** aleph, alef, bailiff, calif, caliph **3.** bumbailiff.

AL′ij– **2.** bailage, scalage, sailage **3.** *retailage*, curtailage.

AL′ik– **2.** Gaelic, malic, Salic.

AL′iks– **2.** calix, calyx, Salix **4.** epicalyx.

AL′ing– **2.** ailing, bailing, failing, hailing, jailing, scaling, mailing, paling, railing, grayling, trailing, sailing, tailing, veiling, wailing, whaling **3.** unfailing, regaling, inhaling, exhaling, *blackmailing*, impaling, *wholesaling*, detailing, retailing, entailing, curtailing, *dovetailing*, availing, prevailing, bewailing **4.** countervailing.

AL′ish– **2.** palish, frailish, stalish.

AL′less– **2.** aleless, bailless, failless, jailless, scaleless, maleless, mailless, nailless, trailless, sailless, tailless, veilless, whaleless.

AL′li– **2.** halely, palely, frailly, stalely; *see* also **AL′i–** aly etc. above.

AL′ment– **2.** ailment, bailment **3.** regalement, impalement, derailment, assailment, retailment, entailment, curtailment, availment, bewailment.

AL′o– **2.** halo **3.** Canelo, canelo.

AL′ya– **5.** regalia, Centralia, Australia, azalea **6.** paraphernalia; *see* also **AL′i–a–** galea, etc.

AL′yun– **3.** alien **4.** regalian, Centralian, Australian, Pygmalion **5.** bacchanalian, saturnalian **6.** sesquipedalian, tatterdemalion; *see* also **AL′i–an–** alien etc.

AM′a– **2.** Fama, lama, Brahma, drama, krama, squama **3.** kalema, salema, Bahama.

A′man– **2.** dayman, cayman, layman, drayman **3.** *highwayman*; *see* also **AM′en–** amen etc. below.

AM′ant– **2.** claimant, clamant **3.** adhamant, reclaimant.

AM′at– **2.** hamate, squamate **3.** desquamate.

AMB′er– **2.** chamber **3.** bedchamber **4.** antechamber

AMB′rik– **2.** cambric.

AM′en– **2.** amen, Haman, daimen, flamen, Bremen, stamen **3.** velamen, clinamen, foramen, duramen, examen, putamen, gravamen; *see* also **A′man–** dayman etc. above.

AM′ent– **2.** ament, pament, payment, raiment **3.** allayment, repayment, defrayment, betrayment.

AM′er– **2.** aimer, amor, gamer, lamer, blamer, claimer, maimer, namer, framer, shamer, tamer **3.** acclaimer, declaimer, reclaimer, proclaimer, disclaimer, exclaimer, nicknamer, testamur.

AM′est– **2.** gamest, lamest, tamest; and verbs ending in **AM** plus –est.

AM′ful– **2.** aimful, gameful, blameful, shameful.

AM′i– **2.** Amy, gamy, Jamie, flamy, Mamie, rami, zemi.

AM′ing– **2.** aiming, gaming, laming, blaming, flaming, claiming, maiming, naming, framing, shaming, taming **3.** acclaiming, declaiming, reclaiming, proclaiming, disclaiming, exclaiming, inflaming nicknaming, misnaming.

AM'ish– 2. lamish, samish, Samish, tamish.

AM'less– 2. aimless, fameless, gameless, blameless, claimless, flameless, nameless, frameless shameless, tameless 3. *nicknameless.*

AM'li– 2. gamely, lamely, namely, samely, tamely.

AM'ness– 2. gameness, lameness, sameness, tameness.

AM'us– 2. Amos, famous, hamus, hamous, ramus, ramous, samos, shame us etc. squamous 3. mandamus, biramous 4. ignoramus.

AN'a– 2. ana, Dana, Rana, rena, scena 3. arcana, campana 4. Cartagena, omniana, Geoplana 5. Americana.

AN'al– 2. banal, manal, veinal 3. bimanal 4. septimanal, interveinal.

AN'an– 2. Canaan, rainin' etc.

AND'er– 3. remainder, attainder, detainder.

AN'er– 2. chainer, feigner, caner, gainer, plainer, saner, seiner, stainer, vainer 3. urbaner, ordainer, profaner, chicaner, complainer, humaner, inaner, retainer, abstainer.

A'ness– 2. gayness, grayness, greyness; *see* also **AN'ness–** plainness etc. below.

AN'est– 2. plainest, sanest, vainest 3. urbanest, profanest, humanest, inanest; and verbs ending in **AN** plus –est.

AN'ful– 2. baneful, gainful, painful 3. disdainful, ungainful, complainful.

AN'i– 2. cany, Janey, rainy, brainy, grainy, veiny, zany 4. Allegheny, miscellany, castellany.

AN'ij– 2. chainage, drainage, cranage, trainage.

AN'ing– 2. deigning, feigning, caning, planing, paining, reigning, reining, raining, craning, training, straining, seining, waning 3. ordaining, disdaining, complaining, *airplaning*, campaigning, arraigning, unreining, detraining, entraining, restraining, retaining 4. uncomplaining, aquaplaning, ascertaining, entertaining.

AN'ish– 2. Danish, sanish, vainish 3. urbanish.

ANJ'el– 2. angel 3. archangel.

ANJ'er– 2. changer, danger, manger, ranger, stranger 3. exchanger, endanger, arranger, deranger, *bushranger*, estranger 4. money-changer, interchanger, rearranger, disarranger.

ANJ'est– 2. strangest; and verbs ending in **ANJ** plus –est.

ANJ'ez– 2. changes, ranges, granges 3. exchanges, shortchanges, arranges, deranges, estranges 4. rearranges, prearranges, interchanges, disarranges.

ANJ'i– 2. mangy, rangy.

ANJ'ing– 2. changing, ranging 3. unchanging, exchanging, shortchanging, estranging 4. interchanging, rearranging, prearranging, disarranging.

ANJ'less– 2. changeless, mangeless, rangeless, grangeless 3. exchangeless.

ANJ'li– 2. Rangeley, strangely.

ANJ'ling– 2. changeling, strangeling.

ANJ'ment– 2. changement 3. arrangement, derangement, estrangement 4. rearrangement, prearrangement, disarrangement.

ANJ'ness– 2. strangeness.

AN'less– 2. chainless, gainless, maneless, painless, rainless, brainless, grainless, strainless, stainless, vaneless, veinless, waneless, swainless.

AN'li– 2. fainly, plainly, mainly, sanely, vainly 3. urbanely, profanely, ungainly, humanely, insanely 4. inhumanely.

AN'ment– 3. enchainment, ordainment, regainment, arraignment, attainment, detainment, retainment **4.** reordainment, ascertainment, entertainment.

AN'ness– **2.** plainness, saneness, vainness **3.** urbaneness, profaneness, humaneness, inaneness, insaneness; *see* also **A'ness–** gayness etc. above.

AN'o– **2.** Drano **3.** volcano, sereno [Sp.].

ANT'ed– **2.** fainted, feinted, painted, sainted, tainted **3.** ensainted, attainted, acquainted **4.** unacquainted.

ANT'er– **2.** fainter, feinter, painter, quainter.

ANT'est– **2.** faintest, quaintest.

ANT'i– **2.** dainty, fainty.

ANT'if– **2.** plaintiff **3.** coplaintiff.

ANT'ing– **2.** fainting, feinting, painting, sainting, tainting **3.** repainting, attainting, acquainting.

ANT'ish– **2.** faintish, saintish.

ANT'iv– **2.** plaintive **3.** complaintive, constraintive.

ANT'li– **2.** faintly, saintly, quaintly **3.** unfaintly, unsaintly.

ANT'ness– **2.** faintness, quaintness.

AN'um– **3.** Arcanum, Solanum.

AN'us– **2.** heinous, Janus, manus, veinous, pain us **3.** ananas, Silvanus **4.** decumanus.

A'o– **2.** kayo, bleo, Mayo **3.** cacao.

A'on– **2.** rayon, crayon **3.** Lycaon.

A'or– **2.** mayor **3.** mormaor, conveyor, purveyor, surveyor; *see* **A'er–** feyer etc. above.

A'os– **2.** chaos, naos, Naos, Taos **3.** pronaos **4.** epinaos.

AP'en– **2.** shapen, tapen **3.** unshapen, misshapen.

AP'er– **2.** aper, gaper, caper, paper, draper, scraper, sapor, shaper, taper, tapir, vapor **3.** nordcaper, *landscaper*, escaper, *wallpaper*, *gunpaper*, *newspaper*, *skyscraper*, red-taper.

AP'erz– apers etc., *see* **AP'er–** aper etc. above, plus "s" or "'s."

AP'i– **2.** gapy, grapy, crapy, crepy, scrapy **3.** red-tapey.

AP'ing– **2.** aping, gaping, Peiping, draping, scraping, shaping, taping **3.** escaping, *landscaping*, *skyscraping*, reshaping, misshaping, retaping.

AP'is– **2.** apis, tapis **3.** sinapis, Serapis.

AP'ish– **2.** apish, gapish, papish **3.** red-tapish.

AP'ist– **2.** papist, tapist **3.** *landscapist*, escapist, red-tapist.

AP'izm– **2.** apism, papism **3.** red-tapism.

AP'l– **2.** capel, maple, papal, staple **3.** nonpapal **4.** antipapal.

AP'less– **2.** capeless, grapeless, shapeless, tapeless.

AP'let– **2.** apelet, capelet, grapelet.

AP'li– **2.** shapely **3.** unshapely, *shipshapely.*

AP'lz– **2.** maples, Naples, staples.

AP'on– **2.** capon, tape on etc.

AP'ron– **2.** apron, napron.

AR'a– **2.** Eire, Sara, Sarah, tera **3.** Madeira, caldera, Sahara, cascara, gallera.

AR'ans– **3.** forbearance, appearance **4.** unforbearance.

AR'er– **2.** airer, error, bearer, barer, darer, fairer, farer, carer, scarer, blarer, flarer, glarer, snarer, pairer, parer, sparer, rarer, sharer, tearer, terror, starer, wearer, swearer, squarer **3.** sword-bearer, talebearer, pallbearer, cupbearer, mace-bearer, outdarer, wayfarer, seafarer, declarer, ensnarer, repairer, preparer, impairer, comparer, despairer, awarer, forswearer **4.** standard-bearer, armor-bearer.

AR'erz– airers etc., *see* **AR'er–** airer etc. above, plus "s" or "'s."

AR'ess– **2.** heiress, bearess **3.** coheiress.

AR'est– **2.** barest, fairest, rarest, squarest **3.** unfairest; and verbs ending in **AR** plus -est.

AR'ez– **2.** Ares, Aries, Dares, caries, Lares, nares, paries **4.** Buenos Aires.

AR'ful– **2.** dareful, careful, prayerful **3.** uncareful, despairful.

AR'i– **2.** airy, aerie, chary, dairy, fairy, faerie, Gary, hairy, Carey, scary, lairy, blary, flary, glary, glairy, clary, Mary, nary, snary, prairie, seri, stary, vary, wary; *see* also **AR'i–** scarry etc.; **AR'i–** Barrie etc.; **ER'i–** berry etc. **3.** *quandary*, vagary, *rosemary*, canary, contrary, unwary **4.** syllabary, columbary, dromedary, lapidary, prebendary, legendary, secondary, nucleary, tertiary, formicary, persicary, tutelary, mammilary, capillary, ancillary, axillary, maxillary, corollary, medullary, formulary, scapulary, titulary, calamary, lachrymary, customary, millenary, parcenary, mercenary, centenary, ordinary, culinary, seminary, luminary, doctrinary, sanguinary, legionary, regionary, pulmonary, coronary, sublunary, stationary, cautionary, missionary, dictionary, functionary, pensionary, passionary, questionary, visionary, numerary, vulnerary, Tipperary, literary, honorary, temporary, arbitrary, *accessary*, necessary, emissary, commissary, janissary, adversary, dietary, proletary, planetary, monetary, secretary, military, solitary, sanitary, dignitary, sedentary, fragmentary, commentary, momentary, voluntary, tributary, salutary, reliquary, antiquary, January, February, statuary, actuary, sanctuary, sumptuary, mortuary, estuary, salivary, cassowary **5.** subsidiary, stipendiary, incendiary, pecuniary, fiduciary, apothecary, hypothecary, epistolary, vocabulary, constabulary, accustomary, bicentenary, tercentenary, imaginary, disciplinary, preliminary, veterinary, ganglionary, probationary, precautionary, discretionary, processionary, additionary, traditionary, seditionary, petitionary, tuitionary, reactionary, confectionary, ablutionary, revisionary, divisionary, provisionary, itinerary, contemporary, extemporary, unnecessary, proprietary, depositary, prothonotary, contributary, residuary, obituary, tumultuary, voluptuary **6.** beneficiary, intermediary, accidentiary, adminiculary, prolegomenary, valetudinary, latitudinary, multitudinary, eleemosynary, insurrectionary, elocutionary, evolutionary, revolutionary, supernumerary **7.** consuetudinary, vicissitudinary.

AR'id– **2.** varied **3.** unvaried; *see* also **AR'id–** carried etc.; **ER'id–** berried etc.

AR'ing– **2.** airing, baring, bearing, daring, faring, haring, herring, caring, chairing, scaring, blaring, flaring, glaring, pairing, paring, sparing, sharing, tearing, staring, wearing, Waring, swearing, squaring **3.** *talebearing*, *seafaring*, declaring, repairing, impairing, despairing, outstaring, outwearing, outswearing, forswearing **4.** overbearing, undeclaring.

AR'is– **2.** naris **3.** Polaris' **4.** cucullaris.

AR'ish– **2.** bearish, barish, fairish, garish, cherish, rarish, squarish **3.** nightmarish **4.** debonairish.

AR'less– **2.** airless, heirless, hairless, careless, chairless, glareless, snareless, pairless, spareless, prayerless, shareless, tareless, stairless.

AR'li– **2.** barely, fairly, rarely, squarely, yarely **3.** unfairly.

AR'line– **2.** airline, hairline.

AR'man– **2.** airman, chairman.

AR'ness– **2.** bareness, fairness, spareness, rareness, thereness, squareness, whereness **3.** *threadbareness*, unfairness, awareness **4.** debonairness, unawareness.

AR'o– **2.** aero, faro, Pharaoh **3.** ranchero, cochero, vaquero, bolero, llanero, dinero, sombrero, torero [all Sp.] **4.** sudadero, matadero, hacendero, caballero, bandolero, campanero, zapatero [all Sp.]; *see* also **AR'o–** arrow etc.

AR'u– **2.** Meru, Nehru.

AR'um– **2.** arum, garum, harem, carrom, scare 'em etc. **4.** harumscarum **9.** scientia scientiarum.

AS'a– **2.** Asa, mesa, presa [It.], vasa [L.] **3.** cabeza [Sp.].

AS'al– **2.** basal, casal, vasal **3.** oasal.

AS'eez– **2.** bases **3.** oases.

AS'en– **2.** basin, facin' etc., hasten, Jason, chasten, mason, sasin **3.** *washbasin*, enchasten, freemason, *stonemason*; *see* also **AS'on–** caisson etc. below.

AS'ens– **3.** abaisance, obeisance, adjacence, complaisance, complacence, renascence, connascence **4.** interjacence, uncomplaisance.

AS'ent– **2.** jacent, nascent, naissant **3.** obeisant, subjacent, adjacent, complacent, renascent, renaissant, connascent **4.** circumjacent, interjacent, uncomplacent.

AS'er– **2.** Acer, baser, chaser, facer, caser, lacer, placer, macer, pacer, spacer, racer, bracer, tracer **3.** abaser, debaser, defacer, effacer, eraser, horse racer, embracer, begracer, disgracer, retracer, encaser, belacer, enlacer, unlacer, grimacer, outpacer, replacer, misplacer, displacer **4.** steeplechaser, interlacer

AS'ez– aces, etc. *see* **AS–** ace etc. above, plus "s" or "'s."

AS'ful– **2.** spaceful, graceful **3.** ungraceful, disgraceful.

ASH'a– **2.** Asia, geisha **3.** Acacia, Dalmatia.

ASH'al– **2.** facial, glacial, spatial, racial **3.** abbatial, palatial, prelatial, primatial **4.** unifacial, interspatial, interracial.

ASH'an– **2.** Asian **3.** predacean, phocacean, cetacean, testacean, crustacean; *see* also **ASH'un–** nation etc. below.

ASH'ens– **2.** facients, patience, patients **3.** impatience, outpatients.

ASH'ent– **2.** facient, patient **3.** impatient, outpatient **4.** sorbefacient, rubefacient, calefacient, tumefacient, stupefacient, somnifacient, liquefacient.

ASH'un– **2.** nation, ration, station **3.** cibation, libation, limbation, jobation, probation, placation, vacation, peccation, plication, sulcation, truncation, location, vocation, furcation, piscation, gradation, foundation, laudation, sudation, creation, legation, ligation, rogation, purgation, jugation, striation, alation, halation, ablation, oblation, sublation, elation, delation, gelation, relation, velation, deflation, sufflation, inflation, conflation, dilation, vallation, illation, collation, prolation, cremation, sigmation, himation, gemmation, commation, summation, formation, planation, adnation, enation, agnation, signation, cognation, damnation, conation, donation, phonation, pronation, lunation, libration, vibration, hydration, ceration, spheration, migration, liration, oration, moration, nitration, titration, filtration, curation, duration, neuration, gyration, cessation, causation, pausation, natation, jactation, lactation, tractation, dictation, nictation, citation, saltation, peltation, cantation, plantation, dentation, mentation, tentation, floatation, notation, potation, rotation, quotation, votation, captation, septation, flirtation, hortation, curtation, substation, gestation, testation, crustation, gustation, guttation, lutation, mutation, nutation, putation, equation, lavation, ovation, novation, starvation, nervation, servation, curvation, laxation, taxation, vexation, fixation, luxation, fluxation **4.** reprobation, approbation, perturbation, accubation, incubation, titubation, intubation, desiccation, exsiccation, deprecation, imprecation, comprecation, albication, radication, abdication, dedication, medication, predication, indication, vindication, syndication, replication, triplication, implication, complication, application, supplication, duplication, explication, varication, fabrication, imbrication, lubrication, rubrication, lorication, extrication, vesication, mastication, rustication, toxication, allocation, collocation, dislocation, embrocation, avocation, convocation, provocation, demarcation, altercation, bifurcation, confiscation, obfuscation, coruscation, degradation, aggradation, depredation, validation, lapidation, trepidation, liquidation, emendation, commendation, inundation, retardation, denudation, desudation, transudation, trabeation, ideation, nucleation, permeation, lineation, recreation, procreation, propagation, divagation, delegation, relegation, allegation, abnegation, segregation, aggregation, congregation, obligation, fumigation, irrigation, litigation, mitigation, castigation, instigation, fustigation, elongation, prolongation, abrogation, derogation, objurgation, expurgation, subjugation, conjugation, corrugation, fasciation, radiation, mediation, ciliation, filiation, palliation, foliation, spoliation, expiation, variation, seriation, satiation, vitiation, aviation, obviation, deviation, debarkation, embarkation, demarkation, inhalation, exhalation, congelation, correlation, revelation, insufflation, sibilation, jubilation, strigilation, vigilation, depilation, compilation, ventilation, mutilation, installation, flabellation, cancellation, flagellation, lamellation, crenellation, compellation, appellation, tessellation, castellation, constellation, vacillation, oscillation, fibrillation, titillation, scintillation, distillation, instillation, decollation, percolation, violation, immolation, desolation, isolation, insolation, consolation, avolation, legislation, contemplation, tabulation, tribulation, ambulation, peculation, speculation, calculation, circulation, osculation, adulation, undulation, stridulation, modulation, nodulation, regulation, angulation, ululation, emulation, simulation, stimulation, nummulation, formulation, cumulation, granulation, crenulation, annulation, population, stipulation, sporulation, insulation, pustulation, ovulation, defamation, acclamation, declamation, reclamation, proclamation, exclamation, desquamation, racemation, decimation, sublimation, acclimation, collimation, animation, intimation, estimation, inflammation, consummation, affirmation, confirmation, deformation, reformation, malformation, information, conformation, transformation, inhumation, exhumation, lachrymation, profanation, explanation, emanation, impanation, hyphenation, alienation, catenation, impregnation, indignation, obsignation, designation, resignation, assignation, consignation, combination, turbination, vaccination, fascination, ordination, pagination, machination, declination, reclination, inclination, pollination, lamination, gemination, semination, culmination, fulmination, commination, domination, nomination, germination, termination, vermination, lumination, rumination, supination, fibrination, destination, glutination, ruination, divination, condemnation, carbonation, condonation, coronation, personation, detonation, intonation, incarnation, hibernation, alternation, consternation, subornation, eburnation, dissipation, inculpation, exculpation, syncopation, extirpation, usurpation, occupation, nuncupation, declaration, reparation, preparation, separation, celebration, palpebration, cerebration, terebration, vertebration, calibration, adumbration, lucubration, obsecration, desecration, consecration, execration, dehydration, liberation, verberation, laceration, maceration, ulceration, carceration, federation, ponderation, moderation, toleration, numeration, generation, veneration, cineration, operation, asperation, desperation, iteration, literation, alteration, severation, integration, emigration, remigration, immigration, transmigration, admiration, aspiration, respiration, transpiration, inspiration, perspiration, suspiration, expiration, decoration, adoration, perforation, coloration, imploration, exploration, pignoration, corporation, peroration, restoration, aberration, saburration, susurration, penetration, impetration, perpetration, arbitration, infiltration, concentration, orchestration, fenestration, sequestration, registration, ministration, demonstration, remonstration, illustration, procuration, obduration, induration, figuration, fulguration, objuration, conjuration, depuration, suppuration, mensuration, maturation, saturation, trituration, suturation, condensation, compensation, dispensation, conversation, endorsation, incrassation, inspissation, succussation, decussation, dilatation, delactation, affectation, delectation, humectation, expectation, reluctation, eructation, hebetation, vegetation, habitation, dubitation, recitation, incitation, oscitation, excitation, meditation, agitation, digitation, cogitation, gurgitation, militation, imitation, limitation, sanitation, capitation, crepitation, palpitation, irritation, hesitation, visitation, nictitation, gravitation, levitation, invitation, exaltation, occultation, auscultation, consultation, exultation, decantation, recantation, incantation, implantation, transplantation, indentation, lamentation, segmentation, pigmentation, augmentation, commentation, fomentation, fermentation, frumentation, presentation, ostentation, sustentation, frequentation, confrontation, denotation, annotation, connotation, compotation, misquotation, adaptation, impartation, dissertation, dehortation, exhortation, deportation, importation, transportation, exportation, devastation, infestation, molestation, forestation, detestation, intestation, contestation, protestation, attestation, reinstation, degustation, incrustation, confutation, refutation, salutation, immutation, commutation, permutation, transmutation, deputation, reputation, amputation, imputation, computation, disputation, graduation, valuation, adequation, actuation, punctuation, fluctuation, fructuation, situation, excavation, aggravation, depravation, elevation, salivation, derivation, deprivation, cultivation, motivation, captivation, estivation, renovation, innovation, enervation, innervation, observation, reservation, preservation, conservation, decurvation, incurvation, relaxation, annexation, prefixation, affixation, suffixation, solmization **5.** disapprobation, exacerbation, hypothecation, syllabication, eradication, revindication, adjudication, albification, pacification, specification, calcification, dulcification, edification, nidification, codification, modification, deification, salification, qualification, vilification, mellification, jollification, mollification, nullification, prolification, amplification, simplification, magnification, dignification, signification, damnification, unification, aerification, clarification, verification, nigrification, glorification, petrification, thurification, purification, falsification, versification, classification, ossification, ratification, gratification, lactification, rectification, sanctification, notification, certification, fortification, mortification, testification, justification, mystification, vivification, republication, multiplication, misapplication, reduplication, quadruplication, communication, prevarication, authentication, domestication, sophistication, prognostication, intoxication, reciprocation, equivocation, retrogradation, invalidation, consolidation, intimidation, delapidation, recommendation, accomodation, enucleation, delineation, allineation, variegation, investigation, interrogation, emaciation, depreciation, appreciation, officiation, enunciation, denunciation, renunciation, annunciation, pronunciation, excruciation, eradiation, irradiation, remediation, repudiation, retaliation, conciliation, affiliation, humiliation, defoliation, exfoliation, despoliation, calumniation, columniation, inebriation, excoriation, appropriation, expropriation, repatriation, expatriation, infuriation, luxuriation, expatiation, ingratiation, initiation, propitiation, novitiation, substantiation, nogotiation, alleviation, abbreviation, lixiviation, exuviation, asphyxiation, disembarkation, intercalation, interrelation, invigilation, annihilation, assimilation, horripilation, circumvallation, interpellation, vitriolation, etiolation, interpolation, disconsolation, confabulation, somnambulation, perambulation, noctambulation, ejaculation, fasciculation, vermiculation, matriculation, reticulation, denticulation, articulation, gesticulation, miscalculation, tuberculation, emasculation, triangulation, dissimulation, accumulation, manipulation, depopulation, repopulation, congratulation, capitulation, expostulation, amalgamation reanimation, approximation, reaffirmation, misinformation, malconformation, hydrogenation, alienation, concatenation, rejuvenation, hallucination, subordination, preordination, coordination, imagination, origination, disinclination, contamination, insemination, dissemination, elimination, recrimination, incrimination, discrimination, abomination, predomination, denomination, renomination, prenomination, determination, extermination, acumination, illumination, peregrination, indoctrination, assassination, procrastination, predestination, agglutination, conglutination, impersonation, anticipation, participation, emancipation, preoccupation, exhilaration, deliberation, reverberation, incarceration, evisceration, confederation, desideration, consideration, preponderation, immoderation, vociferation, proliferation, exaggeration, refrigeration, acceleration, deceleration, intoleration, concameration, agglomeration, conglomeration, enumeration, renumeration, degeneration, regeneration, incineration, itineration, exoneration, remuneration, co-operation, exasperation, depauperation, recuperation, vituperation, commiseration, reiteration, obliteration, alliteration, transliteration, adulteration, asseveration, redintegration, elaboration, collaboration, corroboration, imperforation, invigoration, amelioration, deterioration, discoloration, commemoration, incorporation, expectoration, recalcitration, administration, prefiguration, transfiguration, inauguration, commensuration, circumgyration, intravasation, extravasation, improvisation, tergiversation, interpretation, inhabitation, capacitation, felicitation, solicitation, resuscitation, premeditation, exagitation, recogitation, precogitation, regurgitation, habilitation, debilitation, facilitation, delimitation, exploitation, decapitation, decrepitation, precipitation, revisitation, necessitation, ornamentation, supplementation, sedimentation, regimentation, alimentation, documentation, argumentation, instrumentation, representation, inadaptation, coadaptation, manifestation, deforestation, reforestation, circumnutation, evaluation, revaluation, attenuation, extenuation, insinuation, continuation, effectuation, perpetration, habituation, accentuation, insalivation, recaptivation, ostracization, hybridization, iridization, oxidization, aggrandization, standardization, syllogization, eulogization, catechization, focalization, vocalization, feudalization, vandalization, idealization, realization, legalization, racialization, socialization, alkalization, formalization, normalization, penalization, moralization, centralization, neutralization, vitalization, tantalization, totalization, equalization, chattelization, stabilization, mobilization, sterilization, fertilization, utilization, tranquilization, civilization, crystallization, verbalization, symbolization, idolization, formulization, minimization, victimization, atomization, urbanization, vulcanization, organization, Christianization, humanization, galvanization, pollenization, scrutinization, solemnization, columnization, carbonization, ionization, colonization, mnemonization, harmonization, canonization, synchronization, patronization, modernization, fraternization, polarization, summarization, mercerization, mesmerization, pauperization, cauterization, pulverization, arborization, theorization, authorization, vaporization, temporization, proctorization, phosphorization, pasteurization, sulphurization, dramatization, stigmatization, magnetization, monetization, sensitization, amortization, analyzation, paralyzation **6.** contraindication, decalcification, solidification, disqualification, exemplification, indemnification, saponification, personification, transmogrification, electrification, emulsification, intensification, diversification, beatification, identification, excommunication, unsophistication, interlineation, supererogation, mispronunciation, intermediation, domiciliation, reconciliation, misappropriation, transubstantiation, consubstantiation, circumstantiation, differentiation, tintinnabulation, circumambulation, recapitulation, abalienation, ratiocination, insubordination, inco-ordination, indiscrimination, predetermination, indetermination, reconsideration, inconsideration, maladministration, incapacitation, unpremeditation, prestidigitation, interdigitation, rehabilitation, experimentation, misrepresentation, individuation, discontinuation, superannuation, deoxidization, devocalization, commercialization, materialization, decimalization, nationalization, liberalization, generalization, demoralization, decentralization, naturalization, capitalization, devitalization, revitalization, immortalization, visualization, caramelization, demobilization, remobilization, monopolization, legitimization, economization, anatomization, epitomization, reorganization, inorganization, disorganization, antagonization, recolonization, familiarization, depolarization, formularization, popularization, militarization, polymerization, characterization, deodorization, categorization, systematization, acclimatization, aromatization, alphabetization, anesthetization, arithmetization, demonetization, desensitization **7.** intercommunication, intercolumniation, denationalization, denaturalization, universalization, spiritualization, Americanization **8.** internationalization, individualization, intellectualization.

ASH′und– **2.** rationed, stationed **3.** vacationed.

ASH′unz– nations etc., *see* **ASH′un–** nation etc. above, plus "s" or "'s."

ASH′us– **2.** caseous, spacious, gracious **3.** sebaceous, bibacious, bulbaceous, herbaceous, edacious, predaceous, mendacious, bodacious, smordacious, audacious, safacious, fugacious, salacious, fallacious, fumacious, tenacious, pugnacious, capacious, rapacious, rampacious, feracious, veracious, ungracious, disgracious, voracious flirtatious, setaceous, rutaceous, sequacious, loquacious, vivacious, vexatious **4.** efficacious, perspicacious, pervicacious, contumacious, pertinacious, incapacious, orchidaceous, corallaceous, liliaceous, scoriaceous, capillaceous, farinaceous, carbonaceous, saponaceous, camphoraceous, pulveraceous, frumentaceous, ostentatious, disputatious **5.** inefficacious.

AS′i– **2.** lacy, racy, Gracie, precis, Tracy **4.** contumacy, Betsy-Tacy.

AS′ik– **2.** basic, phasic **3.** tribasic, aphasic **4.** diabasic, polybasic, monophasic, carapacic, diastasic.

AS′in– **2.** basin, sasin, facin' etc. **3.** washbasin; *see* also **AS′on–** caisson etc. below.

AS′ing– **2.** acing, basing, chasing, facing, casing, lacing, placing, pacing, spacing, racing, bracing, tracing **3.** abasing, debasing, effacing, defacing, refacing, encasing, belacing, enlacing, unlacing, shoe lacing, replacing, misplacing, outpacing, horseracing, embracing, grimacing, displacing, erasing, disgracing, retracing **4.** steeplechasing, interlacing.

AS′is– **2.** basis, phasis, glacis, crasis, stasis **3.** oasis.

AS′iv– **2.** suasive **3.** occasive, abrasive, assuasive, dissuasive, persuasive, evasive, invasive, pervasive.

AS′less– **2.** aceless, baseless, faceless, caseless, laceless, placeless, maceless, paceless, spaceless, raceless, graceless, braceless, traceless, vaseless **3.** embraceless.

AS′let– **2.** lacelet, bracelet.

AS′li– **2.** basely **4.** commonplacely.

AS′ment– **2.** basement, casement, placement **3.** abasement, effacement, defacement, encasement, enlacement, replacement, emplacement, displacement, misplacement, embracement, retracement.

AS′o– **2.** peso, say-so **3.** Congreso.

AS′on– **2.** caisson, lace on, *meson*; *see* also **AS′en–** basin etc. above.

AST′ed– **2.** basted, hasted, pasted, tasted, wasted, waisted **3.** unbasted, unpasted, untasted, unwasted, long-waisted, high-waisted, short-waisted.

AST′er– **2.** baster, chaster, paster, taster, waster **3.** foretaster.

AST′ful– **2.** tasteful, wasteful **3.** distasteful, unwasteful.

AST′i– **2.** hasty, pasty, tasty **3.** unhasty, untasty.

AST′ij– **2.** wastage.

AST′ing– **2.** basting, hasting, pasting, tasting, wasting **3.** unbasting, untasting, foretasting, unwasting.

AST′ingz– bastings etc., *see* **AST′ing–** basting etc. above, plus "s" or "'s"; 2. Hastings.

AST′less– **2.** basteless, hasteless, pasteless, tasteless, wasteless, waistless.

AST′ri– **2.** pastry.

AS′um– **3.** omasum **4.** abomasum.

AT′a– **2.** Eta, Beta, data, Theta, rata, strata, Zeta **3.** albata, Caudata, relata, Squamata, pro rata **4.** Vertebrata, ultimata **5.** Invertebrata, desiderata.

AT′al– **2.** datal, fatal, natal, ratal, stratal, statal **3.** prenatal, postnatal, substratal.

AT′e– Ate etc., *see* **AT′i–** Ate etc. below.

AT′ed– **2.** bated, baited, dated, fated, fêted, gated, gaited, hated, plated, plaited, mated, pated, rated, grated, prated, sated, stated, waited, weighted **3.** abated, debated, rebated, predated, postdated, outdated, created, ill-fated, elated, belated, related, deflated, inflated, checkmated, stalemated, cremated, berated, frustrated, instated, awaited **4.** antedated, validated, liquidated, inundated, ideated, permeated, re-created, procreated, propagated, delegated, relegated, abnegated, aggregated, segregated, obligated, fumigated, irrigated, litigated, mitigated, instigated, subjugated, corrugated, radiated, mediated, predicated, indicated, vindicated, syndicated, implicated, complicated, duplicated, supplicated, fabricated, lubricated, extricated, rusticated, advocated, altercated, confiscated, educated, unrelated, correlated, ventilated, scintillated, mutilated, percolated, contemplated, tabulated, modulated, regulated, speculated, circulated, osculated, emulated, formulated, granulated, stipulated, acclimated, animated, intimated, estimated, consummated, emanated, hyphenated, designated, terminated, ruminated, fascinated, carbonated, intonated, hibernated, addle-pated, dissipated, syncopated separated, celebrated, desecrated, consecrated, federated, moderated, tolerated, generated, venerated, operated, emigrated, perforated, decorated, underrated, penetrated, arbitrated, concentrated, demonstrated, illustrated, saturated, compensated, meditated, agitated, cogitated, imitated, palpitated, irritated, hesitated, gravitated, reinstated, amputated, graduated, situated, antiquated, actuated, punctuated, fluctuated, aggravated, elevated, cultivated, captivated, renovated **5.** elucidated, invalidated, consolidated, intimidated, dilapidated, accommodated, repudiated, retaliated, affiliated, humiliated, appropriated, emaciated, ingratiated, appreciated, depreciated, initiated, enunciated, negotiated, associated, annihilated, assimilated, matriculated, articulated, gesticulated, inoculated, accumulated, manipulated, congratulated, capitulated, approximated, subordinated, coordinated, originated, contaminated, disseminated, illuminated, opinionated, impersonated, anticipated, participated, emancipated, exaggerated, accelerated, enumerated, exonerated, remunerated, cooperated, recuperated, commiserated, reiterated, obliterated, disintegrated, elaborated, collaborated, corroborated, commemorated, evaporated, incorporated, inaugurated, premeditated, debilitated, facilitated, precipitated, necessitated, felicitated, resuscitated, orientated, evaluated, devaluated, insinuated, infatuated, accentuated **6.** circumstantiated, differentiated, recapitulated, incapacitated.

AT′en– **2.** datin′ etc., straighten, straiten, Satan.

AT′ent– **2.** latent, blatant, natant, patent **3.** inflatant, dilatant.

AT′er– **2.** bater, baiter, cater, dater, gaiter, hater, skater, later, plater, slater, mater, pater, rater, crater, frater, greater, grater, prater, traitor, satyr, sater, waiter, ′tater, stater **3.** abater, debater, rebater, placater, vacatur, Decatur, elater, delater, relater, Dis pater, confrater, barrater **4.** allocatur, deleatur, imprimatur, annotater, exequatur; *see* also **AT′or–** traitor below.

AT′erz– baiters etc., *see* **AT′er–** baiter etc. above, plus "s" or "′s."

AT′est– **2.** latest, greatest; and verbs ending in **AT** plus –est.

AT′ez– **2.** vates **3.** Primates, penates, Euphrates.

AT′ful– **2.** fateful, hateful, plateful, grateful **3.** ungrateful.

ATH′er– **2.** bather, lather, swather.

ATH′ing– **2.** bathing, scathing, lathing, swathing.

ATH′os– **2.** bathos, pathos.

AT′i– **2.** Ate, eighty, Haiti, Katie, Leyte, slaty, maty, paty, weighty **4.** Jubilate, literati [both L.].

AT′im– **3.** verbatim, gradatim [L.] **4.** seriatim, literatim [both L.].

AT′ime– **2.** daytime, Maytime, playtime, pay time.

AT′ing– **2.** baiting, bating, dating, fêting, hating, skating, plating, plaiting, slating, mating, rating, grating, crating, prating, sating, waiting **3.** abating, debating, postdating, relating, inflating, awaiting **4.** antedating, emanating, reinstating, understating, overstating; and other verbs ending in **AT** plus -ing.

AT′ish– **2.** latish, slatish, straightish.

AT′iv– **2.** dative, native, stative **3.** creative, elative, prolative, dilative, frustrative **4.** approbative, reprobative, desiccative, exsiccative, deprecative, dedicative, medicative, vindicative, judicative, vellicative, replicative, implicative, complicative, duplicative, explicative, suffocative, invocative, educative, recreative, uncreative, procreative, propagative, abnegative, segregative, aggregative, irrigative, mitigative, abrogative, radiative, mediative, palliative, variative, nomenclative, ventilative, oscillative, violative, contemplative, legislative, speculative, calculative, circulative, modulative, regulative, emulative, simulative, stimulative, cumulative, animative, estimative, emanative, designative, geminative, dominative, nominative, germinative, terminative, ruminative, lacerative, federative, generative, operative, decorative, pignorative, ministrative, illustrative, suppurative, compensative, dispensative, vegetative, meditative, cogitative, qualitative, imitative, limitative, irritative, hesitative, quantitative, gravitative, facultative, innovative, punctuative **5.** eradicative, adjudicative, significative, multiplicative, communicative, prognosticative, elucidative, consolidative, accommodative, investigative, depreciative, appreciative, enunciative, denunciative, renunciative, pronunciative, associative, dissociative, retaliative, conciliative, appropriative, initiative, alleviative, gesticulative, coagulative, accumulative, manipulative, congratulative, expostulative, approximative, subordinative, imaginative, originative, contaminative, disseminative, recriminative, discriminative, denominative, determinative, illuminative, opinionative, anticipative, participative, exhilarative, deliberative, confederative, desiderative, exaggerative, accelerative, enumerative, exonerative, remunerative, inoperative, co-operative, recuperative, vituperative, reiterative, alliterative, corroborative, invigorative, ameliorative, deteriorative, commemorative, evaporative, administrative, interpretative, inhabitative, necessitative, resuscitative, premeditative, authoritative, insinuative, continuative **6.** insignificative, uncommunicative, excommunicative, unappreciative, recapitulative, unimaginative, unremunerative.

AT'less– **2.** baitless, dateless, fateless, gateless, gaitless, hateless, mateless, ateless, freightless, grateless, traitless, sateless, stateless, weightless **3.** estateless.

AT'li– **2.** lately, greatly, straitly, straightly, stately **3.** oblately, sedately, striately, prolately, truncately, palmately, innately, pinnately, ternately, ornately, irately, dentately, unstately, privately **4.** delicately, intricately, mediately, desolately, ultimately, intimately, proximately, obstinately, passionately, biternately, triternately, alternately, fortunately, separately, moderately, temperately, desperately, corporately, accurately, obdurately, insensately, decussately, adequately **5.** indelicately, immediately, appropriately, inviolately, disconsolately, immaculately, legitimately, approximately, subordinately, inordinately, co-ordinately, effeminately, discriminately, determinately, impassionately, compassionately, dispassionately, affectionately, proportionately, unfortunately, importunately, deliberately, considerately, immoderately, degenerately, intemperately, illiterately, elaborately, inaccurately, commensurately, precipitately, inadequately **6.** intermediately, inappropriately, unappropriately, illegitimately, insubordinately, indiscriminately, indeterminately, unaffectionately, disproportionately, inconsiderately, incommensurately.

AT'ness– **2.** lateness, greatness, straightness, straitness **3.** sedateness, oblateness, innateness, ornateness, irateness **5.** considerateness, appropriateness.

AT'o– **2.** Cato, Plato **3.** abeto [Sp.], pomato, tomato, potato.

AT'or– **2.** traitor **3.** abator, probator, plicator, locator, piscator, mandator, laudator, creator, legator, negator, ligator, viator, elator, delator, relator, dilator, collator, translator, cremator, senator, signator, spinator, donator, vibrator, migrator, orator, barrator, narrator, curator, gyrator, pulsator, natator, tractator, spectator, dictator, punctator, potator, rotator, portator, testator, equator, levator **4.** incubator, desiccator, exsiccator, deprecator, imprecator, abdicator, dedicator, predicator, indicator, vindicator, judicator, duplicator, explicator, fabricator, lubricator, rubricator, extricator, masticator, rusticator, inculcator, advocator, evocator, invocator, convocator, demarcator, confiscator, educator, depredator, liquidator, emendator, commendator, recreator, procreator, caveator, propagator, abnegator, obligator, alligator, fumigator, irrigator, litigator, mitigator, castigator, instigator, navigator, promulgator, compurgator, expurgator, subjugator, corrugator, gladiator, radiator, mediator, palliator, spoliator, expiator, vitiator, aviator, deviator, escalator, inhalator, nomenclator, revelator, depilator, ventilator, scintillator, mutilator, flagellator, vacillator, oscillator, desolator, percolator, violator, immolator, isolator, contemplator, tabulator, ambulator, speculator, calculator, inoculator, circulator, adulator, modulator, regulator, emulator, simulator, stimulator, granulator, stipulator, insulator, decimator, estimator, consummator, emanator, designator, propugnator, vaccinator, buccinator, fascinator, machinator, comminator, dominator, nominator, terminator, ruminator, divinator, cachinnator, personator, detonator, intonator, alternator, extirpator, separator, celebrator, lucubrator, desecrator, consecrator, execrator, Pantocrator, liberator, moderator, numerator, generator, venerator, operator, integrator, emigrator, immigrator, transmigrator, aspirator, respirator, inspirator, cospirator, decorator, perforator, perpetrator, arbitrator, concentrator, demonstrator, remonstrator, illustrator, instaurator, procurator, depurator, obturator, condensator, compensator, dispensator, meditator, agitator, cogitator, imitator, commentator, annotator, devastator, reinstator, commutator, amputator, valuator, elevator, cultivator, captivator, innovator, enervator, conservator, renovator, malaxator **5.** hypothecator, adjudicator, pacificator, edificator, modificator, qualificator, significator, purificator, classificator, multiplicator, communicator, prevaricator, sophisticator, prognosticator, reciprocator, equivocator, elucidator, invalidator, consolicator, intimidator, delineator, investigator, variegator, interrogator, depreciator, appreciator, officiator, enunciator, annunciator, pronunciator, repudiator, conciliator, calumniator, initiator, propitiator, negotiator, alleviator, abbreviator, asphyxiator, annihilator, assimilator, interpellator, interpolator, perambulator, gesticulator, emasculator, coagulator, accumulator, pedipulator, manipulator, congratulator, expostulator, amalgamator, rejuvenator, originator, contaminator, disseminator, eliminator, denominator, exterminator, illuminator, peregrinator, assassinator, procrastinator, predestinator, impersonator, anticipator, participator, emancipator, deliberator, vociferator, exaggerator, refrigerator, decelerator, accelerator, enumerator, regenerator, incinerator, remunerator, vituperator, commiserator, disintegrator, elaborator, collaborator, corroborator, invigorator, incorporator, administrator, inaugurator, improvisator, tergiversator, resuscitator, habilitator, facilitator, decapitator, evacuator, extenuator, insinuator, continuator, totalizator, catalyzator **6.** excommunicator, circumnavigator, supererogator, prestidigitator.

AT'oz– Cato's etc., *see* **AT'o–** Cato etc. above, plus "s" or "'s."

AT'ress– **2.** traitress, waitress **3.** oratress, dictatress **4.** imitatress.

AT'rik– **2.** matric, phratric.

AT'riks– **2.** matrix, patrix **3.** fundatrix, cicatrix, quadratrix, dictatrix, testatrix **4.** mediatrix, aviatrix, indicatrix, legislatrix, osculatrix, gubernatrix, nominatrix **5.** administratrix.

AT'ron– **2.** matron, natron, patron **3.** salnatron.

AT'um– **2.** datum, stratum **3.** relatum pomatum, quadratum, erratum, substratum, testatum **4.** seriatim, petrolatum, postulatum, ultimatum, Ageratum, capitatum **5.** desideratum.

AT'ur– **2.** nature **3.** denature **4.** nomenclature, legislature.

AT'us– **2.** date us, latus, flatus, stratus, stratous, status **3.** beatus, hiatus, afflatus, inflatus, senatus, conatus, postnatus, quadratus **4.** apparatus, saleratus, literatus, comitatus.

AV'a– **2.** Ava, deva.

AV'al– **2.** naval, navel **3.** precaval, octaval.

AV'en– **2.** haven, raven, graven, craven, shaven **3.** engraven, unshaven.

AV'er– **2.** laver, flavor, slaver, paver, raver, braver, graver, craver, saver, savor, shaver, waver, waiver, quaver, suaver **3.** cadaver, disfavor, enslaver, Papaver, engraver, depraver, *livesaver, time saver* **4.** demiquaver, semiquaver.

AV'erd– **2.** favored, flavored, wavered, quavered **3.** ill-favored, disfavored, unflavored.

AV'est– **2.** bravest, gravest, suavest.

AV'i– **2.** ave, Davy, Devi, cavy, cavie, slavey, navy, pavy, gravy, wavy **3.** agave, peccavi **4.** Mahadevi.

AV'id– **2.** David, flavid.

AV'ing– **2.** caving, laving, paving, raving, braving, craving, saving, shaving, staving, waving, waiving **3.** behaving, enclaving, enslaving, engraving, depraving, *lifesaving, timesaving* **4.** misbehaving, unenslaving.

AV'is– **2.** Avis, Davis, clavis, mavis, pavis **4.** rara avis [L.].

AV'ish– **2.** slavish, knavish, bravish.

AV'it– **2.** davit **3.** cessavit **4.** affidavit, indicavit, devastavit.

AV'less– **2.** caveless, slaveless, graveless, waveless.

AV'li– **2.** knavely, bravely, gravely, suavely.

AV'ment– **2.** lavement, pavement **3.** enslavement, engravement, depravement.

AV'ness– **2.** braveness, graveness, suaveness.

AV'o– **2.** Pavo, bravo **3.** octavo, centavo.

AV'or– **2.** favor, flavor, savor **3.** disfavor; *see* also **AV'er–** laver.

AV'ur– **2.** gravure **4.** pyrogravure, photogravure, autogravure.

AV'yer– **2.** clavier, pavior, savior, saviour, Xavier **3.** behavior **4.** misbehavior.

AZ'el– **2.** basil, gazel, Hazel, nasal **3.** witch-hazel, appraisal, Azazel **4.** reappraisal.

AZ'en– **2.** raisin, glazen, brazen.

AZ'er– **2.** gazer, hazer, lazar, blazer, mazer, raser, raiser, razor, phraser, grazer, praiser **3.** *stargazer*, upraiser, appraiser, self-praiser, dispraiser **4.** paraphraser.

AZ'ez– baizes etc., *see* **AZ–** baize etc. above, plus "s" or "'s."

AZH'al– **2.** basial **3.** gymnasial.

AZH'an– **2.** Asian **3.** Caucasian, Eurasian, equation **4.** Australasian; *see* also **AZH'un–** rasion etc. below.

AZH'er– **2.** azure, glazier, rasure, frasier, brazier, grazier **3.** embrasure, erasure.

AZH'un– **2.** rasion, suasion **3.** occasion, abrasion, corrosion, equation, persuasion, dissuasion, evasion, invasion, pervasion; *see* also **AZH'an–** Asian etc. above.

AZ'i– **2.** daisy, gazy, hazy, jasey, lazy, glazy, sleazy, mazy, phrasy, crazy **3.** patesi **4.** lackadaisy.

AZ'ing– **2.** dazing, gazing, hazing, lazing, blazing, glazing, braising, phrasing, grazing, praising.

AZ'iz– **2.** daisies.

AZ'less– **2.** hazeless, phraseless, praiseless.

AZ'ment– **3.** amazement, appraisement **4.** reappraisement.

AZ'o– **2.** Mazo **4.** Valparaiso.

AZ'on– **2.** scazon, blazon **3.** emblazon, Malmaison **4.** diapason.

AZ'ur– **2.** azure, rasure **3.** embrasure, erasure; *see* also **AZH'er–** azure etc. above.

A (ay)

3.

TRIPLE RHYMES IN A (pay'ab-le)

Primary or Secondary Accent Falls on Second from Last Syllable.

A'a-bl- 3. playable, payable, sayable, weighable, swayable 4. repayable, prepayable, impayable, unpayable, defrayable, portrayable, unsayable, unswayable, conveyable, surveyable 5. unportrayable, unconveyable.

AB'i-a- 3. labia, trabea, Swabia 4. Arabia.

AB'i-an- 3. Fabian, Sabian, Swabian 4. Arabian.

AB'i-ez- 2. abies, scabies, rabies.

AB'l-ness- 3. ableness, stableness 4. unableness, unstableness.

AB'or-er- 3. laborer, taborer.

AB'or-ing- 3. laboring, neighboring, taboring 4. belaboring, unlaboring.

AD'a-bl- 3. gradable, tradable, shadable, wadable 4. retradable, persuadable, evadable 5. unpersuadable, undissuadable.

AD'ed-li- 3. fadedly, jadedly 4. degradedly.

AD'ed-ness- 3. fadedness, jadedness, shadedness 4. cockadedness, degradedness.

AD'i-a- 3. stadia 4. Acadia, Arcadia, Palladia.

AD'i-al- 3. radial 5. uniradial, multiradial, interstadial.

AD'i-an- 3. radian 4. Barbadian, Palladian, Acadian, Akkadian, Arcadian, nomadian, Canadian.

AD'i-ans- 3. radiance 4. irradiance.

AD'i-ant- 3. radiant, gradient 4. irradiant.

AD'i-at- 3. radiate 4. eradiate, irradiate.

AD'ing-li- 3. fadingly 4. degradingly, pervadingly.

AD'i-um- 3. radium, stadium 4. Palladium, vanadium.

AD'i-us- 3. gladius, radius 4. adradius 5. hyporadius.

A'er-at- 2. aerate.

A'et-on- 3. phaeton.

AG'ran-si- 3. flagrancy, fragrancy, vagrancy.

A'ik-al- 3. laical 4. archaical, Hebraical 5. algebraical, pharisaical 6. paradisaical.

A'it-i- 3. gaiety, laity.

AJ'a-bl- 3. gaugeable, stageable 4. assuageable, dissuageable.

AJ'i-a- 3. Hagia 4. aphagia, dysphagia, Panagia 5. polyphagia.

AJ'i-an- 3. Magian 4. pelagian, contagion 5. Brobdignagian 6. archipelagian.

AJ'i-li- 3. cagily, stagily.

AJ'us-li- 4. rampageously, outrageously, courageously, contagiously 5. advantageously 6. disadvantageously.

AJ'us-ness- 4. rampageousness, outrageousness, courageousness, contagiousness, 5. advantageousness 6. disadvantageousness.

AK'a-bl– 3. acheable, placable, slakable, pacable, breakable, shakable, takable 4. implacable, unslakable, unbreakable, unshakable, mistakable, awakable 5. undertakable, unmistakable.

AK'at-ed– 3. placated, vacated 4. unplacated, revacated.

AK'er-i– 3. bakery, fakery, snakery, rakery, Quakery 5. undertakery.

AK'er-izm– 4. fakirism, Lakerism, Shakerism, Quakerism.

AK'i-a– 3. trachea 4. Batrachia.

AK'i-al– 3. rachial, brachial, tracheal.

AK'i-an– 3. trachean 4. Noachian, batrachian, Eustachian.

AK'i-ness– 3. fakiness, shakiness, flakiness, snakiness, quakiness.

AK'we-us– 3. aqueous 4. subaqueous, terraqueous.

AL'a-bl– 3. bailable, mailable, salable, sailable 4. inhalable, exhalable, unmailable, wholesalable, unsalable, assailable, unsailable, available, retailable 5. unassailable, unavailable.

AL'i-a– 3. galea, palea, Thalia 4. Sedalia, idalia, Westphalia, regalia, Eulalia, Mammalia. Massalia, azalea, sponsalia, Psoralea, Arctalia 5. Lupercalia, paralalia, pseudolalia, echolalia, Bacchanalia, marginalia, Terminalia, Saturnalia, Antarctalia 6. Marsupialia, paraphernalia; *see* also **AL'ya–** regalia etc.

AL'i-an– 3. alien 4. Daedalian, Idalian, regalian, mammalian, Castalian 5. phantasmalian, bacchanalian, saturnalian 6. sesquipedalian, Episcopalian; *see* also **AL'yum–** alien etc.

AL'i-as– 3. alias 4. Sibelius, Ortelius.

AL'i-ness– 3. dailiness, scaliness, wailiness 4. tridailiness.

AL'i-um– 3. Galium, kalium 4. Idalium.

AL'yen-at– 4. alienate.

AL'yen-izm– 5. alienism 6. bacchanalianism 7. sesquipedalianism, Episcopalianism, universalianism.

AM'a-bl– 3. blamable, claimable, namable, framable, tamable 4. unblamable, reclaimable, unnamable, unframable, untamable.

AM'ful-ness– 3. gamefulness, blamefulness, shamefulness 4. unshamefulness.

AM'i-a– 3. lamia 5. adynamia 6. Mesopotamia.

AM'less-ness– 3. aimlessness, famelessness, blamelessness, namelessness, shamelessness, tamelessness.

AN'a-bl– 3. gainable, chainable, planable, drainable, sprainable, trainable, strainable 4. ordainable, profanable, explainable, untrainable, restrainable, constrainable, attainable, obtainable, maintainable, sustainable 5. inexplainable, unexplainable, unobtainable, unattainable, ascertainable.

AN'a-bli– 4. explainably 5. unexplainably, unrestrainably, unattainably, unobtainably.

AN'e-a– 4. Castanea 5. succedanea, miscellanea, collectanea; *see* also **AN'i-a–** mania etc. below.

AN'e-an– 4. terranean, castanean 5. subterranean 6. Mediterranean, circumforanean, contemporanean, extemporanean; *see* also **AN'i-an–** Albanian etc. below.

AN'e-us– 4. siccaneous, araneous, terraneous, spontaneous, castaneous, cutaneous 5. succedaneous, miscellaneous, temporaneous, subterraneous, coetaneous, simultaneous, instantaneous, consentaneous, dissentaneous, subcutaneous 6. antecedaneous, contemporaneous, extemporaneous.

AN'ful-i– 3. banefully, gainfully, painfully 4. disdainfully, ungainfully.

AN'ful-ness– 3. gainfulness, painfulness 4. disdainfulness, ungainfulness.

AN'i-a- 3. mania 4. Albania, amania, Tasmania, Rumania, Ukrainia, Urania, Titania, Castanea 5. succedanea, miscellanea, florimania, theomania, Gallomania, melomania, Anglomania, monomania, hydromania, pyromania, nosomania, kleptomania, dipsomania, potomania, Pomerania, Aquitania, Lithuania, Transylvania, Pennsylvania, collectanea 6. bibliomania, decalcomania, megalomania, demonomania, Tripolitania.

AN'i-ak- 3. maniac 5. egomaniac, ergomaniac, Gallomaniac, Anglomaniac, monomaniac, pyromaniac, dipsomaniac, kleptomaniac 6. bibliomaniac, curiomaniac, megalomaniac.

AN'i-al- 3. cranial 4. domanial, acranial, cutaneal 5. subterraneal.

AN'i-an- 4. Albanian, volcanian, Vulcanian, Tasmanian, Rumanian, Iranian, Ukrainian, Uranian. 5. Pomeranian, Lithuanian, Transylvanian, Pennsylvanian; *see* also **AN'e-an-** terranean etc. above.

AN'i-ness- 3. raininess, braininess, graininess, veininess.

AN'ing-li- 4. complainingly 5. uncomplainingly, entertainingly.

AN'i-um- 3. cranium 4. germanium, geranium, uranium, titanium 5. succedaneum.

ANJ'a-bl- 3. changeable 4. unchangeable, exchangeable, arrangeable, derangeable 5. interchangeable, rearrangeable.

ANJ'a-bli- 3. changeably 4. unchangeably, exchangeably 5. interchangeably.

ANJ'i-ness- 3. manginess, ranginess.

ANT'a-bl- 3. paintable, taintable 4. acquaintable.

ANT'i-li- 3. daintily, saintily.

AP'a-bl- 3. capable, papable, drapable, shapable 4. incapable, escapable, reshapable, unshapable 5. inescapable.

AP'a-bli- 3. capably 4. incapably 5. inescapably, unescapably.

AP'er-er- 3. caperer, naperer, paperer, taperer, vaporer.

AP'er-i- 3. apery, apiary, japery, napery, papery, drapery, grapery, vapory.

AP'er-ing- 3. capering, papering, tapering, vaporing.

AP'i-an- 3. Apian 5. Aesculapian.

AR'a-bl- 3. arable, airable, bearable, pairable, parable, sparable, sharable, tearable, wearable, squarable, swearable 4. unbearable, repairable, unsparable, unwearable, unsquarable.

AR'a-bli- 3. bearably 4. unbearably.

AR'ful-i- 3. carefully, sparefully, prayerfully 4. uncarefully.

AR'ful-ness- 3. carefulness, sparefulness, prayerfulness 4. uncarefulness.

AR'i-a- 3. aria, area, pariah 4. herbaria, Bulgaria, Icaria, cercaria, malaria, talaria, solaria, ranaria, dataria, cataria, wistaria, aquaria, Bavaria 5. topiaria, urticaria, honoraria, adversaria, planetaria.

AR'i-al- 3. aerial, areal, Ariel, ariel, narial 4. diarial, vicarial, malarial, riparial, glossarial, bursarial, nectarial, sectarial, notarial, ovarial 5. calendarial, commissarial, secretarial, actuarial.

AR'i-an- 3. Arian, Aryan, Parian 4. barbarian, gregarian, Bulgarian, vulgarian, Icarian, lunarian, riparian, librarian, agrarian, Caesarian, rosarian, nectarean, sectarian, Bavarian, ovarian 5. millenarian, centenarian, septenarian, Sabbatarian, nonsectarian, vegetarian, proletarian, Trinitarian, Unitarian, antiquarian 6. abecedarian, quinquagenarian, septuagenarian, octogenarian, honegenarian, disciplinarian, predestinarian, totalitarian, utilitarian, humanitarian, necessitarian, ubiquitarian, parliamentarian, sacramentarian, veterinarian, alphabetarian 7. valetudinarian, latitudinarian, platitudinarian.

AR'i-ans- 3. variance 4. invariance.

AR'i-ant- 3. variant 4. bivariant, invariant, covariant, contrariant.

AR'i–at– **4.** salariat **5.** commissariat, proletariat, secretariat.

AR'i–er– **3.** airier, charier, hairier, glarier, varier, warier.

AR'i–est– **3.** airiest, chariest, hairiest, glariest, wariest.

AR'i–ez– **3.** Aries, caries, paries.

AR'i–form– **3.** aeriform, nariform, variform **4.** scalariform.

AR'i–ness– **3.** airiness, chariness, hairiness, glariness, wariness **4.** contrariness **5.** sanguinariness, temporariness, arbitrariness, solitariness, sedentariness, momentariness, voluntariness.

AR'ing–li– **3.** daringly, blaringly, flaringly, glaringly, sparingly **4.** forbearingly.

AR'i–ti– **3.** rarity **5.** debonairity.

AR'i–um– **3.** barium **4.** herbarium, verbarium, solarium, fumarium, ranarium, terrarium, sacrarium, rosarium, lactarium, aquarium, vivarium **5.** columbarium, cinerarium, honorarium, cometarium, planetarium, sanitarium.

AR'i–us– **3.** carious, scarious, various **4.** nefarious, gregarious, precarious, Icarius, vicarious, calcareous, vagarious, hilarious, senarius, riparious, setarious, nectareous, octarius, Aquarius **5.** septenarius, quaternarius, confessarius, Sagittarius, Januarius, Februarius, Stradivarius.

AS'a–bl– **3.** faceable, placeable, traceable **4.** effaceable, defaceable, replaceable, unplaceable, erasable **5.** irreplaceable, unerasable; *see* also **AS'i–bl–** suasible etc. below.

AS'ed–ly– **4.** shamefacedly, barefacedly.

AS'en–si– **4.** adjacency, complacency.

ASH'al–i– **3.** facially, glacially, racially **5.** interracially.

ASH'i–a– **3.** Asia **4.** Sabbatia, acacia, solatia, Dalmatia, Alsatia, Cetacea, Crustacea.

ASH'i–al– **3.** basial, spatial **4.** abbatial, palatial, primatial **5.** interspatial.

ASH'i–an– **3.** Asian, Haitian, Thracian **4.** Sabbatian, Dalmatian, Horatian, Alsatian, Eustachian.

ASH'i–at– **3.** glaciate, satiate **4.** sagaciate, emaciate, expatiate, ingratiate, insatiate.

ASH'i–ent– *see* **ASH'ent–** facient etc.

ASH'i–o– **3.** ratio **4.** locatio [L.], Horatio **7.** Nova Constellatio.

ASH'un–al– **3.** stational **4.** probational, vocational, relational, translational, vibrational, gyrational, sensational, rotational, quotational, equational **5.** incubational, recreational, congregational, conjugational, variational, convocational, educational, revelational, informational, combinational, inclinational, terminational, occupational, inspirational, condensational, compensational, gravitational, presentational, salutational, deputational, derivational, observational **6.** interrogational, denominational, commemorational, representational.

ASH'un–er– **3.** stationer **4.** probationer, foundationer, oblationer **5.** restorationer.

ASH'un–ist– **4.** creationist, deflationist, inflationist, salvationist **5.** convocationist, federationist, moderationist, tolerationist, emigrationist, inspirationist, restorationist, conversationist, imitationist, annotationist, innovationist, transmutationist **6.** repudiationist, annihilationist, emancipationist, colonizationist.

ASH'un–less– **3.** nationless, rationless, stationless **4.** foundationless, vibrationless, temptationless **3.** educationless, inspirationless, conversationless, imitationless; *see* also **ASH'un–** nation etc., plus –less.

ASH'us–ness– **3.** spaciousness, graciousness **4.** edaciousness, audaciousness, mendaciousness, sagaciousness, fugaciousness, fallaciousness, salaciousness, pugnaciousness, tenaciousness, capaciousness, rapaciousness, ungraciousness, veraciousness, voraciousness, sequaciousness, loquaciousness, vivaciousness, vexatiousness **5.** efficaciousness, contumaciousness, pertinaciousness, incapaciousness, perspicaciousness, ostentatiousness, disputatiousness.

AS'i-bl- 3. suasible **4.** evasible, persuasible **5.** unpersuasible; *see* also **AS'a-bl-** faceable etc. above.

AS'i-ness- 3. laciness, raciness.

AS'iv-ness- **4.** abrasiveness, assuasiveness, dissuasiveness, persuasiveness, evasiveness, invasiveness, pervasiveness.

AST'ful-i- **3.** tastefully, wastefully **4.** distastefully.

AST'i-li- **3.** hastily, pastily, tastily.

AT'a-bl- **3.** baitable, hatable, matable, ratable, gratable, satable, statable **4.** abatable, debatable, creatable, relatable, inflatable, dilatable, translatable, beratable **5.** unrelatable, regulatable.

AT'a-bly- **3.** ratably **5.** untranslatably.

AT'a-li- **3.** fatally **4.** prenatally.

AT'en-si- **3.** latency, patency.

AT'ful-i- **3.** fatefully, hatefully, gratefully **4.** ungratefully.

AT'ful-ness- **3.** fatefulness, hatefulness, gratefulness **4.** ungratefulness.

AT'i-ness- **3.** slatiness, weightiness.

AT'ing-li- **3.** gratingly **5.** deprecatingly, nauseatingly, mediatingly, contemplatingly, calculatingly, fascinatingly, alternatingly, penetratingly, meditatingly, irritatingly, hesitatingly, aggravatingly, captivatingly **6.** accommodatingly, interrogatingly, excruciatingly, alleviatingly, discriminatingly, premeditatingly, insinuatingly.

AT'iv-li- **3.** natively **4.** creatively **5.** predicatively, implicatively, legislatively, speculatively, emulatively, simulatively, cumulatively, germinatively, terminatively, operatively, decoratively, dubitatively, meditatively, cogitatively, qualitatively imitatively, hesitatively, quantitativel **6.** significatively, multiplicatively, gesticulatively, accumulatively, manipulatively imaginatively, determinatively, opinionatively, anticipatively, participatively co-operatively, vituperatively, commiseratively, reiteratively, alliteratively, corroboratively, invigoratively, commemoratively, administratively, interpretatively authoritatively, insinuatively **7.** incommunicatively.

AT'iv-ness- 3. nativeness **5.** penetrativeness, imitativeness **6.** imaginativeness.

AT'ron-al- **3.** matronal, patronal.

AT'ron-ij- **3.** matronage, patronage.

AV'a-bl- **3.** lavable, savable, shavable **4** unsavable, unshavable.

AV'er-er- 3. favorer, laverer, flavorer waverer, quaverer.

AV'er-i- **3.** Avery, slavery, knavery bravery, wavery, quavery, savory **4** unsavory **5.** antislavery.

AV'er-ing- **3.** favoring, flavoring, savoring, wavering, quavering **4.** unwavering.

AV'er-us- **3.** favorous, flavorous, quaverous, savorous **4.** papaverous.

AV'i-a- **3.** Moravia, Belgravia, Batavia Octavia **5.** Jugoslavia, Scandinavia.

AV'i-al- **3.** gavial, clavial.

AV'i-an- **3.** avian **4.** Moravian, Belgravian, Batavian, Octavian **5.** Scandinavian.

AV'i-er- **3.** clavier, wavier.

AV'ish-ness- **3.** slavishness, knavishnes

AZ'a-bl- 3. raisable, praisable **4.** appraisable, persuasible **5.** unpersuasible.

AZH'i-a- 3. Asia **4.** abasia, aphasia, e gasia, aplasia, gymnasia, Eurasia, acrasia Acrasia, fantasia, astasia **5.** paraphasia hemostasia.

AZH'i-al- **3.** basial **4.** gymnasial.

AZH'i–an– **3.** Asian **4.** Caucasian, Eurasian **5.** Australasian.

AZ'i–ness– **3.** haziness, laziness, maziness, craziness.

AZ'ing–li– **3.** dazingly, gazingly, blazingly **4.** amazingly.

AZ'on–ing– **3.** blazoning **4.** emblazoning.

A (ah)

1.

SINGLE (MASCULINE) RHYMES IN A (ah)

Primary or Secondary Accent Falls on Last Syllable; Imperfect Rhymes Are in Italics.

A– **1.** ah, baa, bah, da, fa, ha, hah, la, blah [slang], ma, na, nah [both slang], pa, pas [F.], spa, rah, Ra, bra [slang], fra [It.], kra, saa, shah, ta, t'a, taa, va [F.], qua, foi [F.], moi [F.], roi [F.], froid [F.], ya, yah, ja **2.** dada, *howdah, lowdah,* aha, haha, raca, éclat [F.], amah, mama, sama, *grandma,* papa, *grandpa,* faux pas [F.], *Para,* hurrah, état [F.], bourgeois [F.], patois [F.], chaud-froid [F.], huzza **3.** oh and ah, alala, Panama, elema, Parana, acara, baccarat, abaca, Bogota, tiers état [F.], vive le roi [F.].

AB– **1.** ab [Heb.], squab, swab **2.** kitab, *gabgab*; *see* also **OB–** bob etc.

AD– **1.** ahed, baaed, had, wad, quad [slang] **2.** aubade [F.], ballade, roulade, pomade, charade, estrade, hurrahed, façade, glissade, metad **3.** ohed and ahed, esplanade, promenade; *see* also **OD–** odd etc.

AF– **1.** half, Kaf, calf, laugh, Graf [G.], strafe, quaff **2.** behalf, *moon calf, horse-laugh* **3.** better half, half and half.

AFT– **1.** laughed, strafed, quaffed, waft.

AG– **1.** Dag, blague [F.], Prague; *see* also **OG–** bog etc.

AJH– **1.** raj, saj, taj **2.** coupage [F.], barrage, garage, mirage, massage, corsage, potage [F.], lavage [F.] **3.** entourage [F.], repoussage [F.], sabotage, esclavage [F.].

AK– **1.** ach [G.], lac [F.], plaque [F.] **2.** macaque, Iraq, chittak **3.** Sarawak.

AL– **1.** Baal, dal, râle [F.], kraal [D.], salle [F.], Taal, Saal [G.] **2.** Yigdal, *Heimdall,* agal, mahal, locale, *Landsmaal,* *choral,* chorale, morale, cheval [F.], Transvaal, étoile [F.], quetzal **3.** Taj Mahal, laical, farcical, radical, medical, codical, magical, tragical, nymphical, ethical, mythical, biblical, cyclical, helical, comical, technical, ethnical, finical, cynical, conical, apical, epical, topical, typical, centrical, vesical, whimsical, classical, musical, physical, optical, cryptical, vertical, cortical, vortical, mystical, nautical, silvical, cardial, cordial, genial, splenial, finial, hernial, aerial, ferial, serial, ambrosial, tertial, bestial, animal, minimal, lachrymal, decanal, bacchanal, tympanal, turbinal, carcinal, marginal, virginal, machinal, echinal, staminal, matinal, pectinal, retinal, inguinal, regional, torsional, missional, synchronal, seasonal, cantonal, principal, cerebral, vertebral, visceral, general, mineral, funeral, vesperal, geyseral, several, integral, admiral, anchoral, doctoral, cantoral, pastoral, mayoral, magistral, scriptural, sculptural, pastural, gestural, postural, guttural, sutural, textural, Provençal, palatal, vegetal, skeletal, orbital, digital, capital, hospital, marital, nepotal, pivotal, pedestal, gradual, casual, visual, usual, punctual, virtual, sexual, carnival, interval **4.** sporadical, unethical, encyclical, dynamical, inimical, tyrannical, dominical, ironical, electrical, eccentrical, nonclassical, antarctical, despotical, erotical, synoptical, majestical, Apocryphal, microbial, connubial, commercial, fiducial, novendial, gerundial, primordial, collegial, vestigial, conjugial, congenial, marsupial, colloquial, indigenal, phenomenal, intestinal, matutinal, adhesional, convulsional, expansional, partitional, precautional, municipal, Episcopal, preceptoral, carnivoral, continual, ventriloqual, unusual, perpetual, spiritual **5.** lackadaisical, participial, entente cordiale [F.]; *see* also **AL–** Al etc.

AM– **1.** âme [F.], balm, calm, malm, palm, psalm, Guam, qualm **2.** embalm, madame, Baham, salaam, imam, hammam, impalm **3.** Amsterdam, Rotterdam **4.** ad nauseam [L.]; *see* also **OM–** bomb etc.

AMZ– balms etc., *see* **AM–** balm etc. above, plus "s" or "'s."

AN– **1.** âne [F.], crâne [F.], wan, g'wan [slang], swan **2.** cabane [F.], Iban, liane, macan, pecan, Iran, Koran, Bataan **3.** balmacaan, Yucatan, capitan [Sp.], Turkestan, Pakistan **4.** Baluchistan; *see* also **ON–** on etc.

ANCH– stanch; *see* also **ONCH–** haunch etc.

ANS– **2.** séance, nuance **3.** Renaissance **4.** insouciance.

ANT– **1.** aunt, can't, shan't, want **2.** grandaunt, great-aunt **3.** debutante; *see* also **ONT–** font etc.

ANTS– aunts etc., *see* **ANT–** aunt etc. above, plus "s" or "'s."

ANZ– swans etc., *see* **AN–** âne etc. above, plus "s" or "'s"; *see* also **ANZ–** bonze etc.

AP– **1.** gape, swap, yahp [slang] **2.** étape [F.]; *see* also **OP–** bop etc.

AR– **1.** are, aar [D.], bar, dar [slang], far, gar, jar, car, char, scar, mar, gnar, gnarr, par, spar, tsar, tar, star, guar, boire [F.], foire [F.], poire [F.], Loire, gloire [F.], czar **2.** debar, rebar, embar, unbar, disbar, *crossbar*, *crowbar*, sirdar, afar, Safar, segar, cigar, bahar, ajar, evejar, nightjar, *sidecar*, *tramcar*, sircar, *forecar*, Bakar, shicar, *Lascar*, *Kedar*, *streetcar*, simar, canard [F.], *feldspar*, hussar, catarrh, katar, guitar, sitar, kantar, *daystar*, *lodestar*, *polestar*, *earthstar*, *evestar*, pour boire [F.], espoir [F.], savoir [F.], bazaar, bizarre **3.** gangliar, foliar, caviar, jaguar, Malabar, cinnabar, centibar, Zanzibar, saddle bar, axle bar, deodar, calendar, insofar, vinegar, *Trafalgar*, railroad car etc., gyrocar, autocar, tutelar, flagellar, lamellar, tessellar, similar, tonsillar, axillar, tabular, nebular, globular, tubular, schedular, glandular, modular, Cagoulard [F.], regular, angular, singular, jugular, stellular, secular, ocular, jocular, circular, torcular, vascular, scapular, popular, spherular, insular, consular, capsular, spatular, titular, ovular, uvular, valvular, tintamarre, laminar, seminar, columnar, sublunar, registrar, commissar, avatar, scimitar, boulevard [F.], Bolivar, samovar, abatoir [F.], escritoire [F.], repertoire [F.], evening star etc. **4.** Excalibar, dissimilar, somnambular, irregular, triangular, quadrangular, spectacular, vernacular, molecular, vehicular, funicular, particular, binocular, crepuscular **5.** perpendicular.

ARB– **1.** barb, darb [slang], garb, carb [slang], marb [slang], yarb **2.** coarb, *rhubarb*.

ARCH– **1.** arch, larch, march, parch, starch **2.** inarch, remarch, outmarch, cornstarch **3.** overarch, countermarch.

ARD– **1.** bard, barred, chard, charred, fard, hard, guard, jarred, card, scarred, lard, marred, knarred, nard, pard, sparred, sard, shard, tarred, starred, yard **2.** debarred, bombard, regard, *safeguard*, *lifeguard*, *blackguard*, *vanguard*, *placard*, discard, unscarred, foulard, poulard, Reynard, canard, Girard, *spikenard*, Bernard, petard, retard, bestarred, *churchyard*, back yard, *dockyard*, *steelyard*, *barnyard*, *foreyard*, front yard, *courtyard*, *graveyard* **3.**

disregard, bodyguard, avant-garde [F.], interlard, boulevard **4.** camelopard.

ARF– **1.** scarf, sharf, zarf.

ARJ– **1.** barge, charge, large, marge, sparge, sarge, targe **2.** surcharge, discharge, LaFarge, enlarge **3.** countercharge, overcharge, re-enlarge.

ARK– **1.** arc, ark, bark, barque, dark, hark, cark, lark, Clark, clerk, mark, marque, nark [slang], snark [slang], park, spark, sark, shark, stark **2.** *shagbark, snakebark, shellbark,* embark, *tanbark, woodlark, skylark, titlark, landmark,* remark, *hallmark, thumbmark, Denmark, earmark, reichsmark, postmark, birthmark,* impark, dispark, *whitesark, aardvark, Ozark* **3.** disembark, watermark, countermark, hierarch **4.** ecclesiarch.

ARKS– arcs etc., *see* **ARK–** arc etc. above, plus "s" or "'s"; **1.** Marx.

ARKT– **1.** arced, barked, harked, carked, larked, clerked, marked, parked, sparked **2.** embarked, skylarked, remarked, thumbmarked, earmarked, postmarked, birthmarked **3.** disembarked, watermarked.

ARL– **1.** harl, jarl, carl, Carl, Karl, marl, gnarl, snarl, parle **2.** imparl **3.** Albemarle.

ARLZ– harls etc.; *see* **ARL–** harl etc. above, plus "s" or "'s"; **1.** Arles, Charles.

ARM– **1.** arm, barm, charm, farm, harm, larm, larme [F.], marm, tharm **2.** *yardarm,* rearm, inarm, *firearm,* forearm, disarm *crossarm,* gendarme [F.], alarm, schoolmarm **3.** underarm, overarm.

ARN– **1.** barn, darn, larn [slang], Marne, tarn, yarn **2.** lucarne [F.], goldarn, consarn [both slang].

ARND– **1.** darned, yarned **2.** goldarned, consarned [both slang].

ARP– **1.** harp, carp, scarp, sharp, tarp [slang], yarp [slang], zarp **2.** *syncarp,* escarp, *cardsharp* **3.** claviharp, epicarp, pericarp, endocarp, monocarp, counterscarp.

ARS– **1.** arse, farce, garce, parse, sparse, sarse [dial.].

ARSH– **1.** harsh, marsh, warsh [slang] **2.** démarche.

ART– **1.** art, Bart, chart, dart, hart, heart, cart, carte, quarte [F.], blart [dial.], mart, smart, part, Sart, tart, start **2.** *sweetheart, faintheart, dogcart, gocart, dumpcart,* apart, depart, repart, impart, *rampart,* dispart, *forepart,* assart, astart, *redstart,* restart, upstart **3.** a la carte, counterpart, apple tart, sugar tart.

ARTH– **1.** garth, hearth **2.** fishgarth.

ARV– **1.** carve, larve, starve, varve.

ARZ– bars etc., *see* **AR–** are etc. above, plus "s" or "'s"; Lars, Mars.

AS– **2.** en masse **3.** coup de grâce [F.].

ASH– **1.** lache [F.], tache [F.], quash, squash, wash.

AT– **1.** pâte [F.], what, squat, swat, watt, boite [F.], yacht **2.** salat, berat, Duat, *kumquat* **3.** Al Sirat; *see* also **OT–** dot etc.

ATH– **1.** bath, path, rath, wrath **3.** isobath.

ATZ– squats etc., *see* **AT–** pâte [F.] etc. above, plus "s" or "'s"; **1.** batz **2.** ersatz.

AV– **1.** gav, halve, calve, slav, salve, suave **2.** Zouave **3.** Jugoslav, Yugoslav.

AVD– **1.** halved, calved, salved.

AZ– ahs etc., *see* **A–** ah etc. above, plus "s" or "'s"; **1.** vase, yahzz [slang] **2.** namaz, Shiraz, Françoise **3.** Vichyssoise.

AZH– **2.** chauffage [F.], menage, barrage, garage, mirage **3.** bavardage [F.], fuselage, persiflage, camouflage, badinage, cabotage, sabotage **4.** espionage.

A (ah)

2.

DOUBLE (FEMININE) RHYMES IN A (a'ba)

Primary or Secondary Accent Falls on Next to Last Syllable; Imperfect Rhymes Are in Italics.

AB'a- 2. aba, baba, haba [Sp.], Caaba, Kaaba 3. casaba, aftaba 4. piassaba, Ali Baba 5. Addis Ababa.

AB'i- 2. rabi, tabi [Jap.], wabe 3. Wahabi, kohlrabi.

AB'ra- 2. abra 4. candelabra 5. abracadabra.

AD'a- 2. dada, sraddha 3. Haggada, cicada, Colada, armada, granada, Grenada, panada, contrada, Nevada, shahzada 6. Sierra Nevada.

AD'en- 2. Baden 4. Baden-Baden; *see* also **OD'en-** hodden etc.

AD'i- 2. cadi, Mahdi, wadi 3. abadi [Hind.], irade.

AD'o- 2. dado, Prado 3. Mikado, sticcado, stoccado, strappado, dorado, passado, pintado, bravado 4. avocado, desperado, Eldorado, Colorado 5. amontillado 6. incommunicado.

A'e- 2. kai, blahy [slang], tai, sai 4. kaikai.

A'ek- 2. kaik, saic.

AF'a- 2. Daffa, Jaffa, Yafa.

AF'ing- 2. laughing, strafing, quaffing.

AF'l- 2. faffle, taffle, tafel [G.], waffle.

AF'ter- 2. after, laughter.

AG'a- 2. aga, gaga [F.], glaga, Naga, saga.

AG'ar- 2. agar, laager, lager 4. agar-agar.

AG'o- 2. drago 3. Iago, Chicago, sago, farrago 4. Santiago; *see* also **ARG'o-** Argo etc.

AG'wa- 2. agua, jagua, Yagua 3. Managua, piragua.

A'ha- 2. kaha, maha, taha 3. *taiaha.*

A'hu- 2. kahu, Mahu, Rahu, sahu, wahoo, Yahoo 3. Oahu.

A'ing- 2. ahing, baaing, blahing [slang] 3. blah-blahing [slang] 5. ohing and ahing.

AJ'a- 2. rajah 4. maharajah.

AJ'e- 2. haje, hagi, Bragi.

AK'a- 2. haka [Maori], Hakka, raca 3. Karaka, Osaka, pataca 4. Titicaca.

AK'as- 3. Caracas.

AK'en- 2. Aachen, Achen, baken [D.], kraken.

AK'er- 3. fiacre, polacre.

AK'i- 2. kaki, khaki, sake, saki 4. Anunnaki, sukiyaki.

AK'o- 2. hako, Chaco, mako, caco, paco, guaco, huaco 3. cheechako, fondako, guanaco 4. makomako.

AK'wa- 2. aqua 3. namaqua, anaqua.

AL'a- 2. Allah, gala, hala, kala, wallah 3. koala, impala, Marsala, Patala, owala.

AL'et- 2. wallet, swallet; *see* also **OL'et-** collet etc.

AL'i- 2. Ali, Bali, dali, gali, galee, Kali, pali, tali, Vali 3. Bengali, tahali, tamale, Somali, finale 4. Mexicali, pastorale.

AL'o- 2. calo, lalo, malo, palo, swallow, wallow 3. hog wallow; *see* also **OL'o-** follow etc.

AL'u- 2. baloo, balu.

AL'yo– **3.** caballo, seraglio, intaglio.

AM'a– **2.** ama, gama, jama, caama, Kama, lama, llama, mama, mamma, Rama, Brahma, drama, grama, shama, Tama **3.** Bahama, pajama, pyjama **4.** Alabama, Yokohama, ramarama, melodrama, monodrama, diorama, cyclorama, cosmorama, panorama, Fujiyama **5.** myriorama, polyorama.

AM'an– **2.** Brahman, saman, shaman, zaman **4.** Parabrahman.

AM'as– Brahmas etc., *see* **AM'a–** ama etc. above, plus "s" or " 's."

AM'ba– **2.** samba **3.** caramba [Sp.].

AM'er– **2.** calmer, Kammer [D.], palmer **3.** embalmer.

AM'i– **2.** balmy, jami, calmy, malmy, palmy, pahmi, qualmy, swami **3.** palame, salami.

AM'ing– **2.** calming, malming, palming, qualming **3.** embalming, becalming, salaaming, empalming.

AM'ish– **2.** calmish, qualmish.

AM'ist– **2.** palmist, psalmist **3.** embalmist.

AN'a– **2.** Bana, kana, mana, rana, prana, tana, thana **3.** nagana, Guiana, liana, gymkhana, banana, mañana [Sp.], kerana, zenana, purana, Etana, Sultana, lantana, Montana, Curtana, nirvana, iguana **4.** apadana, tramontana, marijuana **5.** Americana **6.** cassabanana, Shakespeariana.

AND'o– **2.** bando **3.** tardando, calando, Orlando, Fernando, Hernando, ritando, lentando, scherzando **4.** ritardando, declamando, lacrimando, recitando, allentando, rallentando.

AN'i– **2.** ani, rani **4.** frangipani, Maharani, Hindustani.

AN'o– **2.** ano, mano, grano **3.** piano, solano, soprano, gitano **4.** pudiano, castellano, altiplano, bonamano, capitano, Montesano **9.** mens sana in corpore sano [L.].

ANT'a– **2.** danta **3.** Vedanta, Infanta.

ANT'ay– **2.** Dante, sante **3.** andante, volante **5.** pococurante.

ANT'i– **2.** aunty, Dante, tanti **3.** Chianti, andante, Kiranti.

A'o– **2.** ao, dao, tao **3.** cacao, macao, talao, Karao [Hind.], parao **4.** carabao, Mindanao.

AP'a– **2.** apa, capa, kapa, papa, tapa **5.** anapanapa.

AP'i– **2.** Hapi **3.** okapi, serape.

AR'a– **2.** cara, Mara, narra, Tara, vara **3.** tiara, ziara, fugara, Sahara, vihara, Sakkara, kaikara, cascara, mascara, Damara, Gemara, apara, arara, chitarra **4.** caracara, tantarara, Demerara, solfatara **5.** Guadalajara, taratantara.

ARB'er– **2.** arbor, barber, Barbour, harbor **3.** enharbor.

ARB'ij– **2.** garbage.

ARB'l– **2.** barbel, garble, garbill, marble **3.** enmarble.

ARB'lz– **2.** barbels, garbles, marbles.

ARB'on– **2.** charbon, carbon **4.** hydrocarbon.

ARB'ord– **2.** arbored, harbored, larboard, starboard.

ARCH'er– **2.** archer, marcher, parcher, starcher **4.** countermarcher.

ARCH'ez– arches etc., *see* **ARCH–** arch etc., plus "es" or " 's."

ARCH'i– **2.** Archie, archy, larchy, starchy.

ARCH'ing– **2.** arching, marching, parching, starching **3.** outmarching **4.** overarching, countermarching.

ARCH'ment– **2.** archment, parchment **3.** emparchment.

ARD'ant– **2.** ardent, gardant, guardant **3.** regardant, retardant.

ARD'ed– **2.** farded, guarded, carded, larded, sharded **3.** bombarded, safeguarded, placarded, discarded, regarded, retarded **4.** disregarded, interlarded, unretarded.

ARD'el– 2. bardel, fardel, sardel, sardelle.

ARD'en– 2. Arden, garden, harden, Varden 3. tea garden, enharden 4. Dolly Varden [Dickens].

ARD'end– 2. gardened, hardened, pardoned 3. unhardened, unpardoned.

ARD'er– 2. ardor, guarder, harder, carder 3. discarder, retarder 4. disregarder.

ARD'i– 2. hardy, lardy, mardy, tardy 3. *Lombardy*, foolhardy.

ARD'ij– 2. yardage.

ARD'ik– 2. bardic 3. Lombardic, Sephardic 4. anacardic, pericardic.

ARD'ing– 2. farding, guarding, Harding, carding, larding 3. unguarding, discarding, retarding 4. disregarding.

ARD'less– 2. fardless, guardless, cardless, lardless, shardless 3. regardless, retardless.

ARD'ment– 3. bombardment, retardment.

ARD'ship– 2. guard ship, hardship.

AR'e– 2. bari, lari, pari, sari 3. safari, shikari, kanari, curare 4. Karharbari, aracari, Carbonari; *see* also **AR'i–** barry etc. below.

AR'er– 2. barrer, marrer, sparrer, tarrer 3. debarrer, bizarrer.

AR'fish– 2. barfish, garfish, starfish 3. cigarfish, guitarfish.

ARG'et– 2. target.

ARG'l– 2. argal, argol, gargle.

ARG'o– 2. Argo, argot, Fargo, cargo, largo, Margo, Margot, pargo, sargo 3. embargo, botargo 4. supercargo.

ARG'on– 2. argon, jargon.

ARG'u– 2. argue 3. reargue, redargue.

AR'i– 2. barry, scarry, charry, jarry, parry, sparry, tarry, starry 4. Carbonari; *see* also **AR'e–** bari etc. above.

AR'ik– 3. Amharic, Gemaric, tartaric.

AR'ing– 2. barring, scarring, charring, jarring, marring, parring, sparring, tarring, starring 3. debarring, disbarring, bestarring.

ARJ'ent– 2. argent, margent, sergeant, Sargent 3. minargent.

ARJ'er– 2. barger, charger, larger, sparger 3. surcharger, discharger, enlarger.

ARJ'ez– 2. barges, charges, marges 3. recharges, surcharges, discharges, enlarges 4. countercharges, overcharges.

ARJ'ik– 3. pelargic, lethargic.

ARJ'in– 2. bargin', chargin', margin.

ARJ'ing– 2. barging, charging 3. discharging, enlarging 4. overcharging.

ARK'a– 2. Charca, parka, markka 3. bidarka.

ARK'al– 3. anarchal, monarchal 4. oligarchal, matriarchal, patriarchal, hierarchal.

ARK'asm– 2. sarcasm.

ARK'en– 2. barken, darken, hearken, starken 3. bedarken, endarken.

ARK'er– 2. barker, darker, harker, carker, larker, marker, markhor, parker, sparker, starker 3. embarker, skylarker.

ARK'est– 2. darkest, starkest.

ARK'et– 2. market 3. newmarket.

ARK'i– 2. arky, barky, darky, larky, Markey, sparky, starky 3. malarkey [slang] 4. oligarchy, hagiarchy, chiliarchy, matriarchy, patriarchy, hierarchy.

ARK'ik– 3. anarchic, monarchic 4. oligarchic, matriarchic, patriarchic.

ARK'ing– 2. barking, harking, carking, larking, marking, parking, sparking, sarking, starking 3. embarking, disbarking, *skylarking*, *earmarking*.

ARK'ish– 2. darkish, carkish, larkish, parkish, sparkish, starkish 3. skylarkish.

ARK'ist– 4. oligarchist, matriarchist, patriarchist, hierarchist.

ARK'l– 2. barkle, darkle, sparkle 3. besparkle.

ARK'ld– 2. barkled, darkled, carkled, sparkled 3. besparkled.

ARK'less– 2. barkless, carkless, larkless, markless, parkless, sparkless.

ARK'let– 2. parklet, sparklet.

ARK'li– 2. Barkley, Berkeley, darkly, sparkly, starkly.

ARK'ling– 2. darkling, larkling, sparkling.

ARK'ner– 3. darkener, hearkener.

ARK'ness– 2. darkness, starkness.

ARK'o– 2. Marco, charco [Sp.].

ARK'tik– 2. Arctic 3. subarctic, Nearctic, Holarctic, Antarctic 4. Palearctic.

ARK'us– 2. Barkis [Dickens], carcass, Marcus.

ARL'and– 2. garland 3. engarland.

ARL'ans– 2. parlance.

ARL'er– 2. gnarler, snarler, parlor 3. sunparlor.

ARL'es– 2. barless, carless, scarless, jarless, marless, tarless, starless, czarless 3. cigarless, catarrhless.

ARL'et– 2. carlet, scarlet, marlet, starlet, varlet; *see* also **ARL'ot–** harlot etc. below.

ARL'i– 2. barley, Charlie, Farley, marly, marli, gnarly, snarly, parley 3. bizarrely.

ARL'ik– 2. garlic, sarlyk 3. pilgarlic.

ARL'ike– 2. barlike, carlike, scarlike, tarlike, starlike, czarlike 3. cigarlike, catarrhlike.

ARL'in– 2. carlin, marlin, marline.

ARL'ing– 2. darling, carling, harling, marling, gnarling, snarling, parling, sparling, starling.

ARL'ot– 2. harlot, carlot, Charlotte; *see* also **ARL'et–** carlet etc. above.

ARL'us– 2. parlous, snarl us etc.; *see* also **ARL'es–** barless etc. above.

ARM'a– 2. dharma, karma 3. adharma.

ARM'ent– 2. garment, sarment 3. debarment, disbarment.

ARM'er– 2. armer, armor, charmer, farmer, harmer 3. disarmer, snake charmer, dirt farmer, alarmer.

ARM'ful– 2. armful, harmful, charmful 3. unharmful.

ARM'i– 2. army, barmy, farmy.

ARM'ik– 2. pharmic, ptarmic 4. polypharmic 5. alexipharmic.

ARM'in– 2. harmine, carmine, charmin' 3. encarmine.

ARM'ing– 2. arming, charming, farming, harming 3. uncharming, forearming, alarming, disarming.

ARM'less– 2. armless, charmless, harmless 3. alarmless.

ARM'let– 2. armlet, charmlet.

ARM'ot– 2. carmot, marmot.

ARN'a– 2. arna, sarna.

ARN'al– 2. charnel, darnel, carnal 3. uncarnal.

ARN'at– 2. carnate 3. incarnate, discarnate 4. reincarnate.

ARN'el– 2. charnel, darnel.

ARN'er– 2. darner, garner, yarner.

ARN'erd– 2. Barnard, garnered.

ARN'ess– 2. farness, harness 3. reharness, unharness, bizarreness.

ARN'i– 2. barny, carney, blarney 3. Killarney.

ARN'ij– 2. carnage.

ARN'ing– 2. darning, yarning 3. goldarning, consarning [both slang].

ARN'ish– 2. garnish, tarnish, varnish.

ARN'isht– 2. garnished, tarnished, varnished 3. ungarnished, untarnished, unvarnished.

AR'o– 2. karo, claro, taro 3. denaro, cantaro, saguaro 4. carbonaro.

ARP'al– 2. carpal 4. metacarpal, intercarpal.

ARP'er– 2. harper, carper, sharper 3. cardsharper.

ARP'et– 2. carpet.

ARP'i– 2. harpy, carpy, sharpy, sharpie.

ARP'ing– 2. harping, carping, sharping 3. cardsharping.

ARS'al– 2. carcel, parcel, tarsal 4. metatarsal.

ARS'er– 2. carcer [L.], parser, sparser, Sarsar.

ARS'ez– 2. farces, parses, sarses.

ARSH'al– 2. martial, marshal, Marshall, partial 3. field marshal, impartial.

ARSH'an– 2. Martian.

ARS'li– 2. parsley, sparsely.

ARS'on– 2. arson, Carson, Larson, parson, squarson.

ARS'us– 2. tarsus 3. protarsus 4. metatarsus.

ART'a– 2. charta [L.], Sparta, cuarta 4. Magna Charta.

ART'an– 2. partan, Spartan, tartan, Tartan; *see* also **ART'en**– hearten etc. below.

ART'ay– 3. ex parte, Astarte 4. colla parte [It.].

ART'ed– 2. darted, hearted, carted, charted, smarted, parted, started 3. kindhearted, hardhearted, freehearted, weakhearted, warmhearted, downhearted, falsehearted, softhearted, lighthearted, fainthearted, stouthearted, truehearted, uncharted, outsmarted, departed, imparted, upstarted 4. stonyhearted, heavyhearted, simplehearted, singlehearted, gentlehearted, chickenhearted, brokenhearted, openhearted, lionhearted, ironhearted, tenderhearted.

ART'en– 2. barton, Barton, hearten, carton, marten, smarten, tarten 3. enhearten, dishearten 4. Tiergarten, kindergarten; *see* also **ART'an**– partan etc. above.

ART'er– 2. arter, barter, charter, darter, garter, carter, parter, martyr, smarter, tartar, tarter, starter 3. departer, imparter, bemartyr, restarter, self-starter 4. protomartyr, cream-of-tartar.

ART'erd– 2. bartered, chartered, gartered, martyred.

ART'ful– 2. artful, heartful, startful.

ART'i– 2. arty, darty, hearty, smarty, party, tarty, starty 3. McCarty, tea party, ex parte, Astarte.

ART'ing– 2. charting, darting, carting, smarting, parting, starting 3. sweethearting, departing, imparting, disparting, restarting, self-starting, upstarting.

ART'ist– 2. artist, chartist, Chartist 4. Bonapartist.

ART'l– 2. dartle, spartle, startle 4. Rosa Dartle [Dickens].

ART'less– 2. artless, dartless, cartless, chartless, heartless, smartless, partless, startless.

ART'let– 2. artlet, Bartlett, heartlet, partlet, martlet, tartlet.

ART'li– 2. smartly, partly, tartly.

ART'ling– 2. dartling, spartling, startling.

ART'ment– 3. apartment, department, impartment, compartment.

ART'ness– 2. smartness, tartness.

ART'o– 3. lagarto, esparto.

ART'on– 2. barton, Barton, carton 4. set one's heart on; *see* also **ART'en**– barton etc. above.

ART'rij– 2. cartridge, partridge.

AR'u– 2. baru, maru.

AR'um– 2. garum, larum 3. alarum.

ARV'a– 2. arva, larva.

ARV'al– 2. Arval, arval, barvel, carval, larval, marvel.

ARV'er– 2. carver, marver, starver.

AS'a– 2. casa [Sp., It., Pg., L.], pasa [Sp.], guasa.

AS'ta– 2. basta, hasta, pasta [It.].

AT'a– 2. bata, data, gata, rata 3. reata [Sp.], regatta, riata, toccata, stoccata, camata, sonata, batata, patata, cantata **4.** alpargata [Sp.], boniata, matamata, carromata, serenata **5.** enamorata, inamorata.

AT'er– **2.** mater, pater, quatre **3.** Dis Pater **4.** alma mater, Stabat Mater.

AT'i– **2.** Sati, zati **3.** piatti, coati, Amati **4.** Jubilate, Cincinnati **5.** illuminati.

AT'o– **2.** dato, datto [both Tag. & Sp.] **3.** legato, staccato, spiccato, marcato [It.], pomato, tomato, annatto, barato [Sp.], vibrato, ritratto [It.] **4.** moderato, obbligato, pizzicato, passionato [It.], disperato [It.], allentato [It.] **5.** demilegato, appassionato.

AT'ra– **2.** matra **3.** Sumatra **4.** Cleopatra.

AT'um– **2.** datum **3.** pomatum.

AV'a– **2.** Java, kava, lava, Brava, guava **3.** cassava **4.** kavakava, piassava.

AV'er– **2.** halver, calver, salver, suaver **3.** palaver.

AV'i– **2.** Ave, Kavi **3.** Mohave, Mojave, peccavi **6.** Rikki-tikki-tavi [Kipling].

AV'ing– **2.** halving, calving, salving.

AV'o– **2.** bravo **3.** octavo, centavo.

A'wa– **2.** awa, tawa **3.** Chihuahua.

A'ya– **2.** aya, Maya, raya, saya **3.** kabaya, papaya, karaya, Hawaii **4.** Surabaya.

AZ'a– **2.** plaza, maza [Sp.].

AZH'ing– **3.** barraging, garaging **4** persiflaging, camouflaging.

AZ'i– **2.** ghazi **3.** Benghazi.

A (ah)

3.

TRIPLE RHYMES IN A (art'less-ly)

Primary or Secondary Accent Falls on
Second from Last Syllable.

AB'i-la- **4.** cantabile **5.** lamentabile.

AK'i-a- **4.** Slovakia **6.** Czechoslovakia.

AM'ist-ri- **3.** palmistry, psalmistry.

ARB'er-ing- **3.** barbering, harboring.

ARD'en-ing- **3.** gardening, hardening, pardoning.

ARD'i-li- **3.** hardily, tardily **4.** foolhardily.

AR'i-ness- **3.** barriness, tarriness, starriness.

AR'i-o- **4.** scenario, Cesario **5.** impresario.

ARK'i-kal- **3.** archical **4.** hylarchical, anarchical, monarchical, tetrarchical **5.** hierarchical.

ARL'a-tan- **3.** charlatan, tarlatan.

ARM'a-bl- **3.** farmable, armable, harmable, charmable, **4.** disarmable, unfarmable, unharmable, uncharmable, alarmable.

ARM'ing-li- **3.** farmingly, harmingly, charmingly **4.** disarmingly, alarmingly.

ARN'ish-er- **3.** garnisher, tarnisher, varnisher.

ARN'ish-ing- **3.** garnishing, tarnishing, varnishing **4.** revarnishing.

ARS'en-er- **3.** larcener, parcener **4.** coparcener.

ARS'en-i- **3.** larceny **4.** coparceny.

ART'ed-li- **4.** halfheartedly, lighheartedly, faintheartedly, stoutheartedly.

ART'ed-ness- **4.** kindheartedness, hardheartedness, downheartedness, lightheartedness **5.** simpleheartedness, openheartedness, lionheartedness.

ART'er-er- **3.** barterer, charterer.

ART'er-i- **3.** artery, bartery, martyry.

ART'i-kl- **3.** article, particle.

ART'i-zan- **3.** artisan, bartizan, partisan.

ART'less-li- **3.** artlessly, heartlessly.

A (cab)

1.

SINGLE (MASCULINE) RHYMES IN A (cab)

Primary or Secondary Accent Falls on Last Syllable; Imperfect Rhymes Are in Italics.

AB– **1.** ab, abb, Bab, dab, gab [coll.], cab, scab, lab, blab, slab, Mab, nab, snab [slang], rab, brab, drab, grab, crab, tab, stab **2.** *Joab*, *confab*, *lablab*, Queen Mab, *eartab* **3.** baobab, taxicab.

ACH– **1.** batch, bach [slang], hatch, catch, latch, slatch, match, natch, snatch, patch, ratch, brach, cratch, scratch, thatch **2.** *nuthatch*, *seecatch*, *potlatch*, mismatch, *tolpatch*, dispatch, *Wasatch*, attach, detach **3.** overmatch.

ACHD– **1.** batched, bached [slang], hatched, latched, matched, snatched, patched, scratched, thatched **2.** mismatched, dispatched, attached, detached.

AD– **1.** ad, add, bad, bade, dad, fad, gad, had, cad, Chad, Tchad, scad, lad, blad [Scot.], glad, clad, plaid, mad, pad, rad [dial.], brad, grad [slang], sad, shad, tad **2.** readd, *Sindbad*, forbade, aubade [F.], egad, begad, *mailclad*, unclad, kneepad **3.** Iliad, chiliad, myriad, Trinidad, ironclad, winter clad, heavy clad, ivy clad, reculade [F.], Leningrad, undergrad, Olympiad, little tad.

ADZ– ads etc., *see* **AD–** ad etc. above, plus "s" or "'s."

AF– **1.** aff [Scot.], baff, chaff, daff, faff, gaff, half, calf, laugh, laff [slang], raff, Wraf, draff, graph, staff, quaff **2.** *chiffchaff*, behalf, *mooncalf*, *horselaugh*, carafe, *riffraff*, agraffe, giraffe, *gibstaff*, *flagstaff*, *distaff*, *Falstaff*, *forestaff* **3.** shandygaff, anagraph, paragraph, telegraph, melograph, phonograph, monograph, dictograph, autograph, photograph, lithograph, epitaph, cenotaph, better half, quarter staff **4.** mimeograph, stereograph, radiograph, cardiograph, heliograph.

AFT– **1.** aft, baffed, daft, daffed, gaffed, haft, laughed, raft, draft, graft, craft, shaft, Taft, staffed, waft, quaffed **2.** abaft, engraft, *witchcraft*, *woodcraft*, *seacraft*, *folkcraft*, *aircraft*, awaft **3.** overdraft, handicraft, metalcraft **4.** antiaircraft.

AG– **1.** ag [slang], bag, dag, fag, gag, jag, cag [slang], scag, skag, lag, flag, slag, mag [coll. and slang], nag, knag, snag, rag, brag, drag, crag, scrag, sag, shag, tag, stag, vag [slang], wag, quag, swag, zag **2.** *handbag*, *gasbag*, *shagrag*, *ragtag*, *wigwag*, *zigzag* **3.** moneybag, saddlebag, demihag, scalawag, chew the rag [slang], Brobdingnag.

AGD– **1.** bagged, fagged, gagged, cagged, lagged, flagged, nagged, snagged, dragged, sagged, tagged, wagged **2.** betagged, *wigwagged*, *zigzagged*.

AJ– **1.** badge, fadge, hadj, cadge, Madge.

AK– **1.** back, bac, hack, jack, kak, kack, cack [all slang], lack, lac, black, clack, claque, plaque, slack, mack, mac [both slang], smack, knack, snack, pack, pac, rack, crack, track, wrack, sack, sac, sacque, shack, tac, tack, stack, Waac, wack [slang], quack, whack, thwack, yak **2.** *ack-ack*, aback, *wayback*, *pinchback*, *hunchback*, *switchback*, *holdback*, *halfback*, *puffback*, *crookback*, *quillback*, *fullback*, *comeback*, *drawback*, *throwback*, *humpback*, *horseback*, *kiack, blackjack, flapjack, slapjack, skipjack, bootjack, muntjak,* alack, shellac, *flicflac, lampblack, bootblack, knickknack,* repack, unpack, *calpac, woolpack, wisecrack,* retrack, *backtrack, racetrack,* tesack, *sicsac, woolsack,* ransack, *rucksack,* attack, *hardtack, ticktack, thumbtack, haystack, bullwhack, Anzac* **3.** zodiac, cardiac, maniac, Pontiac, piggyback, pickaback, huckaback, saddleback, turtleback, quarterback, leatherback, razorback, Union Jack, natterjack, almanac, bric-a-brac, tamarack, cul-de-sac, haversack, bivouac, paddywhack, cattleyak **4.** tacamahac, yakkity-yak [slang].

AKS– **1.** ax, axe, backs, jacks, lax, lacks, flax, slacks, Max, max, snacks, pax, packs, tracks, Thrax, sax, sacks, tax, tacks, stacks, wax, yaks, zax **2.** *addax, pickax, poleax, greenbacks,* relax, *toadflax, climax, backtracks,* ransacks, *haystacks,* dewax, *chaffwax, beeswax, paxwax* **3.** battle-ax, Halifax, parallax, supertax, overtax, income tax.

AKST– **1.** axed, flaxed, taxed, waxed **2.** relaxed, dewaxed **3.** supertaxed, overtaxed.

AKT– **1.** act, fact, lacked, pact, packed, racked, wracked, bract, cracked, tract, tact, tacked, quacked, whacked **2.** react, triact, coact, redact, *hunchbacked, humpbacked, confact,* enact, epact, impact, compact, unpacked, defract, diffract, entr'acte, *sidetracked,* ransacked, transact, intact, *contact,* exact **3.** saddle-backed, cataract, interact, counteract, overact, re-enact, retroact, cataphract, inexact **4.** matter-of-fact.

AKTS– acts etc., *see* **AKT–** act etc. above, plus "s" or "'s."

AL– **1.** Al, dalle, gal [slang], Cal, mal, pal, sal [slang], salle, shall **2.** cabal, locale, canal, corral, morale, La Salle, *aval* **3.** musicale, chaparral, pastorale, entresalle; *see* also **AL–** Baal etc.

ALD– **1.** palled **2.** caballed, corralled **3.** emerald.

ALK– **1.** alk, calk, calc, talc **3.** catafalque.

ALKS– **1.** falx, calks, calx.

ALP– **1.** alp, scalp, palp **3.** auriscalp.

ALPS– **1.** Alps, scalps, palps **3.** auriscalps.

ALT– **1.** alt, shalt.

ALV– **1.** salve, valve **2.** bivalve.

AM– **1.** am, bam, Cham, cham [dial.], dam, damn, gam, gamb, ham, jam, jamb, cam, camm [slang], lam, lamb, clam, flam, slam, ma'am, pam, rhamn, ram, dram, drachm, dramme, gram, gramme, cram, pram, tram, Sam, sham, tam, swam, wham, yam, zam [slang] **2.** madame, *beldam, grandam,* Siam, *jimjam,* enjamb, *flimflam,* Assam, *tamtam, whimwham,* Khayyam **3.** Alabam', cofferdam, Abraham, Birmingham, Nottingham, choriamb, demijambe, diaphragm, diagram, anagram, telegram, milligram, epigram, centigram, cablegram, kilogram, melogram, monogram, cryptogram, marjoram, dithyramb, petersham, Uncle Sam **4.** ad nauseam [L.], The Great I Am **5.** parallelogram.

AMB– **1.** amb, gamb **3.** choriamb, dithyramb.

AMD– **1.** damned, dammed, gammed, jammed, lambed, lammed [slang], clammed, flammed, slammed, rammed, crammed, shammed, whammed.

AMP– **1.** amp [slang], champ, damp, gamp, guimpe, camp, scamp, lamp, clamp, ramp, cramp, tramp, samp, tamp, stamp, vamp, yamp **2.** *chokedamp, firedamp,* decamp, encamp, *slampamp,* restamp, *backstamp,* revamp **3.** Davy lamp, safety lamp, signal lamp.

AMPS– amps etc., *see* **AMP–** amp etc. above, plus "s" or "'s."

AN– **1.** Ann, Anne, ban, Chan, Dan, dan, fan, gan [slang], khan, can, scan, clan, plan, man, pan, Pan, panne, span, ran, bran, Fran, fran [slang], gran, cran, scran, san, tan, than, van **2.** cabane, redan, sedan, Sudan, began, bahan, pecan, *oilcan, cancan, ashcan*, Milan, replan, *madman*, reman, *seaman, cabman, jibman, clubman, subman, tubman, headman, leadman, madman, oddman, bandman, sandman, bondman, hodman, woodman, rodman, wardman, birdman, iceman, freeman, cageman, bargeman, dirgemar, brakeman, lineman, tapeman, fireman, wireman, shoreman, horseman, Norseman, flagman, ragman, dragman, swagman, pegman, yeggman, hangman, songman, cogman, tugman, coachman, Welchman, ranchman, henchman, Frenchman, churchman, watchman, switchman, Scotchman, Dutchman, ploughman, freshman, Welshman, Bushman, Northman, packman, checkman, lockman stockman, milkman, bankman, bookman, workman, oilman, bellman, billman, millman, stillman, tollman, Pullman, dolman, schoolman, penman, trainman, gunman, yeoman, Roman, woman, capman, chapman, shipman, tipman, shopman, topman, barman, carman, spearman, German, Herman, Sherman, merman, airman, Norman, floorman, beadsman, headsman, leadsman, oddsman, bandsman, landsman, bondsman, woodsman, guardsman, herdsman, swordsman, tribesman, tradesman, desman, spokesman, salesman, talesman, dolesman, shoresman, statesman, dragsman, gangsman, marksman, bailsman, spoilsman, almsman, helmsman, groomsman, clansman, kinsman, townsman, oarsman, passman, messman, pressman, batsman, craftsman, draftsman, yachtsman, huntsman, Scotsman, sportsman, batman, meatman, boatman, pitman, footman, postman, Truman, crewman, bowman, cowman, showman, plowman, cayman, layman, playman, drayman, wayman, flyman*, Japan, *lapin*, sapan, *sapin, hardpan*, trepan, *sampan*, Chopin, *inspan, outspan*, Iran, outran, Bataan, rattan, *gratin, fantan*, divan **3.** Marianne, Caliban, balmacaan, barbican, rubican, indican, Anglican, Gallican, pemmican, African, Vatican, Mexican, Oppidan, harridan, orlean, joulean, tinean, Marnean, Etnean, Kordofan, suffragan, cardigan, Michigan, mulligan, hooligan, ptarmigan, wanigan, origan, larrigan, Jonathan, astrakhan, Serbian, Lesbian, Nubian, Indian, guardian, Gordian, Lydian, saffian, ruffian, Belgian, Georgian, Pythian, Fijian, Anglian, Tullian, Julian, simian, Marnian, Appian, Caspian, Thespian, Marian, Austrian, Elysian, Tahitian, Egyptian, Servian, Latvian, Chinaman, husbandman, *policeman*, Orangeman, nobleman, middleman, rifleman, gentleman, longshoreman, signalman, Mussulman, dragoman, midshipman, alderman, fisherman, superman, waterman, peterman, slaughterman, quarterman, overman, sailorman, backwoodsman, Irishman, talisman, *frontiersman*, aircraftsman, *selectman*, merchantman, highwayman, clergyman, tallyman, liveryman, dairyman, ferryman, merryman, countryman, vestryman, marzipan, tragopan, Lutheran, veteran, Alcoran, Parmesan, courtesan, Powhatan, Yucatan, *Tibetan*, Puritan, rheotan, Turkestan, Pakistan, caravan, cordovan, Libyan, Wesleyan **4.** militiaman, jinrikiman, artilleryman, deliveryman, infantryman, catamaran, Baluchistan, Afghanistan, orangutan.

ANCH– **1.** ganch, canch [slang], Blanche, blanch, flanch, ranch, branch, stanch **3.** avalanche.

AND– **1.** and, band, banned, dand [slang], fanned, hand, canned, scanned, land, bland, gland, planned, manned, panned, spanned, brand, grand, strand, sand, tanned, stand **2.** *headband, neckband*, disband, *breastband, wristband*, offhand, *backhand*, unhand, *shorthand*, firsthand, *headland, midland woodland, eland, mainland, dreamland, Greenland, Rhineland, inland, lowland, Lapland, upland, moorland, grassland, Queensland, wasteland, northland*, demand, remand, command, expand, *firebrand, quicksand, greensand, lampstand*, withstand **3.** saraband, contraband, bellyband, four-in-hand, behindhand, secondhand, evenhand, underhand, afterhand, overhand, upper hand, samarcand, fairyland, wonderland, borderland, hinterland, fatherland, motherland, overland, reprimand, confirmand, countermand, Rio Grande, ampersand, understand **4.** multiplicand, Chateaubriand, misunderstand.

ANG– **1.** bang, bhang, dang [dial.], fang, gang, hang, lang [Scot. and dial.], clang, slang, pang, spang [coll.], rang, sprang, sang, tang, swang, twang, whang, vang **2.** shebang, *gambang*, gobang, *holmgang*, *ingang*, *sirgang*, *outgang*, *oxgang*, *boomslang*, Penang, trepang, harangue, meringue, serang, *mustang* **3.** overhang, boomerang, burrawang **4.** orangoutang.

ANGD– **1.** banged, danged [dial.], fanged, ganged [coll.], hanged, clanged, twanged, whanged **2.** bifanged, harangued **3.** boomeranged.

ANGZ– bangs etc., *see* **ANG–** bang etc. above, plus "s" or "'s."

ANJ– **1.** banj [slang], gange, flange **2.** *phalange*, *sporange*.

ANK– **1.** ank [slang], bank, banc, dank, hank, lank, blank, flank, clank, plank, spank, rank, frank, Frank, franc, crank, prank, sank, shank, tank, thank, swank, yank **2.** embank, point-blank, outflank, *gangplank*, disrank, outrank, *redshank*, *foreshank* **3.** mountebank, riverbank, savings bank.

ANKS– banks etc., *see* **ANK–** bank etc. above, plus "s" or "'s"; **1.** Manx, thanx [slang], Yanks **2.** *Fairbanks*, *phalanx*, *longshanks* **3.** bonyshanks.

ANKT– **1.** banked, blanked, flanked, clanked, planked, spanked, ranked, franked, cranked, sanct, tanked, thanked, swanked, yanked **2.** outflanked, outranked **3.** sacrosanct, spindle-shanked.

ANS– **1.** anse, chance, dance, hanse, lance, glance, manse, nance [slang], France, prance, trance, stance **2.** bechance, perchance, mischance, seance, enhance, askance, romance, finance, expanse, entrance, *brilliance*, advance **3.** *disturbance*, *impedance*, *misguidance*, *avoidance*, *ascendance*, permeance, elegance, arrogance, radiance, *allegiance*, *appliance*, variance, nonchalance, sibilance, jubilance, vigilance, ambulance, simulance, petulance, maintenance, countenance, sustenance, prévenance [F], provenance, convenance [F.], *repugnance*, ordinance, dominance, resonance, consonance, assonance, dissonance, governance, *remembrance*, *encumbrance*, sufferance, furtherance, tolerance, temperance, utterance, severance, ignorance, aberrance, penetrance, *remonstrance*, *defeasance*, *malfeasance*, *complaisance*, *obeisance*, *conversance*, *expectance*, *inductance*, *conductance*, *reluctance*, oscitance, hesitance, *repentance*, *acceptance*, circumstance, *inconstance*, *pursuance*, issuance, relevance, *clairvoyance* **4.** significance, extravagance, inelegance, insouciance, irradiance, luxuriance, discountenance, appurtenance, preordinance, predominance, inconsonance, vociferance, intemperance, deliverance, recalcitrance, reconnoisance, reconnaissance, exorbitance, concomitance, precipitance, inheritance, continuance, perpetuance, irrelevance **5.** insignificance, disinheritance, discontinuance.

ANST– **1.** chanced, danced, lanced, glanced, pranced, tranced **2.** enhanced, romanced, financed, entranced, advanced.

ANT– **1.** ant, aunt, bant [slang], gant [slang], hant [slang], chant, cant, can't, scant, plant, slant, pant, rant, grant, shan't **2.** enchant, decant, recant, askant, descant, gallant, replant, *eggplant*, *pieplant*, implant, transplant, supplant, aslant, courant, courante, extant, levant, bezant **3.** Corybant, agacant, desiccant, exsiccant, dodecant, imprecant, albicant, radicant, abdicant, dedicant, mendicant, indicant, applicant, formicant, fabricant, lubricant, vesicant, toxicant, coruscant, confidant, permeant, recreant, procreant, miscreant, elegant, congregant, obligant, irrigant, litigant, mitigant, arrogant, elephant, oliphant, *triumphant*, sycophant, resiant, otiant, nonchalant, libelant, revelant, sibilant, jubilant, vigilant, tremolant, circulant, osculant, stridulant, undulant, ululant, stimulant, cumulant, petulant, postulant, *informant*, revenant, covenant, ordinant, culminant, dominant, consonant, assonant, dissonant, mancipant, Sacripant, celebrant, tolerant, alterant, cauterant, integrant, emigrant, immigrant, odorant, colorant, cormorant, ignorant, penetrant, registrant, ministrant, obscurant, figurant, fulgurant, hebetant, vegetant, dilettant, habitant, oscitant, militant, comitant, crepitant, irritant, hesitant, visitant, *important*, *inconstant*, debutant, menstruant, issuant, fluctuant, gallivant, innovant, cognizant **4.** communicant, intoxicant, consolidant, extravagant, inelegant, depreciant, officiant, renunciant, insouciant, circumvolant, matriculant, coagulant, articulant, congratulant, impetulant, capitulant, appurtenant, discriminant, determinant, aggultinant, conglutinant, horrisonant, reverberant, protuberant, exuberant, preponderant, refrigerant, intolerant, agglomerant, itinerant, deodorant, ameliorant, decolorant, expectorant, recalcitrant, administrant, resuscitant, incogitant, regurgitant, concomitant, continuant, attenuant, irrelevant, incognizant.

ANTS– ants etc., *see* **ANT–** ant etc. above, plus "s" or "'s."

ANZ– Ann's etc., *see* **AN–** Ann etc. above, plus "s" or "'s"; **1.** banns.

AP– **1.** chap, dap, gap, hap, Jap, cap, lap, Lapp, flap, clap, slap, map, nap, knap, snap, pap, rap, wrap, crap, scrap, trap, strap, sap, tap, yap, yapp **2.** *stopgap*, mayhap, *mishap*, *madcap*, *redcap*, becap, *kneecap*, recap, *skullcap*, uncap, *icecap*, *nightcap*, *whitecap*, *foolscap*, *bluecap*, *catlap*, *dewlap*, *flyflap*, *flip-flap*, beclap, *backslap*, genapp, genappe, surnap, resnap, unsnap, enwrap, *mantrap*, entrap, *claptrap*, bestrap, *checkstrap*, *rattrap*, *winesap*, *heeltap*, lagniappe **3.** handicap, overlap, thunderclap, afterclap, photomap, rattletrap.

APS– chaps etc., *see* **AP–** chap etc. above, plus "s" or "'s"; **1.** apse, lapse, schnapps **2.** perhaps, elapse, relapse, collapse, prolapse, synapse **3.** pettichaps.

APST– **1.** lapsed **2.** elapsed, relapsed, collapsed.

AR– through **ARZ–**, *see* long **A** (ay): **AR–** through **ARZ–**; also broad **A** (ah): **AR–** through **ARZ–**.

AS– **1.** ass, bass, fas, gas, lass, blas, glass, class, mass, pass, wrasse, brass, brasse, grass, crass, strass, sass [dial. and slang], tass, vas **2.** *jackass*, rubasse, *fracas*, *Dorcas*, *Midas*, *nefas* [L.], bagasse, fougasse, alas, *Hellas*, *eyeglass*, *hourglass*, declass, reclass, outclass, amass, remass, *Lammas*, en masse, *Thomas*, *Christmas*, *pampas*, *compass*, impasse, surpass, *trespass*, *upas*, *arras*, harass, *Madras*, *Mithras*, terras, terrass, cuirass, morass, *dronkgrass*, *eelgrass*, *Kansas*, kavass, crevasse, *Texas* **3.** anabasse, contrabass, octobass, pancreas, Boreas, isinglass, looking glass, galloglass, weatherglass, middle class, working class, sonderclass, underclass, upper-class, superclass, bonny lass, Nicholas, Pythias, alias, Elias, Candlemas, Michaelmas, Martinmas, Hallowmas, underpass, overpass, Khyber Pass, *encompass*, sassafras, coup-de-grâce [F.], peppergrass, sparrowgrass, Alcatras, *Honduras*, demitasse, tarantass.

ASH– **1.** ash, bash, dash, gash, hash, hache, cash, cache, lash, lâche [F.], flash, clash, plash, splash, slash, mash, smash, gnash, pash [dial.], rash, brash, crash, thrash, sash, stash [dial. and slang], vache **2.** abash, rondache, *slapdash*, rehash, encash, *eyelash*, *backlash*, *pearlash*, *mishmash*, panache, apache, patache [F.], pistache, moustache, soutache [F.] **3.** calabash, balderdash, spatterdash, sabretache.

ASHT– **1.** bashed, dashed, gashed, hashed, cashed, cached, lashed, flashed, clashed, splashed, slashed, mashed, smashed, gnashed, crashed, thrashed, sashed, stashed **2.** abashed, moustached.

ASK– **1.** ask, bask, Basque, casque, cask, flask, mask, task **2.** unmask **3.** antimask.

ASP– **1.** asp, gasp, hasp, clasp, rasp, grasp **2.** agasp, unhasp, enclasp, unclasp.

AST– **1.** bast, dast [dial], fast, gassed, gast [slang], hast, cast, caste, last, blast, mast, massed, nast, past, passed, sassed, vast **2.** *bombast*, *broadcast*, *molecast*, recast, forecast, *dicast*, *downcast*, upcast, miscast, outcast, *steadfast*, *holdfast*, *handfast*, *breakfast*, aghast, *ballast*, *portlast*, outlast, outclassed, amassed, remast, *foremast*, *mainmast*, *durmast*, unmast, dismast, *gymnast*, *dynast*, repast, repassed, *mainpast*, *trispast*, surpassed, harassed, *contrast*, *peltast*, *phantast*, avast **3.** undercast, overcast, scholiast, counterblast, unsurpassed, antispast, pederast, paraphrast, metaphrast, flabbergast **4.** elegiast, bucoliast, ecclesiast, symposiast, enthusiast, iconoclast.

AT– **1.** at, bat, chat, fat, gat, hat, cat, scat, skat, lat, blat, flat, plat, plait, splat, slat, mat, matte, gnat, pat, patte, spat, rat brat, drat, frat [slang], prat, sprat, sat, tat, that, vat **2.** hereat, thereat, whereat, *brickbat*, *hurlbat*, begat, highhat, top hat, *woodchat*, *whinchat*, *stonechat*, *grasschat*, *chitchat*, *bobcat*, *wildcat*, *hellcat*, *polecat*, *tipcat*, *bearcat*, plakat, *muscat*, surat, cravat **3.** caveat, acrobat, flitterbat, tabby cat, kittycat, pussycat, waterchat, lariat, diplomat, pitapat, tokopat, Ararat, democrat, monocrat, bureaucrat, autocrat, plutocrat, thermostat, Rubaiyat **4.** Magnificat, aristocrat, heliostat **5.** commissariat, proletariat, secretariat.

ATCH– batch etc., *see* **ACH–** batch etc. above.

ATH– **1.** bath, Gath, hath, lath, math, snath, path, rath, wrath, strath **2.** *bypath*, *towpath*, *warpath*, *footpath* **3.** demibath, isobath, polymath, misomath, aftermath, philomath, allopath **4.** homeopath, osteopath, physiopath.

AV– **1.** bave [F.], have, halve, calve, lav [slang], Slav, salve **2.** épave [F.] **3.** Jugoslav.

AVZ– **1.** halves, calves, Slavs, salves **3.** Jugoslavs.

AZ– **1.** as, chaz [slang], has, jazz, razz [slang], yazz [slang] **2.** thereas, whereas **3.** razzmatazz.

AZM– **1.** phasm, chasm, plasm, spasm **2.** *sarcasm*, *orgasm*, *miasm*, *empasm*, *phantasm* **3.** idiasm, schediasm, chiliasm, cataclasm, metaplasm, pseudoplasm, neoplasm, protoplasm, pleonasm **4.** enthusiasm, demoniasm, iconoclasm.

A (cab)

2.

DOUBLE (FEMININE) RHYMES IN A (gab'ber)

Primary or Secondary Accent Falls on Next to Last Syllable: Imperfect Rhymes Are in Italics.

AB'er– **2.** dabber, gabber, jabber, blabber, clabber, slabber, nabber, grabber, stabber.

AB'erd– **2.** gabbard, jabbered, scabbard, blabbered, clabbered, tabard.

AB'i– **2.** abbey, Abbie, gabby, cabby, scabby, blabby, flabby, rabbi, crabby, shabby, tabby.

AB'id– **2.** rabid, tabid.

AB'ij– **2.** cabbage.

AB'ik– **2.** rabic **3.** syllabic, cannabic **4.** asyllabic, bisyllabic, trisyllabic **5.** polysyllabic, multisyllabic, monosyllabic.

AB'il– **2.** habile; *see* also **AB'l–** babble etc. below.

AB'in– **2.** cabin, dabbin' etc. **3.** log cabin.

AB'ing– **2.** dabbing, gabbing, jabbing, cabbing, blabbing, nabbing, slabbing, stabbing **3.** confabbing **4.** taxicabbing.

AB'it– **2.** Babbitt, habit, rabbet, rabbit, drabbet **3.** inhabit, cohabit.

AB'l– **2.** babble, dabble, gabble, habile, jabble, cabble, scabble, rabble, brabble, drabble, grabble, scrabble, !yabble **3.** bedabble, bedrabble **4.** applicable, duplicable, explicable, amicable, despicable, extricable, practicable, masticable, educable, manducable, formidable, noticeable, serviceable, balanceable, marriageable, damageable, manageable, knowledgeable, challangeable, *dischargeable*, malleable, permeable, *unliveable*, propagable, refragable, segregable, obligable, irrigable, mitigable, navigable, publishable, perishable, amiable, expiable, variable, leviable violable, calculable, regulable, estimable, fathomable, terminable, pardonable, fashionable, pensionable, actionable, sanctionable, mentionable, questionable, poisonable, personable, governable, exculpable, separable, execrable, renderable, ponderable, preferable, offerable, sufferable, tolerable, numerable, venerable, vulnerable, temperable, superable, miserable, alterable, utterable, conquerable, severable, answerable, admirable, gibble-gabble, ribble-rabble, memorable, honorable, favorable, pleasurable, measurable, exorable, censurable, mensurable, purchasable, marketable, covetable, habitable, dubitable, creditable, *forgettable*, profitable, limitable, hospitable, charitable, irritable, equitable, evitable, comfortable, valuable, *inequable*, issuable **5.** eradicable, multiplicable, inapplicable, inexplicable, inextricable, impracticable, prognosticable, unnoticeable, disserviceable, unmanageable, acknowledgeable, unchallengeable, impermeable, immitigable, interrogable, distinguishable, extinguishable, enunciable, remediable, affiliable, inexpiable, invariable, imperviable, inviolable, incalculable, inoculable, coagulable, inestimable, unfathomable, inalienable, imaginable, disciplinable, contaminable, examinable, abominable, determinable, interminable, unpardonable, companionable, impassionable, impressionable, objectionable, exceptionable, proportionable, unquestionable, developable, inseparable, rememberable, considerable, imponderable, insufferable, decipherable, intolerable, innumerable, invulnerable, insuperable, unalterable, inseverable, deliverable, recoverable, discoverable, unanswerable, commemorable, dishonorable, unfavorable, immeasurable, impenetrable, incensurable, immensurable, commensurable, interpretable, inhabitable, indubitable, discreditable, hereditable, unprofitable, illimitable, inimitable, indomitable, decapitable, precipitable, inhospitable, uncharitable, inequitable, inevitable, uncomfortable, contributable, distributable, attributable, invaluable, perpetuable **6.** ineradicable, indistinguishable, inextinguishable, irremediable, inalienable, unimaginable, indeterminable, disproportionable, undevelopable, inconsiderable, undecipherable, irrecoverable, incommensurable, uninhabitable; *see* also **IB'l–** bibble etc.

AB'ler– **2.** babbler, dabbler, gabbler, cabbler, scabbler, brabbler, grabbler, scrabbler **3.** bedabbler.

AB'let– **2.** crablet, tablet.

AB'li– **2.** babbly, dabbly, drably.

AB'ling– **2.** babbling, dabbling, gabbling, scabbling, brabbling, grabbling.

AB'lish– **2.** babblish **3.** establish **4.** reestablish, disestablish.

AB'o– **2.** jabot, sabot.

AB'ot– **2.** abbot, Abbot, Cabot.

ACH'el– **2.** hatchel, ratchel, satchel.

ACH'er– **2.** batcher, hatcher, catcher, latcher, matcher, snatcher, patcher, scratcher, thatcher **3.** *dogcatcher*, *flycatcher*, dispatcher, *back-scratcher*.

ACH'et– **2.** hatchet, latchet, matchet, ratchet, brachet.

ACH'ez– **2.** batches, baches, hatches, catches, latches, Natchez, patches, matches **3.** *nuthatches*, mismatches, *crosspatches*, dispatches, attaches, detaches **4.** Kaffee Klatches.

ACH'i– **2.** catchy, matchy, machi, snatchy, patchy, scratchy **3.** seecatchie.

ACH'ing– **2.** batching, baching, hatching, catching, latching, matching, snatching, patching, scratching, thatching **3.** dispatching, rematching, mismatching, attaching, detaching, back-scratching.

ACH'less– **2.** batchless, hatchless, catchless, latchless, matchless, patchless, scratchless, thatchless **3.** dispatchless.

ACH'ment– **2.** hatchment, ratchment **3.** attachment, detachment, dispatchment.

AD'a– **2.** adda, dada, stadda.

AD'am– **2.** Adam, madam **3.** macadam.

AD'ed– **2.** added, gadded, plaided, padded, bradded **3.** readded, unadded, unpadded.

AD'en– **2.** gladden, madden, sadden **3.** engladden, Macfadden.

AD'er– **2.** adder, badder, gadder, ladder, bladder, gladder, madder, sadder **3.** stepladder.

AD'est– **2.** baddest, gladdest, maddest, saddest.

AD'i– **2.** daddy, faddy, caddy, caddie, laddie, gladdy, maddy, paddy **4.** sugar daddy, finnanhaddie.

AD'ij– **2.** adage.

AD'ik– **3.** decadic, haggadic, triadic, Helladic, nomadic, monadic, faradic, sporadic, octadic, Sotadic, dyadic, nexadic.

AD'ing– **2.** adding, gadding, padding, bradding.

AD'ish– **2.** faddish, caddish, gladdish, plaidish, maddish, radish, saddish.

AD'l– **2.** addle, paddle, raddle, straddle, saddle, staddle [dial.] **3.** skedaddle [coll.], astraddle, bestraddle, unsaddle **4.** fiddle-faddle.

AD'ld– **2.** addled, paddled, raddled, straddled, saddled, staddled [dial.] **3.** skedaddled [coll.], unsaddled **4.** fiddle-faddled.

AD'li– **2.** badly, gladly, madly, sadly.

AD'ling– 2. addling, paddling, straddling, saddling, spraddling, staddling [dial.] skedaddling, unsaddling 4. fiddle-faddling.

AD'lz– addles etc., *see* **AD'l–** addle etc. above, plus "s" or "'s"; 4. Thomas Traddles [Dickens].

AD'ness– 2. badness, gladness, madness, sadness.

AD'o– 2. shadow 3. foreshadow 4. Colorado, overshadow.

AD'ok– 2. baddock, haddock, paddock, shaddock.

AF'er– 2. chaffer, gaffer, Kaffir, laugher quaffer, piaffer, zaffer.

AF'i– 2. baffy, chaffy, daffy, faffy, draffy, taffy.

AF'ik– 2. maffick, graphic, traffic, Sapphic 3. seraphic, engraphic 4. diagraphic, paragraphic, telegraphic, choregraphic, calligraphic, geographic, melographic, zoographic, lithographic, orthographic, biographic, holographic, stylographic, demographic, homographic, seismographic, cosmographic, chromographic, stenographic, ethnographic, phonographic, chronographic, topographic, typographic, macrographic, micrographic, chirographic, chorographic, neurographic, pyrographic, isographic, pantographic, photographic, cryptographic, cartographic, histographic, autographic, polygraphic 5. paleographic, oleographic, ethneographic, idiographic, bibliographic, heliographic, crystallographic, dactylographic 6. autobiographic, cinematographic.

AF'ing– 2. chaffing, faffing, gaffing, laughing, staffing, quaffing 4. telegraphing, autographing, paragraphing, photographing, lithographing.

AF'l– 2. baffle, daffle [dial.], gaffle, snaffle, raffle, scraffle, yaffle.

AF'ling– 2. baffling, calfling, haffling, snaffling, raffling.

AFT'ed– 2. rafted, drafted, grafted, shafted, wafted 3. engrafted, ingrafted.

AFT'er– 2. after, dafter, laughter, rafter, drafter, draughter, grafter, wafter 3. hereafter, thereafter, whereafter 4. hereinafter, thereinafter.

AFT'i– 2. rafty, drafty, grafty, crafty, wafty.

AFT'ij– 2. draftage, draughtage, graftage, waftage.

AFT'ing– 2. hafting, rafting, drafting, draughting, grafting, shafting, wafting 3. engrafting, ingrafting.

AFT'less– 2. draftless, graftless, craftless, shaftless.

AG'a– 2. Agha, dagga, saga, quagga.

AG'ed– 2. jagged, knagged, ragged, cragged, scragged.

AG'er– 2. bagger, dagger, fagger, gagger, jagger, lagger, flagger, nagger, snagger, ragger, bragger, dragger, sagger, tagger, stagger, wagger, swagger 3. two-bagger. *wigwagger*, *zigzagger* 4. agar-agar, carpetbagger.

AG'erd– 2. haggard, laggard, blackguard, staggard, staggered, swaggered.

AG'ert– 2. braggart, staggart.

AG'i– 2. Aggie, baggie, baggy, faggy, gaggy, haggy [Scot. and dial. Eng.], jaggy, laggy, flaggy, slaggy, Maggie, naggy knaggy, snaggy, raggy, raggee, braggy, draggy, craggy, scraggy, saggy, shaggy, taggy, staggy, quaggy, waggy, swaggy.

AG'ij– 2. baggage.

AG'ing– 2. bagging, gagging, lagging, flagging, nagging, ragging, bragging, tagging, stagging 3. *zigzagging*.

AG'is– 2. haggis.

AG'ish– 2. haggish, flaggish, naggish, braggish, waggish.

AG'it– 2. agate 3. moss agate.

AG'l– 2. daggle, gaggle, haggle, draggle, straggle, waggle, waggel 3. bedraggle 4. raggle-taggle.

AG'ler– 2. daggler, gaggler, haggler, straggler, waggler 3. bedraggler.

AG'ling– 2. daggling, gaggling, haggling, raggling, draggling, straggling, waggling 3. bedraggling.

AG'ma– 2. magma 3. malagma.

AG'nat– 2. agnate, magnate, stagnate.

AG'nes– 2. Agnes, Sphagnous, magnus.

AG'net– 2. magnet, dragnet.

AG'num– 2. Sphagnum, magnum.

AG'on– 2. agon, flagon, dragon, wagon 3. pendragon, *snapdragon.*

AG'ot– 2. fagot, faggot, maggot.

AJ'ent– 2. pageant.

AJ'er– 2. agger, badger, cadger.

AJ'i– 2. hadji, cadgy 3. koradji.

AJ'ik– 2. magic, tragic 3. pelagic, choragic 4. theophagic, sarcophagic, theomagic, hemorrhagic, antitragic 5. archipelagic.

AJ'il– 2. agile, fragile.

AJ'in– 3. imagine.

AK'a– 2. bacca, lacca 3. sifaka, Malacca, alpaca.

AK'ard– 2. placard, Packard.

AK'at– 2. baccate, placate, saccate.

AK'en– 2. blacken, slacken, bracken, kraken.

AK'er– 2. backer, hacker, lacquer, blacker, clacker, slacker, smacker, knacker, packer, cracker, tracker, sacker, tacker, stacker, whacker 3. *whinchacker, hijacker,* shellacker, polacre, *clamcracker, corncracker, firecracker,* ransacker, *bushwhacker.*

AK'est– 2. blackest, slackest.

AK'et– 2. jacket, flacket, placket, packet, racket, rackett, bracket, sacket, tacket 3. *redjacket, bluejacket.*

AK'i– 2. hacky, Jacky, blackie, khaki, lackey, blacky, maki, knacky, raki, cracky, sake, tacky, quacky, wacky 3. *gimcracky* 4. Nagasaki.

AK'ij– 2. backage, package, wrackage, trackage, sackage, stackage.

AK'ing– 2. backing, lacking, blacking, clacking, smacking, packing, racking, cracking, tracking, sacking, tacking, quacking, whacking 3. shellacking, unpacking, ransacking, attacking.

AK'ish– 2. blackish, slackish, knackish, brackish, quackish.

AK'l– 2. hackle, cackle, mackle, macle, grackle, crackle, shackle, tackle, quackle 3. debacle, *piacle, manacle, pinnacle, barnacle, miracle, oracle, coracle, ramshackle,* unshackle, *spectacle, obstacle* 4. tabernacle, hibernacle.

AK'ler– 2. cackler, hackler, crackler, shackler, tackler.

AK'less– 2. backless, hackless, lackless, clackless, slackless, knackless, crackless, trackless, sackless, tackless, stackless.

AK'li– 2. cackly, blackly, slackly, crackly 3. ramshackly.

AK'ling– 2. cackling, crackling, shackling, tackling.

AK'ma– 2. chacma, drachma 4. tetradrachma.

AK'ness– 2. blackness, slackness.

AK'o– 2. jako, shako, squacco 3. tobacco, icaco, goracco.

AK'rid– 2. acrid.

AK'sen– 2. flaxen, waxen.

AK'sent– 2. accent.

AK'ser– 2. taxer, waxer 3. relaxer.

AK'ses– 2. access.

AK'sez– 2. axes, laxes, taxes, waxes 3. relaxes, dewaxes, rewaxes 4. battle-axes.

AK'shun– 2. action, faction, fraction, traction, taction 3. abaction, subaction, reaction, enaction, coaction, compaction, refraction, diffraction, infraction, contraction, protraction, attraction, abstraction, distraction, extraction, transaction, contaction, exaction 4. interaction, counteraction, rubefaction, calefaction, malefaction, putrefaction, liquefaction, satisfaction **5.** dissatisfaction, counterattraction.

AK'shus– **2.** factious, fractious.

AK'si– **2.** flaxy, Maxie, braxy, taxi, taxy, waxy **4.** biotaxy, zootaxy, homotaxy.

AK'sing– **2.** axing, taxing, waxing **3.** relaxing, rewaxing.

AK'sis– **2.** axis, praxis, taxis, staxis **3.** synaxis, syntaxis **4.** prophylaxis, parapraxis, chiropraxis, parataxis, hypotaxis, epistaxis.

AK'son– **2.** axon, Jackson, klaxon, Saxon **3.** diaxon, dendraxon **4.** Anglo-Saxon.

AKT'a– **2.** acta, facta.

AKT'ed– **2.** acted, pacted, fracted **3.** enacted, coacted, redacted, reacted, impacted, defracted, diffracted, attracted, subtracted, detracted, retracted, contracted, protracted, abstracted, distracted, extracted, transacted, contacted, exacted **4.** retroacted, abreacted, arefacted.

AKT'er– **2.** acter, actor, factor, tractor, tactor **3.** abactor, redactor, attracter, diffractor, subtracter, contracter, contractor, protracter, protractor, abstracter, extractor, exacter, exactor **4.** calefactor, malefactor, benefactor.

AKT'ful– **2.** tactful **3.** distractful.

AKT'ik– **2.** lactic, practic, tactic **3.** didactic, galactic, stalactic, malactic, phylactic, climactic, synactic, emphractic, syntactic, protactic **4.** parallactic, catallactic, prophylactic, chiropractic.

AKT'iks– **2.** tactics **3.** didactics **4.** catallactics.

AKT'il– **2.** dactyl, fractile, tractile, tactile **3.** adactyl, didactyl, syndactyl, retractile, contractile, protractile.

AKT'ing– **2.** acting **3.** redacting, enacting, defracting, attracting, retracting, contracting, abstracting, distracting, transacting, exacting **4.** double-acting, counteracting, retroacting.

AKT'is– **2.** practice, practise **3.** malpractice.

AKT'iv– **2.** active, factive **3.** reactive, enactive, inactive, olfactive, refractive, diffractive, attractive, subtractive, detractive, retractive, contractive, protractive, abstractive, distractive, extractive **4.** radioactive, retroactive, counteractive, calefactive, benefactive, rarefactive, putrefactive, liquefactive, unattractive.

AKT'less– **2.** factless, bractless, pactless, tractless, tactless **3.** *compactless*, *abstractless.*

AKT'li– **3.** compactly, abstractly, intactly, exactly **5.** matter-of-factly.

AKT'ment– **3.** enactment, impactment, extractment **4.** re-enactment.

AKT'ness– **3.** compactness, intactness, exactness **4.** inexactness **5.** matter-of-factness.

AKT'o– **2.** acto, facto **3.** de facto.

AKT'or– **2.** actor, acter, factor, tractor, tactor **3.** enacter, diffractor, extractor, exactor **4.** benefactor; *see* also **AK'ter–** acter etc. above.

AKT'ress– **2.** actress **3.** exactress **4.** malefactress, benefactress.

AKT'um– **2.** actum, factum, pactum.

AKT'ur– **2.** facture, fracture **3.** compacture, contracture **4.** manufacture.

AKT'us– **2.** actus, cactus, tactus **4.** Ferocactus.

AL'a– **2.** alla, Allah, galla, gala, calla, palla, pallah **3.** *cabala*, emgalla, Valhalla, mashallah, cavalla.

AL'ad– **2.** ballad, salad.

AL'ans– **2.** balance, valance **3.** unbalance **4.** counterbalance, overbalance.

AL'ant– **2.** gallant, callant, talent **3.** ungallant.

AL'as– **2.** balas, Dallas, Pallas.

ALB'a– **2.** alba, galba **3.** xibalba.

ALB'e– **2.** albe, halbe.

ALB'ert– 2. Albert, halbert.

AL'eed– 2. dallied, rallied, sallied, tallied 4. dilly-dallied, shilly-shallied.

AL'ent– 2. talent; *see* also **AL'ant–** gallant etc. above.

AL'er– 2. pallor, valor 3. caballer.

AL'et– 2. ballot, gallet, mallet, palate, pallet, palette, sallet, valet.

ALF'a– 2. alfa, alpha 3. alfalfa, pentalpha.

AL'i– 2. ally, bally, dally, gally, pally, rally, sally, Sallie, challie, challis, tally, valley 3. Bengali, tamale 4. dilly-dally, Mexicali, shilly-shally, hot tamale.

AL'id– 2. calid, pallid, valid 3. impallid, invalid.

AL'ik– 2. Aleck, Gallic, phallic, malic, grallic, Salic, thallic 3. cabalic, vocalic, vandalic, Uralic, medallic, metallic, italic, Tantalic, smart aleck [coll.], oxalic 4. encephalic, misogallic, intervallic.

AL'is– 2. Alice, allice, chalice, malice, palace 4. digitalis.

ALJ'e– 2. algae, Algy 3. neuralgy, nostalgy.

ALJ'ik– 2. algic 3. gastralgic, neuralgic, antalgic, nostalgic.

ALM'a– 2. Alma, halma 3. agalma.

ALM'ud– 2. almud, Talmud.

AL'o– 2. aloe, fallow, hallow, callow, mallow, sallow, shallow, tallow 3. Allhallow, unhallow, dishallow, marshmallow.

AL'on– 2. gallon, kalon, salon, talon.

AL'op– 2. galop, gallop, scallop, shallop 3. escallop.

AL'or– 2. pallor, valor 3. caballer.

AL'ot– 2. ballot; *see* also **AL'et–** gallet etc. above.

AL'oz– 2. aloes, gallows, hallows 3. Allhallows, dishallows, marshmallows.

ALP'in– 2. Alpine 3. subalpine, Cisalpine, transalpine.

ALP'ing– 2. scalping, palping.

ALT'o– 2. alto 3. Rialto, contralto.

AL'u– 2. value 3. evalue, devalue, revalue 4. undervalue.

AL'um– 2. alum, vallum 3. chloralum, catallum.

AL'us– 2. phallus, Gallus, callus, callous, thallus 4. aryballus.

AL'ya– 2. Alya, dahlia.

AL'yant– 2. valiant.

AL'yun– 2. scallion, pallion, stallion 3. medallion, rapscallion, battalion, Italian.

AM'a– 2. amma, chamma, Gamma, drama, Shammah, Yama 3. Digamma, pajama, pyjama, programma 4. Alabama, panorama, melodrama, monodrama, duodrama.

AM'al– 2. Hamal, mammal; *see* also **AM'el–** camel etc. below.

AMB'er– 2. amber, camber, clamber, sambar, tambour 3. grisamber 4. liquidamber.

AMB'ik– 3. Iambic 4. galliambic, choliambic, choriambic, Pythiambic.

AMB'ist– 2. gambist, cambist 3. iambist.

AMB'it– 2. ambit, gambit.

AMB'l– 2. amble, gamble, gambol, ramble, bramble, scramble, shamble, wamble 3. *preamble*, unscramble.

AMB'ler– 2. ambler, gambler, rambler, scrambler, shambler.

AMB'ling– 2. ambling, gambling, rambling, brambling, scrambling.

AMB'lz– 2. ambles, gambles, gambols, rambles, brambles, scrambles, shambles 3. preambles, unscrambles.

AMB'o– 2. ambo, jambeau, flambeau, crambo, sambo, Sambo, zambo.

AMB'ol– 2. gambol; *see* also **AMB'l–** amble etc. above.

AMB'us– 3. iambus 4. dithyrambus.

AM'ed– 3. Mohammed.

AM'el– 2. camel, Hamal, mammal, trammel 3. enamel, entrammel, untrammel.

AM'er– 2. ammer, dammer, damner, gammer, hammer, jammer, lamber, glamor, clamor, slammer, rammer, grammar, crammer, shammer, stammer, yammer 3. *sledgehammer*, exhammer, *windjammer*, enamor 4. yellowhammer.

AM'fer– 2. camphor, chamfer.

AM'i– 2. gammy, hammy, jammy, clammy, mammy, sammy, chamois, shammy, tammy 3. Miami.

AM'ij– 2. damage, ramage 3. endamage.

AM'ik– 2. amic, gamic 3. Adamic, agamic, syngamic, cinnamic, dynamic, ceramic, engrammic, balsamic, potamic, Benthamic 4. preadamic, polygamic, homogamic, monogamic, Abrahamic, dioramic, cycloramic, cosmoramic, panoramic, telegrammic, monogrammic.

AM'in– 2. amine, famine, gamin, lamin, stamin 3. prolamine, examine 4. reexamine, cross-examine.

AM'ing– 2. damming, damning, gamming, jamming, lambing, lamming [slang], flamming, clamming, slamming, ramming, cramming, shamming, whamming.

AM'is– 2. amice, chlamys, tamis 3. dynamis.

AM'ish– 2. famish, lambish, clammish, rammish 3. enfamish.

AM'let– 2. hamlet, Hamlet, camlet, samlet.

AM'ok– 2. hammock, cammock, mammock.

AM'on– 2. ammon, Ammon, gammon, mammon, salmon, shaman 3. backgammon.

AM'oth– 2. mammoth.

AMP'an– 2. jampan, sampan, tampan.

AMP'ant– 2. rampant.

AMP'as– 2. lampas, pampas.

AMP'er– 2. champer, damper, hamper, camper, scamper, clamper, pamper, pampre, ramper, tramper, tamper, stamper, vamper 3. decamper, revamper.

AMP'i– 2. dampy, crampy, vampy.

AMP'ing– 2. damping, camping, scamping, clamping, ramping, tramping, tamping, stamping, vamping 3. decamping, revamping.

AMP'ish– 2. dampish, campish, scampish, trampish, vampish.

AMP'l– 2. ample, trample, sample 3. ensample, example.

AMP'ler– 2. ampler, trampler, sampler 3. exampler.

AMP'li– 2. amply, damply.

AMP'ling– 2. sampling, trampling 3. ensampling.

AMP'ment– 3. decampment, encampment.

AMP'us– 2. campus, grampus 4. hippocampus.

AM'ut– 2. gamut, Mammut.

AMZ'el– 2. amsel, damsel.

AMZ'un– 2. damson, ramson.

AN'a– 2. ana, Ana, anna, Anna, Hannah, canna, Lana, manna 3. bandanna, Diana, Guiana, liana, banana, sultana, lantana, Montana, ruana, Havana, savanna, Savannah, hosanna, Susanna 4. Indiana, Georgiana, Pollyanna, Marianna, dulciana, Gloriana, tertiana, Susquehanna, Poinciana, Texarkana 5. Louisiana.

AN'al– 2. annal; *see* also **AN'el–** channel etc. below.

ANCH'er– 2. blancher, plancher, rancher, brancher, stancher.

ANCH'ez– 2. blanches, ranches, branches, stanches 4. avalanches.

ANCH'i– 2. ranchy, branchy.

ANCH'ing– 2. blanching, planching, ranching, branching, stanching.

ANCH'less– 2. ranchless, branchless, stanchless.

AND'a– 2. panda, vanda 3. Uganda, Amanda, veranda, Miranda 4. propaganda, jacaranda, memoranda, observanda.

AND'al– 2. scandal, pandal, sandal, Randall, crandall, vandal, Vandal; *see* also **AND'l–** dandle etc. below.

AND'ant– 2. mandant 3. demandant, commandant.

AND'ed– 2. banded, handed, candid, landed, glanded, branded, stranded, sanded 3. disbanded, red-handed, freehanded, three-handed, highhanded, backhanded, blackhanded, fullhanded, cleanhanded, unhanded, forehanded, fourhanded, closehanded, neat-handed, lefthanded, light-handed, right-handed, shorthanded, two-handed, unlanded, demanded, remanded, commanded, expanded, unbranded 4. contrabanded, empty-handed, heavy-handed, singlehanded, openhanded, evenhanded, overhanded, underhanded, reprimanded, countermanded.

AND'eed– 2. bandied, candied, brandied.

AND'er– 2. bander, dander, gander, candor, Landor, lander, blander, slander, pandar, pander, brander, grander, stander, zander 3. disbander, Leander, meander, *backhander*, left-hander, right-hander, philander, *Icelander*, *inlander*, *outlander*, demander, remander, commander, pomander, germander, Menander, expander, Isander, goosander, dittander, *bystander*, *outstander*, withstander 4. oleander, coriander, Afrikander, Newfoundlander, salamander, gerrymander, reprimander, Alexander, understander.

AND'erd– 2. pandered, slandered, standard.

AND'erz– 2. Flanders, glanders, sanders 4. oleanders, salamanders.

AND'ez– 2. Andes 3. Hernandez.

AND'i– 2. Andy, bandy, dandy, handy, candy, Mandy, pandy, randy, brandy, sandy, shandy 3. unhandy, Jim Dandy 4. sugar-candy, jack-a-dandy, spick-and spandy, Rio Grande, jaborandi 6. Yankee Doodle Dandy.

AND'ij– 2. bandage, standage.

AND'ik– 3. Icelandic 4. propagandic.

AND'ing– 2. banding, handing, landing, stranding, sanding, standing 3. disbanding, unhanding, expanding, demanding, remanding, commanding, outstanding, withstanding 4. understanding, notwithstanding 5. misunderstanding.

AND'ish– 2. blandish, brandish, grandish, standish 3. outlandish, Myles Standish.

AND'ist– 4. contrabandist, propagandist.

AND'it– 2. bandit, Pandit.

AND'l– 2. dandle, candle, scandle, handle, pandle, pandal, sandal, vandal 3. manhandle, mishandle; *see* also **AND'al–** scandal etc. above.

AND'ler– 2. chandler, dandler, handler, candler 3. panhandler.

AND'less– 2. bandless, handless, landless, glandless, brandless, strandless, sandless 3. demandless, commandless.

AND'li– 2. blandly, grandly.

AND'ling– 2. bandling, candling, handling, brandling 3. manhandling, mishandling.

AND'ment– 3. disbandment, remandment, commandment.

AND'ness– 2. blandness, grandness.

AND'o– 2. bandeau, landau 3. Orlando, commando, Fernando, Hernando, lentando 4. Ferdinando.

AND'on– 2. Landon, Brandon 3. abandon.

AND'ra– 2. mandra, Sandra 3. Cassandra 4. Alessandra, Alexandra.

AND'stand– 2. bandstand, handstand, grandstand.

AND'um– 2. mandom, random, tandem 3. notandum 4. memorandum, observandum, avizandum 10. de gustibus non est disputandum [L.].

ANDZ'man– 2. bandsman, landsman.

AN'eed– **2.** nannied, grannied, crannied **3.** benannied, begrannied, becrannied.

AN'el– **2.** annal, channel, cannel, flannel, panel, scrannel, stannel **3.** empanel, impanel.

AN'elz– annals, etc. *see* **AN'el–** annal etc. above, plus "s" or "'s."

AN'er– **2.** banner, fanner, canner, scanner, planner, manner, manor, panner, spanner, tanner, vanner **3.** japanner, trepanner.

AN'erd– **2.** bannered, mannered **3.** unmannered, well-mannered, ill-mannered.

AN'et– **2.** gannet, Janet, cannet, planet, vannet; *see* also **AN'it–** granite etc. below.

ANG'er– **2.** banger, ganger, hanger, hangar, clangor, whanger, sanger **3.** haranguer **4.** paper hanger.

ANG'ger– **2.** anger, angor, Bangor, hangar, languor, clangor.

ANG'i– **2.** bangy, fangy, clangy, slangy, tangy, twangy, whangy.

ANG'ing– **2.** banging, hanging, clanging, slanging, twanging, whanging **3.** haranguing **4.** paper hanging, overhanging.

ANG'l– **2.** angle, bangle, dangle, fangle, gangle, jangle, mangle, spangle, strangle, wrangle, tangle, wangle **3.** fandangle, quadrangle, leeangle, triangle, rectangle, pentangle, septangle, sexangle, bespangle, entangle, untangle **4.** jingle-jangle, interjangle, intertangle, disentangle.

ANG'ler– **2.** angler, dangler, gangler, jangler, spangler, wrangler **3.** entangler, untangler.

ANG'less– **2.** bangless, dangless, fangless, gangless, clangless, pangless, twangless.

ANG'li– **2.** bangly, dangly, gangly, jangly, spangly, tangly.

ANG'ling– **2.** angling, dangling, gangling, jangling, mangling, spangling, strangling, wrangling, tangling, wangling.

ANG'man– **2.** hangman, gangman.

ANG'o– **2.** mango, tango **3.** fandango, Cipango, contango **4.** Pago Pago, Pangopango.

ANG'ster– **2.** bangster, gangster, slangster.

ANG'win– **2.** anguine, sanguine **3.** ensanguine, consanguine, exsanguine.

ANG'wish– **2.** anguish, languish.

AN'i– **2.** Annie, Danny, Fanny, canny, clanny, nanny, branny, granny, cranny **3.** Aani, afghani, uncanny, tin-panny **4.** frangipani.

AN'ij– **2.** manage, pannage, crannage, tannage **3.** mismanage.

AN'ik– **2.** phanic, panic, tannic, stannic **3.** neanic, paganic, organic, cyanic, mechanic, volcanic, vulcanic, Brahmanic, Germanic, tympanic, Hispanic, Iranic, tyrannic, Koranic, uranic, satanic, tetanic, Britannic, titanic, sultanic, botanic, Spartanic, galvanic **4.** oceanic, diaphanic, lexiphanic, theophanic, inorganic, exorganic, cosmorganic, opianic, Messianic, porcelanic, aldermanic **5.** hydrocyanic, transoceanic, Aristophanic.

AN'ing– **2.** banning, fanning, canning, scanning, flanning, clanning, planning, manning, panning, spanning, tanning **3.** japanning, trepanning, replanning, remanning, unmanning, outspanning.

AN'ish– **2.** banish, fannish, clannish, planish, mannish, Spanish, vanish **3.** evanish.

AN'ist– **2.** tanist **3.** picanist, sopranist **4.** Alcoranist.

AN'it– **2.** granite **4.** pomegranate.

ANJ'ent– **2.** plangent, frangent, tangent **3.** refrangent, bitangent, cotangent.

ANJ'ez– **2.** Ganges, flanges **3.** phalanges.

ANK'a– **2.** tanka **3.** Bianca, barranca **4.** Casablanca.

ANK'er– **2.** anchor, banker, danker, hanker, canker, chancre, lanker, blanker, flanker, clanker, planker, spanker, ranker, rancor, franker, cranker, pranker, shanker, tanker, thanker, yanker **3.** unanchor, up-anchor, sheet anchor, embanker, encanker, outflanker, outranker.

ANK'erd– 2. anchored, cankered, brancard, tankard **3.** unanchored, uncankered.

ANK'est– 2. dankest, lankest, blankest, rankest, frankest.

ANK'et– 2. banket, blanket.

ANK'ful– 2. prankful, tankful, thankful **3.** unthankful.

ANK'i– 2. ankee, banky, hanky, hankie, lanky, clanky, planky, cranky, pranky, tanky, swanky, Yankee **4.** hanky-panky [coll.].

ANK'ing– 2. banking, blanking, flanking, clanking, planking, spanking, ranking, franking, cranking, tanking, thanking, yanking **3.** embanking, outflanking, unclanking, outranking.

ANK'ish– 2. dankish, lankish, blankish, frankish, prankish.

ANK'l– 2. ankle, hankle, rankle, crankle, tankle.

ANK'less– 2. bankless, hankless, blankless, flankless, clankless, plankless, spankless, rankless, frankless, francless, crankless, prankless, shankless, tankless, thankless.

ANK'li– 2. dankly, lankly, blankly, rankly, frankly.

ANK'ment– 2. bankment **3.** embankment.

ANK'ness– 2. dankness, lankness, blankness, rankness, frankness.

ANK'ok– 2. Bangkok, Hancock.

ANK'or– 2. anchor, rancor; *see* also **ANK'er–** anchor, banker etc. above.

AN'less– 2. banless, fanless, canless, clanless, planless, manless, panless, spanless, tanless.

AN'li– 2. manly **3.** unmanly, *statesmanly* **4.** gentlemanly.

AN'o– 2. piano, soprano **5.** melopiano, mezzo-soprano.

AN'ok– 2. bannock, Bannock, jannock.

AN'on– 2. fanon, canon, cannon, Shannon **3.** Rhiannon, colcannon.

ANS'a– 2. hansa, Hansa.

ANS'el– 2. chancel, Handsel, handsel, cancel.

ANS'er– 2. Anser, answer, chancer, dancer, cancer, lancer, glancer, prancer **3.** fan dancer, merganser, enhancer, romancer, entrancer, advancer **4.** hula dancer, bubble dancer, geomancer, chiromancer, necromancer.

ANS'ez– chances etc., *see* **ANS–** chance etc. plus "s" or "'s."

ANSH'al– 3. ganancial, financial, substantial **4.** transubstantial, insubstantial, unsubstantial, circumstantial.

ANSH'ent– 2. transient.

ANSH'un– 2. scansion, mansion, panchion, stanchion **3.** expansion.

ANS'i– 2. Ancy, chancy, dancy, fancy, Nancy, prancy, Sancy **3.** mischancy, unfancy, *nomancy*, *romancy*, *vacancy*, *peccancy*, *verdancy*, *mordancy*, *infancy*, *brilliancy*, *vallancy*, *tenancy*, *stagnancy*, *regnancy*, *pregnancy*, *sonancy*, *flagrancy*, *fragrancy*, *vagrancy*, *errancy*, *blatancy*, *constancy*, *piquancy*, *truancy*, *buoyancy* **4.** mendicancy, *redundancy*, *accordancy*, *discordancy*, recreancy, termagancy, elegancy, arrogancy, sycophancy, sibilancy, petulancy, chalcomancy, sycomancy, pedomancy, podomancy, geomancy, theomancy, psychomancy, lithomancy, halomancy, belomancy, xylomancy, onomancy, capnomancy, oomancy, ceromancy, necromancy, hydromancy, aeromancy, chiromancy, aldermancy, gyromancy, pyromancy, cartomancy, lithomancy, *lieutenancy*, *repugnancy*, consonancy, dissonancy, *discrepancy*, occupancy, penetrancy, *incessancy*, *recussancy*, *expectancy*, *reluctancy*, habitancy, oscitancy, militancy, irritancy, hesitancy, exultancy, *accountancy*, *inconstancy*, relevancy, conservancy **5.** ornithomancy, bibliomancy, theriomancy, cephalomancy, selenomancy, icthyomancy, aleuromancy, sideromancy, hieromancy, oneiromancy, diathermancy, significancy, extravagancy, predominancy, preponderancy, recalcitrancy, inhabitancy, exorbitancy, precipitancy, irrelevancy **6.** dactyliomancy, logarithmomancy, insignificancy.

ANS'id– **2.** fancied, rancid.

ANS'ing– **2.** chancing, dancing, Lansing, glancing, prancing, trancing **3.** enhancing, romancing, financing, entrancing, advancing **4.** necromancing.

ANS'iv– **3.** enhancive, expansive, advancive **4.** inexpansive.

ANS'ment– **3.** enhancement, entrancement, advancement **4.** nonadvancement.

ANS'um– **2.** hansom, handsome, ransom, transom.

ANT'a– **2.** anta, planta, manta, Santa **3.** Vedanta, infanta, Atlanta **4.** Atalanta.

ANT'al– **2.** antal **3.** gigantal, atlantal, quadrantal, octantal **4.** consonantal; *see* also **ANT'l–** cantle etc. below.

ANT'e– **2.** ante, Dante **3.** andante, bacchante, chianti, durante **4.** Rosinante, Hypapante, dilettante **5.** pococurante, non obstante [L.]; *see* also **ANT'i–** aunty etc. below.

ANT'ed– **2.** hanted, chanted, canted, scanted, planted, slanted, panted, ranted, granted **3.** enchanted, recanted, descanted, implanted, supplanted.

ANT'er– **2.** banter, hanter, chanter, canter, cantor, scanter, planter, slanter, panter, ranter, granter, grantor **3.** enchanter, decanter, trochanter, descanter, supplanter, transplanter, instanter, levanter.

ANT'ez– **2.** Dantes **3.** atlantes **4.** Corybantes.

ANTH'er– **2.** anther, panther.

ANTH'us– **2.** canthus **3.** Dianthus, acanthous, ananthous, synanthous, monanthous, epanthous, chrysanthous **4.** polyanthus, amianthus.

ANT'i– **2.** aunty, anti, banty, chanty, scanty, slanty, panty, ranty, Santy, shanty, tanti **3.** chianti; *see* also **ANT'e–** ante etc. above.

ANT'ij– **2.** chantage, plantage, vantage **3.** advantage **4.** disadvantage.

ANT'ik– **2.** antic, antick, mantic, frantic **3.** pedantic, Vedantic, gigantic, Atlantic, semantic, romantic **4.** corybantic, elephantic, sycophantic, cisatlantic, transatlantic, geomantic, theomantic, chiromantic, pyromantic, necromantic, consonantic.

ANT'in– **2.** plantain **3.** *Levantine*, *Byzantine* **4.** elephantine, adamantine.

ANT'ing– **2.** hanting, chanting, canting, scanting, slanting, planting, panting, ranting, granting **3.** enchanting, decanting, recanting, descanting, implanting, supplanting.

ANT'ist– **2.** Kantist, Vedantist **4.** Esperantist, noncurantist, ignorantist, dilettantist.

ANT'l– **2.** cantle, mantle, mantel **3.** dismantle, immantle; *see* also **ANT'al–** antal etc. above.

ANT'ler– **2.** antler, mantler, pantler **3.** dismantler.

ANT'let– **2.** gantlet, cantlet, plantlet, mantelet.

ANT'li– **2.** scantly, slantly **3.** *gallantly*, aslantly.

ANT'ling– **2.** bantling, scantling, plantling, mantling **3.** dismantling.

ANT'ment– **2.** chantment **3.** enchantment **4.** disenchantment.

ANT'o– **2.** canto, manteau **3.** portmanteau, pro tanto **4.** Esperanto.

ANT'ress– **2.** chantress **3.** enchantress.

ANT'ri– **2.** chantry, gantry, pantry.

ANT'rum– 2. antrum, tantrum 3. hypantrum.

ANT'um– 2. Antum, bantam, phantom 4. adiantum.

AN'yel– 2. Daniel, Haniel, spaniel 3. Nathaniel, field spaniel, toy spaniel 4. springer spaniel, water spaniel.

AN'yun– 2. banian, banyan, fanion, canyon 3. companion.

ANZ'a– 2. stanza 3. bonanza 5. extravaganza.

ANZ'i– 2. pansy, tansy 3. chimpanzee.

AP'a– 2. cappa, Kappa, kappa.

AP'er– 2. chapper, dapper, capper, flapper, clapper, slapper, mapper, napper, knapper, wrapper, scrapper, trapper, strapper, tapper, yapper 3. didapper, *kidnapper*, entrapper, unwrapper, wiretapper, backslapper 4. handicapper, overlapper, snippersnapper, whippersnapper.

AP'et– 2. lappet, scrappet, tappet.

AP'i– 2. chappie, chappy, gappy, happy, mappy, nappy, snappy, pappy, crappie, scrappy, trappy, sappy 3. unhappy, serape.

AP'id– 2. rapid, sapid, vapid.

AP'ij– 2. lappage, scrappage, wrappage.

AP'ing– 2. chapping, dapping, gapping, capping, lapping, clapping, flapping, slapping, mapping, napping, knapping, snapping, rapping, wrapping, scrapping, trapping, strapping, tapping, yapping 3. entrapping, enwrapping 4. handicapping, overlapping.

AP'is– 2. lapis, tapis.

AP'ish– 2. gappish, knappish, snappish, yappish.

AP'ist– 2. mappist, Trappist.

AP'l– 2. apple, chapel, dapple, capple, grapple, scrapple 3. *Whitechapel*, *pineapple*, love apple 4. antechapel.

AP'less– 2. hapless, gapless, capless, lapless, clapless, flapless, slapless, mapless, napless, snapless, papless, rapless, wrapless, scrapless, trapless, strapless, sapless, yapless 4. handicapless.

AP'let– 2. chaplet, taplet.

AP'ling– 2. dappling, lapling, grappling, sapling.

AP'nel– 2. grapnel, shrapnel.

APSH'un– 2. caption 3. recaption, elapsion, collapsion, contraption 4. usucaption.

APS'ing– 2. lapsing 3. relapsing, collapsing.

APT'er– 2. apter, chapter, captor, rapter, raptor 3. adapter, recaptor.

APT'est– 2. aptest, raptest 3. inaptest, unaptest.

APT'ist– 2. Baptist 4. Anabaptist.

APT'iv– 2. captive 3. adaptive 4. unadaptive.

APT'ur– 2. capture, rapture 3. recapture, enrapture 4. manucapture.

AR'a– 2. Eire, Clara 3. Sahara, tiara.

AR'ab– 2. Arab, scarab.

AR'ans– 2. bearance, Clarence 3. forbearance, apparence, transparence.

AR'ant– 2. arrant, parent 3. forbearant, declarant, apparent, stepparent, transparent 4. unapparent, nontransparent.

AR'as– 2. arras, barras, harass, terrace 3. debarras, embarras, embarrass 4. disembarrass.

AR'el– 2. barrel, carrell, carol, parrel 3. pork-barrel, apparel 4. disapparel.

AR'eld– barreled etc., *see* **AR'el–** barrel etc. above plus -ed.

AR'en– 2. barren, Karen; *see* also **AR'on–** Aaron etc. below.

AR'ent– 2. parent 3. apparent, stepparent, transparent 4. unapparent; *see* also **AR'ant–** arrant etc. above.

AR'er– 2. barer, bearer, darer, farer, snarer, parer, sparer, sharer, tearer, starer, wearer, swearer, squarer **3.** wayfarer, seafarer, forswearer.

AR'est– **2.** barest, rarest, sparest, squarest.

AR'et– **2.** garret, carat, caret, claret; *see* also **AR'ot–** garrot etc. below.

AR'i– **2.** airy, ary [dial.], Barrie, Barry, berry, bury, fairy, harry, Harry, carry, Carrie, Larry, marry, nary [dial.], tarry **3.** Du Barry, shooldarry, Glengarry, miscarry, remarry **4.** hari-kari, intermarry, charivari; *see* also **AR'i–** scarry etc.; **ER'i–** berry etc.

AR'id– **2.** arid, harried, carried, married, parried, tarried **3.** Polarid, miscarried, unmarried **4.** intermarried.

AR'ij– **2.** carriage, marriage **3.** miscarriage, disparage **4.** intermarriage.

AR'ik– **2.** baric **3.** barbaric, Pindaric, agaric, Bulgaric, saccharic, polaric, tartaric **4.** cinnabaric, centrobaric, isobaric, Balearic.

AR'ing– **2.** airing, bearing, baring, daring, faring, haring, herring, caring, scaring, blaring, glaring, flaring, paring, pairing, sparing, sharing, tearing, staring, wearing, waring, swearing, squaring **3.** tale bearing, seafaring, declaring, repairing, impairing, despairing, outstaring, forswearing, outwearing **4.** overbearing, undeclaring.

AR'is– **2.** arris, baris, Harris, Clarice, Paris **3.** Polaris.

AR'ish– **2.** bearish, garish, marish, parish, squarish **4.** debonairish.

AR'li– **2.** barely, fairly, rarely, quarely. **3.** awarely **4.** debonairly.

AR'ness– **2.** bareness, fairness, rareness, quareness **3.** awareness **4.** debonairness.

AR'o– **2.** arrow, barrow, farrow, faro, harrow, marrow, narrow, sparrow, yarrow **3.** wheelbarrow, restharrow; *see* also **AR'o–** aero etc.

AR'on– **2.** Aaron, baron, barren, Charon, Karen, Sharon.

AR'ot– **2.** garrot, carrot, parrot; *see* also **AR'et–** garret etc. above.

AR'um– **2.** arum, carom, harem, larum **3.** alarum **4.** harum-scarum.

AS'a– **2.** massa **3.** Hadassah, Manasseh, madrasah, oquassa **4.** Missa bassa [L.].

AS'en– **2.** fasten, casson **3.** assassin.

AS'er– **2.** gasser, hassar, placer, masser, passer **3.** Macassar, amasser, surpasser, harasser **5.** antimacassar.

AS'et– **2.** asset, basset, facet, placet, brasset, tacet, tacit.

AS'ez– **2.** asses, gases, lasses, glasses, classes, masses, passes, brasses, grasses, sasses **3.** declasses, reclasses, outclasses, *eyeglasses*, *hourglasses*, molasses, amasses, surpasses, harasses, cuirasses, morasses **4.** underclasses, superclasses, looking glasses, underpasses, overpasses.

ASH'en– **2.** ashen; *see* **ASH'un–** ashen etc. below.

ASH'er– **2.** Asher, basher, dasher, gasher, hasher, casher, lasher, clasher, flasher, splasher, slasher, masher, smasher, rasher, brasher, crasher, thrasher, stasher **3.** abasher, rehasher **4.** haberdasher, baggage-smasher.

ASH'ez– **2.** ashes, bashes, dashes, gashes, hashes, cashes, caches, lashes, flashes, clashes, splashes, mashes, smashes, nashes, gnashes, pashes, rashes, crashes, thrashes **3.** abashes, rehashes, *eyelashes*, *backlashes*, mustaches **4.** spatterdashes.

ASH'i– **2.** ashy, dashy, hashy, flashy, clashy, plashy, slashy, splashy, mashie, trashy.

ASH'ing– **2.** bashing, dashing, hashing, cashing, caching, lashing, flashing, clashing, splashing, slashing, mashing, gnashing, crashing **3.** backlashing, mishmashing **4.** balderdashing.

ASH'less– **2.** dashless, hashless, cashless, lashless, flashless, clashless, splashless, mashless, crashless.

ASH'un– 2. ashen, fashion, passion, ration 3. refashion, disfashion, Circassian, Parnassian, impassion, compassion, dispassion.

ASH'und– 2. fashioned, passioned, rationed 3. old fashioned, unfashioned, impassioned, unrationed 4. unimpassioned.

AS'i– 2. dassie, gassy, Cassie, lassie, glassy, classy, massy, brassie, brassy, grassy, sassy, chassis 3. morassy 4. Malagasy, Tallahassee.

AS'id– 2. acid, placid 3. subacid, antacid.

AS'ij– 2. passage, brassage.

AS'ik– 2. classic 3. Liassic, Triassic, thalassic, postclassic, boracic, thoracis, Jurassic, potassic 4. pseudoclassic, neoclassic.

AS'il– 2. facile, gracile; *see* also **AS'l–** castle etc. below.

AS'in– 3. assassin; *see* also **AS'en–** fasten etc. above.

AS'ing– 2. gassing, classing, massing 3. reclassing, amassing, surpassing, harassing 4. underclassing, underpassing, overpassing.

AS'is– 2. assis, fascis, chassis, Cassis.

AS'it– 2. tacit; *see* also **AS'et–** asset etc. above.

AS'iv– 2. massive, passive 3. impassive.

ASK'a– 3. Alaska, marasca, Nebraska 4. Athabasca, baked Alaska.

ASK'al– 2. paschal, mascle, rascal, tascal.

ASK'er– 2. asker, basker, lascar, flasker, masker, masquer, tasker 3. unmasker 4. Madagascar, antimasker.

ASK'et– 2. basket, gasket, casket, casquet, lasket, flasket, taskit 3. breadbasket.

ASK'ing– 2. asking, basking, casking, flasking, masking, tasking 3. bemasking, unmasking.

ASK'o– 2. casco, tasco 3. Tabasco, verbasco, fiasco, Belasco.

AS'l– 2. castle, tassel, wrastle, vassal 3. forecastle, Newcastle, envassal; *see* also **AS'il–** facile etc. above.

AS'man– 2. gasman, glassman, classman, passman, grassman, Tassman 4. underclassman, upperclassman.

AS'o– 2. basso, lasso, Tasso 3. Sargasso.

AS'ok– 2. hassock, cassock.

ASP'er– 2. asper, gasper, Jasper, Casper, clasper, rasper, grasper.

ASP'ing– 2. gasping, clasping, rasping, grasping 3. enclasping, unclasping.

AST'a– 2. Shasta 3. shikasta, canasta, catasta.

AST'ed– 2. fasted, lasted, blasted, masted 3. bombasted, broad-lasted, outlasted, three-masted, contrasted 4. flabbergasted.

AST'er– 2. aster, Astor, faster, gaster, caster, castor, blaster, plaster, master, pastor, vaster 3. cadaster, piaster, broadcaster, forecaster, pilaster, Stylaster, paymaster, cubmaster, taskmaster, schoolmaster, choirmaster, bushmaster, postmaster, pinaster, disaster 4. Zoroaster, alabaster, oleaster, criticaster, burgomaster, quartermaster, overmaster, poetaster.

AST'erd– 2. bastard, dastard, plastered, mastered 3. pilastered, beplastered, unmastered.

AST'est– 2. fastest, vastest.

AST'i– 2. blasty, masty, nasty, vasty 3. dynasty 4. anaplasty, dermoplasty, epinasty, hyponasty, pederasty.

AST'ik– 2. clastic, plastic, mastic, rastic, spastic, drastic 3. bombastic, dichastic, sarcastic, elastic, gelastic, scholastic, dynastic, gymnastic, monastic, tetrastich, fantastic 4. inelastic, anaclastic, cataclastic, protoplastic, pederastic, paraphrastic 5. ecclesiastic, iconoclastic, enthusiastic.

AST'iks– 2. plastics, mastics, spastics 3. elastics, gymnastics 5. Ecclesiastics.

AST'ing– 2. fasting, casting, lasting, blasting 3. bombasting, *broadcasting*, forecasting, outlasting, contrasting. **4.** flabbergasting, everlasting.

AST'li– **2.** ghastly, lastly, vastly **3.** steadfastly.

AST'ness– **2.** fastness, vastness **3.** steadfastness.

AST'ral– **2.** astral, castral **3.** subastral, cadastral.

AST'ric– **2.** gastric **3.** digastric **4.** perigastric, hypogastric.

AST'rum– **2.** castrum, plastrum **4.** alabastrum, periastrum.

AS'us– **2.** bassus, passus **3.** Parnassus.

AT'a– **2.** atta, batta **3.** regatta **4.** matamata, yerbamata, paramatta.

AT'ed– **2.** batted, chatted, fatted, hatted, blatted, flatted, platted, plaited, slatted, matted, ratted, patted, spatted, dratted, tatted, vatted **3.** high-hatted, top-hatted, cravatted **4.** caryatid.

AT'en– **2.** Aten, batten, fatten, flatten, platan, platen, patten, paten, ratten, gratten **3.** Manhattan; *see* also **AT'in-Latin** etc. below.

AT'er– **2.** attar, batter, chatter, fatter, hatter, quatre, latter, blatter, flatter, clatter, platter, splatter, matter, smatter, patter, spatter, ratter, dratter, satyr, shatter, tatter, vatter **3.** hamfatter, bespatter.

AT'ern– **2.** slattern, pattern, Saturn.

ATH'er– **2.** gather, lather, blather, slather, rather **3.** foregather, forgather.

ATH'ik– **2.** bathic, spathic **3.** agnathic, apathic, empathic **4.** philomathic, telepathic, antipathic, psychopathic, allopathic, cosmopathic, hydropathic, neuropathic **5.** homeopathic, osteopathic, idiopathic.

AT'i– **2.** batty, chatty, fatty, Hattie, catty, matty, Mattie, natty, gnatty, patty, ratty, yati **3.** chapatty **4.** Cincinnati.

AT'ik– **2.** attic, Attic, platic, static vatic **3.** Sabbatic, ecbatic, creatic, phreatic, sulphatic, emphatic, lymphatic, phosphatic, sciatic, viatic, villatic, dramatic, hematic, schematic, rheumatic, thematic, sematic, pragmatic, judgmatic, phlegmatic, smegmatic, stigmatic, dogmatic, zeugmatic, asthmatic, climatic, dalmatic, pelmatic, grammatic, commatic, gromatic, chromatic, somatic, stomatic, termatic, plasmatic, osmatic, traumatic, unstatic, pneumatic, fanatic, enatic, agnatic, un-Attic, hepatic, pancratic, Socratic, quadratic, geratic, piratic, erratic, astatic, ecstatic, aquatic, lavatic **4.** anabatic, catabatic, metabatic, acrobatic, enneatic, cuneatic, pancreatic, ischiatic, opiatic, Adriatic, mydriatic, psoriatic, muriatic, Asiatic, aviatic, fluviatic, unthematic, emblematic, problematic, kinematic, systematic, astigmatic, dilemmatic, zygomatic, diplomatic, monomatic, aromatic, achromatic, symptomatic, automatic, miasmatic, aseismatic, numismatic, porismatic, diprismatic, macrosmatic, microsmatic, onymatic, morganatic, aplanatic, Pherecratic, theocratic, ochlocratic, democratic, timocratic, gynocratic, androcratic, autocratic, plutocratic, bureaucratic, polycratic, hieratic, operatic, diastatic, anastatic, catastatic, metastatic, geostatic, hemostatic, thermostatic, apostatic, hydrostatic, aerostatic, gyrostatic, photostatic, caryatic **5.** melodramatic, anathematic, theorematic, episematic, anallagmatic, synallagmatic, diaphragmatic, apothegmatic, paradigmatic, diagrammatic, anagrammatic, chronogrammatic, cryptogrammatic, polygrammatic, idiomatic, axiomatic, undiplomatic, iconomatic, monochromatic, isochromatic, polychromatic, cataclysmatic, empyreumatic, physiocratic, arithmocratic, hierocratic, pantisocratic, aristocratic, idiostatic, heliostatic **6.** paleoclimatic, idiosyncratic **7.** parallelogrammatic.

AT'iks– **2.** attics, statics **3.** dramatics, pneumatics, quadratics **4.** aerobatics, acrobatics, kinematics, mathematics, systematics, biostatics.

AT'in– **2.** Latin, matin, Patine, gratin [F.], satin **3.** au gratin [F.]; *see* also AT'en– Aten etc. above.

AT'ing– **2.** batting, chatting, fatting, plaiting, platting, matting, patting, spatting, ratting, dratting, pratting, tatting, vatting **3.** high-hatting, cravatting **4.** cotton batting.

AT'is– **2.** lattice, brattice, gratis.

AT'ish– **2.** battish, fattish, cattish, flattish.

AT'l– **2.** battle, battel, chattel, cattle, rattle, brattle, prattle, tattle **3.** Seattle, embattle **4.** tittle-tattle.

AT'ler– **2.** battler, rattler, prattler, tattler, Statler.

AT'less– **2.** atlas, Atlas, batless, fatless, hatless, catless, flatless, matless, patless, ratless, vatless **3.** cravatless.

AT'li– **2.** fatly, flatly, patly, rattly.

AT'ling– **2.** battling, batling, catling, fatling, Gatling, rattling, prattling, tattling.

AT'ness– **2.** fatness, flatness, patness.

AT'o– **2.** *chateau, gateau, plateau* **3.** mulatto, tomato.

AT'rik– **2.** Patrick **3.** theatric, iatric **4.** pediatric, psychiatric, hippiatric, physiatric.

AT'riks– **3.** theatrics **4.** pediatrics, cyniatrics, phoniatrics, physiatrics.

AT'um– **2.** atom, stratum.

AV'a– **2.** Java, lava.

AV'el– **2.** gavel, cavil, ravel, gravel, travel, tavell **3.** unravel.

AV'er– **2.** haver, claver **3.** cadaver, palaver.

AV'ern– **2.** cavern, tavern.

AV'i– **2.** slavey, navvy, savvy.

AV'id– **2.** avid, pavid, gravid **3.** impavid.

AV'ij– **2.** scavage, ravage, savage.

AV'ik– **2.** Slavic **3.** atavic, octavic Jugoslavic.

AV'ing– **2.** having, halving, calving, salving.

AV'ish– **2.** lavish, ravish **3.** enravish.

AZ'a– **2.** Ghazze, plaza **3.** piazza.

AZ'ard– **2.** hazard, mazzard **3.** haphazard.

AZH'er– **2.** azure.

AZ'l– **2.** Basil, dazzle, razzle, frazzle **3.** bedazzle **4.** razzle-dazzle.

AZ'ling– **2.** dazzling, jazzling **3.** bedazzling **4.** razzle-dazzling.

AZ'ma– **2.** asthma, phasma, plasma **3.** chiasma, miasma, empasma, phantasma **4.** bioplasma, photoplasma.

AZ'mal– **2.** chasmal **3.** miasmal, phantasmal **4.** protoplasmal.

AZ'mik– **2.** chasmic, plasmic, spasmic **3.** miasmic, marasmic, phantasmic **4.** bioplasmic, protoplasmic.

A (cab)

3.

TRIPLE RHYMES IN A (rab'id-ness)

Primary or Secondary Accent Falls on Second from Last Syllable.

AB'a-bl– 2. nabbable, grabbable, tabbabble.

AB'a-sis– 4. anabasis, parabasis, catabasis, metabasis.

AB'id-ness– 3. rabidness, tabidness.

AB'i-er– 3. gabbier, scabbier, blabbier, flabbier, crabbier, shabbier.

AB'i-est– 3. gabbiest, scabbiest, blabbiest, flabbiest, crabbiest, shabbiest.

AB'i-fi– 3. labefy, tabefy 4. syllabify 5. dissyllabify.

AB'i-kal– 3. syllabical, Arabical 6. polysyllabical, monosyllabical, multisyllabical.

AB'i-li– 3. gabbily, blabbily, scabbily, flabbily, crabbily, shabbily.

AB'i-ness– 3. gabbiness, scabbiness, blabbiness, flabbiness, slabbiness, crabbiness, shabbiness.

AB'i-net– 3. cabinet, tabinet.

AB'it-i– 3. Babbitty, rabbity.

AB'it-ing– 3. Babbitting, rabbiting 4. inhabiting, cohabiting.

AB'la-tiv– 3. ablative, babblative.

AB'l-ment– 3. babblement, dabblement, gabblement, rabblement, brabblement, scrabblement.

AB'o-la– 4. parabola, Metabola.

AB'o-rat– 4. elaborate, collaborate.

AB'u-la– 3. fabula, tabula 4. cunabula 5. incunabula.

AB'u-lar– 3. fabular, pabular, tabular 4. confabular, vocabular, conabular 5. acetabular, tintinnabular.

AB'u-lat– 3. fabulate, tabulate 4. confabulate 5. tintinnabulate.

AB'u-list– 3. fabulist 4. vocabulist 5. incunabulist, tintinnabulist.

AB'u-lum– 3. pabulum 5. incunabulum, acetabulum, tintinnabulum.

AB'u-lus– 3. fabulous, pabulous, sabulous 5. tintinnabulous.

ACH'a-bl– 3. batchable, hatchable, catchable, latchable, matchable, snatchable, patchable, scratchable, thatchable 4. unhatchable, uncatchable, rematchable, immatchable, unmatchable, unpatchable, dispatchable, attachable, detachable.

ACH'er-i– 3. hatchery, patchery.

ACH'i-ness– 3. catchiness, snatchiness, patchiness, scratchiness.

AD'a-bl– 3. addable 4. unaddable.

AD'i-kal– 3. radical 4. sporadical.

AD'ish-ness– 3. faddishness, caddishness.

AD'i-tiv– 3. additive, traditive 4. readditive.

AD'o-ing– 3. shadowing 4. foreshadowing 5. overshadowing.

AF'a-bl– 3. affable 4. inaffable, unaffable.

AF'i-a– 3. maffia, mafia, raffia, tafia 4. agraphia, asaphia.

AF'i-kal– 3. graphical 4. seraphical 5. diagraphical, paragraphical, calligraphical, lexigraphical, geographical, biographical, orthographical, cosmographical, ethnographical, telegraphical, pornographical, glossographical, topographical, typographical, photographical, cartographical, phytographical, epitaphical **6.** bibliographical, physiographical, anthropographical, lexicographical **7.** autobiographical, paleontographical.

AF'l-ment- 3. bafflement, snafflement, rafflement, scrafflement.

AFT'i-li- 3. draftily, craftily.

AFT'less-li- 3. draftlessly, graftlessly, craftlessly, shaftlessly.

AG'a-bl- 3. faggable, gaggable, flaggable, naggable, snaggable, draggable, saggable, taggable, waggable.

AG'ed-li- 3. jaggedly, raggedly, scraggedly.

AG'ed-ness- 3. jaggedness, raggedness, craggedness, scraggedness.

AG'er-er- 3. staggerer, swaggerer.

AG'er-i- 3. faggery, jaggery, raggery, staggery, waggery **4.** zigzaggery.

AG'er-ing- 3. staggering, swaggering.

AG'i-li- 3. baggily, raggily, craggily, scraggily, shaggily.

AG'i-ness- 3. bagginess, flagginess, knagginess, bragginess, cragginess, scragginess, shagginess.

AG'ish-li- 3. haggishly, braggishly, waggishly.

AG'on-ist- 3. agonist **4.** antagonist, protagonist **5.** deuteragonist.

AG'on-iz- 3. agonize **4.** antagonize.

AG'on-izm- 4. antagonism, protagonism.

AG'ot-i- 3. fagoty, faggoty, maggoty.

AJ'er-i- 4. menagerie, potagerie.

AJ'ik-al- 3. magical, tragical **5.** theomagical.

AJ'il-ness- 3. agileness, fragileness.

AJ'in-al- 3. paginal **4.** imaginal.

AJ'in-us- 4. farraginous, voraginous **5.** oleaginous, mucilaginous, cartilaginous.

AJ'u-tant- 3. adjutant **4.** coadjutant.

AK'en-ing- 3. blackening, slackening.

AK'er-el- 3. cackerel, mackerel.

AK'er-i- 3. hackery, knackery, Thackeray, quackery, Zachary **4.** hijackery, knickknackery, gimcrackery.

AK'et-ed- 3. jacketed, placketed, packeted, racketed, bracketed.

AK'et-ing- 3. jacketing, packeting, racketing, bracketing.

AK'i-ness- 3. hackiness, tackiness, wackiness **4.** gimcrackiness.

AK'ish-ness- 3. blackishness, slackishness, knackishness, brackishness, quackishness.

AK'rit-i- 3. acrity **4.** alacrity.

AK'ron-ism- 4. anachronism, metachronism.

AKS'a-bl- 3. taxable **4.** relaxable, nontaxable, untaxable.

AKSH'un-al- 3. actional, factional, pactional, fractional, tractional **4.** reactional, redactional **5.** interactional, rarefactional.

AKSH'us-ness- 3. factiousness, fractiousness.

AKS'i-al- 3. axial **4.** abaxial, biaxial, coaxial.

AKT'a-bl- 3. actable, tractable, tactable **4.** olfactable, refractable, attractable, retractable, intractable, extractable, intactable; *see* **AKT'i-bl-** olfactible etc. below.

AKT'e-al- 3. lacteal, bracteal.

AKT'ed-ness- 4. impactedness, contractedness, protractedness, abstractedness, distractedness.

AKT'er-i- 3. factory, lactary, tractory **4.** olfactory, phylactery, enactory, refractory, detractory **5.** calefactory, malefactory, benefactory, manufactory, satisfactory **6.** dissatisfactory.

AKT'i-bl- 4. olfactible, compactible, detractible, contractible, distractible; *see* **AKT'a-bl-** actable etc. above.

AKT'i-kal- 3. practical, tactical **4.** didactical, stalactical, impractical, unpractical, syntactical.

AKT'iv–ness– 3. activeness 4. defractiveness, attractiveness, detractiveness, contractiveness, protractiveness, abstractiveness, distractiveness.

AKT'or–i– factory etc., *see* **AKT'er–i–** factory etc. above.

AKT'or–ship– 3. actorship, factorship 4. contractorship.

AKT'u–al– 3. actual, factual, tactual 4. impactual, contractual, contactual.

AKT'ur–ing– 3. fracturing 4. refracturing 5. manufacturing.

AK'u–at– 3. acuate 4. evacuate.

AK'u–la– 3. bacula, facula, macula, Dracula 4. tentacula.

AK'u–lar– 4. piacular, vernacular, oracular, spectacular, jentacular, tentacular 5. tabernacular, supernacular.

AK'u–lat– 3. jaculate, maculate 4. ejaculate, bimaculate, immaculate 5. interjaculate.

AK'u–lum– 4. piaculum, tentaculum.

AK'u–lus– 3. baculus, sacculus 4. abaculus, miraculous, oraculous, vernaculous.

AL'ans–ing– 3. balancing 4. unbalancing 5. counterbalancing, overbalancing.

AL'ant–ed– 3. talented 4. begallanted.

AL'a–ri– 3. alary, gallery, salary, vallary 4. subalary 5. intercalary.

AL'er–ji– 3. allergy 4. *metallurgy.*

AL'et–ed– 3. balloted, valeted 4. unvaleted.

AL'i–ans– 3. dalliance, ralliance, valiance.

AL'i–at– 3. malleate, palliate, talliate 4. retaliate.

AL'ib–er– 3. caliber, calibre, calabur 4. Excalibur.

AL'id–li– 3. pallidly, validly 4. invalidly.

AL'id–ness– 3. callidness, pallidness, validness 4. impallidness, invalidness.

AL'i–er– 3. dallier, rallier, sallier, tallier.

AL'i–fi– 3. calefy, salify 4. alkalify.

AL'i–ing– 3. dallying, rallying, sallying, tallying.

AL'ik–ly– 3. Gallicly 4. vocalicly, metallicly, smart-aleckly [coll.].

AL'i–ped– 3. aliped, taliped.

AL'i–sis– 4. dialysis, analysis, paralysis, catalysis 6. psychoanalysis.

AL'i–son– 3. alison, Alison, malison.

AL'i–ti– 4. verbality, locality, vocality, rascality, pedality, modality, sodality, feudality, reality, egality, legality, regality, frugality, lethality, formality, normality, banality, venality, signality, finality, tonalty, zonality, carnality, spirality, morality, spectrality, dextrality, plurality, rurality, nasality, fatality, natality, vitality, mentality, totality, mortality, brutality, duality, rivality 5. farcicality, laicality, radicality, Biblicality, comicality, technicality, finicality, clericality, whimsicality, classicality, practicality, verticality, bipedality, ideality, lineality, unreality, illegality, prodigality, conjugality, speciality, sociality, cordiality, filiality, geniality, seriality, spatiality, partiality, bestiality, triviality, joviality, informality, abnormality, feminality, criminality, nationality, rationality, personality, internality, externality, principality, liberality, generality, laterality, literality, severality, integrality, immorality, temporality, corporality, pastorality, naturality, gutturality, commensality, vegetality, hospitality, immortality, visuality, sensuality, actuality, punctuality, virtuality, mutuality, sexuality, coevality 6. inimicality, theatricality, nonsensicality, pragmaticality, impracticality, fantasticality, reciprocality, sesquipedality, ethereality, corporeality, proverbiality, connubiality, provinciality, primordiality, parochiality, congeniality, perenniality, imperiality, materiality, substantiality, prudentiality, essentiality, potentiality, sequentiality, impartiality, colloquiality, conviviality, originality, irrationality, conditionality, conventionality, devotionality, exceptionality, proportionality, tripersonality, impersonality, municipality, illiberality, ephemerality, collaterality, conjecturality, universality, orientality, fundamentality, elementality, sentimentality, instrumentality, horizontality, effectuality, unpunctuality, conceptuality, asexuality **7.** artificiality, superficiality, immateriality, territoriality, confidentiality, insubstantiality, consubstantiality, unsubstantiality, circumstantiality, consequentiality, septentrionality, unconditionality, unconventionality, constitutionality, preternaturality, individuality, ineffectuality, intellectuality **8.** exterritoriality, inconsequentiality, unconstitutionality **9.** extraterritoriality.

ALJ'i-a- **4.** myalgia, gastralgia, neuralgia, dentalgia, nostalgia.

AL'o-er- **3.** hallower, callower, sallower, shallower, tallower.

AL'o-est- **3.** callowest, sallowest, shallowest.

AL'o-ish- **3.** callowish, sallowish, shallowish, tallowish.

AL'o-ji- **4.** mammalogy, analogy, paralogy, oralogy, petralogy, tetralogy, crustalogy **5.** genealogy, mineralogy, pyroballogy **6.** genethlialogy.

AL'o-jist- **4.** dialogist, Decalogist, mammalogist, analogist, penalogist **5.** genealogist, mineralogist.

AL'o-jiz- **4.** dialogize, analogize, penalogize, paralogize **5.** genealogize, mineralogize.

AL'o-jizm- **3.** alogism **4.** dialogism, analogism, paralogism.

AL'o-ness- **2.** callowness, fallowness, sallowness, shallowness.

AL'op-er- **3.** galoper, galloper, scalloper **4.** escalloper.

AL'op-ing- **3.** galoping, galloping, scalloping **4.** escalloping.

AL'u-at- **3.** valuate **4.** devaluate, revaluate **5.** re-evaluate.

AL'us-ez- **3.** phalluses, galluses, calluses.

AL'yun-ish- **3.** scallionish, stallionish **4.** medallionish, rapscallionish.

AM'a-bl- **3.** Amabel, flammable **4.** inflammable.

AM'a-tist- **3.** dramatist, grammatist **5.** melodramatist, anagrammatist, epigrammatist, lipogrammatist **6.** hierogrammatist.

AM'a-tiv- **3.** amative **4.** exclamative.

AM'a-tiz- **3.** dramatize **5.** diagrammatize, anagrammatize, epigrammatize.

AMB'u-lans- **3.** ambulance **4.** somnambulance.

AMB'u-lant- **3.** ambulant **4.** somnambulant, noctambulant.

AMB'u-lat- **3.** ambulate **4.** deambulate, somnambulate, funambulate, perambulate **5.** circumambulate.

AMB'u-list- **4.** somnambulist, funambulist, noctambulist.

AM'er-a- **3.** camera **4.** incamera, Pentamera.

AM'er-al- **3.** cameral **4.** decameral, bicameral, hexameral, tetrameral, pentameral.

AM'er-er- **3.** hammerer, clamorer, stammerer, yammerer.

AM'er-ing- **3.** hammering, clamoring, stammering, yammering **4.** enamoring, beglamouring.

AM'er-on- **4.** Decameron, hexameron, Heptameron.

AM'er-us- **3.** amorous, glamorous, clamorous **4.** unglamorous, hexamerous, heptamerous.

AM'et-er- **4.** diameter, decameter, dynameter, parameter, tetrameter, octameter, pentameter, hexameter, heptameter, voltameter.

AM'ik-al- **3.** amical **4.** dynamical, balsamical.

AM′in-a– **3.** lamina, stamina **4.** foramina.

AM′in-at– **3.** laminate, staminate **4.** foraminate, contaminate.

AM′i-ness– **3.** hamminess, jamminess, clamminess.

AM′it-i– **3.** amity **4.** calamity.

AM′on-it– **3.** Ammonite, mammonite, Shamanite.

AM′on-izm– **3.** mammonism, Shamanism.

AM′or-ing– clamoring etc., *see* **AM′er-ing–** hammering etc. above.

AM′or-us– amorous etc., *see* **AM′er-us–** amorous etc. above.

AMP′er-er– **3.** hamperer, scamperer, pamperer, tamperer.

AMP′er-ing– **3.** hampering, scampering, pampering, tampering.

AMP′i-li– **3.** crampily, vampily.

AMP′i-on– **3.** Campion, champion, lampion, tampion.

AM′u-la– **3.** ammula, mammula.

AM′u-lus– **3.** famulus, hamulus, ramulus, ramulous.

AN′a-ble– **3.** Annabel, bannable, cannable, cannibal, mannable, pannable, sanable, tannable **4.** insanable, untannable; *see* also **AN′i-bal–** Hannibal etc. below.

AN′ar-i– **3.** panary, granary; *see* also **AN′er-i–** cannery etc. below.

AND′a-ble– **3.** bandable, handable, mandible, sandable, standable **4.** demandable, commandable, unstandable **5.** reprimandable, countermandable, understandable **6.** misunderstandable.

AND′al-iz– **3.** scandalize, vandalize.

AND′ed-li– **3.** candidly **4.** highhandedly, backhandedly **5.** openhandedly, underhandedly.

AND′ed-ness– **3.** candidness **4.** highhandedness, backhandedness, lefthandedness **5.** openhandedness, underhandedness.

AND′er-er– **3.** slanderer, panderer **4.** meanderer, philanderer.

AND′er-ing– **3.** slandering, pandering **4.** meandering, philandering.

AND′er-us– **3.** slanderous, panderous.

AND′i-al– **3.** prandial **4.** postprandial **5.** anteprandial.

AND′i-er– **3.** bandier, dandier, handier, randier, sandier **4.** unhandier.

AND′i-fi– **3.** dandify, candify.

AND′i-ing– **3.** bandying, candying, randying.

AND′i-li– **3.** bandily, dandily, handily, randily, sandily **4.** unhandily.

AND′i-ness– **3.** bandiness, dandiness, handiness, randiness, sandiness **4.** unhandiness.

AND′ing-li– **4.** demandingly, commandingly, outstandingly **5.** understandingly.

AND′ing-ness– **4.** demandingness, commandingness, outstandingness **5.** understandingness.

AND′ish-ing– **3.** blandishing, brandishing.

AND′ish-ment– **3.** blandishment, brandishment.

AN′el-ing– **3.** channelling, flannelling, panelling.

AN′er-et– **3.** banneret, lanneret.

AN′er-i– **3.** cannery, panary, granary, tannery.

ANG′gling-li– **3.** anglingly, danglingly, ganglingly, janglingly, manglingly, spanglingly, stranglingly, tanglingly, wranglingly, wanglingly.

ANG′gl-som– **3.** anglesome, janglesome, wranglesome, tanglesome.

ANG′gu-lar– **3.** angular, slangular **4.** triangular, quadrangular, rectangular, octangular, pentangular.

ANG′gu-lat– **3.** angulate, strangulate **4.** triangulate.

ANG′i-li– 3. bangily, clangily, slangily, tangily, twangily.

ANG′ing-li– 3. bangingly, hangingly, clangingly, slangingly, twangingly, whangingly 4. haranguingly.

AN′i-bal– 3. Hannibal, cannibal; *see* also **AN′a-bl–** Annabel etc. above.

AN′i-el– 3. Daniel, Haniel, spaniel, Saniel, 4. Nathaniel.

AN′i-est– 3. canniest, clanniest 4. uncanniest.

AN′i-fi– 3. sanify 4. humanify.

AN′i-form– 3. Janiform, raniform, graniform 4. campaniform.

AN′i-kal– 3. manacle 4. organical, mechanical, Brahmanical, tyrannical, botanical, galvanical 5. charlatanical, puritanical; *see* also **AN′i-kl–** panicle etc. below.

AN′i-kin– 3. Anniekin, cannikin, manikin, pannikin.

AN′i-kl– 3. panicle, sanicle 4. mechanical, tyranical, botanical; *see* also **An′i-kal–** manacle etc. above.

AN′i-mat– 3. animate 4. reanimate, inanimate, exanimate.

AN′i-mus– 3. animous, animus 4. magnanimous, unanimous, multanimous 5. pusillanimous.

AN′i-ness– 3. canniness, clanniness.

AN′ish-ing– 3. banishing, planishing, vanishing.

AN′ish-ment– 3. banishment, vanishment 4. evanishment.

AN′ist-er– 3. banister, ganister, canister.

AN′it-i– 3. sanity, vanity 4. inanity, urbanity, mundanity, profanity, paganity, organity, volcanity, gigmanity, immanity, humanity, insanity 5. inurbanity, inorganity, Christianity, inhumanity, subterranity.

ANJ′en-si– 3. plangency, tangency.

ANJ′er-i– 3. lingerie, singerie.

ANJ′i-a– 3. cangia 4. hydrangea, sporangia.

ANJ′i-bl– 3. frangible, tangible 4. refrangible, infrangible, intangible.

ANK′er-er– 3. anchorer, hankerer.

ANK′er-ing– 3. anchoring, hankering, cankering 4. reanchoring, encankering.

ANK′er-us– 3. cankerous 4. cantankerous.

ANS′i-li– 3. chancily, fancily, prancily.

ANS′ing-li– 3. dancingly, glancingly, prancingly, trancingly 4. entrancingly.

ANS′it-iv– 3. transitive 4. intransitive.

ANS′iv-ness– 4. expansiveness, advanciveness 5. inexpansiveness, unexpansiveness.

ANS′om-er– 3. handsomer, ransomer.

ANT′a-bl– 3. plantable, grantable 4. transplantable, ungrantable.

ANT′el-op– 3. antelope, cantaloupe.

ANT′er-er– 3. banterer, canterer.

ANT′er-ing– 3. bantering, cantering.

ANTH′ro-pi– 4. theanthropy, lycanthropy, philanthropy, psilanthropy, misanthropy, zoanthropy 5. aphilanthropy 6. theophilanthropy.

ANTH′ro-pist– 4. theanthropist, philanthropist, psilanthropist, misanthropist 6. theophilanthropist.

ANTH′ro-pizm– 4. theanthropism, philanthropism, psilanthropism 6. theophilanthropism.

ANT′ik-li– 3. anticly, franticly 4. pedanticly, giganticly, romanticly.

ANT′ik-ness– 3. anticness, franticness 4. pedanticness, giganticness, romanticness.

ANT′i-li– 3. bantily, scantily, slantily, rantily.

ANT′i-ness– 3. bantiness, scantiness, slantiness, rantiness.

ANT′ing-li– 3. cantingly, slantingly, pantingly, rantingly 4. enchantingly.

ANT'u-a- 3. mantua 4. Gargantua.

AN'u-al- 3. annual, manual, Manuel 4. biannual, bimanual, Immanuel 5. semiannual.

AN'u-la- 3. cannula, ranula, granula 4. Campanula.

AN'u-lar- 3. annular, cannular, ranular, granular 4. penannular, campanular.

AN'u-lat- 3. annulate, granulate 4. campanulate.

AN'u-let- 3. annulet, granulet.

AP'a-bl- 3. mappable, snappable, strappable, tappable 4. unmappable.

AP'id-li- 3. rapidly, sapidly, vapidly.

AP'id-ness- 3. rapidness, sapidness, vapidness.

AP'i-er- 3. happier, gappier, lappier, nappier, snappier, scrappier, sappier.

AP'i-est- 3. happiest, gappiest, lappiest, nappiest, snappiest, scrappiest, sappiest 4. unhappiest.

AP'i-li- 3. happily, gappily, snappily, scrappily, sappily 4. unhappily.

AP'o-lis- 4. Annapolis, tetrapolis, pentapolis 5. Minneapolis 6. Indianapolis.

AP'tur-ing- 3. capturing, rapturing 4. recapturing, enrapturing.

AR'a-bl- 3. arable, bearable, parable, sparable, tearable, wearable 4. unbearable, declarable, repairable, unwearable 5. undeclarable, unrepairable.

AR'a-blz- 3. parables, wearables.

AR'a-gon- 3. paragon, tarragon.

AR'ant-li- 3. arrantly 4. apparently, transparently.

AR'as-ing- 3. harassing, terracing 4. embarrassing 5. disembarrassing.

AR'as-ment- 3. harassment 4. embarrassment.

AR'at-iv- 3. narrative 4. declarative, reparative, preparative, comparative.

AR'el-ing- 3. barreling, caroling 4. pork-barreling, appareling.

AR'i-at- 3. lariat 4. salariat 5. commissariat, proletariat, secretariat.

AR'i-er- 3. barrier, charier, farrier, harrier, carrier, marrier, parrier, tarrier, warier.

AR'i-fi- 3. scarify, clarify 4. saccharify.

AR'i-form- 3. nariform, variform 4. scalariform.

AR'i-ing- 3. harrying, carrying, marrying, parrying, tarrying 5. intermarrying.

AR'i-li- 3. airily, fairily; *see* also **ER'i-li-** merrily etc.

AR'in-at- 3. carinate, marinate.

AR'i-ness- 3. chariness, wariness; *see* also **AR'i-ness-** airiness etc.

AR'i-o- 4. Philario, scenario, Lothario 5. impresario.

AR'i-on- 3. carrion, clarion, Marion, Marian 4. Maid Marian.

AR'i-ot- 3. chariot 4. Iscariot.

AR'ish-li- 3. bearishly, garishly.

AR'ish-ness- 3. bearishness, garishness.

AR'is-on- 3. garrison, Harrison, parison 4. caparison, comparison.

AR'it-i- 3. charity, clarity, parity, rarity 4. barbarity, vagarity, vulgarity, uncharity, hilarity, molarity, polarity, imparity, disparity 5. solidarity, similarity, capillarity, bipolarity, exemplarity, globularity, secularity, jocularity, circularity, vascularity, muscularity, regularity, angularity, singularity, granularity, popularity, insularity, debonairity, gemmiparity, omniparity, fissiparity, multiparity, oviparity 6. familiarity, peculiarity, dissimilarity, piacularity, vernacularity, orbicularity, molecularity, particularity, irregularity, triangularity, rectangularity, unpopularity, peninsularity, ovoviparity 7. rectilinearity, curvilinearity, perpendicularity.

AR'-o-er- 3. harrower, narrower 4. wheelbarrower.

AR'o-i- 3. arrowy, marrowy, sparrowy.

AR'o-ing– 3. arrowing, farrowing, harrowing, narrowing 4. wheelbarrowing.

AR'o-lik– 3. arrowlike, barrowlike, farrowlike, farolike, harrowlike, marrowlike, sparrowlike.

AR'ot-ing– 3. garroting, parroting.

AS'a-bl– 3. classable, passable 4. amassable, impassable, surpassable; *see* also **AS'i-bl**– passible etc. below.

AS'a-bli– 3. classably, passably 4. unclassably, impassibly, unpassably, surpassably 5. unsurpassably; *see* also **AS'i-bli**– passibly etc. below.

AS'er-at– 3. lacerate, macerate 4. emaserate.

AS'et-ed– 3. faceted.

ASH'er-i– 3. ashery, fashery, hashery, trashery, sashery 5. haberdashery.

ASH'i-a– 3. fascia, cassia, quassia 4. Circassia, parnassia.

ASH'i-an– 4. Circassian, Parnassian.

ASH'i-er– 3. ashier, dashier, hashier, flashier, plashier, splashier, trashier.

ASH'i-est– 3. ashiest, dashiest, hashiest, flashiest, plashiest, splashiest, trashiest.

ASH'i-ness– 3. ashiness, flashiness, splashiness, trashiness.

ASH'un-al– 3. national, passional, rational 4. irrational 5. international.

ASH'un-at– passionate etc., *see* **ASH'un-it**– passionate etc. below.

ASH'un-ing– 3. fashioning, rationing 4. refashioning, disfashioning.

ASH'un-it– 3. passionate, fashion it 4. impassionate, compassionate, unpassionate, dispassionate.

AS'i-bl– 3. passible 4. impassible, renascible, irascible; *see* also **AS'a-bl**– classable etc. above.

AS'i-bli– 3. passibly 4. impassibly, irascibly; *see* also **AS'a-bli**– classably etc. above.

AS'i-fi– 3. classify, pacify 4. reclassify.

AS'i-kl– 3. fascicle, classical 4. nonclassical 5. neoclassical.

AS'i-nat– 3. fascinate 4. abacinate, deracinate, assassinate.

AS'i-ness– 3. gassiness, classiness, glassiness, massiness, brassiness, grassiness.

AS'it-i– 4. bibacity, dicacity, procacity, edacity, mendacity, mordacity, audacity, sagacity, fugacity, salacity, tenacity, pugnacity, minacity, capacity, rapacity, opacity, feracity, veracity, voracity, sequacity, loquacity, vivacity 5. perspicacity, pervicacity, contumacity, pertinacity, saponacity, incapacity.

AS'iv-li– 3. massively, passively 4. impassively.

AS'iv-ness– 3. massiveness, passiveness 4. impassiveness.

ASP'er-at– 3. asperate, aspirate 4. exasperate.

ASP'ing-li– 3. gaspingly, raspingly, graspingly.

AST'er-i– 3. plastery, mastery 4. dicastery, self-mastery.

AST'er-ing– 3. plastering, mastering, pastoring 4. beplastering 5. overmastering, poetastering.

AST'ik-al– 4. elastical, gymnastical, monastical, fantastical 6. ecclesiastical, enthusiastical.

AST'ik-li– 3. plasticly, drasticly 4. bombasticly, sarcasticly, elasticly, scholasticly, gymnasticly, monasticly, fantasticly.

AST'i-li– 3. ghastily, nastily.

AST'i-sizm– 4. plasticism 5. scholasticism, monasticism, fantasticism.

AST'ri-an– 4. Lancastrian 5. Zoroastrian, alabastrian.

AST'ro-fe– 4. diastrophe, anastrophe, catastrophe 5. epanastrophe.

AT'a-bl– 3. atabal, battable, hattable, mattable, pattable, rattable, vattable 4. combatable, come-at-able, get-at-able; *see* also **AT'i-bl**– patible etc. below.

AT'en-ing- 3. battening, fattening, flattening.

AT'er-al- 3. lateral 4. collateral 5. unilateral, quadrilateral, plurilateral.

AT'er-er- 3. batterer, chatterer, scatterer, flatterer, clatterer, splatterer, smatterer, patterer, shatterer 4. bespatterer.

AT'er-i- 3. battery, hattery, scattery, flattery, slattery, shattery, tattery.

AT'er-ing- 3. battering, chattering, scattering, flattering, clattering, smattering, pattering, spattering, shattering 4. bespattering, unflattering.

ATH'er-er- 3. gatherer, latherer, blatherer, slatherer 4. woolgatherer, ingatherer, foregatherer.

ATH'er-ing- 3. gathering, lathering, blathering, slathering 4. woolgathering, ingathering, foregathering.

ATH'e-sis- 4. diathesis, parathesis, metathesis.

ATH'ik-al- 5. philomathical 6. idiopathical.

AT'i-bl- 3. patible 4. combatable, impatible, compatible 5. incompatible, uncompatible; *see* also **AT'a-bl-** atabal etc. above.

AT'i-fi- 3. ratify, gratify, stratify 4. beatify.

AT'ik-a- 3. Attica 4. sciatica, hepatica.

AT'ik-al- 3. statical, vatical 4. abbatical, sabbatical, emphatical, dramatical, pragmatical, dogmatical, grammatical, climatical, somatical, asthmatical, Socratical, schismatical, prismatical, fanatical, erratical, piratical, ecstatical, aquatical 5. acrobatical, mathematical, emblematical, problematical, systematical, enigmatical, ungrammatical, diplomatical, automatical, symptomatical, numismatical, democratical, bureaucratical, autocratical, apostatical, hypostatical, hydrostatical 6. anagrammatical, idiomatical, axiomatical, aristocratical, unsystematical, anagrammatical, epigrammatical, axiomatical, aristocratical, aerostatical 7. anidiomatical, idiosyncratical.

AT'in-at- 3. patinate 4. Palatinate, gelatinate.

AT'i-ness- 3. battiness, cattiness, chattiness, fattiness, nattiness, rattiness.

AT'in-iz- 3. Latinize, platinize 4. gelatinize.

AT'in-us- 3. Latinus, platinous 4. gelatinous.

AT'is-ing- 3. latticing, bratticing.

AT'i-sizm- 5. pragmaticism, grammaticism, fanaticism 6. Asiaticism.

AT'i-tud- 3. attitude, latitude, platitude, gratitude 4. beatitude, ingratitude.

AT'l-ment- 3. battlement, prattlement, tattlement 4. embattlement.

AT'o-mi- 3. atomy 4. anatomy 5. tesseratomy.

AT'o-mist- 3. atomist 4. anatomist.

AT'rik-al- 3. matrical 4. theatrical, iatrical 5. psychiatrical, idolatrical.

AT'ri-sid- 3. matricide, patricide, fratricide.

AT'ron-ij- 3. matronage, patronage.

AT'ron-iz- 3. matronize, patronize.

AT'ul-a- 3. scatula, spatula 4. comatula.

AT'ul-at- 3. spatulate, gratulate 4. congratulate.

AT'ur-al- 3. natural 4. unnatural 5. supernatural, preternatural.

AT'ur-at- 3. maturate, saturate 5. supersaturate.

AV'aj-er- 3. scavager, ravager, savager.

AV'aj-est- 3. savagest.

AV'aj-ing- 3. scavaging, ravaging.

AV'an-ez- 3. Havanese, Javanese.

AV'el-er- 3. caviler, raveler, traveler 4. unraveler.

AV'el-in- 3. javelin, ravelin.

AV'el-ing- 3. caviling, raveling, graveling, traveling 4. unraveling.

AV'end-er- **3.** chavender, lavender.

AV'er-ij- **3.** average.

AV'er-ing- **3.** havering, clavering **4.** palavering.

AV'er-us- **4.** cadaverous, papaverous.

AV'ish-er- **3.** lavisher, ravisher.

AV'ish-ing- **3.** lavishing, ravishing **4.** enravishing.

AV'ish-ment- **3.** lavishment, ravishment, **4.** enravishment.

AV'i-ti- **3.** cavity, gravity, pravity, suavity **4.** concavity, depravity.

AZ'ard-us- **3.** hazardous.

AZ'i-a- **3.** razzia.

AZ'l-ment- **3.** dazzlement, frazzlement **4.** bedazzlement.

E (bee)

1.

SINGLE (MASCULINE) RHYMES IN E (bee)

Primary or Secondary Accent Falls on Last Syllable; Imperfect Rhymes Are in Italics.

E– **1.** e, E, ee, 'ee.

BE– **1.** b, B, be, bee **2.** A.B., *bawbee*, Bebe, bribee **3.** honeybee, bumblebee, humblebee, scarabee, Niobe, wallaby, Barnaby, Araby, sassaby, jacoby, cenoby.

CHE– **1.** chee **2.** *chee-chee*, litchi, vouchee **3.** debauchee.

DE– **1.** d, D, dee, Dee, dit [F.] **2.** D.D., M.D., Didi, deedee, Chaldee, killdee, grandee, spondee, vendee **3.** C.O.D., Ph.D., chickadee, tragedy, remedy, comedy, perfidy, subsidy, tweedledee, organdy, Normandy, dispondee, arrondi [F.], Burgundy, theody, melody, psalmody, threnody, hymnody, monody, dipody, tripody, parody, prosody, rhapsody, custodee, custody, Lombardy, jeopardy, bastardy **4.** fiddlededee.

FE– **1.** fee, phi **2.** feoffee, Fifi **4.** telegraphy, geography, biography, biographee, anaglyphy, xylography, photography, catastrophe, antistrophe, apostrophe **5.** paleography **6.** dactyliography.

GE– **1.** ghee **2.** whangee **3.** Portugee.

HE– **1.** he **2.** hehee, tehee, bohea.

JE– **1.** g, G, gee **2.** agee, geegee, Gigi, squeegee, pledgee, N.G., pongee, bargee, burgee **3.** mortgagee, elegy, strategy, prodigy, effigy, obligee, perigee, elogy, apogee, dilogy, trilogy, dyslogy, eulogy, allergy, synergy, theurgy, telurgy, zymurgy, liturgy, refugee, syzygy **4.** biology, zoology.

KE– **1.** key, cay, quay, ski, skee **2.** raki, croquis [F.], marquee **3.** colicky, garlicky, panicky, finicky, hillocky, hummocky, Cherokee, master key **4.** synecdoche.

LE– **1.** Lee, lea, li, Leigh, flea, flee, glee, clee **2.** alee, bailee, belee, peelee, pili, folie [F.] **3.** Thessaly, Rosalie, Italy, Castaly, libelee, fleur-de-lis, appellee, enrollee **4.** anomaly, Annabel Lee; *also all adverbs composed of adjective-plus-suffix "-ly"* (e.g. toothsomely, longingly); *also adjectives composed of noun-plus-suffix "-ly"* (e.g. brotherly, sisterly).

ME– **1.** me, smee **2.** ami [F.] **3.** infamy, balsamy, jessamy, dittamy, alchemy, blasphemy, Ptolemy, enemy, bonhomie, confirmee.

NE– **1.** nee, knee, snee **2.** trainee, Beni, Chinee, donee, pawnee, Pawnee, Shawnee **3.** bargainee, distrainee, designee, assignee, consignee, alienee, domine, nominee, internee, optionee, snickersnee, Tuscany, tiffany, Romany, Germany, larceny, eugeny, kitcheny, villainy, tyranny, dysphony, euphony, cushiony, oniony, felony, colony, barony, crimsony, Antony, cottony, gluttony, muttony, Saxony **4.** mahogany, Epiphany, accompany, examinee, illuminee, abandonee, petitionee, Gethsemane.

PE– **1.** p, P, pe, pee **2.** rappee, *earthpea*, *cowpea*, wampee, topee, toupee, rupee **3.** canopy, escapee, agape, calipee, recipe, epopee **4.** Calliope, Penelope.

RE– **1.** re, ree, bree [dial.], Brie, dree [Scot. & dial.], free, pre [slang], spree, tree, three **2.** karree, Marie, in re [L.], debris, broderie [F.], enfree, unfree, *care-free*, *germ-free*, *heart-free*, *dust-free*, agree, degree, puggree, machree, doree, choree, épris [F.], esprit [F.] **3.** Barbary, quandary, boundary, vagary, beggary, sangaree, stingaree, dungaree, pugaree, sugary, diary, chickaree, salary, bain-marie, summary, rapparee, library, contrary, notary, rotary, votary, rosary, Calvary, ribaldry, husbandry, bribery, robbery, treachery, archery, witchery, thundery, prudery, referee, transferee, waggery, roguery, snuggery, drudgery, forgery, bakery, trickery, mockery, rookery, raillery, gallery, flummery, mummery, scenery, finery, fernery, drapery, slippery, trumpery, foppery, popery, tracery, passerie, chancery, sorcery, nursery, battery, flattery, watery, lottery, wintery, artery, mastery, mystery, cautery, feathery, heathery, slavery, knavery, bravery, reverie, thievery, livery, shivery, silvery, equerry, misery, fancy-free, duty-free, imagery, savagery, mimicry, disagree, cavalry, chivalry, rivalry, jugglery, hostelry, revelry, jewelry, devilry, yeomanry, demonry, masonry, jamboree, theory, priory, chicory, hickory, pillory, memory, armory, honoree, vapory, factory, rectory, victory, history, savory, ivory, seigniory, doubletree, whiffletree, Christmas tree, forestry, ancestry, augury, injury, perjury, mercury, penury, potpourri, treasury, usury, century, luxury **4.** infirmary, debauchery, commandery, sculduddery, skulduggery, diablerie, artillery, tomfoolery, gendarmery, perfumery, chicanery, machinery, rotisserie, phylactery, adultery, effrontery, upholstery, delivery, recovery, discovery, corroboree, Terpsichore, extempore, compulsory, precursory, elusory, illusory, refractory, directory, perfunctory, unsavory **5.** anniversary, parliamentary, testamentary, elementary, rudimentary, complimentary, Saulte Sainte Marie, passementerie, satisfactory, contradictory, valedictory.

SE– **1.** c, C, see, sea, cee, si **2.** asea, assis, besee, lessee, précis, sycee **3.** fricassee, releasee, Tennessee, addressee, assessee, promisee, licensee, Sadducee, surfacy, legacy, fallacy, prelacy, primacy, pharmacy, Christmasy, lunacy, papacy, piracy, Holy See, euphrasy, fantasy, prophecy, courtesy, secrecy, pleurisy, marshalcy, colonelcy, minstrelsy, captaincy, surgeoncy, vacancy, peccancy, mordancy, infancy, romancy, nomancy, stagnancy, regnancy, pregnancy, sonancy, blatancy, piquancy, truancy, buoyancy, lambency, lucency, cadency, pendency, ardency, tangency, pungency, cogency, saliency, cliency, valency, nascency, latency, fluency, leprosy, abbacy, embassy, unforesee, undersea, oversea, oversee, endorsee, bankruptcy, Dubussy, jealousy, Argosy, autopsy **4.** celibacy, delicacy, intricacy, advocacy, candidacy, delegacy, supremacy, intimacy, obstinacy, federacy, literacy, magistracy, accuracy, obduracy, adequacy, intestacy, sibilancy, petulancy, consonancy, discrepancy, oscitancy, irritancy, hesitancy, accountancy, acceptancy, inconstancy, relevancy, conservancy, impudency, negligency, excellency, succulency, truculency, corpulency, flatulency, inclemency, permanency, prominency, pertinency, abstinency, competency, penitency, delinquency, idiocy **5.** inefficacy, prolificacy, indelicacy, immediacy, inebriacy, immaculacy, legitimacy, effeminacy, episcopacy, illiteracy, inaccuracy, inadequacy, irradiancy, preponderancy, recalcitrancy, irrelevancy, expediency, incipiency, equivalency, impermanency, impertinency, belligerency, incompetency, impenitency, omnipotency, constituency.

SHE– **1.** she, shee, ski **2.** hachis [F.], Vichy, *banshee*, *banshie* **3.** garnishee, rubbishy, flourishy, debauchee.

TE– **1.** t, T, tee, tea **2.** settee, titi, draftee, high tea, grantee, goatee, coatee, mestee, mustee, trustee, bootee, suttee,

Q.T. [slang] **3.** legatee, remittee, permittee, electee, inductee, guarantee, warrantee, absentee, presentee, patentee, appointee, picottee, allottee, devotee, repartee, deportee, amputee, nicety, fidgety, hatchety, witchety, crotchety, trinkety, subtlety, trumpety, snippety, russety, velvety, laity, crudity, deity, jollity, amity, dimity, enmity, comity, sanity, dignity, trinity, charity, purity, scarcity, falsity, density, sparsity, sanctity, entity, chastity, cavity, gravity, levity, brevity, laxity, spiralty, casualty, cruelty, faculty, occulty, guaranty, sovereignty, warranty, certainty, maggoty, carroty, liberty, puberty, property, poverty, dynasty, contrasty, majesty, amnesty, sacristy, deputy **4.** acerbity, cupidity, arridity, acridity, acidity, avidity, commodity, absurdity, anxiety, dedicatee, morality, fatality, mortality, brutality, equality, ability, debility, agility, facility, docility, fertility, hostility, utility, futility, civility, credulity, calamity, deformity, conformity, amenity, benignity, affinity, infinity, divinity, eternity, community, barbarity, disparity, celebrity, celerity, asperity, sincerity, austerity, dexterity, alacrity, authority, audacity, capacity, felicity, duplicity, complicity, ferocity, atrocity, adversity, diversity, annuity, fatuity, depravity, acclivity, declivity, passivity, activity, captivity, festivity, iniquity, antiquity, complexity, convexity, dishonesty **5.** actuality, affability, changeability, capability, anonymity, Christianity, consanguinity, similarity, animosity, curiosity, electricity, authenticity, elasticity, domesticity, ambiguity, assiduity, contiguity.

THĒ– **1.** the, thee **2.** prithee **3.** apathy, empathy, sympathy, dyspathy, eupathy, timothy.

VĒ– **1.** v, V, vee, vie [F.] **3.** vis-à-vis, joie de vie [F.], eau de vie [F.], Muscovy, anchovy.

WĒ– **1.** wee, we, whee, puy [F.] **2.** ennui, pui [F.], etui, etwee, drawee **3.** mildewy, meadowy, shadowy, sallowy, yellowy, billowy, pillowy, willowy, arrowy, furrowy, point d'appui [F.].

YĒ– **1.** ye **2.** payee, bouilli [F.] **3.** employee.

ZĒ– **1.** z, Z, zee **2.** razee, fusee **3.** bourgeoisie [F.], cognizee, advisee, devisee, chimpanzee, Zuyder Zee **4.** recognizee.

ĒB– **1.** dieb, feeb [slang], glebe, plebe, reeb [slang], grebe **2.** ephebe, tanjib, caraibe.

ĒBZ– diebs etc., *see* **ĒB–** dieb etc. above, plus "s" or "'s"; **1.** Thebes.

ĒCH– **1.** each, beach, beech, keach, keech, leach, leech, bleach, fleech, pleach, sleech, peach, speech, reach, breach, breech, screech, preach, teach, queach **2.** appeach, impeach, outreach, beseech **3.** overreach.

ĒD– **1.** Ede, bead, Bede, deed, feed, gied [dial.], heed, he'd, geed, keyed, lead, bleed, flead, gleed, glede [Scot.], plead, mead, meed, Mede, need, knead, snead, peed, speed, read, reed, rede, Reid, breed, brede, freed, greed, creed, screed, treed, threed, seed, cede, teed, teaed, steed, weed, Swede, tweed, yede **2.** Candide, indeed, misdeed, unfeed, *Lockheed*, unkeyed, *nosebleed*, implead, mislead, knock-kneed, stampede, impede, Godspeed, jereed, reread, misread, outread, inbreed, crossbreed, enfreed, agreed, degreed, decreed, *hayseed*, reseed, *linseed*, *flaxseed*, recede, precede, secede, accede, succeed, concede, *seaweed*, *chickweed*, *milkweed*, *pokeweed*, ennuied **3.** underfeed, overfeed, interplead, millepede, centipede, interbreed, refereed, disagreed, pedigreed, filigreed, cottonseed, epicede, antecede, aniseed, retrocede, supersede, intercede, guaranteed, tumbleweed, locoweed **4.** velocipede, unpedigreed, unguaranteed.

ĒDZ– beads etc., *see* **ĒD–** Ede etc. above, plus "s" or "'s."

EF– 1. beef, chief, feoff, fief, Lif, leaf, lief, neif, reef, reif, brief, grief, sheaf, thief 2. naif, redif, enfeoff, belief, relief, *flyleaf*, *broadleaf*, hanif, shereef, tashrif, motif 3. handkerchief, neckerchief, unbelief, disbelief, misbelief, bas-relief, interleaf, overleaf, velvetleaf, Teneriffe 4. apéritif [F.].

EG– 1. digue [F.], league, skeeg, kleig, peag, Grieg, Teague 2. enleague, *colleague*, banig, renege, intrigue, fatigue, squeteague.

EJ– 1. liege, siege 2. besiege.

EK– 1. eke, beak, beek, cheek, Deke, deek, deak [both slang], feke [slang], geek, geke [both slang], keek [slang], leek, leak, bleak, gleek, clique, cleek, sleek, meek, sneak, pique, peak, peek, Peke, speak, reek, freak, Greek, creek, creak, shriek, streak, wreak, seek, Sikh, chic, sheik, teak, weak, week, tweak, squeak, Zeke 2. saic, caique, *halfbeak*, *grosbeak*, aleak, *houseleek*, oblique, silique, comique [F.], clinique [F.], technique, unique, apeak, repique, *forepeak*, forspeak, areek, perique, cacique, reseek, batik, critique, antique, bezique, physique 3. Mosambique, Martinique, demipique, fenugreek, Politique, novantique, Holy Week, yesterweek 5. Realpolitik [G.], Geopolitik.

EKS– ekes etc., *see* **EK–** eke etc. above, plus "s" or "'s."

EKT– 1. eked, beaked, cheeked, leaked, sneaked, peaked, peeked, piqued, cliqued, reeked, shrieked, streaked, wreaked, tweaked, squeaked 2. pink-cheeked, unpiqued, antiqued 3. eagle-beaked, apple-cheeked, rosy-cheeked.

EL– 1. eel, beal, deal, dele, feal, feel, heal, heel, jeel, jheel, jhil, keel, skeel, leal, leel, Lille, meal, mil, neele, kneel, peal, peel, speel, spiel, reel, creel, seal, seel, ceil, sheel [Scot.], teal, teil, til, steal, steel, veal, weal, weel, squeal, wheal, wheel, twille, zeal 2. abele, Mobile, redeal, ideal, ordeal, misdeal, refeel, forefeel, congeal, *clownheal*, vakil, coquille, Camille, *inchmeal*, *cornmeal*, *piecemeal*, *oatmeal*, landmil, *fistmele*, anneal, anele, chenille, appeal, repeal, *kriegspiel*, *Singspiel*, *Festspiel* [G.], *bonspiel*, enseal, conceal, unseal, baril, datil, manteel, genteel, Bastille, castile, pastille, aiguille, *cogwheel* 3. dishabille, immobile, unideal, Guayaquil, havermeal, camomile, manchineel, cochineal, glockenspiel, difficile, goldenseal, endocoele, neurocoele, commonweal, paddle wheel, balance wheel, alguazil, cacozeal 4. locomobile, automobile.

ELD– 1. eeled, field, heeled, keeled, kneeled, peeled, spieled, sealed, shield, steeled, squealed, weald, wield, wheeled, yield 2. afield, *Sheffield*, *Springfield*, *Canfield*, *infield*, *cornfield*, *airfield*, *Garfield*, *Warfield*, *Mansfield*, *outfield*, congealed, annealed, aneled, appealed, repealed, *windshield*, revealed 3. battlefield, Copperfield, Chesterfield, unrepealed, unrevealed.

ELZ– eels etc., *see* **EL–** eel etc. above, plus "s" or "'s."

EM– 1. eme, beam, deme, deem, scheme, leam, gleam, neem, reem, ream, riem, rheme, bream, dream, fream, cream, scream, stream, seam, seem, teem, team, steam, theme, yeme 2. abeam, *moonbeam*, *hornbeam*, *sunbeam*, *crossbeam*, adeem, addeem, redeem, misdeem, blaspheme, regime, hakeem, agleam, supreme, extreme, *daydream*, ice-cream, escrime [F.], *millstream*, downstream, upstream, raceme, Nashim, beseem, unseam, centime, esteem 3. academe, hyporcheme, disesteem, self-esteem, anatheme.

EMD– 1. beamed, deemed, schemed, gleamed, reamed, dreamed, creamed, screamed, streamed, seamed, seemed, teemed, teamed, steamed 2. redeemed, blasphemed, daydreamed, beseemed, esteemed.

EMZ– emes etc., *see* **EM–** eme etc. above, plus "s" or "'s."

EN– **1.** ean, e'en, been, bean, dean, dene, gean, jean, Jean, Jeanne, gene, Keene, keen, skean, lean, lien, glean, clean, spleen, mean, mien, mesne, pean, peen, breen [slang], green, screen, preen, threne, seen, scene, sheen, teen, 'steen, visne, wean, ween, queen, quean, yean **2.** shebeen, gombeen, ich dien [G.], sardine, dudeen, caffeine, morphine, phosphene, Beguine, sagene, Valjean, Eugene, sakeen, nankeen, buckeen, baleen, scalene, maline, *Hellene*, colleen, Pauline, moulleen, unclean, Kathleen, bemean, demean, demesne, Benin, treneen, shoneen, alpeen, scalpeen, spalpeen, careen, marine, serene, terrene, Irene, pyrene, Dorine, toureen, shagreen, *peagreen*, *sea-green*, *gangrene*, bescreen, rescreen, unscreen, Racine, obscene, Essene, Nicene, piscine, unseen, foreseen, dasheen, machine, eighteen, lateen, ratteen, sateen, fifteen, canteen, nineteen, umpteen, thirteen, fourteen, sixteen, costean, routine, ravine, subvene, prevene, convene, May queen, atween, between, cuisine, benzine **3.** Capuchin, Aberdeen, gabardine, Josephine, carrageen, polygene, photogene, supergene, palanguin, palankeen, damaskeen, Magdalene, opaline, philhellene, mousseline, crinoline, gasolene, mezzanine, Philippine, atropine, submarine, bismarine, cismarine, transmarine, candareen, nectarine, mazarine, Nazarene, tangerine, kittereen, smithereen, wolverine, tambourine, figurine, aquagreen, peregrine, mythogreen, wintergreen, evergreen, Hippocrene, damascene, Damascene, kerosene, overseen, unforeseen, velveteen, turbiteen, quarantine, Byzantine, Constantine, serpentine, seventeen, Argentine, Florentine, Celestine, guillotine, libertine, contravene, supervene, intervene, Halloween, harvest queen, go-between, therebetween, bombazine, magazine, limousine **4.** heterogene, ultramarine, aquamarine; *also many other feminine names ending in the suffix "-ine"* (e.g. Georgine, Albertine).

END– **1.** eaned, beaned, fiend, keened, leaned, gleaned, cleaned, screened, weaned, weened, queened, teind, yeaned **2.** archfiend, demeaned, careened **3.** guillotined, contravened, intervened.

ENTH– **1.** greenth, 'steenth **2.** eighteenth, fifteenth, nineteenth, thirteenth, fourteenth, sixteenth **3.** seventeenth.

ENZ– eans etc., *see* **EN–** ean etc. above, plus "s" or "'s."

EP– **1.** cheep, cheap, deep, heap, jeep, keep, leap, leep, clepe, sleep, neap, neep, sneap, peep, reap, creep, threap, threep, seep, sepe [slang], sheep, teap, steep, weep, sweep **2.** aheap, upkeep, asleep, bopeep, la grippe [F.], estrepe, upsweep **3.** overleap, unasleep, oversleep, chimney sweep.

EPS– cheeps etc., *see* **EP–** cheep etc. above, plus "s" or "'s."

EPT– **1.** cheeped, heaped, jeeped, leaped, neaped, peeped, reaped, seeped, steeped **3.** overleaped.

ER– **1.** ear, beer, bier, cheer, deer, dear, fear, sphere, gear, here, hear, jeer, skeer [dial.], leer, lear, blear, flear, clear, sclere, mere, mir, smear, near, neer, sneer, peer, pier, pear, pir, spear, rear, drear, seer, sear, sere, ser, cere, shear, sheer, tear, teer, tier, Tyr, stere, steer, vire, veer, weir, queer, year **2.** *wheatear*, *killdeer*, reindeer, endear, ensphere, *headgear*, *footgear*, adhere, inhere, cohere, Mynheer, fakir, King Lear, unclear, amir, emir, emeer, premier, besmear, anear, denier, veneer, appear, compeer, outpeer, arrear, career, uprear, plancier, sincere, cashier, frontier, austere, revere, brevier, severe, *midyear*, brassiere, vizier **3.** shillibeer, ginger beer, brigadier, grenadier, bombardier, commandeer, interfere, hemisphere, atmosphere, pedalier, cavalier, lavaliere, chevalier, chandelier, fusilier, chanticleer, gondolier, pistoleer, buccaneer, souvenir, jardiniere, engineer, domineer, mountaineer, mutineer, scrutineer, chiffonier, cannoneer, pioneer, auctioneer, reappear, disappear, agricere, financier, insincere, caboceer, tabasheer, privateer, targeteer, musketeer, sonneteer, profiteer, gazetteer, volunteer, persevere, yesteryear.

ERD– **1.** eared, beard, cheered, feared, sphered, geared, jeered, leered, bleared, cleared, smeared, neared, sneered, peered, reared, seared, sheared, sheered, tiered, steered, veered, weird, queered **2.** uneared, lop-eared, *graybeard*, *treebeard*, *Bluebeard*, endeared, afeared, unfeared, ensphered, adhered, veneered, revered, appeared, outpeered, careered, upreared, cashiered, brassiered **3.** commandeered, interfered, engineered, domineered, mountaineered, pioneered, reappeared, disappeared, privateered, profiteered, volunteered, persevered.

ERS– **1.** Bierce, fierce, pierce, tierce **2.** transpierce.

ERZ– ears etc., *see* **ER–** ear etc. above, plus "s" or "'s"; **2.** Algiers, Tangiers.

ES– **1.** geese, lease, lis, lisse [F.], fleece, Nice, niece, peace, piece, grease, Greece, crease, creese, Kris, cease **2.** obese, esquisse [F.], sublease, release, valise, Felice, pelisse, police, coulisse, Bernice, apiece, *endpiece*, repiece, *neckpiece*, *timepiece*, *crosspiece*, *mouthpiece*, Clarice, cerise, decrease, recrease, increase, Lucrece, Maurice, caprice, cassis, decease, surcease, atis, métis **3.** prerelease, mantelpiece, cornerpiece, centerpiece, afterpiece, masterpiece, frontispiece, ambergris, predecease.

ESH– **1.** biche [F.], fiche, leash, sneesh, riche [F.] **2.** affiche [F.], unleash, potiche [F.], schottische, schottish, pastiche, postiche **3.** nouveau riche [F.].

EST– **1.** east, beast, feast, geest, least, leased, fleeced, sneest, piste, pieced, greased, creased, priest, triste [F.], ceased, teest, queest, yeast **2.** northeast, southeast, modiste, subleased, released, policed, decreased, recreased, increased, archpriest, deceased, batiste, artiste **3.** wildebeest, hartebeest, aubergiste.

ET– **1.** eat, beat, beet, cheat, cheet, feat, feet, Geat, heat, keet, skeet, scete, skete, leat, leet, bleat, fleet, gleet, cleat, pleat, sleet, meat, meet, mete, neat, peat, Pete, reit, freit, greet, Crete, treat, street, cete, seat, sheet, teat, queet, vite [F.], weet, sweet, suite, tweet, wheat **2.** *deadbeat*, *offbeat*, *drumbeat*, *upbeat*, *heartbeat*, *browbeat*, escheat, effete, defeat, reheat, munjeet, mesquite, elite, delete, deplete, replete, complete, *athlete*, *helpmeet*, *mincemeat*, *forcemeat*, *sweetmeat*, repeat, compete, terete, afreet, congreet, accrete, secrete, concrete, discreet, excrete, retreat, maltreat, entreat, estreat, mistreat, downstreet, upstreet, reseat, receipt, disseat, conceit, unseat, *broadsheet*, *clipsheet*, mansuete, unsweet, tout de suite [F.], *peetweet*, *buckwheat* **3.** overeat, parrakeet, lorikeet, incomplete, uncomplete, marguerite, Marguerite, indiscreet, county seat, mercy seat, judgment seat, balance sheet, tout de suite [F.], bittersweet.

ETH– **1.** heath, Keith, 'neath, sneath, sneeth, wreath, sheath, teeth **2.** beneath, eyeteeth, bequeath **3.** underneath.

ETHE– **1.** sneathe, wreathe, breathe, seethe, sheathe, teethe, quethe **2.** enwreathe, imbreathe, inbreathe, outbreathe, ensheathe, bequeath.

ETS– eats, etc., *see* **ET–** eat etc. above, plus "s" or "'s"; **1.** Keats.

EV– **1.** eve, Eve, eave, beeve, cheve, deave, gieve [slang], heave, keeve, leave, lieve, cleave, cleve, cleeve, sleave, sleeve, nieve, peeve, reave, reeve, reve, breve, greave, grieve, screeve, seave, sheave, steeve, Steve, thieve, weave, we've, queeve **2.** naïve, achieve, khedive, upheave, believe, relieve, bereave, aggrieve, reprieve, retrieve, *portreeve*, deceive, receive, conceive, perceive, qui vive [F.], reweave, inweave, unweave **3.** make-believe, unbelieve, disbelieve, interleave, semibreve, reconceive, preconceive, misconceive, apperceive, reperceive, preperceive, interweave **4.** recitative.

EVD– **1.** eaved, cheved, deaved, heaved, keeved, leaved, cleaved, sleaved, sleeved, peeved, reaved, greaved, grieved, screeved, sheaved, steeved, thieved **2.** achieved, upheaved, believed, relieved, bereaved, aggrieved, reprieved, retrieved, deceived, received, conceived, perceived **3.** unbelieved, disbelieved, interleaved, reconceived, preconceived, unconceived, misconceived, apperceived, reperceived, preperceived, unperceived.

EVZ– eves etc., *see* **EV–** eve etc. above, plus "s" or "'s"; **1.** Jeeves.

EZ– E's etc., *see* **E–** E etc. through **ZE–** zee etc. above, plus "s" or "'s"; **1.** ease, bise [F.], cheese, feaze, feeze, heeze, Geez [slang], Jeez [slang], please, mease, mise, neeze, neese, sneeze, pease, pes, Spes, reese, res [L.], breeze, freeze, frieze, grease, seize, tease, these, squeeze, weeze, tweeze, wheeze **2.** unease, heartsease, nipcheese, marquise, valise, Belize, displease, demise, chemise, remise, Burmese, Chinese, appease, trapeze, cerise, enfreeze, unfreeze, imprese, assise, reseize, disseize, bêtise [F.], sottise [F.], Maltese, disease, Louise **3.** Annamese, Portuguese, Singhalese, journalese, Pericles, Damocles, Androcles, Tyrolese, Herculese, Siamese, Assamese, manganese, Japanese, Havanese, Viennese, Pekinese, Cantonese, antifreeze, indices, vortices, overseas, Genevese **4.** Atlantides, Hesperides, antipodes, parentheses, hypotheses, analyses, Xenocrates **5.** Mephistopheles.

EZH– **1.** tige **2.** prestige.

E (bee)

2.

DOUBLE (FEMININE) RHYMES IN E (Le'ah)

Primary or Secondary Accent Falls on Next to Last Syllable; Imperfect Rhymes Are in Italics.

E'a– **2.** chia, Dea, deah [slang], hia, Lea, Leah, rhea, Rea, Rhea, Sia, Thea, via, Zea **3.** Rabia, rebia, obeah, Lucia, badia, Medea, idea, Chaldea, Judea, bahia, ohia, Hygeia, Mammea, Crimea, Carnea, Tarpeia, Maria, Sharia, Spiraea, spirea, Korea, Althea, Hosea **4.** ratafia, Eogaea, Neogaea, Arctogaea, energeia, melopoeia, pathopoeia, diarrhea, logorrhea, pyorrhea, panacea, fantasia, Galatea, Dorothea **5.** Antarctogea, Ave Maria, pharmacopoeia, peripeteia **7.** onomatopoeia; *see* also **E'ya–** Hygeia etc. below.

E'ad– **2.** Pleiad **3.** ideaed **4.** unideaed; *see* also **E'id–** Aeneid etc. below.

E'al– **1.** feal, pheal, real **2.** ideal, unreal, correal **3.** unideal, beau ideal, epigeal, perigeal, meningeal, laryngeal, Arctogaeal, hymeneal, empyreal.

E'an– **2.** lien, paean **3.** Sabaean, plebeian, Chaldean, Andean, Pandean, Shandean, Judean, Orphean, Aegean, Hygeian, trachean, Archean, Crimean, pampean, Korean, petrean, lyncean, Dantean, protean, Lethean, Pantheian, pantheon **4.** Maccabean, amoebean, Caribbean, Niobean, Jacobean, amphigean, perigean, phalangean, laryngean, apogean, Achillean, Galilean, Antillean, Sophoclean, Herculean, European, Eritrean, Tennessean, Pharisean, Sadducean, gigantean, Atlantean **5.** Archimedean, antipodean, terpsichorean, Epicurean **6.** Mephistophelean.

E'ant– **4.** philogeant.

E'as– Aeneas; *see* also **E'us–** Deus etc. below.

EB'a– **2.** iba, peba, Reba, Seba, Sheba **3.** amoeba, zareba, tiriba, Bath-sheba **4.** Jehosheba.

EB'an– **2.** Sheban, Theban **3.** amoeban.

EB'e– **2.** Phoebe, Hebe, TB **4.** heeby-jeeby, heebee-jeebee [both slang].

EB'er– **2.** Eber, Heber, weber.

EB'ez– **4.** heeby-jeebies, heebee-jeebees [both slang].

EB'ic– **3.** amoebic, amebic.

EB'l– **2.** feeble **3.** enfeeble.

EB'o– **2.** eboe, Ibo, Nebo **3.** placebo, gazebo.

EB'ra– **2.** libbra, zebra.

EB'us– **2.** Phoebus, glebous, rebus **3.** ephebus.

ECH'er– **2.** beacher, Beecher, feature, leacher, leecher, bleacher, peacher, reacher, breacher, breecher, creature, screecher, preacher, teacher **3.** defeature, impeacher, beseecher.

ECH'ez– beaches, etc., *see* **ECH–** each etc., plus "s" or "'s."

ECH'i– **2.** beachy, beechy, leachy, leechy, litchi, bleachy, sleechy, peachy, speechy, reachy, reechy, breachy, screechy, preachy, teachy **3.** campeachy.

ECH'ing– **2.** beaching, leaching, leeching, bleaching, fleeching, pleaching, peaching, reaching, breeching, screeching, preaching, teaching **3.** impeaching, outreaching, farreaching, beseeching **4.** overreaching.

ECH'less– 2. beachless, beechless, leachless, peechless, bleachless, sleechless, peachless, speechless, reachless, breechless, breachless, screechless, preachless, teachless.

ECH'ment– 2. preachment **3.** appeachment, impeachment, beseechment.

ED'a– 2. Leda, Theda, Veda, Vida, Ouida **3.** Aïda, kasida, reseda **4.** alameda **5.** olla-podrida.

ED'al– 2. daedal, creedal.

ED'ay– 2. bidet, D-day, fee day.

ED'ed– 2. beaded, deeded, heeded, pleaded, needed, kneaded, reeded, seeded, ceded, weeded, tweeded **3.** unheeded, stampeded, impeded, receded, preceded, seceded, acceded, exceeded, succeeded, conceded, proceeded, unweeded **4.** anteceded, retroceded, superseded, interceded.

ED'en– 2. Eden, reeden, Sweden.

ED'ens– 2. credence **3.** recedence, precedence, concedence **4.** antecedence, antecedents, retrocedence, supersedence.

ED'ent– 2. needn't, credent, cedent, sedent **3.** decedent, recedent, precedent **4.** antecedent, retrocedent, intercedent.

ED'ents– 3. precedents **4.** antecedents.

ED'er– 2. beader, feeder, heeder, leader, bleeder, pleader, needer, kneader, speeder, reader, cedar, ceder, cedre, seeder, weeder **3.** bandleader, ringleader, misleader, impleader, stampeder, impeder, receder, preceder, seceder, acceder, exceeder, succeeder, conceder, proceeder **4.** interpleader, superseder, interceder.

ED'ez– 2. aedes, greedies **4.** Palamedes, Archimedes, Dolomedes.

ED'ful– 2. deedful, heedful, needful, speedful, seedful **3.** unheedful, unneedful.

ED'i– 2. beady, deedy, heedy, Midi, needy, speedy, reedy, greedy, creedy, seedy, sidi, weedy, tweedy **3.** indeedy, unheedy, seaweedy **4.** orthopaedy.

ED'ik– 2. Vedic **3.** comedic **4.** talipedic, cyclopedic, orthopedic **5.** encyclopedic.

ED'ing– 2. beading, deeding, feeding, heeding, leading, bleeding, pleading, kneading, needing, speeding, reeding, reading, breeding, seeding, sheading, weeding **3.** unheeding, misleading, stampeding, impeding, rereading, misreading, inbreeding, cross breeding, reseeding, receding, preceding, seceding, acceding, succeeding, conceding **4.** underfeeding, overfeeding, anteceding, retroceding, superceding, interceding.

ED'l– 2. beadle, daedal, needle, pedal, wheedle, tweedle **3.** bi-pedal, conquedle **4.** semipedal, centipedal.

ED'ler– 2. needler, wheedler.

ED'less– 2. beadless, Bedeless, deedless, feedless, heedless, leadless, needless, speedless, readless, breedless, greedless, creedless, seedless, steedless, weedless, tweedless.

ED'ling– 2. needling, reedling, seedling, wheedling, tweedling.

ED'o– 2. Ido, Lido, credo **3.** albedo, libido, Toledo, torpedo, Laredo, teredo, Bushido [Jap.].

ED'ra– 3. exedra, cathedra **4.** ex cathedra.

ED'ral– 3. dihedral, trihedral, cathedral **4.** decahedral, polyhedral, hemihedral.

ED'rik– 3. diedric **4.** polyhedric, holohedric.

ED'ron– 2. cedron **3.** dihedron, trihedron **4.** polyhedron.

ED'rus– 2. Cedrus **4.** polyhedrous.

ED'um– 2. Ledum, pedum, freedom, Sedum.

ED'ur– 3. procedure **4.** supersedure.

E'er– 2. fleer, freer, seer 3. agreer, decreer, foreseer, sight-seer 4. disagreer, overseer.

E'est– 2. freest, weest.

EF'e– 2. Fifi 3. Afifi; *see* also **EF'i**– beefy etc. below.

EF'er– 2. beefer, chiefer, liefer, reefer, briefer.

EF'i– 2. beefy, Fifi, leafy, reefy, sheafy; *see* also **EF'e**– Fifi etc. above.

EF'less– 2. beefless, chiefless, leafless, reefless, briefless, griefless, sheafless, thiefless 3. beliefless, motifless.

EF'li– 2. chiefly, briefly.

EG'a– 2. Riga, Vega, ziega 3. bodega, omega.

EG'al– 2. legal, regal, gregal 3. illegal, unlegal, vice-regal; *see* also **EG'l**– eagle etc. below.

EG'er– 2. eager, eagre, leaguer, meager, meagre, zieger 3. beleaguer, intriguer, fatiguer 4. overeager, major leaguer, minor leaguer.

EG'ing– 2. leaguing 3. enleaguing, intriguing, fatiguing.

EG'l– 2. eagle, beagle, kleagle, teagle, veigle 3. bald eagle, sea eagle, porbeagle, espiegle, inveigle 4. double eagle, golden eagle; *see* also **EG'al**– legal etc. above.

EG'ler– 2. beagler 3. inveigler.

EG'o– 2. ego, grego 3. Otsego, Oswego.

EG'ress– 2. egress, negress, regress.

EG'ro– 2. Negro 4. Montenegro.

E'hi– 2. Lehigh, kneehigh.

E'hol– 2. keyhole, kneehole, frijol, frijole.

E'id– 3. Aeneid; *see* also **E'ad**– Pleiad etc. above.

E'ik– 2. rheic 3. caffeic, Palaeic, oleic, tropeic, choreic, caseic, proteic 4. mythopoeic 5. xanthoproteic 6. onomatopoeic.

E'ing– 2. being, feeing, geeing, skiing, fleeing, freeing, spreeing, treeing, seeing, teeing 3. well-being, nonbeing, teheeing, agreeing, decreeing, unseeing, foreseeing, sight-seeing 4. refereeing, disagreeing, overseeing, unforeseeing, guaranteeing.

E'ist– 2. deist, theist, zeist 3. ideist 4. Manicheist, polytheist, antitheist, monotheist.

E'it– 3. albeit, sobeit, howbeit.

E'izm– 2. deism, theism, weism 3. Parseeism, sutteeism 4. Manicheism, Phariseeism, Sadduceeism, absenteeism, polytheism, philotheism, cosmotheism, misotheism.

EJ'an– 3. collegian, Norwegian, Glaswegian; *see* also **EJ'un**– legion etc. below.

EJ'ans– 3. allegiance.

EJ'e– 2. Fiji, Gigi, squeegee.

EJ'er– 2. aeger [L.], Aegir, leger, sieger 3. besieger.

EJ'ik– 3. strategic 4. hemiplegic, cycloplegic 5. bibliopegic.

EJ'is– 2. aegis, egis 3. St. Regis.

EJ'un– 2. legion, region 3. collegian, Norwegian, Glaswegian.

EK'a– 2. chica, quica, sika, theca 3. Topeka, Areca, paprica, eureka, zotheca 4. Dominica, Salonika, Costa Rica, endotheca, Tanganyika 5. bibliotheca.

EK'al– 2. fecal, faecal, caecal, thecal, treacle 4. intrathecal 5. bibliothecal; *see* also **EK'l**– chicle etc. below.

EK'an– 3. Mahican, Mohican; *see* also **EK'en**– bleaken etc. below.

EK'ant– 2. piquant, precant, secant 3. cosecant 4. intersecant.

EK'ed– 2. beaked, peaked, streaked.

EK'en– 2. bleaken, sleeken, meeken, weaken 3. Mahican, Mohican; *see* also **EK'on**– beacon etc. below.

EK'er– 2. beaker, bleaker, Bleecker, sleeker, meeker, sneaker, peaker, peeker, speaker, reeker, creacker, krieker, shrieker, weaker, squeaker, tweaker.

EK'erz– beakers etc., *see* **EK'er–** beaker etc. above, plus "s" or "'s."

EK'est– 2. bleakest, sleekest, meekest, weakest.

EK'i– 2. beaky, cheeky, leaky, cliquey, sneaky, peaky, peeky, reeky, creaky, creeky, streaky, shieky, squeaky 6. veni, vidi, vici (L.).

EK'ing– 2. eking, beaking, cheeking, leaking, cliquing, sleeking, sneaking, peaking, peeking, piquing, speaking, reeking, wreaking, creaking, shrieking, streaking, seeking, squeaking, tweaking 3. bespeaking, unspeaking, self-seeking.

EK'ish– 2. bleakish, cliquish, meekish, sneakish, peakish, freakish, Greekish, weakish.

EK'l– 2. chicle, treacle 3. Ezek'l; *see* also **EK'al–** fecal etc. above.

EK'li– 2. bleakly, sleekly, meekly, treacly, weakly, weekly 3. obliquely, uniquely, biweekly, triweekly 4. semiweekly.

EK'ling– 2. weakling.

EK'ness– 2. bleakness, sleekness, meekness, weakness 3. obliqueness, uniqueness, antiqueness.

EK'o– 2. fico, mico, Nico, pico, pekoe 3. Tampico, matico 4. orange pekoe.

EK'ok– 2. Leacock, meacock, peacock, sea cock.

EK'on– 2. beacon, deacon 3. archdeacon; *see* also **EK'en–** bleaken etc. above.

EK'und– 2. fecund 3. infecund.

EK'wal– 2. equal, sequel 3. subequal, inequal, unequal, coequal.

EK'wens– 2. frequence, sequence 3. infrequence.

EK'went– 2. frequent, sequent 3. infrequent.

EL'a– 2. Bela, belah, gila, Leila, Leilah, selah, Shelah, Sheila, Stela 3. tequila, palila, sequela 4. Philomela, Venezuela.

EL'and– 2. eland, Zeeland 3. New Zealand.

ELD'ed– 2. fielded, shielded, wielded, yielded 3. unfielded, unshielded, unwielded, unyielded.

ELD'er– 2. fielder, shielder, wielder, yielder 3. infielder, outfielder, nonyielder.

ELD'i– 2. wieldy, yieldy 3. unwieldy.

ELD'ing– 2. fielding, shielding, wielding, yielding 3. enshielding, unyielding.

EL'e– 2. dele, peele, pili, stele 3. Belili 4. campanile, monostele, protostele; *see* also **EL'i–** eely etc. below.

EL'er– 2. eeler, dealer, feeler, healer, heeler, keeler, kneeler, pealer, peeler, spieler, reeler, sealer, seeler, stealer, stelar, velar, wheeler, squealer 3. misdealer, congealer, annealer, appealer, repealer, concealer, revealer, two-wheeler.

EL'est– 2. lealest 3. genteelest.

EL'i– 2. eely, Ealey, Ely, feally, mealy, freely, Greeley, seely, steely, squealy, wheely 3. genteelly; *see* also **EL'e–** dele etc. above.

EL'ij– 2. keelage, stealage, wheelage.

EL'ik– 2. velic 3. parhelic.

EL'iks– 2. Felix, helix 4. antihelix.

EL'in– 2. beeline, feline, tree line, sea line.

EL'ing– 2. eeling, Ealing, dealing, feeling, healing, heeling, keeling, kneeling, pealing, peeling, reeling, ceiling, sealing, seeling, shealing, steeling, stealing, wheeling, squealing 3. misdealing, unfeeling, congealing, Darjeeling, annealing, appealing, repealing, concealing, unsealing, revealing 4. double dealing 5. automobiling.

EL'ment– 3. congealment, repealment, concealment, revealment.

EL'ness– 2. lealness 3. genteelness.

EL'os– 2. Delos, melos, telos.

EL'um– 2. Caelum, velum.

EL'ya– 2. Delia, Lelia, Celia 3. lobelia,

Bedelia, Cordelia, Orphelia, Amelia, Camellia, Cornelia, Aurelia, Cecelia.

EL'yan– 2. Delian 3. Mendelian, chameleon, carnelian, cornelian, aurelian.

EL'yus– 2. Delius 3. Cornelius, Aurelius.

EM'a– 2. bema, chima, schema, Lima, Pima, rima, rhema, thema, Xema 3. edema, emblema, sclerema, sorema, blastema, Fatima, enthema, eczema 4. seriema, epiblema, hyporchema.

EM'al– 2. demal, hemal, lemel 3. blastemal 4. pseudohemal.

EM'an– 3. beeman, freeman, G–man, he–man, leman, seaman, semen, T–man, Teman, teaman; *see* also **EM'on–** demon etc. below.

EM'ent– 3. agreement, decreement 4. disagreement.

EM'er– 2. beamer, deemer, femur, schemer, lemur, reamer, dreamer, creamer, screamer, streamer, seemer, seamer, teemer, steamer 3. redeemer, blasphemer, *daydreamer*, supremer, extremer.

EM'est– 3. supremest, extremest.

EM'ful– 2. beamful, schemeful, dreamful, teemful.

EM'i– 2. beamy, gleamy, Mime, Mimi, mneme, dreamy, creamy, screamy, streamy, seamy, teemy, steamy 3. *daydreamy.*

EM'ik– 2. phemic, hemic, semic 3. anemic, phonemic, eremic, racemic 4. polyhemic, monoschemic, octasemic, septicemic, monosemic.

EM'ing– 2. beaming, deeming, scheming, gleaming, reaming, dreaming, creaming, screaming, streaming, seeming, seaming, teeming, steaming, theming 3. redeeming, blaspheming, *daydreaming*, beseeming, esteeming 4. unredeeming, unbeseeming.

EM'ish– 2. beamish, squeamish.

EM'ist– 2. schemist, Rhemist 3. extremist.

EM'less– 2. beamless, schemeless, dreamless, gleamless, creamless, streamless, seamless, seemless, teemless, steamless, themeless.

EM'let– 2. beamlet, streamlet, themelet.

EM'li– 2. seemly 3. unseemly, supremely, extremely.

EM'o– 2. hemo, Nemo, primo [It.].

EM'on– 2. demon, daemon, leman, seaman, semen 3. eudemon 4. cacodemon; *see* also **EM'an–** beeman etc. above.

EM'ster– 2. deemster, seamster, teamster.

EM'us– 2. Remus 3. oremus [L.] 4. Academus, Nicodemus.

EN'a– 2. ina [Tag.], gena, Gina, keena, quina, lena, Lena, lina, Lina, Nina, crena, cena [L.], scena, Tina, vina 3. pembina, verbena, *modena*, hyena, Georgina, galena, Salina, Paulina, guapena, subpoena, arena, farina, marina, Marina, tsarina, czarina, Andrena, cassena, Messina, piscina, encina, catena, poltina, cantina, sestina, Christina, Faustina, flutina, Athena, Avena, novena, Rowena 4. quintadena, contadina [It.], Cartagena, melongena, marikina, Magdalena, Catalina, cantilena, semolina, Wilhelmina, philopena, ocarina, ballerina, signorina [It.], orchestrina, sonatina, cavatina, Argentina, Clementina, concertina, Celestina, aguavina.

EN'al– 2. plenal, penal, renal, venal 3. marinal, adrenal, machinal 4. duodenal.

EN'at– 2. enate, crenate.

EN'e– 2. genie. lene, mene [Aram.], Nini, visne 3. Selene, Silene, Camenae, Irene, Rossini 4. fantoccini, campanini, Hippocrene; *see* also **EN'i–** eeny etc. below.

EN'er– 2. keener, leaner, gleaner, cleaner, meaner, greener, screener, weaner, wiener 3. demeanor, serener, obscener, machiner, convener 4. misdemeanor, contravener, supervener, intervener, magaziner.

EN'est– 2. keenest, leanest, cleanest, meanest, greenest 3. serenest, obscenest.

EN'i– 2. eeny, beany, pleny, spleeny, meeny, meanie, sheeny, greeny, teeny, weeny, Queenie, sweeny, Sweeney 3. galeeny; *see* also **EN'e–** genie etc. above.

EN'id– 2. Enid, maenad.

EN'ij– 2. greenage, teenage 3. careenage.

EN'ik– 2. phenic, splenic, Menic, scenic.

EN'iks– 2. phoenix, phenix.

EN'ing– 2. eaning, beaning, deaning, keening, leaning, gleaning, cleaning, meaning, greening, screening, preening, weaning, weening, queening, yeaning 3. bemeaning, demeaning, well-meaning, unmeaning, careening, unscreening, machining, costeaning, subvening, advening, convening 4. double meaning, quarantining, intervening, supervening, overweaning.

EN'ish– 2. beanish, deanish, keenish, leanish, cleanish, spleenish, meanish, greenish, queenish.

EN'ist– 2. plenist 3. machinist, routinist 4. magazinist.

EN'li– 2. keenly, leanly, cleanly, meanly, greenly, queenly 3. serenely, obscenely.

EN'ling– 2. weanling, yeanling.

EN'ness– 2. keenness, leanness, cleanness, meanness, greenness 3. uncleanness, sereneness, obsceneness.

EN'o– 2. beano, keno, leno, mino, Nino, Reno 3. albino, bambino [It.], tondino, camino [Sp.], comino, Merino, casino 4. palombino, baldachino, maraschino, pianino, sopranino, Filipino, San Marino, peacherino, vetturino [It.], andantino, Valentino.

EN'um– 2. plenum, frenum, fraenum 4. duodenum.

EN'us– 2. Enos, genus, Venus, venous 3. scalenus, Silenus.

EN'ya– 2. piña, Niña.

EN'yal– 2. genial, menial 3. congenial 4. uncongenial; *see* also **EN'i–al–** genial etc.

EN'yens– 2. enience 3. prevenience, convenience 4. inconvenience, intervenience.

EN'yent– 2. lenient 3. convenient 4. inconvenient, intervenient.

EN'yor– 2. senior, signor, seignior 3. monsignor.

EN'yus– 2. genius 3. ingenious.

E'o– 2. Eo, Leo, Cleo, neo, Reo, Rio, trio, Theo 3. bohio [Sp.].

E'ol– 2. Creole, Sheol.

E'on– 2. eon, aeon, pheon, Leon, pleon, neon, peon, Creon 3. pantheon 4. Ponce de Leon.

EP'a– 2. Nepa, nipa, niepa, pipa, cepa.

EP'al– 2. ipil, pipal, sepal; *see* also **EP'l–** people etc. below.

EP'en– 2. cheapen, deepen, steepen 3. alipin [Tag.].

EP'er– 2. deeper, cheeper, cheaper, heaper, keeper, leaper, sleeper, Dnieper, peeper, reeper, reaper, creeper, tepor, steeper, weeper, sweeper 3. *beekeeper, bookkeeper, timekeeper, innkeeper, shopkeeper, barkeeper, doorkeeper, horsekeeper, housekeeper, gatekeeper, mooncreeper.*

EP'est– 2. deepest, cheapest, steepest.

EP'i– 2. cheepy, heapy, sleepy, creepy, seepy, sheepy, tepee, steepy, weepy, sweepy 5. Fra Lippo Lippi.

EP'ij– 2. seepage, sweepage.

EP'ing– 2. cheeping, cheaping, deeping, heaping, jeeping, keeping, leaping, sleeping, neaping, peeping, reaping, creeping, threaping, seeping, steeping, weeping, sweeping 3. beekeeping, safekeeping, shopkeeping, housekeeping 4. overleaping, oversleeping, oversteeping.

EP'ish– 2. cheapish, deepish, sheepish, steepish.

EP'l– 2. people, steeple, wheeple 3. repeople, empeople, unpeople, merpeople, dispeople, townspeople; *see* also **EP'al–** ipil etc. above.

EP'less– 2. cheepless, deepless, jeepless, keepless, leapless, sleepless, peepless, seepless, sheepless, weepless.

EP'li– 2. cheaply, deeply, steeply.

EP'ness– 2. cheapness, deepness, steepness.

EP'oi– 2. sepoy, teapoy.

ER'a– 2. era, gerah, Hera, quira, lira, sclera, sera, Terah, Vera 3. Madeira, galera, chimera, chimaera, lempira, Sarira, Sharira, asherah, hetaera 4. rangatira.

ER'ay– 4. Miserere.

ER'al– 2. eral, feral, scleral, spheral, ceral 3. vicegeral 4. hemispheral.

ER'ans– 2. clearance 3. adherence, inherence, coherence, appearance, arrearance 4. interference, incoherence, reappearance, nonappearance, disappearance, perseverance.

ER'ant– 3. sederunt 4. perseverant; *see* also **ER'ent–** gerent etc. below.

ER'e– Erie etc., *see* **ER'i–** aerie etc below.

ER'ens– 3. adherence, inherence, coherence 4. interference, incoherence; *see* also **ER'ans–** clearance etc. above.

ER'ent– 2. gerent, querent 3. adherent, inherent, coherent, vicegerent 4. nonadherent, incoherent, perseverant.

ER'er– 2. cheerer, dearer, fearer, hearer, jeerer, leerer, clearer, smearer, nearer, sneerer, peerer, spearer, rearer, teerer, steerer, veerer, queerer 3. endearer, adherer, coherer, besmearer, appearer, austerer, reverer, severer 4. interferer, overhearer, disappearer, perseverer 5. electioneerer.

ER'ess– 2. peeress, seeress.

ER'est– 2. dearest, merest, nearest, drearest, sheerest, queerest 3. sincerest, austerest, severest.

ER'ez– 2. heres, Ceres, series; *see* also **ER'iz–** dearies etc. below.

ER'ful– 2. earful, cheerful, fearful, sneerful, tearful 3. uncheerful, unfearful.

ER'i– 2. aerie, eerie, Erie, beery, cheery, deary, sphery, jeery, keiri, kiri, leary, leery, bleary, smeary, sneery, peri, peery, speary, dreary, seri, teary, veery, weary, quaere [L.], query 3. uncheery, hetaery, aweary, world-weary 4. hara-kiri, overweary, Miserere.

ER'id– 2. wearied, queried 3. unwearied, world-wearied, unqueried.

ER'ij– 2. clearage, peerage, pierage, steerage 3. arrearage.

ER'ing– 2. earing, beering, dearing, Bering, cheering, fearing, gearing, hearing, jeering, leering, blearing, clearing, nearing, sneering, peering, spearing, rearing, searing, shearing, tiering, steering, veering, queering 3. endearing, adhering, inhering, cohering, besmearing, veneering, appearing, careering, cashiering, revering 4. interfering, overhearing, engineering, domineering, mountaineering, pioneering, cannoneering, auctioneering, reappearing, disappeaering, privatering, profiteering, volunteering 5. electioneering.

ER'iz– 2. dearies, series, wearies, queries; *see* also **ER'ez–** heres etc. above.

ER'less– 2. earless, beerless, cheerless, dearless, deerless, fearless, gearless, jeerless, leerless, Learless, mereless, peerless, spearless, tearless, yearless.

ER'li– 2. dearly, clearly, merely, nearly, drearly, queerly, yearly 3. sincerely, austerely, severely 4. cavalierly, insincerely.

ER'ling– 2. shearling, steerling, yearling.

ER'ment– 2. cerement 3. endearment.

ER'ness– 2. dearness, clearness, nearness, queerness 3. sincereness, austereness, severeness.

ER'o– 2. hero, Nero, Piro, cero, sero, Ciro, zero 5. lillibullero.

ERS′er– 2. fiercer, piercer 3. ear piercer.

ERS′ing– 2. piercing 3. transpiercing.

ER′us– 2. sclerous, serous, cirrus, cirrhous.

ERZ′man– 2. steersman 3. frontiersman 4. privateersman.

ES′a– 3. camisa [Sp.], Theresa.

ES′eez– 2. preces, praeses [L.], theses.

ES′ens– 2. decence 3. obeisance, indecence.

ES′ent– 2. decent, recent 3. obeisant, indecent, unrecent.

ES′ept– 2. precept.

ES′er– 2. leaser, fleecer, piecer, greaser, creaser 3. releaser, decreaser, increaser.

ES′ez– 2. leases, fleeces, nieces, pieces, peaces, greases, creases, ceases 3. subleases, releases, pelisses, valises, repieces, decreases, increases, caprices 4. mantelpieces, centerpieces, masterpieces, frontispieces.

ES′ful– 2. peaceful 3. unpeaceful, capriceful.

ESH′a– 3. silesia, magnesia.

ESH′an– 2. Decian, Grecian 3. Silesian, Venetian, magnesian, Lutetian, Helvetian 4. Polynesian.

ESH′ing– 2. leashing, sneeching 3. unleashing.

ESH′un– 3. deletion, depletion, repletion, impletion, completion, accretion, secretion, incretion, excretion 4. incompletion, internecion.

ESH′us– 2. Decius, specious 3. facetious.

ES′i– fleecy, greasy, creasy.

ES′ik– 2. mnesic 3. algesic, gynecic 4. polynesic.

ES′ing– 2. leasing, fleecing, piecing, greasing, creasing, ceasing 3. releasing, policing, decreasing, increasing, unceasing, surceasing.

ES′is– 2. schesis, tmesis, rhesis, [Gr.], thesis 3. deësis [N.L.], algesis, orchesis, ochlesis, mimesis, kinesis, phonesis, phromesis, noesis [Gr.], ascesis, [N.L.], ecesis, centesis, mathesis, anthesis, esthesis 4. exegesis, catechesis, hyporchesis, anamnesis, Anamnesis, synteresis, hysteresis, catachresis, antichresis, erotesis, anesthesis 5. diaphoresis, perichoresis, hyperesthesis.

ES′iv– 3. adhesive, cohesive 4. inadhesive, monadhesive, incohesive, noncohesive.

ES′less– 2. leaseless, fleeceless, nieceless, peaceless, pieceless, greaseless, creaseless, ceaseless 3. valiseless, capriceless.

EST′a– 4. buena vista [Sp.] 5. hasta la vista [Sp.].

EST′ed– 2. easted, beasted, feasted, yeasted.

EST′er– 2. Easter, easter, feaster 3. down-Easter, northeaster, southeaster.

EST′ern– 2. eastern 3. northeastern, southeastern.

EST′i– 2. beastie, bheesty, bheestie, sneesty, reasty, yeasty.

EST′ing– 2. easting, beasting, feasting, queesting, yeasting.

EST′li– 2. beastly, priestly 3. nonpriestly, unpriestly.

ES′us– 2. Esus, rhesus, Rhesus, Croesus.

ET′a– 2. eta, beta, cheetah, dita, keta, Fleta, meta, Meta, Nita, pita, Rita, Greta, creta, theta, seta, zeta 3. pandita, Chiquita, Marquita, tablita [Sp.], mulita, Anita, planeta, Juanita, magneta, kareeta, amreeta, amrita, rasceta, partita, sortita [It.] 4. palameta, manzanita, margarita, Señorita [Sp.], Carmencita, chirivita 5. Isabelita.

ET′al– 2. fetal, foetal, ketal, Setal 3. decretal; *See* also **ET′l–** beetle etc. below.

ET′am– 2. retem, raetam 3. Antietam.

ET′an– 2. Cretan, teetan; *see* also **ET′en** eaten etc. below; also **ET′on–** Eton etc. below.

ET'e– 2. rete [L.] 3. lanete; *ssee* alo **ET'i**– beety etc. below.

ET'ed– 2. cheated, fetid, heated, bleated, fleeted, gleeted, cleated, pleated, sleeted, meated, meted, neated, greeted, treated, seated, sheeted, teated 3. escheated, defeated, reheated, preheated, unheated, deleted, depleted, repleted, completed, unmeted, repeated, competed, accreted, secreted, concreted, excreted, retreated, maltreated, entreated, mistreated, reseated, receipted, conceited, unseated 4. undefeated, overheated, underheated, uncompleted, unreceipted, unconceited, self-conceited.

ET'en– 2. eaten, beaten, keten, sweeten, wheaten 3. uneaten, worm-eaten, motheaten, unbeaten, browbeaten 4. weatherbeaten; *see* also **ET'an**– Cretan etc. above; also **ET'on**– Eton etc. below.

ET'ens– 2. pretence.

ET'er– 2. eater, beater, cheater, heater, liter, litre, bleater, fleeter, pleater, meter, metre, meeter, neater, Peter, peter, rhetor, greeter, praetor, pretor, treater, seater, teeter, sweeter 3. beefeater, eggeater, fogeater, frogeater, cake-eater, anteater, fire-eater, drum beater, browbeater, escheator, depleter, completer, Demeter, repeater, competer, saltpeter, propretor, retreater, entreater, reseater, receiptor, two-seater 4. overeater, decaliter, hectoliter, centimeter, kilometer.

ET'est– 2. fleetest, meetest, neatest, sweetest 3. effetest, elitest, repletest, completest, discreetest 4. honey-sweetest.

ETH'al– 2. ethal, lethal 3. bequeathal 4. preterlethal.

ETH'an– 2. Ethan 5. Elizabethan.

ETH'e– 2. Lethe.

ETH'en– 2. heathen, wreathen.

ETH'er– 2. either, neither, wreather, breather, seether, sheather 3. enwreather, inbreather, outbreather, bequeather.

ETH'ez– 2. Lethe's 4. cacoëthes.

ET'i– 2. beety, sleety, meaty, peaty, treaty, sweety, sweetie 3. entreaty 4. spermaceti; *see* also **ET'e**– rete etc. above.

ET'ij– 2. eatage, cheatage, cleatage, metage 3. escheatage.

ET'ik– 2. cetic, cretic, Cretic, Rhaetic 3. acetic.

ET'ing– 2. eating, beating, cheating, heating, bleating, fleeting, gleeting, cleating, pleating, sleeting, meting, meeting, neating, greeting, treating, seating, sheeting 3. browbeating, escheating, defeating, reheating, preheating, deleting, depleting, repleting, completing, repeating, competing, accreting, secreting, concreting, excreting, retreating, maltreating, ill-treating, entreating, mistreating, receipting, unseating 4. overeating, nonrepeating, overheating, underheating.

ET'is– 2. Metis, treatise, Thetis 4. diabetes.

ET'ish– 2. beetish, fetish, fetich, sweetish.

ET'ist– 3. defeatist, decretist.

ET'iv– 3. depletive, repletive, completive, accretive, decretive, secretive, concretive, discretive, excretive.

ET'iz– 2. treaties, sweeties 3. entreaties.

ET'l– 2. beetle, betel, baetyl, fetal, wheetle 3. decretal, acetyl 4. chalchihuitl.

ET'li– 2. featly, fleetly, meetly, neatly, sweetly 3. completely, concretely, discreetly 4. obsoletely, incompletely, indiscreetly.

ET'ment– 2. treatment 3. defeatment, maltreatment, ill-treatment, entreatment, mistreatment.

ET'ness– 2. featness, fleetness, meetness, neatness, sweetness 3. effeteness, repleteness, completeness, concreteness, discreetness, petiteness 4. obsoleteness, incompleteness, indiscreetness.

ET′o– 2. keto, Leto, Tito, veto **3.** Chiquito, mosquito, magneto, Benito, bonito, Negrito **4.** angelito, sanbenito.

ET′on– 2. Eton, Eaton, seton, Teton; *see* also **ET′an–** Cretan etc. above; also **ET′en–** eaten etc. above.

ET′um– 2. fretum **3.** zibetum, pinetum, decretum, floretum, rosetum, quercetum **4.** arboretum, Tanacetum, salicetum, tilicetum, viticetum.

ET′ur– 2. feature, creature **3.** defeature, refeature.

ET′us– 2. fetus, foetus, Cetus **3.** quietus, acetous.

E′um– 2. Chiam, meum [L.], Meum **3.** Te Deum [L.], odeum, trophaeum, nymphaeum, nympheum, Iseum, lyceum, bronteum, notaeum, museum **4.** amoebaeum, hypogeum, mausoleum, athenaeum, atheneum, gorgoneum, coliseum, Colosseum **5.** peritoneum.

E′us– 2. Deus [L.], deus [L.], free us **3.** plumbeous, Zaccheus, Aeneas, choreus, gluteus **4.** scarabaeus, Amadeus, coryphеus.

EV′a– 2. Eva, diva, jiva, kiva, Siva, viva **3.** khediva, Geneva, Yeshiva **4.** Mahadeva.

EV′al– 2. eval, shrieval **3.** coeval, grandeval, upheaval, longeval, primeval, retrieval, equaeval **4.** medieval; *see* also **EV′il–** evil etc. below.

EV′ans– 2. grievance **3.** achievance, aggrievance, retrievance, perceivance.

EV′en– 2. even, Stephen, Steven **3.** uneven, bereaven, good even.

EV′er– 2. beaver, fever, heaver, keever, leaver, lever, liever, livre, cleaver, reaver, reever, reiver, griever, sheaver, weaver, weever **3.** naïver, achiever, enfever, hay fever, spring fever, coalheaver, believer, reliever, aggriever, repriever, retriever, deceiver, receiver, conceiver, perceiver **4.** jungle fever, yellow fever, cantilever, make believer, nonbeliever, unbeliever, disbeliever, misbeliever, preconceiver, misconceiver, interweaver, Danny Deever.

EV′i– 2. levee, Levy, leavy, peevey, peevy, peavey, peavy, Stevie, Suevi **4.** Mahadevi.

EV′ij– 2. leavage, cleavage.

EV′il– 2. evil, weevil **3.** boll weevil; *see* also **EV′al–** eval etc. above.

EV′ing– 2. heaving, leaving, cleaving, grieving, sheaving, steeving, thieving, weaving **3.** achieving, upheaving, believing, relieving, bereaving, aggrieving, reprieving, retrieving, deceiving, receiving, conceiving, perceiving, inweaving **4.** disbelieving, misbelieving, unbelieving, preconceiving, interweaving.

EV′ish– 2. peevish, thievish.

EV′less– 2. Eveless, heaveless, leaveless, sleeveless, sheaveless, weaveless.

EV′ment– 3. achievement, relievement, bereavement, retrievement.

EV′ning– 2. evening.

EV′u– 2. kivu.

EV′us– 2. nevus, grievous **3.** longevous, primevous **4.** ambilevous.

E′wa– 2. leeway, seaway.

E′ward– 2. leeward, seaward.

E′ya– 3. Hygeia, Tarpeia **4.** energeia, Barranquilla **6.** onomatopoeia; *see* also **E′a–** chia etc. above.

E′yan– 3. Hygeian, Tarpeian, Pantheian.

EZ′a– 2. pesa, Pisa, tiza, visa **3.** Louisa.

EZ′ans– 3. defeasance, malfeasance, nonfeasance, misfeasance.

EZ′ant– 3. malfeasant.

EZ′er– 2. easer, beezer, cheeser, geezer, pleaser, sneezer, freezer, friezer, greaser, Caesar, seizer, seizor, teaser, squeezer, tweezer, wheezer **3.** misfeasor, appeaser, displeaser, Sharezer, disseizor **4.** Ebenezer.

EZH′a– 3. Rhodesia, magnesia, esthesia; *see* also **EZH′i–a–** Zambesia etc.

EZH'er– 2. leisure, seizure 3. reseizure.

EZH'un– 2. lesion 3. adhesion, inhesion, cohesion, Silesian, trapezian 4. inadhesion, incohesion.

EZ'i– 2. easy, cheesy, sleazy, sneezy, breezy, freezy, greasy, teasy, queasy 3. Zambesi, speakeasy, pachisi, parchesi, uneasy.

EZ'in– 2. seisin, seizin.

EZ'ing– 2. easing, feazing, feezing, pleasing, sneezing, breezing, freezing, friezing, greasing, seizing, teasing, squeezing, wheezing 3. unpleasing, displeasing, appeasing, reseizing.

EZ'ingz– 2. feasings, greasings.

EZ'l– 2. easel, mesel, teasel, weasel.

EZ'lz– 2. easels, measles, weasels.

EZ'ment– 2. easement 3. appeasement.

EZ'on– 2. reason, treason, season 3. unreason, unseason.

EZ'us– 2. Jesus.

E (bee)

3.

TRIPLE RHYMES IN E (see'a-ble)

Primary or Secondary Accent Falls on Second from Last Syllable.

E'a-bl- **3.** feeable, fleeable, freeable, treeable, seeable, skiable **4.** agreeable, decreeable, unseeable **5.** disagreeable.

E'a-bli- **4.** agreeably **5.** disagreeably.

E'al-i- **3.** leally, really **4.** ideally.

E'al-ist- **3.** realist **4.** idealist, surrealist.

E'al-iz- **3.** realise **4.** idealize.

E'al-izm- **3.** realism **4.** idealism.

E'al-ti- **3.** fealty, lealty, realty.

E'an-izm- **3.** peanism **4.** plebeianism, Sebaeanism **6.** Epicureanism.

E'az-on- **3.** liaison.

EB'ri-us- **3.** ebrious **4.** tenebrious, inebrious, funebrious.

ECH'a-bl- **3.** bleachable, reachable, preachable, teachable **4.** impeachable, unreachable, unteachable **5.** unimpeachable.

ECH'i-ness- **3.** peachiness, screechiness, preachiness.

ED'a-bl- **3.** deedable, feedable, heedable, leadable, pleadable, kneadable, readable, seedable, weedable **4.** impedible, unreadable, exceedable **5.** unexceedable, supersedable.

ED'en-si- **4.** precedency **5.** antecedency.

ED'er-ship- **3.** leadership, readership.

ED'ful-i- **3.** heedfully, needfully **4.** unheedfully, unneedfully.

ED'ful-ness- **3.** heedfulness, needfulness **4.** unheedfulness, unneedfulness.

ED'i-a- **3.** media **4.** comedia, acedia **5.** Fissipedia, cyclopedia, epicedia **6.** pharmacopedia, encyclopedia.

ED'i-al- **3.** medial, praedial **4.** admedial, remedial, immedial, comedial **5.** irremedial, intermedial, epicedial.

ED'i-an- **3.** median **4.** tragedian, symmedian, comedian **5.** cosymmedian **6.** encyclopedian.

ED'i-at- **3.** mediate **4.** immediate **5.** intermediate.

ED'i-ens- **4.** obedience, expedience, expedients, ingredients **5.** nonobedience, disobedience, inexpedience.

ED'i-ent- **4.** obedient, impedient, expedient, digredient, ingredient **5.** unobedient, disobedient, inexpedient.

ED'i-er- **3.** beadier, needier, speedier, reedier, greedier, seedier, weedier.

ED'i-est- **3.** beadiest, neediest, speediest, reediest, greediest, seediest, weediest.

ED'i-it- **3.** mediate **4.** immediate **5.** intermediate.

ED'i-li- **3.** beadily, needily, speedily, reedily, greedily, seedily, weedily.

ED'i-ness- **3.** beadiness, neediness, speediness, reediness, greediness, seediness, weediness.

ED'ing-li- **3.** heedingly, pleadingly **4.** unheedingly, misleadingly, exceedingly.

ED'i-um- **3.** medium, tedium **4.** soredium **5.** intermedium, epicedium.

ED′i–us– 3. medius, tedious 5. intermedius.

ED′less–ly– 3. heedlessly, needlessly.

EF′i–ness– 3. beefiness, leafiness.

EG′al–i– 3. legally, regally 4. illegally.

EG′al–ness– 3. legalness, regalness 4. illegalness.

EG′er–li– 3. eagerly, meagerly 4. uneagerly.

EG′er–ness– 3. eagerness, meagerness 4. uneagerness 5. overeagerness.

E′it–i– 3. deity, seity 4. plebeity, tableity, velleity, omneity, aseity, gaseity, ipseity, multeity 5. extraneity, spontaneity, femineity, personeity, corporeity 6. simultaneity, instantaneity, momentaneity, incorporeity 7. contemporaneity.

EJ′ens–i– 3. regency 4. vice-regency.

EJ′i–an– 4. collegian, Fuegian, Norwegian.

EJ′i–um– 4. collegium 5. florilegium.

EJ′us–ness– 4. egregiousness 5. sacrilegiousness.

EK′a–bl– 3. speakable 4. unspeakable.

EK′i–li– 3. beakily, cheekily, leakily, sleekily, sneakily, creakily, squeakily.

EK′i–ness– 3. beakiness, cheekiness, leakiness, sneakiness, creakiness, squeakiness.

EK′ish–ness– 3. cheekishness, cliquishness, sneakishness, freakishness.

EK′wen–si– 3. frequency, sequency 4. infrequency.

EK′wi–al– 4. obsequial, exequial.

EL′a–bl– 3. dealable, feelable, healable, peelable, reelable, sealable, stealable 4. unhealable, congealable, annealable, appealable, repealable, concealable, revealable 5. unconcealable, unrevealable.

EL′i–a– 3. Elia, Delia, Lelia, Celia, Caelia, coelia 4. lobelia, Bedelia, Ophelia, Amelia, Hamelia, cimelia, Cordelia, Cornelia, Karelia, Aurelia; *see* also **EL′ya–** Delia etc.

EL′i–an– 3. Elian, Delian, Caelian 4. Hegelian, carnelian, Karelian, aurelian 6. Mephistophelean, Aristotelian.

EL′i–on– 3. Pelion 4. aphelion, parhelion, chameleon, anthelion 5. perihelion.

EL′i–us– 3. Delius, Helios 4. Cornelius, Aurelius 5. contumelius.

EM′a–bl– 3. beamable, reamable, dreamable, creamable, seamable, steamable 4. redeemable, esteemable.

EM′a–tist– schematist, thematist.

EM′er–i– 3. dreamery, creamery.

EM′i–a– 3. Nemea 4. Euphemia, Bohemia, leukemia, anemia, paroemia, toxemia 5. diarhemia, diarrhaemia.

EM′i–al– 3. cnemial, gremial 4. endemial, vindemial, proemial, paroemial.

EM′i–an– 4. Bohemian 5. academian.

EM′i–er– 3. beamier, gleamier, dreamier, creamier, premier, steamier.

EM′i–li– 3. beamily, gleamily, dreamily, creamily, steamily.

EM′i–ness– 3. beaminess, gleaminess, dreaminess, creaminess, steaminess.

EM′ing–li– 3. beamingly, gleamingly, dreamingly, seemingly 4. beseemingly, unseemingly.

EM′i–um– 3. premium 4. proemium, gelsemium.

EM′i–us– 4. abstemious.

EN′a–bl– 3. gleanable, leanable, meanable, weanable 4. amenable, convenable, unweanable.

EN′er–i– 3. deanery, plenary, greenery, scenery 4. machinery.

EN′i–a– 3. taenia, xenia 4. gardenia, Eugenia, Birkenia, Armenia 5. neomenia, neurasthenia, schizophrenia.

EN′i–al– 3. genial, splenial, menial, taenial, venial, xenial 4. congenial, demesnial 5. uncongenial, primigenial, homogeneal.

EN'i-an- 3. Fenian 4. Hellenian, Armenian, Cyrenian, sirenian, Athenian, parthenian, Ruthenian 5. Esselenian, neomenian.

EN'i-ens- 3. lenience 4. prevenience, convenience 5. inconvenience, intervenience.

EN'i-ent- 3. lenient 4. advenient, prevenient, convenient 5. inconvenient, supervenient, intervenient.

EN'i-er- 3. beanier, spleenier, sheenier, teenier, weenier.

EN'i-um- 3. rhenium, xenium 4. selenium, solenium, proscenium, postscenium 5. calistheneum.

EN'i-us- 3. genius, splenius 4. ingenious, arsenious 5. homogeneous, pergameneous 6. heterogeneous.

EN'yen-si- 3. leniency 4. conveniency 3. inconveniency.

EN'yent-li- 3. leniently 4. conveniently 5. inconveniently.

E'o-krat- 3. rheocrat, theocrat.

E'o-la- 4. areola, roseola, alveola, foveola.

E'o-lus- 3. Aeolus 4. malleolus, nucleolus, alveolus.

EP'i-a- 3. sepia.

EP'i-ad- 4. asclepiad, Asclepiad.

EP'i-li- 3. sleepily, creepily, weepily.

EP'i-ness- 3. sleepiness, creepiness, steepiness, weepiness.

ER'e-al- 3. cereal 4. sidereal, funereal, ethereal; *see* also **ER'i-al-** ferial etc. below.

ER'en-si- 4. adherency, inherency, coherency 5. incoherency.

ER'ful-i- 3. cheerfully, fearfully, tearfully.

ER'ful-ness- 3. cheerfulness, fearfulness, tearfulness.

ER'i-a- 3. eria, feria, Scleria 4. Iberia, Liberia, Siberia, Egeria, Nigeria, Algeria, Hesperia, bacteria, criteria, asteria, hysteria, wisteria, diphtheria 5. cafeteria, acroteria, Anthesteria, Eleutheria.

ER'i-ad- 4. anteriad, posteriad.

ER'i-al- 3. ferial, serial, cereal 4. aerial, sidereal, funereal, imperial, biserial, material, bacterial, arterial, asterial, ethereal, diphtherial 5. managerial, immaterial, monasterial, magisterial, ministerial, presbyterial.

ER'i-an- 3. Erian 4. aerian, Iberian, Liberian, Siberian, Algerian, Pierian, valerian, Cimmerian, Wagnerian, Shakespearean, Hesperian, vesperian, Spencerian, Spenserian, psalterian, trouserian 5. Luciferian, Presbyterian, philotherian, Eleutherian; *see* also **ER'i-on-** allerion etc. below.

ER'i-ens- 4. experience 5. inexperience.

ER'i-er- 3. eerier, beerier, cheerier, blearier, drearier, tearier, wearier; *see* also **ER'i-or-** inferior etc. below.

ER'i-est- 3. eeriest, beeriest, cheeriest, bleariest, dreariest, teariest, weariest.

ER'i-form- 3. spheriform, Seriform 4. viperiform.

ER'i-li- 3. eerily, beerily, cheerily, blearily, drearily, tearily, wearily.

ER'i-ness- 3. eeriness, beeriness, cheeriness, bleariness, dreariness, teariness, weariness.

ER'ing-li- 3. cheeringly, fearingly, jeeringly, peeringly 4. endearingly 5. domineeringly.

ER'i-o- 3. cheerio, serio.

ER'i-on- 4. allerion, Hyperion, criterion; *see* also **ER'i-an-** Erian etc. above.

ER'i-or- 4. inferior, superior, ulterior, anterior, interior, exterior, posterior; *see* also **ER'i-er-** eerier etc. above.

ER'i-um- 3. cerium 4. imperium, bacterium, psalterium 5. desiderium, elaterium, acroterium, magisterium.

ER'i-us- 3. Cereus, cereous, serious 4. imperious, mysterious, ethereous 5. jocoserious, deleterious.

ER′less–li– 3. beerlessly, cheerlessly, fearlessly, peerlessly.

ER′less–ness– 3. beerlessness, cheerlessness, fearlessness, peerlessness.

ES′a–bl– 3. leasable, peaceable, creasable, ceasable 4. releasable, increasable, unceasable.

ES′en–si– 3. decency, recency 4. indecency.

ES′ent–li– 3. decently, recently 4. indecently.

ESH′i–a– 4. silesia, Silesia, telesia, Helvetia 5. Polynesia, alopecia.

ESH′i–an– 3. Decian, Grecian 4. Silesian, Venetian, Lutetian, Helvetian.

ESH′i–at– 4. appreciate, depreciate.

ESH′un–al– 4. secretional, concretional.

ESH′us–ness– 3. speciousness 4. facetiousness.

ES′i–er– 3. fleecier, greasier, creasier.

ES′ing–li– 4. decreasingly, increasingly, unceasingly.

ES′it–i– 4. obesity.

ES′iv–li– 4. adhesively, inhesively, cohesively.

EST′i–ness– 3. reastiness, yeastiness.

EST′li–ness– 3. beastliness, priestliness.

ET′a–bl– 3. eatable, beatable, cheatable, heatable, treatable, seatable 4. uneatable, unbeatable, escheatable, defeatable, deletable, repeatable, entreatable 5. undefeatable, unrepeatable.

ET′ed–li– 3. heatedly 4. repeatedly.

ETH′e–an– 3. Lethean 4. Promethean.

ET′i–an– 3. Tahitian.

ET′i–ness– 3. meatiness, peatiness, sleetiness.

ET′or–i– 4. depletory, repletory, completory, secretory.

EV′a–bl– 3. cleavable, grievable 4. achievable, believable, relievable, retrievable, deceivable, receivable, conceivable, perceivable 5. unbelievable, irretrievable, undeceivable, inconceivable, imperceivable.

EV′a–bli– 4. believably, retrievably, conceivably, perceivably 5. unbelievably, irretrievably, inconceivably, imperceivably.

EV′i–at– 3. deviate 4. alleviate, abbreviate.

EV′ish–li– 3. peevishly, thievishly.

EV′ish–ness– 3. peevishness, thievishness.

EV′i–us– 3. devious, previous.

EZ′a–bl– 3. feasible, freezable, seizable, squeezable 4. defeasible, cohesible 4. appeasable 5. indefeasible, inappeasable, unappeasable.

EZH′i–a– 3. Freesia 4. Zambesia, parrhesia, ecclesia, amnesia, trapezia, esthesia 5. anesthesia; *see* also **EZH′a–** Rhodesia etc.

EZH′i–an– 4. Ephesian, trapezian, ecclesian, etesian, artesian; *see* also **EZH′un–** lesion etc.

EZ′i–a– 4. algesia, esthesia.

EZ′i–er– 3. easier, cheesier, sleazier, breezier, greasier, queasier, wheezier 4. uneasier.

EZ′i–est– 3. easiest, cheesiest, sleaziest, breeziest, greasiest, queasiest, wheeziest 4. uneasiest.

EZ′i–li– 3. easily, cheesily, sleazily, breezily, greasily, queasily, wheezily 4. uneasily.

EZ′i–ness– 3. easiness, cheesiness, sleaziness, breeziness, greasiness, wheeziness, queasiness 4. uneasiness.

EZ′ing–li– 3. pleasingly, freezingly, teasingly, wheezingly 4. displeasingly, appeasingly.

EZ′on–al– 3. seasonal 4. unseasonal.

EZ′on–er– 3. reasoner, seasoner.

EZ′on–ing– 3. reasoning, seasoning 4. unreasoning.

E (heh)

1.

SINGLE (MASCULINE) RHYMES IN E (heh)

Primary or Secondary Accent Falls on Last Syllable; Imperfect Rhymes Are in Italics.

E– **1.** heh, yeh [slang].

EB– **1.** ebb, deb [coll.], Deb, Geb, keb, Keb, bleb, pleb, Sleb, neb, reb, theb, web **2.** zibeb [obs.], cubeb, subdeb [coll.], *blackneb*, *cobweb* **3.** coulterneb.

EBD– **1.** ebbed, kebbed, blebbed, nebbed, webbed **2.** *cobwebbed.*

EBZ– **1.** ebbs, debs [coll.], Debs, blebs, plebs, nebs, rebs, thebs, webs **2.** cubebs, subdebs [coll.], *cobwebs.*

ECH– **1.** etch, fetch, ketch, sketch, letch, fletch, cletch, retch, wretch, stretch, tech, tetch [both dial.], quetch [obs. exc. dial.], vetch **2.** outstretch **3.** photoetch, bitter vetch.

ECHD– **1.** etched, fetched, sketched, fletched, retched, stretched, teched [dial.], quetched [obs. exc. dial.] **2.** farfetched, outstretched **3.** photoetched.

ED– **1.** Ed, ed [slang], bed, dead, fed, ged, gedd, Ged, head, jed, ked, led, lead, bled, fled, gled [Scot.], plead, pled, sled, *Ned*, snead, t'nead [Scot.], *ped*, *sped*, *red*, *redd*, med [slang], read, bred, bread, dread, Fred, spread, shred, tread, thread, said, shed, ted, Ted, stead, wed, 'stead, zed **2.** co-ed, abed, embed, imbed, *hotbed*, well-fed, unfed, ahead, *deadhead*, *redhead*, *roundhead*, *godhead*, behead, *blockhead*, *bulkhead*, *ramhead*, *drumhead*, *bonehead*, *towhead*, *drophead*, *spearhead*, *forehead*, *sorehead*, *hogshead*, *hothead*, bebfed, *bobsled*, mislead, pre-med [slang], *biped*, reread, misread, outread, *highbred*, *homebred*, inbred, *lowbred*, *purebred*, *crossbred*, *sweetbread*, *shortbread*, *truebred*, widespread, bespread, well-spread, outspread, retread, rethread, unthread, resaid, gainsaid, unsaid, *bloodshed*, *bedstead*, *roadstead*, bestead, *homestead*, *farmstead*, instead, rewed, unwed **3.** underfed, marblehead, bufflehead, fountainhead, dragonhead, arrowhead, loggerhead, copperhead, overhead, figurehead, aliped, taliped, cheliped, milliped, soliped, remiped, semiped, palmiped, plumiped, pinniped, uniped, serriped, cirriped, fissiped, multiped, breviped, octoped, quadruped, thoroughbred, underbred, gingerbread, underspread, overspread, *aforesaid*, watershed **4.** maxilliped **6.** parallelepiped; *also the past tense and past participle of regular verbs ending in "d" or "t"* (e.g. garlanded, coveted.)

EDTH– **1.** breadth **2.** hairbreadth, hairsbreadth.

EF– **1.** f, F, ef, eff, deaf, def [slang], feoff, jeff, Jeff, clef, nef, ref [slang], chef **2.** enfeoff.

EFT– **1.** eft, deft, feoffed, heft, jeffed, left, cleft, klepht, reft, theft, weft, wheft **2.** enfeoffed, infeft, aleft, bereft **3.** unbereft.

EG– **1.** egg, beg, keg, skeg, leg, cleg, Meg, sneg, peg, reg [slang], dreg, seg, teg, yegg [slang] **2.** *blackleg*, *bowleg*, *proleg*, *foreleg*, *nutmeg*, unpeg, *goose egg* **3.** philabeg, atabeg, filibeg, beglerbeg, Winnipeg, Silas Wegg [Dickens].

EGZ– eggs, etc., *see* **EG–** egg etc., above, plus "s" or " 's."

EJ– **1.** edge, hedge, kedge, skedge, ledge, fledge, cledge, gledge [Scot.], pledge, sledge, dredge, sedge, tedge, wedge **2.** unedge, allege, impledge **3.** interpledge, sacrilege, privilege.

EJD– **1.** edged, hedged, kedged, ledged, fledged, pledged, sledged, dredged, sedged, wedged **2.** two-edged. unfledged, alleged, impledged, unpledged **3.** double-edged, deckle-edged, privileged.

EK– **1.** ec [slang], beck, checque, check, Czech, deck, feck, geck, heck, haec, keck, lec, leck, lech, lek, fleck, cleck, smeck [slang], neck, sneck, peck, speck, spec [slang], reck, wreck, brek, trek, sec, tec, tech, teck **2.** home-ec [slang], *pinchbeck*, Quebec, recheck, bedeck, *foredeck*, *roughneck*, *wryneck*, *blackneck*, *breakneck*, *crookneck*, *swanneck*, sapek, *henpeck*, *flyspeck*, *shipwreck*, *parsec* **3.** countercheck, bottleneck, rubberneck, leatherneck **4.** bibliothec.

EKS– becks etc., *see* **EK–** beck etc. above, plus "s" or "'s"; **1.** x, X, ex, faex, hex, kex, lex, flex, plex, spex, specs, rex, prex, sex, vex **2.** *index*, *codex*, deflex, *reflex*, *biflex*, inflex, *diplex*, *triplex*, complex, *simplex*, perplex, *duplex*, annex, connex, *apex*, unsex, *vortex*, convex **3.** dorsiflex, circumflex, retroflex, genuflex, contraplex, nulliplex, veniplex, multiplex, disannex.

EKST– **1.** hexed, flexed, next, sexed, sext, text, vexed **2.** annexed, perplexed, unsexed, pretext, context **3.** genuflexed.

EKT– **1.** becked, checked, decked, flecked, flect, necked, pecked, specked, recked, wrecked, trekked, sect **2.** unchecked, bedecked, affect, effect, *defect*, refect, *prefect*, infect, perfect, traject, abject, subject, adject, eject, deject, reject, inject, conject, project, disject, elect, prelect, select, deflect, reflect, inflect, neglect, collect, *crooknecked*, connect, respect, inspect, *prospect*, expect, suspect, arrect, erect, direct, correct, porrect, bisect, dissect, transect, detect, contect, protect **3.** disaffect, misaffect, disinfect, retroject, interject, dialect, analect, re-elect, nonelect, intellect, circumflect, genuflect, recollect, reconnect, disconnect, self-respect, disrespect, circumspect, retrospect, introspect, indirect, misdirect, incorrect, resurrect, insurrect, intersect, architect.

EKTS– **1.** sects **2.** affects, effects, *defects* infects, perfects, trajects, subjects, adjects, ejects, dejects, rejects, injects, conjects, projects, disjects, elects, prelects, selects, deflects, reflects, inflects, neglects, collects, connects, respects, inspects, *prospects*, expects, suspects, arrects, erects, directs, corrects, porrects, bisects, dissects, transects, detects, contects, protects **3.** disaffects, misaffects, disinfects, retrojects, interjects, dialects, analects, re-elects, intellects, circumflects, genuflects, recollects, reconnects, disconnects, disrespects, retrospects, introspects, misdirects, resurrects, insurrects, intersects, architects.

EL– **1.** l, L, el, El, ell, bel, Bel, bell, belle, Belle, dell, fell, hell, Hel, jell, gel, kell, mel, mell, smell, Nell, knell, snell, schnell [G.], pell, spell, rel, cell, sell, shell, tell, well, dwell, swell, quell, yell, zel **2.** gabelle, rebel, *dumbbell*, Nobel, *harebell*, *corbeil*, *bluebell*, *cowbell*, rondell, *sardelle*, cordelle, befell, refel, miel [F.], pall-mall, pell-mell, Carmel, quenelle, spinel, Cornell, prunelle, noel, Noel, appel [F.], lapel, rappel [F.], repel, *scalpel*, impel, compel, propel, dispel, expel, respell, misspell, morel, nacelle, resell, ficelle, pucelle, excel, encell, Moselle, marcel, échelle [F.], *bombshell*, *sea shell*, unshell, *nutshell*, retell, bretelle, hotel, artel, cartel, foretell, cuartel [Sp.], unwell, farewell, indwell, gazelle **3.** Annabel, Annabelle, Isabel, Jezebel, bonnibel, citadel, infidel, hirondelle, hydrogel, aguamiel [Sp.], parallel, caramel, bechamel, philomel, fontanel, fustanelle, sentinel, jargonelle, personnel, pimpernel, ritornel, mackerel, pickerel, nonpareil, aquarelle, chanterelle [F.], pipistrel, unicell, undersell, oversell, carrousel, cockleshell, bagatelle, brocatel, muscatel, Neufchâtel, immortelle, caravel, demoiselle **4.** matériel, mademoiselle.

ELB– **1.** elb, skelb.

ELCH– **1.** belch, keltch [slang], welsh, Welsh, quelch, squelch [both slang].

ELD– **1.** eld, belled, felled, geld, held, helled, jelled, keld, meld, smelled, knelled, shelled, pelled, spelled, celled, shelled, welled, weld, dwelled, swelled, quelled, yeld, yelled, fjeld **2.** rebelled, beheld, upheld, withheld, repelled, impelled, compelled, propelled, dispelled, expelled, respelled, misspelled, excelled, marcelled, unquelled **3.** unicelled, parallelled **4.** unparallelled.

ELF– **1.** elf, delf, pelf, self, shelf, Guelph **2.** *didelph*, myself, thyself, himself, oneself, herself, ourself, yourself, itself.

ELFT– **1.** delft, Delft, pelfed, selfed.

ELFTH– **1.** twelfth.

ELK– **1.** elk, whelk, yelk.

ELM– **1.** elm, helm, realm, whelm **2.** unhelm, dishelm, Anselm **3.** overwhelm.

ELP– **1.** help, kelp, skelp, whelp, swelp, yelp **2.** self-help.

ELS– **1.** else **2.** how else, where else, what else.

ELT– **1.** elt, belt, dealt, felt, gelt, kelt, Celt, Kelt, melt, smelt, knelt, pelt, spelt, celt, Celt, veld, veldt, svelte, welt, dwelt **2.** unbelt, misdealt, *homefelt*, unfelt, *heartfelt*, remelt, undwelt.

ELTH– **1.** health, stealth, wealth **3.** commonwealth.

ELV– **1.** delve, helve, shelve, twelve.

ELVD– **1.** delved, helved, shelved.

ELVZ– **1.** elves, delves, helves, selves, shelves, twelves **2.** themselves, ourselves, yourselves.

ELZ– l's, ells, etc., *see* **EL–** l etc. above, plus "s" or "'s"; **1.** Welles, Wells **2.** Lascelles **3.** Dardanelles.

EM– **1.** m, M, em, 'em, Em, Emm, Dem., fem, feme, hem, gem, kemb, chem [slang], Lem, phlegm, Flem, Clem, clem, mem, crème [F.], sem [slang], Shem, Tem, stem, them **2.** condemn, begem, ahem, in rem [L.], *semsem*, contemn, protem, *pipestem*, *Zemzem* **3.** anadem, diadem, Bethlehem, requiem, stratagem, theorem, apothegm **4.** ad hominem [L.].

EMP– **1.** hemp, kemp, Kemp, temp **2.** *kohemp*.

EMPT– **1.** empt, kempt, dreamt, tempt **2.** pre-empt, coempt, adempt, unkempt, undreamt, perempt, attempt, retempt, contempt, exempt.

EMZ– m's, ems etc., *see* **EM–** m etc. above, plus "s" or "'s"; **1.** Thames, temse.

EN– **1.** n, N, en, ben, Ben, benn, Chen, den, fen, hen, gen [slang], Jen, ken, Ken, Len, glen, men, pen, wren, sen, Shen, ten, then, wen, when, yen, Zen **2.** Big Ben, *benben*, again, *peahen*, beken, amen, *seamen*, *horsemen*, *Norsemen*, *Bushmen*, *Northmen*, *pigpen*, impen, *cowpen*, marraine [F.], cayenne, Cheyenne **3.** oxygen, endogen, halogen, nitrogen, cyclamen, specimen, partimen, gentlemen, aldermen, Englishmen, Darien, julienne, brevipen, fountain pen, poison pen, denizen, citizen **4.** tragedienne, comedienne, sicilienne, éolienne [F.], Tyrolienne, equestrienne, Valenciennes, Parisienne [F.].

ENCH– **1.** bench, kench, blench, flench, clench, drench, French, trench, wrench, tench, stench, wench, quench, squench **2.** unbench, disbench, unclench, bedrench, retrench, intrench **3.** monkey wrench.

END– **1.** end, bend, fend, kenned, lend, blend, blende, mend, pend, penned, spend, rend, friend, trend, send, shend, tend, vend, wend, Zend **2.** upend, rebend, *prebend*, unbend, *addend*, defend, offend, forfend, *pitchblende*, *hornblende*, amend, emend, remend commend, append, depend, *stipend*, impend, *compend*, perpend, misspend, expend, suspend, befriend, ascend, descend, *godsend*, transcend, attend, subtend, pretend, intend, contend, portend, extend, distend, ostend, Ostend 3. dividend, subtrahend, apprehend, reprehend, comprehend, recommend, discommend, vilipend, reverend, condescend, repetend, coextend, minuend 4. misapprehend, miscomprehend, superintend.

ENDZ– ends etc., *see* **END–** end etc. above, plus "s" or " 's."

ENG– 1. dreng, drengh, kreng, sheng 2. *thameng, ginseng, banteng.*

ENGTH– 1. length, strength 2. full length, full strength.

ENJ– 2. *Stonehenge*, avenge, revenge.

ENK– 1. renk.

ENS– 1. dense, fence, hence, flense, mense [Scot. and N. of Eng.], pence, pense [obs.], Spence, cense, sense, tense, thence, vence [slang], whence 2. condense, defense, defence, offense, herehence, immense, commence, prepense, threepence, propense, sixpence, twopence, dispense, expense, suspense, incense, nonsense, subtense, pretense, intense 3. accidence, incidence, diffidence, confidence, subsidence, residence, dissidence, evidence, providence, impudence, recondense, self-defense, indigence, negligence, diligence, exigence, audience, prurience, excellence, prevalence, pestilence, redolence, indolence, condolence, violence, somnolence, insolence, turbulence, flocculence, succulence, truculence, fraudulence, opulence, corpulence, virulence, purulence, flatulence, lutulence, vehemence, recommence, immanence, permanence, eminence, imminence, prominence, continence, pertinence, abstinence, recompense, deference, reference, preference, difference, inference, conference, reverence, reticence, innocence, frankincense, commonsense, competence, appetence, penitence, impotence, refluence, affluence, effluence, influence, confluence, subsequence, consequence, eloquence, congruence 4. coincidence, improvidence, malevolence, preeminence, obedience, expedience, ebulience, experience, subservience, intelligence, equivalence, insomnolence, benevolence, impermanence, incontinence, impertinence, indifference, circumference, belligerence, irreverence, beneficence, magnificence, munificence, incompetence, inappetence, impenitence, omnipotence, inconsequence, incongruence, grandiloquence, magniloquence.

ENST– 1. fenced, flensed, mensed, sensed, censed, tensed 2. against, condensed, commenced, anenst, fornenst, dispensed, incensed 3. evidenced, recommenced, recompensed, reverenced, influenced 4. experienced 5. inexperienced.

ENT– 1. bent, dent, fent, Ghent, hent, gent, Kent, kent, lent, Lent, leant, blent, meant, pent, spent, rent, brent, Trent, sent, cent, scent, tent, stent, vent, went 2. unbent, indent, relent, Ament, fornent, lament, dement, cement, augment, foment, ferment, torment, anent, repent, misspent, unspent, resent, present, assent, ascent, descent, present, dissent, concent, consent, docent, detent, intent, content, distent, extent, ostent, event, prevent, invent, frequent 3. accident, occident, incident, diffident, confident, subsident, evident, provident, impudent, indigent, negligent, diligent, dirigent, corrigent, transigent, exigent, attrahent, contrahent, ambient, gradient, audient, salient, lenient, sapient, prevalent, excellent, somnolent, insolent, turbulent, flocculent, succulent, esculent, luculent, muculent, truculent, fraudulent, opulent, corpulent, querulent, virulent, purulent, flatulent, lutulent, ligament, parliament, armament, firmament, ornament, tournament, sacrament, testament, management, implement, complement, supplement, tenement, increment, excrement, cerement, banishment, garnishment, punishment, nourishment, lavishment, ravishment, pediment, sediment, condiment, rudiment, regiment, aliment, compliment, liniment, merriment, worriment, flurriment, detriment, nutriment, sentiment, revelment, devilment, government, wonderment, document, tegument, argument, monument, instrument, remanent, immanent, permanent, thereanent, eminent, imminent, prominent, continent, pertinent, abstinent, overspent, deferent, preferent, afferent, efferent, different, reverent, Millicent, reticent, innocent, competent, appetent, penitent, malcontent, affluent, effluent, refluent, subsequent, circumvent, underwent, represent **4.** coincident, improvident, intelligent, aperient, parturient, subservient, lineament, medicament, predicament, disarmament, temperament, disablement, ennoblement, bemuddlement, inveiglement, entanglement, accoutrement, acknowledgment, replenishment, admonishment, relinquishment, presentiment, bedevilment, enlightenment, abandonment, apportionment, environment, imprisonment, dismemberment, bewilderment, embitterment, beleaguerment, encompassment, embarrassment, impermanent, incontinent, impertinent, indifferent, belligerent, irreverent, Privatdocent [G.], misrepresent, beneficent, magnificent, munificent, incompetent, impenitent, omnipotent, mellifluent, inconsequent, grandiloquent, magniloquent **5.** circumambient, impoverishment, accompaniment, disillusionment.

ENTH– **1.** tenth **2.** *seventh*, *dozenth* **3.** *eleventh.*

ENTS– bents etc., *see* **ENT–** bent etc. above, plus "s" or " 's"; **2.** Coblentz.

ENZ– ens etc., *see* **EN–** n etc. above, plus "s" or " 's"; **1.** ense, gens, lens, cleanse **3.** Valenciennes.

ENZD– **1.** lensed, cleansed.

EP– **1.** chep [slang], dep [slang], hep [slang], skep, clep, slep, nep, pep, rep, prep [slang], strep [slang], step, steppe, yep [slang], zep [slang] **2.** *madnep*, *catnep*, *instep*, unstep, *stairstep*, misstep, *catstep*, *footstep* **3.** demirep, overstep.

EPT– **1.** kept, slept, pepped, crept, sept, stepped, wept, swept **2.** adept, unkept, y-clept, inept, accept, *precept*, *concept*, *percept*, discept, except, suscept, unswept **3.** preconcept, intercept **4.** biblioklept, intussuscept.

EPTH– **1.** depth.

ER– through **ERZ–**, *see* short **U** (tub): **UR–** through **URZ–**.

ES– **1.** s, S, es, ess, Bes, Bess, chess, dess, fess, fesse, 'fess, guess, Hess, jess, less, bless, mess, ness, pess, dress, cress, press, tress, stress, cess, sess, Tess, yes **2.** frondesce, confess, profess, quiesce, largesse, turgesce, noblesse, unless, kermess, finesse, caress, address, *headdress*, redress, undress, egress, regress, digress, ingress, progress, transgress, accresce, depress, repress, impress, compress, oppress, express, suppress, distress, duress, assess, obsess, success, recess, precess, princesse, *princess*, possess, comtesse [F.], tristesse [F.] **3.** SOS, incandesce, stewardess, shepherdess, acquiesce, recalesce, coalesce, opalesce, convalesce, nonetheless, luminesce, baroness, readdress, maladdress, allegress [F.], retrogress, water cress, phosphoresce, effloresce, fluoresce, recompress, overstress, reassess, repossess, prepossess, disposses, poetess, effervesce, deliquesce **4.** nevertheless, rejuvenesce, ambassadress; *also adjectives composed of noun-plus-suffix "-less"* (e.g. motionless, passionless); *also nouns composed of adjective-plus-suffix "-ness"* (e.g. tardiness, toothsomeness); *also nouns made feminine by addition of the suffix "-ess"* (e.g. stewardess, manageress).

ESH– **1.** hesh [slang], flesh, flèche, mesh,

spesh [slang], fresh, crèche, thresh, sesh [slang] 2. calèche [F.], *horseflesh*, enmesh, secesh, afresh, unfresh, refresh, rethresh.

ESK– 1. esk [slang], desk 2. burlesque, Moresque, grotesque 3. arabesque, Romanesque, barbaresque, picaresque, chivalresque, humoresque, plateresque, picturesque, scuplturesque, statuesque.

EST– 1. est, best, chest, fessed, fest, guest, guessed, hest, gest, geste, jest, lest, blest, blessed, nest, pest, rest, wrest, Brest, breast, dressed, crest, pressed, tressed, stressed, cest, cessed, test, vest, west, quest, yessed, zest 2. Trieste, infest, behest, suggest, digest, ingest, congest, beau geste [F.], celeste, Celeste, molest, unblest, funnest, impest, arrest, caressed, *headrest*, *bookrest*, unrest, *footrest*, abreast, *redbreast*, *blackbreast*, addressed, redressed, undressed, regressed, digressed, transgressed, progressed, *firecrest*, depressed, repressed, impressed, compressed, oppressed, suppressed, expressed, distressed, prestressed, assessed, alceste, obsessed, recessed, possessed, attest, obtest, detest, retest, pretest, contest, protest, divest, invest, bequest, request, inquest, Midwest, northwest, southwest 3. S O S-ed, incandesced, manifest, counterfessed, acquiesced, redigest, predigest, recalesced, coalesced, opalesced, convalesced, luminesced, Budapest, anapest, Bucharest, readdressed, interest, Everest, retrogressed, phosphoresced, effloresced, fluoresced, recompressed, uncompressed, unimpressed, raven-tressed, overstressed, reassessed, unassessed, repossessed, prepossessed, self-possessed, unpossessed, dispossessed, palimpsest, effervesced, deliquesced 4. j'y suis, j'y reste [F.]; *also the superlative degree of all adjectives composed of adjective-plus-suffix -est* (e.g. steadiest, giddiest, windiest, shoddiest, sturdiest, dowdiest, rowdiest, darlingest, laughingest, belovedest, horridest).

ET– 1. et, bet, Chet, debt, fet, get, het, jet, ket, khet, let, Lett, blet, flet, plet, met, net, pet, ret, bret, fret, frette, pret, tret, threat, set, sett, shet [dial.], stet, vet, wet, quet, sweat, whet, yet 2. layette, abet, Tibet, barbette, cadet, vedette, bidet, indebt, Claudette, Odette, baguette, baguet, beget, forget, plaquette, coquette, coquet, croquette, casquette, ailette, alette, galette [F.], sublet, Gilette, toilette, roulette, plumette, Nanette, Jeannette, *genet*, dinette, cornet, lunette, brunette, pipette, aret, barrette, umbrette, soubrette, aigrette, *egret*, regret, curette, chevrette, beset, reset, *thickset*, *quickset*, dancette, *inset*, pincette, *onset*, *moonset*, *sunset*, *upset*, *farset*, *outset*, flechette, clochette, brochette, plushette, duet, revet, brevet, bewet, vignette, lorgnette, gazette, rosette, musette 3. Juliette, ariette, storiette, serviette, suffragette, etiquette, tourniquet, flannelette, novelette, landaulet, rigolette, quadruplet, quintuplet, epaulette, cassolette, pianette, villanette, castanet, cravenette, bobbinet, stockinet, clarinet, bassinet, martinet, Antoinette, minionette, mignonette, maisonette, saxcornet, tabaret, cigarette, Margaret, collaret, minaret, lazaret, pierrette [F.], farmerette, banneret, leatherette, interfret, vinaigrette, taboret, anisette, marmoset, overset, silhouette, minuet, pirouette, statuette.

ETH– 1. eth, Beth, death, breath, saith, Seth, teth, steth [slang] 2. Macbeth 3. shibboleth, twentieth, thirtieth, fortieth, fiftieth, sixtieth, eightieth, ninetieth 4. seventieth.

ETZ– bets etc., *see* **ET–** bet etc. above, plus "s" or "'s."

EV– 1. Bev, chev, rev, [slang].

EZ– 1. Ez, fez, mezz [slang], knez, prez [slang], says, sez, yez [both slang] 2. Juarez, cortez, Suez.

EZH– 1. beige, greige 2. manége, barége, cortége.

E (heh)

2.

DOUBLE (FEMININE) RHYMES IN E (web′by)

Primary or Secondary Accent Falls on Next to Last Syllable: Imperfect Rhymes Are in Italics.

EB′er– 2. ebber, blebber [dial.], nebber [dial.], webber.

EB′i– 2. debby [slang], Debby, kebbie, kebby [both Scot. & N. of Eng.], blebby, nebby, webby 3. *cobwebby.*

EB′ing– 2. ebbing, kebbing, blebbing [dial.], nebbing [dial.], webbing 3. unebbing, *cobwebbing.*

EB′it– 2. debit 3. redebit.

EB′l– 2. debile, pebble, rebel, treble 3. archrebel.

EB′li– 2. pebbly, trebly.

ECH′ed– 2. wretched.

ECH′er– 2. etcher, fetcher, sketcher, lecher, fletcher, retcher, stretcher, quetcher.

ECH′i– 2. fetchy, sketchy, stretchy, techy, tetchy, vetchy.

ECH′ing– 2. etching, fetching, sketching, fletching, retching, stretching, quetching 3. outstretching.

ED′a– 2. Edda, khedda, Ledda, Nedda, Vedda.

ED′al– 2. medal, pedal 3. bipedal, tripedal 4. fissipedal, equipedal; *see* also **ED′l–** heddle etc. below.

ED′ant– 2. pedant.

ED′ed– 2. bedded, headed, leaded, sledded, redded, breaded, dreaded, shredded, threaded, tedded, wedded 3. embedded, imbedded, hardheaded, beheaded, pigheaded, longheaded, thickheaded, coolheaded, bullheaded, bareheaded, clearheaded, flat-headed, lightheaded, softheaded, hotheaded, unshredded, unthreaded, unwedded 4. puddingheaded, manyheaded, double-headed, rattleheaded, levelheaded, arrowheaded, Janus-headed, interthreaded.

ED′en– 2. deaden, leaden, redden, threaden 4. Armageddon.

ED′er– 2. edder, bedder, Cheddar, deader, header, leader, sledder, nedder, redder, dreader, spreader, shredder, threader, treader, shedder, tedder 3. embedder, beheader, unthreader, retreader, *homesteader* 4. double-header.

ED′est– 2. deadest, reddest, dreadest.

ED′ful– 2. headful, dreadful.

ED′head– 2. deadhead, redhead.

ED′i– 2. eddy, Eddie, beddy, heady, leady, neddy, ready, reddy, bready, Freddie, spready, shreddy, thready, Teddy, steady 3. already, unready, unsteady.

ED′ing– 2. bedding, heading, leading, sledding, redding, breading, dreading, spreading, shredding, treading, threading, shedding, tedding, steading, wedding 3. embedding, imbedding, beheading, bespreading, outspreading, retreading, rethreading, unthreading, *homesteading*, rewedding 4. overspreading, golden wedding.

ED′ish– 2. eddish, deadish, reddish, breadish.

ED′it– 2. edit, credit 3. subedit, reedit, accredit, discredit, miscredit.

ED'l– 2. heddle, meddle, medal, peddle, pedal, reddle, treadle 3. bepedal, tripedal 4. intermeddle.

ED'ler– 2. heddler, meddler, medlar, pedlar, peddler, treadler 4. intermeddler.

ED'less– 2. bedless, headless, leadless, sledless, redless, breadless, dreadless, shredless, treadless, threadless, shedless, tedless 3. co-edless, *bulkheadless, bedsteadless, homesteadless.*

ED'li– 2. deadly, medley, redly.

ED'line– 2. deadline, headline, breadline.

ED'ling– 2. heddling, meddling, peddling, reddling, treadling, 4. intermeddling.

ED'lok– 2. deadlock, headlock, kedlock, wedlock.

ED'na– 2. Edna, Sedna.

ED'ness– 2. deadness, redness.

ED'o– 2. eddo, meadow.

ED'on– 4. Armageddon; *see* **ED'en–** deaden etc. above.

ED'ward– 2. Edward, bedward.

ED'wood– 2. deadwood, redwood.

ED'zo– 2. mezzo 4. intermezzo.

EF'en– 2. effen, deafen, Strephon.

EF'er– 2. deafer, feoffor, Pfeffer [G.], heifer, kefir, zephyr 4. Hasenpfeffer [G.].

EF'ik– 2. brephic 3. malefic, benefic 4. peristrephic, isopsephic.

EF'is– 2. preface.

EFT'er– 2. defter, hefter, lefter, clefter 3. berefter.

EFT'est– 2. deftest, leftist, cleftest 3. bereftest.

EFT'i– 2. hefty, Kefti, Lefty.

EFT'li– 2. deftly 3. bereftly.

EFT'ness– 2. deftness, leftness, cleftness 3. bereftness.

EG'er– 2. egger, beggar, skegger, legger, pegger 3. *bootlegger.*

EG'i– 2. eggy, keggy, leggy, Peggy, dreggy, seggy.

EG'ing– 2. egging, begging, kegging, legging, pegging, segging 3. unkegging, bootlegging, unpegging.

EG'nant– 2. regnant, pregnant.

EJ'end– 2. legend.

EJ'er– 2. edger, hedger, kedger, ledger, pledger, sledger, dredger 3. alleger, repledger.

EJ'et– 2. pledget.

EJ'ez– 2. edges, hedges, kedges, ledges, fledges, cledges, pledges, sledges, dredges, sedges, tedges, wedges 3. alleges, repledges, unwedges 4. interpledges, sacrileges, privileges.

EJ'i– 2. edgy, hedgy, ledgy, fledgy, cledgy, sedgy, wedgy.

EJ'ing– 2. edging, hedging, kedging, ledging, fledging, pledging, sledging, dredging, wedging 3. enhedging, alleging, repledging, impledging.

EJ'less– 2. edgeless, hedgeless, kedgeless, ledgeless, pledgeless, sledgeless, dredgeless, sedgeless, tedgeless, wedgeless 3. privilegeless.

EJ'ment– 3. allegement.

EJ'o– 2. seggio [It.]. 3. solfeggio, arpeggio.

EK'a– 2. Écca, ekka, Mecca 3. sabeca, Rebecca.

EK'ant– 2. peccant 3. impeccant.

EK'er– 2. becker, decker, checker, chequer, gecker, flecker, necker, snecker, pecker, trekker, wrecker 3. rechecker, bedecker, exchequer, *woodpecker, henpecker* 4. double-decker.

EK'erd– 2. checkered, record.

EK'et– 2. becket, fecket 5. Thomas à Becket.

EK'i– 2. Becky, checky, kecky, flecky, pecky, specky, wrecky 3. shipwrecky.

EK'ij– 2. wreckage.

EK'ing– 2. becking, decking, checking, flecking, necking, snecking, pecking, specking, recking, wrecking, trekking 3. bedecking, *henpecking*, bewrecking, *shipwrecking*.

EK'ish– 2. heckish, peckish, wreckish.

EK'l– 2. deckle, heckle, Jeckyll, keckle, speckle, brekkle, freckle, Seckel, shekel 3. bespeckle, befreckle.

EK'la– 2. Thecla, Thekla.

EK'ld– 2. deckled, neckled, keckled, fleckled, speckled, freckled 3. bespeckled, befreckled.

EK'ler– 2. heckler, freckler.

EK'less– 2. beckless, checkless, deckless, feckless, geckless, fleckless, necklace, neckless, peckless, speckless, reckless, wreckless.

EK'li– 2. speckly, freckly.

EK'ling– 2. deckling, heckling, keckling, speckling, reckling, freckling.

EK'mate– 2. checkmate, deckmate.

EK'ni– 4. theotechny, agrotechny, pyrotechny.

EK'nik– 2. technic 3. pantechnic 4. polytechnic, theotechnic, philotechnic, pyrotechnic.

EK'niks– 3. eutechnics 4. pyrotechnics.

EK'ning– 3. beckoning, reckoning.

EK'nist– 4. polytechnist, theotechnist, philotechnist, pyrotechnist.

EK'o– 2. echo, bekko, gecko, secco 3. re-echo.

EK'on– 2. beckon, Becken, flecken, reckon.

EK'ond– 2. beckoned, fleckened, reckoned, second.

EKS'a– 3. annexa, adnexa.

EKS'al– 2. nexal, plexal 3. adnexal.

EKS'as– Texas; *see* also **EKS'us–** nexus etc. below.

EKS'er– 2. hexer, flexor, vexer 3. *indexer*, annexer, perplexer 4. dorsiflexor.

EKSH'un– 2. lection, flection, section, vection 3. affection, defection, refection, effection, infection, confection, profection, perfection, abjection, adjection, trajection, ejection, dejection, rejection, injection, projection, election, prelection, selection, deflection, reflection, inflection, dilection, collection, bolection, complexion, connection, inspection, prospection, erection, direction, correction, resection, bisection, trisection, dissection, insection, exsection, detection, protection, evection, invection, convection, provection 4. disaffection, reinfection, disinfection, imperfection, insubjection, interjection, dorsiflexion, circumflexion, genuflection, predilection, intellection, recollection, reconnection, disconnection, circumspection, retrospection, introspection, redirection, indirection, misdirection, insurrection, venesection, hemisection, vivisection, intersection.

EKSH'ur– 2. flexure, plexure 3. deflexure, inflexure, complexure 4. contraflexure.

EKSH'us– 3. infectious, selectious.

EKS'i– 2. ecce, kexy, prexy, sexy 4. cataplexy, apoplexy.

EKS–il– 2. exile, flexile.

EKS'ing– 2. X-ing, hexing, flexing, sexing vexing 3. inflexing, complexing, perplexing, *duplexing*, annexing, unsexing, convexing.

EKS'is– 3. Alexis, orexis, syntexis, cathexis 4. catalexis, epiplexis.

EKS'li– 3. complexly, convexly.

EKS'tant– 2. extant, sextant.

EKS'til– 2. sextile, textile 3. bissextile.

EKS'us– 2. nexus, plexus, Texas 3. connexus, complexus 4. solar plexus.

EKT'al– 2. ectal, tectal 4. dialectal.

EKT'ant– 3. infectant, reflectent, amplectant, humectant, annectent, aspectant, respectant, expectant, suspectant 4. disinfectant, unexpectant.

EKT'ed– 2. sected 3. affected, effected, infected, confected, perfected, objected, subjected, ejected, dejected, rejected, injected, projected, elected, selected, deflected, reflected, biflected, inflected, neglected, collected, complected, connected, respected, expected, inspected, suspected, erected, directed, corrected, bisected, dissected, detected, protected, invected 4. unaffected, disaffected, disinfected, interjected, re-elected, pre-elected, retroflected, recollected, disconnected, unexpected, unsuspected, redirected, misdirected, uncorrected, resurrected, intersected.

EKT'er– 2. hector, Hector, lector, nectar, specter, rector, sector, vector 3. affecter, effecter, effector, infector, perfecter, objector, ejector, injector, projector, elector, prelector, selector, deflector, reflector, inflector, neglecter, collector, connector, respecter, expecter, inspector, prospector, erector, director, corrector, bisector, dissector, detector, protector, bivector 4. disinfecter, interjecter, dialector, nonreflector, genuflector, disrespecter, resurrecter, vivisector.

EKT'erd– 2. hectored, nectared, spectered, sectored.

EKT'ern– 2. lectern.

EKT'est– 3. abjectest, selectest, directest.

EKT'ful– 3. neglectful, respectful, suspectful 4. unrespectful, disrespectful.

EKT'ik– 2. hectic, pectic 3. ephectic, eclectic, synectic, orectic, syntectic 4. dialectic, analectic, catalectic, epiplectic, apoplectic, isopectic, orthotectic 5. acatalectic 6. hypercatalectic.

EKT'il– 2. sectile 3. insectile, projectile.

EKT'ing– 3. affecting, effecting, infecting, confecting, perfecting, objecting, subjecting, ejecting, dejecting, rejecting, injecting, conjecting, projecting, electing, selecting, deflecting, reflecting, inflecting, neglecting, collecting, connecting, respecting, expecting, inspecting, suspecting, erecting, directing, correcting, bisecting, dissecting, detecting, protecting 4. disinfecting, interjecting, re-electing, recollecting, disconnecting, self-respecting, unsuspecting, redirecting, misdirecting, resurrecting, intersecting, vivisecting.

EKT'iv– 3. affective, effective, defective, refective, infective, perfective, objective, subjective, ejective, rejective, conjective, projective, elective, selective, deflective, reflective, inflective, collective, connective, respective, inspective, prospective, perspective, erective, directive, corrective, detective, protective, invective 4. ineffective, imperfective, intellective, recollective, disconnective, irrespective, circumspective, retrospective, introspective.

EKT'li– 3. abjectly, selectly, suspectly, erectly, directly, correctly 4. circumspectly, indirectly, incorrectly.

EKT'ment– 3. ejectment, dejectment, rejectment, projectment.

EKT'ness– 3. abjectness, subjectness, selectness, erectness, directness, correctness 4. circumspectness, indirectness, incorrectness.

EKT'or– 2. hector, lector, rector, sector, vector; *see* also **EKT'er–** hector etc. above.

EKT'ral– 2. spectral.

EKT'ress– 2. lectress, rectress 3. electress, inspectress, directress, protectress.

EKT'rik– 3. electric 4. dielectric, anelectric 5. hydroelectric.

EKT'riks– 2. rectrix 3. directrix, bisectrix, trisectrix.

EKT'rum– 2. plectrum, spectrum 3. electrum.

EKT'ur– 2. lecture 3. confecture, subjecture, conjecture, projecture, belecture 4. architecture.

EKT'us– 2. pectous, rectus 3. praefectus, delectus, conspectus, prospectus.

EL'a– 2. Ella, Bella, Della, fella, fellah, kella, kellah, cella, sella, Stella, yella [slang] 3. glabella, tabella, rubella, umbella, padella, predella, lamella, canella, prunella, Prunella, Capella, Kapelle [G.], umbrella, corella, doncella, osella, rosella, Marcella, patella 4. Arabella, clarabella, Isabella, villanella, fustanella, tiarella, Cinderella, agacella, varicella, navicella, panatela, tarantella, fenestella.

EL'an– 3. Magellan, Atellan; *see* also **EL'en–** Helen etc. below; also **EL'on–** felon below.

EL'ant– 3. flagellant, appellant, repellent, impellent, propellent, propellant, expellent, expellant, revellent, divellent.

EL'ar– 2. cellar, sellar, stellar 3. glabellar, lamellar, patellar 4. interstellar; *see* also **EL'er–** Eller, etc. below.

EL'as– 2. Hellas, pellas 3. procellas; *see* also **EL'us–** Hellas etc. below.

EL'at– 2. pellate, prelate, cellate, stellate 3. debellate, flabellate, appellate, ocellate, patellate, constellate, scutellate 4. interpellate.

EL'ay– 2. melee, mele.

ELB'a– 2. Elba, Melba 3. peach Melba.

ELCH'er– 2. belcher, welsher, squelcher.

ELCH'ing– 2. belching, welshing, squelching.

ELD'ed– 2. gelded, melded, welded.

ELD'er– 2. elder, gelder, skelder [old slang], melder, welder.

ELD'est– 2. eldest.

ELD'ing– 2. gelding, melding, welding.

EL'een– 2. Hellene, melene.

EL'en– 2. Ellen, Helen 3. Llewellyn; *see* also **EL'an–** Magellan etc. above; also **EL'on–** felon etc. below.

EL'ent– 3. repellent, impellent, propellent, expellent, revellent, divellent; *see* also **EL'ant–** flagellant etc. above.

EL'er– 2. Eller, beller, feller, heller, Keller [G.], smeller, kneller, speller, seller, cellar, sheller, teller, stellar, weller, dweller, queller, sweller, yeller 3. rebeller, lamellar, appellor, repeller, impeller, compeller, propeller, dispeller, expeller, exceller, foreteller, nonstellar, cave dweller 4. Rockefeller, underseller, storyteller, fortuneteller, interstellar.

EL'est– 2. swellest.

ELF'ik– 2. Delphic, Guelphic 3. didelphic 4. diadelphic, monodelphic.

ELF'in– 2. elfin, Delphin, delphine.

ELF'ish– 2. elfish, pelfish, selfish, shellfish 3. unselfish.

ELF'ri– 2. belfry, pelfry.

EL'i– 2. Elly, belly, delly, Delhi, felly, jelly, kelly, Kelly, melee, smelly, Nelly, shelly, Shelley 3. *shadbelly, redbelly, slowbelly, gorbelly, whitebelly, potbelly,* nice Nelly, cancelli 4. checkerbelly, vermicelli, Botticelli.

EL'id– 2. bellied, gelid, jellied 3. *slowbellied, gorbellied, potbellied.*

EL'ik– 2. bellic, fellic, skelic, melic, relic, telic 3. angelic, scalpelic, Pentelic 4. infidelic, evangelic, sapropelic, philatelic, autotelic.

EL'ing– 2. belling, Delling, felling, knelling, smelling, spelling, selling, shelling, telling, welling, dwelling, swelling, quelling, yelling 3. rebelling, repelling, impelling, compelling, propelling, dispelling, misspelling, expelling, outspelling, outselling, excelling, taletelling, foretelling, indwelling 4. parallelling, uncompelling, underselling, storytelling, fortunetelling.

EL'is– 2. Ellis, trellis.

EL'ish– 2. hellish, relish, wellish, swellish 3. embellish, disrelish.

EL'ist– 2. cellist, trellised.

EL'it– 2. prelate, sell it, tell it 3. appellate.

ELM'a– 2. Elma, pelma, Selma, Thelma, Velma.

ELM'et– 2. helmet, pelmet.

ELM'ing– 2. helming, whelming 3. unhelming, dishelming 4. overwhelming.

EL'ness– 2. fellness, wellness, swellness 3. unwellness 4. caramelness.

EL'o– 2. bellow, cello, fellow, Jello, mellow, melo [slang], yellow 3. *playfellow*, niello, prunello, morello, martello, Othello duello, scrivello 4. violoncello, punchinello, albarello, saltarello, Monticello, brocatello, Donatello.

EL'od– 2. bellowed, mellowed, yellowed 3. unmellowed.

EL'on– 2. felon, melon 3. *muskmelon, mushmelon* 4. watermelon; *see* also **EL'an**– Magellan etc. above and **EL'en**– Ellen etc. above.

EL'op– 3. develop, envelop.

EL'opd– 3. developed, enveloped 4. undeveloped, unenveloped.

EL'ot– 2. helot, zealot.

EL'oz– 2. bellows, cellos, fellows, mellows, yellows.

ELP'er– 2. helper, yelper.

ELP'ful– 2. helpful 3. self-helpful, unhelpful.

ELP'i– 2. kelpie.

ELP'ing– 2. helping, whelping, yelping.

ELP'less– 2. helpless, kelpless, whelpless, yelpless.

ELT'a– 2. delta, pelta, shelta.

ELT'ed– 2. belted, felted, melted, smelted, pelted, spelted, welted 3. unbelted, unmelted.

ELT'er– 2. belter, felter, kelter, melter, smelter, pelter, spelter, shelter, welter, swelter 4. helter-skelter.

ELTH'i– 2. healthy, stealthy, wealthy 3. unhealthy, unwealthy.

ELT'i– 2. beltie, felty, kelty.

ELT'ing– 2. belting, felting, melting, smelting, pelting, spelting, welting.

ELT'less– 2. beltless, feltless, peltless, weltless.

ELT'ri– 2. peltry, sweltry.

EL'um– 2. bellum [L.], vellum 3. labellum, flabellum, prebellum, cribellum, flagellum, sacellum 4. cerebellum, ante bellum.

EL'us– 2. Hellas, jealous, pellas, Tellus, zealous 3. tassellus, ocellus, procellas, Marcellus, vitellus, entellus 4. overzealous.

ELV'er– 2. delver, helver, shelver.

ELV'ing– 2. delving, helving, shelving.

EL'yun– 2. hellion, selion 3. rebellion.

EL'yus– 3. rebellious.

EM'a– 2. Emma, gemma, lemma, nema, stremma, stemma 3. dilemma, trilemma, maremma 4. analemma, tetralemma, neurilemma.

EM'an– 2. leman, lemman.

EMB'er– 2. ember, member 3. remember, dismember, December, September, November 4. disremember.

EMB'l– 2. tremble, semble 3. atremble, assemble, dissemble, resemble 4. reassemble.

EMB'lans– 2. semblance 3. assemblance, dissemblance, resemblance.

EMB'lant– 2. semblant 3. resemblant.

EMB'ld– 2. trembled, sembled 3. assembled, dissembled, resembled 4. reassembled, unassembled, undissembled.

EMB'lem– 2. emblem.

EMB'ler– 2. trembler, tremblor 3. assembler, dissembler, resembler.

EMB'li– 2. trembly, Wembley 3. assembly, dissembly.

EMB'lij– 3. assemblage.

EMB'lik– 2. emblic.

EMB'ling– 2. trembling, sembling 3. assembling, dissembling, resembling 4. reassembling.

EMB'ral– 2. membral 3. bimembral, trimembral, Septembral.

EMB'rans– 3. remembrance 4. unremembrance.

EM'ent– 2. clement, Clement 3. inclement.

EM'er– 2. emmer, hemmer, tremor, stemmer 3. condemner, begemmer, contemner.

EM'i– 2. Emmy, demi-, gemmy, hemi-, jemmy, phlegmy, tremie, semi-, stemmy.

EM'ik– 2. chemic 3. ecdemic, pandemic, endemic, alchemic, ischemic, polemic, totemic, systemic 4. academic, epidemic, polydemic, stratagemic, theoremic.

EM'ing– 2. hemming, gemming, kembing, lemming, Fleming, clemming, stemming 3. condemning, begemming, contemning.

EM'ish– 2. blemish, Flemish, flemish.

EM'ishd– 2. blemished, Flemished, flemished 3. unblemished.

EM'ist– 2. chemist 4. biochemist.

EM'lin– 2. gremlin, Kremlin.

EM'on– 2. lemon.

EMP'er– 2. semper [L.], temper 3. attemper, untemper, distemper.

EMP'erd– 2. tempered 3. attempered, ill-tempered, distempered.

EMP'est– 2. tempest.

EMP'l– 2. Hempel, temple, stemple, stempel.

EMP'lar– 2. templar 3. Knight Templar, exemplar.

EMP'ra– 2. sempre [It.].

EMP'shun– 2. emption 3. ademption, redemption, pre-emption, co-emption, exemption.

EMP'ted– 2. empted, tempted 3. adempted, pre-empted, attempted, untempted, exempted 4. unattempted, unexempted.

EMP'ter– 2. emptor, tempter 3. preemptor, coemptor, unkempter, attempter.

EMP'ti– 2. empty.

EMP'ting– 2. empting, tempting 3. pre-empting, attempting, exempting.

EMP'tiv– 3. redemptive, pre-emptive.

EMP'tress– 2. temptress 3. redemptress.

EN'a– 2. bena, henna, jenna, senna 3. Gehenna, Alhenna, Siena, sienna, Vienna, antenna, duenna, Ravenna.

EN'ant– 2. pennant, tenant 3. lieutenant.

EN'as– 2. menace, tenace; *see* also **EN'is–** Dennis etc. below.

EN'at– 2. pennate 3. tripennate, impennate, antennate 4. latipennate.

ENCH'ant– 2. penchant, trenchant 3. intrenchant.

ENCH'er– 2. bencher, blencher, flencher, clencher, wrencher, drencher, trencher, censure, quencher 3. retrencher, intrencher.

ENCH'ing– 2. benching, blenching, flenching, clenching, wrenching, drenching, trenching, quenching 3. bedrenching, retrenching, unquenching.

ENCH'less– 2. benchless, trenchless, quenchless.

ENCH'man– 2. henchman, Frenchman.

ENCH'ment– 3. retrenchment, entrenchment, intrenchment.

END'a– 2. benda, denda, Brenda, Zenda 3. addenda, credenda, agenda, legenda, delenda, commenda [L.] 4. referenda, hacienda, corrigenda.

END'al– 2. trendle, sendal, sendle 3. prebendal 4. referendal.

END'ans– 2. tendance 3. ascendance, descendance, attendance; *see* also **END'ens–** resplendence etc. below.

END'ant– 2. pendant, tendant 3. defendant, appendant, dependant, ascendant, descendant 4. codefendant, codescendant; *see* also **END'ent–** splendent etc. below.

END'ed– 2. ended, bended, fended, blended, mended, friended, trended, tended, vended, wended 3. upended, defended, offended, unblended, amended, emended, commended, appended, depended, impended, expended, suspended, befriended, unfriended, ascended, descended, transcended, attended, pretended, intended, contended, portended, extended, distended 4. undefended, apprehended, reprehended, comprehended, interblended, recommended, condescended, unattended, unintended, unextended 5. misapprehended, miscomprehended, unrecommended, superintended.

END'ens– 3. resplendence, dependence, impendence, transcendence, intendence 4. independence, condescendence 5. interdependence, superintendence; *see* also **END'ans–** tendance etc. above.

END'ent– 2. splendent, pendent, tendent 3. resplendent, transplendent, dependent, impendent, ascendent, descendent, transcendent 4. independent, undependent, equipendent, condescendent 5. interdependent, superintendent; *see* also **END'ant–** pendant etc. above.

END'er– 2. ender, bender, fender, gender, lender, blender, splendor, slender, mender, spender, render, trender, sender, tender, vender, vendor, wender 3. defender, offender, engender, amender, commender, depender, expender, suspender, befriender, surrender, ascender, descender, pretender, contender 4. apprehender, reprehender, comprehender, moneylender, interblender, recommender.

END'erz– fenders etc., *see* **END'er–** ender etc. above plus "s" or " 's."

END'i– 2. bendy, fendy, Mendi, Wendy 3. effendi 5. modus vivendi [L.].

END'ing– 2. ending, bending, fending, lending, blending, mending, pending, spending, rending, trending, sending, tending, vending, wending 3. unending, upending, unbending, defending, offending, amending, commending, depending, impending, perpending, expending, misspending, suspending, befriending, heart-rending, ascending, descending, transcending, attending, pretending, contending, portending, distending, extending 4. unoffending, apprehending, reprehending, comprehending, interblending, moneylending, recommending, overspending, condescending, unpretending 5. superintending.

END'less– 2. endless, bendless, mendless, trendless, friendless.

END'li– 2. friendly 3. unfriendly.

END'ment– 3. amendment, commendment, befriendment, intendment.

END'o– 3. reddendo, crescendo 4. decrescendo, diluendo [It.], innuendo 5. diminuendo.

END'or– 2. splendor, vendor; *see* also **END'er–** ender etc. above.

END'um– 3. habendum, addendum, dedendum, reddendum, credendum, agendum, commendam, tenendum 4. corrigendum, referendum.

END'us– 3. tremendous, stupendous.

EN'el– 2. bennel, fennel, kennel, vennel.

EN'ent– tenent; *see* also **EN'ant–** pennant etc. above.

EN'er– 2. penner, tenner, tenor, Venner 4. countertenor.

EN'et– 2. Bennett, bennet, dennet, jennet, genet, rennet, sennet, senate, tenet.

ENG'then– 2. lengthen, strengthen.

ENG'thi– 2. lengthy, strengthy.

EN'i– 2. any, benne, beni, benny, Benny, fenny, henny, jenny, Jennie, Lenny, blenny, many, penny, wenny 3. Kilkenny, *catchpenny*, *halfpenny*, *passpenny*, *sixpenny*, *twopenny*.

EN'ik– 2. phenic, genic, splenic, phrenic, scenic, sthenic 3. Edenic, hyphenic, dysgenic, eugenic, lichenic, Galenic, galenic, selenic, Hellenic, irenic, *arsenic*, parthenic, asthenic 4. metagenic, polygenic, oxygenic, authigenic, Diogenic, cacogenic, psychogenic, chromogenic, thermogenic, monogenic, nitrogenic, photogenic, pathogenic, philhellenic, Panhellenic, proselenic, paraphrenic, neurasthenic, calisthenic, Demosthenic.

EN'iks– 3. dysgenics, eugenics, poimenics, irenics.

EN'im– 2. denim.

EN'in– 2. Lenin, rennin, venin.

EN'ing– 2. denning, fenning, kenning, penning.

EN'is– 2. Dennis, menace, tenace, tennis, Venice.

EN'ish– 2. hennish, plenish, Rhenish, wennish 3. deplenish, replenish, displenish.

EN'it– 2. jennet, senate, sennit, sennet, sennight.

EN'iz– 2. bennies, jennies, pennies.

ENJ'er– 3. avenger, revenger.

ENJ'in– 2. engine.

ENJ'ing– 2. venging 3. avenging, revenging.

ENJ'ment– 3. avengement, revengement.

ENK'i– 2. renky [dial. Eng.].

EN'li– 2. Henley, cleanly 3. uncleanly.

EN'lik– 2. denlike, fenlike, henlike, penlike, wrenlike.

EN'om– 2. venom, mennom 3. envenom.

EN'on– 2. mennon, pennon, tenon.

ENS'al– 2. mensal 3. bimensal, commensal, forensal.

ENS'at– 2. sensate 3. condensate, compensate, insensate, intensate.

ENS'eez– 2. menses 4. Albigenses 5. amanuenses.

ENS'en– 2. ensign, densen.

ENS'er– 2. denser, fencer, flenser, menser [Scot. & N. of Eng.], spencer, Spencer, Spenser, censer, censor, senser, sensor, tenser, tensor 3. condenser, prehensor, commencer, dispenser, extensor, intenser 4. recompenser.

ENS'est– 2. densest, tensest 3. intensest.

ENS'ez– 2. fences, flenses, menses [Scot. & N. of Eng.], censes, senses, tenses 3. condenses, commences, dispenses, incenses 4. recompenses, quartertenses, influences.

ENS'forth– 2. henceforth, thenceforth, whenceforth.

ENS'ful– 2. penseful [obs. exc. dial.], senseful.

ENSH'al– 3. credential, rodential, prudential, agential, bigential, tangential, torrential, essential, sentential, potential, Provencial, sequential 4. precedential, confidential, residential, presidential, evidential, sapiential, pestilential, deferential, referential, preferential, differential, inferential, conferential, transferential, reverential, inessential, nonessential, penitential, influential, subsequential, consequential 5. jurisprudential, expediential, intelligential, circumferential, unreverential, irreverential, equipotential, inconsequential.

ENSH'alz– 3. credentials, essentials, potentials.

ENSH'ent– 2. sentient 3. assentient, presentient, dissentient, insentient, consentient.

ENSH'er– 2. censure.

ENSH'un– 2. gentian, mention, pension, tension 3. indention, prehension, declension, dimension, repension, propension, suspension, ascension, descension, recension, presention, dissension, accension, incension, consension, attention, obtention, detention, retention, pretension, intention, intension, contention, portention, abstention, extention, distention, ostension, obvention, subvention, prevention, invention, convention 4. apprehension, reprehension, comprehension, reascension, condescension, inattention, hypotension, hypertension, contravention, circumvention, supervention, intervention 5. inapprehension, misapprehension, incomprehension, uncondescension, nonintervention.

ENSH′unz– gentians etc., *see* **ENSH′un-** gentian etc. above, plus "s" or "'s."

ENSH′us– **3.** tendentious, silentious, licentious, dissentious, pretentious, sententious, contentious **4.** conscientious, unpretentious.

ENS′i– **2.** pensy [Scot. & dial. Eng.].

ENS′il– **2.** bensel [Scot. & dial. Eng.], pencil, pencel, pensile, sensile, tensile, stencil **3.** prehensile, depencil, blue-pencil, extensile, utensil **4.** hyperpencil.

ENS′ild– **2.** pencilled, tensiled, stencilled **3.** blue-pencilled, utensilled.

ENS′ing– **2.** fencing, flensing, censing, mensing [Scot. & N. of Eng.], tensing **3.** condensing, commencing, dispensing, incensing, pretensing **4.** recompensing, influencing.

ENS′is– **5.** amanuensis.

ENS′iv– **2.** pensive, tensive **3.** defensive, offensive, prehensive, expensive, suspensive, intensive, extensive, distensive, ostensive **4.** inoffensive, apprehensive, comprehensive, recompensive, inexpensive, condescensive, inextensive **5.** inapprehensive, incomprehensive.

ENS′less– **2.** fenceless, penceless, senseless **3.** defenseless, offenseless, expenseless **4.** recompenseless.

ENS′li– **2.** densely, tensely **3.** immensely, propensely, intensely.

ENS′ment– **3.** commencement, incensement.

ENS′ness– **2.** denseness, tenseness **3.** immenseness, propenseness, intenseness.

ENS′um– **2.** pensum, sensum.

ENS′us– **2.** census **3.** consensus.

ENT′a– **2.** nenta, Senta **3.** magenta, polenta, Pimenta, pimienta, cuarenta, placenta **4.** pedimenta **5.** rejectamenta, impedimenta.

ENT′ad– **2.** entad, pentad **4.** ectoentad.

ENT′al– **2.** ental, dental, gentle, mental, rental, trental, cental **3.** edental, bidental, tridental, postdental, ungentle, amental, fragmental, amental, segmental, tegmental, pigmental, momental, parental, percental **4.** accidental, incidental, transcendental, interdental, oriental, fundamental, ligamental, firmamental, ornamental, tournamental, sacramental, atramental, testamental, elemental, complemental, supplemental, tenemental, recremental, incremental, pedimental, condimental, rudimental, regimental, alimental, complimental, detrimental, nutrimental, sentimental, governmental, apartmental, departmental, compartmental, documental, tegumental, argumental, monumental, instrumental, continental, componental, grandparental, biparental **5.** antecedental, coincidental, medicamental, predicamental, temperamental, impedimental, experimental, developmental; *see* also **ENT′il–** dentil etc. below.

ENT′alz– **2.** rentals, trentals **4.** incidentals, regimentals.

ENT′ans– **2.** sentence **3.** repentance **4.** unrepentance.

ENT′ant– **3.** repentant **4.** unrepentant, representant.

ENT′at– **2.** dentate **3.** edentate, bidentate, tridentate **4.** testamentate.

ENT′ay– **3.** dolente **4.** presidente, tardamente [It.], lentamente [It.], cognoscente [It.] **5.** aguardiente [Sp.] **6.** dolce far niente [It.].

ENT′e– diapente; *see* also **ENT′i–** Henty etc. below.

ENT′ed– **2.** dented, rented, scented, tented, vented **3.** indented, relented, lamented, demented, cemented, augmented, fermented, tormented, repented, unrented, assented, dissented, consented, unscented, contented, frequented, prevented, invented **4.** precedented, unindented, unlamented, ornamented, complimented, supplemented, battlemented, unrepented, represented, discontented, unfrequented, circumvented **5.** unprecedented, unornamented, misrepresented, unrepresented.

ENT′en– 2. Lenten.

ENT′ens– 2. sentence 3. repentance 4. unrepentance.

ENT′er– 2. enter, denter, renter, center, tenter, venter 3. re-enter, indenter, lamenter, cementer, augmenter, commenter, fomenter, fermenter, tormenter, tormentor, repenter, assenter, absenter, decenter, recenter, precentor, dissenter, incenter, incentor, consenter, retentor, frequenter, preventer, inventor, resenter, presenter 4. unrelentor, ornamenter, supplementer, epicenter, barycenter, circumventor, representer 5. experimenter, misrepresenter; *see* also **ENT′or–** lentor etc. below.

ENT′erd– 2. entered, centered, tentered 3. re-entered, self-centered.

ENT′ez– 2. flentes [L.], twenties.

ENT′ful– 2. scentful 3. lamentful, contentful, resentful, eventful, inventful 4. unresentful, uneventful, uninventful.

ENT′i– 2. Henty, Lenty, plenty, twenty 3. Amenti, aplenty 4. diapente, cognoscenti [It.].

ENT′ij– 2. ventage 3. percentage.

ENT′ik– 3. identic, argentic, crescentic, authentic.

ENT′il– 2. dentil, dentile, lentil, centile, ventil 3. percentile; *see* also **ENT′al–** ental etc. above; also **ENT′l–** gentle etc. below.

ENT′ile– 2. gentile, centile.

ENT′in– 2. dentin, dentine, Quentin 3. Tridentine, San Quentin.

ENT′ing– 2. denting, renting, scenting, tenting, venting 3. indenting, relenting, lamenting, cementing, augmenting, fomenting, fermenting, tormenting, repenting, accenting, assenting, absenting, dissenting, consenting, contenting, preventing, inventing, frequenting, resenting, presenting 4. unrelenting, ornamenting, supplementing, complimenting, circumventing, representing 5. experimenting, misrepresenting.

ENT′is– 2. prentice 3. apprentice 5. non compos mentis [L.].

ENT′ist– 2. dentist, prenticed 3. apprenticed, trecentist, preventist, presentist.

ENT′iv– 3. pedentive, lamentive, assentive, incentive, attentive, detentive, retentive, adventive, preventive, presentive 4. inattentive, unretentive, circumventive, interventive.

ENT′l– 2. gentle 3. ungentle; *see* also **ENT′al–** ental etc. above; also **ENT′il–** dentil etc. above.

ENT′less– 2. bentless, dentless, Lentless, rentless, scentless, centless, tentless, ventless 3. relentless, lamentless, cementless, fermentless, tormentless, repentless, descentless, consentless, contentless, eventless, resentless.

ENT′li– 2. gently 3. ungently, intently 4. confidently, evidently, excellently, insolently, eminently, innocently, impotently.

ENT′ment– 3. relentment, contentment, resentment, presentment 4. discontentment, representment.

ENT′ness– 2. bentness, lentness, meantness, pentness, spentness 3. intentness 4. confidentness, evidentness, excellentness, insolentness.

ENT′o– 2. lento, cento 3. memento, pimento, pimiento, fomento, Sorrento, trecento 4. Sacramento, portamento, pentimento, quattrocento 6. pronunciamento.

ENT′oid– 2. dentoid.

ENT′or– 2. lentor, mentor, centaur, stentor 3. fermentor, tormentor, precentor, succentor, incentor, bucentaur, retentor 4. unrelentor, circumventor; *see* also **ENT′er–** enter etc. above.

ENT′os– 2. pentose.

ENT'ral– 2. central, ventral **3.** subcentral, precentral, biventral **4.** paracentral, metacentral, dorsiventral.

ENT'rans– 2. entrance, entrants **3.** re-entrance, re-entrants.

ENT'ri– 2. entry, gentry, sentry.

ENT'rik– 2. centric 3. acentric, eccentric, concentric 4. paracentric, metacentric, barycentric, geocentric, egocentric, homocentric 5. Saturnicentric, heliocentric, anthropocentric.

ENT'rum– 2. centrum 3. precentrum, epicentrum, pseudocentrum.

ENT'um– 2. mentum 3. amentum, ramentum, cementum, tegmentum, momentum, sarmentum, fermentum, tormentum, frumentum [L.], percentum, unguentum 4. fundamentum [L.], velamentum, sacramentum, testamentum **5.** paludamentum.

ENT'ur– 2. denture, tenture, venture 3. debenture, indenture, rudenture, adventure, reventure 4. maladventure, peradventure, misadventure.

ENT'us– 3. pigmentous, momentous, sarmentous, portentous, unguentous 4. ligamentous, filamentous, immomentous pedetentous.

EN'um– 2. venom, mennom 3. envenom.

EN'vi– 2. envy.

ENZ'a– 3. cadenza 4. influenza.

ENZ'ez– 2. lenses, cleanses.

ENZ'i– 2. frenzy 3. Rienzi.

ENZ'iz– 2. frenzies, Menzies.

EP'er– 2. hepper, leper, pepper, strepor, tepor, stepper 3. high-stepper.

EP'erd– 2. jeopard, leopard, peppered, shepherd.

EP'i– 2. kepi, peppy, tepee 3. Apepi.

EP'id– 2. lepid, trepid, tepid 3. intrepid.

EP'ik– 2. epic 3. monepic 4. orthoëpic.

EP'ing– 2. pepping, stepping 3. high-stepping 4. overstepping.

EP'it– 3. decrepit.

EP'o– 2. Beppo, depot.

EP'od– 2. epode, depoted.

EP'ok– 2. epoch.

EP'on– 2. weapon.

EP'shun– 3. ereption, surreption, deception, reception, preception, exception, inception, conception, perception, susception 4. beneception, antiseption, preconception, misconception, apperception, preperception, imperception, interception 5. nociperception, introsusception, intussusception.

EP'si– 3. apepsy, dyspepsy, eupepsy 4. catalepsy, epilepsy.

EP'sis– 2. pepsis, sepsis, scepsis 3. syllepsis, prolepsis, asepsis 4. analepsis, paralepsis, metalepsis, antisepsis.

EPT'al– 2. heptal, septal.

EPT'ans– 3. acceptance, exceptance.

EPT'ant– 2. reptant 3. acceptant, exceptant.

EPT'ed– 3. accepted, excepted 4. unaccepted, unexcepted, intercepted.

EPT'er– 2. scepter, sceptre 3. adepter, receptor, preceptor, accepter, excepter, inceptor, susceptor 4. intercepter; *see* also **EPT'or**– receptor etc. below.

EPT'ik– 2. skeptic, kleptic, peptic, threptic, septic, sceptic 3. sylleptic, proleptic, apeptic, dyspeptic, eupeptic, aseptic 4. analeptic, cataleptic, metaleptic, epileptic, nympholeptic, bradypeptic, antiseptic 5. epanaleptic, acataleptic.

EPT'il– 2. reptile, septile.

EPT'ing– 3. accepting, excepting, incepting 4. intercepting.

EPT'iv– 3. acceptive, deceptive, receptive, preceptive, exceptive, inceptive, conceptive, perceptive, susceptive 4. nociceptive, autoceptive, apperceptive, imperceptive, interceptive, insusceptive 5. intussusceptive.

EPT'li– 3. adeptly, ineptly.

EPT'ness– 3. adeptness, ineptness.

EPT'or– 3. receptor, preceptor, inceptor, susceptor 4. beneceptor; *see* also **EPT'er–** scepter, etc. above.

EPT'um– 2. septum 3. perceptum.

ER'a– 2. serra, terra [It.] 3. sierra, acerra.

ER'af– 2. seraph, teraph; *see* also **ER'if–** serif etc. below.

ER'ald– 2. Gerald, herald, Herrold, perilled 3. imperilled.

ER'and– 2. errand.

ER'ant– 2. errant 3. aberrant.

ER'ens– 2. Terence 3. aberrance.

ER'er– 2. error, terror.

ER'et– 2. ferret, lerret, terret, wherret; *see* also **ER'it–** merit etc. below.

ER'i– 2. berry, bury, cherry, derry, ferry, jerry, Kerry, skerry, flerry, merry, perry, serry, sherry, terry, very, wherry 3. *bayberry, dayberry, burberry, redberry, breadberry, chokeberry, baneberry, wineberry, oneberry, Juneberry, youngberry, bogberry, dogberry, hackberry, blackberry, inkberry, pinkberry, bilberry, mulberry, cranberry, snowberry, crowberry, strawberry, squawberry, barberry, deerberry, mossberry, raspberry, catberry, dewberry, blueberry, gooseberry, chokecherry* 4. chinaberry, guavaberry, coffeeberry, beriberi, partridgeberry, orangeberry, thimbleberry, bumbleberry, dangleberry, tangleberry, huckleberry, loganberry, rowanberry, checkerberry, winterberry, Christmasberry, lotusberry, locustberry, Pondicherry, millinery, stationery, lamasery, cemetery, presbytery, mesentery, monastery.

ER'id– 2. berried, buried, cherried, ferried, serried, wherried 3. unburied, unserried.

ER'if– 2. serif, sheriff 4. undersheriff; *see* also **ER'af–** seraph etc. above.

ER'ik– 2. Eric, deric, derrick, ferric, spheric, Herrick, cleric, ceric, Seric, pteric, terek, steric, queric 3. suberic, valeric, dimeric, chimeric, Homeric, mesmeric, generic, piperic, glyceric, icteric, enteric, hysteric 4. peripheric, helispheric, hemispheric, perispheric, atmospheric, metameric, isomeric, polymeric, neoteric, esoteric, exoteric.

ER'iks– 2. derricks, clerics 3. hysterics 4. esoterics.

ER'il– 2. beryl, ferrule, peril, sterile 3. imperil, unsterile 4. chrysoberyl.

ER'in– 2. Serin.

ER'ing– 2. erring, herring.

ER'is– 2. Eris, derris, ferris, terrace.

ER'ish– 2. cherish, perish.

ER'it– 2. merit 3. inherit, demerit 4. disinherit.

ER'iz– 2. berries, buries, cherries, ferries, sherries, wherries, queries.

ER'on– 2. heron.

ER'or– 2. error, terror.

ER'ul– 2. ferule, ferrule, spherule, perule.

ER'und– 2. errand, gerund.

ER'us– 2. ferrous 3. nonferrous.

ES'a– 2. dessa, sessa, Tessa 3. Odessa, Marpessa, Duessa 4. dogaressa.

ES'al– 2. quezal, vessel 3. redressal, processal; *see* also **ES'il–** decile etc. below; also **ES'l–** deasil etc. below.

ES'ant– 2. jessant 3. confessant, caressant, depressant, incessant.

ES'ay– 2. esse [L.], essay.

ESCH'al– 2. bestial 3. celestial, agrestial.

ESCH'un– 2. question 3. suggestion, digestion, ingestion, congestion, requestion 4. indigestion.

ES'ed– 2. essed, blessed.

ES'en– 2. Essen, lessen, lesson.

ES'ens– 2. essence, crescents 3. albescence, rubescence, candescence, quiescence, calescence, mollescence, tumescence, senescence, accrescence, excrescence, concrescence, nigrescence, virescence, florescence, floressence, vitrescence, putrescence, latescence, lactescence, quintessence, mutescence, frutescence, liquescence 4. erubescence, lapidescence, iridescence, viridescence, incandescence, recrudescence, acquiescence, requiescence, decalescence, coalescence, opalescence, convalescence, adolescence, obsolescence, intumescence, evanescence, juvenescence, luminescence, arborescence, phosphorescence, calorescence, efflorescence, deflorescence, inflorescence, sonorescence, fluorescence, deliquescence, effervescence 5. nonacquiescence, rejuvenescence.

ES'ent– 2. crescent 3. albescent, rubescent, candescent, quiescent, calescent, tumescent, senescent, lignescent, accrescent, decrescent, increscent, excrescent, nigrescent, virescent, florescent, horrescent, vitrescent, latescent, frutescent, liquescent, fervescent 4. erubescent, lapidescent, iridescent, viridescent, incandescent, acquiescent, coalescent, opalescent, convalescent, scintellescent, adolescent, obsolescent, luminescent, phosphorescent, efflorescent, sonorescent, fluorescent, deliquescent, effervescent 5. nonacquiescent, rejuvenescent, noneffervescent, uneffervescent.

ES'er– 2. guesser, jessur, lesser, lessor, blesser, plessor, messer, dresser, presser, cesser 3. confessor, professor, sublessor, addressor, redresser, redressor, aggressor, progressor, transgressor, depressor, represser, impresser, compressor, oppressor, suppressor, assessor, obsessor, successor, possessor 4. acquiescer, second guesser, predecessor, antecessor, intercessor, dispossessor.

ES'ez– 2. s's, S's, eses, esses, desses, fesses, 'fesses, guesses, jesses, blesses, messes, dresses, cresses, presses, tresses, stresses, sesses, cesses, yeses 3. confesses, professes, turgesces, kermesses, finenesses, caresses, addresses, redresses, undresses, regresses, digresses, progresses, transgresses, accresces, depresses, represses, impresses, compresses, oppresses, suppresses, expresses, distresses, assesses, obsesses, recesses, possesses, successes 4. SOS's, incandesces, stewardesses, shepherdesses, second guesses, acquiesces, coalesces, convalesces, luminesces, baronesses, readdresses, retrogresses, water cresses, phosphoresces, effloresces, fluoresces, recompresses, overstresses, reassesses, repossesses, prepossesses, dispossesses, poetesses, effervesces, deliquesces 5. rejuvenesces, ambassadresses.

ES'ful– 3. distressful, successful 4. nonsuccessful, unsuccessful.

ESH'al– 2. deasil, special 3. especial.

ESH'ens– 2. nescience, prescience.

ESH'er– 2. mesher, fresher, pressure, thresher, tressure 3. refresher, nonpressure.

ESH'i– 2. fleshy, meshy.

ESH'ing– 2. meshing, threshing 3. refreshing.

ESH'l– 2. deasil, special 3. especial.

ESH'less– 2. fleshless, meshless.

ESH'li– 2. fleshly, freshly 3. unfleshly, unfreshly.

ESH'ment– 3. enmeshment, refreshment.

ESH'un– 2. Hessian, freshen, cession, session 3. confession, profession, aggression, egression, regression, digression, ingression, congression, progression, transgression, depression, repression, impression, compression, oppression, expression, suppression, obsession, recession, precession, secession, accession, succession, concession, possession 4. nonaggression, retrogression, introgression, repossession, prepossession, self-possession, dispossession, retrocession, introcession, supersession, intercession, indiscretion, quarter session.

ESH'unz– Hessians etc., *see* **ESH'un–** Hessian etc. above, plus "s" or "'s."

ESH'us– 2. precious 3. enmesh us, refresh us.

ES'i– 2. esse [L.], Essie, Bessie, Jesse, Jessie, messy, dressy, tressy, Tessie 3. in esse [L.].

ES'ij– 2. message, presage 3. expressage.

ES'il– 2. decile, cresyl, sessile, Cecil; *see* also **ES'l–** deasil etc. below; also **ES'al–** quezal etc. above.

ES'ing– 2. guessing, jessing, blessing, messing, pressing, stressing, yessing 3. confessing, professing, caressing, addressing, redressing, undressing, digressing, progressing, depressing, repressing, impressing, compressing, oppressing, suppressing, expressing, assessing, possessing, distressing 4. acquiescing, coalescing, convalescing, retrogressing, repossessing, prepossessing, unpossessing, dispossessing, effervescing 5. unprepossessing.

ES'iv– 2. crescive 3. caressive, redressive, aggressive, regressive, digressive, ingressive, congressive, progressive, transgressive, depressive, repressive, impressive, compressive, oppressive, suppressive, expressive, obsessive, recessive, accessive, excessive, successive, concessive, possessive 4. unprogressive, retrogressive, inexpressive, unexcessive.

ESK'i– 2. desky, pesky [coll.].

ESK'li– 3. blottesquely, grotesquely 4. picturesquely, statuesquely.

ESK'ness– 3. grotesqueness 4. picturesqueness, statuesqueness.

ESK'o– 2. fresco 3. tedesco [It.], alfresco, grotesco [obs.].

ESK'u– 2. fescue, rescue.

ES'l– 2. deasil, chessel, nestle, pestle, wrestle, trestle, sessile, Cecil, vessel 3. unnestle; *see* also **ES'al–** quezal etc. above; **ES'il–** decile etc. above.

ES'ler– 2. nestler, wrestler.

ES'ling– 2. nestling, wrestling.

ES'man– 2. pressman, yes man [slang].

ES'ment– 3. redressment, impressment, assessment.

ES'on– 2. Essen, lesson, lessen.

ES'or– 2. lessor, plessor 3. confessor, professor, aggressor, possessor; *see* also **ES'er–** guesser etc. above.

EST'a– 2. festa [It.], testa, cuesta, Vesta 3. podesta, egesta, ingesta, fiesta [Sp.], siesta, Avesta.

EST'al– 2. festal, vestal 3. agrestal.

EST'ant– 2. gestant, restant 3. contestant.

EST'ed– 2. bested, chested, jested, nested, rested, wrested, breasted, crested, tested, quested, vested, zested 3. infested, suggested, digested, ingested, congested, molested, arrested, unrested, attested, detested, protested, requested, unquested, divested, invested 4. manifested, predigested, undigested, unmolested, double-breasted, single-breasted, pigeonb-reasted, interested 5. uninterested, disinterested.

EST'er– 2. ester, Esther, bester, Chester, fester, Hester, jester, Lester, Leicester, Nestor, nester, pester, rester, wrester, testar, tester, vester, wester, quester 3. infester, suggester, digester, molester, semester, trimester, arrester, attester, contester, protester, requester, sequester, Sylvestor, northwester, southwester 4. manifester, mid-semester.

EST'ern– 2. hestern [obs.], western, yestern [arch.] 3. midwestern, northwestern, southwestern.

EST'ez– 2. Estes, restes 3. Dermestes, Herpestes, Orestes.

EST'ful– 2. jestful, restful, questful, zestful 3. unrestful.

EST'i– 2. chesty, Feste, resty, cresty, teste, testy, westy, zesty.

EST'ik– 2. gestic 3. asbestic, majestic,

orchestic, telestic, telestich, domestic, amnestic, agrestic 4. anapestic, catachrestic.

EST'in– 2. destine, sestine 3. predestine, clandestine, intestine.

EST'ind– 2. destined 3. predestined, undestined.

EST'ing– 2. besting, guesting, jesting, nesting, resting, wresting, breasting, cresting, testing, vesting, westing, questing 3. infesting, suggesting, digesting, ingesting, congesting, arresting, attesting, detesting, contesting, protesting, divesting, investing, requesting 4. manifesting, interesting 5. disinteresting, uninteresting.

EST'is– 2. restis 3. Alcestis; *see* also **EST'us–** Festus etc. below.

EST'iv– 2. estive, festive, restive 3. infestive, suggestive, digestive, congestive, tempestive, attestive 4. manifestive.

EST'less– 2. guestless, jestless, restless, breastless, crestless, questless.

EST'ling– 2. nestling.

EST'ment– 2. vestment 3. arrestment, divestment, investment.

EST'o– 2. presto 4. manifesto.

EST'ral– 2. kestrel 3. orchestral, palestral, semestral, trimestral, fenestral, campestral, ancestral.

EST'ri– 2. vestry.

EST'ur– 2. gesture, vesture 3. revesture, divesture, investure.

EST'us– 2. Festus, restis, cestus 3. asbestos, Alcestis.

ET'a– 2. eta, Etta, geta, meta, Greta, stretta 3. vendetta, codetta [It.], Valetta, burletta, lametta, Minetta, Egretta, biretta, Rosetta, mozzetta 4. arietta, Henrietta, animetta [It.], operetta 5. comedietta.

ET'al– 2. metal, petal 3. abettal, begettal; *see* also **ET'l–** ettle etc. below.

ET'ed– 2. betted, jetted, netted, petted, retted, fretted, stetted, vetted, wetted, whetted, sweated 3. abetted, indebted, coquetted, unfretted, regretted, brevetted, curvetted, gazetted 4. epauletted, coronetted, bayonetted, interfretted, unregretted, pirouetted.

ET'en– 2. Breton, threaten, whetten 3. rethreaten.

ET'er– 2. better, debtor, fetter, getter, letter, netter, petter, retter, fretter, wetter, sweater, whetter 3. abettor, enfetter, unfetter, begetter, go-getter, forgetter, dead letter, red-letter, black-letter, regretter, besetter, typesetter, upsetter.

ET'est– 2. wettest.

ET'ful– 2. netful, fretful 3. forgetful, regretful 4. unforgetful.

ETH'el– 2. Ethel, ethal, Bethel.

ETH'er– 2. feather, heather, leather, blether, mether, nether, tether, weather, wether, whether 3. tail feather, pinfeather, together, whitleather, comether, aweather, bellwether 4. altogether, patent leather.

ETH'erd– 2. feathered, heathered, leathered, tethered, weathered 3. pinfeathered, unfeathered, untethered, unweathered.

ET'i– 2. betty, Betty, chetty, Hetty, jetty, Letty, netty, Nettie, petty, petit, fretty, pretty, sweaty 3. confetti, spaghetti, libretti, sunsetty, Rossetti 4. spermaceti, Donizetti.

ET'ik– 2. Lettic, metic 3. ascetic, syndetic, algetic, Gangetic, aphetic, Japhetic, prophetic, bathetic, pathetic, synthetic, prothetic, aesthetic, poietic, ochletic, athletic, phyletic, gametic, emetic, mimetic, cometic, hermetic, seismetic, cosmetic, genetic, splenetic, phrenetic, threnetic, magnetic, kinetic, phonetic, goetic, noetic, Noetic, poetic, zoetic, herpetic, paretic, syncretic, heretic, heuretic, pyretic, Ossetic, zetetic, Helvetic, auxetic 4. alphabetic, diabetic, asyndetic, geodetic, cynegetic, exegetic, analgetic, energetic, synergetic, syzygetic, diathetic, apathetic, sympathetic, epithetic, antithetic, epenthetic, parenthetic, nomothetic, cosmothetic, hypothetic, anesthetic, rabietic, homiletic, arithmetic, Baphometic, hypnoetic, theoretic, anchoretic, diuretic, apatetic, erotetic, synartetic **5.** apologetic, antipathetic, polysynthetic, polyprothetic, hyperesthetic, cosmopoietic, monophyletic, polyphyletic, metagenetic, psychogenetic, morphogenetic, pathogenetic, homogenetic, thermogenetic, monogenetic, oogenetic, pyrogenetic, polygenetic, diamagnetic, parakinetic, telekinetic, autokinetic, dianoetic, mythopoetic, chrysopoetic, diaphoretic, antipyretic, peripatetic **6.** heterophyletic, paleogenetic, parthenogenetic, heterogenetic **7.** onomatopoetic.

ET′iks– **3.** athletics, Hermetics, cosmetics, magnetics, kinetics, phonetics, poetics, aesthetics **4.** cynegetics, exegetics, homiletics, theoretics, dietetics.

ET′ing– **2.** betting, getting, jetting, letting, bletting, netting, petting, retting, fretting, setting, wetting, sweating, whetting **3.** abetting, begetting, forgetting, coquetting, regretting, besetting, upsetting, brevetting, curvetting, gazetting **4.** unforgetting, somersetting, intersetting, minuetting **5.** mosquito netting.

ET′ish– **2.** fetish, fetich, Lettish, pettish, wettish **3.** coquettish.

ET′ist– **3.** cornettist, librettist, motettist, duettist, vignettist **4.** clarinettist.

ET′l– **2.** ettle [dial.], fettle, kettle, metal, mettle, nettle, petal, Gretel, settle, cetyl **3.** abettal, unmettle, resettle, unsettle **4.** centripetal **6.** Popocatepetl.

ET′ld– **2.** fettled, mettled, petalled, settled **3.** high mettled, unsettled **4.** double petalled.

ET′ler– **2.** nettler, settler.

ET′less– **2.** debtless, threatless.

ET′ling– **2.** fettling, nettling, settling **3.** unsettling.

ET′ment– **3.** abetment, indebtment, besetment, revetment.

ET′ness– **2.** setness, wetness.

ET′o– **2.** ghetto, stretto **3.** concetto [It.], zucchetto, stiletto, palmetto, rispetto [It.], libretto, falsetto, terzetto **4.** lazaretto, allegretto, amoretto.

ET′rad– **2.** retrad, tetrad.

ET′rik– **2.** metric **3.** dimetric, symmetric **4.** diametric, dynametric, asymmetric, pedometric, geometric, logometric ergometric, thermometric, chronometric, barometric, micrometric, hydrometric, hygrometric, isometric, photometric, autometric, tautometric **5.** trigonometric, magnetometric.

ET′sal– **2.** quetzal, pretzel.

ET′so– **2.** pezzo [It.]. **4.** intermezzo.

ET′work– **2.** network, fretwork.

EV′an– **2.** Evan, Bevan, Devon; *see* also **EV′en–** heaven etc. below.

EV′el– **2.** bevel, kevel, level, nevel, revel **3.** sea level, dishevel **4.** water level, spirit level; *see* also **EV′il–** devil etc. below.

EV′eld– **2.** bevelled, deviled, levelled, nevelled, revelled **3.** bedevilled, dishevelled.

EV′elz– bevels etc., *see* **EV′el–** bevel etc. above, plus "s" or " 's."

EV′en– **2.** heaven, leaven, seven, chevon, steven, sweven **3.** eleven; *see* also **EV′an–** Evan etc. above.

EV′enth– **2.** seventh **3.** eleventh.

EV′er– **2.** ever, lever, levir, clever, never, sever **3.** whichever, whenever, wherever, forever, whatever, however, whoever, endeavor, assever, dissever **4.** whichsoever, whensoever, whencesoever, wheresoever, whatsoever, whosoever, whosesoever, howsoever, cantilever **5** whithersoever.

EV'i– 2. Evy, bevy, chevy, heavy, levee, levy, clevy, nevvy, Chevvy **3.** top-heavy, replevy.

EV'il– 2. devil, Neville **3.** bedevil, daredevil, she-devil, blue devil, red devil; *see* also **EV'el–** bevel etc. above.

EV'ilz– devils etc., *see* **EV'il–** devil etc. above, plus "s" or " 's."

EV'in– **2.** levin **3.** replevin.

EV'is– **2.** chevise, clevis, brevis [L.], crevice **3.** Ben Nevis **7.** ars longa, vita brevis [L.].

EZ'ans– **2.** pleasance, peasants, presence, presents **4.** omnipresence.

EZ'ant– **2.** pheasant, pleasant, peasant, bezant **3.** unpleasant **4.** omnipresent.

EZH'er– **2.** leisure, pleasure, measure, treasure **3.** displeasure, admeasure, re-measure, commeasure, entreasure.

EZH'erz– **2.** pleasures, measures, treasures.

EZ'l– **2.** bezel, bezzle **3.** embezzle.

EZ'ler– **3.** embezzler.

E (heh)

3.

TRIPLE RHYMES IN E (eb′on-y)

Primary or Secondary Accent Falls on Second from Last Syllable.

EB′i–er– **2.** blebbier, nebbier, webbier **4.** cobwebbier.

EB′i–est– **3.** blebbiest, nebbiest, webbiest **4.** cobwebbiest.

EB′on–i– **3.** ebony.

EB′ri–ti– **4.** celebrity, tenebrity.

EB′u–lar– **3.** nebular.

ECH′a–bl– **3.** fetchable, sketchable, stretchable.

ECH′er–i– **3.** lechery, treachery.

ECH′er–us– **3.** lecherous, treacherous.

ECH′i–ness– **3.** sketchiness, stretchiness, tetchiness.

ED′a–bl– dreadable; *see* also **ED′i–bl–** edible etc. below.

ED′en–ing– **3.** deadening, leadening, reddening.

ED′er–al– **3.** federal.

ED′i–bl– **3.** edible, dreadable, credible **4.** unedible, impedible, incredible.

ED′i–er– **3.** headier, readier, breadier, spreadier, shreddier, threadier, steadier **4.** unreadier, unsteadier.

ED′i–est– **3.** headiest, readiest, breadiest, spreadiest, shreddiest, threadiest, steadiest **4.** unreadiest, unsteadiest.

ED′i–ing– **3.** eddying, readying, steadying.

ED′i–kant– **3.** dedicant, medicant, predicant.

ED′i–kat– **3.** dedicate, medicate, predicate **4.** rededicate, depredicate.

ED′i–kl– **3.** medical, pedicle **4.** premedical.

ED′i–li– **3.** readily, steadily **4.** unreadily, unsteadily.

ED′i–ment– **3.** pediment, sediment **4.** impediment.

ED′i–ness– **3.** headiness, readiness, breadiness, spreadiness, shreddiness, threadiness, steadiness **4.** unreadiness, unsteadiness.

ED′it–ed– **3.** edited, credited **4.** re-edited, unedited, accredited, discredited, miscredited **5.** unaccredited, undiscredited.

ED′it–er– **3.** editor, creditor.

ED′it–i– **4.** rubedity, heredity.

ED′it–ing– **3.** editing, crediting **4.** accrediting, discrediting, miscrediting.

ED′it–iv– **3.** redditive, creditive, sedative **4.** impeditive.

ED′it–or– **3.** editor, creditor **4.** subeditor.

ED′u–lus– **3.** credulous, sedulous **4.** incredulous, unsedulous.

EF′a–lus– **3.** Cephalus **4.** acephalus, acephalous, encephalous, Bucephalus.

EF′er–ens– **3.** deference, reference, preference **4.** cross-reference.

EF′er–ent– **3.** efferent, deferent, referent, preferent.

EF'in–it– 3. definite 4. indefinite, undefinite.

EF'is–ens– 4. maleficence, beneficence.

EF'is–ent– 4. maleficent, beneficent.

EF'lu–ent– 3. effluent, defluent, refluent.

EG'a–bl– 3. beggable, legable, peggable.

EG'ar–i– 3. beggary, Weggery.

EG'a–si– 3. legacy.

EG'a–sus– 3. Pegasus.

EG'i–ness– 3. egginess, legginess, dregginess.

EG'nan–si– 3. regnancy, pregnancy.

EG'raf–i– 4. telegraphy, choregraphy.

EG'u–lar– 3. regular, tegular 4. irregular, unregular.

EJ'i–bl– 3. legible 4. allegeable, illegible.

EJ'i–bli– 3. legibly 4. illegibly.

EJ'i–o– 4. solfeggio, arpeggio.

EK'a–bl– 3. checkable, peccable, secable 4. impeccable.

EK'ond–li– 3. fecundly, secondly.

EK'on–ing– 3. beckoning, reckoning 4. dead reckoning.

EK're–ment– 3. decrement, recrement.

EKS'a–bl– 3. vexable 4. annexable; *see* also **EKS'i–bl–** flexible etc. below.

EKS'ed–li– 3. vexedly 4. perplexedly, convexedly.

EKS'el–ent– 3. excellent.

EKSH'un–al– 3. flectional, sectional 4. affectional, objectional, projectional, reflectional, inflectional, collectional, complexional, connectional, directional, correctional, resectional, bisectional, dissectional, protectional, convectional 5. interjectional, resurrectional, insurrectional, vivisectional.

EKSH'un–er– 4. confectioner, perfectioner, correctioner.

EKSH'un–ist– 4. perfectionist, projectionist, protectionist 3. resurrectionist, insurrectionist, vivisectionist 6. antiprotectionist 7 antivivisectionist.

EKS'i–bl– 3. flexible 4. deflexible, reflexible, inflexible; *see* also **EKS'a–bl–** vexable etc. above.

EKS'i–kal– 3. lexical 4. indexical, pyrexical.

EKS'i–ti– 4. complexity, perplexity, duplexity, convexity.

EKS'iv–ness– 4. reflexiveness, perplexiveness.

EKT'a–bl– 4. subjectable, objectable, rejectable, delectable, deflectable, respectable, expectable, suspectable, erectable, detectable 5. indelectable; *see* also **EKT'i–bl–** affectible etc. below.

EKT'a–bli– 4. delectably, respectably 5. undelectably, unsuspectably.

EKT'a–kl– 3. spectacle 4. bespectacle; *see* also **EKT'i–kl–** dialectical etc. below.

EKT'a–ri– 3. nectary, sectary; *see* also **EKT'o–ri–** rectory etc. below.

EKT'ed–li– 4. affectedly, subjectedly, dejectedly, reflectedly, neglectedly, collectedly, connectedly, respectedly, protectedly 5. unaffectedly, disaffectedly, recollectedly, disconnectedly, unexpectedly, unsuspectedly.

EKT'ed–ness– 4. affectedness, infectedness, abjectedness, dejectedness, subjectedness, neglectedness, suspectedness 5. unaffectedness, disaffectedness, disconnectedness, unexpectedness, unsuspectedness.

EKT'ful–i– 4. neglectfully, respectfully 5. unrespectfully, disrespectfully.

EKT'ful–ness– 4. neglectfulness, respectfulness, suspectfulness 5. disrespectfulness.

EKT'i–bl– 4. affectible, effectible, defectible, infectible, perfectible, subjectible, reflectible, connectible, suspectible, dissectible 5. unaffectible; *see* also **EKT'a–bl–** subjectable etc. above.

EKT'i–fi– 3. rectify 4. objectify, subjectify.

EKT'i-kl- 5. dialectical, apoplectical; *see* also **EKT'a-kl-** spectacle etc. above.

EKT'ing-li- 4. affectingly, objectingly, reflectingly.

EKT'i-tud- 3. rectitude 4. senectitude.

EKT'i-vist- 4. objectivist, collectivist.

EKT'iv-li- 4. affectively, effectively, defectively, infectively, perfectively, objectively, subjectively, projectively, electively, selectively, deflectively, reflectively, inflectively, neglectively, collectively, connectively, respectively, prospectively, perspectively, directively, correctively, protectively, invectively 5. ineffectively, unreflectively, irreflectively, recollectively, irrespectively, retrospectively, introspectively.

EKT'iv-ness- 4. effectiveness, defectiveness, perfectiveness, objectiveness, subjectiveness, reflectiveness, collectiveness, prospectiveness, protectiveness 5. unobjectiveness, irreflectiveness, unreflectiveness, recollectiveness.

EKT'or-al- 3. pectoral, rectoral, sectoral 4. prefectoral, electoral, inspectoral, directoral, protectoral.

EKT'or-at- 3. rectorate 4. electorate, expectorate, directorate, protectorate.

EKT'or-i- 3. rectory 4. refectory, trajectory, directory, correctory, protectory 5. interjectory; *see* also **EKT'ar-i-** nectary etc. above.

EKT'u-al- 3. lectual 4. effectual, prefectual 5. ineffectual, intellectual.

EKT'ur-al- 4. prefectural, conjectural 5. architectural.

EKT'ur-er- 3. lecturer 4. conjecturer.

EK'u-lar- 3. specular, secular 4. trabecular, vallecular, molecular.

EK'u-lat- 3. peculate, speculate.

EK'und-li- 3. fecundly, secondly.

EK'u-tiv- 4. executive, subsecutive, consecutive 5. unconsecutive.

EL'a-bl- 3. bellable, delible, fellable, gelable, spellable, sellable, tellable, quellable 4. indelible, compellable, expellable, unspellable, foretellable, unquellable.

EL'a-tin- gelatin, gelatine, skeleton.

EL'a-tiv- 3. relative 4. appellative, compellative, irrelative, correlative.

EL'e-gat- 3. delegate, relegate.

EL'er-i- 3. celery, cellary, stellary.

EL'et-on- 3. skeleton, gelatin, gelatine.

ELF'i-a- 4. Didelphia 5. Philadelphia, Monodelphia 6. Polyadelphia.

ELF'i-an- 4. didelphian 5. Philadelphian, Christadelphian.

ELF'ish-li- 3. elfishly, selfishly 4. unselfishly.

ELF'ish-ness- 3. elfishness, selfishness 4. unselfishness.

EL'i-bl- 3. delible 4. indelible; *see* also **EL'a-bl-** bellable etc. above.

EL'i-ing- 3. bellying, jellying.

EL'i-ka- 3. Melica 4. Angelica.

EL'i-kan- 3. pelican, belly can, jelly can.

EL'i-kl- 3. bellical, helical, pellicle 4. angelical, vitellicle 5. evangelical.

EL'ing-ly- 3. tellingly, quellingly, wellingly 4. compellingly.

EL'ish-ing- 3. relishing 4. embellishing.

EL'ish-ment- 3. relishment 4. embellishment.

EL'i-ti- 3. pellety 4. fidelity 5. infidelity.

EL'o-er- 3. bellower, mellower, yellower.

EL'o-est- 3. mellowest, celloist, yellowest.

EL'o-i- 3. mellowy, yellowy.

EL'o-ing- 3. bellowing, mellowing, yellowing.

EL'on-i- 3. felony, melony.

EL'op-ing- 4. developing, enveloping 5. undeveloping.

EL'op-ment- 4. development, envelopment.

ELT′er–i– 3. smeltery, sheltery, sweltery.

ELT′er–ing– 3. sheltering, weltering, sweltering.

ELTH′i–er– 3. healthier, stealthier, wealthier.

ELTH′i–est– 3. healthiest, stealthiest, wealthiest.

ELTH′i–li– 3. healthily, stealthily, wealthily.

EL′u–lar– 3. cellular, stellular 4. bicellular 5. unicellular, interstellular.

EL′us–li– 3. jealously, zealously.

EL′us–ness– 3. jealousness, zealousness.

EM′an–e– 4. anemone, Gethsemane 5. pantanemone, Agapemone.

EM′as–i– 4. supremacy.

EM′a–tist– 4. emblematist 5. theorematist.

EMB′er–i– 3. embery 4. Decembery, Septembery, Novembery.

EMB′er–ing– 3. membering 4. remembering, dismembering.

EMB′er–ish– 3. emberish 4. Septemberish, Decemberish, Novemberish.

EM′en–si– 3. clemency.

EM′er–al– 3. femerell, femoral, nemoral 4. ephemeral, trihemeral.

EM′er–ald– 3. emerald.

EM′er–i– 3. emery, gemmary, memory.

EM′e–sis– 3. emesis, Nemesis.

EM′i–kal– 3. chemical 4. endemical, alchemical, polemical 5. academical, epidemical 6. electrochemical.

EM′i–li– 3. Emily, gemmily.

EM′in–al– 3. feminal, geminal, seminal 4. bigeminal, tergeminal.

EM′in–at– 3. feminate, geminate 4. effeminate, ingeminate, tergeminate, disseminate, inseminate.

EM′in–ent– 3. eminent 4. pre-eminent 5. supereminent.

EMN′i–ti– 4. indemnity, solemnity.

Em′o–ne– 4. anemone, Gethsemane 5. pantanemone, Agapemone.

EM′o–ra– 3. femora, remora 4. ephemera.

EM′o–ral– 3. femoral, nemoral; *see* also **EM′er–al–** femerell etc. above.

EM′o–ri– 3. emery, Emory, gemmary, memory.

EMP′er–er– 3. emperor, temperer.

EMP′er–i– 3. empery, tempery, tempore [L.] 4. extempore.

EMP′or–al– 3. temporal 4. atemporal, extemporal 5. supertemporal.

EMP′to–ri– 4. redemptory, peremptory.

EM′u–lent– 3. emulant, tremulant, temulent.

EM′u–lus– 3. emulous, tremulous.

EN′ar–i– 3. denary, hennery, plenary, senary 4. decennary, centenary, septennary.

EN′at–or– senator; *see* also **EN′i–tor–** genitor etc. below.

END′a–bl– 3. endable, lendable, mendable 4. defendable, amendable, emendable, commendable, dependable, ascendable, descendable 5. recommendable, independable, undependable, unascendable; *see* also **END′i–bl–** rendible etc. below.

END′an–si– 4. appendancy, ascendancy, attendancy, intendancy; *see* also **END′en–si–** splendency etc. below.

END′en–si– 3. splendency, pendency, tendency 4. transcendency, resplendency, transplendency, dependency, impendency, intendency 5. independency, ambitendency, countertendency; *see* also **END′an–si–** appendancy etc. above.

END′er–er– 3. genderer, slenderer, renderer, tenderer 4. engenderer, surrenderer.

END′er–est– 3. slenderest, tenderest.

END'er-ing- 3. gendering, rendering, tendering 4. engendering, surrendering.

END'er-li- 3. slenderly, tenderly.

END'er-ness- 3. slenderness, tenderness.

END'i-bl- 3. rendible, vendible 4. ascendible, accendible, extendible, invendible 5. comprehendible; *see* also **END'a-bl-** endable etc. above.

END'i-us- 4. compendious, dispendious.

END'less-li- 3. endlessly, bendlessly, mendlessly, friendlessly.

END'less-ness- 3. endlessness, bendlessness, mendlessness, friendlessness.

END'us-li- 4. tremendously, stupendously.

END'us-ness- 4. tremendousness, stupendousness.

EN'er-at- 3. generate, venerate 4. degenerate, regenerate, ingenerate, progenerate, intenerate.

EN'es-is- 3. genesis 4. regenesis, pangenesis, parenesis 5. paragenesis, catagenesis, metagenesis, epigenesis, neogenesis, psychogenesis, morphogenesis, pathogenesis, biogenesis, homogenesis, monogenesis, oogenesis, zoogenesis, pyrogenesis, ectogenesis, ontogenesis, histogenesis, polygenesis 6. osteogenesis, organogenesis, parthenogenesis, anthropogenesis, heterogenesis.

ENGTH'en-ing- 3. strengthening, lengthening.

EN'i-a- 4. millennia, quadrennia, decennia.

EN'i-al- 4. biennial, triennial, millennial, perennial, plurennial, decennial, tricennial, vicennial, sexennial, centennial, quotennial, septennial, novennial, quinquennial 5. bicentennial, tricentennial, tercentennial 6. duodecennial.

EN'i-form- 3. penniform 4. bipenniform, antenniform.

EN'i-kal- 3. scenical 4. Galenical, sirenical, arsenical 5. hygienical, ecumenical 6. catechumenical.

EN'i-ti- 3. lenity 4. amenity, serenity, terrenity, obscenity.

EN'i-tiv- 3. genitive, lenitive, splenitive 4. progenitive 5. primogenitive.

EN'i-tor- 3. genitor, senator 4. progenitor 5. primogenitor.

EN'i-tud- 3. lenitude, plenitude 4. serenitude.

EN'i-tur- 3. geniture 4. progeniture 5. primogeniture 6. ultimogeniture.

EN'i-um- 4. biennium, millenium, quadrennium, decennium, sexennium, septennium.

EN'i-zon- 3. benison, denizen, venison 4. endenizen.

ENS'a-bl- 4. condensable, dispensable 5. incondensable, indispensable; *see* also **ENS'i-bl-** sensible etc. below.

ENS'a-ri- dispensary; *see* also **ENS'o-ri-** sensory etc. below.

ENS'a-tiv- 3. pensative, sensitive 4. condensative, compensative, dispensative, insensitive, intensative.

ENSH'a-ri- 4. sententiary 5. residentiary, penitentiary.

ENSH'i-at- 4. essentiate, licentiate, potentiate 5. differentiate.

ENSH'i-ent- 3. sentient 4. assentient, presentient, dissentient, insentient, consentient.

ENSH'u-al- 3. mensual, censual, sensual 4. trimensual, consensual.

ENSH'un-al- 3. tensional 4. dimensional, ascensional, descensional, attentional, intentional, contentional, extensional, preventional, conventional 5. unintentional, unconventional.

ENSH'un-er- 3. mentioner, pensioner 4. conventioner.

ENSH'un-ing- 3. mentioning, pensioning, tensioning.

ENSH'un–ist– 4. ascentionist, descentionist, recensionist, extensionist, preventionist, conventionist.

ENSH'us–ness– 4. licentiousness, pretentiousness, sententiousness, contentiousness 5. conscientiousness, unpretentiousness.

ENS'i–bl– 3. sensible, tensible 4. condensible, defensible, insensible, unsensible, distensible, ostensible 5. indefensible, apprehensible, reprehensible, comprehensible, inostensible 6. irreprehensible, incomprehensible; *see* also **ENS'a–bl–** condensable etc. above.

ENS'i–bli– 3. sensibly 4. defensibly, insensibly, ostensibly 5. reprehensibly, comprehensibly 6. incomprehensibly.

ENS'i–fi– 3. densify, sensify 4. intensify.

ENS'i–kal– 4. forensical, nonsensical.

ENS'i–ti– 3. density, tensity 4. condensity, immensity, propensity, attensity, intensity.

ENS'i–tiv– 3. sensitive 4. condensitive, insensative; *see* also **ENS'a–tiv–** pensative etc. above.

ENS'iv–li– 3. pensively 4. defensively, offensively, expensively, intensively, extensively 5. inoffensively, apprehensively, reprehensively, comprehensively, inexpensively 6. incomprehensively.

ENS'iv–ness– 3. pensiveness 4. offensiveness, expensiveness, intensiveness, extensiveness 5. comprehensiveness 6. incomprehensiveness.

ENS'less–li– 3. senselessly, tenselessly 4. defenselessly, offenselessly.

ENS'less–ness– 3. senselessness, tenselessness 4. defenselessness.

ENS'o–ri– 3. sensory 4. condensery, defensory, prehensory, dispensary, suspensory, incensory, ostensory 5. reprehensory.

ENT'a–bl– 3. rentable, tentable 4. lamentable, fermentable, repentable, contentable, preventable, inventable, frequentable, presentable 5. uncontentable, representable, unpresentable.

ENT'a–bli– 4. lamentably, preventably, presentably 5. unpreventably, unpresentably.

ENT'a–kl– 3. pentacle, tentacle.

ENT'a–li– 3. mentally 4. fragmentally, segmentally, pigmentally, momentally, parentally 5. accidentally, occidentally, incidentally, orientally, fundamentally, ornamentally, elementally, supplementally, regimentally, alimentally, complimentally, detrimentally, sentimentally, governmentally, monumentally, instrumentally, continentally 6. temperamentally, developmentally.

ENT'al–ist– 5. Occidentalist, transcendentalist, Orientalist, fundamentalist, sentimentalist, instrumentalist 6. experimentalist.

ENT'al–izm– 5. Occidentalism, transcendentalism, Orientalism, elementalism, fundamentalism, sentimentalism.

ENT'a–ri– 3. dentary 4. fragmentary, segmentary, pigmentary 5. filamentary, sacramentary, testamentary, elementary, complementary, supplementary, sedimentary, rudimentary, alimentary, complimentary, documentary, tegumentary 6. uncomplimentary, integumentary, emolumentary.

ENT'a–sis– 3. entasis.

ENT'a–tiv– 3. tentative 4. augmentative, fermentative, presentative, pretentative, sustentative, frequentative 5. alimentative, complimentative, argumentative, representative 6. experimentative, misrepresentative.

ENT'ed–li– 4. dementedly, tormentedly, contentedly 5. unlamentedly, discontentedly, unfrequentedly 6. unprecedentedly.

ENT'ed–ness– 3. scentedness 4. dementedness, fermentedness, tormentedness, contentedness, frequentedness, inventedness 5. discontentedness, unfrequentedness 6. unprecedentedness.

ENT'er–ing– 3. entering, centering 4. re-entering, self-centering.

ENT'ful–li– 4. resentfully, eventfully, inventfully 5. unresentfully, uneventfully.

ENT'ful–ness– 4. resentfulness, eventfulness, inventfulness 5. uneventfulness.

ENTH'e–sis– 4. epenthesis, parenthesis.

ENT'i–bl– 4. inventible; *see* also **ENT' a–bl–** rentable etc. above.

ENT'i–kal– 3. dentical, denticle 4. identical, authentical, conventical, conventicle.

ENT'i–kul– 3. denticule, lenticule.

ENT'i–ment– 3. sentiment 4. presentiment.

ENT'i–nel– 3. dentinal, sentinel.

ENT'ing–li– 4. relentingly, lamentingly, augmentingly, tormentingly, repentingly, assentingly, dissentingly, consentingly 5. unrelentingly.

ENT'i–ti– 3. entity 4. identity, nonentity.

ENT'iv–li– 4. presentively, attentively, retentively, preventively, inventively.

ENT'iv–ness– 4. attentiveness, retentiveness, preventiveness, inventiveness, presentiveness 5. inattentiveness, uninventiveness.

ENT'l–ness– 3. gentleness 4. ungentleness 5. Occidentalness, transcendentalness, Orientalness, elementalness, fundamentalness, sentimentalness.

ENT'ral–i– 3. centrally, ventrally 4. subcentrally, uncentrally 5. dorsiventrally.

ENT'rik–al– 3. centrical, ventricle 4. eccentrical, concentrical.

ENT'u–al– 4. accentual, percentual, adventual, eventual, conventual.

ENT'u–at– 4. accentuate, eventuate.

ENT'us–li– 4. momentously, portentously.

ENT'us–ness– 4. momentousness, portentousness.

EN'u–at– 3. tenuate 4. attenuate, extenuate.

EN'u–us– 3. tenuous, strenuous 4. ingenuous 5. disingenuous.

EP'a–rat– 3. reparate, separate.

EP'er–us– 3. leperous, streperous 4. obstreperous.

EP'ik–al– 3. epical 5. orthoëpical.

EP'it–ant– 3. crepitant, strepitant.

EPSH'un–al– 4. exceptional, conceptional 5. unexceptional.

EPS'i–a– 4. apepsia, dyspepsia, eupepsia 5. monoblepsia.

EPT'i–bl– 4. deceptible, receptible, acceptable, perceptible, susceptible 5. imperceptible, insusceptible, unsusceptible.

EPT'i–bli– 4. perceptibly, susceptibly 5. indeceptibly, imperceptibly, unsusceptibly.

EPT'ik–al– 3. skeptical, septical 4. syleptical, aseptical, receptacle, conceptacle 5. antiseptical.

EPT'iv–ness– 4. deceptiveness, receptiveness, perceptiveness, susceptiveness 5. imperceptiveness.

EPT'u–al– 4. preceptual, conceptual, perceptual 5. preconceptual.

ER'a–fim– 3. seraphim, teraphim.

ER'an–si– 3. errancy 4. aberrancy, inerrancy.

ER'a–pi– 3. therapy 5. theotherapy, psychotherapy, hydrotherapy, autotherapy 6. balneotherapy, radiotherapy.

ER'i–bl– 3. errable, terrible.

ER'i–dez– 4. Pierides, Hesperides.

ER'i-er- 3. berrier, burier, ferrier, merrier, terrier.

ER'i-est- 3. merriest.

ER'i-fi- 3. spherify, terrify, verify.

ER'i-ing- 3. berrying, burying, ferrying, serrying, wherrying 4. cranberrying, strawberrying, blueberrying 5. huckleberrying.

ER'i-ka- 3. erica, erika 4. America.

ER'i-kal- 3. spherical, sphericle, clerical 4. chimerical, Homerical, mesmerical, numerical, generical, hysterical 5. hemispherical, atmospherical, rhinocerical, climacterical, esoterical, exoterical.

ER'i-li- 3. merrily, verily.

ER'i-ment- 3. merriment 4. experiment.

ER'ish-ing- 3. cherishing, perishing 4. uncherishing, unperishing.

ER'it-ans- 3. heritance 4. inheritance 5. disinheritance.

ER'it-ed- 3. ferreted, merited 4. inherited, disherited, emerited, unmerited 5. disinherited.

ER'it-er- 3. ferreter, meriter 4. inheritor, coheritor.

ER'it-i- 3. verity 4. legerity, celerity, temerity, asperity, prosperity, sincerity, alterity, dexterity, austerity, posterity, severity 5. insincerity, indexterity 6. ambidexterity.

ER'it-ing- 3. ferreting, meriting 4. inheriting, unmeriting 5. disinheriting.

ER'it-iv- 4. aperitive, imperative, preteritive.

ER'o-gat- 3. derogate 4. interrogate 5. supererogate.

ERJ- through **ERZ-**, *see* short **U** (tub): **URJ'en-si** through **URZH'un-ist.**

ES'a-bl- 3. guessable, pressable 4. unguessable, assessable, possessable 5. unredressable, unassessable, unpossessable.

ES'a-ri- 4. confessary; *see* also **ES'o-ri-** professory etc. below.

ES'en-si- 4. acescency, quiescency, turgescency, excrescency, liquescency 5. erubescency, incandescency, acquiescency, convalescency, adolescency, efflorescency, delitescency, effervescency.

ES'ful-i- 3. blessfully, stressfully 4. successfully, distressfully.

ES'i-bl- 4. concrescible, redressible, transgressible, depressible, repressible, impressible, compressible, suppressible, expressible, vitrescible, putrescible, accessible, concessible 5. irrepressible, insuppressible, unexpressible, inaccessible, unconcessible, fermentescible, effervescible 6. ineffervescible.

ES'i-bli- 4. expressibly, accessibly 5. irrepressibly, inexpressibly, inaccessibly.

ES'i-kat- 3. desiccate, vesicate, exsiccate.

ES'i-ma- 3. decima 5. Quadragesima, Sexagesima, Quinquagesima 6. Septuagesima.

ES'i-mal- 3. decimal 4. trigesimal, vigesimal, millesimal, centesimal 5. duodecimal, nonagesimal, quadragesimal sexagesimal 6. septuagesimal, infinitesimal.

ES'i-mo- 5. octodecimo, sextodecimo, duodecimo.

ES'ing-li- 3. pressingly 4. caressingly, depressingly, distressingly 5. prepossessingly.

ES'i-ti- 4. obesity, necessity.

ES'iv-li- 4. aggressively, regressively, digressively, progressively, transgressively, depressively, repressively, impressively, oppressively, expressively, excessively, successively, possessively.

ES'iv-ness- 4. aggressiveness, progressiveness, depressiveness, impressiveness, oppressiveness, expressiveness, excessiveness, successiveness, possessiveness.

ES'o-ri- 4. professory, confessary, accessory, successory, concessory, possessory 5. intercessory.

ESH'i-ens- 3. nescience, prescience.

ESH'i-ness- 3. fleshiness, meshiness.

ESH'un-al- 3. sessional 4. confessional, professional, digressional, congressional, progressional, transgressional, discretional, impressional, compressional, expressional, recessional, precessional, accessional, successional, possessional, processional 5. retrocessional, intercessional.

ESH'un-er- 3. sessioner 4. secessioner, possessioner, processioner.

ESH'un-ist- 4. confessionist, progressionist, impressionist, suppressionist, expressionist, secessionist, concessionist, successionist, processionist.

EST'a-bl- 3. testable, 4. detestable, intestable, contestable 5. incontestable.

EST'a-bli- 3. testably 4. detestably, contestably 5. incontestably, uncontestably.

EST'a-ment- 3. testament, vestiment.

EST'er-ing- 3. festering, pestering, westering 4. sequestering.

EST'ful-i- 3. restfully, questfully.

EST'i-al- 3. bestial 4. celestial, agrestial 5. uncelestial 6. supercelestial.

EST'i-bl- 4. digestible, suggestible, comestible, divestible 5. indigestible; *see* also EST'a-bl- testable etc. above.

EST'i-kal- 4. majestical 5. anapaestical, catachrestical.

EST'in-al- 3. destinal 4. intestinal.

EST'i-ness- 3. restiness, testiness.

EST'ing-li- 3. jestingly, testingly 4. protestingly 5. interestingly 6. uninterestingly.

EST'iv-li- 3. festively, restively 4. suggestively.

EST'iv-ness- 3. festiveness, restiveness 4. suggestiveness.

EST'ri-al- 4. pedestrial, bimestrial, trimestrial, terrestrial 5. decimestrial 6. superterrestrial.

EST'ri-an- 4. pedestrian, palaestrian, campestrian, rupestrian, sylvestrian, equestrian.

EST'ri-us- 4. pedestrious, terrestrious.

EST'ur-al- 3. gestural, vestural.

EST'u-us- 4. tempestuous, incestuous.

ET'a-bl- 3. gettable, lettable, nettable, pettable, settable 4. forgettable, regrettable, upsettable 5. unforgettable, unregrettable.

ET'a-bli- 4. regrettably 5. unforgettably.

ET'a-lus- 3. petalous 4. apetalous 5. polypetalous.

ET'er-a- 4. et cetera.

ET'er-er- 3. betterer, fetterer, letterer.

ET'er-ing- 3. bettering, fettering, lettering.

ET'er-it- 3. preterit, preterite 4. inveterate.

ET'ful-i- 3. fretfully 4. forgetfully, regretfully.

ET'ful-ness- 3. fretfulness 4. forgetfulness, regretfulness.

ETH'er-i- 3. feathery, heathery, leathery, tethery, weathery.

ETH'er-ing- 3. feathering, leathering, tethering, weathering 4. untethering.

ETH'i-kal- 3. ethical 4. nonethical, unethical.

ETH'less-li- 3. deathlessly, breathlessly.

ETH'less-ness- 3. deathlessness, breathlessness.

ET'i-kal- 4. ascetical, prophetical, pathetical, synthetical, hermetical, cosmetical, planetical, genetical, threnetical, noetical, poetical, syncretical, heretical 5. alphabetical, diabetical, exegetical, energetical, catechetical, apathetical, metathetical, epithetical, antithetical, parenthetical, nomothetical, hyperthetical, homiletical, arithmetical, unpoetical 6. apologetical, antipathetical, homogenetical.

ET'i–ness– 3. jettiness, pettiness, sweatiness.

ET'i–nu– 3. detinue, retinue.

ET'ish–li– 3. pettishly 4. coquettishly.

ET'ish–ness– 3. pettishness 4. coquettishness.

ET'i–sizm– 4. athleticism, phoneticism, asceticism, aestheticism.

ET'i–tiv– 3. vetitive 4. repetitive, competitive 5. noncompetitive, uncompetitive.

ET'ri–fi– 3. metrify, petrify.

ET'ri–kal– 3. metrical 4. symmetrical, nonmetrical, unmetrical, obstetrical 5. diametrical, dynametrical, heptametrical, hexametrical, perimetrical, asymmetrical, pedometrical, geometrical, stichometrical, graphometrical, biometrical, thermometrical, clinometrical, chronometrical, barometrical, hydrometrical, horometrical, isometrical 6. craniometrical, trigonometrical, electrometrical 7. isoperimetrical.

ET'ri–ment– 3. detriment.

EV'a–lent– 3. prevalent 4. unprevalent.

EV'el–er– 3. beveler, deviler, leveler, reveler.

EV'el–ing– 3. beveling, deviling, leveling, reveling 4. bedeviling, disheveling.

EV'el–ment– 3. devilment, revelment 4. bedevilment, dishevelment.

EV'el–ri– 3. devilry, revelry.

EV'er–ans– 3. reverence, severance 4. irreverence, disseverance.

EV'er–er– 3. leverer, cleverer, severer 4. endeavorer.

EV'er–est– 3. Everest, cleverest.

EV'er–et– 3. Everett, leveret.

EV'er–ij– 3. beverage, leverage.

EV'er–ing– 3. severing 4. endeavoring.

EV'i–ti– 3. levity, brevity 4. longevity.

EV'o–lens– 4. benevolence, malevolence 5. unbenevolence.

EV'o–lent– 4. benevolent, malevolent 5. unbenevolent.

EV'o–lus– 4. benevolous, malevolous.

EV'o–lut– 3. evolute, devolute, revolute.

EZ'ant–ri– 3. pheasantry, pleasantry, peasantry.

EZH'er–er– 3. pleasurer, measurer, treasurer.

EZH'er–ing– 3. pleasuring, measuring, treasuring.

EZ'i–dens– 3. residents, residence, presidents 4. vice-presidents.

EZ'i–dent– 3. resident, president 4. nonresident, vice-president.

EZ'i–tant– 3. hesitant 4. unhesitant.

EZ'o–nant– 3. resonant 4. unresonant.

I (eye)

1.

SINGLE (MASCULINE) RHYMES IN I (eye)

Primary or Secondary Accent Falls on Last Syllable; Imperfect Rhymes Are in Italics.

I– 1. i, I, ay, aye, ai, eye 2. *redeye, frog-eye, black-eye, black eye, pink-eye, cockeye, buckeye, peepeye, fisheye, cat's-eye, oxeye* 3. weather eye.

BI– 1. by, bye, buy 2. good-bye, bye-bye, *go-by, hereby, thereby, whereby,* forby, foreby 3. by-and-by, rockaby, lullaby, hushaby, by the by, by the bye, underbuy, overbuy, alibi, passer-by, incubi.

DI– 1. die, dye 2. bedye, redye, undye.

FI– 1. fie, phi 2. defy, fie-fie [coll.] 3. labefy, tabefy, tumefy, tepefy, stupefy, arefy, rarefy, torrefy, putrefy, pinguefy, liquefy, verbify, rubify, ladify, edify, nidify, dandify, mundify, codify, modify, deify, preachify [coll.], speechify, Frenchify, churchify, mythify, qualify, steelify, vilify, jellify, mollify, nullify, amplify, simplify, duplify, ramify, mummify, humify, sanify, magnify, dignify, minify, damnify, bonify, carnify, unify, torpify, typify, scarify, clarify, lubrify, micrify, spherify, verify, terrify, nigrify, horrify, glorify, petrify, nitrify, vitrify, aurify, purify, pacify, specify, calcify, classify, falsify, ossify, rectify, versify, crucify, ratify, gratify, sanctify, fructify, stultify, quantify, daintify, notify, certify, fortify, mortify, testify, justify, mystify, prettify, beautify, sanguify, vivify, satisfy, argufy [coll. & dial.], ladyfy, monkeyfy 4. syllabify, decalcify, remodify, disqualify, exemplify, divinify, indemnify, personify, saccharify, transmogrify, electrify, objectify, emulsify, beatify, identify, revivify, complexify 5. diabolify.

GI– 1. guy, Guy 2. fall guy, wise guy [both slang].

HI– 1. hie, high, heigh, hi [slang] 2. knee-high, sky-high.

KI– 1. chi, sky, Skye 2. haikai, kai-kai, ensky, blue sky 3. starry sky.

LI– 1. lie, lye, cly [cant], fly, ply, sly 2. ally, *Ely,* belie, rely, outlie, *dayfly, bobfly, gadfly, gallfly, jarfly, firefly, horsefly, housefly, botfly, shoofly,* apply, reply, imply, comply, supply, unsly, July 3. really, alkaly, disally, misally, dragonfly, butterfly, reapply, misapply, multiply, reimply, underlie, overlie, lazuli 4. oversupply 5. lapis lazuli.

MI– 1. my 2. demi, demy.

NI– 1. nigh, nye, sny 2. deny, well-nigh 3. redeny, termini, *alumni.*

PI– 1. pi, pie, spy 2. *magpie, nanpie, mincepie, potpie,* espy, bespy 3. humble pie, apple pie, occupy 4. preoccupy.

RI– 1. rye, wry, dry, fry, gri, gry [both Gypsy], cry, scry, pry, spry, try 2. awry, adry, *roughdry, fish fry,* decry, descry, *outcry,* atry.

SI– 1. sigh, scye 2. *armscye, Versailles* 3. prophesy.

SHI– 1. shy 2. unshy.

TI– 1. tie, ty, tye, Tai, Thai, sty, stye 2. *hogtie,* untie, *necktie, pigsty.*

THI– **1.** thigh, thy.

VI– **1.** vie **2.** outvie.

WI– **1.** y, Y, wye, Wye, why.

IB– **1.** gibe, jibe, kibe, libe [slang], bribe, scribe, tribe **2.** imbibe, ascribe, subscribe, describe, prescribe, transcribe, inscribe, conscribe, proscribe, perscribe **3.** circumscribe, superscribe, diatribe.

IBD– **1.** gibed, jibed, kibed, bribed **2.** imbibed, ascribed, subscribed, described, prescribed, transcribed, inscribed, conscribed, proscribed, perscribed **3.** circumscribed, superscribed.

IBZ– gibes etc., *see* **IB–** gibe etc. above, plus "s" or " 's."

ID– **1.** ide, I'd, eyed, bide, chide, died, dyed, guide, guyed, hide, Hyde, lied, Clyde, glide, slide, nide, snide, pied, spied, ride, bride, cried, scried, dried, gride, pride, pried, tried, stride, side, sighed, tide, tied, vied, wide **2.** *red-eyed, calf-eyed, pie-eyed, black-eyed, snake-eyed, meek-eyed, pink-eyed, cock-eyed, hawk-eyed, pale-eyed, wall-eyed, owl-eyed, dull-eyed, green-eyed, pop-eyed, blear-eyed, clear-eyed, cat-eyed, soft-eyed, squint-eyed, blue-eyed, dove-eyed, lynx-eyed, ox-eyed,* abide, carbide, redyed, defied, sulphide, confide, misguide, *rawhide, cowhide, bromide,* denied, espied, arride, child bride, undried, *hydride,* deride, descried, *boride, chloride, nitride,* night ride, untried, astride, bestride, outstride, outride, aside, *wayside,* subside, *bedside, broadside,* beside, decide, *seaside,* reside, preside, offside, *lakeside, brookside, hillside,* inside, *topside, fireside, foreside, white-side,* outside, *excide, ebb tide, flood tide, high tide, low tide, neap tide,* betide, retied, *Yuletide, springtide, noon tide, Shrovetide,* divide, provide, world-wide **3.** iodide, almond-eyed, bonafide, tumefied, tepefied, stupefied, rarefied, torrefied, putrefied, liquefied, pacified, specified, calcified, dulcified, crucified, edified, modified, deified, qualified, mollified, nullified, magnified, dignified, bonified, evrified, glorified, terrified, petrified, vitrified, purified, falsified, versified, ossified, ratified, gratified, stratified, rectified, sanctified, fructified, stultified, notified, certified, fortified, mortified, testified, justified, mystified, beautified, vivified, satisfied, disulphide, eagle-eyed, goggle-eyed, evil-eyed, unallied, misallied, unbelied, unapplied, misapplied, multiplied, cyanide, arsenide, occupied, saccharide, fluoride, override, telluride, prophesied, Barmecide, alongside, herbicide, verbicide, regicide, fungicide, homicide, germicide, vermicide, lapicide, parricide, matricide, patricide, fratricide, countryside, vaticide, suicide, larvicide, slickenside, oceanside, mountainside, coincide, glucoside, peroxide, genocide, underside, waterside, riverside, unbetide, eventide, Whitsuntide, Hallowtide, undertide, Eastertide, Lammastide, Christmastide, subdivide, nation-wide **4.** microbicide, tyrannicide, sororicide, uxoricide, insecticide, infanticide, giganticide, parenticide, liberticide, nematocide, decalcified, solidified, unqualified, saponified, unverified, electrified, emulsified, intensified, diversified, beatified, unsanctified, identified, revivified, dissatisfied, formaldehyde, preoccupied, unoccupied, Allhallowtide, Michaelmastide **5.** parasiticide.

IDZ– ides etc., *see* **ID–** ide etc. above, plus "s" or " 's"; **3.** Ironsides, sobersides.

IF– **1.** fife, kife [slang], life, knife, rife, strife, wife **2.** *jackknife, midwife, oldwife, goodwife, alewife, housewife, fishwife* **3.** afterlife, bowie knife, pocket knife, puddingwife.

IJ– **1.** Lige, 'blige **2.** oblige **3.** reoblige, disoblige.

IK– **1.** Ike, bike, dike, fyke, hike [coll.], haik, Haikh, like, Mike, mike [slang], Smike, pike, pyke, spike, grike, shrike, trike [slang], strike, sike, tyke, tike, wike [obs.] **2.** Vandyke, *hitchhike* [slang], alike, *seedlike, childlike, godlike,* belike, *lifelike,* *wifelike, flamelike, homelike, dovelike, elflike, kinglike, winglike, manlike, swanlike, queenlike, hornlike,* unlike, *apelike, earlike, starlike, warlike, airlike,* dislike, mislike, *catlike, ghostlike, deathlike, toothlike, earthlike, screwlike, rampike, turnpike* **3.** unalike, womanlike, tigerlike, Quakerlike, fatherlike, motherlike, brotherlike, sisterlike, peasantlike, ladylike, fairylike, marlinspike.

IKS– dikes etc., *see* **IK–** Ike etc. above, plus "s" or " 's."

IL– **1.** aisle, isle, I'll, bile, file, guile, gyle, Heil, chyle, lisle, mile, smile, Nile, pile, spile, rile, tile, stile, style, vile, wile, weil, while **2.** Kabyle, defile, *profile,* beguile, enisle, *senile,* repile, compile, unpile, resile, *exile,* ensile, *centile, gentile, reptile, septile, fertile, turnstile, hostile, futile, rutile,* revile, awhile, meanwhile, erstwhile, worthwhile, therewhile **3.** atrabile, crocodile, photofile, Francophile, rheophile, theophile, ergophile, halophile, Anglophile, Gallophile, thermophile, Sinophile, hippophile, typophile, psychrophile, Negrophile, gastrophile, pyrophile, mesophile, Russophile, Slavophile, camomile, juvenile, recompile, thermopile, domicile, reconcile, volatile, vibratile, versatile, mercantile, infantile, decastyle, pentastyle, peristyle, monostyle, polystyle, otherwhile **4.** Italophile, aelurophile, dodecastyle.

ILD– **1.** aisled, child, filed, mild, smiled, piled, spiled, styled, wild, whiled **2.** *grandchild, godchild,* defiled, beguiled, enisled, compiled, self-styled, reviled.

ILZ– aisles etc., *see* **IL–** aisle etc. above, plus "s" or " 's."

IM– **1.** I'm, chime, dime, disme, chyme, lime, clime, climb, slime, mime, rhyme, grime, crime, prime, sime, cyme, time, thyme, zyme **2.** sublime, *birdlime, quicklime, brooklime,* beslime, berhyme, begrime, *daytime, playtime, bedtime,* betime, *lifetime, springtime,* meantime, *noontime,* sometime, mistime **3.** paradigm, maritime, pantomime, summertime, aftertime, overtime.

IMD– **1.** chimed, limed, climbed, mimed, rhymed, primed, timed **2.** berhymed, unrhymed, well-timed, ill-timed.

IMZ– chimes etc., *see* **IM–** chime etc. above, plus "s" or " 's"; **2.** betimes, sometimes, ofttimes **3.** oftentimes.

IN– **1.** eyn, eyne [both arch. & dial.], ein [G.], bine, chine, dine, dyne, fine, kine [arch. & dial.], line, spline, mine, nine, pine, spine, Rhine, brine, shrine, trine, sine, tsine, shine, tine, Tyne, stein, thine, vine, wine, swine, twine, whine **2.** *Sabine, woodbine,* combine, *carbine, turbine, Aldine,* indign, condign, *nundine,* define, refine, confine, trephine, porcine, aline, align, malign, *saline, headline, beeline, tapeline, fishline, carline, airline, hairline, crossline, outline, bowline,* decline, recline, incline, feline, moline, *cauline, Pauline, damine, gold mine, carmine, canine, ranine,* benign, *quinine,* repine, *Alpine, vulpine,* opine, *vespine, lupine, supine, cedrine, ferine,* enshrine, *caprine, Petrine, murrhine,* assign, design, resign, piscine, calcine, langsyne, sinsyne, consign, *cosine, phocine, hircine, ursine,* beshine, *shoeshine, moonshine, sunshine,* outshine, *equine,* divine, *ovine, bovine, cervine, corvine,* entwine **3.** cannabine, columbine, concubine, muscadine, monodyne, anodyne, hirundine, paludine, superfine, realign, alkaline, tourmaline, sepaline, opaline, disalign, petaline, hyaline, disincline, monocline, angeline, musteline, aniline, aquiline, inquiline, caballine, coralline, metalline, crystalline, suilline, sibylline, berylline, Caroline, underline, interline, figuline, Ursuline, vituline, sycamine, calamine, calcimine, undermine, countermine, asinine, leonine, pavonine, eburnine, saturnine, elapine, porcupine, catarrhine, saccharine, viperine, anserine, passerine, riverine, peregrine, sapphirine, viberrine, platyrrhine, lemurine, azurine, soricine, reconsign, undersign, countersign, monkeyshine [slang], palatine, cisplatine, anatine, infantine, Constantine, argentine, Argentine, valentine, serpentine, turpentine, Aventine, lacertine, Palestine, Celestine, Ernestine, Philistine, brandywine, interwine, Auld Lang Syne 4. incarnadine, heterodyne, antalkaline, Evangeline, Capitoline, accipitrine, elephantine, hyacinthine, labyrinthine, aberdevine.

IND– 1. bind, dined, find, fined, hind, kind, lined, blind, mind, pined, rynd, rind, rined, grind, signed, tined, vined, wind, twined, whined 2. combined, unbind, *bearbind*, defined, refined, ahind, behind, mankind, unkind, aligned, maligned, unlined, declined, reclined, inclined, purblind, opined, *millrynd*, unwind, entwined 3. undefined, unrefined, unconfined, gavelkind, womankind, humankind, realigned, disinclined, color-blind, underlined, interlined, undermined, master mind, unresigned, undersigned, countersigned, interwind, intertwined 4. incarnadined.

INT– 1. jint [dial.], pint 2. ahint, behint [both Scot. & N. of Eng.], half pint.

INTS– 1. Heintz, pints 2. half pints.

INZ– dines etc., *see* **IN–** eyn etc. above, plus "s" or "'s."

IP– 1. hipe, kipe, hyp [dial.], slipe [Scot. & dial.], slype, snipe, pipe, ripe, gripe, tripe, stripe, type, stipe, vipe [slang], wipe, wype, swipe 2. *pitchpipe*, *windpipe*, *bagpipe*, *hornpipe*, *blowpipe*, *rareripe*, unripe, retype, *ectype*, *tintype*, *piewipe*, *sideswipe* 3. guttersnipe, overripe, megatype, teletype, antitype, linotype, phototype 4. stereotype 5. daguerreotype.

IPS– hipes etc., *see* **IP–** hipe etc. above, plus "s" or "'s."

IPT– 1. hiped, sliped [Scot. & dial.], sniped, piped, griped, striped, typed, stiped, wiped, swiped 2. retyped, *sideswiped* 4. stereotyped.

IR– 1. ire, byre, dire, fire, hire, gyre, lyre, mire, pyre, pyr, spire, sire, shire, tire, Tyre, wire, quire, choir, squire 2. afire, *backfire*, *blackfire*, *needfire*, *wildfire*, *hell-fire*, *shellfire*, *bonfire*, misfire, *spitfire*, rehire, admire, bemire, aspire, respire, expire, transpire, inspire, conspire, perspire, suspire, *grandsire*, desire, *gudesire*, *belsire*, attire, retire, envire, barbwire, rewire, unwire, acquire, require, inquire, esquire 3. overtire; *see* also **I'er–** eyer etc.

IRD– 1. fired, hired, mired, spired, sired, tired, wired, squired 2. backfired, misfired, admired, bemired, aspired, respired, expired, transpired, inspired, conspired, perspired, desired, attired, retired, rewired, acquired, required, inquired 3. overtired, uninspired.

IS– 1. ice, bice, dice, lice, splice, slice, mice, nice, gneiss, pice, spice, speiss, rice, rais, grice, price, trice, thrice, sice, syce, vice, vise, twice 2. suffice, resplice, *titmice*, bespice, *allspice*, reprice, precise, concise, entice, advice, device 3. paradise, sacrifice, overnice, camphor ice, edelweiss.

IST– 1. iced, diced, feist [loc.], Geist [G.], spliced, riced, Christ, priced 2. uniced, Weltgeist [G.], Zeitgeist [G.], bespiced, repriced, enticed 3. poltergeist, antichrist 4. emparadised.

IT– 1. ite [slang], bite, bight, dite, dight, fight, hight, height, kite, skite [dial.], light, lite [slang], blight, blite, flight, plight, slight, sleight, mite, might, smite, night, knight, snite [Scot. & dial.], spite, rite, right, write, wright, bright, fright, krait, sprite, trite, sight, site, cite, tight, tite [dial.], wight, quite, white 2. *Sadite*, bedight, *lyddite*, *endite*, indict, indite, condite, *podite*, *cordite*, sea fight, *graphite*, *cockfight*, *bullfight*, *sulphite*, *ophite*, *Ophite*, *turfite*, fist fight, *Shiite*, alight, *halite*, *daylight*, red light, *floodlight*, delight, relight, *twilight*, *skylight*, *stylite*, green light, *moonlight*, *sunlight*, *go-light*, polite, *lamplight*, *hoplite*, *stoplight*, *marlite*, *starlite*, flashlight, *footlight*, *Hamite*, *Semite*, *bromite*, *somite*, *termite*, *Danite*, *Tanite*, *midnight*, good night, benight, beknight, ignite, *lignite*, *ichnite*, *finite*, *crinite*, *Stannite*, *sennight*, unknight, *Sunnite*, tonight, *bornite*, *fortnight*, unite, despite, aright, *barite*, *playwright*, *dendrite*, *bookwright*, *wheelwright*, downright, *shipwright*, upright, *cartwright*, outright, birthright, forthright, *plowwright*, *pyrite*, eyebright, affright, contrite, attrite, eyesight, accite, *calcite*, *felsite*, *insight*, incite, *townsite*, *foresight*, excite, *latite*, *ratite*, *partite*, airtight, requite, *Levite*, invite, *Servite*, bobwhite, snow-white, lintwhite, *quartzite* **3.** Rechabite, Moabite, Jacobite, Niobite, trilobite, cenobite, anthracite, boracite, plebiscite, extradite, expedite, recondite, incondite, troglodyte, erudite, hanifite, epiphyte, neophyte, lithophyte, dermophyte, zoophyte, microphyte, hydrophyte, aerophyte, mesophyte, ectophyte, entophyte, Fahrenheit, malachite, hyalite, corallite, crystallite, Ishmaelite, Israelite, proselyte, candlelight, satellite, nephelite, Carmelite, ampelite, menilite, acolyte, impolite, zoolite, chrysolite, Loyolite, kimberlite, spherulite, lazulite, Adamite, Gothamite, calamite, Elamite, Islamite, dynamite, wolframite, Hiramite, Moslemite, eremite, stalagmite, hellgrammite, Edomite, dolomite, widow's mite, vulcanite, manganite, melanite, Canaanite, sylvanite, reignite, ebonite, aconite, Mammonite, Maronite, overnight, day and night, reunite, disunite, Sybarite, Lazarite, siderite, dolerite, copyright, anchorite, Laborite, Minorite, underwrite, overwrite, azurite, lazurite, marcasite, pargasite, parasite, leucocyte, phagocyte, oversight, second sight, hematite, stalactite, magnetite, appetite, tripartite, celestite, Ballistite, muscovite **4.** meropodite, Amalekite, Ishmaelite, Israelite, Raphaelite, gastrophilite, toxophilite, monophylite, theodolite, cosmopolite, siderolite, novaculite, ventriculite, Bethlehemite, labradorite, meteorite, Monophysite, Dyophysite.

ĪTH– **1.** lithe, blithe, writhe, sithe, scythe, tithe, stythe, withe.

ĪTHD– **1.** writhed, scythed, tithed, withed.

ĪTS– bites etc., *see* **ĪT–** bite etc. above, plus "s" or " 's."

ĪV– **1.** I've, chive, dive, five, hive, gyve, jive [slang], skive, live, clive, rive, drive, shrive, strive, thrive, shive, stive [Scot. & dial. Eng.], wive **2.** redive, *high dive*, *swan dive*, *nose dive*, ungyve, *ogive*, *beehive*, alive, connive, arrive, derive, deprive, contrive, revive, convive, survive **3.** overdrive.

ĪVD– **1.** dived, hived, gyved, skived, knived, rived, shrived, strived, thrived, shived, stived, wived **2.** long-lived, short-lived, connived, arrived, derived, deprived, contrived, revived, survived.

ĪVZ– chives, etc., *see* **ĪV–** chive, etc. above, plus "s" or " 's"; **1.** Ives **2.** St. Ives.

ĪZ– i's, ayes etc., *see* **Ī–** i etc. through **WĪ–** y etc. above, plus "s" or " 's"; **1.** guise, rise, prize, prise, size, sice, vise, wise **2.** sheep's eyes, *brighteyes*, disguise, demise, remise, premise, *bromize*, surmise, despise, arise, *moonrise*, *sunrise*, apprise, reprise, emprise, comprise, uprise, misprize, surprise, assize, resize, excise, incise, capsize, baptize, chastise, advise, devise, revise, *sidewise*, *endwise*, *edgewise*, *likewise*, *clockwise*, unwise, *nowise*, *crosswise* **3.** Judaize, archaize, Hebraize, hybridize, iridize, chloridize, subsidize, liquidize, oxidize, gormandize, aggrandize, iodize, melodize, psalmodize, rhapsodize, standardize, jeopardize, elegize, syllogize, eulogize, energize, catechize, empathize, sympathize, verbalize, feudalize, legalize, racialize, specialize, socialize, martialize, alkalize, penalize, signalize, journalize, papalize, opalize, moralize, centralize, neutralize, vitalize, tantalize, dualize, equalize, royalize, obelize, angeleyes, novelize, stabilize, sterilize, fossilize, fertilize, utilize, tranquilize, civilize, metallize, crystallize, symbolize, idolize, fabulize, formulize, euphemize, itemize, minimize, pilgrimize, victimize, compromise, presurmise, urbanize, vulcanize, paganize, mechanize, Christianize, Romanize, Germanize, humanize, galvanize, heathenize, Hellenize, recognize, pollinize, feminize, Latinize, glutinize, scrutinize, solemnize, tyrannize, ebonize, carbonize, agonize, symphonize, euphonize, unionize, lionize, fractionize, colonize, demonize, harmonize, sermonize, canonize, synchronize, patronize, platonize, peptonize, modernize, fraternize, immunize, communize, syncopize, philippize, barbarize, vulgarize, plagiarize, burglarize, summarize, notarize, mercerize, tenderize, etherize, mesmerize, pauperize, cauterize, pulverize, satirize, theorize, authorize, memorize, vaporize, temporize, terrorize, proctorize, enterprise, pasteurize, sulphurize, martyrize, emphasize, synthesize, ostracize, laicize, ethicize, Gothicize, publicize, Anglicize, Gallicize, Sinicize, classicize, criticize, synopsize, exorcise, dramatize, pragmatize, dogmatize, magnetize, monetize, sensitize, narcotize, egotize, iotize, hypnotize, amortize, deputize, colloquize, zigzagwise, anywise, corner wise, weather-wise, otherwise **4.** italicize, catholicize, politicize, domesticize, deoxidize, apostrophize, theosophize, philosophize, radicalize, provincialize, commercialize, substantialize, potentialize, decimalize, nationalize, rationalize, sectionalize, personalize, liberalize, federalize, generalize, demoralize, decentralize, naturalize, capitalize, devitalize, immortalize, visualize, actualize, ritualize, mutualize, sexualize, evangelize, caramelize, solubilize, diabolize, metabolize, monopolize, macadamize, epitomize, dehumanize, rejuvenize, antagonize, philanthropize, misanthropize, plagiarize, familiarize, circularize, regularize, singularize, formularize, popularize, militarize, characterize, deodorize, allegorize, categorize, extemporize, desulphurize, panegyrize, metastasize, hypostasize, parenthesize, emblematize, systematize, acclimatize, democratize, apostatize, alphabetize, anesthetize, demagnetize, demonetize, desensitize, Protestantize, proselytize, contrariwise **5.** phenomenalize, professionalize, denationalize, irrationalize, conventionalize, impersonalize, denaturalize, spiritualize, Americanize, deoxygenize, platitudinize, attitudinize, revolutionize, particularize, apotheosize, anathematize, legitimatize **6.** testimonialize, participialize, internationalize, institutionalize, constitutionalize, individualize, cosmopolitanize.

IZD– **1.** prized, sized, wised [slang] **2.** disguised, demised, surmised, despised, apprised, comprised, surprised, incised, capsized, baptized, chastised, advised, devised, revised; *also past tense of all verbs ending in verbal suffix "-ize"* (*see* Judaize etc. above).

I (eye)

2.

DOUBLE (FEMININE) RHYMES IN I (li'ar)

Primary or Secondary Accent Falls on Next to Last Syllable; Imperfect Rhymes Are in Italics.

I'a– 2. ayha, dia, pia, chria, praya, stria, via, Zia **3.** Tobiah, Sophia, Thalia, Maria, latria, Uriah, messiah, Josiah, Isaiah, Keziah **4.** Obadiah, Zebediah, asaphia, Hezekiah, Jeremiah, Black Maria, Zachariah, callisteia **5.** hyperdulia, Hippodamia, Iphigenia.

I'ad– 2. dyad, Pleiad, naiad, dryad, triad **4.** jeremiad, hamadryad.

I'adz– dyads etc., *see* **I'ad–** dyad etc. above, plus "s" or "'s"; 2. Hyads.

I'ak– 2. Dyak, kayak, guaiac **4.** elegiac.

I'al– 2. dial, phial, gayal, myall, pial, spial, ryal, trial, vial, viol **3.** sundial, defial, supplial, denial, genial, espial, decrial, retrial, mistrial, bass viol **4.** self-denial, intrapial, interstrial.

I'am– 2. I am, lyam, Priam, Siam.

I'amb– 2. iamb **3.** diiamb.

I'an– 2. Ian, Chian, Ryan, Bryan **3.** thalian, genian, Orion **4.** Jeremian; *see* also **I'on–** ion etc. below.

I'ans– 2. fiance [obs.], science **3.** affiance, defiance, alliance, reliance, appliance, compliance, suppliance **4.** misalliance, self-reliance, incompliance, noncompliance; *see* also **I'ants–** fiants etc. below.

I'ant– 2. fiant, giant, client, pliant, riant, Bryant, scient **3.** affiant, defiant, reliant, appliant, repliant, compliant **4.** self-reliant, uncompliant.

I'ants– fiants etc., *see* **I'ant–** fiant etc. above plus "s" or "'s."

I'ar– 2. liar, briar, friar; *see* also **I'er–** eyer etc. below.

I'as– 2. eyas, bias, Lias, drias, Trias **3.** unbias, Tobias, Elias, Messias, Josias, Marrhias **4.** Jeremias, Ananias; *see* also **I'us–** pious etc. below.

I'at– fiat; *see* also **I'et–** diet etc. below.

IB'al– 2. Bible, libel, scribal, tribal **4.** intertribal.

IB'eks– 2. ibex, vibex.

IB'er– 2. fiber, giber, liber, Liber, briber, scriber, Tiber **3.** imbiber, subscriber, describer, prescriber, transcriber, inscriber, proscriber **4.** circumscriber.

IB'ing– 2. gibing, jibing, bribing, scribing **3.** imbibing, ascribing, subscribing, describing, prescribing, transcribing, inscribing, conscribing, proscribing, perscribing **4.** circumscribing, superscribing.

IB'l– 2. Bible, libel, scribal, tribal **3.** intertribal.

IB'ol– 2. eyeball, highball, fly ball.

IB'rant– 2. vibrant.

IB'rat– 2. librate, vibrate **4.** equilibrate.

IB'rid– 2. hybrid, Librid **4.** polyhybrid.

ICH'us– 2. righteous **3.** unrighteous **4.** superrighteous, overrighteous.

ID'a– 2. Ida, Haida, Lida, cnida, Vida **3.** Oneida.

ID'al– 2. bridal, tidal **3.** cotidal **4.** regicidal, fungicidal, homicidal, germicidal, vermicidal, parricidal, matricidal, patricidal, fratricidal, septicidal, suicidal **5.** tyrannicidal, sororicidal, insecticidal, infanticidal; *see* also **ID'l–** idle etc. below.

ID'ans– 2. guidance **3.** abidance, misguidance, subsidence.

ID'ed– 2. bided, chided, guided, glided, prided, sided, tided, tidied **3.** abided, confided, misguided, elided, collided, derided, decided, lopsided, one-sided, both-sided, two-sided, betided, divided, presided **4.** undecided, many-sided, coincided, subdivided, unprovided.

ID'en– 2. Leyden, Dryden, widen **3.** rewiden; *see* also **ID'on–** guidon etc. below.

ID'ent– 2. bident, rident, trident, strident **3.** subsident.

ID'er– 2. eider, bider, chider, guider, hider, glider, slider, nidor, spider, rider, strider, stridor, sider, cider, wider **3.** abider, confider, misguider, backslider, derider, roughrider, outrider, decider, insider, East-sider, outsider, provider, resider, presider **4.** coincider, subdivider.

ID'est– 2. piedest, widest.

ID'ful– 2. prideful.

ID'i– 2. didy, Friday, sidy, tidy, vide **3.** untidy **4.** bonafide.

ID'ij– 2. guidage, hidage, sideage.

ID'il– 2. idyl, idyll.

ID'ing– 2. biding, chiding, guiding, hiding, gliding, sliding, niding, riding, priding, striding, siding, tiding **3.** abiding, confiding, misguiding, eliding, colliding, *backsliding*, deriding, subsiding, betiding, dividing, providing, residing, presiding **4.** law-abiding, coinciding, redividing, subdividing.

ID'ingz– 2. ridings, sidings, tidings.

ID'l– 2. idle, idol, bridle, bridal, sidle, tidal **3.** unbridle; *see* also **ID'al–** bridal etc. above.

ID'led– 2. idled, bridled, sidled **3.** unbridled.

ID'ler– 2. idler, bridler, sidler.

ID'less– 2. guideless, rideless, brideless, sideless, tideless **4.** suicideless.

ID'li– 2. idly. bridely, widely.

ID'ling– 2. idling, bridling, sidling **3.** unbridling.

ID'ness– 2. piedness, wideness.

ID'o– 2. Dido, dido, Fido.

ID'on– 2. guidon, Sidon **3.** Poseidon; *see* also **ID'en–** Leyden etc. above.

ID'or– 2. nidor, stridor; *see* also **ID'er–** eider etc. above.

ID'rat– 2. hydrate **3.** dehydrate **4.** carbohydrate.

ID'us– 2. Didus, Midas, nidus.

I'ens– 2. clients, science; *see* also **I'ans–** fiance etc. above.

I'ent– 2. client, scient; *see* also **I'ant–** fiant etc. above.

I'er– 2. eyer, buyer, dyer, dier, higher, liar, lier, flier, flyer, plier, plyer, slyer, nigher, spyer, wrier, briar, brier, drier, friar, fryer, frier, crier, prier, pryer, prior, spryer, trier, trior, sigher, shier, tier, vier **3.** defier, applier, implier, complier, supplier, denier, greenbrier, sweetbrier, decrier, descrier **4.** stupefier, liquefier, speechifier, edifier, modifier, deifier, vilifier, qualifier, amplifier, simplifier, nullifier, ramifier, dignifier, signifier, unifier, typifier, clarifier, terrifier, verifier, glorifier, classifier, pacifier, falsifier, versifier, crucifier, ratifier, gratifier, rectifier, sanctifier, certifier, fortifier, testifier, justifier, beautifier, satisfier, multiplier, underlier, occupier, prophesier **5.** disqualifier, exemplifier, indemnifier, personifier, calorifier, intensifier, diversifier, identifier.

I'ern– 2. iron **3.** sadiron, gridiron, andiron, flatiron **4.** grappling iron, curling iron.

I'est– 2. highest, slyest, nighest, wriest, driest, shyest, spryest, shiest.

I'et– 2. diet, fiat, piet, riot, quiet **3.** inquiet, unquiet, disquiet; *see* also **I'ot–** eyot etc. below.

IF'a– 2. Haifa, typha.

IF'en– 2. hyphen, siphon, Typhon.

IF'er– 2. bifer, fifer, lifer, knifer, rifer, cipher, sypher 3. decipher.

IF'est– 2. rifest.

IF'id– 2. bifid, trifid.

IF'ing– 2. fifing, knifing, wifing.

IF'l– 2. Eiffel, rifle, trifle, stifle.

IF'ler– 2. rifler, trifler, stifler.

IF'less– 2. fifeless, lifeless, knifeless, strifeless, wifeless.

IF'li– 2. rifely, wifely 3. *housewifely.*

IF'lik– 2. lifelike, knifelike, wifelike.

IF'ling– 2. rifling, trifling, stifling.

IG'a– 2. biga, striga, saiga 3. quadriga.

IG'al– 2. pygal, zygal.

IG'at– 2. ligate, strigate.

IG'er– 2. geiger, tiger.

I'glas– 2. eyeglass, spyglass.

I'glif– 2. diglyph, triglyph 4. monotriglyph.

IG'o– 3. caligo, fuligo [L.], lentigo, vertigo 4. impetigo.

IG'rant– 2. migrant 3. transmigrant.

IG'ress– 2. tigress, Tigris.

I'i– 2. eyey, skyey, criey.

I'id– 2. sly-eyed, pie-eyed, dry-eyed.

I'ing– 2. eyeing, buying, bying, dying, dyeing, guying, hieing, skying, lying, flying, plying, pieing, piing, spying, drying, frying, crying, prying, trying, sighing, shying, tying, stying, vying 3. undying, defying, allying, belying, relying, applying, replying, implying, complying, supplying, outlying, denying, espying, decrying, descrying, outcrying, outsighing, untying, outvying 4. alibiing, stupefying, putrefying, liquefying, edifying, dandifying, modifying, deifying, preachifying [coll.], speechifying, qualifying, vilifying, mollifying, nullifying, amplifying, simplifying, ramifying, magnifying, dignifying, signifying, unifying, typifying, clarifying, terrifying, verifying, horrifying, glorifying, petrifying, purifying, classifying, pacifying, specifying, falsifying, versifying, crucifying, ratifying, gratifying, rectifying, stultifying, notifying, certifying, fortifying, prettifying, mortifying, testifying, mystifying, justifying, beautifying, vivifying, satisfying, argufying [coll. & dial.], multiplying, occupying, prophesying 5. solidifying, disqualifying, exemplifying, humanifying, indemnifying, personifying, emulsifying, electrifying, objectifying, beatifying, identifying, revivifying, self-satisfying, unsatisfying, oversupplying, preoccupying.

I'ish– 2. slyish, dryish, shyish.

IJ'a– 3. Abijah, Elijah 4. Jehudijah.

IJ'er– 2. Niger 3. obliger.

IJ'ing– 2. obliging 4. unobliging, disobliging.

IK'a– 2. plica, mica, Micah, pica, pika, spica, Spika, styca 3. nagaika, lorica, vesica [L.] 4. balalaika, hydromica.

IK'al– 2. plical, Michal, Michael, pical 4. interplical.

IK'at– 2. plicate, spicate.

IK'en– 2. liken, lichen 3. unliken, disliken, misliken.

IK'er– 2. ichor, diker, hiker [coll.], liker, piker, spiker, striker 3. *hitchhiker* [slang], disliker.

IK'i– 2. ikey, piky, spiky, Psyche 4. phytopsyche.

IK'ik– 2. psychic 3. nonpsychic, unpsychic.

IK'ing– 2. diking, liking, piking, spiking, striking, viking 3. hitchhiking [slang], disliking, misliking.

IK'l– 2. Michael, pical, cycle, psychal 3. recycle, bicycle, tricycle 4. interplical, hemicycle, epicycle, monocycle, multicycle, motorcycle.

IK'li– 2. likely 3. belikely, unlikely.

IK'lik– 2. cyclic 3. acyclic, bicyclic, encyclic 4. polycyclic, epicyclic.

IK'ling– 2. cycling 3. bicycling 4. motorcycling.

IK'on– 2. icon.

IK'us– 2. Ficus, Picus, spicous 3. anticous, anticus [L.], posticous, posticus [L.] 4. umbilicus, Andronicus.

IL'a– 2. Ila, Hyla, Lila, pyla 3. strobila, Delilah.

IL'aks– 2. lilacs, smilax.

IL'and– 2. island, highland, Thailand 3. Rhode Island, Long Island.

IL'ar– 2. filar, pilar, stylar 3. bifilar, trifilar; *see* also **IL'er**– filer etc. below.

IL'ark– 2. phylarch, skylark.

ILD'er– 2. milder, wilder.

ILD'est– 2. mildest, wildest.

ILD'ish– 2. childish, mildish, wildish.

ILD'li– 2. mildly, riledly [coll.], wildly 3. beguiledly.

ILD'lik– 2. childlike, mild-like [dial.], riled-like [dial.], wild-like [dial.] 3. beguiled-like [dial.].

ILD'ness– 2. mildness, riledness [coll.], wildness 3. beguiledness, unwildness.

IL'e– 2. hyle 3. sedile, ancile; *see* also **IL'i**– highly etc. below.

IL'eks– 2. ilex, silex.

IL'ent– 2. silent 3. unsilent.

IL'er– 2. filer, filar, Schuyler, miler [slang], smiler, piler, pilar, Tyler, tiler, styler, stylar, viler 3. defiler, bifilar, trifilar, beguiler, compiler, reviler 4. reconciler.

IL'est– 2. vilest.

IL'et– 2. eyelet, islet, smilet, stylet.

IL'ful– 2. guileful, smileful, wileful.

IL'i– 2. highly, hyle, slyly, smily, wryly, riley [coll.], Riley, dryly, shyly, wily 3. sedile, ancile.

IL'ij– 2. mileage, smileage, silage.

IL'ing– 2. filing, smiling, piling, spiling, riling, tiling, styling, wiling, whiling 3. defiling, beguiling, compiling, exiling, restyling, reviling 4. domiciling, reconciling.

IL'is– 3. Aprilis, Quintilis, Sextilis.

IL'ish– 2. stylish 3. unstylish.

IL'less– 2. guileless, smileless, styleless, wileless.

IL'ment– 3. defilement, beguilement, compilement, resilement, exilement 4. domicilement, reconcilement 5. irreconcilement.

IL'o– 2. high-low, milo, silo, Shiloh, stilo.

IL'oid– 2. styloid, xyloid.

IL'on– 2. phylon, nylon, pylon.

IL'ot– 2. Nilot, pilot 3. sky pilot.

IL'um– 2. filum [L.], phylum, hilum, pilum 3. asylum.

IL'us– 2. hilus, Nilous, Silas, stylus.

IM'a– 2. Phyma, Lima, mima, rima, tryma, sima, cyma 3. Tellima, Jemima 4. arapaima.

IM'aks– 2. Limax, climax 4. anti-climax.

IM'al– 2. rimal, primal, shtreimel 4. isocheimal, isocrymal.

IM'an– 2. pieman, shy man, Wyman.

IM'at– 2. primate, my mate, shy mate.

IM'en– 2. daimon, Hymen, limen, crimen [L.], Simon, taimen, Timon, vimen.

IM'er– 2. chimer, limer, climber, mimer, rimer, primer, timer, timor 3. sublimer, begrimer, reprimer, old-timer.

IM'est– 2. primest 3. sublimest.

IM'i– 2. limy, limey [slang], blimy, slimy, rimy, rhymy, primy, stymie, stimy, thymy 3. beslimy, old-timy.

IM'ik– 2. rhymic, thymic, zymic 3. enzymic 4. isocheimic, catathymic.

IM'ing– 2. chiming, climbing, sliming, rhyming, griming, priming, timing 3. begriming, berhyming, pump priming, two-timing [slang].

IM'ish– 2. chimish, rhymish, timish.

IM'ist– 2. rhymist, timist.

IM'it– 2. climate, time it 3. acclimate.

IM'less– 2. chimeless, dimeless, limeless, climbless, slimeless, mimeless, rhymeless, rimeless, grimeless, timeless.

IM'li– 2. primely, timely 3. sublimely, untimely.

IM'ness– 2. primeness 3. sublimeness.

IM'us– 2. rimous, primus, simous, cymous, timeous [Scot. & Ir.], thymus.

IN'a– 2. Ina, China, Dinah, Heine, Jaina, mina, myna, vina [L.] 3. Sabina, Medina, Regina, Shekinah, trichina, Salina, salina, farina, Sabrina, piscina, Lucina, glucina 4. Adelina, Angelina, Evelina, Carolina, Platyrrhina.

IN'aks– 2. pinax, Thrinax.

IN'al– 2. binal, final, spinal, rhinal, crinal, trinal, sinal, vinal 3. acclinal, declinal, synclinal, caninal, prorhinal 4. semifinal, isoclinal, periclinal, interspinal, endocrinal, matutinal 5. cerebrospinal.

IN'an– 2. Hainan, Tainan 3. Salinan.

IN'at– 2. binate, spinate, quinate.

IND'ed– 2. blinded, minded, rinded, winded 3. snow-blinded, reminded, free-minded, strong-minded, high-minded, weak-minded, like-minded, low-minded, fair-minded, light-minded 4. unreminded, carnal-minded, feeble-minded, double-minded, evil-minded, simple-minded, bloody-minded, worldly-minded, earthly-minded, even-minded, narrow-minded, sober-minded.

IND'er– 2. binder, finder, hinder, kinder, blinder, minder, grinder, winder 3. *bookbinder*, *spellbinder*, *faultfinder*, *pathfinder*, reminder, sidewinder, stem-winder 4. organ grinder.

IND'est– 2. kindest, blindest.

IND'ful– 2. mindful 3. remindful, unmindful.

IND'hand– 3. behindhand.

IND'ing– 2. binding, finding, blinding, minding, grinding, winding 3. rebinding, bookbinding, unbinding, reminding, unwinding.

IND'less– 2. bindless, mindless, rindless, grindless, windless.

IND'li– 2. kindly, blindly 3. unkindly, purblindly.

IND'ness– 2. kindness, blindness 3. unkindness, snow blindness 4. color blindness.

IN'er– 2. diner, finer, liner, miner, minor, piner, Shriner, signer, shiner, winer, twiner, whiner 3. combiner, definer, refiner, confiner, maligner, headliner, streamliner, recliner, incliner, outliner, benigner, repiner, supiner, assigner, resigner, consigner, diviner, entwiner, designer, resigner 4. underliner, underminer, intertwiner.

IN'ess– 2. highness, nighness, slyness, wryness, dryness, spryness, shyness.

IN'est– 2. finest 3. benignest, supinest, divinest 4. superfinest.

IN'i– 2. Heinie, liny, miny, piny, spiny, briny, tiny, viny, winy, whiny 3. sunshiny, moonshiny.

IN'ing– 2. dining, fining, lining, mining, pining, signing, shining, Vining, wining twining, whining 3. combining, defining, refining, confining, relining, declining, reclining, inclining, outlining, repining, opining, resigning, designing, outshining, entwining 4. unconfining, underlining, interlining, undermining, countersigning, intertwining.

IN'is– 2. finis 3. Erinys.

IN'it– 2. finite, crinite.

IN'land– 2. Rhineland, Vineland.

IN'less– 2. fineless, lineless, pineless, spineless, signless, tineless, vineless, wineless.

IN'li– 2. finely 3. condignly, malignly, benignly, supinely, divinely 4. superfinely, unbenignly, saturninely, undivinely.

IN'lik– 2. binelike, finelike, linelike, pinelike, spinelike, signlike, tinelike, vinelike, winelike.

IN'ment– 3. refinement, confinement, alignment, malignment, enshrinement, assignment, designment, resignment, entwinement 4. unrefinement, realignment, interlinement, intertwinement.

IN'ness– 2. fineness 3. condignness, benignness, supineness, divineness 4. superfineness.

IN'o– 2. Aino, rhino, Taino 3. sabino, albino.

IN'um– 2. Linum, vinum [L.] 3. tablinum 4. Antirrhinum.

IN'us– 2. dinus, Linus, minus, Minos, Pinus, spinous, sinus, vinous 3. echinus, Lupinus.

I'o– 2. io, Io, Clio, trio 3. Ohio.

I'ol– 2. viol 3. bass viol; *see* also **I'al–** dial etc. above.

I'on– 2. ion, lion, scion, Zion 3. Arion, Orion, Ixion, sea lion 4. dandelion; *see* also **I'an–** Ian etc. above.

I'or– 2. prior, trior; *see* also **I'er–** eyer etc. above.

I'ot– 2. eyot, piot, riot, Sciot; *see* also **I'et–** diet etc. above.

IP'a– 2. nipa, pipa, ripa, Stipa.

IP'al– 2. ripal, typal 4. archetypal; *see* also **IP'l–** stipel etc. below.

IP'ed– 2. biped, striped 6. parallelepiped.

IP'end– 2. ripened, stipend.

IP'er– 2. hyper, niper [obs.], sniper, piper, riper, griper, striper, typer, viper, wiper, swiper 3. *sandpiper*, *bagpiper*, *sideswiper* 4. linotyper, windshield wiper 5. stereotyper 6. daguerreotyper.

IP'est– ripest; *see* also **IP'ist–** typist etc. below.

IP'i– 2. pipy, stripy, swipy 4. polytypy, antitypy, chromotypy, phonotypy 6. daguerreotypy.

IP'ing– 2. piping, Peiping, griping, striping, typing, wiping, swiping 3. retyping, restriping, sideswiping 4. linotyping 5. electrotyping 6. daguerreotyping.

IP'ist– 2. typist, ripest 4. linotypist, phonotypist 5. electrotypist 6. daguerreotypist.

IP'l– 2. stipel 3. disciple; *see* also **IP'al–** ripal etc. above.

IP'less– 2. pipeless, gripeless, stripeless, typeless, wipeless, swipeless.

IP'o– 2. hypo, typo.

IP'rus– 2. Cyprus, cypress, Cypris.

IR'a– 2. Ira, eyra, beira, daira, lira, Lyra, Mira, Myra 3. hegira, Almira, almirah, palmyra, Elmira, hetaira, Elvira.

IR'al– 2. gyral, chiral, pyral, spiral, styryl 3. papyral, retiral 4. polygyral, allochiral.

IR'ant– 2. gyrant, spirant, tyrant 3. aspirant, expirant, conspirant, archtyrant; *see* also **IR'ent–** virent etc. below.

IR'at– 2. pirate 3. archpirate.

IR'ate– 2. irate, gyrate, lyrate, lirate 3. agyrate 4. circumgyrate, dextrogyrate 5. sinistrogyrate.

IR'e– 2. daire, kairi [Jap.] 3. venire 4. praemunire, Dies Irae [L.]; *see* also **IR'i–** eyrie etc. below.

IR'een– 2. Irene, kyrene, kairine, pyrene, styrene, squireen.

IR'en– 2. kairine, siren 5. lepidosiren; *see* also **IR'on–** Byron etc. below.

IR'ent– 2. virent 3. inquirent 4. sempervirent; *see* also **IR'ant–** gyrant etc. above.

IR'er– 2. direr, firer, hirer, mirer, tirer, wirer 3. admirer, bemirer, aspirer, respirer, expirer, inspirer, conspirer, perspirer, suspirer, attirer, retirer, haywirer [slang], rewirer, acquirer, requirer, enquirer, inquirer, desirer.

IR'est– 2. direst 3. *haywirest* [slang].

IR'ful– 2. ireful, direful 3. desireful.

IR'i– 2. eyrie, dairi, fiery, miry, spiry, wiry, squiry 3. expiry, perspiry, enquiry, inquiry.

IR'id– 2. irid, Lyrid, xyrid 3. mormyrid, Osiride 4. sempervirid.

IR'ik– 2. gyric 3. oneiric, epeiric 4. photogyric.

IR'ing– 2. firing, hiring, miring, spiring, tiring, wiring, squiring 3. admiring, bemiring, aspiring, respiring, expiring, inspiring, conspiring, perspiring, attiring, retiring, untiring, unwiring, acquiring, requiring, inquiring, desiring 4. unaspiring, uninspiring, reacquiring, uninquiring, undesiring.

IR'is– 2. iris, Iris, Siris 3. Osiris.

IR'ish– 2. Irish, squirish.

IR'ist– 2. irised, lyrist.

IR'less– 2. tireless, wireless, squireless.

IR'li– 2. direly, squirely 3. entirely.

IR'lik– 2. byrelike, firelike, lyrelike, mirelike, pyrelike, spirelike, tirelike, wirelike, choirlike.

IR'ling– 2. hireling, squireling.

IR'ment– 3. bemirement, attirement, retirement, acquirement, requirement.

IR'ness– 2. direness 3. entireness.

IR'o– 2. gyro, Cairo, pyro, tyro 4. Autogiro.

IR'on– 2. Byron, gyron, Chiron, myron, Myron, siren 3. environ.

IR'one– 2. pyrone, Tyrone.

IR'os– 2. gyrose, virose.

IR'sum– 2. iresome, tiresome 3. desiresome.

IR'us– 2. gyrus, Pyrus, spirous, Cyrus, virus 3. Epirus, apyrous, papyrus, desirous.

IS'a– 2. beisa, Meissa.

IS'al– 2. sisal 4. paradisal; *see* also **IZ'al–** sizal etc. below.

IS'ens– 2. license, licence 3. dog license 4. marriage license, driver's license 5. poetic license.

IS'er– 2. icer, dicer, geyser, slicer, splicer, nicer, spicer, ricer, pricer, cicer 3. preciser, conciser, enticer 4. sacrificer 5. self-sacrificer.

IS'est– 2. nicest 3. precisest, concisest.

IS'ez– 2. ices, dices, slices, splices, spices, rices, prices, vices 3. suffices, entices, advices, devices 4. sacrifices.

IS'ful– 3. enticeful, deviceful.

IS'i– 2. icy, nisi, spicy, ricey.

IS'ing– 2. icing, dicing, slicing, splicing, spicing, pricing 3. sufficing, enticing 4. sacrificing 5. self-sacrificing.

IS'is– 2. Isis, physis, lysis, crisis, phthisis; *see* also **IS'us–** nisus etc. below.

IS'iv– 3. collisive, derisive, decisive, precisive, incisive, divisive 4. cicatrisive, indecisive, undivisive.

IS'less– 2. iceless, diceless, sliceless, spliceless, spiceless, riceless, priceless, viceless 3. adviceless 4. sacrificeless.

IS'li– 2. nicely 3. precisely, concisely 4. overnicely.

IS'man– 2. iceman, viseman, viceman.

IS'ment– 3. sufficement, enticement.

IS'ness– 2. niceness 3. preciseness, conciseness 4. overniceness.

IS'on– 2. bison, hyson, grison, vison.

IST'er– 2. Meister [G.], shyster [coll.] 4. Kapellmeister [G.].

IST'lik– 2. Christlike.

IST'ro– 2. maestro.

IS'us– 2. nisus, Nisus, risus [L.] 4. Dionysus; *see* also **IS'is–** Isis etc. above.

IT'a– 2. vita 3. baryta, Nerita 4. amalaita.

IT'al– **2.** dital, title, vital **3.** detrital, recital, entitle, mistitle, requital **4.** microphytal, parasital.

IT'ant– **3.** incitant.

IT'e– **2.** rite **3.** Venite **4.** Aphrodite, Amphitrite, arborvitae; *see* also **IT'i**–blighty etc. below.

IT'ed– **2.** bighted, dited, dighted, heighted, kited, lighted, blighted, plighted, slighted, knighted, nighted [rare], spited, righted, frighted, sighted, cited, sited, whited **3.** indited, indicted, alighted, delighted, relighted, unlighted, benighted, beknighted, unknighted, ignited, united, despited, affrighted, attrited, recited, excited, incited, long-sighted, farsighted, clear-sighted, nearsighted, shortsighted, requited, invited **4.** candlelighted, satellited, reunited, ununited, disunited, copyrighted, eagle-sighted, oversighted, uninvited, unrequited.

IT'em– **2.** item, bite 'em.

IT'en– **2.** heighten, chitin, chiton, lighten, brighten, frighten, triton, Triton, tighten, Titan, whiten **3.** enlighten, retighten, untighten.

IT'er– **2.** iter, biter, fighter, kiter, lighter, blighter, flighter, plighter, slighter, miter, mitre, smiter, niter, righter, writer, brighter, triter, sighter, citer, tighter, whiter **3.** *backbiter*, indicter, inditer, indictor, *bullfighter*, alighter, delighter, politer, *lamplighter*, unmiter, igniter, uniter, rewriter, *typewriter*, exciter, inviter, requiter **4.** candlelighter, impoliter, dynamiter, reuniter, copy writer, underwriter.

IT'est– **2.** lightest, slightest, rightest, brightest, tritest, tightest, whitest **3.** politest, *uprightest* **4.** impolitest.

IT'ez– **2.** nighties **3.** barytes, pyrites, sorites.

IT'ful– **2.** mightful, spiteful, rightful, frightful, sprightful **3.** delightful, despiteful, unrightful.

ITH'er– **2.** either, blither, neither, writher, tither.

ITH'est– **2.** lithest, blithest.

ITH'ful– **2.** litheful, blitheful.

ITH'ing– **2.** nithing, writhing, trithing, scything, tithing.

ITH'li– **2.** lithely, blithely.

ITH'nes– **2.** litheness, blitheness.

ITH'on– **2.** python.

ITH'sum– **2.** lithesome, blithesome.

IT'i– **2.** blighty, flighty, mighty, mity, nighty, nightie, whity **3.** almighty **4.** Aphrodite, highty-tighty; *see* also **IT'e**–rite etc. above.

IT'ing– **2.** biting, diting, fighting, kiting, skiting [dial.], lighting, blighting, plighting, slighting, smiting, knighting, spiting, writing, righting, frighting, citing, sighting, whiting **3.** *backbiting*, inditing, indicting, *cockfighting*, *bullfighting*, alighting, delighting, beknighting, uniting, affrighting, *handwriting*, reciting, inciting, exciting, inviting, requiting **4.** proselyting, dynamiting, reuniting, disuniting, expediting, copywriting, copyrighting, underwriting, uninviting.

IT'is– **3.** phlebitis, carditis, rachitis, nephritis, iritis, arthritis, neuritis **4.** meningitis, laryngitis, tonsillitis, dermatitis **5.** pericarditis, appendicitis, peritonitis.

IT'ish– **2.** lightish, slightish, spitish, brightish, tritish, tightish, whitish **4.** eremitish, anchoritish.

IT'iv– **3.** attritive, excitive **4.** expeditive, appetitive.

IT'l– **2.** title, vital **3.** recital, betitle, entitle, mistitle, requital; *see* also **IT'al**–dital etc. above.

IT'less– **2.** bightless, fightless, heightless, kiteless, lightless, miteless, mightless, nightless, knightless, spiteless, riteless, rightless, frightless, sprightless, sightless **3.** delightless **4.** proselyteless, dynamiteless, copyrightless.

IT'li– 2. lightly, slightly, nightly, knightly, rightly, brightly, sprightly, tritely, sightly, tightly, whitely 3. politely, *fortnightly*, uprightly, contritely, unsightly 4. eruditely, impolitely.

IT'ment– 3. indictment, affrightment, incitement, excitement, invitement.

IT'ner– 2. heightener, lightener, brightener, frightener, whitener.

IT'ness– 2. lightness, slightness, rightness, brightness, triteness, whiteness 3. politeness, uprightness 4. eruditeness, impoliteness.

IT'ning– 2. heightening, lightning, lightening, tightening, brightening, frightening, whitening 3. streak lightning, chain lightning, sheet lightning.

IT'oid– 2. cytoid.

IT'on– 2. chiton, Triton, cyton, Titan.

IT'um– 2. item, Blitum 5. ad infinitum.

IT'us– 2. litus, ritus [L.], situs, Titus 3. attritus, detritus, St. Vitus.

I'us– 2. pious, Pius, prius 3. bacchius, unpious, Darius 4. nisi prius 5. antibacchius; *see* also **I'as–** eyas etc. above.

IV'a– 2. iva, Iva, daiva, Siva, Saiva 3. saliva 4. conjunctiva.

IV'al– 2. nival, rival, thivel 3. ogival, archival, salival, arrival, corrival, deprival, outrival, estival, revival, survival 4. nonarrival, relatival, genitival, adjectival, conjunctival 5. imperatival.

IV'an– 2. Ivan, divan; *see* also **IV'en–** liven etc. below.

IV'ans– 3. connivance, arrivance, contrivance, survivance.

IV'ant– 2. trivant 3. connivant, survivant.

IV'at– 2. private 3. unprivate.

IV'en– 2. liven 3. enliven; *see* also **IV'an–** Ivan etc. above.

IV'er– 2. diver, fiver [slang], hiver, jiver [slang], skiver, liver, livor, sliver, river, driver, shriver, striver, thriver, stiver 3. pearl diver, conniver, depriver, arriver, slave driver, contriver, survivor 4. deep sea diver.

IV'est– 2. livest 3. alivest.

IV'i– 2. ivy, jivy [slang], skivie [Scot.], stivy 4. poison ivy.

IV'ing– 2. diving, hiving, jiving [slang], skiving, riving, driving, striving, shriving, thriving, stiving [Scot. & dial. Eng.], wiving 3. conniving, arriving, deriving, contriving, reviving, surviving.

IV'li– 2. lively, shively 3. unlively.

IV'ment– 3. deprivement, revivement.

IV'us– 2. divus, clivus 3. salivous, acclivous, declivous, proclivous.

I'way– 2. byway, highway, skyway.

IZ'a– 2. Isa, Liza 3. Eliza, coryza.

IZ'al– 2. sizal 3. surmisal, despisal, arrhizal, apprizal, reprisal, comprisal, surprisal, incisal, capsizal, advisal, revisal 4. paradisal.

IZ'en– 2. bison, dizen, greisen 3. bedizen, horizon 4. spiegeleisen, Blut und eisen [G.].

IZ'er– 2. geyser, Kaiser, miser, riser, prizer, sizer, sizar, visor, vizor, wiser 3. disguiser, elisor, remiser, surmiser, apprizer, surpriser, assizer, incisor, excisor, capsizer, baptizer, chastiser, deviser, devisor, reviser, divisor 4. gormandizer, aggrandizer, eulogizer, catechizer, vocalizer, analyzer, paralyzer, vitalizer, moralizer, neutralizer, tantalizer, totalizer, equalizer, sterilizer, fertilizer, civilizer, symbolizer, idolizer, itemizer, atomizer, organizer, humanizer, scrutinizer, solemnizer, lionizer, colonizer, harmonizer, sermonizer, canonizer, synchronizer, patronizer, modernizer, fraternizer, mesmerizer, cauterizer, pulverizer, theorizer, temporizer, terrorizer, authorizer, enterpriser, exerciser, exorciser, magnetizer, appetizer, sympathizer, improviser, supervisor 5. apologizer, generalizer, demoralizer, monopolizer, economizer, epitomizer, deodorizer, extemporizer, nonsympathizer.

IZ'est– 2. wisest 3. unwisest.

IZ'i– 2. sizy 3. capsizy.

IZ'ing– 2. rising, prizing, sizing, wising 3. disguising, surmising, despising, arising, comprising, surprising, uprising, chastising 4. gormandizing, standardizing, jeopardizing, enfranchising, disfranchizing, merchandizing, eulogizing, realizing, localizing, vocalizing, penalizing, moralizing, neutralizing, specializing, tantalizing, mobilizing, sterilizing, compromising, enterprising, ostracising, publicizing, criticizing, advertising, sympathizing, improvising, supervising 5. philosophizing, materializing, demoralizing, generalizing, capitalizing, devitalizing, revitalizing, immortalizing, monopolizing, visualizing, uncompromising, familiarizing, characterizing, italicizing, systematizing; *also all other verbs ending in "ize" plus "ing."*

IZ'ment– 3. franchisement, apprizement, assizement, baptizement, chastisement, advisement 4. aggrandizement, enfranchisement, disfranchisement.

IZ'mik– 2. seismic 3. aseismic, coseismic.

IZ'nes– 2. wiseness 3. unwiseness.

IZ'o– 3. aviso, proviso 4. Valparaiso, improviso.

IZ'on– 2. bison 3. horizon.

IZ'or– 2. visor, vizor 3. elisor, incisor, devisor, divisor 4. supervisor; *see* also **IZ'er–** geyser etc. above.

I (eye)

3.

TRIPLE RHYMES IN I (eye'a-ble)

Primary or Secondary Accent Falls on Second from Last Syllable.

I'a-bl- 3. eyeable, liable, pliable, friable, triable, viable 4. reliable, appliable, impliable, compliable, deniable 5. modifiable, qualifiable, undeniable, verifiable, classifiable, pacifiable, falsifiable, rectifiable, fortifiable, justifiable, satisfiable, unreliable, multipliable, undeniable 6. solidifiable, exemplifiable, electrifiable, diversifiable, identifiable, unjustifiable, unsatisfiable.

I'a-bli- 3. pliably 4. reliably, appliably, compliably, deniably 5. justifiably, unreliably, undeniably 6. unjustifiably, unsatisfiably.

I'a-dez- 3. Hyades, Pleiades, naiades, dryades 5. hamadryades.

I'a-gram- 3. diagram, skiagram, viagram.

I'a-kal- 3. piacle 4. dandiacal, zodiacal, heliacal, maniacal 5. prosodiacal, elegiacal, demoniacal, simoniacal 6. pyromaniacal, dipsomaniacal, kleptomaniacal, hypochondriacal, paradisiacal 7. encyclopediacal, bibliomaniacal.

I'al-lik- 3. dial-like, phial-like, trial-like, vial-like, viol-like 4. sundial-like.

I'an-si- 3. cliency, pliancy, riancy 4. compliancy.

I'ant-li- 3. pliantly 4. defiantly, reliantly, compliantly.

I'ar-i- 3. diary, briary, friary; *see* also **I'er-i-** fiery etc. below.

I'ar-ist- 3. diarist, Piarist.

I'ark-i- 3. diarchy, triarchy.

I'as-is- 4. psychiasis, psoriasis 5. odontiasis 6. hypochondriasis, elephantiasis.

I'at-er- 4. psychiater, archiater, hippiater.

I'at-ri- 4. podiatry, psychiatry, phoniatry, hippiatry.

I'at-rist- 4. podiatrist, psychiatrist, hippiatrist.

IB'a-bl- 3. bribable, scribable 4. ascribable, subscribable, describable, prescribable, inscribable, proscribable 5. indescribable, undescribable, circumscribable.

IB'a-bli- 4. describably 5. indescribably, undescribably.

IB'er-i- 3. bribery.

ID'a-bl- 3. guidable, hidable, ridable 4. unguidable, elidable, unridable, bestridable, decidable, dividable, providable 5. undecidable, subdividable, undividable, unprovidable.

ID'ed-li- 4. unguidedly, misguidedly, decidedly, lopsidedly 5. undecidedly, undividedly, unprovidedly.

ID'ful-li- 3. pridefully.

ID'ing-li- 3. chidingly, guidingly, hidingly, glidingly, slidingly, stridingly, sidingly 4. abidingly, confidingly, misguidingly, unhidingly, unchidingly.

I'en-si- 3. cliency, pliancy, riancy 4. compliancy.

I'er-i- 3. fiery, lyery, briery, priory; *see* also **I'ar-i-** diary etc. above.

I'et–al– 3. dietal, hyetal 4. parietal, varietal, societal 5. isohyetal.

I'et–ed– 3. dieted, rioted, quieted. 4. unquieted, disquieted.

I'et–er– 3. dieter, rioter, quieter 4. proprietor, disquieter.

I'et–est– 3. quietest 4. unquietest.

I'et–i– 3. piety 4. ubiety, dubiety, filiety, impiety, variety, ebriety, sobriety, propriety, society, satiety, anxiety 5. contrariety, inebriety, insobriety, notoriety, impropriety.

I'et–ing– 3. dieting, rioting, quieting 4. unquieting, disquieting.

I'et–ist– 3. dietist, pietist, quietist 4. varietist.

I'et–izm– 3. pietism, quietism 4. varietism.

IF'en–at– 3. hyphenate, siphonate.

IF'er–ing– 3. ciphering, syphering 4. deciphering.

IF'ling–li– 3. triflingly, stiflingly.

I'il–at– 4. annihilate.

I'il–ist– 3. nihilist.

I'ing–li– 3. lyingly, flyingly, pryingly, sighingly, vyingly 4. defyingly 5. gratifyingly, mystifyingly, satisfyingly.

IK'a–bl– 3. likeable, spikeable 4. unlikeable, dislikeable.

IK'li–hud– 3. likelihood 4. unlikelihood.

IK'lik–al– 3. cyclical 4. bicyclical, encyclical.

IL'a–bl– 3. smilable, rilable, filable, stylable, wilable, whilable 4. defilable, beguilable 5. reconcilable 6. irreconcilable, unreconcilable.

IL'and–er– 3. islander, highlander, Thailander.

IL'er–i– 3. guilery, pilary.

IL'ful–i– 3. guilefully, wilefully 4. beguilefully.

IL'ful–ness– 3. guilefulness, wilefulness 4. beguilefulness.

IL'ing–li– 3. smilingly 4. beguilingly.

IM'er–i– 3. rhymery, primary.

IM'i–ness– 3. liminess, sliminess, riminess, griminess.

IN'a–bl– 3. finable, linable, signable 4. combinable, definable, declinable, inclinable, opinable, assignable, designable, divinable 5. undefinable, undeclinable, unassignable, undivinable.

IN'a–bli– 4. definably, assignably 5. undefinably, undeclinably, unassignably.

IN'a–li– 3. finally, spinally.

IND'er–i– 3. bindery, grindery.

IN'er–i– 3. binary, finery, finary, minery, pinery, vinery, winery, quinary, swinery 4. refinery, alpinery.

IN'i–er– 3. spinier, brinier, shinier, tinier, winier.

IN'i–est– 3. spiniest, briniest, shiniest, tiniest, winiest.

IN'les–li– 3. spinelessly, winelessly.

I'ol–a– 3. viola, Viola 4. variola.

I'ol–et– 3. triolet, striolet, violet.

I'ol–ist– 3. sciolist, violist.

I'ol–us– 3. sciolous 4. gladiolus, modiolus, variolous.

I'on–iz– 3. ionize, lionize.

I'op–i– 3. myopy 4. presbyopy, Calliope.

I'or–i– priory; *see* also **I'ar–i–** diary etc. above; and **I'er–i–** fiery etc. above.

I'os–en– 3. Pliocene, Miocene 4. post-Pliocene.

I'ot–er– 3. rioter, quieter.

IP'ing–li– 3. pipingly, gripingly.

IP'les–li– 3. pipelessly, gripelessly, stripelessly, typelessly.

IR'a–bl– 3. fireable, hirable 4. respirable, expirable, inspirable, transpirable, perspirable, untirable, acquirable, requirable, inquirable, desirable 5. uninspirable, undesirable.

IR'as–i– 3. piracy 4. retiracy.

IR'ful–ness– **3.** irefulness, direfulness **4.** desirefulness.

IR'ing–li– **4.** admiringly, aspiringly, conspiringly, retiringly, inquiringly, desiringly.

IR'on–i– **3.** irony, sireny.

IS'a–bl– **3.** sliceable, spiceable, riceable, priceable **4.** enticeable.

IS'er–i– **3.** spicery **4.** irrisory, derisory, incisory.

IS'i–er– **3.** icier, spicier.

IS'i–est– **3.** iciest, spiciest.

IS'i–kl– **3.** icicle, bicycle, tricycle.

IS'i–li– **3.** icily, spicily.

IS'iv–li– **4.** derisively, decisively, incisively **5.** indecisively, undecisively.

IS'iv–ness– **4.** derisiveness, decisiveness, incisiveness **5.** undecisiveness.

IS'or–i– derisory etc., *see* **IS'er–i–** spicery etc. above.

IT'a–bl– **3.** lightable, writable, sightable, citable **4.** indictable, ignitable, unitable, recitable, excitable, incitable, requitable **5.** extraditable.

IT'a–bli– **4.** indictably, unitably, excitably.

IT'al–iz– **3.** vitalize **4.** devitalize, revitalize.

IT'at–iv– **3.** writative **4.** recitative, excitative, incitative, requitative.

IT'en–er– **3.** heightener, lightener, brightener, frightener, tightener, whitener **4.** enlightener.

IT'ful–i– **3.** spitefully, rightfully, frightfully, sprightfully **4.** delightfully.

ITH'som–li– **3.** lithesomely, blithesomely.

ITH'som–ness– **3.** lithesomeness, blithesomeness.

IT'i–er– **3.** flightier, mightier **4.** almightier.

IT'il–i– **3.** flightily, mightily, sprightily **4.** almightily.

IT'i–ness– **3.** flightiness, mightiness **4.** almightiness.

IT'ing–li– **3.** bitingly, blightingly, slightingly **4.** excitingly, invitingly.

IT'less–ness– **3.** nightlessness, sightlessness.

IT'li–ness– **3.** knightliness, sprightliness, sightliness **4.** unsightliness.

IV'a–bl– **3.** drivable **4.** undrivable, deprivable, derivable, contrivable, revivable **5.** unrevivable.

IV'an–si– **4.** connivancy, contrivancy, survivancy.

IV'as–i– **3.** privacy.

IV'ing–li– **3.** jivingly [slang], drivingly, strivingly, thrivingly.

IZ'a–bl– **3.** prizable, sizable **4.** demisable, surmisable, despisable, comprisable, excisable, advisable, devisable **5.** subsidizable, oxidizable, realizable, analyzable, crystallizable, utilizable, civilizable, organizable, recognizable, incognizable, exercisable, inadvisable.

IZ'a–bli– **3.** sizeably **4.** advisably **5.** inadvisably.

IZ'ed–li– **4.** surmisedly, advisedly **5.** unadvisedly, improvisedly, unprovisedly.

IZ'ing–li– **4.** despisingly, surprisingly **5.** enterprisingly, tantalizingly, scrutinizingly, agonizingly, appetizingly.

IZ'or–i– **4.** advisory, revisory, provisory **5.** supervisory.

I (bib)

1.

SINGLE (MASCULINE) RHYMES IN I (bib)

Primary or Secondary Accent Falls on Last Syllable; Imperfect Rhymes Are in Italics.

IB– **1.** bib, bibb, chib, dib, fib, gib, jib, Lib, lib [slang], glib, mib [dial.], nib, snib, rib, drib, crib, sib, Tib, tib [slang], quib, squib, zib [slang] **2.** Adib, ad lib [slang], renib, *midrib.*

IBD– **1.** bibbed, dibbed, fibbed, jibbed, ribbed, cribbed, squibbed **3.** rock-ribbed.

IBZ– bibs etc., *see* **IB–** bib etc. above, plus "s" or "'s"; **2.** his nibs.

ICH– **1.** itch, bitch, ditch, dich, fitch, hitch, skitch [slang], lich, flitch, miche, smitch [slang], niche, snitch, pitch, rich, britch [dial.], stitch, witch, quitch, switch, twitch, which **2.** unhitch, enrich, restitch, *seamstitch, hemstitch, chainstitch, whipstitch, catstitch,* bewitch **3.** featherstitch, czarevitch.

ICHD– **1.** itched, bitched [vulgar], ditched, hitched, niched, snitched, pitched, stitched, switched, twitched **2.** unhitched, enriched, restitched, bewitched **3.** featherstitched.

ID– **1.** id, bid, chid, did, fid, gid, hid, kid, Kidd, skid, lid, slid, mid, rid, grid, strid, Sid, Cid, quid, squid **2.** rebid, forbid, outbid, undid, outdid, *bifid, trifid, eyelid,* amid, *Enid, aphid,* Madrid, *Muphrid, Astrid* **3.** underbid, overbid, overdid, katydid, invalid, pyramid.

IDST– **1.** didst, midst **2.** amidst.

IDTH– **1.** width.

IF– **1.** if, biff, diff [slang], pfiff, jiff [slang], skiff, glyph, cliff, miff [dial. & slang], sniff, piff, spiff [slang], riff, griffe, griph, Sif, tiff, stiff, wiff [slang], quiff, whiff **2.** *Saiph, midriff* **3.** handkerchief, neckerchief, logogriph, hippogriff, Teneriffe, bindle stiff [slang] **4.** hieroglyph.

IFS– **1.** ifs, cliffs, sniffs, tiffs, whiffs, ziffs, etc.

IFT– **1.** biffed, gift, lift, miffed [dial. & slang], sniffed, snift, spiffed [slang], rift, drift, shrift, thrift, sift, shift, tiffed, tift, squiffed [slang], swift, whiffed **2.** relift, uplift, adrift, *spindrift, spoondrift, snowdrift, spendthrift, muckthrift,* reshift, *makeshift, gearshift* **3.** chimney swift.

IFTH– **1.** fifth.

IG– **1.** big, bigg, dig, fig, gig, jig, skig [slang], nig, snig [slang], pig, spig [slang], rig, wrig, brig, Frigg, grig, crig, prig, sprig, trig, cig [slang], tyg, wig, swig, twig, Whig, zig **2.** fishgig, fizgig, renege, bigwig, earwig **3.** Mr. Big, infra dig [coll.], caprifig, whirligig, Guinea pig, thimblerig, periwig **4.** thingumajig [coll.].

IGD– **1.** figged, rigged, grigged, wigged, swigged, twigged, zigged **2.** reneged, full-rigged, square-rigged, bewigged.

IGZ– bigs etc., *see* **IG–** big etc. above, plus "s" or "'s"; **1.** Biggs, Briggs, digs [slang], Jiggs, Riggs **3.** Mrs. Wiggs.

IJ– **1.** fidge [dial.], midge, smidge, nidge, ridge, bridge, whidge [slang], squidge **2.** enridge, abridge, *cabbage, cribbage, bondage, yardage, cordage, leafage, roofage, package, leakage, coinage, carnage, dumpage, stoppage, moorage, storage, dosage, message, sausage, usage, shortage, hostage, postage,* *language, selvage, drayage, voyage* **3.** brigandage, *appendage, impoundage,* lineage, verbiage, foliage, vassalage, *assemblage,* tutelage, mucilage, cartilage, pilgrimage, appanage, vicinage, alienage, badinage, peonage, siphonage, baronage, patronage, parsonage, personage, *equipage,* vicarage, plunderage, brokerage, cooperage, porterage, quarterage, fosterage, average, beverage, leverage, flowerage, saxifrage, anchorage, harborage, tutorage, hemorrhage, arbitrage, pasturage, surplusage, armitage, hermitage, heritage, clientage, parentage **4.** espionage.

IJD– **1.** fidged [dial.], nidged, ridged, bridged **2.** unridged, abridged, unbridged **3.** unabridged.

IK– **1.** ich [G.], ick [slang], chic, chick, tchick, Dick, dick [slang & dial.], hic, hick, kick, lick, flick, click, slick, mick, nick, snick, pick, pic [slang], spick, rick, wrick, brick, Frick, crick, cric, creek [coll.], scrick [slang], prick, trick, sick, sic, tick, tic, stick, stich, thick, Vic, vic [slang], wick, quick **2.** *dabchick, peachick, cowlick, nutpick, toothpick, hayrick, firebrick, landsick, seasick, homesick, brainsick, moonsick, heartsick, lovesick, knobstick, yardstick, broomstick, drumstick, chopstick, metestick,* Old Vic, *lampwick, Warwick, Brunswick* **3.** Benedick, benedick, Catholic, arsenic, chivalric, choleric, limerick, turmeric, whitterick, maverick, plethoric, rhetoric, bishopric, lunatic, heretic, politic, walking stick, fiddlestick, candlestick, bailiwick, candlewick, double quick **4.** allocochick, ich liebe dich [G.], kinnikinnick, archbishopric, arithmetic, impolitic **5.** cosmopolitic.

IKS– chicks etc., *see* **IK–** ich [G.] etc. above, plus "s" or "'s"; **1.** Bix, chix [slang], Dix, fix, mix, nix, Pnyx, pyx, pix, rix, Trix, six, Styx **2.** affix, adfix, refix, prefix, infix, confix, transfix, postfix, suffix, prolix, admix, immix, commix **3.** antefix, crucifix, intermix, undermix, overmix, cicatrix, Beatrix, twenty-six **4.** aviatrix, executrix.

IKST– **1.** fixed, mixed, nixed [slang], sixte, 'twixt **2.** affixed, adfixed, refixed, prefixed, infixed, confixed, transfixed, postfixed, suffixed, admixed, immixed, commixed, betwixt **3.** antefixed, dorsifixed, intermixed, undermixed, overmixed.

IKT– **1.** dict [arch.], kicked, licked, clicked, picked, Pict, bricked, tricked, strict, sicked, ticked, wicked **2.** addict, *edict,* predict, delict, *relict,* afflict, inflict, conflict, depict, astrict, restrict, constrict, evict, convict, two-wicked **3.** contradict, benedict, Benedict, interdict, overstrict, preconvict.

IL– **1.** ill, bill, Bill, chill, chil, dill, fill, Phil, phil [slang], gill, hill, jill, kil, kill, kiln, skil, skill, lill, li'l [dial.], Lil, mill, mil, nil, pill, spill, rill, brill, drill, frill, grill, grille, prill, shrill, trill, thrill, sill, shil, shill, til, till, still, thill, vill, ville, will, Will, quill, squill, swill, twill **2.** *playbill, waybill, redbill, handbill, broadbill, ringbill, wrybill, cockbill, hornbill, thornbill, spoonbill, waxbill, crossbill, boatbill, shortbill, bluebill, shoebill,* spadille, refill, fulfill, *scrodgill, bluegill, molehill,* downhill, uphill, *anthill,* sijill, *limekiln, treadmill, windmill,* quadrille, befrill, *footrill, headsill, groundsill,* retill, until, bestill, standstill, distill, instill, coutil, Seville, goodwill, ill will, Brazil, frazil **3.** dishabille, dollar bill, razorbill, piccadill, daffodil, Francophil, Gallophil, Anglophil, demophil, Sinophil, chlorophyll, astrophil, Negrophil, chrysophyll, Celtophil, phytophil, underfill, overfill, cement mill, juvenile, puerile, imbecile, codicile, domicile, verticil, window sill, Mother Sill, volatile, vibratil, pulsatile, versatile, mercantile, infantile, reinstill, thereuntil, intertill, undertill, overtill, Faneuil, Louisville, Evansville, whippoorwill.

ILCH– **1.** filch, milch, pilch, zilch [slang].

ILD– **1.** build, billed, chilled, filled, gilled, gild, guild, killed, skilled, milled, pilled, spilled, frilled, trilled, stilled, quilled, willed **2.** rebuild, rebilled, unfilled, fulfilled, begild, *wergild*, *Brunhild*, unskilled, untilled, distilled, instilled, unstilled, self-willed, strong-willed **3.** unfulfilled, octogild, undistilled.

ILK– **1.** ilk, bilk, milk, silk, whilk **2.** sour milk, spilt milk, spun silk.

ILN– **1.** kiln, Milne **2.** limekiln.

ILT– **1.** built, gilt, guilt, hilt, jilt, kilt, lilt, milt, spilt, silt, tilt, stilt, wilt, quilt **2.** rebuilt, unspilt, atilt, uptilt **3.** Vanderbilt, clipper built.

ILTS– **1.** gilts, guilts, hilts, jilts, kilts, lilts, silts, tilts, stilts, wilts, quilts **3.** Vanderbilts.

IM– **1.** Bim, bim [slang], dim, him, hymn, gym, Jim, jim [slang], Kim, skim, limn, limb, flim [slang], glim, Clim, Klim, slim, mim, nim, Nym, rim, brim, grim, grimme, scrim, prim, trim, Sim, shim, Tim, vim, swim, whim, zimb **2.** bedim, enlimn, corymb, betrim **3.** cherubim, paradigm, seraphim, pseudonym, synonym, antonym, undernim, interim, hexastigm, Tiny Tim.

IMD– **1.** dimmed, hymned, skimmed, limbed, slimmed, rimmed, brimmed, trimmed **2.** bedimmed, untrimmed.

IMF– **1.** lymph, nymph **2.** wood nymph **3.** endolymph, paranymph, water nymph.

IMP– **1.** imp, bimp [slang], gimp, jimp, skimp, scimp, limp, blimp, mimp, pimp, grimp [slang], crimp, scrimp, primp, shrimp, simp [slang], tymp.

IMZ– Bim's etc., *see* **IM–** Bim etc. above, plus "s" or " 's."

IN– **1.** in, inn, bin, been, chin, tchin, din, fin, Finn, finn [slang], gin, jinn, kin, skin, Lynn, lin, Glynn, min, Min, pin, spin, brin, grin, crin, sin, shin, tin, thin, win, twin, whin, Yin **2.** herein, therein, wherein, within, *nubbin*, *globin*, *robin*, *rubin*, *has-been*, *Cochin*, *urchin*, *Odin*, Baffin, Boffin, *redfin*, *threadfin*, *blackfin*, *elfin*, *dolphin*, *dauphin*, *bowfin*, *Fagin*, begin, *piggin*, *noggin*, *pidgin*, *Elgin*, *engine*, *margin*, *virgin*, akin, Pekin, blood kin, *lambkin*, *bodkin*, *princekin*, *welkin*, *napkin*, *catkin*, reskin, *redskin*, *calfskin*, *pigskin*, *sealskin*, *doeskin*, *lambskin*, *sharkskin*, *moleskin*, *sheepskin*, *bearskin*, *deerskin*, *maudlin*, *mafflin*, *mufflin*, *Franklin*, *collin*, *colin*, *Kremlin*, *drumlin*, *dunlin*, *poplin*, *carline*, *marlin*, Berlin, *merlin*, *Merlin*, *muslin*, *villain*, *chaplain*, *stamin*, *vermin*, *Lenin*, *lignin*, *tannin*, *rennin*, *lapin*, repin, *inchpin*, *pippin*, unpin, *tenpin*, *ninepin*, *kingpin*, *pushpin*, *hatpin*, *sculpin*, *respin*, *Crispin*, *fibrin*, agrin, chagrin, corinne, *caprin*, *dextrin*, Turin, *tocsin*, *rosin*, *trypsin*, Tientsin, *Latin*, *pectin*, *glutin*, *Swithin*, *penguin*, *pinguin*, *sequin* **3.** carabin, jacobin, Jacobin, colobin, paladin, amidin, morindin, *Alladin*, paraffin, Micky Finn, origin, waringin, Capuchin, absinthine, manakin, baldachin, ramekin, bodikin, birdikin, spilikin, billikin, manikin, cannikin, pannikin, bootikin, *grimalkin*, kilderkin, tigerkin, nipperkin, tigerskin, hyaline, caballine, alkaline, tourmaline, coralline, crystalline, ptyalin, Gobelin, gobelin, capelin, Zeppelin, javelin, sibylline, aniline, aquiline, bandoline, mandolin, violin, lanoline, crinoline, Caroline, *tarpaulin*, globulin, capulin, insulin, discipline, masculine, Ursuline, Benjamin, jessamine, vitamin, *albumin*, *illumine*, mezzanine, Fescennine, feminine, pavonine, heroine, wankapin, terrapin, chinquapin, calepin, underpin, saccharine, whipper-in, margarin, tamarin, nectarine, Sanhedrin, viperine, aspirin, anserine, peregrine, glycerin, Catherine, Lohengrin, tambourin, moccasin, *Wisconsin*, damassin, mortal sin, agatine, bulletin, Byzantine, *asbestine*, *intestine*, *Rasputin*, thick and thin, brodequin, harlequin, mannequin, lambrequin, *Algonquin*, genuine **4.** hemoglobin, ragamuffin, digitalin, Evangeline, tuberculin, elaterin, alabastrine, highfalutin **5.** nitroglycerin.

INCH– **1.** inch, chinch, finch, kinch, linch, lynch, flinch, clinch, minch [slang], pinch, cinch, squinch **2.** redfinch, goldfinch, bullfinch, greenfinch, grass finch, hawfinch, unclinch, bepinch.

INCHT– **1.** inched, lynched, flinched, clinched, pinched, cinched **2.** unclinched, uncinched.

IND– **1.** binned, chinned, finned, ginned, lind, lynde, pinned, grinned, sind, scind, sinned, thinned, wind **2.** thick-skinned, thin-skinned, unskinned, abscind, rescind, exscind, whirlwind **3.** disciplined, tamarind, Amerind **4.** undisciplined.

ING– **1.** ing, Ing, Inge, bing, ching, ding, ging, hing, king, ling, fling, cling, Kling, pling [slang], Ming, ping, ring, wring, bring, dring, spring, string, sing, singh, ting, sting, thing, wing, swing, zing **2.** beking, Chungking, Nanking, *fledgeling, changeling, weakling, dukeling, stripling, Riesling, princeling*, Peiping, enring, aspring, *offspring, mainspring, latchstring, checkstring, hamstring, bowstring, shoestring, Singsing, Storting, something, nothing*, bewing, *redwing, pinwing, lapwing, waxwing, whitewing* **3.** scaffolding, rescinding, rewarding, horseshoeing, triumphing, pillaging, managing, foraging, à la king, mafficking, trafficking, dialing, rivaling, caviling, toweling, sanderling, underling, fingerling, easterling, maddening, widening, deafening, stiffening, roughening, toughening, strengthening, slackening, thickening, sickening, opening, happening, lessening, threatening, sweetening, softening, fastening, hastening, moistening, fattening, leavening, evening, rationing, pensioning, auctioning, questioning, echoing, larruping, sugaring, soldering, murdering, differing, suffering, angering, ushering, weathering, soldiering, hankering, hollering, summering, centering, sauntering, quartering, blistering, answering, doctoring, motoring, licquoring, conjuring, murmuring, featuring, fracturing, lecturing, picturing, culturing, posturing, purchasing, solacing, menacing, latticing, financing, promising, witnessing, publishing, famishing, ravishing, fidgeting, blanketing, coveting, surfeiting, limiting, fagoting, balloting, adapting, ballasting, Odelsting, anything, everything, arguing, issuing, elbowing, swallowing, yellowing, billowing, merrywing, climaxing, lobbying, fancying, monkeying, volleying, journeying, moseying, curtseying, bullying, whinnying, copying, wearying, varying, querying, dairying, curtsying, emptying, partying, puttying, envying. **4.** mismanaging, disparaging, encouraging, discouraging, awakening, imagining, determining, occasioning, envisioning, beleaguering, continuing, mutinying **5.** administering, accompanying; *and present participle of all other verbs ad infinitum.*

INGD– **1.** dinged, pinged, ringed, stringed, tinged, winged, zinged **2.** beringed, *webwinged*, bewinged.

INJ– **1.** binge, dinge, hinge, pinge, fringe, cringe, scringe, springe, singe, tinge, swinge, twinge **2.** unhinge, impinge, infringe, *syringe*, astringe, attinge, atwinge.

INK– **1.** ink, Inc., inc [slang], chink, dink, Fink, fink [slang], gink [slang], jink, kink, skink, link, blink, clink, slink, mink, smink [slang], pink, spink, rink, brink, drink, prink, shrink, trink, sink, cinque, stink, think, wink, quink [slang], twink, zinc **2.** perjink, *iceblink*, relink, enlink, unlink, pincpinc, Sintsink, bethink, forethink, *hoodwink* **3.** bobolink, interlink, countersink, tiddlywink, jinniwink.

INKS– inks etc., *see* **INK–** ink etc. above, plus "s" or "'s"; **1.** sphinx, jinx, lynx, minx **2.** methinks **3.** criosphinx.

INKT– **1.** inked, chinked, kinked, linked, blinked, clinked, minked, pinked, rinked, prinked, tinct, winked **2.** beminked, succinct, discinct, instinct, distinct, extinct, *hoodwinked* 3. indistinct.

INS– 1. chinse, mince, rinse, prince, since, wince, quince 2. evince, convince 3. merchant prince; *see* also **INTS–** bints etc. below.

INT– 1. bint, dint, hint, lint, blint [slang], flint, glint, splint, mint, print, sprint, tint, stint, vint, quint, squint. 2. *skinflint*, *gunflint*, *capmint*, *spearmint*, *catmint*, reprint, *hoofprint*, imprint, misprint, *footprint*, *blueprint* 3. sodamint, calamint, peppermint, gingerprint, aquatint, monotint, mezzotint 4. septuagint.

INTH– 1. plinth 2. *Corinth* 3. terebinth, labyrinth, hyacinth, colocynth.

INTS– bints etc., *see* **INT–** bint etc. above, plus "s" or "'s"; 1. chintz.

INZ– ins etc., *see* **IN–** in etc. above, plus "s" or "'s."

IP– 1. chip, dip, fip [slang], gip, hip, gyp, jip, jipp [both slang], kip, skip, lip, blip [slang], flip, glip [slang], clip, slip, nip, snip, pip, rip, drip, grip, grippe, scrip, trip, strip, thrip, sip, ship, tip, quip, whip, yip, zip 2. redip, inclip, unclip, *harelip*, *cowslip*, *catnip*, adrip, unrip, unstrip, outstrip, sibship, *headship*, midship, *friendship*, *hardship*, *lordship* *wardship*, reship, *flagship*, *judgeship*, *clanship*, transship, *queenship*, *kinship*, *sonship*, *township*, *troopship*, *airship*, *heirship*, *worship*, *warship*, *lightship*, *saintship*, *courtship*, equip, *coachwhip*, *horsewhip* 3. pogonip, comradeship, amidship, stewardship, *trusteeship*, ladyship, battleship, seamanship, workmanship, penmanship, horsemanship, chairmanship, statesmanship, sportsmanship, fellowship, scholarship, membership, leadership, partnership, ownership, censorship, sponsorship, authorship 4. guardianship, partisanship, citizenship, companionship, relationship, survivorship, acquaintanceship, apprenticeship.

IPS– chips etc., *see* **IP–** chip etc. above, plus "s" or "'s"; 1. Phipps 2. ellipse, eclipse 4. Apocalypse.

IPT– 1. chipped, gipped, gypped, skipped, lipped, clipped, clipt, slipped, dripped, crypt, script, whipped 2. *harelipped*, *thin-lipped*, *stiff-lipped*, *red-lipped*, *close-lipped*, *subscript*, *transcript*, conscript, proscript, *postscript*, *horsewhipped* 3. eucalypt, antescript, superscript, manuscript 4. apocalypt.

IR– through **IRZ–**, *see* short **U** (tub): **UR–** through **URZ–**.

IS– 1. bis, Dis, diss, hiss, kiss, lis, liss, bliss, gliss [slang], miss, Chris, priss [coll.], Tris, sis, siss, this, vis, wis [arch. or obs.], quis, cuisse, Swiss 2. abyss, dehisce, amiss, remiss, dismiss, iwis, ywis [both arch.] 3. magadis, cowardice, prejudice, benefice, edifice, sacrifice, orifice, artifice, Judas kiss, chrysalis, fortalice, Salamis, Artemis, reminisce, precipice, avarice, dentifrice, verdigris, mistigris, ambergris, licorice, Beatrice, cockatrice, emphasis, synthesis, emesis, Nemesis, genesis, abatis, clematis, armistice, interstice 4. Gallipolis, acropolis, necropolis, metropolis, anabasis, metabasis, psoriasis, periphrasis, metastasis, hypostasis, antithesis, parenthesis, diaeresis, analysis, paralysis 5. fideicommiss, sui generis [L.], biogenesis, metamorphosis 6. elephantiasis, abiogenesis, adipogenesis.

ISH– 1. ish, dish, fish, gish, lish, mish [slang], pish, wish, cuish, squish, swish 2. mayfish, crayfish, redfish, goldfish, swordfish, kingfish, clingfish, stingfish, dogfish, hogfish, frogfish, blackfish, creekfish, weakfish, inkfish, sailfish, shellfish, filefish, tilefish, greenfish, queenfish, pinfish, jawfish, crawfish, sawfish, garfish, starfish, batfish, catfish, flatfish, ratfish, whitefish, jewfish, bluefish, cowfish, plowfish, anguish 3. jellyfish, killifish, candlefish, devilfish, squirrelfish, tasselfish, cuttlefish, ribbonfish, surgeonfish, cigarfish, guitarfish, amberfish, barberfish, thunderfish, niggerfish, triggerfish, silverfish, babyish, dowdyish, devilish, womanish, heathenish, yellowish, willowish, ogreish, Quakerish, feverish, cleverish.

ISK– **1.** bisque, disc, disk, fisc, Fiske, lisk [dial.], pisk, risk, brisk, frisk, tisk! [coll.], whisk **2.** *lutfisk*, francisc **3.** odalisque, obelisk, basilisk, tamarisk, asterisk.

ISM– *see* **IZM–**.

ISP– **1.** lisp, risp, crisp, wisp, whisp.

IST– **1.** ist, fist, fyst, hissed, hist, gist, jist, kissed, list, missed, mist, rist, frist [slang], wrist, grist, prissed [coll.], tryst, sist, sissed, cist, cyst, schist, wist, twist, whist **2.** puckfist, dehisced, agist, bekissed, unkissed, alist, enlist, bemist, unmissed, dismissed, assist, subsist, desist, resist, encyst, insist, consist, exist, persist, atwist, entwist, untwist **3.** Judaist, archaist, ultraist, prosaist, Arabist, methodist, psalmodist, threnodist, monodist, synodist, parodist, rhapsodist, concordist, Talmudist, atheist, tritheist, pacifist, specifist, elegist, strategist, eulogist, liturgist, monachist, catechist, anarchist, monarchist, apathist, amethyst, cymbalist, pedalist, feudalist, racialist, specialist, socialist, martialist, formalist, annalist, analyst, catalyst, journalist, choralist, moralist, pluralist, ruralist, fatalist, vitalist, novelist, pugilist, nihilist, libellist, duellist, symbolist, Aeolist, sciolist, fabulist, querulist, dynamist, ceramist, alchemist, pessimist, optimist, ophthalmist, undismissed, lachrymist, urbanist, Urbanist, vulcanist, organist, mechanist, Shamanist, Romanist, botanist, alienist, Hellenist, reminisced, terminist, Alpinist, Latinist, Calvinist, columnist, trombonist, hedonist, unionist, visionist, actionist, factionist, fictionist, notionist, Zionist, colonist, mnemonist, mammonist, harmonist, canonist, modernist, saturnist, communist, Taoist, egoist, jingoist, banjoist, soloist, Shintoist, landscapist, syncopist, Eucharist, diarist, solarist, summarist, glossarist, Lazarist, mesmerist, preterist, satirist, theorist, aphorist, colorist, amorist, armorist, humorist, terrorist, motorist, symmetrist, Scripturist, synthesist, pharmacist, solecist, mythicist, biblicist, publicist, classicist, physicist, exorcist, hydrocyst, colipsist, progressist, prelatist, schematist, stigmatist, dogmatist, pietist, quietist, magnetist, phonetist, syncretist, occultist, scientist, presentist, Adventist, narcotist, egotist, hypnotist, nepotist, despotist, altruist, casuist, bolshevist, archivist, passivist, activist, pre-exist, coexist, intertwist, essayist, hobbyist, lobbyist, copyist **4.** mosaicist, polemicist, empiricist, romanticist, chiropodist, telegraphist, telepathist, commercialist, nominalist, nationalist, liberalist, federalist, literalist, naturalist, capitalist, Scripturalist, ritualist, revivalist, evangelist, philatelist, parabolist, hyperbolist, monopolist, legitimist, epitomist, zootomist, accompanist, hygienist, alienist, determinist, protagonist, tobacconist, religionist, opinionist, communionist, revisionist, extensionist, delusionist, illusionist, reactionist, perfectionist, obstructionist, eudaemonist, misogynist, emancipist, plagiarist, apiarist, secularist, ocularist, singularist, militarist, psychiatrist, hexametrist, pedometrist, problematist, systematist, enigmatist, diplomatist, automatist, numismatist, separatist **5.** bibliopegist, industrialist, conventionalist, Universalist, transcendentalist, spiritualist, automobilist, indeterminist, revolutionist, particularist, caricaturist, experimentist, apocalyptist; *and many other agent nouns ending in the suffiz "-ist."*

IT– **1.** it, bit, bitt, chit, dit, ditt [both dial.], fit, phit, git [dial.], hit, jit [slang], kit, skit, lit, flit, split, slit, mit, mitt, smit, nit, knit, pit, spit, writ, rit, brit, frit, grit, sprit, sit, cit, tit, wit, whit, quit, twit, zit [slang] **2.** *tidbit*, *titbit*, *forebitt*, befit, unfit, misfit, *outfit*, alit, unlit, *twilit*, *moonlit*, *sunlit*, submit, admit, emit, demit, remit, commit, omit, permit, transmit, reknit, unknit, *cockpit, coalpit, armpit, ashpit, lickspit, turnspit, pitpit, daywrit,* outsit, tomtit, *godwit, chickwit,* outwit, acquit **3.** counterfeit, compromit, intromit, pretermit, intermit, manumit, Messerschmitt, definite, infinite, interknit, preterit, hypocrite, favorite, apposite, opposite, requisite, exquisite, perquisite, Jesuit **4.** indefinite, prerequisite, inapposite, unopposite.

ITH– **1.** kith, lith, myth, smith, smyth, pith, frith, crith. sith **2.** *trilith, goldsmith, locksmith, tinsmith, gunsmith* **3.** megalith, neolith, monolith, acrolith, coppersmith, silversmith, Arrowsmith **4.** paleolith, anthropolith.

ITHE– **1.** with, withe **2.** bewith, hamewith, herewith, therewith, wherewith, forthwith.

ITS– its etc., *see* **IT–** it etc. above, plus "s" or "'s"; **1.** Fitz, blitz, spitz, Ritz, Fritz, sitz.

IV– **1.** chiv [slang], div [slang], give, live, fliv [slang], spiv [slang], sieve, shiv [slang] **2.** forgive, misgive, relive, outlive **3.** combative, negative, sedative, quiddative, purgative, talkative, ablative, amative, sanative, narrative, curative, causative, fixative, auditive, quietive, expletive, fugitive, primitive, dormitive, nutritive, tortitive, partitive, substantive **4.** figurative, intensative, consultative, impeditive **5.** conciliative; *and many other adjectives ending in the suffiz "-ive."*

IVD– **1.** lived, sieved **2.** relived, unlived, outlived, long-lived, short-lived **3.** negatived.

IZ– **1.** is, biz [slang], Diz, fizz, phiz [slang], his, gizz [Scot. & N. of Eng.], Liz, riz [dial.], friz, sizz, 'tis, viz, wiz [slang], quiz, whiz, zizz **2.** Cadiz, gin fizz, befriz, requiz, gee whizz [coll.].

IZM– **1.** ism, schism, chrism, prism **2.** abysm **3.** Judaism, archaism, Lamaism, Hebraism, ultraism, Mosaism, prosaism, Methodism, Yankeeism, atheism, bitheism, pacifism, dandyism, Toryism, rowdyism, syllogism, eulogism, energism, synergism, liturgism, catechism, anarchism, monarchism, Baalism, cabalism, tribalism, verbalism, vandalism, feudalism, realism, legalism, regalism, frugalism, localism, vocalism, carnalism, journalism, papalism, moralism, centralism, pluralism, ruralism, racialism, socialism, fatalism, vitalism, dualism, loyalism, royalism, nihilism, pugilism, servilism, cataclysm, embolism, symbolism, idolism, botulism, euphemism, animism, pessimism, optimism, peanism, paganism, organism, Romanism, Satanism, Brahmanism, feminism, cretinism, destinism, Calvinism, Darwinism, lionism, Zionism, demonism, Mormonism, Platonism, modernism, communism, unionism, Taoism, egoism, heroism, Shintoism, barbarism, plagiarism, solarism, Quakerism, mesmerism, mannerism, pauperism, theorism, aphorism, humorism, terrorism, historism, pasteurism, ostracism, solecism, Gallicism, Biblicism, publicism, Anglicism, synicism, Sinicism, stoicism, lyricism, classicism, criticism, witticism, skepticism, mysticism, paroxysm, sabbatism, dogmatism, grammatism, pietism, quietism, magnetism, syncretism, Semitism, occultism, egotism, hypnotism, nepotism, despotism, Hinduism, altruism, untruism, atavism, Bolshevism, nativism, powwowism, Kukluxism **4.** theosophism, philosophism, cannibalism, surrealism, radicalism, rationalism, liberalism, federalism, commercialism, capitalism, teetotalism, ritualism, evangelism, catabolism, metabolism, hyperbolism, alcoholism, monopolism, somnambulism, Confucianism, Puritanism, determinism, impressionism, infusionism, plagiarism, peculiarism, militarism, allegorism, Epicurism, amateurism, Italicism, Catholicism, empiricism, grammaticism, fanaticism, phoneticism, asceticism, romanticism, neuroticism, agnosticism, astigmatism, automatism, democratism, conservatism, favoritism, patriotism, absolutism, progressivism, subjectivism, collectivism, somniloquism, ventriloquism **5.** proverbialism, imperialism, materialism, colloquialism, phenomenalism, sensationalism, professionalism, conventionalism, municipalism, universalism, controversialism, sentimentalism, instrumentalism, spiritualism, republicanism, Americanism, Mohammedanism, microorganism, multitudinism, indeterminism, restorationism, prohibitionism, exhibitionism, evolutionism, revolutionism, incendiarism, peculiarism, particularism **6.** supernaturalism, individualism, cosmopolitanism **7.** humanitarianism, parliamentarianism **8.** valetudinarianism, establishmentarianism; *and many other nouns ending in the suffiz "ism."*

I (bib)

2.

DOUBLE (FEMININE) RHYMES IN I (bib′ber)

Primary or Secondary Accent Falls on Next to Last Syllable; Imperfect Rhymes Are in Italics.

IB–ald– ribald; *see* also **IB′ld–** bibbled etc. below.

IB′er– **2.** bibber, dibber, fibber, gibber, jibber, glibber, nibber, ribber, cribber, squibber **3.** winebibber, ad libber [slang].

IB′est– **2.** glibbest.

IB′et– **2.** gibbet, libbet, ribbet, zibet **3.** inhibit, prohibit, exhibit **5.** flibbertigibbet.

IB′i– **2.** gibby, skibby [loc.], Libby, nibby [Scot. & N. of Eng.], ribby, fribby, tibby **4.** nibby-jibby, nibby-gibby.

IB′ij– **2.** cribbage.

IB′ing– **2.** bibbing, fibbing, jibbing, ribbing, cribbing, squibbing **3.** winebibbing, ad libbing [slang].

IB′it– **3.** adhibit, inhibit, prohibit, exhibit; *see* also **IB′et–** gibbet etc. above.

IB′l– **2.** bibble, dibble, gibel, kibble, nibble, ribble, dribble, fribble, gribble, scribble, tribble, thribble, sibyl, cibol, quibble **3.** transcribble **4.** ishkabibble [slang].

IB′ld– **2.** bibbled, dibbled, ribald, dribbled, scribbled, quibbled.

IB′ler– **2.** bibbler, dibbler, kibbler, nibbler, dribbler, cribbler, scribbler, quibbler **3.** transcribbler.

IB′let– **2.** giblet, riblet, driblet, triblet.

IB′li– **2.** glibly, nibbly, dribbly, scribbly, quibbly.

IB′lik– **2.** Biblic, niblick **4.** philobiblic.

IB′ling– **2.** bibbling, dibbling, kibbling, nibbling, dribbling, fribbling, cribbling, scribbling, sibling, quibbling **3.** transcribbling.

IB′on– **2.** gibbon, ribbon **3.** blue ribbon.

IB′onz– **2.** bibbons, gibbons, Gibbons, ribbons.

IB′sen– **2.** Ibsen, Gibson.

IB′ut– **2.** tribute **3.** attribute, retribute, contribute, distribute.

ICH′el– **2.** Mitchell, switchel.

ICH′en– **2.** kitchen.

ICH′er– **2.** itcher, ditcher, hitcher, snitcher [slang], pitcher, richer, stitcher, switcher, twitcher **3.** enricher, bewitcher.

ICH′est– **2.** richest.

ICH′et– **2.** fitchet, witchet, twitchet.

ICH′ez– **2.** itches, bitches, ditches, hitches, flitches, niches, snitches [slang], pitches, riches, britches, breeches, stitches, witches, switches, twitches **3.** enriches, bewitches.

ICH′i– **2.** itchy, bitchy, fitchy, hitchy, pitchy, stitchy, witchy, switchy, twitchy.

ICH′ing– **2.** itching, ditching, hitching, pitching, stitching, witching, switching, twitching **3.** enriching, bewitching.

ICH′less– **2.** itchless, ditchless, hitchless, pitchless, stitchless, witchless, switchless, twitchless.

ICH′li– **2.** richly.

ICH′ment– **3.** enrichment, bewitchment.

ID′ans– **2.** biddance, riddance **3.** forbiddance, good riddance.

ID'ed– 2. kidded, skidded, lidded, ridded 4. invalided, pyramided.

ID'en– 2. bidden, hidden, midden, slidden, ridden, stridden 3. unbidden, forbidden, beridden, bedridden, childridden, hagridden, plague-ridden, unthridden 4. unforbidden, kitchen midden, fever-ridden, overridden.

ID'er– 2. bidder, kidder, Kidder, skidder, slidder, ridder 3. rebidder, forbidder, outbidder, consider 4. overbidder, reconsider, disconsider.

ID'erd– 3. considered 4. reconsidered, ill-considered, well-considered, unconsidered.

ID'i– 2. biddy, diddy [dial.], giddy, kiddy, skiddy, middy, tiddy, widdy 3. Dinwiddie 4. chickabiddy.

ID'ik– 3. rubidic, iridic, juridic, acidic, fatidic, druidic 4. pyramidic.

ID'ing– 2. bidding, kidding, skidding, ridding 3. forbidding, outbidding 4. underbidding, overbidding, unforbidding, pyramiding.

ID'ish– 2. kiddish, Yiddish.

ID'l– 2. diddle, fiddle, middle, niddle [Scot. & Ir.], piddle, riddle, riddel, griddle, quiddle, twiddle 3. flumdiddle, condiddle, unriddle 4. flummadiddle, tarradiddle.

ID'ler– 2. diddler, fiddler, piddler, riddler, twiddler 4. tarradiddler.

ID'ling– 2. diddling, fiddling, kidling, middling, piddling, riddling, griddling twiddling.

ID'ni– 2. kidney, Sidney, Sydney.

ID'o– 2. kiddo [slang], widow.

IF'en– 2. striffen, stiffen; *see* also **IF'in–** biffin etc. below.

IF'er– 2. differ, niffer, sniffer, stiffer, squiffer [slang], whiffer.

IF'est– 2. stiffest.

IF'i– 2. iffy [slang], jiffy, Liffey, cliffy, miffy, sniffy, spiffy [slang], squiffy [slang], whiffy.

IF'ik– 2. glyphic 3. morbific, rubific, deific, algific, triglyphic, prolific, magnific, somnific, terrific, aurific, horrific, classific, pacific, Pacific, specific, sensific, ossific, lucific, mucific, lactific, pontific, vivific 4. diaglyphic, anaglyphic, geoglyphic, logogriphic, calorific, dolorific, humorific, honorific, sonorific, saporific, soporific, beatific, scientific 5. hieroglyphic 6. dactylioglyphic.

IF'iks– 3. significs, specifics 4. calorifics, colorifics 5. hieroglyphics, dermatoglyphics.

IF'in– 2. biffin, griffin, striffen, tiffin, stiffen; *see* also **IF'on–** griffon etc. below.

IF'ing– 2. biffing, miffing [dial. & slang], sniffing, spiffing, tiffing, whiffing.

IF'ish– 2. sniffish, tiffish, stiffish.

IF'l– nifle [dial.], sniffle, piffle, riffle, whiffle.

IF'ler– 2. sniffler, piffler, riffler, whiffler.

IF'li– 2. sniffly, stiffly.

IF'ling– 2. sniffling, piffling, riffling, whiffling.

IF'on– 2. griffon, chiffon.

IFT'ed– 2. gifted, lifted, rifted, drifted, sifted, shifted 3. ungifted, uplifted.

IFT'er– 2. lifter, drifter, sifter, shifter, swifter 3. uplifter, *shoplifter*, *sceneshifter*.

IFT'est– 2. swiftest.

IFT'i– 2. fifty, clifty, nifty [slang], snifty, rifty, drifty, thrifty, shifty 4. fifty-fifty.

IFT'ij– 2. driftage, siftage, shiftage.

IFT'ing– 2. gifting, lifting, snifting, rifting, drifting, sifting, shifting 3. *shoplifting*, uplifting, resifting, *sceneshifting*.

IFT'less– 2. giftless, liftless, riftless, driftless, thriftless, shiftless.

IFT'ness– 2. miffedness, swiftness.

IG'an– 2. wigan 3. balbriggan.

IG′and– 2. brigand 3. balbrigganed.

IG′er– 2. bigger, chigger, digger, gigger, jigger, ligger, nigger, snigger, rigger, rigor, prigger, sprigger, trigger, sigger, wigger, swigger, twigger, vigor 3. gold digger, gravedigger, reneger, outrigger 4. thimblerigger.

IG′erd– 2. jiggered, niggard, sniggered, triggered 3. unniggard, bejiggered.

IG′ers– chiggers etc., *see* **IG′er–** bigger etc. above, plus "s" or "'s."

IG′est– 2. biggest, triggest.

IG′i– 2. biggy, piggy, spriggy, wiggy, twiggy 4. piggy-wiggy.

IG′ing– 2. digging, gigging, jigging, rigging, trigging, wigging, swigging, twigging 3. redigging, reneging, unrigging 4. thimblerigging.

IG′ish– 2. giggish, jiggish, riggish, priggish, wiggish, Whiggish.

IG′it– 2. giggit, jigget, jiggit [both coll.], Brigit, frigate.

IG′izm– 2. priggism, wiggism, Whiggism.

IG′l– 2. giggle, higgle, jiggle, niggle, sniggle, wriggle, striggle [coll. Eng.], wiggle, swiggle [dial.], squiggle 3. *porwigle.*

IG′ler– 2. giggler, higgler, jiggler, niggler, sniggler, wriggler, wiggler, squiggler [slang].

IG′let– 2. giglet, piglet, wiglet, Whiglet.

IG′li– 2. bigly, giggly, jiggly, niggly, pigly, wiggly, wriggly, squiggly 4. Uncle Wiggly.

IG′ling– 2. giggling, higgling, jiggling, niggling, pigling, wriggling, wiggling, swiggling [dial.], squiggling.

IG′ma– 2. sigma, stigma 3. enigma, kerygma, sterigma 4. hypostigma.

IG′me– 2. pigmy, stigme.

IG′ment– 2. figment, pigment.

IG′nant– 3. indignant, malignant, benignant.

IG′net– 2. signet, cygnet.

IG′num– 2. lignum, rignum, signum, tignum.

IG′or– 2. rigor, vigor; *see* also **IG′er–** bigger etc. above.

IG′ot– 2. bigot, gigot, spigot, riggot, frigate.

IG′ur– 2. figure, ligure 3. refigure, prefigure, configure, disfigure, transfigure.

IJ′er– 2. ridger, bridger 3. abridger.

IJ′et– 2. fidget, midget, nidget, Bridget, digit.

IJ′i– 2. gidgee, midgy, ridgy, squidgy.

IJ′id– 2. rigid, frigid 3. unrigid, unfrigid.

IJ′il– 2. strigil, sigil, vigil.

IJ′ing– 2. fidging [dial.], nidging, ridging, bridging 3. abridging, enridging.

IJ′it– digit; *see* also **IJ′et–** fidget etc. above.

IJ′on– 2. smidgen, pigeon, pidgin, widgeon, wigeon 3. religion 4. irreligion, gyropigeon.

IJ′us– 3. prodigious, religious, litigious 4. irreligious, unreligious, sacrilegious 5. overreligious, unsacrilegious.

IK′a– 2. licca, sicca, ticca, tikka.

IK′ed– 2. wicked.

IK′en– 2. chicken, Rikken, stricken, sicken, thicken, quicken 4. wonder-stricken, terror-stricken, horror-stricken.

IK′enz– chickens etc., *see* **IK′en–** chicken etc. above, plus "s" or "'s"; 2. Dickens.

IK′er– 2. icker [Scot.], bicker, dicker, kicker, licker, liquor, flicker, clicker, slicker, smicker, nicker, knicker, snicker, picker, ricker, pricker, tricker, sicker, ticker, tikker, sticker, thicker, vicar, wicker, quicker 3. *bootlicker.*

IK′erz– ickers etc., *see* **IK′er–** icker etc. above, plus "s" or "'s."

IK′est– 2. slickest, sickest, thickest, quickest.

IK′et– 2. clicket, smicket, snicket, picket, spicket, cricket, pricket, siket [dial.], ticket, thicket, wicket **3.** reticket, midwicket **4.** walking ticket.

IK'ets– 2. pickets, rickets, crickets, tickets, wickets.

IK'i– 2. icky [slang], dicky, dickey, hickey, Micky, Nicky, snickey, picky, rickey, bricky, crickey [slang], pricky, tricky, tickey, sticky, Vicky, wicky **3.** doo hickey [slang], jinriki, gin rickey.

IK'ing– 2. kicking, licking, flicking, clicking, slicking, nicking, snicking, picking, ricking, bricking, cricking, tricking, ticking, wicking **3.** bootlicking, hand picking **4.** pocket-picking.

IK'ish– 2. slickish, hickish [slang], pickish, prickish, trickish, sickish, stickish, thickish.

IK'l– 2. chicle, fickle, mickle [dial.], nickel, pickle, pikle, prickle, trickle, strickel, sickle, tickle **3.** renickel, depickle **4.** cupronickel, pumpernickel.

IK'ler– 2. fickler, pickler, prickler, strickler, tickler, stickler.

IK'let– 2. chiclet, tricklet.

IK'li– 2. slickly, prickly, trickly, sickly, tickly, stickly, thickly, quickly.

IK'ling– 2. chickling, pickling, prickling, trickling, tickling, stickling.

IK'lish– 2. pricklish, ticklish.

IK'ness– 2. slickness, sickness, thickness, quickness **3.** *homesickness*, *heartsickness*, *lovesickness*.

IK'nik– 2. picnic, pyknic, strychnic **4.** isopycnic.

IK'ning– 3. sickening, thickening, quickening.

IKS'a– 2. Bixa.

IKS'en– 2. Bixin, mixen, vixen.

IKS'er– 2. fixer, mixer, sixer **3.** affixer, prefixer, transfixer, elixir **4.** intermixer.

IKSH'a– 2. ricksha **3.** jinricksha **4.** jinrickisha.

IKSH'un– 2. diction, fiction, friction, striction **3.** addiction, prediction, indiction, affixion, prefixion, transfixion, suffixion, reliction, affliction, infliction, confliction, depiction, obstriction, restriction, constriction, eviction, conviction **4.** contradiction, malediction, valediction, benediction, interdiction, jurisdiction, crucifixion, dereliction.

IKS'i– 2. Dixie, dixie, dixy, jixie, mixy, nixie, nixy [cant], pixy, pixie, rixy [loc., Eng.], tricksy, Trixie.

IKS'ing– 2. fixing, mixing **3.** affixing, prefixing, admixing, commixing **4.** intermixing.

IKS'it– 2. dixit **4.** ipse dixit.

IKS'tur– 2. fixture, mixture **3.** affixture, immixture, commixture **4.** intermixture.

IKT'al– 2. rictal **3.** edictal.

IKT'at– 2. dictate, nictate.

IKT'ed– 3. addicted, predicted, relicted, afflicted, inflicted, conflicted, depicted, restricted, constricted, evicted, convicted **4.** contradicted, interdicted, self-inflicted, unrestricted, unconstricted.

IKT'er– 2. fictor, lictor, Pictor, stricter, victor **3.** predictor, afflicter, inflicter, conflicter, depicter, depictor, constrictor, evictor, convictor **4.** contradicter, contradictor **5.** boa constrictor.

IKT'est– 2. lickedest, strictest.

IKT'i– 5. corpus delicti.

IKT'ik– 2. ictic **3.** deictic **4.** apodictic, endeictic.

IKT'im– 2. victim, kicked him.

IKT'ing– 3. addicting, predicting, afflicting, inflicting, conflicting, depicting, restricting, constricting, evicting, convicting **4.** contradicting, unconflicting, unconstricting.

IKT'iv– 2. fictive **3.** addictive, predictive, indictive, afflictive, inflictive, conflictive, depictive, astrictive, restrictive, constrictive, convictive **4.** contradictive, maledictive, benedictive, apodictive, interdictive, jurisdictive, nonrestrictive.

IKT'or– 2. fictor, lictor, Pictor, victor 3. depictor, convictor 4. interdictor 5. boa constrictor.

IKT'um– 2. dictum 3. delictum.

IKT'ur– 2. picture, stricture 3. depicture, impicture, word picture.

IKT'us– 2. ictus, rictus 3. Invictus 4. Benedictus, acronyctous.

IK'up– 2. dikkop, hiccup, hiccough, pickup.

IL'a– 2. Scylla, villa, squilla, Squilla, Zilla 3. chincilla, cedilla, camilla, Camilla, armilla, Manila, manilla, vanilla, papilla, guerrilla, spirilla, gorilla, Priscilla, Drusilla, mantilla, scintilla, flotilla, axilla, maxilla 4. sabadilla, granadilla, cascarilla, camarilla 5. sarsaparilla.

IL'an– 2. Villain, villein 3. archvillain.

IL'ar– 2. pillar 4. caterpillar, camarilla; *see* also **IL'er–** iller etc. below.

ILB'ert– 2. filbert, Gilbert.

ILCH'er– 2. filcher, milcher, pilcher.

ILD'a– 2. Hilda, tilde 3. Brünnhilde, Matilda, Mathilda.

ILD'ed– 2. builded, gilded 3. begilded, ungilded.

ILD'er– 2. builder, gilder, guilder, wilder 3. rebuilder, shipbuilder, housebuilder, begilder, bewilder.

ILD'ing– 2. building, gilding 3. begilding, shipbuilding 4. castle-building.

ILD'u– 2. mildew, will do.

IL'er– 2. iller, biller, chiller, filler, giller, hiller, killer, miller, pillar, spiller, driller, friller, griller, shriller, triller, thriller, siller, schiller, tiller, stiller, thiller, willer, quiller, swiller 3. fulfiller, painkiller, man-killer, befriller, pralltriller, distiller, instiller 4. killer-diller [slang], giant-killer, lady-killer [slang], caterpillar.

IL'est– 2. illest, chillest, shrillest, stillest.

IL'et– 2. billet, fillet, skillet, millet, pillet, rillet, drillet, trillet, willet, quillet 3. pilwillet.

IL'fer– 2. pilfer 4. Bella Wilfer [Dickens].

IL'ful– 2. skillful, willful 3. unskillful, unwillful.

IL'grim– 2. pilgrim.

IL'i– 2. billy, Billie, chilly, chili, Chile, dilly, dilli, filly, gillie, hilly, lily, Millie, rilly, frilly, grilly, shrilly, thrilly, silly, Scilly, tilly, tilley, Tillie, Willie, willy, willey, quilly, twilly 4. Piccadilly, daffodilly, piccalilli, tiger lily, water lily, willy-nilly 5. daffydowndilly; *see* also **IL'li–** illy etc. below.

IL'id– 2. gillied, lilied.

IL'ij– 2. pillage, grillage, tillage, stillage, village.

IL'ik– 3. idyllic, odylic, vanillic, Cyrillic, basilic, dactylic, exilic 4. hemophilic, zoophilic, imbecilic, salicylic 5. homodactylic.

IL'ing– 2. billing, chilling, filling, killing, milling, spilling, drilling, frilling, grilling, trilling, thrilling, shilling, schilling, tilling, stilling, willing, quilling, swilling 3. fulfilling, befrilling, distilling, instilling, unwilling 4. unfulfilling, overwilling.

IL'ip– 2. fillip, Philip.

IL'is– 2. Phyllis, cilice, Willis 4. amaryllis.

IL'iz– 2. billies, dillies, fillies, gillies, lilies, sillies, Scillies, willies 3. Achilles.

ILK'en– 2. milken, silken.

ILK'er– 2. bilker, milker, silker.

ILK'i– 2. milky, silky, Willkie.

ILK'ing– 2. bilking, milking, silking.

IL'li– 2. illy, skilly, stilly, willy; *see* also **IL'i–** billy etc. above.

IL'man– 2. billman, Gilman, hill man, millman, pillman, grillman, Stillman.

IL'ment– 3. fulfilment, distillment, instillment.

IL'mi– 2. filmy.

IL'ness– 2. illness, chillness, shrillness, stillness.

IL'o– 2. billow, kilo, pillow, willow 3. Camillo, lapillo, Negrillo 4. peccadillo, armadillo, grenadillo, tabardillo, weeping willow.

IL'ok– 2. fillock, hillock, sillock.

ILT'ed– 2. hilted, jilted, kilted, lilted, silted, tilted, stilted, wilted, quilted 3. tip-tilted, unwilted 4. crazy-quilted.

ILT'er– 2. filter, philter, jilter, kilter, milter, tilter, stilter, wilter, quilter 3. refilter, infilter.

ILT'i– 2. guilty, silty, tilty, stilty.

ILT'ing– 2. jilting, kilting, lilting, silting, tilting, stilting, wilting, quilting 3. tip-tilting, unwilting 4. crazy quilting.

IL'um– 4. aspergillum.

IL'us– 2. gryllus, villus, villous 3. camillus, capillus, lapillus, arillus, fibrillous, bacillus, favillous, pulvillus 4. aspergillus.

ILV'er– 2. silver 3. resilver, quicksilver.

IL'yans– 2. brilliance 3. non-brilliance, resilience, consilience; *see* also **IL'i–ens**– resilience etc.

IL'yant– 2. brilliant 3. unbrilliant, resilient 4. overbrilliant; *see* also **IL'i–ent**– resilient etc.

IL'yar– 3. familiar, auxiliar 4. unfamiliar 5. overfamiliar.

IL'yard– 2. billiard, milliard.

IL'yun– 2. billion, million, pillion, prillion, trillion, stillion 3. tourbillion, mandilion, modillion, vermilion, nonillion, carillon, quadrillion, decillion, octillion, centillion, quintillion, cotillion, septillion, sextillion, postilion, pavilion, civilian.

IL'yus– 2. bilious 4. atrabilious; *see* also **IL'i–us**– punctilious etc.

IM'aj– 2. image, scrimmage 3. archimage.

IM'ba– 2. simba 3. marimba.

IMB'al– 2. gimbol, cymbal, symbol, simball, timbal 4. clavicymbal.

IMB'er– 2. limber, timber, timbre 3. unlimber, retimber.

IMB'l– 2. bimbil, fimble, nimble, cymbal, simbil, symbol, simball, timball, thimble, wimble.

IMB'o– 2. kimbo, limbo 3. akimbo.

IMB'us– 2. limbus, limbous, nimbus.

IM'el– 2. Himmel [G.], heml, kümmel; *see* also **IM'l**– gimmal etc. below.

IM'er– 2. dimmer, gimmer, hymner, skimmer, limmer, glimmer, slimmer, nimmer, brimmer, grimmer, krimmer, primer, primmer, trimmer, simmer, shimmer, swimmer 3. aglimmer, asimmer, ashimmer 4. trihemimer.

IM'est– 2. dimmest, slimmest, grimmest, primmest, trimmest.

IM'i– 2. gimme [slang], jimmy, skimmy, limby, shimmy, whimmy, zimme.

IM'id– 2. imid, jimmied, shimmied, timid.

IM'ij– 2. image, scrimmage 3. arch image.

IM'ik– 2. gimmick [slang], mimic, wimick, zymic 3. alchimic, etymic 4. cherubimic, zoomimic, pantomimic, pseudonymic, homonymic, synonymic, eponymic, patronymic, metronymic, metonymic.

IM'ing– 2. dimming, skimming, limbing, blimbing, slimming, brimming, trimming, swimming 3. bedimming, retrimming.

IM'it– 2. limit.

IM'l– 2. gimmal, Himmel [G.], heml, kümmel, Friml.

IM'less– 2. hymnless, limbless, rimless, brimless, vimless, whimless.

IM'li– 2. dimly, slimly, grimly, primly, trimly.

IM'ner– 2. hymner, limner.

M'ness– 2. dimness, slimness, grimness, primness, trimness.

M'ni– 2. chimney 3. lamp chimney.

MP'er– 2. skimper, limper, crimper, scrimper, shrimper, simper, whimper.

MP'est– 2. limpest.

IMP'i– 2. impi, impy, skimpy, limpy, crimpy, scrimpy, shrimpi, shrimpy.

IMP'ing– 2. imping, skimping, limping, crimping, scrimping, primping, shrimping.

IMP'ish– 2. impish, limpish, shrimpish.

IMP'l– 2. dimple, pimple, rimple, crimple, simple, wimple 3. bewimple, unwimple.

IMP'ler– 2. dimpler, rimpler, simpler, wimpler.

IMP'lest– 2. simplest.

IMP'li– 2. dimply, limply, pimply, simply.

IMP'ling– 2. impling, dimpling, pimpling, rimpling, crimpling.

IMZ'i– 2. flimsy, slimsy, mimsey, whimsey.

IMZ'on– 2. crimson 3. encrimson.

IN'a– 2. binna, Mina, pinna 3. meminna, Corinna.

IN'as– 2. inness, pinnace 3. Erinys.

IN'at– 2. innate, pinnate 3. bipinnate.

INCH'er– 2. lyncher, flincher, clincher, pincher, cincher 4. penny pincher [slang].

INCH'ing– 2. inching, lynching, flinching, clinching, pinching, cinching 4. penny-pinching [slang].

IND'a– 2. Linda, pinda 3. Belinda, Lucinda 4. Ethelinda.

IND'ed– 2. brinded, sinded, winded 3. abscinded, rescinded, exscinded, longwinded.

IND'en– 2. linden 5. Unter den Linden.

IND'er– 2. dinder, hinder, linder, flinder, pinder, Pindar, cinder, tinder, winder 3. unhinder, rescinder.

IND'i– 2. Lindy, pindy [dial.], Sindhi, Cindy, shindy [slang & loc.], windy 3. Lucindy.

IND'ik– 2. indic, Indic, syndic.

IND'l– 2. dindle, kindle, Mindel, spindle, rindle, brindle, sindle, dwindle, swindle 3. rekindle, enkindle.

IND'ler– 2. kindler, swindler 3. enkindler.

IND'ling– 2. kindling, dwindling, swindling 3. rekindling, enkindling.

IND'o– 2. lindo, window 3. show window, shopwindow.

IND'rans– 2. hindrance.

IND'red– 2. kindred.

IND'u– 2. Hindu.

IND'us– 2. Indus.

IN'en– 2. linen 4. Irish linen.

IN'er– 2. inner, dinner, finner, ginner, skinner, pinner, spinner, grinner, sinner, shinner, tinner, thinner, winner, twinner 3. beginner, breadwinner 4. afterdinner.

IN'est– 2. innest, thinnest.

IN'et– 2. linnet, minute, pinnet, spinet.

IN'fant– 2. infant.

IN'ful– 2. skinful, sinful 3. unsinful.

ING'er– 2. dinger, blinger [slang], flinger, slinger, ringer, wringer, springer, stringer, singer, stinger, winger, swinger, whinger 3. humdinger, night-winger, klipspringer, left-winger 4. Minnesinger, Meistersinger.

ING'ger– 2. finger, linger 3. forefinger, malinger.

ING'gerz– 2. fingers, lingers 4. butterfingers.

ING'i– 2. bingey, binghi, bingy, dingy, dinghy, flingy, clingy, pingy, ringy, springy, stringy, wingy, swingy.

ING'ing– 2. dinging, flinging, clinging, slinging, ringing, wringing, bringing, springing, stringing, singing, stinging, winging, swinging 3. enringing, upbringing, outwinging.

ING'l– 2. dingle, jingle, lingel, lingle, mingle, pingle, cringle, pringle, tringle, single, shingle, tingle, swingle 3. swingdingle, immingle, commingle, Kriss Kringle, surcingle, reshingle 4. intermingle.

ING'ler– 2. jingler, mingler, pingler, shingler, tingler 3. commingler.

ING'less– 2. kingless, pingless, ringless, springless, stingless, wingless.

ING'let– 2. jinglet, kinglet, ringlet, springlet, winglet.

ING'li– 2. dingly, jingly, kingly, mingly, springly, singly, shingly, tingly.

ING'ling– 2. dingling, jingling, kingling, mingling, Ringling, singling, shingling, wingling, swingling 3. immingling, commingling 4. intermingling.

ING'lish– 2. English, tinglish 3. non-English.

ING'lz– dingless etc., *see* **ING'l**– dingle etc. above, plus "s" or "'s."

ING'o– 2. bingo, dingo, jingo, lingo, gringo, stingo 3. flamingo, eryngo.

IN'i– 2. chinny, finny, guinea, hinny, ginny, jinni, Jinny, jinny, skinny, Pliny, Minnie, Minne, ninny, pinny, spinney, shinny, tinny, vinny, Winnie, squinny, whinny 3. New Guinea 4. ignominy, pickaninny, Ol' Virginny.

IN'ik– 2. dinic, finick, Finnic, clinic, pinic, Sinic, cynic, vinic, quinic 3. Rabbinic, Odinic, delphinic, aclinic, triclinic, pollinic, Brahminic, encrinic, succinic, platinic 4. Jacobinic, polyclinic, mandarinic, narcotinic.

IN'ing– 2. inning, chinning, dinning, ginning, skinning, pinning, spinning, grinning, sinning, shinning, tinning, thinning, winning 3. beginning, unpinning, breadwinning 4. underpinning, overthinning.

IN'is– 2. pinnace 3. Erinys.

IN'ish– 2. finish, Finnish, tinnish, thinnish 3. refinish, diminish.

IN'ist– 4. violinist.

INJ'ens– 3. attingence, contingence, contingents.

INJ'ent– 2. fingent, ringent, fringent, stringent, tingent 3. impingent, refringent, astringent, restringent, constringent, attingent, contingent.

INJ'er– 2. injure, hinger, ginger, fringer, cringer, singer, tinger, swinger 3. impinger, infringer.

INJ'ez– 2. binges, dinges, hinges, cringes, scringes, fringes, singes, tinges, swinges, twinges 3. unhinges, befringes, infringes, impinges, constringes, perstringes.

INJ'i– 2. dingy, cringy, fringy, stingy, twingy.

INJ'ing– 2. dingeing, hinging, cringing, fringing, singeing, tingeing, swingeing, twinging 3. unhinging, impinging, refringing, infringing, constringing, perstringing.

INJ'ment– 3. unhingement, impingement, infringement, perstringement.

INK'a– 2. Inca, Dinka, Xinca 3. Katinka, Katrinka, stotinka.

INK'er– 2. inker, skinker, linker, blinker, clinker, slinker, pinker, drinker, prinker, shrinker, sinker, tinker, stinker, thinker, winker, swinker 3. enlinker, bethinker, freethinker, *hoodwinker*.

INK'est– 2. pinkest.

INK'i– 2. inky, chinky, dinky, dinkey, kinky, linky, blinky, pinky, sinky, stinky, zincky.

INK'ij– 2. linkage, shrinkage.

INK'ing– 2. inking, chinking, kinking, skinking, linking, blinking, clinking, slinking, pinking, rinking, drinking, shrinking, sinking, stinking, thinking, winking 3. enlinking, unlinking, freethinking, unthinking, hoodwinking.

INK'l– 2. inkle, kinkle, wrinkle, crinkle, sprinkle, strinkle, tinkle, winkle, winkel 3. besprinkle, unwrinkle 4. intersprinkle, periwinkle.

INK'ler– 2. wrinkler, sprinkler, tinkler, twinkler.

INK'li– 2. pinkly, wrinkly, crinkly, tinkly, twinkly.

INK'ling– 2. inkling, wrinkling, crinkling, sprinkling, tinkling, twinkling.

INKT'iv– 3. distinctive, extinctive, instinctive 4. indistinctive, undistinctive.

INKT'li– 3. succinctly, distinctly 4. indistinctly 5. contradistinctly.

INKT'ness– 3. succinctness, distinctness 4. indistinctness, undistinctness.

INKT'ur– 2. cincture, tincture 3. pollincture, encincture.

INK'went– 3. delinquent, relinquent.

INK'wish– 3. relinquish.

IN'land– 2. inland, Finland.

IN'less– 2. dinless, finless, ginless, kinless, skinless, pinless, sinless, tinless, winless.

IN'let– 2. inlet, tinlet.

IN'li– 2. inly, thinly, twinly 3. McKinley.

IN'ness– 2. inness, thinness.

IN'o– 2. minnow, winnow.

INS'el– 2. tinsel.

INS'ens– 2. incense 3. St. Vincent's.

INS'er– 2. mincer, rinser, wincer 3. convincer.

INS'ic– 3. intrinsic, extrinsic.

INS'ing– 2. mincing, rinsing, wincing 3. evincing, convincing 4. unconvincing.

INS'ment– 3. evincement, convincement.

INST'er– 2. minster, spinster 3. Axminster, Westminster.

INST'rel– 2. minstrel.

INT'ed– 2. dinted, hinted, flinted, glinted, splinted, minted, printed, sprinted, tinted, stinted, squinted 3. reprinted, imprinted, misprinted, footprinted, unstinted, rosetinted 4. fingerprinted, rosy tinted.

INT'er– 2. hinter, linter, splinter, minter, printer, sprinter, tinter, stinter, winter, squinter, twinter 3. imprinter, midwinter 4. mezzotinter.

INTH'in– 3. absinthin, absinthine 4. terebinthine, labyrinthine, hyacinthine.

INT'i– 2. Dinty, linty, flinty, glinty, splinty, minty, shinty, tinty, squinty 3. McGinty.

INT'ij– 2. splintage, mintage, tintage, vintage.

INT'ing– 2. dinting, hinting, glinting, splinting, minting, printing, sprinting, tinting, stinting, squinting 3. imprinting, misprinting.

INT'l– 2. lintel, pintle, scintle, quintal 3. trigintal.

INT'o– 2. pinto, Shinto 4. mezzotinto.

INT'ri– 2. vintry, wintry.

IN'u– 2. sinew 3. unsinew, continue 4. discontinue.

IN'yun– 2. minion, mignon, minyan, pinion, pignon 3. Virginian, dominion, opinion.

IP'ant– 2. flippant, trippant 3. unflippant 4. countertrippant.

IP'er– 2. chipper, dipper, kipper, skipper, lipper, flipper, clipper, slipper, nipper, snipper, ripper, dripper, gripper, tripper, stripper, sipper, shipper, tipper, whipper 3. Big Dipper, Yom Kippur, outstripper, horsewhipper 4. lady's-slipper, gallinipper.

IP'erd– 2. kippered, skippered, slippered.

IP'erz– chippers etc., *see* **IP'er–** chipper etc. above, plus "s" or " 's."

IP'est– 2. flippest.

IP'et– 2. skippet, snippet, pipit, rippet, rippit, trippet, sippet, tippet, whippet.

IP'i– 2. chippy, dippy, hippy, lippy, klippe, slippy, nippy, snippy, pippy, drippy, grippy, shippy, tippy, zippy 3. Xanthippe 4. Aganippe, Mississippi.

IP'id– 3. insipid.

IP'ij– 2. chippage, kippage, slippage, scrippage, strippage.

IP'ik– 2. hippic, typic **3.** adipic, philhippic, Philippic, atypic **4.** polytypic, stenotypic **5.** electrotypic **6.** daguerreotypic.

IP'in– 2. pippin.

IP'ing– 2. chipping, dipping, skipping, flipping, clipping, slipping, nipping, snipping, ripping, dripping, gripping, stripping, sipping, shipping, tipping, quipping, whipping, zipping 3. outstripping, equipping, horse whipping.

IP'ish– 2. hippish, hyppish, snippish, grippish, quippish.

IP'it– 2. pipit, rippit; *see* also **IP'et–** skippet etc. above.

IP'l– 2. nipple, ripple, cripple, gripple, grippal, triple, sipple, tipple, tiple, stipple **3.** becripple **4.** participle.

IP'ler– 2. rippler, crippler, strippler, tippler, stippler.

IP'let– 2. chiplet, liplet, ripplet, triplet, striplet, tiplet.

IP'li– 2. ripply, cripply, triply, stipply.

IP'ling– 2. chipling, Kipling, rippling, crippling, stripling, tippling, stippling.

IP'ment– 2. gripment, shipment **3.** equipment, reshipment, transhipment.

IP'o– 2. gippo, hippo, shippo 3. filippo.

IP'on– 2. slip-on, Nippon.

IPSH'un– 2. scription 3. Egyptian, conniption [coll.], ascription, subscription, description, prescription, transcription, inscription, proscription **4.** circumscription, superscription.

IPS'i– 3. ipse [L.], gypsy, tipsy **3.** Poughkeepsie.

IP'sis– 2. krypsis, tripsis, stypsis 3. ellipsis.

IPST'er– **2.** tipster, quipster, whipster.

IPT'ik– 2. diptych, glyptic, cryptic, kryptic, triptych, styptic 3. ecliptic, elliptic, syncryptic **4.** diaglyptic, anaglyptic, holocryptic, hypostyptic **5.** apocalyptic.

IPT'iv– 3. descriptive, prescriptive, transcriptive, inscriptive, conscriptive, proscriptive 4. circumscriptive.

IPT'ur– 2. scripture.

IP'us– 2. hippus 3. philippus **4.** Epihippus, Protohippus.

IR– through **IRZ–**, *see* also short **U** (tub): **UR'a** through **URZ'i.**

IR'a– 2. Irra, lira, sirrah **4.** tirralirra.

IR'er– 2. dearer, clearer, mirror, nearer, sneerer, peerer.

IR'ik– 2. lyric, pyrrhic, Pyrrhic **3.** argyric, vampiric, empiric, satiric, satyric, butyric 4. panegyric.

IR'il– 2. Cyril, squirrel, virile **3.** unvirile.

IR'ist– 2. lyrist 4. panegyrist.

IR'it– 2. spirit 3. dispirit, inspirit **4.** party spirit.

IRK– through **IRT–**, *see* short **U** (tub): **URK'a** through **URT'um.**

IR'up– 2. chirrup, syrup, stirrup.

IR'us– 2. byrrus, cirrus, cirrous, cirrhous.

IS'a– 2. lyssa, Missa [L.] **3.** Melissa, Clarissa, vibrissa, Nerissa, abscissa, mantissa **4.** paterissa.

IS'al– 2. missal 3. abyssal, dismissal.

ISCH'an– 2. Christian 3. non-Christian, unchristian 4. anti-Christian.

IS'eez– 2. Pisces, sissies 3. Ulysses.

IS'el– 2. missel, rissel, scissel, wissel [Scot.] **3.** dickcissel; *see* also **IS'l–** fissile etc. below.

IS'en– 2. listen, glisten, christen **3.** relisten, rechristen.

IS'ens– 3. dehiscence **4.** indehiscence, reminiscence, obliviscence, reviviscence.

IS'ent– 3. dehiscent **4.** indehiscent, reminiscent, reviviscent.

IS'er– 2. hisser, kisser, misser, risser **3.** remisser, dismisser 4. reminiscer.

IS'ez– hisses etc., *see* **IS–** bis etc. plus "es" or " 's"; 2. Mrs.

IS'ful– 2. blissful 3. unblissful, remissful.

ISH'a– 3. militia, Letitia 4. Aloysia.

ISH'al– 3. judicial, official, comitial, initial, solstitial 4. prejudicial, unjudicial, beneficial, edificial, sacrificial, artificial, unofficial, superficial, postcomitial, interstitial 5. extrajudicial, unbeneficial, unsuperficial.

ISH'an– 2. Priscian, Titian 3. magician, logician, technician, patrician, optician, physician, musician 4. rhetorician, politician, statistician 5. mathematician; *see* also **ISH'un–** fission etc. below.

ISH'ens– 3. efficience, deficience, proficience, sufficience, omniscience 4. inefficience, self-sufficience, unsufficience.

ISH'ent– 3. efficient, deficient, proficient, sufficient, objicient, volitient, omniscient 4. inefficient, self-sufficient, insufficient, unproficient.

ISH'er– 2. disher, fisher, fissure, wisher, swisher 3. kingfisher, well-wisher.

ISH'ful– 2. dishful, fishful, wishful 3. unwishful.

ISH'i– 2. fishy, Vichy, squishy, swishy.

ISH'ing– 2. dishing, fishing, wishing, swishing 3. well-wishing, ill-wishing.

ISH'na– 2. Mishna, Krishna.

ISH'op– 2. bishop 3. archbishop.

ISH'pan– 2. Ishpan, dishpan.

ISH'u– 2. issue, fichu, tissue 3. reissue.

ISH'un– 2. fission, mission, Priscian, Titian 3. ambition, addition, tradition, edition, dedition, reddition, sedition, rendition, vendition, condition, audition, perdition, magician, logician, volition, submission, admission, emission, demission, remission, commission, omission, permission, dismission, transmission, ignition, cognition, technician, munition, punition, suspicion, attrition, patrician, detrition, metrician, contrition, nutrition, petition, tactician, optician, partition, sortition, fruition, tuition, physician, transition, position, musician 4. inhibition, prohibition, exhibition, readdition, extradition, recondition, precondition, erudition, coalition, abolition, demolition, ebullition, insubmission, readmission, preadmission, intromission, intermission, manumission, mechanician, inanition, recognition, definition, admonition, premonition, ammunition, apparition, rhetorician, electrician, malnutrition, tralatition, repetition, competition, politician, statistician, superstition, intuition, acquisition, requisition, inquisition, perquisition, disquisition, apposition, deposition, preposition, imposisupposition, disposition, exposition 5. superaddition, preadmonition, mathematician, contraposition, juxtaposition, anteposition, decomposition, predisposition, indisposition.

ISH'us– 2. vicious 3. ambitious, seditious, judicious, officious, flagitious, malicious, delicious, pernicious, puniceous, propitious, auspicious, suspicious, capricious, nutritious, factitious, fictitious 4. expeditious, injudicious, unofficious, unpropitious, inauspicious, unsuspicious, avaricious, meretricious, tralatitious, repetitious, adventitious, surreptitious, suppositious 5. supposititious.

IS'i– 2. missy, nisse, prissy [coll.], sissy [coll.].

IS'ik– 2. lyssic 3. silicic, anisic, masticic.

IS'il– 2. fissile, missile, scissile; *see* also **IS'l–** fissile, missal etc. below.

IS'ing– 2. hissing, Gissing, kissing, missing, sissing [chiefly dial.] 3. dehiscing, dismissing 4. prejudicing, reminiscing.

IS'it– 2. licit 3. elicit, illicit, solicit, implicit, explicit 4. inexplicit.

IS'iv– 2. fissive, missive 3. submissive, admissive, emissive, remissive, omissive, commissive, promissive, permissive, dismissive, transmissive 4. unsubmissive, intermissive.

ISK'a– 3. francisca.

ISK'al– 2. discal, fiscal, friscal 4. obeliscal.

ISK'an– 2. priscan 3. Franciscan 4. San Franciscan.

ISK'er– 2. risker, brisker, frisker, whisker 3. bewhisker.

ISK'est– 2. briskest, friskest.

ISK'et– 2. biscuit, brisket, frisket, wisket 3. Sea Biscuit.

ISK'i– 2. pisky [dial.], risky, frisky, whiskey.

ISK'in– 2. griskin, siskin, whiskin.

ISK'ing– 2. risking, brisking, frisking, whisking.

ISK'it– 2. biscuit 3. Sea Biscuit; *see* also **ISK'et–** biscuit, brisket etc. above.

ISK'o– 2. Frisco, cisco 3. San Francisco.

ISK'us– 2. discus, discous, fiscus [L.], viscous 3. hibiscus, trochiscus, meniscus, lemniscus, lentiscus 4. calathiscus, abaciscus.

IS'l– 2. fissile, missal, missel, missile, missle, rissel, rissle, bristle, gristle, sistle, scissel, scissile, thistle, wissel [Scot.], whistle 3. abyssal, dismissal, epistle, dickcissel 4. cacomistle.

IS'ler– 2. bristler, whistler 3. epistler.

IS'li– 2. bristly, gristly, thistly.

IS'ling– 2. bristling, brisling, whistling.

IS'mus– 2. isthmus, Christmas.

IS'n– 2. listen, glisten, christen 3. relisten, rechristen.

IS'ness– 2. thisness 3. remissness.

IS'ning– 3. listening, glistening, christening.

ISP'er– 2. lisper, risper, crisper, whisper 3. stage whisper.

ISP'est– 2. crispest.

ISP'i– 2. crispy, wispy.

ISP'ing– 2. lisping, crisping, wisping.

ISP'ness– 2. crispness.

IST'a– 2. vista 3. ballista, genista, Baptista.

IST'al– 2. distal, crystal, cystal, vistal; *see* also **IST'l–** istle etc. below.

IST'ans– 2. distance 3. outdistance, assistance, desistance, resistance 4. equidistance, unresistance.

IST'ant– 2. distant 3. assistant, resistant 4. coassistant, equidistant, nonresistant, unresistant; *see* also **IST'ent–** subsistent etc. below.

IST'ed– 2. fisted, listed, misted, wristed, trysted, cysted, twisted 3. hardfisted, closefisted, tightfisted, two-fisted, enlisted, black-listed, white-listed, strong-wristed, thin-wristed, assisted, subsisted, desisted, resisted, encysted, insisted, consisted, existed, persisted, untwisted 4. ironfisted, unassisted, unresisted, intertwisted.

IST'em– 2. system 4. solar system, nervous system, railroad system.

IST'en– 2. pristine, Sistine 3. Philistine 4. amethystine.

IST'ens– 3. subsistence, existence, insistence, consistence, persistence 4. preexistence, nonexistence, unexistence, coexistence, inconsistence.

IST'ent– 3. subsistent, existent, insistent, consistent, persistent 4. pre-existent, nonexistent, coexistent, inconsistent; *see* also **IST'ant–** distant etc. above.

IST'er– 2. bister, bistre, lister, blister' glister, mister, sister, twister, xyster 3. agister, agistor, magister, enlister, assister, sob sister, subsister, resister, exister, insister, stepsister, persister 4. water blister, foster sister.

IST'ful– 2. listful, mistful, wistful.

IST'i– 2. listy, misty, gristy.

IST'ik– 2. distich, fistic, mystic, pistic, cystic, schistic 3. Buddhistic, deistic, theistic, sophistic, logistic, ballistic, stylistic, monistic, eristic, poristic, juristic, puristic, touristic, statistic, baptistic, artistic, linguistic 4. atheistic, pantheistic, syllogistic, eulogistic, catechistic, anarchistic, cabalistic, feudalistic, realistic, formalistic, annalistic, journalistic, moralistic, socialistic, fatalistic, vitalistic, dualistic, royalistic, pugilistic, symbolistic, euphemistic, alchemistic, pessimistic, optimistic, Romanistic, humanistic, Hellenistic, Calvanistic, agonistic, canonistic, communistic, Taoistic, egoistic, eucharistic, egotistic, hypnotistic, inartistic, altruistic, casuistic, atavistic, Jehovistic **5.** polytheistic, antiphlogistic, cannibalistic, naturalistic, capitalistic, ritualistic, evangelistic, monopolistic, antagonistic, impressionistic, anachronistic, characteristic, allegoristic, romanticistic, Anabaptistic **6.** imperialistic, materialistic, phenomenalistic, universalistic **7.** supernaturalistic, individualistic.

IST'iks– **2.** mystics **3.** sphragistics, logistics, ballistics, statistics, linguistics **4.** syllogistics, agonistics, solaristics.

IST'ing– **2.** listing, misting, gristing, trysting, twisting **3.** enlisting, assisting, subsisting, desisting, resisting, existing, insisting, consisting, persisting, entwisting, untwisting **4.** pre-existing, nonexisting, intertwisting.

IST'iv– **3.** assistive, desistive, resistive, persistive.

IST'l– **2.** istle, distal, listel, pistil, pistol, Bristol, crystal, cystal, vistal.

IST'less– **2.** listless, mistless, twistless **3.** resistless.

IST'ment– **3.** agistment, enlistment.

IST'o– **3.** Mephisto, Callisto.

IST'us– **2.** cistus, schistous, xystus **3.** anhistous, rockcistus.

IS'um– **2.** lissome **3.** Alyssum **4.** sweet alyssum **5.** fideicommissum.

IS'us– **2.** Issus, byssus, missis, missus **3.** narcissus.

IT'a– **2.** Pitta, pitta, Sitta, shittah, vitta **3.** sagitta, Mylitta.

IT'al– **2.** victual **3.** remittal, committal, transmittal, acquittal; *see* also **IT'l–** kittle etc. below.

IT'an– **2.** Britain, Briton, witan **3.** Great Britain; *see* also **IT'en–** bitten etc. below.

IT'ans– **2.** pittance, quittance **3.** admittance, remittance, omittance, permittance, transmittance, acquittance.

IT'ed– **2.** bitted, fitted, flitted, slitted, knitted, pitted, spitted, ritted, gritted, witted, quitted, twitted **3.** unbitted, befitted, refitted, unfitted, submitted, admitted, emitted, demitted, remitted, omitted, committed, transmitted, unpitted, half-witted, acquitted, quick-witted, sharp-witted, short-witted, outwitted **4.** benefited, counterfeited, unremitted, recommitted, interknitted, ready-witted, nimble-witted.

IT'en– **2.** bitten, kitten, litten, mitten, smitten, written, Britain, Briton **3.** flea-bitten fly-bitten, frost-bitten, unsmitten, Great Britain, unwritten **4.** conscience-smitten, terror-smitten, underwritten.

IT'ent– **3.** emittent, remittent **4.** unremittent, intromittent, intermittent.

IT'er– **2.** bitter, fitter, hitter, jitter [slang], skitter, litter, flitter, glitter, splitter, slitter, knitter, pitter, spitter, Ritter, fritter, gritter, critter, [dial. & coll.], sitter, titter, quitter, twitter **3.** embitter, befitter, refitter, outfitter, pinch hitter, rail splitter, submitter, admitter, emitter, remitter, omitter, committer, permitter, transmitter, outsitter, atwitter, outwitter, acquitter **4.** benefiter, counterfeiter, recommitter, manumitter, baby sitter.

IT'ern– **2.** bittern, gittern, flittern, cittern.

IT'erz– bitters etc., *see* **IT'er–** bitter etc. above, plus "s" or "'s."

IT'est– **2.** fittest, flittest.

IT'ful– **2.** fitful, witful.

ITH'er– **2.** dither, hither, blither, slither, tither, thither, wither, swither, whither, zither.

ITH'i– 2. pithy, smithy, stithy, withy 3. twigwithy.

ITH'ik– 2. lithic, mythic 3. trilithic, ornithic 4. megalithic, eolithic, neolithic, monolithic, polymythic, philornithec 5. archaeolithic, palaeolithic.

ITH'm– 2. rhythm 3. logarithm, algorithm.

ITH'mik– 2. rhythmic, 4. logarithmic, polyrhythmic.

IT'i– 2. bitty, bittie, chitty, ditty, kitty, skitty, flitty, slitty, pity, gritty, grittie, pretty, city, witty, twitty 3. ambitty, poditty, committee, self-pity.

IT'id– 2. dittied, pitied, citied 3. unpitied, uncitied.

IT'ik– 2. lytic, critic 3. rachitic, graphitic, enclitic, proclitic, politic, Hamitic, Semitic, granitic, lignitic, nephritic, pyritic, arthritic, neuritic, Levitic 4. Jacobitic, neophytic, zoophytic, dialytic, analytic, paralytic, granulitic, spherulitic, Adamitic, Islamitic, dynamitic, eremitic, stalagmitic, tympanitic, Sybaritic, Nazaritic, diacritic, hypercritic, parasitic, anthracitic, hematitic.

IT'ing– 2. bitting, chitting, fitting, hitting, skitting, flitting, splitting, slitting, knitting, pitting, spitting, gritting, sitting, witting, quitting, twitting 3. befitting, outfitting, hard-hitting, pinch-hitting, hairsplitting, earsplitting, submitting, admitting, emitting, remitting, omitting, committing, permitting, transmitting, unwitting, acquitting, outwitting 4. unbefitting, benefiting.

IT'ish– 2. skittish, British.

IT'l– 2. kittle, kittel, skittle, little, spittle, brittle, grittle, tittle, victual, whittle 3. belittle, remittal, committal, transmittal, lickspittle, acquittal 4. noncommittal, nonacquittal.

IT'ler– 2. skittler, littler, brittler, tittler, victualer. whittler 3. belittler.

IT'less– 2. bitless, fitless, hitless, pitless, spitless, gritless, witless.

IT'lest– 2. littlest, brittlest.

IT'li– 2. fitly 3. unfitly.

IT'ling– 2. kitling, brittling, titling, victualing, witling, whittling, whitling.

IT'lz– kittles etc., *see* **IT'l–** kittle etc. above, plus "s" or "'s."

IT'ment– 2. fitment 3. refitment, remitment, commitment, acquitment 4. recommitment.

IT'ness– 2. fitness, witness 3. unfitness, eyewitness.

IT'ni– 2. jitney, witney, Whitney 3. Mt. Whitney.

IT'zi– 2. Mitzy, ritzy, Fritzy.

IV'el– 2. snivel, drivel, swivel.

IV'en– 2. given, riven, driven, shriven, striven, thriven 3. forgiven, wind-driven, rain-driven, undriven, unshriven 4. unforgiven, overdriven.

IV'er– 2. giver, liver, flivver [slang], sliver, river, shiver, stiver, quiver 3. forgiver, life-giver, deliver, outliver, Spoon River 4. Indian giver.

IV'erd– 2. livered, flivvered [slang], slivered, shivered, quivered 3. delivered, pale-livered, white-livered 4. undelivered, lily-livered, pigeon-livered, yellow-livered.

IV'et– 2. rivet, grivet, privet, trivet, civet.

IV'id– 2. livid, vivid.

IV'ik– 2. civic 3. uncivic.

IV'ing– 2. giving, living, sieving 3. lawgiving, forgiving, misgiving, Thanksgiving, outliving 4. unforgiving, everliving.

IV'l– 2. snivel, rivel, drivel, frivol, shrivel, civil, swivel 3. uncivil.

IV'ling– 2. sniveling, driveling, shriveling, swiveling.

IV'ness– 3. forgiveness 4. unforgiveness.

IV'ot– 2. divot, pivot.

IZ'ard– 2. izard, gizzard, blizzard, lizard, vizard, wizard 3. lounge lizzard [slang]; *see* also **IZ'erd–** scissored etc. below.

IZ'dom– 2. wisdom.

IZ'en– 2. dizen, mizzen, risen, ptisan, wizen 3. bedizen, arisen.

IZ'er– 2. rizzar, frizzer, scissor, quizzer, whizzer, visor, vizor 3. befrizzer.

IZ'erd– 2. scissored, visored, vizored; *see* also **IZ'ard–** izard etc. above.

IZH'un– 2. Frisian, scission, vision 3. elision, allision, illision, collision, Parisian, derision, misprision, abscission, decision, recission, rescission, precision, incision, concision, excision, revision, prevision, provision, division, envision 4. paradisian, aphrodisian, prodelision, television, subdivision, audivision, supervision.

IZ'i– 2. busy, dizzy, frizzy, Lizzie, mizzy, nizy, frizzy, tizzy, quizzy.

IZ'ik– 2. physic, phthisic 4. paradisic, metaphysic, biophysic.

IZ'iks– 2. physics 4. metaphysics, geophysics, biophysics, zoophysics.

IZ'ing– 2. fizzing, frizzing, quizzing, whizzing 3. befrizzing.

IZ'it– 2. visit 3. revisit, exquisite.

IZ'l– 2. chisel, fizzle, mizzle, drizzle, frizzle, grizzle, sizzle, swizzle, twizzle 3. enchisel, rumswizzle.

IZ'ler– 2. chiseler, frizzler, grizzler.

IZ'li– 2. chiselly, mizzly, drizzly, frizzly, grisly, grizzly.

IZ'ling– 2. chiseling, fizzling, mizzling, drizzling, frizzling, grizzling, sizzling, swizzling.

IZ'm– ism etc., *see* **IZM–** ism etc.

IZ'mal– 2. dismal, chrismal, prismal 3. abysmal, strabismal, baptismal 4. catechismal, cataclysmal, asterismal, paroxysmal.

IZ'mik– 2. clysmic, trismic 4. cataclysmic, embolismic, aphorismic, algorismic.

IZ'mus– 2. trismus 3. strabismus, accismus.

IZ'n– 2. dizen, his'n [dial.], mizzen, risen, prison, wizen 3. bedizen, arisen, imprison.

IZ'ness– 2. business 3. nonbusiness 4. monkey business [slang].

IZ'um– rizzom; *see* also **IZM–** ism etc.

I (bib)

3.

TRIPLE RHYMES IN I (Lib'y-a)

Primary or Secondary Accent Falls on Second from Last Syllable.

IB'i-a- 3. Libya, tibia 4. amphibia.

IB'i-al- 3. tibial, stibial.

IB'i-an- 3. Libyan 4. amphibian, bathybian.

IB'ing-li- 3. bibbingly, fibbingly, jibbingly, ribbingly, cribbingly, squibbingly 4. wine bibblingly, ad libbingly [slang].

IB'it-ed- 4. inhibited, exhibited, prohibited 5. uninhibited, unprohibited.

IB'it-er- 4. inhibiter, inhibitor, exhibitor, prohibiter, prohibitor.

IB'it-ing- 4. inhibiting, exhibiting, prohibiting.

IB'it-iv- 4. inhibitive, exhibitive, prohibitive 5. uninhibitive, unprohibitive.

IB'i-us- 3. stibious 4. amphibious, bathybius.

IB'on-lik- 3. gibbonlike, ribbonlike.

IB'u-lar- 3. fibular 4. mandibular, vestibular 5. infundibular.

IB'ut-ed- 3. tributed 4. attributed, contributed, distributed.

IB'ut-er- 4. attributer, contributor, distributer, distributor.

IB'ut-iv- 4. attributive, retributive, contributive, distributive.

ICH'er-i- 3. fitchery, michery, stitchery, witchery 4. bewitchery.

ICH'et-i- 3. witchetty, twitchety.

ICH'i-ness- 3. itchiness, hitchiness, pitchiness, switchiness, twitchiness.

ICH'ing-li- 3. itchingly, pitchingly, witchingly, switchingly, twitchingly 4. enrichingly, bewitchingly.

ICH'ing-ness- 3. itchingness, pitchingness, witchingness, switchingness, twitchingness 4. enrichingness, bewitchingness.

ICH'less-li- 3. itchlessly, hitchlessly, pitchlessly, stitchlessly, switchlessly, twitchlessly.

ID'a-bl- 3. biddable 4. rebiddable, unbiddable, forbiddable.

ID'en-ness- 3. hiddenness 4. forbiddenness 5. unforbiddenness.

ID'i-a- 3. Lydia, Nydia 4. Ophidia, Numidia, Canidia.

ID'i-al- 4. presidial, noctidial.

ID'i-an- 3. Gideon, Lydian, Vidian 4. ophidian, rachidian, Euclidean, Numidian, meridian, obsidian, quotidian, Ovidian 5. nullifidian, taxaspidean, postmeridian 6. antemeridian.

ID'if-i- 3. nidify 4. solidify, humidify, lapidify, acidify, rancidify, fluidify.

ID'ik-al- 4. veridical, juridical, druidical, causidical 5. pyramidical.

ID'it-i- 3. quiddity 4. rabidity, morbidity, turbidity, rigidity, frigidity, algidity, turgidity, calidity, squalidity, validity, gelidity, solidity, stolidity, timidity, humidity, tumidity, rapidity, sapidity, vapidity, trepidity, tepidity, sipidity, limpidity, torpidity, cupidity, stupidity, aridity, hybridity, acridity, viridity, floridity, torridity, putridity, acidity, placidity, flaccidity, rancidity, viscidity, lucidity, pinguidity, fluidity, liquidity, avidity, pavidity, lividity **5.** invalidity, insolidity, intrepidity, insipidity, pellucidity, translucidity, impavidity.

ID'i-um- 3. idiom, Psidium **4.** rubidium, iridium, presidium, cecidium.

ID'i-us- 3. Phidias, hideous **4.** perfidious, lapideous, insidious, fastidious, avidious, invidious.

ID'u-al- 4. residual, dividual **5.** individual.

ID'ul-at- 3. stridulate **4.** acidulate.

ID'ul-us- 3. stridulous **4.** acidulous.

ID'u-us- 3. biduous, viduous **4.** assiduous, deciduous, residuous, dividuous **5.** unassiduous, indeciduous.

IF'an-i- 3. tiffany, Tiffany **4.** Epiphany.

IF'er-us- 4. bulbiferous, limbiferous, herbiferous, morbiferous, nubiferous, splendiferous, frondiferous, tergiferous, branchiferous, conchiferous, lethiferous, aliferous, saliferous, piliferous, velliferous, celliferous, melliferous, stelliferous, foliferous, proliferous, cauliferous, armiferous, comiferous, pomiferous, laniferous, graniferous, igniferous, ligniferous, spiniferous, omniferous, somniferous, stanniferous, penniferous, coniferous, soniferous, pruniferous, umbriferous, ceriferous, floriferous, poriferous, cupriferous, ferriferous, cirriferous, rostriferous, auriferous, thuriferous, bacciferous, calciferous, vociferous, dorsiferous, ossiferous, furciferous, luciferous, muciferous, cruciferous, lactiferous, fructiferous, setiferous, pestiferous, sanguiferous, aquiferous, valviferous, multiferous, oviferous **5.** oleiferous, umbiliferous, coralliferous, metalliferous, papilliferous, petroliferous, maculiferous, ramuliferous, granuliferous, atomiferous, luminiferous, resiniferous, antenniferous, carboniferous, nectariferous, tuberiferous, odoriferous, sudoriferous, saporiferous, boraciferous, corticiferous, calyciferous, argentiferous **6.** aluminiferous, diamondiferous.

IF'ik-al- 4. magnifical, mirifical, pacifical, specifical, lactifical, pontifical, vivifical **5.** saporifical, beatifical.

IF'ik-ant- 4. nidificant, mundificant, significant, sacrificant **5.** insignificant.

IF'ik-at- 4. nidificate, nostrificate, pontificate, certificate, pacificate.

IF'i-sens- 4. magnificence, munificence.

IF'i-sent- 4. magnificent, munificent.

IF'lu-us- 4. fellifluous, mellifluous, sanguifluous.

IF'on-i- 3. triphony **4.** polyphony, antiphony, oxyphony.

IFT'a-bl- 3. liftable, siftable, shiftable.

IFT'il-i- 3. niftily [slang], shiftily, thriftily.

IFT'i-ness- 3. niftiness [slang], shiftiness, thriftiness.

IFT'less-ness- 3. shiftlessness, thriftlessness.

IF'ug-al- 4. vermifugal, febrifugal, centrifugal.

IG'am-i- 3. bigamy, digamy, trigamy **4.** polygamy.

IG'am-ist- 3. bigamist, digamist, trigamist **4.** polygamist.

IG'am-us- 3. bigamous, digamous, trigamous **4.** polygamous.

IG'er-i- 3. piggery, priggery, wiggery, Whiggery.

IG'ish-li- 3. piggishly, priggishly, Whiggishly.

IG'mat-ist- 3. stigmatist **4.** enigmatist.

IG'mat-iz- 3. stigmatize **4.** enigmatize **5.** paradigmatize.

IG'nan-si- 4. indignancy, malignancy, benignancy.

IG'nant-li- 4. indignantly, malignantly, benignantly.

IG'ne-us- 3. igneous, ligneous, cygneous **5.** pyroligneous.

IG'ni-a- 4. insignia.

IG'ni-fi- 3. ignify, dignify, lignify, signify 4. undignify.

IG'ni-ty- 3. dignity 4. indignity, condignity, malignity, benignity.

IG'on-al- 3. trigonal 4. polygonal, ditrigonal.

IG'or-us- 3. rigorous, vigorous.

IG'raf-i- 4. tachigraphy, calligraphy, polygraphy, epigraphy, pasigraphy, stratigraphy, lexigraphy 5. pseudopigraphy.

IG'u-us- 4. ambiguous, irriguous, exiguous, contiguous.

IJ'a-bl- 3. bridgeable 4. abridgable, unbridgeable 5. unabridgable.

IJ'en-us- 4. ambigenous, indigenous, cauligenous, terrigenous, rurigenous, oxygenous 5. alkaligenous, coralligenous, nepheligenous; *see* also **IJ'in-us-** polygynous etc. below.

IJ'er-ent- 4. belligerent, refrigerant 5. hederigerent.

IJ'er-us- 4. pedigerous, armigerous, plumigerous, belligerous, piligerous, cirrigerous, discigerous, cornigerous, crucigerous, setigerous, navigerous, ovigerous.

IJ'et-i- 3. fidgety, midgety.

IJ'i-a- 3. Phrygia 4. Ogygia, fastigia 5. Cantabrigia.

IJ'i-an- 3. Phrygian, Stygian 4. Ogygian, Vestigian 5. Cantabrigian.

IJ'id-li- 3. rigidly, frigidly.

IJ'id-ness- 3. rigidness, frigidness.

IJ'in-al- 4. original 5. unoriginal.

IJ'in-us- 4. polygynous, uliginous, fuliginous, lentiginous, vertiginous, vortiginous; *see* also **IJ'en-us-** ambigenous etc. above.

IJ'i-um- 3. phrygium 4. pterygium, fastigium, syzygium.

IJ'us-li- 4. prodigiously, religiously, litigiously 5. sacrilegiously.

IJ'us-ness- 4. prodigiousness, religiousness, litigiousness 5. sacrilegiousness.

IK'a-ment- 4. medicament, predicament.

IK'ar-us- 3. Icarus, lickerous.

IK'at-iv- 3. fricative, siccative 4. abdicative, predicative, indicative, vindicative, desiccative, exsiccative.

IK'en-er- 3. thickener, quickener.

IK'en-ing- 3. sickening, thickening, quickening.

IK'er-ing- 3. bickering, dickering, flickering, smickering, snickering.

IK'er-ish- 3. lickerish, liquorish, licorice.

IK'et-er- 3. picketer, cricketer, ticketer.

IK'et-i- 3. rickety, crickety, thickety 4. pernickety, persnickety.

IK'et-ing- 3. picketing, cricketing, ticketing.

IK'i-li- 3. trickily, stickily.

IK'i-ness- 3. trickiness, stickiness.

IK'li-ness- 3. prickliness, sickliness.

IK'ol-us- 3. Nicholas 4. urbicolous, sepicolous, terricolous, agricolous, silvicolous.

IK'or-i- 3. chicory, hickory 4. Halicore, Terpsichore.

IKS'a-bl- 3. fixable, mixable 4. prefixable, unfixable, immixable, unmixable.

IKS'ed-li- 3. fixedly, mixedly.

IKSH'un-al- 3. fictional, frictional 4. convictional 5. contradictional, benedictional, jurisdictional.

IKS'it-i- 3. fixity, siccity 4. prolixity.

IKT'a-bl- 4. predictable, convictable 5. contradictable, unpredictable, unrestrictable 6. uncontradictable.

IKT'iv-li- 4. predictively, vindictively, restrictively.

IKT'iv-ness- 4. predictiveness, vindictiveness, restrictiveness.

IKT'or-i- 3. victory 4. serictery 5. contradictory, maledictory, valedictory, benedictory, interdictory 6. uncontradictory.

IK'ul-a- 4. fidicula, Canicula, reticula

IK'ul–ant– 4. matriculant, articulant.

IK'ul–ar– 3. spicular 4. orbicular, vehicular, follicular, canicular, funicular, apicular, matricular, ventricular, auricular, acicular, fascicular, vesicular, versicular, reticular, denticular, lenticular, articular, particular, clavicular 5. appendicular, perpendicular, adminicular, quinquarticular.

IK'ul–at– 3. spiculate 4. orbiculate, pediculate, forficulate, folliculate, vermiculate, paniculate, geniculate, apiculate, turriculate, matriculate, auriculate, aciculate, fasciculate, straticulate, reticulate, denticulate, monticulate, articulate, particulate, gesticulate 5. appendiculate canaliculate, immatriculate, inarticulate, multarticulate, octarticulate.

IK'ul–um– 3. spiculum 4. Janiculum, geniculum, periculum, curriculum, reticulum.

IK'ul–us– 4. ridiculous, folliculous, cauliculus, cauliculous, vermiculous, panniculus, ventriculous, vesiculus, vesiculous, meticulous.

IK'u–us– 4. transpicuous, conspicuous, perspicuous 5. inconspicuous.

IK'wit–i– 4. ubiquity, obliquity, iniquity, antiquity.

IK'wit–us– 4. ubiquitous, obliquitous, iniquitous.

IL'a–bl– 3. billable, fillable, killable, millable, spillable, thrillable, syllable, tillable 4. refillable, unfillable, unkillable, unspillable, unthrillable, untillable, distillable.

IL'aj–er– 3. pillager, villager.

IL'ar–i– 3. phyllary, Hilary, pillary 5. codicillary.

IL'er–i– 3. pillery, pillory, frillery, cilery, Sillery 4. artillery, distillery.

IL'et–ed– 3. billeted, filleted 4. unbilleted, unfilleted.

IL'et–ing– 3. billeting, filleting.

IL'ful–i– 3. skillfully, willfully 4. unskillfully, unwillfully.

IL'ful–ness– 3. skillfulness, willfulness 4. unskillfulness.

IL'i–a– 3. ilia, cilia 4. sedilia, familia, Emilia, similia, Cecilia 5. mirabilia, notabilia, pedophilia, hemophilia, zoophilia, adactylia 6. memorabilia.

IL'i–ad– 3. Iliad, Gilead, chiliad, milliad.

IL'i–ak– 3. iliac 5. sacroiliac, hemophiliac.

IL'i–al– 3. ilial, filial 4. grandfilial, familial.

IL'i–an– 3. Ilian, Ilion, Chilean, Gillian, Lillian 4. Virgilian, Cecilian, Sicilian, reptilian, Castilian, civilian, Brazilian 5. crocodilian, Maximilian.

IL'i–ar– 4. familiar, conciliar, auxiliar 5. domiciliar.

IL'i–at– 3. filiate, ciliate 4. affiliate, humiliate, conciliate 5. domiciliate, reconciliate.

IL'i–ens– 4. resilience, dissilience, transilience, consilience; *see* also **IL'yans–** brilliance etc.

IL'i–ent– 4. resilient, dissilient, transilient, consilient.

IL'i–est– 3. chilliest, hilliest, silliest, stilliest.

IL'i–fi– 3. vilify 4. stabilify, nihilify, fossilify.

IL'i–form– 3. filiform, phylliform, liliform, stilliform 4. papilliform.

IL'ik–a– 3. silica 4. basilica.

IL'ik–al– 3. filical, silicle 4. umbilical, basilical.

IL'ik–in– 3. Billiken, spilikin, spillikin 4. basilican.

IL'ik–um– 3. tilikum, tillicum.

IL'i–ness– 3. chilliness, hilliness, silliness.

IL'ing–li– 3. fillingly, chillingly, killingly, trillingly, thrillingly, willingly 4. unwillingly.

IL'it-at– 3. militate 4. habilitate, stabilitate, debilitate, nobilitate, facilitate 5. rehabilitate, imbecilitate.

IL'it-i– 4. ability, lability, debility, mobility, nobility, nubility, nihility, agility, fragility, humility, senility, febrility, sterility, virility, scurrility, neurility, facility, gracility, docility, tensility, tactility, ductility, gentility, motility, fertility, tortility, hostility, utility, futility, civility, servility, exility, flexility 5. bribability, probability, readability, laudability, affability, changeability, chargeability, liability, pliability, viability, placability, peccability, secability, vocability, workability, saleability, amability, flammability, namability, tenability, inability, capability, culpability, wearability, errability, curability, durability, traceability, disability, versability, ratability, tractability, suitability, notability, quotability, temptability, portability, instability, mutability, suability, solvability, movability, provability, knowability, taxability, vincibility, docibility, miscibility, edibility, credibility, vendibility, audibility, legibility, frangibility, tangibility, fallibility, gullibility, feasibility, risibility, visibility, sensibility, tensibility, passibility, possibility, plausibility, fusibility, partibility, flexibility, fluxibility, immobility, ignobility, solubility, volubility, imbecility, indocility, juvenility, prehensility, volatility, vibratility, versatility, retractility, contractility, inductility, infertility, inutility, incivility 6. describability, improbability, absorbability, implacability, impeccability, applicability, amicability, practicability, masticability, revocability, avoidability, manageability, exchangeability, malleability, permeability, ineffability, navigability, approachability, punishability, perishability, reliability, amiability, variability, insatiability, negotiability, availability, violability, calculability, redeemability, inflammability, reformability, conformability, alienability, amenability, impregnability, attainability, mentionability, questionability, governability, incapability, impalpability, reparability, separability, comparability, ponderability, preferability, transferability, venerability, vulnerability, utterability, integrability, answerability, desirability, acquirability, adorability, meliorability, deplorability, memorability, vaporability, exorability, inerrability, penetrability, demonstrability, incurability, endurability, measurability, censurability, insurability, advisability, condensability, dispensability, reversability, impassability, relatability, dilatability, translatability, retractability, attractability, delectability, respectability, predictability, marketability, habitability, excitability, creditability, imitability, irritability, unsuitability, presentability, accountability, adaptability, acceptability, attemptability, transportability, detestability, adjustability, immutability, commutability, transmutability, imputability, computability, disputability, inscrutability, retrievability, conceivability, resolvability, removability, immovability, improvability, cognizability, invincibility, convincibility, irascibility, immiscibility, cognoscibility, reducibility, conducibility, producibility, inedibility, incredibility, inducibility, seducibility, inaudibility, illegibility, dirigibility, infrangibility, intangibility, indelibility, infallibility, defeasibility, persuasibility, divisibility, invisibility, expansibility, defensibility, insensibility, distensibility, extensibility, invincibility, responsibility, reversibility, collapsibility, impassibility, accessibility, impressibility, compressibility, expressibility, admissibility, remissibility, transmissibility, impossibility, diffusibility, infusibility, compatibility, defectibility, affectibility, effectibility, perfectibility, conductibility, destructibility, deceptibility, perceptibility, susceptibility, contemptibility, corruptibility, impartibility, convertibility, digestibility, resistibility, existibility, exhaustibility, combustibility, inflexibility, insolubility **7.** indescribability, imperturbability, communicability, impracticability, irrevocability, interchangeability, impermeability, irrefragability, irreproachability, imperishability, enunciability, justifiability, invariability, influenciability, reconcilability, assimilability, inviolability, incalculability, coagulability, irredeemability, irreformability, determinability, impressionability, irreparability, inseparability, incomparability, imponderability, innumerability, invulnerability, unutterability, undesirability, inexorability, impenetrability, indemonstrability, immeasurability, commensurability, indispensability, inexcusability, untranslatability, inhabitability, hereditability, incogitability, illimitability, inimitability, inheritability, inevitability, precipitability, insurmountability, incontestability, irrefutability, incommutability, indisputability, irretrievability, inconceivability, irresolvability, recognizability, incognizability, incognoscibility, irreducibility, incorrigibility, indefeasibility, indivisibility, indefensibility, comprehensibility, irresponsibility, irreversibility, inaccessibility, irrepressibility, incompressibility, inexpressibility, irredressibility, inadmissibility, irremissibility, incompatibility, indefectibility, imperfectibility, indestructibility, imperceptibility, incorruptibility, inconvertibility, indigestibility, irresistibility, inexhaustibility, incombustibility **8.** incommunicability, indefatigability, irreconcilability, incommensurability, hyperirritability, incomprehensibility; *and numerous other derived nouns ending in "-ility."*

IL'i-um– 3. ilium, ileum, Ilium, Lilium, Liliom, pileum, trillium **4.** beryllium, auxilium, concilium.

IL'i-us– 4. punctilious **5.** supercilious; *see* also **IL'yus–** bilious etc.

ILK'i-est– 3. milkiest, silkiest.

IL'o-i– 3. billowy, pillowy, willowy.

IL'o-ji– 3. dilogy, trilogy, sylloge **4.** palilogy, fossilogy, antilogy, festilogy.

IL'o-jiz– 3. syllogize 4. epilogize.

IL'o-jizm– 3. syllogism 4. amphilogism, epilogism **5.** pseudosyllogism.

IL'o-kwens– 4. blandiloquence, grandiloquence, magniloquence, somniloquence, multiloquence, stultiloquence, breviloquence.

IL'o-kwent– 4. grandiloquent, melliloquent, magniloquent, somniloquent, veriloquent, flexiloquent, dulciloquent, pauciloquent, altiloquent, sanctiloquent, multiloquent, suaviloquent.

IL'o-kwi– 4. soliloquy, dulciloquy, somniloquy, ventriloquy, pauciloquy, Centiloquy, dentiloquy, multiloquy, stultiloquy **5.** pectoriloquy.

IL'o-kwist– 4. soliloquist, somniloquist, gastriloquist, ventriloquist, dentiloquist.

IL'o-kwiz– 4. soliloquize, ventriloquize.

IL'o-kwizm– 4. somniloquism, ventriloquism, gastriloquism **5.** pectoriloquism.

IL'o-kwus– 4. grandiloquous, tardiloquous, somniloquous, ventriloquous **5.** pectoriloquous.

IL'yan-si– 3. brilliancy **4.** resiliency, transiliency.

IL'yar-i– 3. miliary 4. auxiliary.

IM'er-i– 3. glimmery, simmery, shimmery.

IM'er-ing– 3. glimmering, simmering, shimmering.

IM'er-us– 3. dimerous, glimmerous, trimerous **4.** polymerous.

IM'et-er– 3. dimeter, trimeter, scimiter 4. millimeter, polymeter, perimeter, altimeter, voltimeter, centimeter **5.** alkalimeter, polarimeter, calorimeter.

IM'et-ri– 3. symmetry **4.** perimetry, asymmetry, altimetry, bathymetry **5.** alkalimetry, calorimetry, polarimetry.

IM'i-an- 3. simian, Simeon 4. Endymion.

IM'ik-al- 3. mimical 4. alchymical, inimical 5. homonymical, toponymical, patronymical, metonymical.

IM'il-e- 3. simile 4. dissimile, facsimile.

IM'in-al- 3. biminal, liminal, criminal, Viminal 4. regiminal, subliminal.

IM'in-at- 3. criminate 4. eliminate, recriminate, incriminate, discriminate.

IM'in-i- 3. Bimini, jiminy, crimine, crim-iny [both slang] 4. postliminy 6. nim-iny-piminy.

IM'it-at- 3. imitate, limitate 4. delimitate.

IM'it-er- 3. limiter, scimitar, scimiter.

IM'it-i- 3. dimity, limity 4. sublimity, proximity 5. magnanimity, unanimity, sanctanimity, equanimity, pseudonymity, anonymity, synonymity 6. pusillanimity.

IMP'er-er- 3. simperer, whimperer.

IMP'er-ing- 3. simpering, whimpering.

IM'u-lant- 3. simulant, stimulant.

IM'u-lat- 3. simulate, stimulate 4. assimulate, dissimulate, restimulate.

IM'u-lus- 3. limulus, stimulus.

IN'a-kl- 3. binnacle, binocle, pinnacle.

INCH'ing-li- 3. inchingly, flinchingly, clinchlingly, pinchingly, cinchingly 5. penny pinchingly [slang].

IND'er-i- 3. cindery, tindery.

IND'i-a- 3. India.

IND'i-er- 3. windier.

IND'i-kat- 3. indicate, syndicate, vindicate.

IN'e-a- 3. linea, tinea, vinea 5. Nemertinea; *see* also **IN'i-a-** Inia etc. below.

ĪN'e-al- 3. lineal, pineal, tineal, vineal 4. gramineal, stamineal, pectineal 5. interlineal, consanguineal; *see* also **IN'i-al-** inial etc. below.

IN'e-ar- 3. linear 4. trilinear, collinear 5. rectilinear.

IN'e-ma- 3. kinema, cinema.

IN'e-us- 4. vimineous, fulmineous, sanguineous 5. testudineous, ignominious, consanguineous.

ING'er-er- 3. fingerer, lingerer 4. malingerer.

ING'er-ing- 3. fingering, lingering 4. malingering.

ING'i-ness- 3. ringiness, springiness, stringiness.

ING'ul-a- 3. lingula.

ING'ul-ar- 3. cingular, singular.

ING'ul-at- 3. lingulate, cingulate.

IN'i-a- 3. Inia, linea, tinea, vinea, zinnia 4. Sardinia, Virginia, lacinia, Lavinia 5. anodynia, pleurodynia, Abyssinia, Nemertinea.

IN'i-al- 3. inial, finial, lineal, pineal, tineal, vineal 4. dominial; *see* also **IN'e-al-** lineal etc. above.

IN'i-an- 4. Sardinian, Delphinian, Virginian, Flaminian, Justinian, Darwinian 5. Carthaginian, Carolinian, Abyssinian, Serpentinean, Palestinian, Augustinian 7. anthropophaginian.

IN'i-at- 3. lineate, miniate 4. delineate, laciniate.

IN'i-er- 3. finnier, skinnier, tinnier.

IN'i-kal- 3. finical, clinical, cynical, binocle 4. rabbinical, synclinical, Brahminical, adminicle, dominical; *see* also **IN'a-kl-** binnacle etc. above.

IN'i-kin- 3. finikin, minikin.

IN'ish-er- 3. finisher 4. diminisher.

IN'ish-ing- 3. finishing 4. refinishing, diminishing 5. undiminishing.

IN'ist-er- 3. minister, sinister 4. administer 5. ambisinister.

IN'ist-ral- 3. ministral, sinistral 5. dextrosinistral.

IN'it–i– 3. finity, trinity 4. affinity, diffinity, infinity, confinity, virginity, salinity, felinity, caninity, vicinity, Latinity 5. masculinity, femininity, asininity, peregrinity, exsanguinity, consanguinity, patavinity.

IN'it–iv– 3. finitive 4. affinitive, definitive, infinitive.

IN'it–ud– 3. finitude 4. infinitude.

IN'i–um– 3. minium 4. delphinium, virginium, illinium, perinium, actinium 5. quadricinium, tirocinium, patrocinium.

IN'i–us– 5. ignominious, consanguineous; *see* also **IN'e–us–** vimineous etc. above.

INJ'ens–i– 3. stringency 4. refringency, astringency, constringency, contingency.

INJ'il–i– 3. dingily, stingily.

INJ'i–ness– 3. dinginess, stinginess.

INK'a–bl– 3. drinkable, shrinkable, sinkable, thinkable 4. undrinkable, unshrinkable, unthinkable.

INK'i–ness– 3. inkiness, kinkiness, slinkiness, pinkiness.

INK'ing–ly– 3. slinkingly, thinkingly, winkingly 4. unthinkingly.

INK'wit–i– 4. longinquity, propinquity.

INS'i–bl– 4. evincible, invincible, convincible.

INS'ing–li– 3. mincingly 4. convincingly.

INT'er–est– 3. interest 4. disinterest.

INT'er–i– 3. splintery, printery, wintery.

INT'er–ing– 3. splintering, wintering.

INTH'i–a– 3. Cynthia 4. Carinthia.

INTH'i–an– 3. Cynthian 4. Carinthian, Corinthian, absinthian 5. hyacinthian, labyrinthian.

IN'u–at– 3. sinuate 4. insinuate, continuate.

IN'u–us– 3. sinuous 4. continuous 5. uncontinuous, discontinuous.

IP'a–bl– 3. chippable, dippable, clippable, nippable, rippable, shippable, tippable.

IP'ar–us– 3. biparous 4. ambiparous, deiparous, polyparous, primiparous, gemmiparous, vermiparous, omniparous, criniparous, uniparous, floriparous, pluriparous, fissiparous, fructiparous, multiparous, dentiparous, viviparous, oviparous, larviparous 6. ovoviviparous.

IP'ath–i– 4. somnipathy, antipathy.

IP'er–i– 3. flippery, slippery, pipery, frippery.

IP'i–ent– 4. desipient, incipient, insipient, percipient 5. appercipient.

IP'ik–al– 3. typical 4. atypical, etypical, nontypical, untypical.

IP'i–ness– 3. slippiness, nippiness, snippiness, grippiness.

IP'it–al– 4. centripetal, basipetal, bicipital, occipital, ancipital, sincipital.

IP'ol–e– 3. Tripoli 4. Gallipoli.

IP'ot–ens– 4. armipotence, ignipotence, plenipotence, omnipotence.

IP'ot–ent– 4. deipotent, bellipotent, armipotent, plenipotent, ignipotent, omnipotent, noctipotent, multipotent.

IPSH'un–al– 4. transcriptional, inscriptional, conscriptional.

IPT'er–al– 3. dipteral 4. hemipteral, peripteral.

IPT'er–us– 3. dipterous, dipteros, Dipterus, tripterous 4. peripterous.

IPT'ik–al– 3. cryptical 4. elliptical 6. apocalyptical.

IPT'iv–li– 4. descriptively, prescriptively 5. circumscriptively.

IP'ul–ar– 3. stipular 4. manipular.

IP'ul–at– 3. stipulate 4. pedipulate, manipulate, astipulate.

IR'a–si– through **IR'i–us,** *see* also short **U** (tub): **URB'a–bl** through **URZH'un–ist.**

IR'a–si– 4. deliracy, conspiracy.

IR'i–a– 3. Syria, Styria 4. Valkyria, Elyria, Assyria; *see* also **ER'i–a–** eria etc.

IR'i–an– 3. Syrian, Tyrian, Styrian 4. Valkyrian, Assyrian.

IR'ik-al- 3. lyrical, miracle 4. empirical, satirical, satyrical 5. panegyrical.

IR'is-ist- 3. lyricist 4. empiricist.

IR'is-izm- 3. lyricism 4. empiricism.

IR'i-um- 3. Miriam 4. delirium, imperium.

IR'i-us- 3. Sirius 4. delirious, imperious.

IS'a-bl- 3. kissable, missable 4. dismissable; *see* also **IS'i-bl-** missible etc. below.

IS'en-ing- 3. listening, glistening, christening.

ISH'al-i- 4. judicially, officially 5. prejudicially, beneficially, sacrificially, artificially, unofficially, superficially.

ISH'ar-i- 4. judiciary, justiciary 5. beneficiary.

ISH'ens-i- 4. efficiency, deficiency, proficiency, sufficiency 5. beneficiency, inefficiency, unproficiency, self-sufficiency, insufficiency.

ISH'ent-li- 4. efficiently, deficiently, proficiently, sufficiently 5. inefficiently, unproficiently, insufficiently.

ISH'i-a- 4. indicia, Alicia, Galicia, Felicia, comitia, Tunisia, asitia, Justitia 5. apositia.

ISH'i-at- 3. vitiate 4. officiate, initiate, propitiate, patriciate, novitiate.

ISH'on-al- 3. missional 4. additional, traditional, conditional, volitional, commissional, nutritional, transitional, positional, petitional, tuitional 5. exhibitional, unconditional, recognitional, depositional, prepositional, impositional, compositional, propositional, expositional, suppositional, repetitional, intuitional.

ISH'on-er- 3. missioner 4. conditioner, commissioner, parishioner, petitioner, practitioner 5. exhibitioner, coalitioner, admonitioner.

ISH'on-ing- 4. conditioning, positioning, petitioning.

ISH'on-ist- 4. traditionist 5. prohibitionist, exhibitionist, expeditionist, coalitionist, abolitionist, requisitionist, oppositionist.

ISH'us-li- 3. viciously 4. judiciously, officiously, maliciously, deliciously, perniciously, auspiciously, suspiciously, capriciously 5. injudiciously, inauspiciously, avariciously, meretriciously, adventitiously.

ISH'us-ness- 3. viciousness 4. ambitiousness, seditiousness, judiciousness, officiousness, flagitiousness, deliciousness, perniciousness, propitiousness, auspiciousness, suspiciousness, capriciousness, nutritiousness, fictitiousness 5. injudiciousness, inauspiciousness, avariciousness, meretriciousness, adventitiousness, superstitiousness, supposititiousness.

IS'i-bl- 3. missible, miscible, scissible 4. admissible, remissible, immiscible, omissible, permissible, transmissible 5. unremissible, unpermissible, obliviscible; *see* also **IS'a-bl-** kissable etc. above.

IS'i-bli- 4. admissibly, permissibly.

IS'i-li- 3. prissily [coll.], Sicily.

IS'im-o- 4. dolcissimo [It.], altissimo, fortissimo, prestissimo, bravissimo [It.] 5. pianissimo 6. generalissimo.

IS'in-al- 3. piscinal, vicinal 4. medicinal, fidicinal, officinal, vaticinal.

IS'i-pat- 3. dissipate 4. anticipate, participate.

IS'it-i- 4. cubicity, mendicity, pudicity, publicity, felicity, triplicity, simplicity, complicity, duplicity, conicity, unicity, tonicity, stoicity, lubricity, rubricity, sphericity, centricity, pepticity, septicity, stypticity, verticity, vorticity, plasticity, spasticity, causticity, mysticity, rusticity, toxicity 5. benedicite, immundicity, spheroidicity, impudicity, infelicity, catholicity, multiplicity, accomplicity, quadruplicity, atomicity, endemicity, atonicity, canonicity, caloricity, electricity, eccentricity, concentricity, authenticity, eupepticity, ellipticity, autopticity, elasticity, domesticity **6.** periodicity, egocentricity, inelasticity.

IS'it–ing– **4.** eliciting, soliciting.

IS'it–li– **3.** licitly **4.** illicitly, implicitly, explicitly.

IS'it–ness– **3.** licitness **4.** illicitness, implicitness, explicitness.

IS'it–or– **4.** elicitor, solicitor.

IS'it–ud– **3.** spissitude **4.** solicitude, vicissitude.

IS'it–us– **4.** felicitous, solicitous.

ISK'i–er– **3.** riskier, friskier.

ISK'i–est– **3.** riskiest, friskiest.

ISK'i–li– **3.** riskily, friskily.

ISK'i–ness– **3.** riskiness, friskiness.

IS'or–i– **4.** admissory, remissory, dimissory, dismissory, rescissory.

IST'en–si– **3.** distancy **4.** subsistency, existency, insistency, consistency, persistency **5.** pre-existency, inconsistency.

IST'ent–li– **3.** distantly **4.** existently, insistently, persistently **5.** inconsistently.

IST'er–i– **3.** blistery, mystery **4.** baptistery, commistery; *see* also **IST'or–i–** history etc. below.

IST'er–lik– **3.** blisterlike, sisterlike.

IST'ful–i– **3.** listfully, wistfully.

IST'i–bl– **4.** resistible, existible **5.** irresistible, unresistible.

IST'ik–al– **3.** mystical **4.** deistical, theistical, logistical, sophistical, hemistichal, papistical, eristical, patristical, juristical, puristical, statistical, artistical, linguistical **5.** atheistical, pantheistical, eulogistical, synergistical, catechistical, anarchistical, cabalistical, alchemistical, Calvinistical, canonistical, synchronistical, egoistical, eucharistical, syncretistical **6.** theosophistical, antagonistical, characteristical, hypocoristical.

IST'ik–at– **4.** sophisticate, phlogisticate **5.** unsophisticate, dephlogisticate.

IST'or–i– **3.** history **4.** faldistory, consistory; *see* also **IST'er–i–** blistery etc. above.

IT'a–bl– **3.** fittable, hittable, knittable, pittable, quittable **4.** Mehitable, admittable, remittable, omittable, committable, permittable, transmittable **5.** unremittable, unacquittable.

IT'an–i– **3.** dittany, kitteny, litany, Brittany.

IT'er–al– **3.** literal **4.** presbyteral, alliteral, biliteral, triliteral.

IT'er–at– **3.** iterate **4.** reiterate, presbyterate, alliterate, obliterate, transliterate.

IT'er–er– **3.** bitterer, jitterer [slang], litterer, glitterer, fritterer, titterer, twitterer **4.** embitterer.

IT'er–est– **3.** bitterest.

IT'er–i– **3.** jittery [slang], littery, glittery, tittery, twittery.

IT'er–ing– **3.** jittering [slang], littering, glittering, frittering, tittering, twittering **4.** embittering.

ITH'er–i– **3.** dithery, smithery, withery.

ITH'er–ing– **3.** dithering, blithering, withering.

ITH'es–is– **4.** epithesis, antithesis.

ITH'i–a– **3.** lithia, Pythia **4.** forsythia.

IT'i–er– **3.** flittier, grittier, prettier, wittier, Whittier.

IT'i–est– **3.** grittiest, prettiest, wittiest.

IT'ik–al– **3.** critical **4.** political, hermitical, acritical, soritical, Levitical **5.** eremitical, stalagmitical, diacritical, hypocritical, hypercritical, parasitical, Jesuitical **6.** cosmopolitical, metropolitical, oneirocritical.

IT'il–i– **3.** grittily, prettily, wittily.

IT'i–ness– **3.** fittiness, flittiness, grittiness, prettiness, wittiness.

IT'ing–li– **3.** fittingly, flittingly, wittingly, twittingly **4.** befittingly, unwittingly **5.** unbefittingly, unremittingly.

IT'is–izm– 3. Briticism, criticism, witticism.

IT'l–ness– 3. littleness, brittleness.

IT'u–al– 3. ritual, situal 4. habitual, obitual 5. unhabitual.

IT'ul–ar– 3. titular 4. capitular.

IV'a–bl– 3. givable, livable 4. forgivable, unlivable 5. unforgivable.

IV'al–ent– 3. bivalent, divalent, trivalent 4. polyvalent, omnivalent, univalent, multivalent, equivalent.

IV'at–iv– 3. privative 4. derivative, deprivative.

IV'el–er– 3. sniveller, driveller, civiller.

IV'er–er– 3. sliverer, shiverer, quiverer 4. deliverer.

IV'er–i– 3. livery, slivery, rivery, shivery, quivery 4. delivery.

IV'er–ing– 3. slivering, shivering, quivering 4. delivering.

IV'i–a– 3. trivia 4. Olivia, Bolivia.

IV'i–al– 3. trivial 4. oblivial, quadrivial. lixivial, convivial.

IV'i–an– 3. Vivian 4. Bolivian.

IV'id–li– 3. lividly, vividly.

IV'id–ness– 3. lividness, vividness.

IV'il–i– 3. snivelly, civilly 4. uncivilly.

IV'ing–li– 3. givingly, livingly 4. forgivingly, outgivingly.

IV'it–i– 3. privity 4. acclivity, declivity, proclivity, passivity, nativity, activity, motivity, captivity, festivity 5. impassivity, compassivity, emissivity, negativity, relativity, sensitivity, positivity, inactivity, objectivity, subjectivity, electivity, collectivity, connectivity, inductivity, conductivity, productivity, receptivity, perceptivity, susceptivity 6. correlativity, alternativity, retroactivity, reproductivity.

IV'it–us– 4. acclivitous, declivitous, proclivitous.

IV'i–um– 3. trivium 4. quadrivium, lixivium.

IV'i–us– 3. bivious 4. oblivious, lascivious, lixivious, multivious.

IV'ok–al– 4. univocal, equivocal 5. unequivocal.

IV'ol–i– 3. Rivoli, Tivoli.

IV'ol–us– 3. frivolous 4. unfrivolous.

IV'or–us– 4. herbivorous, frondiverous, amphivorous, frugivorous, mellivorous, vermivorous, panivorous, ranivorous, granivorous, lignivorous, pomivorous, omnivorous, baccivorous, piscivorous, fucivorous, mucivorous, nucivorous, ossivorous, fructivorous, sanguivorous, equivorous 5. graminivorous, insectivorous, vegetivorous, sanguinivorous.

IZ'er–i– 3. misery, quizzery.

IZH'on–al– 3. visional 4. precisional, revisional, previsional, divisional, provisional.

IZ'i–an– 3. Frisian 4. Elysian, Tunisian, Parisian, precisian 5. paradisian.

IZ'i–bl– 3. risible, visible, quizzable 4. derisible, divisible, invisible, acquisible 5. indivisible, undivisible.

IZ'i–er– 3. busier, dizzier, fizzier, frizzier.

IZ'i–est– 3. busiest, dizziest, fizziest, frizziest.

IZ'ik–al– 3. physical, phthisical, quizzical 5. paradisical, metaphysical, cataphysical, geophysical, psychophysical.

IZ'il–i– 3. busily, dizzily, frizzily.

IZ'ing–li– 3. whizzingly, quizzingly.

IZ'it–iv– 4. acquisitive, inquisitive, disquisitive.

IZ'it–or– 3. visitor 4. acquisitor, requisitor, inquisitor, disquisitor.

O (oh)

1.

SINGLE (MASCULINE) RHYMES IN O (oh)

Primary or Secondary Accent Falls on Last Syllable; Imperfect Rhymes Are in Italics.

O– **1.** o, O, oh, oe, owe, eau, eaux [both F.] **2.** K. O. [coll.], kayo [slang] **3.** video, rodeo, studio, Indio [Sp.], Tokyo, oleo, folio, cameo, Romeo, Borneo, Scipio, Scorpio, embryo, cheerio, vireo, histrio, nuncio **4.** presidio, adagio, religio [L.], punctilio, borachio, Borachio, pistachio, portfolio **5.** Montevideo, ex officio, braggadocio, oratorio, impresario.

BO– **1.** bo, boh, 'bo, 'boe [both slang], beau **2.** jabot, sabot, embow, *rainbow*, *oboe*, *hobo*, *crossbow* **3.** saddlebow.

DO– **1.** do, doe, doh, dough **2.** *Dido*, *rondo*, rondeau, Bordeau **3.** Rinaldo, cabildo [Sp.].

FO– **1.** foe, Fo, faux [F.] **2.** *Sappho*, *Morpho*, *bufo*, *buffo* [It.] **3.** comme il faut [F.].

GO– **1.** go **2.** ago, *Margot*, forego, *sorgo*, *outgo* **3.** touch-and-go, long ago, undergo, indigo, vertigo **5.** archipelago.

HO– **1.** ho, hoe, Hoh **2.** mahoe, heigh-ho, oho, *moho*, *roho* [Sp.], soho, *Soho*, yo-ho, *brujo* [Sp.] **3.** Idaho, Navaho, Westward Ho, tallyho **4.** Arapaho.

JO– **1.** Jo, Joe, joe [slang] **2.** banjo **3.** *adagio*.

KO– **1.** ko, Ko, Co., Coe, coe [loc. Eng.] **2.** *unco* [Scot. & N. of Eng.], *coco*, *cocoa*, *moko* **3.** medico [coll.], calico, Sinico, haricot, cantico, portico, Mexico, rococo, *albarco* **4.** magnifico, energico [It.], angelico, simpatico, patetico [both It.].

LO– **1.** lo, low, Lowe, blow, flow, floe, glow, slow, sloe **2.** alow, tableau, bibelot, [F.], *flyblow*, *deathblow*, *pueblo*, below, hello, *inflow*, ice floe, *outflow*, aglow, *moonglow*, *sunglow*, pilau, kolo, matelot [F.], rouleau, hullo **3.** buffalo, bungalow, counterblow, overflow, alpenglow, counterglow, furbelow, pomelo, gigolo, tremolo.

MO– **1.** mo, mho, Moe, mot, mow **2.** bon mot, *twelvemo*, *haymow* **3.** alamo, dynamo, chalumeau, Eskimo, centimo, ultimo, proximo **4.** dolcissimo [It.], altissimo, fortissimo, prestissimo, bravissimo [It.] **5.** pianissimo **6.** generalissimo.

NO– **1.** no, know, snow **2.** tonneau, foreknow, besnow, Gounod **3.** domino.

PO– **1.** Po, Poe, peau [F.], poh **2.** chapeau, drapeau [F.], *depot*, shippo, cachepot [F.] **3.** apropos **4.** malapropos.

RO– **1.** roe, row, Rowe, rho, bro [slang], fro, grow, crow, scrow, pro, trow, strow, throe, throw **2.** arow, carreau [F.], *windrow*, *hedgerow*, ingrow, outgrow, *cockcrow*, *pilcrow*, *scarecrow*, escrow, genro, carot, de trop [F.], bestrow, rethrow, downthrow, upthrow, bureau **3.** to-and-fro, Pierrot, intergrow, Chatellerault, Rotten Row, overthrow.

SO– **1.** so, soh, sow, sew **2.** *soso*, *so-so*, morceau [F.], Rousseau, trousseau, how so **3.** curassow, curacao, so-and-so.

SHO– **1.** show, shew, sho **2.** cachot [F.], *sideshow*, *style show*, foreshow, *horse show* **3.** picture show.

TO– 1. toe, tow, stow 2. bateau, plateau, chateau, molto [It.], manteau, coteau [F.], couteau [F.], tiptoe, bestow, sexto 3. mistletoe, timber toe [slang], undertow, manito, portmanteau 4. incognito.

THO– 1. though 2. although.

VO– 1. Vaux, voe 3. *centaro* 4. de Marivaux.

WO– 1. woe, whoa, quo 3. quid pro quo [L.], status quo [L.] 4. status in quo [L.], in statu quo [L.].

YO– 1. yo, yo' [dial.] 2. *bagnio*, noyau, *yo-yo* 3. *imbroglio*, *seraglio*, *intaglio* 4. *latticinio*.

OB– 1. obe, aube, Job, lobe, globe, robe, probe 2. conglobe, enrobe, unrobe, disrobe.

OCH– 1. coach, loach, poach, roach, broach, brooch, croche 2. encoach, abroach, cockroach, encroach, approach, reproach 3. self-reproach.

OCHT– 1. coached, poached, broached 2. uncoached, unbroached, encroached, approached, reproached.

OD– 1. ode, ohed, owed, bode, goad, hoed, code, lode, load, blowed [slang & dial.], slowed, mode, mowed, node, spode, road, rode, rowed, crowed, strode, sowed, sewed, shoad, shode, towed, toed, toad, stowed, woad, yod 2. unowed, abode, *elbowed*, embowed, unbowed, forebode, unload, explode, commode, unmowed, *epode*, erode, corrode, bestrode, intoed, bestowed 3. overload, a la mode, incommode, discommode, antipode, pigeon-toed, episode, timber-toed [slang].

ODZ– odes etc., *see* **OD–** ode etc. above, plus "s" or "'s"; 1. Rhodes.

OF– 1. oaf, goaf, koph, loaf, toph 2. *breadloaf*, *witloof* 3. half a loaf, sugar loaf, monostrophe.

OG– 1. log, rogue, brogue, drogue, drogh, trogue, togue, vogue 2. embogue, collogue, pirogue, prorogue 3. disembogue, epilogue, apologue.

OJ– 1. doge, loge 2. gamboge, eloge 3. horologe.

OK– 1. oak, oke [slang], boke [slang], choke, folk, hoke [slang], joke, coak, coke, bloak, bloke [both slang], cloak, sloke, moke, moch, smoke, poke, spoke, broke, croak, stroke, soak, toque, stoke, woke, yoke, yolk 2. *seafolk*, *kinfolk*, *townsfolk*, uncloak, besmoke, bespoke, forespoke, forspoke, baroque, *sunstroke*, asoak, evoke, revoke, invoke, convoke, provoke, awoke 3. artichoke, okeydoke [slang], gentlefolk, womenfolk, counterstroke, equivoque.

OKS– oaks etc., *see* **OK–** oak etc. above, plus "s" or "'s"; 1. hoax, coax.

OKT– 1. choked, joked, coaked, coked, cloaked, smoked, poked, spoked, croaked, stroked, soaked, stoked, yoked 2. uncloaked, besmoked, evoked, revoked, invoked, convoked, provoked 3. counterstroked, double yolked.

OL– 1. ol, ole [dial.], ol', bole, boll, bowl, dhole, dole, foal, goal, hole, whole, jowl [dial.], coal, cole, kohl, skoal, mole, knoll, poll, pole, roll, role, droll, drole [F.], scroll, troll, stroll, soul, sole, shoal, shole, toll, stole, thole, vole 2. *Creole*, embowl, *obole*, condole, *segol*, *borehole*, *bunghole*, *manhole*, *kilnhole*, *peephole*, *pinhole*, *loophole*, *porthole*, *heart-whole*, *tophole*, cajole, bricole, *charcoal*, *Maypole*, *tadpole*, *redpole*, *flagpole*, *payroll*, *logroll*, parole, virole, enroll, unroll, furole, enscroll, inscroll, patrol, control, resole, halfsole, rissole [F.], ensoul, insoul, console, citole, *sestole*, pistole, extoll 3. ariole, dariole, aureole, foliole, apiole, variole, cabriole, oriole, gloriole, capriole, petiole, ostiole, vacuole, amphibole, racambole, carambole, farandole, girandole, pigeonhole, buttonhole, cubbyhole, glory hole, caracole, arvicole, septimole, carmagnole, Seminole, rantipole, metropole, barcarole.

rigmarole, escarole, fumarole, fusarole, squatarole, azarole, banderole, casserole, self-control, girasole, camisole **4.** bibliopole, remote control.

OLD– **1.** old, bold, bowled, bolled, fold, foaled, gold, hold, cold, coaled, scold, skoaled, mold, mould, polled, rolled, sold, soled, shoaled, told, tolled, stoled, wold **2.** *blindfold*, *twofold*, *threefold* etc., *bifold*, enfold, infold, unfold, *sheepfold*, spun gold, behold, *freehold*, *stronghold*, uphold, *leasehold*, *household*, *threshold*, *foothold*, withhold, cajoled, remold, *leafmold*, paroled, controlled, half-soled, unsold, retold, untold, foretold, twice-told **3.** overbold, hundredfold, thousandfold, manifold, multifold, interfold, marigold, copyhold, pigeonholed, pudding mold, bullet mold, Leopold, uncontrolled, self-controlled, undersold, oversold, sable-stoled.

OLK– **1.** polk, Polk, yolk, Volk.

OLT– **1.** bolt, dolt, holt, jolt, colt, molt, smolt, poult, volt **2.** rebolt, eyebolt, kingbolt, wringbolt, unbolt, lavolt, revolt **3.** shackle bolt, thunderbolt, millivolt, demivolt.

OLZ– Ol's, bowls etc., *see* **OL–** ol etc. above, plus "s" or "'s."

OM– **1.** ohm, oam, dom, dome, foam, home, holm, haulm, heaume, comb, loam, gloam, glome, mome, Nome, gnome, pome, roam, rom, Rome, drome, chrome, tome **2.** endome, afoam, befoam, megohm, *coxcomb*, aplomb, Jerome **3.** semidome, catacomb, honeycomb, currycomb, evenglome, metronome, gastronome, palindrome, hippodrome, aerodrome, Ethan Frome, polychrome, monochrome, microsome, chromosome.

OMZ– ohms etc., *see* **OM–** ohm etc. above, plus "s" or "'s"; **1.** Holmes, Soames.

ON– **1.** own, bone, Beaune, phone, hone, Joan, cone, scone, lone, loan, blown, flown, mown, moan, known, None, pone, roan, Rhone, drone, groan, grown, crone, prone, throne, thrown, sewn, sown, shown, shone, tone, stone, zone **2.** disown, *aitchbone*, *backbone*, *whalebone*, *trombone*, *jawbone*, *icebone*, *fishbone*, *wishbone*, *breastbone*, condone, alone, cologne, Cologne, full-blown, unblown, high-flown, unflown, bemoan, *hormone*, unknown, foreknown, depone, repone, *corn pone*, propone, dispone, postpone, ladrone, begroan, half-grown, full-grown, ungrown, bestrown, dethrone, unthrown, unsewn, unsown, unshown, foreshown, atone, intone, fronton [Sp.], *curbstone*, *headstone*, *sandstone*, *end stone*, *grindstone*, *lodestone*, *bloodstone*, *keystone*, *freestone*, *flagstone*, *clingstone*, *hailstone*, *millstone*, *milestone*, *tilestone*, *limestone*, *brimstone*, *tombstone*, *rhinestone*, *moonstone*, *soapstone*, *whetstone*, *hearthstone*, enzone, *ozone* **3.** anklebone, knucklebone, cuttlebone, megaphone, vitaphone, dictaphone, telephone, graphophone, gramophone, xylophone, microphone, saxophone, unbeknown, unforeknown, interpone, chaperone, cicerone, overgrown, semitone, baritone, monotone, undertone, overtone, cornerstone, overthrown **4.** radiophone, electrophone, Eau-de-Cologne.

OND– **1.** owned, boned, phoned, honed, coned, loaned, moaned, monde, droned, groaned, throned, toned, zoned **2.** disowned, fine-boned, bemoaned, beau monde, haut monde [F.], postponed, dethroned, atoned, high-toned, intoned, flagstoned, enzoned, unzoned **3.** telephoned, demimonde, chaperoned.

ONT– **1.** don't, conte, won't.

ONZ– owns etc., *see* **ON–** own etc. above, plus "s" or "'s"; **1.** Jones, nones, Nones **3.** lazybones, Davy Jones.

OO–, *see* under **OO** (good) following short **O** (awe).

OP– **1.** ope [dial. or poetic], dope, hope, cope, scope, lope, slope, mope, nope [slang or loc.], pope, rope, grope, trope, soap, tope, taupe, stope 2. elope, aslope, agrope, dragrope, towrope, soft-soap 3. telescope, periscope, seismoscope, gyroscope, microscope, horoscope, spectroscope, stethoscope, cantaloupe, antelope, envelope, interlope, protopope, philanthrope, misanthrope, isotope 4. stereoscope, kaleidoscope, dipleidoscope, polemoscope, heliotrope.

OPS– opes etc., *see* **Op–** ope etc. above, plus "s" or "'s"; 1. Stopes.

OPT– 1. oped [poetic], doped, hoped, coped, loped, sloped, moped, roped, groped, soaped 2. eloped 3. *enveloped.*

OR– through **ORZ–**, *see* also short **O** (awe): **OR–** through **ORZ–**.

OR– 1. ore, oar, o'er, bore, boar, Boer, chore, door, fore, four, gore, hoar, core, corps, score, lore, floor, more, mohr, snore, pour, pore, spore, roar, soar, sore, shore, tore, store, wore, swore, yore 2. forebore, adore, Indore, indoor, outdoor, before, therefore, wherefore, Johore, décor [F.], encore, threescore, fourscore etc., galore [coll.], *folklore*, *booklore*, deplore, implore, explore, ignore, *downpour*, outpour, *uproar*, *eyesore*, *heartsore*, *footsore*, ashore, *seashore*, inshore, foreshore, restore, *drugstore*, forswore 3. troubadour, picador, matador, Isadore, stevedore, Polydore, open door, battledore, Theodore, commodore, two-by-four, semaphore, pinafore, heretofore, albacore, terpsichore, underscore, Sagamore, sycamore, paramour, Barrymore, Baltimore, sophomore, furthermore, evermore, nevermore, Singapore, carnivore 4. hereinbefore.

ORCH– 1. scorch, porch, torch 2. front porch.

ORD– 1. oared, bored, board, doored, ford, gored, gourd, hoard, hoared, horde, cored, scored, floored, snored, poured, pored, toward, stored, sword 2. aboard, *clapboard*, *cupboard*, *switchboard*, *headboard*, *breadboard*, *sideboard*, *cardboard*, *seaboard*, *surfboard*, *springboard*, *blackboard*, *buckboard*, *wallboard*, *inboard*, *clapboard*, *outboard*, adored, *two-doored*, *four-doored*, afford, ungored, encored, uncored, deplored, implored, explored, restored 3. shuffleboard, beaverboard, overboard, ironing board, open-doored, unexplored, unrestored.

ORJ– 1. forge, gorge, porge 2. engorge, disgorge.

ORK– 1. pork 2. *morepork*, salt pork.

ORN– 1. borne, bourn, Doorn, scorn, mourn, morn, shorn, worn, sworn 2. forborne, bemourn, unshorn, betorn, *toilworn*, outworn, unsworn, forsworn 3. unforsworn.

ORND– 1. scorned, mourned 2. unscorned, bemourned, unmourned.

ORS– 1. force, hoarse, coarse, course, source 2. enforce, inforce, perforce, recourse, discourse, resource, divorce 3. reinforce, intercourse, watercourse.

ORT– 1. fort, forte, court, mort, port, sport 2. aport, apport, rapport, deport, report, *seaport*, import, comport, *airport*, *carport*, purport, *passport*, disport, export, transport, support, resort 3. sally port, davenport, nonsupport 4. pianoforte.

ORTH– 1. forth, fourth 2. henceforth, thenceforth.

ORZ– oars etc., *see* **OR–** oar etc. above, plus "s" or "'s"; 2. indoors, outdoors, all fours, plus fours, Azores.

OS– 1. boce, dose, kos, close, gross, socc 2. globose, verbose, nodose, jocose, engross, morose 3. overdose, grandiose, otiose, bellicose, annulose, diagnose, adipose, comatose.

OSH– 1. Boche, cloche, sosh [slang].

OST– 1. oast, boast, dosed, ghost, host, coast, most, post, roast, grossed, toast 2. *seacoast*, *headmost*, *endmost*, *hindmost*, almost, *inmost*, *topmost*, *upmost*, *foremost*, *utmost*, reposte, *milepost*, *signpost*, *outpost*, engrossed 3. bottommost, easternmost, northernmost, hindermost, undermost, innermost, lowermost, uppermost, centermost, outermost, uttermost, nethermost, hithermost, furthermost, diagnosed, whipping post, hitching post, letter post.

OT– **1.** oat, boat, dote, goat, coat, cote, côte [F.], scote, bloat, float, gloat, moat, mote, smote, note, rote, wrote, groat, throat, shoat, shote, tote [coll. & slang], stoat, vote, quote **2.** *lifeboat*, *sailboat*, *showboat*, *houseboat*, *scapegoat*, *redcoat*, *turncoat*, *topcoat*, *waistcoat*, afloat, refloat, emote, demote, remote, promote, denote, *keynote*, connote, *gracenote*, *footnote*, capote, garrote, rewrote, *starthroat*, *whitethroat*, *cutthroat*, aptote, diptote, triptote, devote, outvote, bequote, misquote **3.** ferryboat, river boat, antidote, anecdote, table d'hote, billy goat, nanny goat, mountain goat, redingote, petticoat, overcoat, underwrote, creosote, asymptote.

OTH– **1.** oath, both, loath, sloth, wroth, growth, troth, Thoth, quoth **2.** *outgrowth*, betroth **3.** behemoth, aftergrowth, overgrowth, undergrowth.

OTH– **1.** loathe, clothe **2.** reclothe, unclothe, betroth.

OTHZ– **1.** loathes, clothes **2.** reclothes, bedclothes, betroths **3.** underclothes.

OTS– oats etc., *see* **OT–** oat etc. above, plus "s" or "'s"; **1.** Oates, Coates.

OV– **1.** dove, hove, Jove, cove, loave, clove, mauve, rove, drove, grove, Shrove, trove, strove, throve, tove [Scot.], stove, wove **2.** behove, gemauve, *mangrove*, rewove, inwove **3.** perijove, apojove, treasure-trove, interwove.

OVZ– **1.** Jove's, loaves, cloves, mauves, roves, droves, groves, troves, toves [Scot.], stoves.

OZ– **1.** owes, bows, beaux, chose, doze, does, foes, goes, hose, glows, close, clothes, Mose, nose, knows, snows, pose, spose [slang], rows, rose, brose, froze, croze, prose, pros, sows, sews, toes, tows, toze, those **2.** *rainbows*, *bulldoze*, enclose, unclose, foreclose, disclose, depose, repose, impose, compose, oppose, propose, dispose, expose, transpose, suppose, arose, *tuberose*, *tea rose*, *wild rose*, *dog rose*, *rockrose*, *primrose*, *moss rose*, unfroze, *tiptoes* **3.** dominoes, decompose, recompose, discompose, superpose, interpose, predispose, indispose, presuppose, damask rose, bramble rose, Irish rose, pettitoes.

OZD– **1.** dozed, hosed, closed, nosed, posed, prosed **2.** *bulldozed*, enclosed, unclosed, foreclosed, disclosed, deposed, reposed, imposed, composed, opposed, proposed, disposed, exposed, transposed, supposed **3.** decomposed, discomposed, interposed, predisposed, well-disposed, ill-disposed, indisposed, presupposed.

OZH– **1.** loge **2.** gamboge, éloge.

O (oh)

2.

DOUBLE (FEMININE) RHYMES IN O (bo'a)

Primary or Secondary Accent Falls on Next to Last Syllable; Imperfect Rhymes Are in Italics.

O'a– 2. boa, koa, loa, moa, Noah, noa, proa, Shoa 3. Gilboa, jerboa, aloha, Samoa, anoa, leipoa 4. Kanaloa, Metazoa, Anthozoa, microzoa, Hydrozoa, Sporozoa, entozoa, Protozoa.

O'ab– 2. doab, Joab, Moab.

O'al– 3. bestowal, restowal.

O'an– 2. cowan, rowan 3. eoan, Samoan, Minoan.

OB'a– 2. koba 3. cohoba, arroba 4. algarroba, bona roba [arch.], Manitoba.

OB'al– 2. lobal, global, probal 3. microbal, Cristobal.

OB'at– 2. lobate, globate, probate.

OB'er– 2. rober, robur, prober, sober 3. amobyr, enrober, disrober, October.

OB'i– 2. obi, dobe, Gobi, goby, Kobe, globy, toby [slang], Toby 3. adobe.

OB'ik– 2. phobic, strobic 3. niobic, microbic 4. phobophobic, hydrophobic, claustrophobic, photophobic.

OB'il– 2. mobile 3. immobile 4. locomobile, automobile.

OB'ing– 2. globing, robing, probing 3. englobing, enrobing, unrobing, disrobing.

OB'it– 2. obit, Tobit 3. post-obit.

OB'l– 2. coble, noble 3. ennoble, ignoble, unnoble.

OB'o– 2. oboe, bobo, hobo, lobo, zobo.

OB'ra– 2. dobra, cobra.

OB'ul– 2. lobule, globule.

OB'us– 2. obus, Kobus, lobus [NL.], globus, globous 3. jacobus.

OCH'er– 2. poacher, broacher 3. encroacher, approacher, reproacher.

OCH'ez– 2. coaches, loaches, poaches, roaches, broaches, brooches 3. encoaches cockroaches, encroaches, approaches, reproaches 4. self reproaches.

OCH'ful– 3. reproachful 4. unreproachful, self-reproachful.

OCH'ing– 2. coaching, poaching, broaching 3. encoaching, encroaching, approaching, reproaching.

OCH'ment– 3. encroachment, approachment.

OD'a– 2. oda, coda, Rhoda, soda, Toda 3. pagoda, salsoda 4. baking soda, ice-cream soda, Scotch and soda 5. Chinese pagoda, whisky and soda.

OD'al– 2. odal, modal, nodal, yodel 3. trinodal 4. internodal.

OD'ed– 2. boded, goaded, coded, loaded, noded, woaded 3. foreboded, decoded, unloaded, exploded, outmoded, corroded 4. overloaded, incommoded, discommoded, uncorroded.

OD'el– 2. yodel, yodle.

OD'en– 2. Odin, boden, Woden.

OD'ent– 2. rodent 3. explodent, erodent, corrodent.

OD'er– 2. Oder, odor, boder, goader, loader, roader, woader 3. foreboder, malodor, reloader, unloader, exploder, corroder.

OD'i– 2. Godey, Cody, toady, tody, woady.

OD'ik– 2. odic 4. palinodic.

OD'ing– 2. boding, goading, coding, loading 3. foreboding, decoding, unloading, exploding, outmoding, eroding, corroding 4. overloading, discommoding.

OD'ist– 2. odist, codist, modist 4. palinodist.

OD'ler– 2. yodler, yodeler.

OD'o– 2. dodo, Jodo 3. quomodo [L.] 4. Quasimodo.

OD'ster– 2. goadster, lodestar, roadster.

OD'us– 2. modus [L.], nodus, nodous.

O'e– 2. Chloë, poe, poi, Zoe 3. evoe; *see* also **O'i**– bowie etc. below.

O'ed– 2. co-ed.

O'el– 2. Joel, koel, Lowell, Noel, nowel, Crowell.

O'em– 2. phloem, poem, proem 4. mythopoem, Jeroboam [slang, Eng.].

O'en– 2. Owen, Cohen, rowan.

O'er– 2. o'er, ower, Boer, goer, hoer, lower, blower, glower, slower, mower, knower, rower, grower, crower, sewer, sower, shower, tower, stower 3. foregoer, outgoer, foreknower, cockcrower, foreshower, bestower 4. overthrower.

O'erd– 2. lowered, froward, toward 3. untoward.

O'est– 2. lowest, slowest.

O'et– 2. poet.

OF'a– 2. sofa.

OF'er– 2. Ophir, gopher, gaufre, loafer, chauffeur.

OF'et– 2. tophet.

OF'i– 2. trophy, strophe, Sophie.

OG'a– 2. snoga, toga, yoga 3. Tioga, noyoga 4. Saratoga, Conestoga 5. Ticonderoga.

OG'an– 2. hogan, logan, slogan, rogan, brogan.

OG'er– 2. ogre, drogher.

OG'i– 2. bogy, bogie, dogie, fogy, fogey, logy, pogy, stogy, stogie, voguey, yogi 3. old-fogy, old-fogey 6. cedant arma togae [L.].

OG'ish– 2. roguish, voguish.

OG'l– 2. ogle, bogle, fogle, Vogel [G.], Vogul 3. aasvogel [D.].

OG'o– 2. gogo, mogo, Pogo, zogo.

OG'us– 2. bogus.

O'ha– 2. poha 3. aloha [Hawaian], aloja [Sp.].

O'he– 3. evohe!

O'ho– 2. coho, moho, mojo, Mojo, Moxo, rojo [Sp.], Soho 3. corojo.

O'i– 2. bowie, Bowie, doughy, Joey, blowy, glowy, Chloë, snowy, poe, poi, roi, rowy, showy, towy, Zoë 3. evoe!

O'ij– 2. flowage, towage, stowage.

O'ik– 2. Troic, Stoic, stoic, zoic 3. echoic, diploic, heroic, dichroic, azoic, benzoic 4. authochroic, epizoic, Eozoic, Neozoic, hylozoic, protozoic 5. Archaeozoic, Paleozoic.

O'iks– 2. Coix, stoics 3. heroics.

O'ing– 2. owing, bowing, Boeing, going, hoeing, lowing, glowing, slowing, mowing, knowing, snowing, rowing, growing, crowing, throwing, sowing, sewing, showing, towing, toeing, stowing 3. elbowing, seagoing, ingoing, foregoing, outgoing, helloing, inflowing, outflowing, foreknowing, unknowing, ingrowing, outgrowing, cockcrowing, foreshowing, tiptoeing 4. easygoing, thoroughgoing, undergoing, overthrowing.

OJ'an– 2. Trojan, yojan.

OJ'e– 2. shoji 3. agoge 4. anagoge, apagoge, epagoge, paragoge, isogoge.

OJ'ent– 2. cogent 3. incogent, uncogent.

OJ'urn– 2. sojourn.

OK'a– 2. oka, oca [Sp.], boca [Sp.], choca, phoca, coca, loka, loca, sloka, mocha, polka, trocha [Sp.], stocah 3. jocoque 4. tapioca, curiboca.

OK'al– 2. bocal, focal, phocal, local, trochal, socle, vocal, yokel 3. bifocal, collocal, bivocal 4. hyperfocal, patrilocal, multivocal, equivocal.

OK'e– 2. Loki, loci, moki, troche, trochee 3. jocoqui, ditrochee; *see* also **OK'i–** oaky etc. below.

OK'en– 2. oaken, spoken, broken, soken, token 3. bespoken, freespoken, unspoken, well-spoken, plain-spoken, soft-spoken, short-spoken, outspoken, smooth-spoken, true-spoken, unbroken, *heart-broken*, betoken, foretoken.

OK'er– 2. ochre, choker, joker, coker, cloaker, smoker, poker, roker, spoker, broker, croaker, stroker, soaker, stoker, yoker 3. *stockbroker*, *pawnbroker*, evoker, revoker, invoker, convoker, provoker 4. mediocre.

OK'et– 2. oket, poke it.

OK'i– 2. oaky, choky, hokey, jokey, coky, Loki, loci, moki, smoky, poky, roky, croaky, troche, trochee, soaky, yoky, yolky 3. jocoqui, ditrochee 4. okey-dokey [slang], hokeypokey [coll.].

OK'ij– 2. chokage, cloakage, rokeage [loc.], brokage, soakage.

OK'ing– 2. choking, joking, coking, cloaking, smoking, poking, spoking, croaking, troching, stroking, soaking, stoking, yoking 3. uncloaking, evoking, revoking, invoking, provoking, unyoking.

OK'l– 2. yokel 4. okel-dokel [slang]; *see* also **OK'al–** bocal etc. above.

OK'less– 2. oakless, jokeless, cokeless, blokeless [slang], cloakless, smokeless, pokeless, spokeless, croakless, yokeless, yolkless.

OK'ment– 3. revokement, invokement, provokement.

OK'o– 2. choco, coco, cocoa, koko, Ko-Ko, loco, moko, poco [It.], poco [slang], troco, soco, toco 3. rococo, al loco [It.] 4. locofoco, moko-moko, Orinoco.

OKS'er– 2. hoaxer, coaxer.

OKS'ing– 2. hoaxing, coaxing.

OK'um– 2. oakum, hokum.

OK'us– 2. focus, hocus, locus, crocus 4. hocus-pocus.

OK'ust– 2. focussed, hocussed, locust 3. unfocussed, sweet locust.

OL'a– 2. ola, bola, bowla, gola, kola, schola, Lola, mola, Mola, Nola, sola, stola, vola [L.], Zola 3. crayola, Viola, mandola, Angola, pimola, victrola 4. carambola, Pensacola, pianola, Gorgonzola 5. Savonarola.

OL'an– 2. O-lan, Dolan, Nolan, tolan; *see* also **OL'en–** solen etc. and **OL'on–** colon etc. below.

OL'ar– 2. bolar, molar, polar, solar, volar 4. unipolar, circumpolar, lunisolar, circumsolar; *see* also **OL'er–** Olor etc. below.

OLD'ed– 2. folded, scolded, molded 3. blindfolded, enfolded, unfolded 4. manifolded.

OLD'en– 2. olden, holden, golden 3. embolden, beholden 4. misbeholden.

OLD'er– 2. older, bolder, boulder, folder, holder, colder, scolder, molder, smolder, polder, shoulder 3. enfolder, unfolder, beholder, freeholder, landholder, upholder, shareholder, leaseholder, householder, withholder, slaveholder, cold-shoulder 4. manifolder, copyholder, candleholder, bottleholder.

OLD'erd– 2. bouldered, shouldered 3. broad-shouldered, round-shouldered, stoop-shouldered, square-shouldered 4. narrow-shouldered.

OLD'est– 2. oldest, boldest, coldest.

OLD'i– **2.** oldy, foldy, moldy, mouldy **3.** unmoldy.

OLD'ing– **2.** folding, holding, molding, scolding **3.** enfolding, landholding, beholding, upholding, withholding, slaveholding, non-molding, unmolding **4.** interfolding, overfolding.

OLD'ish– **2.** oldish, boldish, coldish.

OLD'li– **2.** oldly, boldly, coldly **4.** manifoldly.

OLD'ment– **3.** enfoldment, infoldment, withholdment.

OLD'ness– **2.** oldness, boldness, coldness.

OL'en– **2.** solen, stolen, Stollen, swollen; *see* also **OL'an**– O-lan etc. above and **OL'on**– colon etc. below.

OL'ent– **2.** olent, dolent, volant **3.** condolent.

OL'er– **2.** Olor, bowler, bolar, dolor, coaler, koller, molar, knoller, poler, polar, poller, roller, droller, scroller, troller, stroller, soler, solar, shoaler, toller, volar **3.** condoler, cajoler, enroller, patroller, controller, comptroller, consoler, extoller **4.** piegonholer, unipolar, circumpolar, Holy Roller, lunisolar.

OL'est– **2.** drollest.

OL'ful– **2.** bowlful, doleful, soulful.

OL'i– **2.** bowly, bolly, foaly, holy, wholly, coaly, lowly, slowly, moly, knolly, rolly, drolly, scrolly, soli, solely, sholy [dial.], shoaly **3.** unholy, anole, pinole, posole **4.** roly-poly, caracoli.

OL'ing– **2.** bolling, bowling, doling, foaling, goaling, holing, coaling, poling, polling, rolling, drolling, trolling, strolling, toliing **3.** condoling, cajoling, controlling, paroling, enrolling, unrolling, patrolling, half-soling, consoling, extolling **4.** caracoling.

OL'ish– **2.** Polish, drollish, soulish.

OL'jer– **2.** soldier.

OL'ment– **3.** condolement, cajolement, enrollment, controlment.

OL'ness– **2.** wholeness, drollness, soleness.

OL'o– **2.** bolo, Bolo, Cholo, Golo, Lolo, polo, solo, stolo [L.] **3.** barolo **4.** bolobolo.

OL'on– **2.** colon, Solon, stolon **3.** eidolon **4.** semicolon; *see* also **OL'an**– O-lan etc. and **OL'en**– solen etc. above.

OL'or– **2.** Olor, dolor; *see* also **OL'er**– Olor, bowler etc. above.

OL'som– **2.** dolesome, wholesome **3.** unwholesome.

OLST'er– **2.** bolster, holster **3.** upholster.

OLT'ed– **2.** bolted, jolted, molted **3.** unbolted, revolted.

OLT'en– **2.** molten **3.** unmolten.

OLT'er– **2.** bolter, colter, jolter, molter **3.** unbolter, revolter.

OLT'ij– **2.** boltage, voltage.

OLT'ing– **2.** bolting, jolting, molting **3.** unbolting, revolting.

OLT'ish– **2.** doltish, coltish.

OL'um– **2.** solum [L.] **3.** idolum.

OL'us– **2.** bolus, dolose, dolous, dolus [L.], solus [L.] **4.** holus-bolus, gladiolus.

OM'a– **2.** coma, loma, noma, Roma, stroma, soma, stoma **3.** aboma, zygoma, aloma, Tacoma, diploma, aroma, prosoma, phytoma, rhizoma.

OM'ad– **2.** nomad.

OM'al– **2.** domal, bromal, somal, stromal.

OM'an– **2.** bowman, foeman, gnomon, Roman, showman, yeoman.

OM'en– **2.** omen, nomen [L.], gnomon, yeomen **3.** abdomen, praenomen, agnomen, cognomen.

OM'end– **2.** omened **3.** ill omened, badomened **4.** happy-omened.

OM'ent– **2.** foment, loment, moment **3.** bestowment, last moment.

OM'er– 2. omer, gomer, Gomer, homer, Homer, comber, roamer, vomer 3. *beachcomber*, *wool comber*, misnomer.

OM'i– 2. domy, foamy, homy, homey [both coll.], Kome, Komi, loamy 3. Naomi 4. lomi-lomi.

OM'ij– 2. ohmage, homage.

OM'ik– 2. ohmic, domic, gnomic, bromic, chromic 3. achromic, dichromic 4. hydrobromic, polychromic.

OM'ing– 2. doming, foaming, homing, coaming, combing, gloaming, roaming 3. befoaming, Wyoming, *beachcombing*, *wool-combing*.

OM'is– 3. Nokomis, exomis.

OM'ish– 2. domish, foamish, gnomish, Romish, tomish.

OM'less– 2. domeless, foamless, homeless, combless, loamless, gnomeless.

OM'o– 2. homo, Como, momo, chromo, duomo [It.] 3. Pokomo 4. major-domo.

OM'us– 2. domus [L.], Comus, Momus, chromous 3. prodromus, disomus 4. Major Domus.

ON'a– 2. ona, bona [L.], Bona, Dona, Gona, kona, Jonah, Mona, drona, krona, trona, zona [L.] 3. annona, Annona, ancona, Ancona, cinchona, Bellona, Bologna, Ramona, Cremona, kimono 4. Barcelona, Desdemona, Toromona, Arizona.

ON'ad– 2. monad.

ON'al– 2. phonal, chronal, thronal, tonal, zonal 3. coronal, atonal, azonal 4. polytonal, polyzonal, interzonal.

ON'ant– 2. sonant, tonant 4. supersonant, intersonant; *see* also **ON'ent–** opponent etc. below.

ON'at– 2. donate, phonate, pronate, zonate.

ON'e– 3. euphone, Dione, Shoshone 4. abalone, macaroni, lazzaroni, cicerone.

ON'ent– 3. opponent, deponent, component, proponent, disponent, exponent 4. interponent; *see* also **ON'ant–** sonant etc. above.

ON'er– 2. owner, boner, donor, phoner, loaner, moaner, droner, toner, stoner 3. condoner, bemoaner, postponer, atoner, entoner, intoner.

O'ness– 2. lowness, slowness.

ON'i– 2. bony, phony [slang], cony, pony, drony, crony, tony [vulgar], stony 3. bologna, Dione, polony, Shoshone 4. chalcedony, abalone, ceremony, alimony, agrimony, acrimony, matrimony, patrimony, parsimony, sanctimony, antimony, testimony, macaroni, lazzaroni, cicerone.

ON'ij– 2. dronage 4. chaperonage.

ON'ing– 2. owning, boning, phoning, honing, loaning, moaning, droning, groaning, throning, toning, stoning, zoning 3. disowning, condoning, bemoaning, postponing, dethroning, unthroning, atoning, intoning, enzoning 4. telephoning, chaperoning.

ON'is– 3. Adonis, Coronis.

ON'less– 2. boneless, phoneless, loanless, moanless, groanless, throneless, toneless, stoneless, zoneless 4. telephoneless, chaperoneless.

ON'li– 2. only, lonely 3. alonely, unlonely 4. one and only.

ON'ment– 3. disownment, condonement, postponement, dethronement, enthronement, atonement, intonement.

ON'ness– 2. ownness, loneness, proneness 3. unknownness.

ON'o– 2. fono, Nono 3. kimono 4. Johnny Bono.

ON'som– 2. lonesome.

ON'um– 2. bonum [L.].

ON'us– 2. onus, bonus, conus, Cronus, tonus 3. colonus.

OO'– *see* under **OO** (good) following short **O** (awe).

O'on– 2. zoon 3. polyzoon, epizoon.

OP'a– **2.** opah, chopa, copa, scopa **3.** Europa.

OP'al– **2.** opal, copal, nopal **3.** sinople **4.** periople **5.** Adrianople, Constantinople.

OP'er– **2.** doper, hoper, coper, loper, sloper, moper, roper, groper, soaper, toper, stoper **3.** eloper, soft-soaper **4.** interloper.

OP'i– **2.** dopey, Hopi, slopy, mopy, ropy, soapy.

OP'ing– **2.** doping, hoping, coping, loping, sloping, moping, roping, groping, soaping, toping, stoping **3.** eloping, soft-soaping **4.** interloping.

OP'l– **3.** sinople **4.** periople **5.** Adrianople, Constantinople.

OP'less– **2.** hopeless, popeless, soapless.

OP'ment– **3.** elopement.

OP'us– **2.** opus, Propus **3.** lagopous, Lagopus, Canopus, pyropus.

OR'a– through **OR'us,** *see* also short **O** (awe): **OR'a** through **OR'ward.**

OR'a– **2.** ora, Ora, bora, Dora, goura, hora, Cora, kora, Korah, Lora, flora, Flora, Nora, torah, Torah **3.** Eldora, Pandora, rhodora, angora, señora [Sp.], signora [It.], aurora, Masora, totora **4.** Floradora, Theodora, passiflora, Passiflora.

OR'aks– **2.** borax, Dorax, storax, thorax.

OR'al– **2.** oral, horal, choral, loral, floral, chloral, poral, roral, thoral **3.** trifloral, auroral, sororal.

OR'an– **2.** Koran, toran **3.** Sonoran.

OR'at– **2.** orate, borate, florate, chlorate, prorate **3.** deflorate, biflorate.

OR'ay– **2.** foray, moire **3.** signore [It.] **6.** improvvisatore [It.].

ORD'ed– **2.** boarded, forded, hoarded, sworded **3.** afforded, unhoarded.

ORD'er– **2.** boarder, forder, hoarder.

ORD'ing– **2.** boarding, fording, hoarding **3.** affording, unhoarding **4.** beaver-boarding.

OR'er– **2.** borer, gorer, corer, scorer, floorer, snorer, porer, pourer, roarer, sorer, soarer, storer **3.** adorer, encorer, deplorer, implorer, explorer, ignorer, outpourer, restorer.

OR'ez– **2.** mores **3.** Cursores, Raptores **4.** Grallatores.

OR'i– **2.** oary, ory, dory, gory, hoary, kori, Kore, lory, flory, glory, more, snory, pory, shory, Tory, story **3.** Old Glory, vainglory, maggiore [It.], pilori, signore [It.] **4.** hunky-dory [coll.], allegory, category, tautegory, amphigory, counterflory, probatory, piscatory, gradatory, predatory, mandatory, mundatory, laudatory, feudatory, sudatory, prefatory, negatory, rogatory, purgatory, nugatory, oblatory, grallatory, parlatory, amatory, crematory, fumatory, chrismatory, sanatory, signatory, crinatory, donatory, phonatory, culpatory, vibratory, migratory, oratory, curatory, juratory, gyratory, pulsatory, natatory, dictatory, citatory, saltatory, potatory, rotatory, hortatory, gestatory, gustatory, mutatory, lavatory, salvatory, deletory, suppletory, expletory, decretory, excretory, feretory, bibitory, auditory, plauditory, pellitory, olitory, dormitory, fumitory, crinitory, monitory, punitory, territory, transitory, petitory, desultory, inventory, promontory, offertory, repertory, statutory **5.** phantasmagory, approbatory, reverbatory, applicatory, explicatory, vesicatory, masticatory, advocatory, revocatory, invocatory, confiscatory, episcatory, manducatory, depredatory, commandatory, amendatory, emendatory, commendatory, transudatory, obligatory, fumigatory, derogatory, objurgatory, expurgatory, depreciatory, gladiatory, radiatory, mediatory, palliatory, expiatory, revelatory, habilatory, depilatory, flagellatory, constellatory, distillatory, condolatory, consolatory, ambulatory, speculatory, circulatory, osculatory, adulatory, stridulatory, undulatory, regulatory, emulatory, simulatory, postulatory, defamatory, acclamatory, declamatory, proclamatory, exclamatory, desquamatory, sublimatory, inflammatory, affirmatory, confirmatory, reformatory, informatory, lachrymatory, explanatory, designatory, criminatory, fulminatory, comminatory, terminatory, divinatory, condemnatory, cachinnatory, inculpatory, declaratory, preparatory, lucubratory, consecratory, execratory, emigratory, immigratory, transmigratory, aspiratory, transpiratory, inspiratory, perspiratory, expiratory, laboratory, exploratory, demonstratory, remonstratory, procuratory, abjuratory, adjuratory, compulsatory, compensatory, dispensatory, accusatory, excusatory, excitatory, invitatory, auscultatory, consultatory, sussultatory, incantatory, dehortatory, exhortatory, refutatory, salutatory, observatory, preservatory, conservatory, Il Trovatore, inhibitory, prohibitory, exhibitory, recognitory, admonitory, premonitory, depository, repository, suppository, expository, competitory, retributory, contributory, executory, involutory **6.** disapprobatory, significatory, purificatory, certificatory, communicatory, reciprocatory, equivocatory, elucidatory, recommendatory, delineatory, investigatory, interrogatory, enunciatory, denunciatory, pronunciatory, retaliatory, conciliatory, initiatory, propitiatory, negotiatory, alleviatory, abbreviatory, preambulatory, funambulatory, perambulatory, ejaculatory, articulatory, gesticulatory, emasculatory, manipulatory, congratulatory, expostulatory, recriminatory, incriminatory, discriminatory, exterminatory, procrastinatory, anticipatory, emancipatory, reverberatory, exaggeratory, refrigeratory, acceleratory, remuneratory, corroboratory, circumgyratory, improvisatory, circumrotatory, extenuatory, circumlocutory, interlocutory, improvvisatore [It.] **7.** supererogatory, reconciliatory.

OR'ij– **2.** oarage, shorage, storage.

OR'ik– **2.** boric, choric, chloric, roric, psoric **3.** perchloric **4.** hydrochloric.

OR'ing– **2.** oaring, boring, choring, goring, coring, scoring, snoring, poring, roaring, soaring, shoring, storing **3.** adoring, encoring, deploring, imploring, exploring, ignoring, outpouring, restoring.

OR'is– **2.** Boris, Doris, loris **3.** cantoris.

OR'ist– **2.** chorist, florist.

ORJ'er– **2.** forger, gorger **3.** disgorger.

ORJ'ing– **2.** forging, gorging **3.** engorging, disgorging.

ORJ'ment– **3.** engorgement, disgorgement.

OR'less– **2.** oarless, oreless, boreless, doorless, goreless, whoreless, coreless, scoreless, loreless, poreless, pourless, sporeless, roarless, soreless, shoreless.

OR'ment– **3.** adorement, deplorement, implorement, explorement, ignorement, restorement.

ORN'ful– **2.** scornful, mournful.

ORN'ing– **2.** scorning, mourning, morning **3.** a-borning, unscorning, deep mourning.

OR'o– **2.** oro [Sp.], Oro, boro, Boro, loro, Moro, Poro, toro **4.** aposoro, torotoro.

OR'on– **2.** boron, moron.

ORS'er– **2.** forcer, hoarser, coarser, courser **3.** enforcer, discourser, divorcer.

ORS'est– **2.** hoarsest, coarsest.

ORS'ful– **2.** forceful **3.** resourceful **4.** unresourceful.

ORSH'un– **2.** portion **2.** apportion, proportion **4.** disproportion; *see* also **ORSH'un–** torsion etc.

ORSH'und– **2.** portioned **3.** apportioned, unportioned, proportioned **4.** reapportioned, unproportioned, disproportioned.

ORS'ing– 2. forcing, coursing 3. enforcing, discoursing, divorcing 4. reinforcing.

ORS'iv– 3. enforcive, discoursive, divorcive.

ORS'less– 2. forceless, sourceless 3. discourseless, resourceless, divorceless.

ORS'li– 2. hoarsely, coarsely.

ORS'ment– 2. forcement 3. deforcement, enforcement, divorcement 4. reinforcement.

ORS'ness– 2. hoarseness, coarseness.

ORS'o– 2. dorso [ML.], corso [It.], Corso, torso.

ORT'a– 2. forte.

ORT'al– 2. portal 3. transportal.

ORT'ans– 3. comportance, transportance, supportance.

ORT'ed– 2. courted, ported, sported 3. deported, reported, imported, disported, exported, transported, supported.

ORT'ent– 2. portent.

ORT'er– 2. courter, porter, sporter 3. reporter, importer, exporter, transporter, supporter.

ORT'i– 2. forty, porty, sporty.

ORT'ing– 2. courting, sporting, Storting 3. deporting, reporting, importing, exporting, transporting, supporting.

ORT'iv– 2. sportive 3. disportive, transportive.

ORT'li– 2. courtly, portly 3. uncourtly, unportly.

ORT'ment– 3. deportment, comportment, disportment, transportment.

OR'um– 2. forum, jorum [coll.], quorum 3. decorum 4. indecorum, variorum, cockalorum, pittosporum 5. schola cantorum [L.].

OR'us– 2. Horus, chorus, porus, porous, sorous, torus, torose, torous 3. decorous, pelorus, pylorus, canorous, sonorous, imporous 4. indecorous.

OS'a– 2. dosa 3. Mendoza, mimosa, Formosa 4. Mariposa, amorosa [It.].

OS'er– 2. doser, closer, grocer, grosser 3. jocoser, engrosser, greengrocer, moroser.

OS'est– 2. closest, grossest 3. morosest.

OSH'a– 2. Scotia 3. macrotia 4. Nova Scotia.

OSH'al– 2. social 3. precocial, asocial, dissocial 4. antisocial, intersocial.

OSH'er– 2. kosher, clocher.

OSH'un– 2. ocean, Goshen, lotion, motion, notion, potion, groschen 3. Boeotian, nicotian, emotion, demotion, commotion, promotion, devotion 4. braggadocian, locomotion, self-devotion.

OSH'us– 3. precocious, nepotious, ferocious, atrocious.

OS'ij– 2. dosage.

OS'ing– 2. dosing, grossing 3. engrossing.

OS'is– 2. gnosis, ptosis 3. thrombosis, lordosis, morphosis, zygosis, psychosis, zymosis, osmosis, prognosis, hypnosis, necrosis, morosis, sorosis, neurosis 4. psittacosis, ankylosis, cyanosis, diagnosis, adiposis, hematosis 5. pediculosis, tuberculosis.

OS'iv– 3. explosive, erosive, corrosive 4. inexplosive, unexplosive.

OS'li– 2. closely, grossly 3. verbosely, jocosely, morosely 4. bellicosely.

OS'ness– 2. closeness, grossness 3. verboseness, jocoseness, moroseness.

OS'o– 2. soso, so-so, mosso [It.] 3. pomposo [It.], corozo 4. arioso, gracioso, tremoloso [It.], animoso [It.], penseroso [It.], doloroso [It.], amoroso, strepitoso [It.], maestoso [It.], virtuoso.

OST'al– 2. coastal, postal 4. intracoastal, intercoastal.

OST'ed– 2. boasted, ghosted, hosted, posted, roasted, toasted 3. enghosted.

OST'er– 2. boaster, coaster, poster, roaster, toaster 3. four-poster 4. roller coaster.

OST'ij– 2. postage.

OST'ing– 2. boasting, ghosting, hosting, coasting, posting, roasting, toasting 3. riposting, imposting, retoasting.

OST'li– 2. ghostly, mostly.

OT'a– 2. cota [Tag.], lota, lotah, Lota, flota, nota, rota, tota [Amharic], vota, quota 3. iota, Dakota, pelota, nonquota 4. Minnesota.

OT'al– 2. dotal, notal, rotal, total, votal 3. teetotal, sum total, sum-total 4. extradotal, antidotal, anecdotal, sacerdotal.

OT'at– 2. notate, rotate 3. *annotate.*

OT'ed– 2. boated, doted, coated, bloated, floated, gloated, moated, moted, noted, throated, toted [coll.], voted, quoted 3. refloated, demoted, promoted, denoted, connoted, unnoted, red-throated, dry-throated, full-throated, deep-throated, devoted, misquoted 4. petticoated, particoated, sugar-coated, unpromoted, ruby-throated, yellow-throated, undevoted.

OT'en– 2. oaten, crotin, croton 3. verboten [G.].

OT'ent– 2. flotant, potent 3. prepotent 4. counterpotent.

OT'er– 2. boater, doter, coater, scoter, bloater, floater, gloater, motor, noter, poter, roter, Soter, toter, voter, quoter 3. demoter, remoter, promoter, bimotor, trimotor, denoter, devoter, misquoter 4. locomotor, rotomotor.

OT'est– 2. protest 3. remotest.

OTH'ful– 2. loathful, slothful, trothful.

OTH'ing– 2. loathing, clothing, trothing 3. betrothing.

OTH'som– 2. loathsome.

OT'i– 2. doty, dhoti, goaty, bloaty, floaty, throaty 3. coyote.

OT'ij– 2. boatage, dotage, floatage, flotage 4. anecdotage, sacerdotage.

OT'ik– 2. otic, photic, lotic 3. aphotic, dysphotic, parotic.

OT'ing– 2. boating, doting, coating, bloating, floating, gloating, noting, toting [coll.], voting, quoting 3. demoting, promoting, denoting, connoting, devoting, misquoting 4. sugar-coating.

OT'ish– 2. oatish, boatish, dotish, goatish.

OT'ist– 2. scotist, noticed, votist 3. unnoticed 4. anecdotist.

OT'iv– 2. floative, motive, votive 3. emotive, promotive, denotive 4. locomotive 5. electromotive.

OT'o– 2. Oto, Otoe, photo, moto [It.], roto, toto 3. Kioto, De Soto, in toto [L.], divoto, ex voto [L.], ex-voto 4. Mr. Moto.

OT'um– 2. notum, totum, quotum 3. pronotum, teetotum, factotum.

OT'us– 2. Otus, lotus, Notus 3. amotus, macrotous.

OV'a– 2. ova, Ova, nova 3. Jehovah, korova 4. Villanova, Casanova.

OV'al– 2. oval 3. suboval.

OV'en– 2. cloven, woven 3. uncloven, rewoven, inwoven 4. interwoven.

OV'er– 2. over, Dover, clover, plover, drover, shrover, stover, trover 3. walkover, moreover, leftover.

OV'i– 2. grovy 3. anchovy.

OV'ing– 2. coving, roving, shroving, stoving.

OV'um– 2. ovum, novum 3. protovum.

O'yo– 2. coyo, yo-yo 3. arroyo.

OZ'a– 2. boza, rosa [L.], Rosa 3. Mendoza, flindosa, Spinoza, sub rosa [L.].

OZ'al– 2. rosal 3. deposal, reposal, opposal, proposal, disposal, transposal, supposal 4. interposal, presupposal, predisposal.

OZ'en– 2. chosen, frozen 3. unchosen, forechosen, unfrozen.

OZ'er– 2. dozer, glozer, closer, noser, poser, roser, proser 3. *bulldozer*, encloser, incloser, forecloser, discloser, deposer, reposer, imposer, composer, opposer, proposer, disposer, exposer, supposer 4. decomposer, recomposer, interposer, predisposer, presupposer 5. superimposer.

OZ'ez– 2. dozes, closes, Moses, poses, roses 4. indisposes 5. superimposes.

OZH'er– 2. osier, hosier, closure, crosier 3. enclosure, foreclosure, disclosure, reposure, composure, disposure, exposure 4. decomposure, discomposure 5. superimposure.

OZH'un– 3. icosian, applosion, implosion, explosion, ambrosian, erosion, corrosion.

OZ'i– 2. dozy, fozy, cozy, nosy, posy, rosy, prosy, tosy, tozie.

OZ'ing– 2. dozing, closing, nosing, posing, prosing 3. bulldozing, enclosing, apposing, deposing, reposing, imposing, composing, opposing, proposing, disposing, exposing, transposing 4. juxtaposing, unimposing, decomposing, recomposing, interposing, indisposing 5. superimposing.

OZ'o– 2. bozo [slang], kozo.

OZ'on– 2. ozone, slow zone.

OZ'ur– 2. closure 3. enclosure, inclosure, foreclosure, disclosure, reposure, composure, disposure, exposure 4. discomposure.

O (oh)

3.

TRIPLE RHYMES IN O (know'a-ble)

Primary or Secondary Accent Falls on Second from Last Syllable.

O'a-bl- 3. knowable, showable, 4. unknowable, bestowable 5. overthrowable.

OB'i-a- 3. obeah, phobia 4. Zenobia 5. brontephobia, stasiphobia, toxiphobia, cibophobia, phobophobia, neophobia, theophobia, algophobia, ergophobia, Anglophobia, ochlophobia, Gallophobia, dromophobia, cremnophobia,phonophobia, hypnophobia, cynophobia, zoophobia, topophobia, acrophobia, androphobia, hydrophobia, negrophobia, claustrophobia, pyrophobia, nosophobia, lyssophobia, batophobia, nyctophobia, sitophobia, brontophobia, scotophobia, photophobia 6. agoraphobia, batrachophobia, cardiophobia, bibliophobia, hagiophobia, Germanophobia, astrapophobia, anthropophobia, aelurophobia, thalassophobia, thanatophobia.

OB'i-an- 4. Jacobian, cenobian, macrobian, microbian.

OB'il-iz- 3. mobilize 4. demobilize, remobilize, immobilize.

OCH'a-bl- 3. poachable 4. approachable, reproachable 5. unapproachable, irreproachable.

OD'al-er- 3. odaler, yodeler.

OD'i-ak- 3. Kodiak, nodiak, zodiac.

OD'i-al- 3. podial 4. allodial, threnodial, prosodial, custodial 5. palinodial, episodial.

OD'i-an- 3. Rhodian 4. Cambodian, Herodian, prosodian, custodian.

OD'i-on- 4. Triodion, melodion, melodeon, collodion 5. nickelodeon.

OD'i-um- 3. odium, podium, rhodium, sodium 4. allodium, taxodium.

OD'i-us- 3. odious 4. melodious, commodious 5. unmelodious, incommodious, discommodious.

OD'or-us- 3. odorous 4. malodorous, inodorous.

OG'i-izm- 3. bogyism, fogyism.

O'ik-al- 3. stoical 4. heroical, unstoical 5. unheroical.

O'il-i- 3. snowily, showily.

O'ing-li- 3. flowingly, glowingly, knowingly 4. unknowingly.

OJ'i-a- 3. loggia 4. alogia, dyslogia 5. apologia.

OJ'i-an- 4. gambogian 5. geologian, neologian, theologian, philologian, astrologian, mythologian 6. archaeologian.

OK'a-bl- 3. smokable, vocable 4. unsmokable, invocable 5. uninvocable.

OK'al-i- 3. focally, locally, vocally.

OK'al-ist- 3. localist, vocalist.

OK'al-iz- 3. focalize, localize, vocalize.

OK'al-izm- 3. localism, vocalism.

OK'en-li- 3. brokenly 4. outspokenly.

OK'i-er- 3. oakier, chokier, smokier, pokier, croakier, soakier, yolkier.

OK'i-ness- 3. oakiness, chokiness, smokiness, pokinesss, croakiness, soakiness, yolkiness.

OK'ing-li- 3. chokingly, jokingly, croakingly, strokingly, soakingly 4. provokingly.

OK'less–li– 3. jokelessly, smokelessly.

OKS'ing–li– 3. hoaxingly, coaxingly.

OK'us–ing– 3. focusing, hocusing.

OK'us–less– 3. focusless, hocusless, locusless, crocusless.

OL'a–bl– 3. bowlable, goalable, holable, pollable, rollable, tollable 4. unbowlable, ungoalable, unholable, controllable, consolable 5. uncontrollable, unconsolable, inconsolable.

OL'a–bli– 4. consolably, controllably 5. uncontrollably, unconsolably, inconsolably.

OL'ar–i– 3. bolary, molary, polary, solary; *see* also **OL'er–i–** drollery etc. below.

OL'ar–iz– 3. polarize, solarize 4. depolarize.

OLD'a–bl– 3. foldable, scoldable, moldable 4. unfoldable, unscoldable.

OL'er–i– 3. drollery, bolary, molary, polary, solary 4. cajolery 5. rigmarolery.

OL'e–um– 3. oleum 4. linoleum, petroleum, crystoleum; *see* also **OL'i–um–** oleum, folium, etc. below.

OL'ful–ness– 3. dolefulness, soulfulness.

OL'i–a– 4. Mongolia, magnolia, Aetolia 5. melancholia.

OL'i–an– 4. Aeolian, Mongolian, simoleon [slang], Napoleon, Pactolian, Aetolian 5. metabolian, Anatolian, Capitolian.

OL'i–at– 3. foliate, spoliate 4. defoliate, infoliate.

OL'i–er– 3. holier, lowlier, Grolier 4. unholier.

OL'i–est– 3. holiest, lowliest 4. unholiest.

OL'i–ness– 3. holiness, lowliness, shoaliness 4. unholiness.

OL'ing–li– 4. condolingly, cajolingly, consolingly, extollingly.

OL'i–o– 3. oleo, olio, folio, roleo 4. portfolio.

OL'i–um– 3. oleum, folium, scholium 4. trifolium, linoleum, arolium, petroleum, crystoleum 5. Capitolium.

OL'o–ist– 3. poloist, soloist.

OLST'er–er– 3. bolsterer 4. upholsterer.

OM'as–i– 4. diplomacy.

OM'at–izm– 3. chromatism 4. achromatism, diplomatism.

OM'i–al– 3. nomial, tomial 4. binomial, monomial.

OM'i–er– 3. domier, foamier, homier, loamier.

OM'i–est– 3. domiest, foamiest, homiest, loamiest.

OM'i–ness– 3. dominess, foaminess, hominess, loaminess.

OM'ing–li– 3. foamingly, homingly, gloamingly, roamingly.

OM'i–o– 3. Romeo, Dromio.

OM'i–um– 3. chromium, tomium 4. encomium 5. nosocomium.

OM'luv–ing– 3. homeloving, chromeloving.

ON'a–bl– 3. ownable, bonable, phonable, honable, loanable, thronable, tonable, zonable 4. condonable, atonable 5. unatonable.

ON'i–a– 4. Adonia, aphonia, begonia, Ionia, bryonia, Laconia, Franconia, Slavonia, valonia, ammonia, Harmonia, pneumonia, asonia, Ausonia, Antonia 5. Caledonia, Macedonia, Patagonia.

ON'i–al– 3. monial 4. colonial, demonial, harmonial, baronial 5. ceremonial, matrimonial, patrimonial, sanctimonial, testimonial 6. intercolonial.

ON'i–an– 4. aeonian, Gorgonian, Ionian, chelonian, demonian, Simonian, Johnsonian, Ausonian, Shoshonean, Platonian, Etonian, Oxonian, Esthonian, Miltonian, Plutonian, favonian, pavonian, bezonian 5. Caledonian, Patagonian, Thessalonian, Babylonian, Ciceronian, Amazonian, Macedonian, halcyonian.

ON'i–er– 3. bonier, phonier [slang], dronier, tonier [vulgar], stonier.

ON'i–est– 3. boniest, phoniest [slang], toniest [vulgar], stoniest.

ON'i–um– 4. agonium, euphonium, polonium, stramonium, ammonium, harmonium, Plutonium 5. sporogonium, pelargonium, pandemonium, testimonium.

ON'i–us– 4. euphonious, symphonious, felonious, Polonius, harmonious, erroneous, ultroneous, Antonius 5. ceremonious, querimonious, acrimonious, matrimonious, parsimonious, sanctimonious, inharmonious 6. unceremonious, unsanctimonious.

O'o–lit– 3. oolite, zoolite.

O'o–lith– 3. zoolith.

OP'i–a– 3. topia 4. myopia, Utopia 5. Ethiopia, cornucopia, presbyopia, nyctalopia.

OP'i–an– 4. Aesopian, Utopian 5. Ethiopian, cornucopian.

OP'i–ness– 3. dopiness, ropiness, soapiness.

OP'ish–ness– 3. mopishness, popishness.

OR'a–bl– 3. soarable, storable 4. adorable, deplorable, explorable, restorable.

OR'a–bli– 4. adorably, deplorably.

OR'al–i– 3. orally, florally.

OR'at–iv– 4. explorative, restorative.

OR'e–al– 3. boreal 4. arboreal, phosphoreal, marmoreal, corporeal, aequoreal 5. bicorporeal, incorporeal; *see* also **OR'i–al–** boreal etc. below.

OR'e–an– 4. roborean, marmorean, aurorean, Hectorean; *see* also **OR'i–an–** Dorian etc. below.

OR'i–a– 3. doria, scoria, Gloria, noria 4. Peoria, theoria, euphoria, dysphoria, memoria, emporia, Pretoria, Victoria, Astoria 5. Infusoria 6. phantasmagoria, Waldorf Astoria.

OR'i–al– 3. boreal 4. arboreal, phosphoreal, marmoreal, corporeal, aequoreal, Escorial, enchorial, authorial, memorial, armorial, manorial, rasorial, risorial, scansorial, censorial, sensorial, sponsorial, tonsorial, rosorial, cursorial, gressorial fossorial, factorial, rectorial, sectorial, tectorial, vectorial, pictorial, tinctorial doctorial, proctorial, auctorial, praetorial, cantorial, raptorial, scriptorial, sartorial, quaestorial, haustorial, sutorial, tutorial, textorial, uxorial 5. bicorporeal, incorporeal, immemorial, responsorial, insessorial, dismissorial, piscatorial, purgatorial, grallatorial, amatorial, senatorial, oratorial, curatorial, natatorial, spectatorial, dictatorial, saltatorial, gestatorial, equatorial, reptatorial, prefectorial, electorial, inspectorial, directorial, editorial, territorial, sussultorial, inventorial, preceptorial, repertorial, assertorial, consistorial 6. ambassadorial, phantasmagorial, expurgatorial, gladiatorial, mediatorial, legislatorial, gubernatorial, visitatorial, observatorial, proprietorial, exterritorial, conspiratorial, inquisitorial, executorial 7. extraterritorial.

OR'i–an– 3. Dorian 4. roborean, Gregorian, marmorean, aurorean, praetorian, Hectorean, stentorian, Nestorian, historian, Victorian 5. hyperborean, purgatorian, amatorian, senatorian, oratorian, mid-Victorian 6. salutatorian, valedictorian.

OR'i–at– 3. floriate, storiate 4. excoriate 5. professoriate.

OR'i–fi– 3. scorify, glorify, storify.

OR'i–ness– 3. goriness, hoariness, poriness 5. dilatoriness, desultoriness, peremptoriness.

OR'i–ol– 3. oriole, gloriole.

OR'i–um– 3. corium, thorium 4. ciborium, triforium, emporium, sensorium, praetorium, scriptorium, pastorium, haustorium 5. sudatorium, crematorium, fumatorium, sanatorium, moratorium, natatorium, auditorium, digitorium.

OR'i-us– 3. scorious, Lorius, glorious 4. laborious, arboreous, inglorious, vainglorious, unglorious, uproarious, censorious, victorious, stentorious, notorious, sartorius, uxorious 5. accessorius, meritorious, amatorious, saltatorious.

ORS'a-bl– 3. forceable, forcible 4. enforceable, divorceable 5. unenforceable, undivorceable.

ORSH'un-al– 3. portional, torsional 4. proportional 5. disproportional.

ORSH'un-er– 3. portioner 4. apportioner, proportioner, extortioner.

ORT'a-bl– 3. courtable, portable 4. deportable, reportable, importable, exportable, transportable, supportable 5. insupportable.

ORT'li-ness– 3. courtliness, portliness 4. uncourtliness.

OR'us-li– 3. porously 4. decorously, sonorously.

OSH'a-bl– 3. sociable 4. negotiable, dissociable, unsociable.

OSH'i-a– 4. nicotia, anotia, macrotia, microtia; *see* also **OSH'a–** Scotia etc.

OSH'i-an– 4. Boeotian, nicotian 5. braggadocian.

OSH'i-ant– 3. otiant 4. negotiant, dissociant.

OSH'i-at– 4. negotiate, associate, dissociate, consociate.

OSH'un-al– 3. motional, notional 4. emotional, commotional, promotional, devotional 5. unemotional, nondevotional, undevotional.

OSH'us-li– 4. precociously, ferociously, atrociously.

OSH'us-ness– 4. precociousness, ferociousness, atrociousness.

OS'iv-li– 4. explosively, erosively, corrosively 5. inexplosively.

OS'iv-ness– 4. explosiveness, erosiveness, corrosiveness.

OST'ful-i– 3. boastfully, ghostfully.

OST'ing-li– 3. boastingly, coastingly, roastingly, toastingly.

OST'li-ness– 3. ghostliness, hostliness.

OT'a-bl– 3. floatable, notable, potable, votable, quotable 4. unfloatable, denotable, unquotable.

OT'ab-li– 3. notably, quotably.

OT'al-er– 3. totaler 4. teetotaler.

OT'al-izm– 4. teetotalism 5. sacerdotalism.

OT'ar-i– 3. coterie, notary, rotary, votary.

OT'at-iv– 3. flotative, rotative 4. denotative, connotative.

OT'ed-li– 3. bloatedly, notedly 4. devotedly, sweet-throatedly.

OT'er-i– 3. coterie, notary, rotary, votary.

OT'ing-li– 3. dotingly, bloatingly, gloatingly, quotingly.

OT'iv-li– 3. votively 4. emotively.

OV'en-li– 3. clovenly, wovenly 5. interwovenly.

OV'i-a– 3. fovea 4. synovia, Monrovia.

OV'i-al– 3. foveal, jovial 4. unjovial, synovial.

OZ'a-bl– 4. deposable, imposable, opposable, disposable, transposable, supposable 5. decomposable, indisposable, untransposable.

OZ'ar-i– 3. rosary.

OZH'er-i– 3. osiery, hosiery.

OZH'i-a– 4. symposia, ambrosia.

OZ'i-er– 3. dozier, cozier, nosier, rosier, prosier.

OZ'i-est– 3. doziest, coziest, nosiest, rosiest, prosiest.

OZ'il-i– 3. dozily, cozily, nosily, rosily, prosily.

OZ'i-ness– 3. doziness, foziness, coziness, nosiness, rosiness, prosiness.

O (awe)

1.

SINGLE (MASCULINE) RHYMES IN O (awe)

Primary or Secondary Accent Falls on Last Sylllable; Imperfect Rhymes Are in Italics.

O– **1.** awe, aw [slang], chaw [dial.], daw, haw, jaw, caw, scaw, law, flaw, claw, slaw, maw, naw [slang], gnaw, paw, raw, braw, draw, gra, craw, straw, saw, pshaw, taw, tau, thaw, squaw, yaw **2.** *jackdaw*, guffaw, *heehaw*, macaw, pilau, pilaw, *coleslaw*, begnaw, papaw, *pawpaw*, withdraw, hurrah, *seesaw*, foresaw **3.** overawe, overdraw, oversaw **4.** mother-in-law.

OB– **1.** ob, bob, daub, fob, gob, gaub, hob, job, kob, cob, Cobb, scob [Scot. N. of Eng. & Ir.], lob, blob, glob [slang], slob, mob, nob, knob, snob, rob, brob, throb, sob, stob, thob [slang], wob [slang], swab, quab, squab **2.** *cabob*, *nabob*, *earbob*, bedaub, *corncob*, *hoblob*, *hobnob*, carob, athrob, *nawab* **3.** thingumbob **4.** thingumabob; *see* also **AB–** squab etc.

OBZ– gobs etc., *see* **OB–** ob etc. above, plus "s" or " 's."

OCH– **1.** botch, gotch, hotch [slang], cotch, scotch, Scotch, blotch, splotch, notch, nautch, rotch, crotch, watch, swatch **2.** debauch, *hopscotch*, *hotchpotch*, *deathwatch*, *dogwatch*, outwatch.

OCHT– **1.** botched, scotched, blotched, splotched, notched, crotched, watched **2.** debauched, unwatched.

OD– **1.** odd, awed, gaud, God, hod, jawed, cod, cawed, laud, clod, Claude, plod, maud, Maude, nod, gnawed, pod, pawed, rod, broad, fraud, scrod, prod, trod, sod, sawed, shod, tod, tawed, vaude [slang], wad, quad, quod [slang], squad **2.** unawed, *tomcod*, belaud, applaud, maraud, abroad, defraud, *Nimrod*, *Penrod*, hurrahed, roughshod, unshod, *slipshod*, *tightwad*, per quod [L.] **3.** overawed, Ichabod, demigod, underjawed, goldenrod; *see* also **AD–** baaed etc.

ODZ– odds etc., *see* **OD–** odd etc. above, plus "s" or " 's."

OF– **1.** off, doff, goff, koff, cough, coff [slang], scoff, prof [slang], shroff, trough, toff [slang], quaff **2.** *runoff*, *throwoff*, *setoff*, *castoff*, *chincough*, Kharkov, Orloff, Azof **3.** philosoph **4.** bibliosoph.

OFT– **1.** oft, doffed, coughed, scoffed, loft, croft, soft, toft, quaffed **2.** aloft, hayloft.

OG– **1.** Og, bog, dog, fog, gog, Gog, hog, jog, cog, log, blog [slang], flog, clog, slog, mog [slang], smog, nog, brog, frog, grog, sogg [slang], tog, quag **2.** embog, *watchdog*, *bulldog*, *firedog*, befog, agog, *Magog*, *seahog*, *hedgehog*, *quahog*, *shearhog*, *backlog*, *putlog*, *eggnog*, *crannog*, *scuppaug*, *bullfrog*, pishaug, tautog **3.** underdog, prairie dog, megafog, pettifog, pedagogue, Gogmagog, demagogue, xenagogue, synagogue, hydragogue, mystagogue, logogogue, Decalogue, Tagalog, dialogue, trialogue, grammalogue, analogue, catalogue, theologue, melologue, homologue, Sinologue, monologue, apologue, necrologue, apologue, horologue, duologue, Dannebrog, golliwogg, polliwog; *see* also **AG–** blague etc.

OGD– **1.** bogged, dogged, hogged, jogged, cogged, logged, flogged, clogged, slogged **2.** embogged, befogged **3.** catalogued, waterlogged.

OGZ– dogs etc., *see* **OG–** Og etc. above, plus "s" or " 's."

OJ– **1.** bodge, dodge, lodge, podge, stodge **2.** unlodge, dislodge, *hodgepodge* **3.** horologe.

OK– **1.** auk, awk, balk, bock, choc [slang], chock, chalk, doc [slang], dock, gawk, hawk, hock, Jock, jock [slang], calk, cawk, cock, lock, loch, block, flock, clock, mawk [slang], smock, knock, pock, rock, roc, frock, crock, sock, shock, talk, stalk, stock, walk, squak **2.** rhebok, *klipbok*, *blesbok*, ad hoc [L.], *Mohawk*, *sparhawk*, *sorehawk*, *goshawk*, acock, *woodcock*, *peacock*, *Hancock*, Bangkok, *padlock*, *deadlock*, *wedlock*, *Shylock*, *hemlock*, unlock, *gunlock*, *rowlock*, *oarlock*, *forelock*, *Sherlock*, *fetlock*, *flintlock*, *wristlock*, unblock, *bedrock*, unfrock, *traprock*, *ticktock*, restock, unstock, *livestock*, *sidewalk*, outwalk **3.** bontebok, tomahawk, hollyhock, poppycock, shuttlecock, weathercock, Antioch, chockablock, stumbling block, fetterlock, interlock, Little Rock, alpenstock, laughingstock, overstock **4.** Vladivostok; *see* also **AK–** ach etc.

OKS– auks etc., *see* **OK–** auk etc. above, plus "s" or " 's"; **1.** ox, box, fox, cox, phlox, Nox, Knox, pox, vox **2.** abox, bandbox, sandbox, snuffbox, strongbox, workbox, jukebox, mailbox, pillbox, hatbox, princox, Coxcox, smallpox **3.** chatterbox, paradox, philodox, homodox, orthodox, Goldilocks, equinox, chicken pox **4.** heterodox, unorthodox.

OKT– **1.** balked, hawked, calked, blocked, crocked, talked, stalked **2.** decoct, concoct.

OL– **1.** all, awl, ball, bawl, doll, fall, gall, Gaul, gol [slang], hall, haul, call, caul, loll, moll, maul, small, pall, Paul, pawl, pol, poll, spall, brawl, drawl, crawl, scrawl, sprawl, trawl, Saul, Sol, shawl, tall, stall, wall, squall, yawl **2.** *eyeball*, *highball*, *blackball*, *pinball*, *snowball*, *fireball*, *baseball*, *football*, *catchall*, *windfall*, befall, *rainfall*, *downfall*, *snowfall*, *nightfall*, *pitfall*, Bengal, spurgall, dance hall, *birdcall*, recall, miscall, *catcall*, bemaul, appal, epaule, Nepal, bethrall, enthrall, atoll, extol, *boxstall*, *thumbstall*, install, forestall, withal, devall, sea wall, *stonewall*, *Cornwall* **3.** all in all, free-for-all, basketball, Montreal, evenfall, waterfall, alcohol, overhaul, protocol, folderal, disenthrall, parasol, girasol, entresol, reinstall, fingerstall, therewithal, wherewithal, caterwaul.

OLD– **1.** auld, bald, bawled, galled, called, scald, drawled, crawled, walled **2.** blackballed, snowballed, recalled, uncalled, so-called, appalled, enthralled, stone-walled **3.** Archibald, overhauled, unappalled, unenthralled.

OLF– **1.** golf **2.** Rudolph.

OLS– **1.** false, halse, valse, waltz.

OLT– **1.** halt, fault, gault, malt, smalt, salt, vault **2.** *cobalt*, default, assault, *basalt*, envault, exalt **3.** pseudosalt, somersault.

OLTS– halts etc., *see* **OLT–** halt etc. above, plus "s" or " 's."

OLV– **1.** solve **2.** absolve, resolve, dissolve, evolve, devolve, revolve, involve **3.** circumvolve, intervolve.

OLVD– **1.** solved **2.** absolved, resolved, dissolved, evolved, devolved, revolved, involved **3.** circumvolved, intervolved.

OM– **1.** bomb, chom, chawm [both slang], dom, domn, gaum, haulm, glom [slang], plomb [slang], mom [slang], rhomb, from, prom [slang], shawm, Tom, Guam, qualm **2.** Bonhomme, aplomb, coulomb, geom [slang], imaum, *pompom*, therefrom, wherefrom, *pogrom*, *wigwam* **3.** atom bomb, axiom, hecatomb; *see* also **AM–** balm etc.

OMB– **1.** rhomb, stromb.

OMP– **1.** comp [slang], pomp, romp, trompe, stomp, wamp, swamp.

OMPT– **1.** compt, romped, prompt, swamped.

OMZ– bombs etc., *see* **OM–** bomb etc. above, plus "s" or " 's."

ON– **1.** on, awn, bon, bonne [F.], don, Don, dawn, fawn, faun, gone, John, john [slang], con, lawn, mon [Scot.], non [L.], pawn, spawn, brawn, drawn, prawn, shone, wan, swan, yon, yawn **2.** hereon, thereon, whereon, *bonbon*, chiffon, begone, *bygone*, *foregone*, Yukon, salon, Ceylon, anon, impawn, upon, indrawn, undrawn, withdrawn, Tucson, baton, cretonne, Yvonne, chignon, Luzon **3.** hanger-on, hangers-on, Audubon, Celadon, chelidon, myrmidon, mastodon, Corydon, pantheon, galleon, colophon, Xenophon, nonagon, tarragon, tetragon, octagon, pentagon, protagon, heptagon, martagon, hexagon, woebegone, Oregon, perigon, isogon, undergone, polygon, oxygon, gabion, Albion, demijohn, Little John, Prester John, leprechaun, Rubicon, Helicon, silicon, technicon, opticon, lexicon, gonfalon, petalon, Avalon, echelon, Babylon, Pergamon, gonfanon, organon, xoanon, tympanon, noumenon, Parthenon, hereupon, thereupon, whereupon, fanfaron, megaron, Oberon, pentacron, Omicron, balatron, anatron, orison, Alençon, cabochon, abaton, phaeton, trilithon, ornithon, halcyon, Amazon, cabezon, liaison, Barbizon **4.** melodicon, basilicon, catholicon, irenicon, harmonicon, sciopticon, panopticon, lapideon, Napoleon, Anacreon, chiliagon, amphibion, Endymion, Hyperion, oblivion, alluvion, Laocoon, hyperbaton, automaton **5.** acolodicon, synonymicon, stereopticon **6.** etymologicon; *see* also **AN–**ane [F.] etc.

ONCH– **1.** haunch, launch, paunch, craunch, staunch.

OND– **1.** awned, bond, donned, dawned, fond, blond, blonde, monde, pond, spawned, frond, wand, yawned **2.** seconde, abscond, despond, respond, beyond **3.** vagabond, overfond, demimonde, correspond.

ONG– **1.** bong, dong, gong, long, flong, pong, wrong, prong, strong, throng, song, tong, thong, wong **2.** Souchong, *dingdong*, mah-jongg, Hong Kong, along, daylong, headlong, belong, lifelong, prolong, erelong, nightlong, *pingpong*, sarong, *headstrong*, *singsong*, paktong, quantong, *diphthong*, *triphthong*, payong **3.** billabong, underfong, overlong, scuppernong, evensong, undersong, aftersong.

ONK– **1.** gonk [slang], honk, conk, konk [both slang], conch, bronc [slang], cronk, tonk, wonk, squonk [both slang] **2.** triconch **3.** honky-tonk.

ONKS– honks etc., *see* **ONK–** honk etc. above, plus "s" or " 's"; Bronx.

ONS– **1.** bonce, sconce, nonce **2.** ensconce, response, patonce.

ONT– **1.** daunt, font, gaunt, haunt, jaunt, flaunt, pont, taunt, vaunt, want, wont **2.** bouffant, aflaunt, romaunt, Vermont, Dupont, avaunt **3.** Hellespont; *see* also **ANT–** aunt etc.

ONZ– awns etc., *see* **ON–** on etc. above, plus "s" or " 's"; **1.** bonze, fons, fauns, pons [L.], bronze, frons [L.] **2.** bygones.

OP– **1.** op [slang], bop [slang], chop, dop, fop, gaup, gawp [slang], hop, cop, scaup, lop, flop, plop, slop, mop, knop, pop, drop, crop, prop, strop, sop, shop, top, stop, staup, wop, wap, swap, swop [both dial. & coll.], whop [coll.], yawp **2.** alop, aslop, *slipslop*, *raindrop*, *snowdrop*, *teardrop*, *dewdrop*, *eavesdrop*, outcrop, unprop, asop, *milksop*, *soursop*, *sweetsop*, *workshop*, *pawnshop*, *redtop*, *tiptop*, *foretop*, estop, *backstop*, *nonstop*, *shortstop* **3.** soda pop, lollipop, underprop, overtop **4.** flippityflop; *see* also **AP–** gape etc.

OPS– bops [slang] etc., *see* **OP–** bop etc. above, plus "s" or " 's"; **1.** Ops, copse.

OPT– **1.** opt, chopped, hopped, copped, Copt, lopped, flopped, plopped, slopped, mopped, popped, dropped, propped, sopped, stopped **2.** adopt, estopped, unstopped.

OR– through **ORZ–**, *see* also long **O** (oh): **OR–** through **ORZ–**.

OR– **1.** or, dor, for, cor, nor, tor, Thor, war **2.** Alcor, Côte d'Or, whyfor, abhor, décor [F.], señor [Sp.], lessor **3.** mirador, comprador, matador, cantador [Sp.] picador, Labrador, meteor, mortgagor, biophor, pastophor, Ecuador, chancellor, counselor, councillor, Eleanor, alienor, bargainor, emperor, conqueror, promisor, senator, champertor, dinosaur, semitaur, Minotaur, god of war, tug of war, man of war **4.** capeador [Sp.], toreador, conquistador, Corregidor, heliodor, excelsior, deliveror, recoveror, megalosaur, ornithosaur, ichthyosaur.

ORB– **1.** orb, sorb, Sorb **2.** inorb, absorb, resorb, disorb.

ORCH– **1.** scorch, porch, torch.

ORD– **1.** bord, dord, ford, gord [slang], cord, chord, lord, warred, ward, sward, fiord **2.** afford, abhorred, accord, *whipcord, landlord*, belord, milord, award, reward, *greensward* **3.** unaccord, disaccord, octachord, unichord, polychord, lyrichord, harpsichord, clavichord, overlord **4.** harmonichord, misericord.

ORF– **1.** corf, morph [slang], dwarf, swarf, wharf **3.** Dusseldorf.

ORG– **1.** orgue, org [slang], borg, morgue **3.** Swedenborg.

ORJ– **1.** forge, gorge, George, corge **2.** regorge, engorge, disgorge **3.** disengorge, overgorge.

ORK– **1.** orc, ork [slang], fork, cork, corke, torque, stork, York **2.** *pitchfork*, New York.

ORKT– **1.** forked, corked, torqued.

ORL– **1.** orle, ceorl, schorl, whorl.

ORM– **1.** dorm, form, norm, storm, warm, swarm **2.** deform, reform, inform, conform, perform, misform, transform, bestorm, *barnstorm*, rewarm, lukewarm **3.** stelliform, uniform, aeriform, floriform, cruciform, multiform, misinform, chloroform, thunderstorm **4.** trapeziform.

ORMD– **1.** formed, stormed, warmed, swarmed **2.** deformed, well-formed, ill-formed, informed, bestormed, *barnstormed* **3.** unreformed, well-informed, uninformed.

ORN– **1.** born, dorn, horn, corn, scorn, lorn, morn, Norn, shorn, torn, thorn, worn, sworn **2.** suborn, reborn, *freeborn, highborn*, inborn, unborn, *lowborn, first-born, newborn, trueborn*, adorn, dehorn, *staghorn, bighorn, Longhorn, pronghorn, foghorn*, French horn, *greenhorn, shorthorn, shoehorn, popcorn*, forlorn, *lovelorn*, midmorn, untorn, *buckthorn, hawthorn*, rewarn, forewarn **3.** readorn, unadorn, Matterhorn, barleycorn, peppercorn, yestermorn.

ORND– **1.** scorned **2.** suborned, adorned, dehorned, unwarned, forewarned.

ORP– **1.** dorp, gorp [slang], torp [slang], thorp, warp **2.** moldwarp **3.** Oglethorpe.

ORPS– **1.** corpse, warps **2.** moldwarps **3.** Oglethorpes.

ORS– **1.** gorse, horse, corse, Morse, Norse, torse **2.** endorse, sea horse, unhorse, remorse, retrorse, introrse, extrorse, dextrorse **3.** rocking horse, hobbyhorse, Charley horse, sinistrorse.

ORT– **1.** ort, bort, fort, mort, snort, sort, short, tort, wart, quart, swart, thwart **2.** abort, dehort, exhort, escort, amort, assort, resort, consort, retort, intort, contort, distort, extort, cavort, athwart.

ORTH– **1** morth, north, swarth, Jorth **2.** commorth

ORTS– orts etc., *see* **ORT–** ort etc. above, plus "s" or "'s"; **1.** quarts, quartz **2.** biquartz.

ORZ– wars etc., *see* **OR–** or etc. above, plus "s" or "'s"; **2.** quatorze **4.** Louis Quatorze.

OS– **1.** os, Boss, boss, doss, fosse, joss, loss, floss, gloss, moss, ross, dross, cross, sauce, soss, toss, stoss **2.** emboss, vanfoss, kaross, across, lacrosse, recross, incross, *crisscross*, *christcross*, *ringtoss* **3.** albatross, double-cross, applesauce **4.** rhinoceros.

OSH– **1.** bosh, bosch, Boche, gosh, josh, losh, slosh, posh [slang], sposh [slang], frosh [slang], sash, tosh, wash, swash, quash, squash **2.** kibosh, galosh, awash, bewash, rewash, *hogwash*, *eyewash*, *siwash*, *backwash*, *wishwash*, *whitewash*, *musquash* **3.** mackintosh.

OSK– **1.** bosk, Bosc, mosque **2.** kiosk, imbosk **3.** abelmosk.

OSP– **1.** hosp [slang], knosp, wasp **3.** galliwasp.

OST– **1.** bossed, fossed, cost, lost, mossed, frost, crossed, wast **2.** exhaust, cabossed, embossed, imbost, accost, enmossed, defrost, *hoarfrost*, recrossed, uncrossed, *criscrossed*, betossed **3.** Pentecost, holocaust, double-crossed, anagnost, geognost **4.** bibliognost.

OT– **1.** ought, aught, bought, bot [slang], bott, dot, fought, got, ghat, hot, jot, cot, caught, Scot, Scott, lot, Lot, blot, clot, plot, slot, mot, knot, not, naught, snot [slang], pot, pott, spot, rot, wrought, brought, fraught, trot, sot, sought, shot, shott, tot, taught, taut, stot, thought, watt, wot, swat, squat, what, yacht **2.** *abbot*, *Cabot*, *robot*, begot, forgot, *spigot*, *ingot*, *argot*, *Margot*, *ergot*, *eyot*, *ryot*, *riot*, *Sciot*, cocotte, *plumcot*, *mascot*, *wainscot*, *dovecot*, allot, shallot, *Helot*, *zealot*, *pilot*, *simblot*, *diglot*, *billot*, *tillot*, complot, *onslaught*, culotte, *motmot*, cannot, *dreadnought*, unknot, *topknot*, *slipknot*, *love knot*, *whatnot*, repot, *teapot*, *crackpot*, *skilpot*, *trampot*, *despot*, *tosspot*, *fleshpot*, *sunspot*, *garrot*, garrote, *parrot*, inwrought, unwrought, unfraught, *hilltrot*, distraut, besot, besought, resought, *bloodshot*, *foreshot*, *slingshot*, *buckshot*, *gunshot*, *snapshot*, *hipshot*, *upshot*, *earshot*, *grapeshot*, *bowshot*, *potshot*, untaught, methought, *forethought*, gavotte, *kumquat*, loquat, asquat **3.** unforgot, haricot, apricot, persicot, peridot, larigot, idiot, galiot, chariot, heriot, patriot, cheviot, cachalot, Lancelot, ocelot, pentaglot, heptaglot, hexaglot, polyglot, matalotte, counterplot, sans-culotte, bergamot, guillemot, Huguenot, Argonaut, Juggernaut, flowerpot, coffeepot, galipot, talipot, tommyrot, underwrought, overwrought, overshot, Hottentot, afterthought, aforethought, aliquot **4.** forget-me-not, Iscariot **5.** witenagemot.

OTH– **1.** auth [slang], doth, Goth, cloth, moth, broth, froth, troth, swath **2.** *breechcloth*, *broadcloth*, *sackcloth*, *oilcloth*, *loincloth*, betroth **3.** Visigoth, Ostrogoth, saddlecloth, behemoth.

OTS– dots etc., *see* **OT–** ought etc. above, plus "s" or "'s."

OV– **1.** of **2.** hereof, thereof, whereof.

OZ– awes etc., *see* **O–** awe etc. above, plus "s" or "'s"; **1.** oz [slang], Oz, Boz, gauze, hawse, cause, clause, pause, vase, was, 'twas, yaws **2.** because, applause **3.** Santa Claus.

OZM– **3.** macrocosm, microcosm, loxocosm

O (awe)

2.

DOUBLE (FEMININE) RHYMES IN O (daub'er)

Primary or Secondary Accent Falls on Next to Last Syllable; Imperfect Rhymes Are in Italics.

OB'er– 2. dauber, jobber, cobber, lobber, blobber, slobber, knobber, snobber, robber, throbber, sobber, wabber, swabber 3. bedauber, beslobber 5. Mr. Micawber [Dickens].

OB'ern– 2. auburn.

OB'i– 2. bobby, dauby, dobby, gobby, hobby, cobby, scobby, lobby, mobby, nobby, knobby, snobby, wabby, squabby.

OB'in– 2. bobbin, dobbin, robbin, robin 3. round robin.

OB'ing– 2. bobbing, daubing, jobbing, cobbing, lobbing, mobbing, snobbing, robbing, throbbing, sobbing, swabbing 3. hobnobbing.

OB'ish– 2. bobbish, lobbish, mobbish, snobbish, squabbish.

OB'l– 2. bauble, gobble, hobble, cobble, nobble, wobble, squabble.

OB'ler– 2. gobbler, hobbler, cobbler, nobbler, wobbler, squabbler 4. turkey gobbler, cherry cobbler.

OB'let– 2. goblet, squablet.

OB'li– 2. obley, hobbly, cobbly, wobbly, squabbly.

OB'lin– 2. goblin 3. hobgoblin.

OB'ling– 2. gobbling, hobbling, cobbling, snobling, wobbling, squabbling.

OBST'er– 2. daubster, lobster.

OB'ul– 2. lobule, globule.

OCH'er– 2. botcher, notcher, splotcher, watcher, swatcher 3. debaucher, topnotcher, hopscotcher.

OCH'i– 2. botchy, Scotchy, blotchy, splotchy, notchy, crotchy.

OCH'ing– 2. botching, scotching, blotching, splotching, notching, watching 3. debauching, hopscotching.

OD'al– 2. caudal 3. acaudal, subcaudal, bicaudal; *see* also **OD'l–** dawdle etc. below.

OD'ed– 2. lauded, plodded, nodded, podded, prodded, sodded, wadded 3. belauded, applauded, marauded, defrauded.

OD'en– 2. hodden, broaden, trodden, sodden 3. introdden, downtrodden, untrodden.

OD'er– 2. odder, dodder, fodder, nodder, lauder, plodder, broader, prodder, sawder, solder 3. Cape Codder, belauder, applauder, marauder, defrauder.

OD'ern– 2. modern 3. unmodern 4. ultramodern.

OD'ess– 2. bodice, goddess 4. demigoddess.

OD'est– 2. oddest, modest, broadest 3. immodest, unmodest 4. supermodest.

OD'i– 2. body, bawdy, dawdy, gaudy, hoddy, cloddy, noddy, poddy, soddy, shoddy, toddy, wadi, waddy, squaddy 3. embody, somebody, nobody, cum laude 4. anybody, antibody, everybody, busybody, disembody, hoddy-doddy [dial.], coddy-moddy 5. magna cum laude, summa cum laude.

OD'id– 2. bodied, toddied, waddied 3. embodied, unbodied 4. ablebodied, unembodied.

OD'ik– 2. odic 3. geodic, iodic, melodic, spasmodic, anodic, threnodic, synodic, epodic, rhapsodic, methodic 4. periodic, unmelodic, hellanodic, episodic, kinesodic.

OD'ing– 2. codding, lauding, plodding, nodding, podding, prodding, wadding 3. belauding, applauding, marauding, defrauding.

OD'is– 2. bodice, goddess.

OD'ish– 2. oddish, gaudish, cloddish, poddish.

OD'it– 2. audit, plaudit.

OD'l– 2. dawdle, coddle, caudle, caudal, model, noddle, toddle, waddle, swaddle, twaddle 3. acaudal, subcaudal, remodel 4. mollycoddle.

OD'ler– 2. dawdler, coddler, toddler, waddler, swaddler, twaddler 4. mollycoddler.

OD'li– 2. oddly, godly, waddly, twaddly 3. ungodly.

OD'lin– 2. codlin, maudlin.

OD'ling– 2. dawdling, godling, codling, coddling, modeling, toddling, waddling, swaddling, twaddling 4. mollycoddling.

OD'ri– 2. Audrey, bawdry, tawdry.

O'er– 2. gnawer, pawer, rawer, drawer, sawer, tawer 4. overdrawer.

O'est– 2. rawest.

OF'e– 2. coffee, toffee, toffy.

OF'er– 2. offer, doffer, goffer, coffer, cougher, scoffer, proffer.

OF'et– 2. prophet, profit, soffit 3. archprophet 4. weather prophet.

OF'ik– 2. ophic, trophic, strophic 4. hypertrophic, catastrophic, antistrophic, apostrophic, theosophic, philosophic 5. unphilosophic.

OF'in– 2. dauphin, coffin 3. encoffin.

OF'ing– 2. offing, doffing, coughing, scoffing.

OF'is– 2. office 3. post office, War Office 5. employment office.

OF'ish– 2. offish, spoffish, crawfish, sawfish, squawfish 3. standoffish.

OF'it– 2. prophet, profit, soffit.

OF'l– 2. offal, coffle, waffle; *see* also **O'ful–** awful etc. below.

OF'n– 2. often, soften.

OF'ner– 2. oftener, softener.

OFT'er– 2. ofter, lofter, crofter, softer.

OFT'est– 2. oftest, softest.

OFT'i– 2. lofty, softy 3. toplofty.

O'ful– 2. awful, lawful 3. unlawful; *see* also **OF'l–** offal etc. above.

OG'a– 2. gogga.

OG'an– 2. goggan, moggan 3. toboggan 4. pogamoggan.

OG'er– 2. auger, augur, dogger, hogger, jogger, cogger, logger, flogger, clogger, slogger, togger 3. befogger, whole-hogger 4. pettifogger.

OG'i– 2. boggy, doggy, foggy, joggy, loggy, cloggy, moggy, smoggy, poggy, froggy, groggy.

OG'in– 2. loggin, noggin.

OG'ing– 2. bogging, dogging, fogging, hogging, jogging, cogging, logging, flogging, clogging, slogging, frogging 3. befogging, prologuing 4. cataloguing, epiloguing.

OG'ish– 2. doggish, hoggish, froggish.

OG'l– 2. boggle, goggle, joggle, coggle, toggle 3. boondoggle [slang].

OG'ler– 2. boggler, goggler, joggler.

OG'let– 2. boglet, loglet, froglet.

OG'ling– 2. boggling, goggling, joggling 3. boondoggling [slang].

OG'ust– 2. August 3. mid-August.

O'i– 2. jawy, flawy, strawy, thawy, yawy.

O'ing– 2. awing, chawing [inelegant or dial.], hawing, jawing, cawing, flawing, gnawing, pawing, drawing, sawing, pshawing, tawing, thawing, yawing **3.** guffawing, heehawing, outlawing, withdrawing, hurrahing, seesawing **4.** overawing, overdrawing.

OJ′er– **2.** bodger, dodger, codger, lodger, Roger **3.** corndodger, dislodger.

OJ′ez– dodges etc., *see* **OJ–** dodge etc., plus "s" or " 's."

OJ′i– **2.** dodgy, podgy, stodgy **4.** pedagogy, demagogy.

OJ′ik– **2.** logic **3.** choplogic, eulogic, agogic **4.** pedagogic, psychagogic, demagogic, anagogic, hypnagogic, epagogic, paragogic, isagogic, mystagogic, dialogic, catalogic, metalogic, geologic, neologic, psychologic, pathologic, ethologic, mythologic, biologic, philologic, homologic, cosmologic, penologic, ethnologic, chronologic, hypnologic, zoologic, acrologic, necrologic, micrologic, hydrologic, agrologic, astrologic, ontologic, tautologic, cytologic, phytologic, histologic **5.** mineralogic, lexicologic, toxicologic, archaeologic, sociologic, hagiologic, physiologic, entomologic, etymologic, anthropologic, **6.** meteorologic.

OJ′iks– **4.** pedagogics, anagogics, theologics.

OJ′ing– **2.** dodging, lodging **3.** unlodging, dislodging.

OK′a– **2.** bocca, rocca [It.].

OK′er– **2.** balker, chalker, docker, gawker, hawker, calker, cocker, locker, blocker, clocker, mocker, smocker, knocker, rocker, socker, soccer, shocker, talker, stalker, stocker, walker, squawker **3.** jayhawker, jaywalker, sleepwalker, streetwalker, nightwalker **4.** Knickerbocker, tomahawker.

OK′et– **2.** docket, cocket, locket, pocket, rocket, brocket, crocket, krocket, sprocket, socket **3.** pickpocket, impocket, unpocket, hip pocket, air pocket, vest pocket, watch pocket, skyrocket.

OK′i– **2.** balky, chalky, gawky, hawky, hockey, jockey, cocky, locky, lochy, blocky, flocky, pocky, pawky, rocky, crocky, talky, talkie, stocky, stalky, squawky **3.** field hockey, ice hockey, disk jockey [slang], horsejockey, Milwaukee **4.** walkie-talkie.

OK′ij– **2.** dockage, lockage, soccage.

OK′ing– **2.** balking, chalking, docking, gawking, hawking, hocking, calking, cocking, locking, blocking, flocking, clocking, mocking, smocking, knocking, rocking, crocking, socking, shocking, talking, stocking, stalking, walking, squawking **3.** jayhawking, unlocking, unblocking, bluestocking, jaywalking.

OK′ish– **2.** balkish, chalkish, gawkish, hawkish, cockish, mawkish, mockish, stockish **3.** peacockish.

OK′l– **2.** hockle, cockle, strockle, socle.

OK′let– **2.** cocklet, rocklet, stocklet.

OK′ling– **2.** cockling, flockling, rockling.

OK′ni– **2.** cockney, Procne.

OK′o– **2.** jocko, socko [slang], yocco **3.** sirocco, Morocco.

OKS′a– **2.** coxa, moxa, noxa, toxa.

OKS′al– **2.** coxal, noxal **4.** paradoxal.

OKS′en– **2.** oxen, cockswain.

OKS′er– **2.** oxer, boxer **4.** paradoxer, philodoxer.

OKSH′al– **3.** trinoctial **4.** equinoctial.

OKSH′un– **2.** auction, coction **3.** decoction, recoction, concoction.

OKSH′us– **2.** noxious **3.** obnoxious, innoxious.

OKS′i– **2.** boxy, doxy, foxy, poxy, roxy, proxy **3.** Biloxi **4.** paradoxy, cacodoxy, orthodoxy **5.** heterodoxy.

OKS′ik– **2.** toxic **4.** streptococcic, antitoxic.

OKS′in– **2.** toxin, tocsin **4.** antitoxin.

OKS′ing– **2.** boxing, foxing **4.** shadowboxing.

OKT'iv– 2. octave 3. decoctive, concoctive.

OKT'or– 2. auctor, doctor, proctor 3. concoctor.

OKT'rin– 2. doctrine.

OK'us– 2. Daucus, caucus, lochus, floccus, Glaucus, glaucous, raucous 4. pneumococcus, streptococcus 5. staphylococcus.

OL'a– 2. aula, olla, holla, Paula 3. corolla, chuckwalla 4. Guatemala.

OL'ar– 2. dollar, collar, scholar, sollar; *see* also **OL'er–** bawler etc. below.

OL'ard– 2. bollard, collard, collared, pollard, scholard, scholared.

OLD'er– 2. alder, balder, Balder, scalder.

OLD'est– 2. baldest.

OLD'ing– 2. balding, scalding, Spaulding.

OL'ej– 2. college, knowledge 3. acknowledge, foreknowledge.

OL'en– 2. fallen, pollen, Stollen [G.] 3. downfallen, crestfallen.

OL'er– 2. bawler, dollar, faller, hauler, holler, caller, collar, choller, choler, scholar, loller, mauler, smaller, brawler, drawler, crawler, scrawler, sprawler, trawler, sollar, taller, staller, squaller, squalor 3. hog caller, enthraller, extoller, forestaller, potwaller 4. overhauler, dorsicollar, caterwauler.

OL'erd– 2. bollard, collared, collard, dollared, hollered, pollard, scholared.

O'less– 2. awless, aweless, jawless, lawless, flawless, clawless.

OL'est– 2. smallest, tallest.

OL'et– 2. collet, wallet, swallet 3. La-Follette.

OL'fin– 2. dolphin.

OL'i– 2. dolly, folly, golly, holly, jolly, collie, Molly, molle, Polly, poly [slang], rolley, rawly, drawly, crawly, scrawly, sprawly, trolley, squally, volley 3. *loblolly* 4. melancholy.

OL'id– 2. olid, jollied, collied, solid, stolid, squalid, volleyed 4. semisolid.

OL'ij– 2. haulage, college, knowledge, stallage 3. acknowledge, foreknowledge.

OL'ik– 2. aulic, Gaulic, rollick, frolic 3, embolic, symbolic, carbolic, bucolic, hydraulic, petrolic, systolic 4. diabolic, metabolic, hyperbolic, alcoholic, vitriolic, melancholic, diastolic, epistolic, apostolic 5. bibliopolic.

OL'in– 2. colin, collin 3. tarpaulin 4. hemicollin.

OL'ing– 2. balling, bawling, falling, galling, hauling, calling, lolling, mauling, palling, Pawling, brawling, drawling, crawling, scrawling, trawling, thralling, stalling, walling, squalling 3. blackballing, snowballing, befalling, recalling, miscalling, appalling, enthralling, extolling, installing, forestalling 4. overhauling, unenthralling, caterwauling.

OL'is– 2. follis, caulis, solace, Wallace 3. Cornwallis 4. torticollis.

OL'ish– 2. dollish, Gaulish, smallish, polish, tallish, squallish 3. abolish, demolish.

OL'ive– 2. olive 3. green olive, ripe olive.

OL'ment– 3. appallment, epaulement, enthrallment, installment.

OL'ness– 2. allness, smallness, tallness.

OL'o– 2. follow, hollo, hollow, Rollo, wallow, swallow 3. Apollo; *see* also **AL'o–** calo etc.

OL'op– 2. dollop, jollop, collop, scallop, lollop, trollop, wallop [dial, coll. & slang] 3. escalop.

OLS'er– 2. falser, waltzer.

OLT'ed– 2. faulted, halted, malted, salted, vaulted 3. defaulted, assaulted, exalted.

OLT'er– 2. alter, altar, falter, halter, malter, smalter, palter, salter, psalter, vaulter, Walter 3. defaulter, unhalter, Gibraltar, assaulter, exalter.

OLT′ern– 2. altern, saltern 3. subaltern.

OLT′i– 2. faulty, malty, salty, vaulty, volti [It.].

OLT′ij– 2. faultage, maltage, vaultage.

OLT′ik– 2. Baltic 3. cobaltic, basaltic 4. peristaltic.

OLT′ing– 2. faulting, halting, malting, salting, vaulting 3. defaulting, assaulting, exalting.

OLT′less– 2. faultless, haltless, maltless, saltless 3. defaultless, assaultless.

OL′um– 2. column, solemn.

OLV′ent– 2. solvent 3. absolvent, resolvent, dissolvent, insolvent, evolvent.

OLV′er– 2. solver 3. absolver, resolver, dissolver, evolver, revolver, involver.

OLV′ing– 2. solving 3. absolving, resolving, dissolving, evolving, devolving, revolving, involving 4. undissolving, unrevolving.

OLV′ment– 3. evolvement, devolvement, involvement.

OM′a– 2. comma, cauma, momma, trauma.

OM′as– 2. Thomas, promise 4. doubting Thomas.

OMB′a– 2. domba, tromba 3. zambomba, calomba.

OMB′at– 2. combat, wombat.

OMB′er– 2. omber, ombre, Scomber, somber.

OMB′i– 2. Dombey, zombie 4. Abercrombie.

OMB′l– 2. comble, wamble 3. ensemble.

OM′et– 2. comet, domett, grommet 3. Mahomet.

OM′i– 2. mommy, pommy, tommy, Tommy.

OM′ij– 2. homage, pommage.

OM′ik– 2. comic, nomic, dromic, promic 3. encomic, dinomic, syndromic, achromic, dichromic, atomic, entomic, phantomic, dystomic, Suomic 4. tragicomic, quasicomic, pathognomic, pyrognomic, economic, agronomic, chironomic, metronomic, astronomic, gastronomic, isonomic, autonomic, plutonomic, taxonomic, theobromic, hydrobromic, paradromic, palindromic, orthodromic, exodromic, loxodromic, monochromic, bathochromic, xanthochromic, polychromic, diatomic, triatomic, dermatomic, anatomic, monatomic, pentatomic, heptatomic, hexatomic, epitomic, microtomic, orthotomic 5. seriocomic, physiognomic, Deuteronomic, tesseratomic, heroicomic.

OM′iks– 2. comics 4. bionomics, economics, agronomics.

OM′ing– 2. bombing, gloming, glauming [both slang].

OM′is– 2. promise, Thomas 4. doubting Thomas.

OMP′i– 2. Pompey, rompy, swampy.

OMP′ish– 2. rompish, swampish.

OMP′us– 2. pompous 3. unpompous 4. catawampus.

ON′a– 2. donna, fauna 3. madonna 4. belladonna, prima donna, avifauna, piscifauna.

ON′ald– 2. Donald, Ronald.

OND′a– 2. fonda [Sp.], honda, nonda. 3. Golconda 4. anaconda.

OND′e– 2. spondee 3. dispondee.

OND′ed– 2. bonded 3. unbonded, absconded, responded 4. corresponded.

OND′ens– 3. abscondence, despondence, respondence 4. correspondence.

OND′ent– 2. frondent 3. despondent, respondent 4. co-respondent, correspondent.

OND′er– 2. bonder, fonder, condor, launder, blonder, ponder, wander, squander, yonder 3. absconder, responder 4. corresponder.

OND′est– 2. fondest, blondest.

OND′ij– 2. bondage, frondage 4. vagabondage.

OND'ing– 2. bonding 3. absconding, responding 4. vagabonding, corresponding.

OND'l– 2. fondle, rondle, rondel.

OND'li– 2. fondly, blondly 4. overfondly, overblondly.

OND'ness– 2. fondness, blondness.

OND'o– 2. hondo, rondo, tondo [It.].

ON'e– 2. Pawnee, Shawnee, Swanee; *see* also **ON'i**– awny etc. below.

ON'er– 2. awner, honor, fawner, conner, pawner, spawner, wanner, yawner 3. dishonor, *aleconner*.

ON'erd– 2. honored 3. time-honored, unhonored, dishonored.

ON'est– 2. honest, wannest, non est [L.] 3. dishonest.

ON'et– 2. bonnet, sonnet 3. sunbonnet, bluebonnet.

ONG'a– 2. bonga [Tag.], donga, conga, tonga, Tonga, wonga 3. Batonga 4. wonga-wonga.

ONG'er– 2. conger, longer, wronger, stronger, thronger 3. prolonger.

ONG'est– 2. longest, strongest.

ONG'ful– 2. longful, wrongful, throngful, songful.

ONG'i– 2. thongy 3. sing-songy.

ONG'ing– 2. longing, wronging, thronging 3. ding-donging, belonging, prolonging.

ONG'ish– 2. longish, wrongish, prongish, strongish.

ONG'li– 2. longly, wrongly, strongly.

ON'i– 2. awny, bonny, fawny, Johnny, Connie, lawny, Lonnie, pawny, Ronnie, scrawny, prawny, tawny, swanny, yawny 3. gyronny 5. mulligatawny; *see* also **ON'e**– Pawnee etc. above.

ON'ik– 2. phonic, conic, clonic, nonic, chronic, tonic 3. carbonic, bubonic, aconic, laconic, draconic, iconic, zirconic, Adonic, hedonic, sardonic, paeonic, agonic, trigonic, jargonic, aphonic, siphonic, symphonic, euphonic, typhonic, Pyrrhonic, benthonic, pythonic, Brythonic, Ionic, cyclonic, colonic, demonic, mnemonic, pulmonic, gnomonic, harmonic, sermonic, pneumonic, canonic, zoonic, Japonic, Aaronic, Neronic, ironic, Byronic, masonic, parsonic, atonic, Platonic, subtonic, tectonic, Metonic, pretonic, Miltonic, syntonic, protonic, Teutonic, plutonic, Slavonic, acronyc, ozonic 4. Pharaonic, polyconic, chalcedonic, algedonic, chelidonic, pantheonic, geogonic, theogonic, cosmogonic, polygonic, megaphonic, diaphonic, telephonic, antiphonic, cacophonic, xylophonic, microphonic, polyphonic, baryphonic, histrionic, cinnamonic, eudaemonic, hegemonic, Solomonic, philharmonic, anharmonic, enharmonic, etymonic, geoponic, electronic, supersonic, diatonic, hematonic, Housatonic, pentatonic, heptatonic, orthotonic, monotonic, neurotonic, isotonic, hypertonic, intertonic, polytonic, embryonic 5. chameleonic, Napoleonic, architectonic, electrotonic, Neoplatonic, geotectonic.

ON'iks– 2. onyx 3. hedonics, sardonyx, mnemonics, harmonics 4. chalcedonyx, histrionics, geoponics.

ON'ing– 2. awning, dawning, donning, fawning, conning, pawning, spawning, yawning.

ON'is– 3. Adonis.

ON'ish– 2. donnish, monish, tonnish, wannish 3. admonish, premonish, astonish.

ONK'er– 2. honker, conquer, conker 3. reconquer.

ONK'i– 2. donkey, conky.

ONK'ing– 2. honking, conking [slang].

ONK'us– 2. rhonchus, bronchus.

ON'li– 2. wanly.

ONS'al– 2. consul, sponsal, tonsil 3. proconsul, responsal.

ONS'er– 2. sponsor, tonsor 4. chirotonsor.

ONSH'us– 2. conscious, Pontius 3. subconscious, self-conscious, unconscious.

ONS'iv– 3. responsive 4. irresponsive, unresponsive, corresponsive.

ONST'er– 2. monster.

ONS'trans– 2. monstrance 3. demonstrance, remonstrance.

ONS'trant– 3. demonstrant, remonstrant, Premonstrant.

ONS'trus– 2. monstrous.

ONS'ul– 2. consul, sponsal, tonsil 3. proconsul, vice-consul, responsal.

ONT'al– 2. ontal, fontal, pontal 3. gerontal 4. horizontal.

ONT'an– 2. montane 3. tramontane, submontane, cismontane, transmontane 4. ultramontane.

ONT'ed– 2. daunted, fonted, haunted, flaunted, taunted, vaunted, wanted, wonted 3. undaunted, unwanted, unwonted.

ONT'er– 2. daunter, gaunter, haunter, flaunter, saunter, taunter, vaunter, wanter 5. tessaraconter.

ONT'est– 2. gauntest.

ONT'i– 2. haunty, jaunty, flaunty, vaunty.

ONT'ij– 2. pontage, vauntage, wantage.

ONT'ik– 2. pontic, quantic 3. odontic, gerontic 4. mastodontic, uniquantic.

ONT'in– 2. pontine, Pontine 3. dracontine, cispontine, transpontine 4. Hellespontine.

ONT'ing– 2. daunting, haunting, jaunting, flaunting, taunting, vaunting, wanting, wonting.

ONT'less– 2. dauntless, fontless, hauntless, tauntless, vauntless, wantless, wontless.

ONT'o– 2. conto, pronto, Tonto 3. Toronto.

ONZ'i– 2. bronzy.

ONZ'o– 3. Alphonso, Alonzo.

OP'er– 2. chopper, hopper, copper, scauper, lopper, mopper, pauper, popper, dropper, cropper, proper, propper, stropper, sopper, shopper, topper, stopper, swapper [dial. & coll.], whopper [coll.] 3. *clodhopper*, *grasshopper*, *eavesdropper*, improper, tiptopper 4. window shopper.

OP'et– 2. moppet, poppet.

OP'i– 2. choppy, hoppy, copy, loppy, floppy, sloppy, moppy, poppy, droppy, croppy, soppy, shoppy 3. recopy, jaloppy, jalopy [both slang].

OP'ij– 2. proppage, stoppage.

OP'ik– 2. scopic, tropic, topic 3. acopic, syncopic, Cyclopic, diplopic, canopic, Sinopic, hydropic, anthropic, atropic, Aesopic, prosopic, atopic, ectopic, metopic, entopic, syntopic, myopic 4. telescopic, periscopic, geoscopic, rheoscopic, orthoscopic, thermoscopic, lychnoscopic, aposcopic, acroscopic, macroscopic, microscopic, hydroscopic, aeroscopic, hygroscopic, poroscopic, spectroscopic, gyroscopic, pantoscopic, photoscopic, autoscopic, polyscopic, Ethiopic, nyctalopic, lycanthropic, theanthropic, philanthropic, misanthropic, diatropic, ametropic, nyctitropic, isentropic, geotropic, rheotropic, orthotropic, allotropic, monotropic, apotropic, hydrotropic, aerotropic, neurotropic, isotropic, autotropic, exotropic, polytropic, isotopic, polytopic, presbyopic, polyopic 5. kaleidoscopic, hagioscopic, helioscopic, deuteroscopic, fluoroscopic, electroscopic, hemeralopic, paleanthropic, heliotropic, dexiotropic, heterotopic.

OP'ing– 2. chopping, hopping, copping, lopping, flopping, plopping, slopping, mopping, popping, dropping, cropping, propping, stropping, sopping, shopping, topping, stopping, swapping [dial. & coll.], whopping [coll.] 3. *clodhopping*, *eavesdropping*, estopping, clip-clopping 4. overtopping.

OP'ish– 2. foppish, shoppish.

OP'l– 2. hopple, copple, popple, thropple, topple, stopple 3. estoppel.

OP'ling– 2. fopling, toppling, stoppling.

OP'shun– 2. option 3. adoption 4. re-adoption.

OP'si– 2. copsy, Mopsy, dropsy, Topsy.

OP'sis– 3. synopsis 4. thanatopsis.

OPT'ed– 2. opted 3. co-opted, adopted 4. unadopted.

OPT'er– 2. opter 3. adopter, diopter, orthopter 4. helicopter, phenicopter.

OPT'ik– 2. optic, Coptic 3. synoptic, autoptic, orthoptic.

OPT'ing– 2. opting 3. adopting.

OPT'iv– 2. optive 3. co-optive, adoptive.

OR'a– 2. orra, aura, gora, gorah, Laura, sorra 3. Andorra, begorra [dial. Ir.], Camorra, Gomorrah.

OR'al– 2. aural, oral, horral, coral, laurel, moral, sorrel, quarrel 3. amoral, Balmoral, immoral, unmoral, binaural.

OR'anj– 2. orange 3. mock orange 4. navel orange, Osage orange.

ORB'el– 2. orbell, corbeil, corbel, warble.

ORB'ent– 3. absorbent, resorbent 4. nonabsorbent, unabsorbent.

ORB'ing– 2. orbing 3. absorbing, resorbing.

ORB'l– 2. corbel, warble.

ORCH'er– 2. scorcher, torcher, torture.

ORCH'erd– 2. orchard, tortured.

ORCH'ing– 2. scorching, torching.

ORD'al– 2. chordal 3. concordal.

ORD'an– 2. Jordan, warden.

ORD'ans– 3. accordance, concordance, discordance.

ORD'ant– 2. mordant 3. accordant, concordant, discordant 4. disaccordant.

ORD'ed– 2. corded, chorded, lorded, sordid, warded, swarded 3. accorded, recorded, belorded, unlorded, awarded, rewarded 4. unrecorded, unrewarded.

ORD'er– 2. order, border, corder, warder 3. reorder, disorder, emborder, accorder, recorder, awarder, rewarder 4. money order.

ORD'erd– 2. ordered, bordered 3. well-ordered, unordered, disordered, unbordered.

ORD'ij– 2. cordage, wardage.

ORD'ing– 2. cording, chording, lording, warding 3. according, recording, belording, awarding, rewarding; *see* also **ORD'ing–** boarding etc.

ORD'on– 2. Gordon, Jordan, cordon, warden.

OR'el– 2. laurel, saurel, sorrel, quarrel; *see* also **OR'al–** aural etc. above.

OR'en– 2. foreign, sporran, warren.

OR'ens– 2. Lawrence, Florence 3. abhorrence, St. Lawrence.

OR'ent– 2. horrent, torrent, warrant 3. abhorrent, death warrant, search warrant.

OR'er– 2. horror, warrer 3. abhorrer.

OR'est– 2. forest 3. afforest, deforest, reforest, disforest.

OR'fan– 2. orphan 3. half-orphan.

ORF'i– 4. metamorphy, geomorphy, zoomorphy.

ORF'ik– 2. Orphic, morphic 3. amorphic, dimorphic, trimorphic 4. metamorphic, endomorphic, pseudomorphic, geomorphic, theomorphic, monomorphic, zoomorphic, theromorphic, tauromorphic, isomorphic, pantomorphic, automorphic, exomorphic, polymorphic 5. ophiomorphic, theriomorphic, heteromorphic, deuteromorphic 6. ephemeromorphic.

ORF'ing– 2. dwarfing, wharfing.

ORF'it– 2. forfeit 3. reforfeit.

ORF'izm– 2. Orphism, morphism 4. metamorphism, monomorphism, zoomorphism.

ORF'us– 3. amorphous, dimorphous, trimorphous 4. paramorphous, metamorphous, polymorphous **5.** ophiomorphous, anthropomorphous.

ORG′an– 2. organ, Gorgon, Morgan, morgan, morgen **3.** idorgan, biorgan **4.** Demogorgon.

ORG′ij– 2. mortgage.

OR′i– 2. corrie, scaurie, Laurie, lorry, sorry, saury, quarry **4.** Annie Laurie.

OR′id– 2. horrid, florid, torrid, Taurid 3. Centaurid.

OR′ij– 2. borage, forage, porridge.

OR′ik– 2. auric, goric, choric, chloric, tauric, toric, Yorick **3.** sudoric, theoric, phosphoric, enchoric, caloric, pyloric, rhetoric, historic, plethoric **4.** meteoric, semaphoric, cataphoric, metaphoric, allegoric, paregoric, oratoric, androtauric, prehistoric **5.** phantasmagoric; *see* also **OR′ik–** boric etc.

OR′ing– 2. warring **3.** abhorring.

OR′is– 2. orris, Doris, Horace, morris; *see* also **OR′us–** Caurus etc. below.

OR′ist– 2. chorist, florist.

ORJ′er– 2. forger, gorger.

ORJ′i– 2. orgy, Georgie, porgy, storge **4.** Georgy Porgy.

ORJ′us– 2. gorgeous **3.** ungorgeous.

ORK′a– 2. Orca **3.** Majorca, Minorca.

ORK′er– 2. forker, corker, porker, Yorker **3.** New Yorker.

ORK′i– 2. forky, corky.

ORK′id– 2. orchid.

ORK′ing– 2. forking, Dorking, corking 3. uncorking.

ORK′us– 2. Orcus, Dorcas, orchis.

ORM′al– 2. formal, cormel, normal **3.** informal, unformal, abnormal, unnormal, transnormal **4.** uniformal, supernormal.

ORM′an– 2. Mormon, Norman.

ORM′ans– 2. dormance **3.** conformance, performance.

ORM′ant– 2. dormant, formant **3.** undormant, informant, conformant, performant.

ORM′er– 2. ormer, dormer, former, stormer, warmer, swarmer **3.** deformer, reformer, informer, conformer, performer, transformer, barnstormer, chair warmer **4.** misinformer, nonconformer.

ORM′est– 2. warmest.

ORM′i– 2. dormy, forme, horme, stormy, swarmy.

ORM′ing– 2. forming, storming, warming, swarming **3.** deforming, reforming, informing, conforming, performing, transforming, bestorming, barnstorming, housewarming **4.** misinforming, unconforming, nonconforming.

ORM′ist– 3. reformist, conformist **4.** nonconformist, unconformist.

ORM′less– 2. formless, stormless.

ORM′li– 2. warmly **4.** uniformly.

ORM′us– 2. Ormus, cormus, cormous 3. abnormous, enormous.

ORN′a– 2. Lorna **3.** cromorna.

ORN′er– 2. horner, corner, scorner, warner **3.** suborner, adorner, forewarner **4.** chimney corner, catercorner, cattycorner, kittycorner **5.** Little Jack Horner, puss in the corner.

ORN′i– 2. horny, corny, scorny, thorny.

ORN′ing– 2. horning, corning, scorning, morning, warning **3.** suborning, a-borning, adorning, dehorning, good morning, forewarning.

ORN′is– 2. ornis, cornice **3.** Dinornis, Notornis **4.** Ichthyornis.

ORN′ish– 2. hornish, Cornish, Plornish [Dickens], warnish [Scot.].

ORN′less– 2. hornless, cornless, scornless, thornless.

ORN′ment– 3. adornment **4.** unadornment.

OR′o– 2. borrow, morrow, sorrow **3.** tomorrow, good morrow.

ORP'er– 2. scorper, torpor, warper.

ORS'al– 2. dorsal, morsal 3. dextrorsal 4. sinistrorsal.

ORS'el– 2. morsel, norsel, torsel, torcel 3. ensorcell.

ORS'er– 2. horser 3. endorser.

ORS'ful– 2. forceful 3. remorseful, resourceful.

ORSH'un– 2. torsion 3. abortion, consortion, detorsion, retortion, intorsion, contortion, extortion; *see* also **ORSH'un**– portion etc.

ORSH'us– 2. tortious 3. extortious.

ORS'iv– 2. torsive 3. contorsive, extorsive.

ORS'o– 2. dorso [ML.], corso [It.], torso.

ORT'a– 2. torta, Torte [G.] 3. aorta 4. sesquiquarta.

ORT'al– 2. mortal, sortal, chortle 3. aortal, immortal.

ORT'ans– 2. portance 3. importance 4. unimportance.

ORT'ed– 2. snorted, sorted, warted, thwarted 3. aborted, exhorted, escorted, assorted, resorted, consorted, unsorted, detorted, retorted, contorted, distorted, extorted, cavorted, resorted.

ORT'eks– 2. cortex, vortex.

ORT'en– 2. chorten, shorten 3. foreshorten.

ORT'er– 2. mortar, snorter, sorter, shorter, quarter, swarter, thwarter 3. dehorter, exhorter, escorter, hindquarter, forequarter, assorter, resorter, consorter, retorter, contorter, distorter, extorter.

ORT'est– 2. shortest, swartest.

ORT'i– 2. forty, snorty, sortie, Shorty, Torte [G.], warty, swarty.

ORT'ij– 2. shortage.

ORT'ing– 2. snorting, sorting, Storting, thwarting 3. aborting, exhorting, escorting, consorting, retorting, contorting, distorting, extorting, cavorting, resorting.

ORT'is– 2. fortis, mortise, tortoise.

ORT'iv– 2. ortive, tortive 3. abortive, retortive, contortive, distortive, extortive.

ORT'l– 2. chortle; *see* also **ORT'al**– mortal etc. above.

ORT'ment– 2. sortment 3. assortment, consortment.

ORT'un– 2. fortune 3. misfortune, importune.

OR'us– 2. Caurus, Laurus, Taurus 3. thesaurus 4. Brontosaurus, Labrosaurus, Hadrosaurus, Mixosaurus 5. Megalosaurus, Ichthyosaurus, Atlantosaurus, ceratosaurus; *see* also **OR'is**– orris etc. above.

OR'ward– 2. forward, norward 3. henceforward, thenceforward, straightforward.

OS'a– 2. Ossa, ossa [L.], fossa, glossa.

OS'al– 2. ossal, dossal, glossal 3. colossal 4. hypoglossal; *see* also **OS'il**– docile etc. and **OS'l**– jostle etc. below.

OS'er– 2. bosser, Chaucer, dosser, josser, glosser, rosser, crosser, saucer, tosser 3. embosser 4. cup-and-saucer.

OS'et– 2. bosset, faucet, cosset, Nauset, posset.

OSH'er– 2. bosher, josher, cosher, washer, swasher, squasher 3. *whitewasher*.

OSH'i– 2. boshy, sloshy, toshy, washy, swashy, squashy 4. wishy-washy.

OSH'ing– 2. joshing, sloshing, washing, swashing, squashing 3. dishwashing.

OSH'un– 2. caution 3. incaution, precaution.

OS'i– 2. bossy, flossy, Flossie, glossy, mossy, posse, drossy, saucy, tossy.

OS'ij– 2. fossage, gaussage, sausage.

OS'ik– 2. fossick, glossic 3. molossic, banausic.

OS'il– 2. docile, dossil, fossil 3. indocile; *see* also **OS'l**– jostle etc. below; **OS'al**– ossal etc. above.

OS'ing– 2. bossing, dossing, glossing, mossing, crossing, tossing 3. embossing, grade crossing 4. railroad crossing.

OS′ip– 2. gossip.

OS′l– 2. jostle, throstle, tossel, wassail 3. apostle; *see* also **OS′al–** ossal etc. and **OS′il–** docile etc. above.

OS′ler– 2. ostler, hostler, jostler.

OS′li– 2. crossly.

OS′om– 2. blossom, possum 3. reblossom, opossum.

OSP′er– 2. prosper.

OSP′i– 2. waspy.

OST′a– 2. costa, Hosta 3. subcosta.

OST′al– 2. costal 4. Pentecostal, infracostal, supracostal, intercostal.

OST′ed– 2. frosted 3. exhausted, accosted, defrosted.

OST′el– 2. hostel, rostel.

OST′er– 2. Auster, foster, coster, Gloucester, roster, froster, zoster 3. exhauster, accoster, impostor 4. pentecoster, paternoster, Pater Noster.

OST′i– 2. frosty.

OST′ij– 2. hostage.

OST′ik– 2. caustic, gnostic 3. encaustic, agnostic, prognostic, acrostic 4. diacaustic, catacaustic, diagnostic, geognostic, paracrostic, pentacrostic.

OST′il– 2. hostile, postil.

OST′ing– 2. costing, frosting 3. exhausting, accosting.

OST′iv– 2. costive 3. exhaustive 4. inexhaustive, unexhaustive.

OST′ral– 2. austral, costrel, claustral, nostril, rostral 4. longirostral.

OST′rat– 2. rostrate, prostrate.

OST′rum– 2. haustrum, nostrum, rostrum.

OST′ur– 2. posture 3. imposture.

OS′um– 2. blossom, possum 3. emblossom, opossum 4. Geoglossum.

OS′us– 3. colossus, molossus.

OT′a– 2. cotta, pottah, chrotta 3. Carlotta 4. terra cotta, Epicauta, Argonauta.

OT′al– 2. glottal 4. epiglottal; *see* also **OT′l–** bottle etc. below.

OT′ed– 2. dotted, jotted, lotted, blotted, clotted, plotted, slotted, knotted, potted, spotted, rotted, trotted, sotted, shotted, squatted 3. wainscotted, allotted, unknotted, unspotted, garroted 4. juggernauted.

OT′en– 2. gotten, rotten, shotten, tauten 3. begotten, ill-gotten, ungotten, forgotten, misgotten 4. misbegotten, unforgotten; *see* also **OT′on–** cotton etc. below.

OT′er– 2. otter, daughter, dotter, hotter, jotter, cauter, cotter, blotter, clotter, plotter, slaughter, knotter, potter, spotter, rotter, trotter, shotter, water, squatter, swatter, yachter 3. granddaughter, complotter, unknotter, garrotter, globetrotter, bogtrotter, breakwater, limewater, firewater.

OT′est– 2. hottest.

OT′ful– 2. plotful, potful, thoughtful 3. unthoughtful.

OTH′am– 2. Gotham, Jotham.

OTH′er– 2. author, bother, fother, pother, rather, frother, swather.

OTH′ful– 2. slothful, wrathful.

OTH′i– 2. bothy, mothy, frothy, swathy.

OTH′ik– 2. Gothic, Sothic 4. Visigothic, Suigothic, Ostrogothic.

OTH′ing– 2. frothing, trothing 3. betrothing.

OT′i– 2. dotty, haughty, blotty, clotty, naughty, knotty, potty, spotty, shotty, totty, squatty, yachty.

OT′id– 3. carotid, parotid.

OT′ij– 2. cottage, clottage, plottage, pottage, wattage, squattage.

OT′ik– 2. otic, glottic, nautic 3. chaotic, thrombotic, sybotic, helcotic, narcotic, zygotic, argotic, dichotic, psychotic, morphotic, orthotic, xanthotic, biotic, meiotic, diglottic, Nilotic, psilotic, culottic, demotic, thermotic, seismotic, osmotic, zymotic, henotic, kenotic, binotic, pyknotic, monotic, hypnotic, zootic, nepotic, despotic, parotic, acrotic, necrotic, dicrotic, hydrotic, erotic, cerotic, sclerotic, xerotic, porotic, pyrotic, neurotic, entotic, aptotic, exotic, quixotic, loxotic, myotic, rhizotic 4. anecdotic, alloeotic, indigotic, symbiotic, idiotic, semeiotic, periotic, patriotic, epiglottic, polyglottic, endosmotic, exosmotic, enzymotic, melanotic, cyanotic, Argonautic, aeronautic, agrypnotic, escharotic, anacrotic, catacrotic, monocrotic, polycrotic, oneirotic, ichthyotic 5. catabiotic, amphibiotic, antibiotic, halobiotic, macrobiotic, Iscariotic, neurohypnotic, epizootic, rhinocerotic.

OT'iks– 2. nautics 3. biotics, demotics, thermotics 4. aeronautics.

OT'ing– 2. dotting, hotting, jotting, blotting, clotting, plotting, knotting, potting, spotting, rotting, trotting, swatting, squatting, yachting 3. allotting, unknotting, garroting, globe-trotting, besotting 4. juggernauting.

OT'is– 2. glottis 4. epiglottis, hypoglottis.

OT'ish– 2. hottish, Scottish, sottish, schottische, squattish.

OT'l– 2. bottle, dottle, glottal, mottle, pottle, rotl, crottle, throttle, tottle, wattle, twattle 3. bluebottle 4. acocotl, axolotl, epiglottal.

OT'ler– 2. bottler, mottler, throttler, twattler.

OT'less– 2. dotless, cotless, blotless, plotless, knotless, potless, spotless, rotless, totless, thoughtless.

OT'li– 2. hotly, motley, tautly.

OT'ling– 2. bottling, mottling, throttling, wattling, twattling.

OT'ment– 2. squatment 3. allotment, besotment.

OT'o– 2. Otto, lotto, blotto [slang], motto, potto, grotto, sotto [It.] 3. ridotto, fagotto [It.], risotto [It.].

OT'on– 2. cotton, Lawton, frotton, Groton 3. guncotton; *see* also **OT'en–** gotten etc. above.

OT'um– 2. autumn, bottom.

OV'el– 2. hovel, novel, grovel.

OV'er– 2. hover, suaver.

OV'erb– 2. proverb.

O'yer– 2. lawyer, sawyer 3. top sawyer.

OZ'al– 2. causal, pausal, clausal; *see* also **OZ'l–** nozzle etc. below.

OZ'er– 2. hawser, causer, pauser.

OZ'ez– 2. gauzes, causes, clauses, pauses, vases 3. becauses, applauses.

OZ'i– 2. gauzy, causey, lawzy [dial.].

OZ'ing– 2. causing, clausing, pausing.

OZ'it– 2. closet, posit 3. deposit, reposit, composite 4. juxtaposit, oviposit, decomposite, incomposite, interposit.

OZ'iv– 2. plausive 3. applausive 4. unapplausive.

OZ'l– 2. nozzle, snozzle, sozzle; *see* also **OZ'al–** causal etc. above.

OZ'mik– 2. osmic, cosmic 3. aosmic 4. neocosmic, macrocosmic, microcosmic.

OZ'mos– 2. cosmos 4. macrocosmos, microcosmos.

O (awe)

3.

TRIPLE RHYMES IN O (prob'a-ble)

Primary or Secondary Accent Falls on Second from Last Syllable.

OB'a-bl- 3. daubable, robbable, probable 4. improbable.

OB'er-i- 3. bobbery, daubery, jobbery, clobbery, slobbery, snobbery, robbery, strawberry.

OB'er-ing- 3. clobbering, slobbering.

OB'ul-ar- 3. lobular, globular.

OD'a-bl- 3. laudable, plaudable 4. applaudable.

OD'er-er- 3. dodderer, fodderer, solderer.

OD'er-i- 3. doddery, gaudery.

OD'er-ing- 3. doddering, foddering, soldering.

OD'i-fi- 3. codify, modify.

OD'i-ing- 3. bodying 4. embodying, disbodying 5. disembodying.

OD'ik-al- 3. codical, nodical 4. spasmodical, synodical, monodical, prosodical, rhapsodical, methodical 5. periodical, episodical.

OD'i-ness- 3. bawdiness, gaudiness.

OD'it-er- 3. auditor, plauditor.

OD'it-i- 3. oddity, quoddity 4. commodity 5. incommodity, discommodity.

OD'ul-ant- 3. modulant, fraudulent.

OD'ul-ar- 3. modular, nodular.

OF'ag-a- 4. Sarcophaga, Zoophaga.

OF'ag-al- 4. sarcophagal, esophagal.

OF'ag-an- 4. zoophagan, saprophagan.

OF'ag-us- 4. geophagous, theophagous, sarcophagus, sarcophagous, zoophagous, hippophagous, androphagous, necrophagous, esophagus, saprophagous 5. ichthyophagous.

OF'aj-i- 4. theophagy, sarcophagy, hippophagy, phytophagy, pantophagy 5. ichthyophagy, anthropophagy.

OF'aj-ist- 4. geophagist, omophagist, hippophagist, pantophagist 5. ichthyophagist, galactophagist.

OF'el-ez- 5. Mephistopheles.

OF'er-er- 3. offerer, cofferer, profferer.

OF'er-ing- 3. offering, goffering, coffering, proffering 4. thank offering, peace offering 5. freewill offering.

OF'ik-al- 3. trophical, sophical 5. theosophical, philosophical.

OF'il-us- 4. Theophilus, sarcophilous, Sarcophilus, xylophilous, saprophilous, zoophilous 5. acidophilus, heliophilous.

OF'on-i- 4. theophany, cacophony, homophony, photophony, Christophany, tautophony, orthophony.

OF'or-us- 4. zoophorus, phyllophorous, pyrophorous, pyrophorus 5. galactophorous.

OF'ul-i- 3. awfully, lawfully 4. unlawfully.

OF'ul-ness- 3. awfulness, lawfulness 4. unlawfulness.

OG'am-i- 4. endogamy, monogamy, misogamy, exogamy 5. deuterogamy.

OG'am-ist- 4. monogamist, cryptogamist, misogamist 5. deuterogamist.

OG'am-us- 4. endogamous, homogamous, monogamous, idogamous, exogamous 5. heterogamous.

OG'at-iv- 4. derogative, prerogative 5. interrogative.

OG'er-el- 3. doggerel, hoggerel.

OG'er-i- 3. froggery, groggery, toggery 5. pettifoggery.

OG'nom-i- 4. pathognomy 5. craniognomy, physiognomy.

OG'on-i- 4. geogony, theogony, mahogany, homogony, cosmogony, monogony, zoogony, mythogony 5. bibliogony, physiogony, heroogony, heterogony.

OG'raf-er- 4. logographer, lithographer, orthographer, biographer, demographer, mimographer, nomographer, cosmographer, sphenographer, stenographer, hymnographer, chronographer, zoographer, topographer, typographer, chirographer, chorographer, glossographer, photographer, cartographer, cryptographer, doxographer, mythographer 5. lexicographer, celidographer, choreographer, selenographer, bibliographer 6. autobiographer.

OG'raf-i- 4. cacography, chalcography, zincography, macrography, micrography, phycography, geography, logography, psychography, morphography, ethography, lithography, anthography, orthography, mythography, biography, haplography, stylography, xylography, demography, psalmography, mimography homography, nomography, cosmography, planography, scenography, sphenography, stenography, zenography, technography, ichnography, ethnography, hymnography, phonography, chronography, pornography, zoography, lipography, topography, typography, micrography, hydrography, cerography, pterography, chirography, orography, horography, chorography, petrography, neurography, pyrography, isography, nosography, hypsography, glossography, ontography, scotography, photography, glyptography, cryptography, cartography, histography, autography, phytography, myography 5. pharmacography, lexicography, celidography, archaeography, palaeography, ideography, stereography, osteography, radiography, cardiography, semeiography, hagiography, heliography, ophiography, bibliography, physiography, hyalography, metallography, crystallography, sigillography, selenography, iconography, anthropography, siderography, hierography, heterography, papyrography, thalassography, sematography, pneumatography, thanatography, skeletography, cometography, hyetography, odontography, ichthyography 6. zoogeography, pythogeography, chromolithography, autobiography, dactyliography, historiography, ecclesiography, oceanography, Christianography, cinematography, phantasmatography, numismatography, chromophotography.

OG'raf-ist- 4. biographist, stenographist, phonographist, monographist, zoographist, topographist, chirographist, photographist, orthographist 5. metallographist, selenographist, siderographist.

OG'ur-al- 3. augural 4. inaugural.

OJ'en-ez- 4. Diogenes, protogenes.

OJ'en-i- 3. progeny 4. biogeny, homogeny, nomogeny, monogeny, ethnogeny, oögeny, misogyny, zoogeny, autogeny, pathogeny 5. embryogeny, anthropogeny.

OJ'en-ist- 4. biogenist, philogynist, monogenist, misogynist 5. abiogenist, heterogenist.

OJ'en-us- 4. endogenous, biogenous, primogenous, homogenous, thermogenous, hypogenous, hydrogenous, pyrogenous, nitrogenous, exogenous, lithogenous.

OJ'ik-al- 3. logical 4. alogical, illogical, unlogical 5. anagogical, synagogical, apagogical, dialogical, analogical, symbological, geological, theological, neological, psychological, pathological, anthological, ethnological, mythological, biological, homological, cosmological, zymological, technological, penological, technological, ichnological, chronological, zoological, tropological, necrological, micrological, typological, metrological, astrological, neurological, glossological, nosological, histological, tautological, cytological, doxological 6. genealogical, toxicological, archaeological, ideological, sociological, bibliological, physiological, etymological, entomological, terminological, anthropological, climatological, embryological, Egyptological 7. bacteriological, ecclesiological, meteorological, palaeontological.

OJ'in–i– 4. philogyny, monogyny, misogyny; *see* also **OJ'en–i–** progeny etc. above.

OJ'in–ist– 4. biogenist, philogynist, monogenist, misogynist.

OJ'it–at– 3. cogitate 4. recogitate, precogitate, excogitate.

OK'at–iv– 3. locative, talkative, vocative 4. untalkative, invocative, provocative.

OK'er–i– 3. mockery, rockery, crockery.

OK'il–i– 3. chalkily, gawkily, cockily, pawkily, stockily.

OK'i–ness– 3. chalkiness, gawkiness, cockiness, rockiness, talkiness, stockiness.

OK'ing–li– 3. mockingly, shockingly, squawkingly.

OK'ras–i– 4. landocracy, theocracy, theocrasy, neocrasy, ptochocracy, ochlocracy, doulocracy, democracy, timocracy, nomocracy, cosmocracy, technocracy, ethnocracy, monocracy, androcracy, isocracy, chrysocracy, stratocracy, plantocracy, autocracy, plutocracy, bureaucracy 5. gynaecocracy, idiocrasy, hagiocracy, physiocracy, arithmocracy, millionocracy, hierocracy, pantisocracy, thalassocracy, ergatocracy, gerontocracy, despotocracy, aristocracy.

OK'rat–ist– 4. theocratist, democratist, bureaucratist.

OK'rat–izm– 3. Socratism 4. democratism, bureaucratism.

OKS'ik–al– 3. toxical 5. paradoxical, orthodoxical.

OKS'im–al– 3. proximal 4. approximal.

OK'ul–ar– 3. ocular, jocular, locular, vocular 4. binocular, monocular.

OK'ul–at– 3. oculate, flocculate 4. inoculate, binoculate.

OK'ul–us– 3. oculus, loculus 4. monoculus.

OK'ut–or– 4. oblocutor, collocutor, prolocutor 5. interlocutor.

OL'a–bl– 3. callable 4. recallable, enthrallable.

OL'at–er– 4. idolater, pyrolater, artolater 5. bibliolater, heliolater, Mariolater, iconolater.

OL'a–tri– 4. symbolatry, mobolatry, idolatry, lordolatry, litholatry, theolatry, cosmolatry, onolatry, monolatry, zoolatry, topolatry, necrolatry, pyrolatry, Christolatry, plutolatry 5. archaeolatry, hygeiolatry, gynaeolatry, hagiolatry, orphiolatry, bibliolatry, heliolatry, geniolatry, Mariolatry, patriolatry, physiolatry, angelolatry, symbololatry, uranolatry, Parthenolatry, iconolatry, demonolatry, anthropolatry, arborolatry, grammatolatry, thaumatolatry, ichthyolatry 6. ecclesiolatry.

OL'at–rus– 4. idolatrous, zoolatrous 5. heliolatrous, bibliolatrous.

OL'id–li– 3. solidly, stolidly, squalidly.

OL'if–i– 3. jollify, mollify, qualify 4. idolify, disqualify.

OL'i–form– 3. colliform, cauliform 4. emboliform.

OL'i–ing– 3. dollying, follying, jollying.

OL'ik–al– 4. symbolical, catholical 5. diabolical, parabolical, hyperbolical, apostolical 6. bibliopolical.

OL'ik-l- 3. follicle, caulicle.

OL'ik-som- 3. rollicksome, frolicsome.

OL'ing-li- 3. drawlingly, crawlingly 4. appallingly, enthrallingly.

OL'ish-er- 3. polisher 4. abolisher, demolisher.

OL'ish-ing- 3. polishing 4. abolishing, demolishing, repolishing.

OL'is-i- 3. policy 4. impolicy.

OL'is-is- 4. biolysis, hemolysis, hydrolysis, neurolysis, autolysis, histolysis.

OL'it-i- 3. jollity, polity, quality 4. equality, frivolity 5. isopolity, interpolity, inequality, coequality.

OL'it-iks- 3. politics 5. geopolitics, cosmopolitics.

OL'o-er- 3. follower, hollower, wallower, swallower.

OL'og-us- 4. homologous, isologous, tautologous 5. heterologous.

OL'o-ing- 3. following, hollowing, wallowing, swallowing.

OL'oj-er- 4. geologer, theologer, philologer, mythologer, phrenologer, acknowledger, phonologer, chronologer, horologer, astrologer 5. physiologer, etymologer.

OL'oj-i- 3. ology 4. naology, symbology, cacology, ecology, oncology, tocology, sarcology, muscology, phycology, mycology, pedology, tidology, odology, podology, pseudology, geology, rheology, theology, neology, algology, ergology, trichology, conchology, ptochology, archology, euchology, psychology, graphology, nephology, trophology, morphology, pathology, ethology, lithology, mythology, anthology, orthology, biology, philology, typhlology, haplology, hylology, xylology, sphygmology, gemmology, homology, nomology, gnomology, pomology, thermology, desmology, chresmology, seismology, cosmology, pneumology, zymology, phenology, menology, penology, phrenology, technology, ichnology, aphnology, ethnology, kinology, Sinology, limnology, hymnology, phonology, monology, chronology, tonology, hypnology, runology, cynology, oology, noology, zoology, apology, tropology, topology, hippology, carpology, typology, barology, pharology, ambrology, timbrology, ombrology, macrology, necrology, micrology, dendrology, hydrology, therology, pterology, agrology, hygrology, arthrology, chirology, orology, horology, chorology, iatrology, patrology, metrology, petrology, astrology, gastrology, neurology, pyrology, misology, dosology, nosology, posology, threpsology, gypology, glossology, chrysology, battology, cetology, ctetology, dittology, cytology, phytology, sitology, planktology, pantology, ontology, otology, photology, glottology, cryptology, typtology, cartology, pestology, histology, Christology, tautology, plutology, taxology, sexology, doxology, auxology, myology, bryology 5. amphibology, malacology, pharmacology, gynecology, lexicology, toxicology, monadology, acidology, pteridology, dicaeology, archaeology, atheology, palaeology, ideology, pantheology, speleology, teleology, areology, thereology, phraseology, osteology, edaphology, agathology, ornithology, abiology, sociology, radiology, cardiology, semeiology, hagiology, ophiology, sophiology, caliology, bibliology, heliology, mommiology, craniology, koniology, agriology, gnosiology, physiology, etiology, axiology, praxiology, angelology, dactylology, potamology, anemology, ophthalmology, docimology, paromology, atomology, entomology, orismology, etymology, mechanology, volcanology, organology, campanology, uranology, lichenology, selenology, asthenology, arachnology, carcinology, criminology, terminology, eccrinology, actinology, iconology, pogonology, demonology, gnomonology, synchronology, Hibernology, maternology, immunology, heroology, antapology, anthropology, hierology, ponerology, heterology, enterology, oneirology, iatrology, electrology, acyrology, papyrology, martyrology, parisology, piscatology, eschatology, haematology, rhematology, sematology, agmatology, climatology, thremmatology, stomatology, dermatology, thermatology, thaumatology, pneumatology, kymatology, thanatology, geratology, teratology, olfactology, esthetology, hyetology, melittology, semantology, odontology, deontology, neontology, erotology, Egyptology, heortology, aristology, agrostology, ichthyology, embryology **6.** metamorphology, geomorphology, psychopathology, neuropathology, theomythology, amphibiology, microbiology, stoichiology, dactyliology, paroemiology, bacteriology, soteriology, heresiology, hamartiology, diabolology, epistemology, phenomenology, paleethnology, meteorology, universology, emblematology, philematology, systematology, onomatology, numismatology, toreumatology, dialectology, paleontology **7.** paleopsychology, idiopsychology.

ŎL'oj–ist– **4.** geologist, neologist, theologist, echologist, conchologist, psychologist, morphologist, pathologist, lithologist, anthologist, mythologist, biologist, philologist, mimologist, palmologist, homologist, pomologist, seismologist, cosmologist, zymologist, phrenologist, technologist, ethnologist, Sinologist, hymnologist, phonologist, monologist, chronologist, hypnologist, oologist, noologist, zoologist, apologist, necrologist, dendrologist, hydrologist, horologist, petrologist, astrologist, chirologist, neurologist, glossologist, nosologist, gypsologist, battologist, ontologist, otologist, photologist, histologist, tautologist, phytologist, bryologist, myologist **5.** pharmacologist, anthocologist, lexicologist, toxicologist, archaeologist, ideologist, teleologist, phraseologist, ornithologist, sociologist, hagiologist, craniologist, physiologist, ophthalmologist, etymologist, arachnologist, demonologist, anthropologist, hierologist, oneirologist, dermatologist, herpetologist, neontologist, Egyptologist, melittologist, ichthyologist, embryologist **6.** paroemiologist, bacteriologist, ecclesiologist, meteorologist, numismatologist, dialectologist, paleontologist.

OL'oj–iz– **4.** geologize, neologize, theologize, philologize, homologize, monologize, apologize, astrologize, doxologize, battologize, mythologize **5.** sociologize, entomologize, etymologize.

OL'op–er– **3.** scalloper, walloper [dial., coll. & slang].

OLT'er–er– **3.** alterer, falterer, palterer, psalterer.

OLT'er–i– **3.** saltery, psaltery.

OLT'er–ing– **3.** altering, faltering, paltering **4.** unaltering, unfaltering.

OLT'i–est– **3.** faultiest, maltiest, saltiest.

OLT'i–ness– **3.** faultiness, maltiness, saltiness.

OL'ub–li– **3.** solubly, volubly **4.** insolubly **5.** indissolubly.

OLV'a–bl– **3.** solvable **4.** absolvable, resolvable, insolvable, unsolvable, dissolvable **5.** unresolvable, indissolvable.

OLV'en–si– **3.** solvency **4.** insolvency, revolvency.

OM'ak–i– **3.** naumachy **4.** theomachy, logomachy, sciomachy, psychomachy, monomachy, tauromachy, pyromachy, duomachy **5.** iconomachy, centauromachy, gigantomachy **6.** alectryomachy.

OM'ath–i– **4.** philomathy, chrestomathy.

OM'en–a– **4.** phenomena **5.** prolegomena **6.** antilegomena, paralipomena.

OM'et–er– **4.** tribometer, oncometer, pedometer, speedometer, ondometer, udometer, geometer, rehometer, ergometer, tachometer, graphometer, bathometer, stethometer, cyclometer, kilometer, sillometer, bolometer, stylometer, pulmometer, chromometer, tromometer, thermometer, seismometer, osmometer, atmometer, cymometer, zymometer, planometer, manometer, pychometer, clinometer, vinometer, phonometer, monometer, chronometer, sonometer, tonometer, oometer, tropometer, hippometer, barometer, vibrometer, ombrometer, macrometer, micrometer, dendrometer, hydrometer, spherometer, hygrometer, psychrometer, chirometer, spirometer, orometer, horometer, spectrometer, nitrometer, astrometer, pyrometer, gasometer, pulsometer, drosometer, hypsometer, passometer, lactometer, stactometer, hectometer, altometer, pantometer, photometer, comptometer, haptometer, leptometer, optometer, cyrtometer, cryometer **5.** tacheometer, oleometer, areometer, stereometer, heliometer, craniometer, variometer, fluviometer, pluviometer, oscillometer, scintillometer, dynamometer, anemometer, arithmometer, galvanometer, salinometer, declinometer, inclinometer, actinometer, harmonometer, micronometer, respirometer, electrometer, opisometer, thallasometer, climatometer, chromatometer, pneumatometer, thanatometer, olfactometer, refractometer, magnetometer, piezometer, horizometer **6.** diaphanometer, sphygmomanometer.

OM′et–ri– **3.** maumetry **4.** geometry, rheometry, Mahometry, stichometry, pyschometry, morphometry, orthometry, biometry, cyclometry, colometry, thermometry, pneumometry, planometry, phonometry, chronometry, tonometry, typometry, barometry, micrometry, hydrometry, gygrometry, horometry, chorometry, astrometry, pyrometry, gasometry, isometry, hypsometry, photometry, autometry **5.** areometry, stereometry, osteometry, cardiometry, stoichiometry, craniometry, anemometry, uranometry, galvanometry, trigonometry, ozonometry, anthropometry, electrometry, piezometry **6.** historiometry.

OM′ik–al– **3.** domical, comical **4.** atomical, phantomical **5.** tragicomical, economical, agronomical, metronomical, astronomical, anatomical, zootomical **6.** uneconomical.

OM′in–al– **3.** nominal **4.** abdominal, adnominal, praenominal, cognominal, pronominal, surnominal.

OM′in–ans– **3.** dominance, prominence **4.** predominance.

OM′in–ant– **3.** dominant, prominent **4.** subdominant, predominant **5.** superdominant.

OM′in–at– **3.** dominate, comminate, nominate **4.** abominate, predominate, denominate, renominate, prenominate, innominate.

OM′in–i– **3.** dominie, hominy, Romany **5.** Chickahominy.

OM′in–us– **3.** ominous, dominus **4.** abdominous, binominous.

OMN′i–a– **3.** omnia **4.** insomnia.

OM′un–ist– **3.** communist **4.** noncommunist **5.** anticommunist.

OND′en–si– **4.** despondency **5.** correspondency.

OND′er–er– **3.** launderer, ponderer, wanderer, squanderer.

OND′er–ing– **3.** laundering, pondering, wandering, squandering.

OND′er–us– **3.** ponderous **4.** preponderous **5.** equiponderous.

ON′i–er– **3.** bonnier, tawnier, brawnier, scrawnier.

ON′i–est– **3.** bonniest, tawniest, brawniest, scrawniest.

ON′if–i– **3.** bonify **4.** saponify, personify, ozonify.

ON′ik–a– **3.** Monica **4.** harmonica, japonica, Veronica.

ON′ik–al– **3.** conical, chronicle, tonical **4.** euphonical, iconical, mnemonical, harmonical, canonical, ironical, synchronical, thrasonical **5.** cosmogonical, histrionical, diaphonical, tautophonical, geoponical.

ON′im-i- **3.** onymy **4.** homonymy, synonymy, eponymy, toponymy, patronymy, metronymy, metonymy; *see* also **ON′om-i-** morphonomy etc. below.

ON′im-ist- **4.** synonymist, eponymist; *see* also **ON′om-ist-** economist etc. below.

ON′im-us- **3.** onymous **4.** anonymous, pseudonymous, eponymous, homonymous, synonymous, paronymous, autonymous **5.** heteronymous.

ON′ing-li- **3.** fawningly, yawningly.

ON′ish-ing- **3.** monishing **4.** admonishing, premonishing, astonishing.

ON′ish-ment- **4.** admonishment, premonishment, astonishment.

ON′is-izm- **4.** sardonicism, laconicism, teutonicism **5.** histrionicism.

ON′it-or- **3.** monitor **4.** admonitor, premonitor.

ON′o-graf- **3.** phonograph, monograph, tonograph, chronograph.

ON′o-gram- **3.** monogram, chronogram, tonogram.

ON′om-er- **4.** astronomer, gastronomer.

ON′om-i- **4.** morphonomy, economy, agronomy, astronomy, gastronomy, isonomy, taxonomy, nosonomy, autonomy **5.** dactylonomy, anthroponomy, Deuteronomy; *see* also **ON′im-i-** onymy etc. above.

ON′om-ist- **4.** economist, synonymist, eponymist, agronomist, gastronomist, autonomist, plutonomist.

ON′om-iz- **4.** economize, astronomize, gastronomize, autonomize.

ONS′ul-ar- **3.** consular **4.** nonconsular, proconsular, vice-consular.

ONT′ing-li- **3.** dauntingly, hauntingly, tauntingly, vauntingly, wantingly.

OP′ath-i- **4.** theopathy, psychopathy, allopathy, somnopathy, hydropathy, neuropathy, autopathy **5.** homoeopathy, osteopathy, deuteropathy.

OP′ath-ist- **4.** psychopathist, allopathist, hylopathist, somnopathist, hydropathist, neuropathist **5.** homoeopathist, osteopathist.

OP′er-i- **3.** foppery, coppery **4.** zoopery.

OP′i-er- **3.** choppier, copier, floppier, sloppier, soppier.

OP′i-est- **3.** choppiest, hoppiest, floppiest, sloppiest, soppiest.

OP′i-ist- **3.** copyist.

OP′ik-al- **3.** tropical, topical **4.** subtropical **5.** microscopical, philanthropical, misanthropical.

OP′i-ness- **3.** choppiness, floppiness, sloppiness, soppiness.

OP′ol-is- **3.** propolis **4.** cosmopolis, acropolis, necropolis, metropolis **5.** Heliopolis.

OP′ol-ist- **4.** monopolist **5.** bibliopolist, pharmacopolist.

OP′ol-it- **4.** cosmopolite, metropolite.

OPT′ik-al- **3.** optical **4.** autoptical.

OPT′im-ist- **3.** optimist.

OP′ul-us- **3.** opulus, populous **4.** unpopulous.

OR′ak-l- **3.** oracle, coracle; *see* also **OR′ik-al-** oracle etc. below.

OR′al-i- **3.** morally **4.** immorally, unmorally.

OR′al-ist- **3.** coralist, moralist.

ORD′er-ing- **3.** ordering, bordering **4.** reordering, embordering.

ORD′er-li- **3.** orderly **4.** unorderly, disorderly.

ORD′i-al- **3.** cordial **4.** primordial, exordial.

ORD′i-an- **3.** Gordian **4.** accordion, Edwardian.

ORD′in-al- **3.** ordinal **4.** biordinal, diordinal.

ORD′in-at- **3.** ordinate **4.** subordinate, inordinate, co-ordinate, foreordinate **5.** insubordinate, in-co-ordinate, un-co-ordinate.

OR'e-at- **3.** aureate, laureate **5.** baccalaureate, poet laureate.

OR'gan-iz- **3.** organize, gorgonize **4.** reorganize, disorganize.

OR'i-an- **3.** saurian, taurian **4.** centaurian **5.** dinosaurian, morosaurian.

OR'id-er- **3.** corridor.

OR'id-li- **3.** horridly, floridly, torridly.

OR'i-er- **3.** sorrier, warrior, quarrier.

OR'if-i- **3.** aurify, horrify, torrefy **4.** calorify, historify.

OR'i-form- **3.** floriform, moriform, poriform **4.** arboriform, vaporiform.

OR'ik-al- **3.** oracle, coracle **4.** rhetorical, historical **5.** meteorical, anaphorical, metaphorical, allegorical, categorical, tautegorical, oratorical.

OR'it-i- **4.** priority, majority, minority, sonority, sorority, authority **5.** meliority, seniority, juniority **6.** inferiority, superiority, deteriority, anteriority, interiority, exteriority, posteriority.

ORM'a-bl- **3.** formable, warmable, stormable **4.** informable, conformable, performable, transformable, unwarmable.

ORM'al-iz- **3.** formalize, normalize **4.** informalize.

ORM'at-iv- **3.** dormitive, formative **4.** afformative, deformative, reformative, informative, transformative.

ORM'it-i- **4.** deformity, conformity, abnormity, enormity **5.** uniformity, multiformity, nonconformity, inconformity, unconformity.

OR'o-er- **3.** borrower, sorrower.

OR'o-ing- **3.** borrowing, morrowing, sorrowing.

ORS'a-bl- **3.** forcible **4.** endorsable, enforceable, divorceable.

ORSH'un-al- **3.** torsional **4.** abortional, contortional, distortional.

ORSH'un-ist- **4.** contortionist, extortionist.

ORT'a-bl- **3.** sortable **4.** unsortable, distortable; *see* also **ORT'a-bl-** courtable etc.

ORT'at-tiv- **3.** hortative **4.** dehortative, exhortative.

ORT'if-i- **3.** fortify, mortify **4.** defortify, refortify.

ORT'ik-al- **3.** cortical, vortical.

ORT'un-it- **3.** fortunate **4.** unfortunate, misfortunate, importunate.

OS'for-us- **3.** Bosphorus, phosphorus, phosphorous.

OS'i-bl- **3.** possible **4.** impossible, compossible, unpossible.

OS'i-er- **3.** bossier, flossier, glossier, mossier, saucier.

OS'i-est- **3.** bossiest, flossiest, glossiest, mossiest, sauciest.

OS'i-ness- **3.** bossiness, glossiness, mossiness, sauciness.

OS'it-i- **3.** docity, paucity, raucity **4.** gibbosity, globosity, verbosity, precocity, jocosity, hircosity, viscosity, muscosity, mucosity, nodosity, fungosity, regosity, velocity, pilosity, callosity, villosity, gulosity, rimosity, fumosity, venosity, spinosity, vinosity, pomposity, ferocity, serosity, porosity, atrocity, neurocity, aquosity, nivosity **5.** bellicosity, varicosity, vitreosity, dubiosity, graciosity, speciosity, preciosity, grandiosity, seriosity, curiosity, furiosity, vitiosity, otiosity, fabulosity, sabulosity, nebulosity, rugulosity, scrupulosity, animosity, arenosity, luminosity, glutinosity, tenebrosity, tuberosity, ponderosity, generosity, vaporosity, reciprocity, unctuosity, fructuosity, virtuosity, tortuosity, flexuosity **6.** religiosity, ridiculosity, meticulosity, fuliginosity, voluminosity, vociferosity, anfractuosity, infructuosity, impetuosity **7.** impecuniosity.

OSK'op-i- **3.** nauscopy **4.** stethoscopy, necroscopy, microscopy, horoscopy, brontoscopy, spectroscopy, gastroscopy, autoscopy, cryoscopy **5.** stereoscopy, ornithoscopy, radioscopy, cranioscopy, dactyloscopy, ophthalmoscopy, lecanoscopy, organoscopy, uranoscopy, retinoscopy, ceraunoscopy, metoposcopy, hieroscopy, deuteroscopy, fluoroscopy **6.** meteoroscopy.

OSK′op–ist– **4.** microscopist, stethoscopist, misoscopist **5.** stereoscopist, metoposcopist, oneiroscopist, ornithoscopist.

OS′of–er– **4.** theosopher, philosopher, psilosopher, misosopher.

OS′of–i– **4.** gymnosophy, theosophy, philosophy, psilosophy, misosophy.

OS′of–ist– **4.** gymnosophist, theosophist, philosophist, chirosophist, misosophist.

OS′of–iz– **4.** theosophize, philosophize.

OST′ik–al– **4.** agnostical, acrostical.

OST′is–izm– **3.** Gnosticism **4.** agnosticism, acrosticism.

OST′rof–e– **4.** monostrophe, apostrophe.

OT′an–i– **3.** botany, cottony **4.** monotony.

OT′er–er– **3.** slaughterer, totterer, waterer.

OT′er–i– **3.** cautery, lottery, pottery, tottery, watery.

OT′er–ing– **3.** slaughtering, tottering, watering.

OTH′es–is– **3.** prothesis **4.** apothesis, hypothesis.

OT′i–er– **3.** haughtier, naughtier, squattier.

OT′i–est– **3.** haughiest, naughtiest, squattiest.

OT′ik–al– **3.** nautical **4.** biotical, despotical, erotical, exotical **5.** anecdotical, idiotical.

OT′il–i– **3.** dottily, haughtily, naughtily, spottily, squattily.

OT′il–us– **3.** nautilus.

OT′i–ness– **3.** dottiness, haughtiness, naughtiness, knottiness, spottiness, squattiness.

OT′is–izm– **4.** eroticism, neuroticism, exoticism.

OT′om–i– **3.** scotomy **4.** strabotomy, phlebotomy, dichotomy, trichotomy, cyclotomy, helotomy, aplotomy, tenotomy, zootomy, apotome, microtomy, nephrotomy, neurotomy, autotomy, phytotomy, loxotomy **5.** tracheotomy, stereotomy, osteotomy, cardiotomy, herniotomy, pogonotomy, anthropotomy, laparotomy, Caesarotomy, enterotomy, ichthyotomy, Ichthyotomi.

OT′on–i– **4.** homotony, monotony, chirotony.

OV′el–er– **3.** hoveler, groveler.

OV′el–ing– **3.** hoveling, groveling.

OZ′a–bl– **3.** causable, plausible **4.** implausible, unplausible.

OZ′it–iv– **3.** causative, positive **4.** appositive, depositive, prepositive, compositive, expositive, transpositive, suppositive.

OZ′it–or– **4.** depositor, repositor, compositor, expositor, transpositor.

OZ′it–um– **4.** depositum, suppositum.

OO (good)

1.

SINGLE (MASCULINE) RHYMES IN OO (good)

Primary or Secondary Accent Falls on Last Syllable; Imperfect Rhymes Are in Italics.

OOD– **1.** good, hood, could, should, stood, wood, would **2.** *manhood*, unhood, *monkshood*, *knighthood*, withstood, *scrubwood*, *beechwood*, *deadwood*, *wildwood*, *dogwood*, *cordwood*, *plywood*, *wormwood*, *gumwood*, *teakwood*, *greenwood*, *firewood*, *rosewood*, *driftwood* **3.** babyhood, hardihood, likelihood, livelihood, womanhood, maidenhood, widowhood, sisterhood, spinsterhood, fatherhood, motherhood, brotherhood, parenthood, understood, sandalwood, satinwood, cottonwood, underwood **4.** misunderstood.

OOF– **1.** oof, phoof [both slang], woof.

OOK– **1.** book, hook, cook, cuck [dial.], look, lug, lugh, hook, snook, rook, brook, crook, shook, took, zook [slang] **2.** *cookbook*, sambuk, fonduk, unhook, *fishhook*, *outlook*, Chinook, forsook, ursuk, betook, partook, mistook **3.** pocketbook, tenterhook, overlook, inglenook, undertook, overtook.

OOL– **1.** Ull, bull, full, pull, Pul, rull, shul, wool **2.** *bulbul*, *dreadful*, *handful*, *bodeful*, *gleeful*, half-full, *guileful*, *baneful*, *tuneful*, *useful*, *houseful*, *rueful*, *eyeful*, *wrongful*, *watchful*, *bashful*, *wishful*, *loathful*, *wrathful*, *healthful*, *slothful*, *mirthful*, *mouthful*, *sackful*, *bookful*, *forkful*, *soulful*, *brimful*, *roomful*, *manful*, *sinful*, *helpful*, *cupful*, *carful*, *chanceful*, *glassful*, *hatful*, *boatful*, *doubtful*, *tactful*, *artful*, *hurtful*, *boastful*, *joyful*, *wirepull* [coll.], *lamb's-wool* **3.** semibull, chrysobull, tableful, thimbleful, purposeful, meaningful, stomachful, fanciful, merciful, pitiful, plentiful, bountiful, barrelful, shovelful, teaspoonful, worshipful, teacupful, wonderful, tumblerful, masterful, platterful, colorful, overfull, powerful, prayerful, pocketful, bucketful, sorrowful, bellyful [vulgar].

OOLF– **1.** wolf **2.** *aardwolf*, *werewolf* **3.** demiwolf.

OOM– **1.** room, broom, groom, whom **2.** *bedroom*, *tearoom*, *cookroom* *cloakroom*, *ballroom*, *greenroom*, *gunroom*, *spare room*, *wareroom*, *barroom*, *storeroom*, *classroom*, *stateroom*, *coatroom*, *courtroom*, *East room*, *bathroom*, *mushroom*, whisk broom, *bridegroom* **3.** coffeeroom, anteroom, sitting room, elbowroom; *see* also **UM–** boom etc.

OOS– **1.** puss **2.** *couscous*, sour puss [slang].

OOSH– **1.** bush, cush, push **2.** *peabush*, *shadbush*, *spicebush*, *smokebush*, *twinebush*, *sloebush*, *forebush*, *horsebush*, *lotebush*, *dogbush*, *buckbush*, *gallbush*, *pearlbush*, *ambush*, *pinbush*, *hempbush*, *kinksbush*, *goatbush*, *saltbush*, *squawbush*, *jewbush*, *snowbush*, *maybush*, *rosebush*, *kiddush* **3.** coffeebush, hobblebush, bramblebush, needlebush, brittlebush, flannelbush, buttonbush, sugarbush, soldierbush, pepperbush, fetterbush.

OOT– **1.** foot, put, soot **2.** afoot, *webfoot*, *lobefoot*, *clubfoot*, *padfoot*, *spadefoot*, *three-foot*, *Blackfoot*, *foalfoot*, *fanfoot*, *crowfoot*, *barefoot*, *forefoot*, *four-foot*, *two-foot*, *crossfoot*, *plotfoot*, *coltsfoot*, *six-foot* **3.** pussyfoot, tenderfoot, underfoot.

OO (good)

2.

DOUBLE (FEMININE) RHYMES IN OO (hood′ed)

Primary or Secondary Accent Falls on Next to Last Syllable; Imperfect Rhymes Are in Italics.

OOD′ed– 2. hooded, wooded 3. unhooded, unwooded, red-wooded, thick-wooded, well-wooded, dense-wooded, soft-wooded, copsewooded.

OOD′en– 2. wooden.

OOD′i– 2. hoodie, goody, woody 4. goody-goody.

OOD′ing– 2. gooding, hooding, pudding.

OOG′ar– 2. booger [dial.], sugar 3. loaf sugar, cane sugar, spun sugar, brown sugar, beet sugar 4. maple sugar.

OOG′i– 2. boogey, luggie 4. boogey-woogey [slang].

OOK′ed– 2. hooked, crooked.

OOK′er– 2. booker, hooker, cooker, looker, snooker, rooker, stooker 3. on-looker 4. overlooker.

OOK′i– 2. booky, bookie, hooky, cooky, rooky, brooky, stookie.

OOK′ing– 2. booking, hooking, cooking, looking, rooking, brooking, crooking 3. rebooking, unhooking, good-looking, on-looking 4. overlooking.

OOK′ish– 2. bookish, hookish, cookish, rookish.

OOK′let– 2. booklet, nooklet, brooklet.

OOL′en– 2. pullen, woolen.

OOL′er– 2. buller, fuller, puller 3. wire-puller [coll.].

OOL′est– 2. fullest.

OOL′et– 2. bullet, pullet.

OOL′i– 2. bully, fully, mulley, pulley, woolly.

OOL′ing– 2. bulling, pulling 3. wire-pulling [coll.].

OOL′ish– 2. bullish, fullish, woollish.

OOM′an– 2. woman 3. horsewoman, washwoman 4. gentlewoman.

OOSH′er– 2. busher, pusher 3. pen-pusher 4. pedal-pusher.

OOSH′un– 2. cushion 3. recushion.

OOS′i– 2. pussy.

OOST′er– 2. Worcester.

OOT′ed– 2. footed, sooted 3. splayfooted, web-footed, clubfooted, big-footed, wing-footed, dog-footed, duck-footed, lame-footed, one-footed, barefooted, four-footed, sure-footed, catfooted, flat-footed, left-footed, swift-footed, light-footed, right-footed, claw-footed, two-footed 4. nimble-footed, cloven-footed, slender-footed, feather-footed, pussyfooted.

OOT′er– 2. footer, putter 3. webfooter, four-footer, six-footer 4. pussyfooter.

OOT′i– 2. footy, sooty.

OOT′ing– 2. footing, putting, sooting 4. pussyfooting.

OOZ′i– 2. woozy [slang].

OO (good)

3.

TRIPLE RHYMES IN OO (wood′i-ness)

Primary or Secondary Accent Falls on Second from Last Syllable.

OOD′i-ness- **3.** goodiness, woodiness.

OOK′ed-ness- **3.** hookedness, crookedness.

OOK′er-i- **3.** bookery, cookery, nookery, rookery.

OOK′ish-li- **3.** bookishly, cookishly.

OOK′ish-ness- **3.** bookishness.

OOL′i-ness- **3.** wooliness.

OOL′ish-ness- **3.** bullishness.

OOM′an-li- **3.** womanly **4.** unwomanly **5.** gentlewomanly.

OOT′ed-ness- **4.** flat-footedness.

OOT′i-ness- **3.** snootiness, sootiness.

OI (boy)

1.

SINGLE (MASCULINE) RHYMES IN OI (boy)

Primary or Secondary Accent Falls on Last Syllable; Imperfect Rhymes Are in Italics.

OI– **1.** oy, oye [both Scot.], boy, buoy, foy, goy, goi, joy, coy, koi, loy, cloy, moy, Roy, troy, Troy, soy, toy **2.** *playboy, highboy, callboy, schoolboy, tomboy, doughboy, lowboy, messboy, bat boy, postboy, cowboy,* pakchoi, ahoy, *kill-joy,* enjoy, montjoy, decoy, alloy, deploy, employ, annoy, *viceroy,* destroy, travois, travoy, savoy, Savoy, convoy **3.** stableboy, altar boy, overjoy, hoi polloi [Gr.], Illinois, corduroy, Iroquois **4.** hobbledehoy, avoirdupois, padausoy.

OID– **1.** buoyed, joyed, Lloyd, Floyd, cloyed, sloyd, Freud, toyed, void **2.** rebuoyed, unbuoyed, *rhomboid, stromboid, globoid, cuboid,* enjoyed, decoyed, *sarcoid, discoid, muscoid, mycoid, gadoid, lambdoid, algoid, tringoid, spongoid, fungoid, conchoid, trochoid, scaphoid, xiphoid, lymphoid, typhoid,* alloyed, *haloid,* deployed, employed, *maskoid, squaloid, tabloid, cycloid, veloid, styloid, diploid, sigmoid, comoid, prismoid,* annoyed, *nanoid, sphenoid, glenoid, ctenoid, spinoid, crinoid, conoid, lunoid, cynoid, ooid, zooid, trappoid, vespoid, laroid, fibroid, android, dendroid, chondroid, spheroid, theroid, pteroid, Negroid, congroid, ochroid, nephroid, toroid, cuproid, astroid,* destroyed, avoid, devoid, *neuroid, thyroid, ursoid, deltoid, lentoid, mastoid, lithoid, ovoid, equoid, corvoid, hyoid, myoid, rhizoid* **3.** scaraboid, overjoyed, pinacoid, coracoid, helicoid, toxicoid, *didelphoid,* ornithoid, ophioid, cardioid, histioid, cephaloid, omphaloid, alkaloid, unalloyed, sepaloid, opaloid, petaloid, hyaloid, hypsiloid, reptiloid, coralloid, metalloid, crystalloid, mongoloid, unemployed, misemployed, cuculoid, celluloid, condyloid, dactyloid, entomoid, balanoid, melanoid, drepanoid, tetanoid, adenoid, solenoid, catenoid, *arachnoid,* echinoid, cyprinoid, platinoid, belonoid, salmonoid, coronoid, anthropoid, saccharoid, xanthocroid, cylindroid, amberoid, diphtheroid, antheroid, aneroid, bacteroid, asteroid, hysteroid, lemuroid, ankyroid, ellipsoid, prismatoid, rheumatoid, thanatoid, teratoid, planetoid, herpetoid, granitoid, *odontoid,* lacertoid, obovoid, ichthyoid, trapezoid **4.** pyramidoid, encephaloid, *epicycloid, varicelloid,* marioloid, tentaculoid, tuberculoid, albumenoid, gelatinoid, *tetrahedroid, octahedroid, polyhedroid, salamandroid,* rhinoceroid, hemispheroid, Melanochroid, meteoroid, *parathyroid* **5.** pachydermatoid.

OIF– **1.** coif, quoif.

OIK– **1.** hoick, yoick.

OIKS– **1.** hoicks, yoicks.

OIL– **1.** oil, boil, Boyle, Doyle, foil, goyle, goil [slang], coil, Coyle, moil, moyle, noil, poil, spoil, roil, broil, stroil, soil, toil, voile **2.** enoil, aboil, *gumboil, parboil, gargoyle,* accoil, recoil, uncoil, *trefoil, tinfoil,* despoil, *turmoil,* embroil, *subsoil, topsoil,* etoile, entoil, estoile **3.** multifoil, quaterfoil, counterfoil, disembroil, overtoil.

OILD– **1.** oiled, boiled, foiled, coiled,

moiled, spoiled, roiled, broiled, soiled, toiled **2.** unoiled, unboiled, hard-boiled, soft-boiled, parboiled, recoiled, uncoiled, despoiled, embroiled **3.** multifoiled, disembroiled, unembroiled, overtoiled.

OILZ– oils etc., *see* **OIL–** oil etc. above, plus "s" or "'s."

OIN– **1.** foin, join, coin, coign, quoin, loin, groin **2.** sainfoin, sagoin, adjoin, subjoin, rejoin, sejoin, enjoin, conjoin, disjoin, misjoin, recoin, eloign, purloin, sirloin, Des Moines, almoign, essoin **3.** surrejoin, interjoin, tenderloin, frankalmoign.

OIND– **1.** joined, coined, loined, poind **2.** adjoined, rejoined, enjoined, uncoined, purloined, strong-loined.

OINT– **1.** oint, joint, point **2.** unjoint, disjoint, *bluejoint*, anoint, appoint, *standpoint*, repoint, pour point, *pourpoint*, *bluepoint*, *viewpoint* **3.** reappoint, disappoint, needle-point, counterpoint, cover-point.

OIS– **1.** choice, Joyce, Royce, voice **2.** rejoice, Rolls Royce, *invoice* **3.** second choice.

OIST– **1.** foist, hoist, joist, moist, voiced **2.** rejoiced, revoiced, invoiced, unvoiced, *loud-voiced*, *low-voiced*, *weak-voiced*, *clear-voiced*, *harsh-voiced*, *sweet-voiced*, *soft-voiced*, *faint-voiced* **3.** dreamy-voiced, empty-voiced, feeble-voiced, hollow-voiced, silver-voiced, trumpet-voiced **4.** clarion-voiced.

OIT– **1.** doit, skoit [slang], moit, droit, toit, quoit **2.** dacoit, exploit, adroit, Detroit, Introit **3.** maladroit.

OIZ– boys etc. *see* **OI–** boy etc. above, plus "s" or "'s"; **1.** noise, poise, froise [dial.] **3.** Illinois, erminois, centipoise, equipoise, counterpoise, Iroquois **4.** avoirdupois.

OI (boy)

2.

DOUBLE (FEMININE) RHYMES IN OI (joy′ful)

Primary or Secondary Accent Falls on Next to Last Syllable; Imperfect Rhymes Are in Italics.

OI′al– 2. loyal, royal 3. unloyal, disloyal, viceroyal, unroyal, sur-royal 4. pennyroyal, chapel royal.

OI′ans– 2. buoyance, joyance 3. flamboyance, annoyance, chatoyance, prevoyance, clairvoyance.

OI′ant– 2. buoyant 3. flamboyant, unbuoyant, chatoyant, prevoyant, clairvoyant.

OID′al– 3. ooidal, zooidal, rhomboidal, cuboidal, typhoidal, discoidal, colloidal, cycloidal, sigmoidal, spheroidal, ovoidal 4. anthropoidal, asteroidal, saccharoidal 5. paraboloidal, hemispheroidal, elephantoidal, meteoroidal.

OID′ans– 2. voidance 3. avoidance 4. reavoidance.

OID′er– 2. moider, broider, voider 3. embroider, avoider.

OID′ik– 3. diploidic, spheroidic.

OI′er– 2. oyer, Boyer, foyer, coyer, toyer 3. enjoyer, decoyer, deployer, employer, annoyer, destroyer 4. self-employer, self-destroyer.

OI′est– 2. coyest.

OI′ful– 2. joyful 3. unjoyful 4. overjoyful.

OI′ij– 2. buoyage, voyage 3. alloyage.

OI′ing– 2. buoying, joying, coying, cloying, ploying, toying 3. enjoying, decoying, deploying, employing, annoying, destroying, envoying, convoying.

OI′ish– 2. boyish, coyish, toyish.

OIL′er– 2. oiler, boiler, foiler, coiler, moiler, spoiler, broiler, soiler, toiler 3. recoiler, uncoiler, despoiler, embroiler.

OIL′i– 2. oily, doily, coyly, noily, roily.

OIL′ing– 2. oiling, boiling, foiling, coiling, moiling, spoiling, roiling, broiling, soiling, toiling 3. recoiling, despoiling, embroiling.

OIL′ment– 3. despoilment, embroilment, entoilment.

OIL′som– 2. roilsome, toilsome.

OIM′ent– 2. cloyment, ployment 3. enjoyment, deployment, employment 4. unemployment.

OIND′er– 2. joinder, poinder 3. rejoinder, misjoinder 4. surrejoinder.

OIN′er– 2. joiner, coiner 3. rejoiner, enjoiner, conjoiner, purloiner.

OI′ness– 2. coyness.

OIN′ij– 2. coinage.

OIN′ing– 2. foining, joining, coining, groining, quoining 3. adjoining, rejoining, enjoining, disjoining, purloining.

OINT′ed– 2. jointed, pointed 3. unjointed, conjointed, disjointed, anointed, appointed, unpointed 4. unanointed, disappointed.

OINT′er– 2. jointer, pointer 3. unjointer, disjointer, anointer, appointer, appointor 4. disappointer.

OINT′ing– 2. jointing, pointing 3. disjointing, anointing, appointing 4. disappointing.

OINT'less– 2. jointless, pointless.

OINT'ment– 2. ointment 3. disjointment, anointment, appointment 4. reappointment, disappointment.

OIS'er– 2. choicer 3. rejoicer.

OIS'ing– 2. voicing 3. rejoicing, invoicing 4. unrejoicing.

OIS'less– 2. choiceless, voiceless 3. rejoiceless, invoiceless.

OI'som– 2. noisome, cloysome, toysome.

OIST'er– 2. oyster, foister, hoister, cloister, moister, roister 3. encloister.

OIST'ing– 2. foisting, hoisting, joisting.

OIT'ed– 2. doited, quoited 3. exploited 4. unexploited.

OIT'er– 2. goiter, loiter, quoiter 3. exploiter, adroiter 4. reconnoiter.

OIT'i– 3. dacoity 4. hoity-toity.

OI'us– 2. joyous 3. annoyous.

OIZ'ez– 2. noises, poises.

OIZ'on– 2. foison, poison 3. empoison.

OI (boy)

3.

TRIPLE RHYMES IN OI (loy'al-ty)

Primary or Secondary Accent Falls on Second from Last Syllable.

OI'a-bl- 3. buoyable 4. enjoyable, employable 5. unenjoyable.

OI'al-i- 3. loyally, royally 4. disloyally, unroyally.

OI'al-ist- 3. loyalist, royalist.

OI'al-ti- 3. loyalty, royalty 4. unloyalty, disloyalty, viceroyalty.

OI'an-si- 3. buoyancy 4. flamboyancy, chatoyancy, clairvoyancy.

OI'ant-li- 3. buoyantly 4. flamboyantly, clairvoyantly.

OID'a-bl- 3. voidable 4. avoidable 5. unavoidable.

OI'ing-li- 3. cloyingly, toyingly 4. annoyingly.

OI'ing-ness- 3. cloyingness 4. annoyingness.

OI'ish-ness- 3. boyishness, toyishness.

OIL'ing-ly- 3. boilingly, spoilingly, soilingly, toilingly 4. recoilingly.

OIN'a-bl- 3. joinable, coinable 4. unjoinable, disjoinable.

OINT'ed-li- 3. jointedly, pointedly 4. disjointedly.

OI'som-li- 3. noisomely, cloysomely, toysomely.

OIST'er-ing- 3. cloistering, roistering 4. uncloistering.

OIST'er-us- 3. boisterous, roisterous.

OIT'er-er- 3. loiterer 5. reconnoiterer.

OIT'er-ing- 3. loitering 5. reconnoitering.

OIZ'on-ing- 3. poisoning 4. empoisoning.

OU (how)

1.

SINGLE (MASCULINE) RHYMES IN OU (how)

Primary or Secondary Accent Falls on Last Syllable; Imperfect Rhymes Are in Italics.

OU– **1.** ow, bow, bough, chow, dhow, how, gow, ghow [both slang], Howe, jhow, cow, scow, plow, slough, mow, now, pow [slang], row, brow, frau, prow, sow, tau, thou, vow, wow **2.** miaow, Foochow, Soochow, *chowchow*, endow, *hoosegow* [slang], somehow, allow, *snowplow*, *haymow*, enow, erenow, *eyebrow*, *highbrow*, *kowtow*, avow, bowwow, *powwow* **3.** disendow, anyhow, reallow, disallow, reavow, disavow.

OUCH– **1.** ouch, couch, slouch, pouch, grouch, crouch, vouch **2.** avouch **3.** Scaramouch.

OUD– **1.** bowed, foud, cowed, dowd, loud, cloud, plowed, crowd, scrowd [slang], proud, shroud, stroud, vowed, wowed **2.** unbowed, endowed, aloud, allowed, becloud, encloud, replowed, unplowed, beshroud, enshroud, unshroud, avowed, bowwowed **3.** overcloud, overcrowd, unavowed, disavowed.

OUF– **1.** ouf, ouphe.

OUJ– **1.** gouge, scrouge.

OUL– **1.** owl, dowl, fowl, foul, howl, jowl, cowl, cowle, scowl, growl, prowl, yowl **2.** screech owl, afoul, befoul, *peafowl*, *seafowl*, encowl **3.** guinea fowl, waterfowl.

OULD– **1.** owled, fouled, howled, cowled, scowled, growled **2.** befouled, uncowled.

OUN– **1.** down, gown, clown, noun, brown, drown, frown, crown, town **2.** adown, *rubdown*, *touchdown*, *shakedown*, *comedown*, *moondown*, *sundown*, godown, *lowdown*, *showdown*, *nightgown*, renown, *pronoun*, embrown, nutbrown, uncrown, discrown, downtown, uptown, *Charlestown* **3.** upside-down, hand-me-down, tumbledown, eider-down.

OUND– **1.** bound, downed, found, hound, gowned, clowned, mound, pound, round, browned, drowned, frowned, ground, crowned, sound, wound **2.** abound, *hidebound*, rebound, *spellbound*, inbound, *icebound*, *eastbound*, *westbound*, outbound, *northbound*, *southbound*, redound, refound, dumbfound, confound, profound, *greyhound*, *bloodhound*, *wolfhound*, *horehound*, *foxhound*, renowned, impound, compound, propound, expound, around, aground, *background*, uncrowned, surround, resound, unsound, astound, resound **3.** unrenowned, triple-crowned, vantage ground, middle ground, pleasure ground, underground **4.** superabound, merry-go-round, burying ground.

OUNDZ– **1.** bounds, hounds, pounds, rounds, grounds, sounds, wounds, zounds.

OUNJ– **1.** lounge, scrounge.

OUNS– **1.** ounce, bounce, jounce, flounce, pounce, rounce, trounce **2.** announce, enounce, denounce, renounce, pronounce **3.** mispronounce.

OUNT– **1.** fount, count, mount **2.** account, recount, discount, miscount, *viscount*, amount, remount, surmount, dismount **3.** paramount, catamount, tantamount.

OUR– 1. our, hour, gaur, scour, lour, flour, sour 2. bescour, besour, devour.

OUS– 1. bouse, chouse, douse, gauss, house, louse, blouse, mouse, nous, grouse, souse 2. *clubhouse, madhouse, guardhouse, birdhouse, doghouse, workhouse, warehouse, storehouse, poorhouse, lighthouse, penthouse, outhouse, hothouse, dormouse, titmouse* 3. countinghouse, customhouse, summerhouse, slaughterhouse, chapter house, porterhouse, Mickey Mouse, flittermouse.

OUST– 1. oust, doused, bloused, roust, groused, soused.

OUT– 1. out, bout, doubt, gout, scout, lout, flout, clout, snout, pout, spout, rout, kraut, drought, grout, Prout, sprout, trout, shout, tout, stout 2. *hangout* [slang], *dugout, tryout, blackout, knockout, walkout, lookout, hereout, thereout, whereout, shutout,* without, throughout, about, redoubt, misdoubt, boy scout, eelpout, bespout, *downspout,* derout, devout 3. in-and-out, out-and-out, gadabout, roundabout, hereabout, thereabout, whereabout, knockabout, whirlabout, runabout, stirabout, rightabout, roustabout, waterspout, sauerkraut, undevout.

OUTH– 1. mouth, drouth, south 2. *hardmouth, frogmouth, snakemouth, flutemouth* 3. chiselmouth, cottonmouth.

OUTHD– 2. loudmouthed, bigmouthed, closemouthed.

OUTS– outs etc., *see* **OUT–** out etc. above, plus "s" or " 's."

OUZ– bows etc., *see* **OU–** ow etc. above, plus "s" or " 's"; 1. bouse, dowse, house, blouse, mouse, spouse, rouse, browse, drowse, souse, touse 2. rehouse, espouse, arouse, carouse.

OUZD– 1. housed, bloused, browsed, drowsed, soused 2. espoused, aroused, caroused.

OU (how)

2.

DOUBLE (FEMININE) RHYMES IN OU (a-vow'al)

Primary or Secondary Accent Falls on Next to Last Syllable; Imperfect Rhymes Are in Italics.

OU'al– 2. cowal 3. avowal 4. disavowal; *see* also **OU'el–** bowel etc. below.

OU'an– 2. gowan, rowan, rowen.

OU'ans– 3. allowance, avowance 4. disallowance, disavowance.

OU'ard– 2. Howard, coward.

OUCH'er– 2. coucher, sloucher, poucher, groucher, croucher, voucher 3. avoucher.

OUCH'i– 2. slouchy, pouchy, grouchy.

OUCH'ing– 2. couching, slouching, pouching, grouching, crouching, vouching 3. avouching.

OUCH'o– 2. Gaucho.

OUD'ed– 2. clouded, crowded, shrouded 3. beclouded, unclouded, enshrouded, unshrouded 4. unbeclouded, overclouded, overcrowded.

OUD'er– 2. chowder, louder, powder, crowder, prouder 3. clam chowder, gunpowder, face powder 4. baking powder.

OUD'est– 2. loudest, proudest.

OUD'i– 2. dowdy, Goudy, howdie, howdy, cloudy, rowdy, shroudy 3. pandowdy, cum laude 5. magna cum laude, summa cum laude.

OUD'ing– 2. clouding, crowding, shrouding 3. beclouding, enshrouding 4. overclouding, overcrowding.

OUD'ish– 2. loudish, proudish.

OUD'li– 2. loudly, proudly.

OU'el– 2. bowel, dowel, howel, nowel, Powell, rowel, trowel, towel, vowel 3. embowel, avowal 4. disembowel, disavowal, semivowel.

OU'en– 2. gowan, rowen, rowan.

OU'er– 2. bower, dower, cower, lower, flower, glower, plower, plougher, power, rower, shower, tower, vower 3. embower, endower, allower, beflower, deflower, lidflower, windflower, bloodflower, globeflower, fameflower, shoeflower, grapeflower, coneflower, horseflower, tongueflower, safflower, blackflower, snailflower, gallflower, wallflower, fanflower, swanflower, enflower, twinflower, moonflower, unflower, sunflower, cornflower, lampflower, mistflower, dayflower, Mayflower, empower, horse power, manpower, watchtower, church tower, avower 4. cauliflower, coralflower, passionflower, cuckooflower, tulipflower, honeyflower, gillyflower, Julyflower, candlepower, underpower, overpower, water power, overtower, disavower.

OU'es– 2. prowess.

OU'i– 2. dowie, cowy, yowie [slang], zowie [slang].

OU'ing– 2. bowing, cowing, ploughing, plowing, rowing, vowing 3. allowing, avowing 4. disallowing, disavowing.

OUL'er– 2. fouler, fowler, howler, scowler, growler, prowler, yowler.

OUL'est– 2. foulest.

OUL'et– 2. owlet, howlet, rowlet.

OUL'i– 2. owly, Rowley, growly.

OUL'ing– 2. fouling, fowling, howling, cowling, scowling, growling, prowling.

OUL'ish– 2. owlish, foulish.

OU'ment– 3. endowment, allowment, avowment 4. disavowment.

OUND'ed– 2. bounded, founded, hounded, mounded, pounded, rounded, grounded, sounded, wounded 3. abounded, rebounded, unbounded, redounded, dumfounded, confounded, well-founded, ill-founded, unfounded, impounded, compounded, propounded, expounded, surrounded, ungrounded, astounded, resounded 5. superabounded.

OUND'er– 2. bounder, founder, flounder, pounder, rounder, sounder 3. rebounder, dumfounder, confounder, profounder, impounder, compounder, propounder, expounder, surrounder, resounder.

OUND'est– 2. roundest, soundest 3. profoundest.

OUND'i– 2. houndy, woundy.

OUND'ij– 2. poundage, groundage, soundage 3. impoundage.

OUND'ing– 2. bounding, founding, hounding, pounding, rounding, grounding, sounding, wounding 3. abounding, rebounding, unbounding, redounding, dumfounding, confounding, impounding, compounding, propounding, expounding, resounding, loud-sounding, well-sounding, deep-sounding, clear-sounding, high-sounding, surrounding, resounding 4. evil-sounding 5. superabounding.

OUND'ingz– 2. groundings, soundings 3. surroundings.

OUND'less– 2. boundless, groundless, soundless.

OUND'li– 2. roundly, soundly 3. profoundly, unsoundly.

OUND'ling– 2. foundling, groundling.

OUND'ness– 2. roundness, soundness 3. profoundness, unsoundness.

OUND'rel– 2. scoundrel 3. archscoundrel.

OUND'ri– 2. foundry 4. iron foundry.

OUN'er– 2. browner, drowner, frowner, crowner 3. uptowner.

OUN'est– 2. brownest.

OUN'-i 2. downy, brownie, browny, frowny, towny.

OUN'ing– 2. downing, gowning, clowning, browning, Browning, drowning, frowning, crowning 3. encrowning, uncrowning, discrowning.

OUN'ish– 2. clownish, brownish, frownish, townish.

OUNJ'er– 2. lounger, scrounger.

OUNJ'ing– 2. lounging, scrounging.

OUN'less– 2. downless, gownless, frownless, crownless.

OUNS'er– 2. bouncer, flouncer, pouncer, trouncer 3. announcer, denouncer, renouncer, pronouncer.

OUNS'ez– 2. ounces, bounces, flounces, pounces, trounces 3. announces, denounces, pronounces.

OUNS'il– 2. council, counsel 3. recounsel.

OUNS'ing– 2. bouncing, flouncing, pouncing, trouncing 3. announcing, denouncing, renouncing, pronouncing 4. mispronouncing.

OUNS'ment– 3. announcement, enouncement, denouncement, renouncement, pronouncement 4. mispronouncement.

OUNT'ed– 2. counted, mounted 3. accounted, recounted, uncounted, discounted, miscounted, amounted, remounted, surmounted, dismounted.

OUNT'er– 2. counter, mounter 3. accounter, encounter, discounter, remounter, surmounter 4. re-encounter.

OUNT'ess– 2. countess 3. viscountess.

OUNT'i– 2. bounty, county, mounty 3. viscounty.

OUNT'in– 2. fountain, mountain 4. catamountain.

OUNT'ing– 2. counting, mounting 3. accounting, discounting, miscounting, amounting, surmounting, dismounting.

OUN'ward– 2. downward, townward.

OUR'er– 2. scourer, sourer 3. devourer.

OUR'est– 2. dourest, sourest.

OUR'i– 2. houri, dowry, cowrie, floury, flowery 3. avowry.

OUR'ing– 2. scouring, flouring, souring 3. beflouring, devouring.

OUR'li– 2. hourly, dourly, sourly 3. half-hourly.

OUR'ness– 2. dourness, sourness.

OUS'er– 2. douser, mouser, souser.

OUS'ez– 2. douses, louses, blouses, spouses, souses.

OUS'i– 2. blousy, mousey, spousy.

OUS'ing– 2. dousing, blousing, mousing, sousing.

OUST'er– 2. ouster, jouster, rouster.

OUST'ing– 2. ousting, rousting.

OUT'ed– 2. doubted, gouted, scouted, flouted, clouted, pouted, spouted, routed, sprouted, shouted, touted 3. undoubted, misdoubted, derouted, unsprouted.

OUT'er– 2. outer, doubter, douter, jowter, scouter, louter, flouter, clouter, pouter, spouter, router, sprouter, trouter, shouter, touter, stouter 3. devouter 4. in-and-outer, down-and-outer.

OUT'est– 2. stoutest 3. devoutest.

OUTH'i– 2. mouthy, drouthy.

OUTH'ing– 2. mouthing, southing 3. bemouthing.

OUT'i– 2. doughty, gouty, louty, snouty, pouty, spouty, droughty, grouty, trouty.

OUT'ing– 2. outing, doubting, scouting, flouting, clouting, pouting, spouting, routing, grouting, sprouting, shouting, touting 3. undoubting, bespouting, derouting, rerouting, resprouting.

OUT'ish– 2. outish, loutish, stoutish.

OUT'let– 2. outlet, troutlet.

OUT'li– 2. stoutly 3. devoutly 4. undevoutly.

OUT'ness– 2. outness, stoutness 3. devoutness.

OU'wou– 2. bowwow, powwow, wouwou.

OUZ'al– 2. housal, spousal 3. espousal, arousal, carousal; *see* also **OUZ'l–** ouzel etc. below.

OUZ'er– 2. dowser, mouser, Mauser, schnauzer, rouser, browser, trouser, Towser 3. Tannhauser, espouser, arouser, carouser.

OUZ'ez– 2. houses, blouses, spouses, rouses, browses 3. espouses, arouses, carouses.

OUZ'i– 2. bousy, housy, lousy, blowsy, mousy, drowzy, frowzy, grousy.

OUZ'ij– 2. housage, spousage 3. espousage.

OUZ'ing– 2. dowzing, housing, blowzing, mousing, rousing, browsing, drowsing 3. espousing, arousing, carousing.

OUZ'l– 2. ouzel, housal, housel, mousle, spousal, tousle 3. espousal, carousal.

OU (how)

3.

TRIPLE RHYMES IN OU (al-low'a-ble)

Primary or Secondary Accent Falls on Second from Last Syllable.

OU'a-bl- 4. endowable, allowable, avowable 5. unallowable, disallowable, unavowable, disavowable.

OU'a-bli- 4. allowably, avowably 5. unallowably, unavowably.

OUD'ed-ness- 3. cloudedness, crowdedness 4. uncloudedness 5. overcrowdedness.

OUD'il-i- 3. dowdily, cloudily, rowdily.

OUD'i-ness- 3. dowdiness, cloudiness, rowdiness.

OU'er-er- 3. flowerer, glowerer, showerer.

OU'er-i- 3. bowery, Bowery, dowery, lowery, flowery, glowery, showery, towery.

OU'er-ing- 3. dowering, cowering, lowering, flowering, glowering, showering, towering 4. deflowering, empowering 5. overpowering, overtowering.

OU'er-less- 3. dowerless, flowerless, powerless.

OUL'er-i- 3. owlery, fowlery.

OUND'a-bl- 3. groundable, soundable 4. confoundable, impoundable, compoundable, astoundable.

OUND'ed-li- 3. roundedly 4. unboundedly, dumfoundedly, confoundedly 5. unconfoundedly.

OUND'ed-ness- 3. roundedness 4. unboundedness, dumfoundedness, confoundedness, unfoundedness, ungroundedness.

OUND'ing-li- 4. aboundingly, confoundingly, astoundingly.

OUND'less-li- 3. boundlessly, groundlessly, soundlessly.

OUND'less-ness- 3. boundlessness, groundlessness, soundlessness.

OUNT'a-bl- 3. countable, mountable 4. accountable, discountable, uncountable, surmountable 5. unaccountable, insurmountable, unsurmountable.

OUNT'a-bli- 4. accountably 5. unaccountably, insurmountably, unsurmountably.

OUT'i-ness- 3. doughtiness, goutiness, spoutiness, droughtiness.

OUZ'il-i- 3. drowsily, frowsily.

OUZ'i-ness- 3. lousiness, drowziness, frowziness.

OUZ'ing-li- 3. rousingly 4. carousingly.

U (you)

1.

SINGLE (MASCULINE) RHYMES IN U (you)

Primary or Secondary Accent Falls on Last Syllable; Imperfect Rhymes Are in Italics.

U– **1.** u, U, ewe, yew, you **2.** bayou **3.** w, W, double-u.

BU– **1.** boo **2.** Abou, abu, aboo, *baboo*, *babu*, taboo, tabu, yabu, yaboo, debut, bamboo, imbue, *zebu* **3.** bugaboo, peekaboo, marabou, caribou.

CHU– **1.** chew **2.** kachoo, *choo-choo* [slang], kerchoo, eschew **3.** catechu.

DU– **1.** do, due, dew **2.** ado, adieu, subdue, bedew, redo, skiddoo [slang], *mildew*, chandoo, chandu, endew, endue, rendu [F.], vendue, indue, *Hindu*, undo, perdu, perdue, Purdue, fordo, foredo, misdo, outdo, *hoodoo*, to-do, *voodoo* **3.** billet-doux, derring-do, how-dy-do [coll.], honeydew, residue, underdo, overdo, overdue, well-to-do.

FU– **1.** fu, fou [Scot. & dial. Eng.], fou [F.], few, feu, phew, phoo **2.** mafoo, mafu, phoo-phoo, *curfew* **3.** feverfew.

GU– **1.** goo, gout [F.] **2.** ragout [F.], burgoo, burgout, googoo.

HU– **1.** hoo, who, Hu, hue, hew, Hugh **2.** ahu, *wahoo*, *Yahoo*, boohoo, yoohoo **3.** ballyhoo [slang], Elihu.

JU– **1.** Jew **2.** *baju* [Malay], bijou, *juju* **3.** acajou, kinkajou, sapajou.

KU– **1.** coo, coup, q, Q, cue, queue, skew **2.** *aku*, *baku*, *cuckoo*, *coo-coo* [slang], askew **3.** barbecue.

LU– **1.** loo, Lu, Lou, lieu, blue, blew, flu, flue, flew, glue, clue, clew, slue, slew **2.** halloo, sky-blue, true-blue, *igloo*, unglue, *tolu*, *curlew*, *purlieu*, *Lulu*, *Sulu*, *Zulu* **3.** ululu **4.** hullabaloo.

MU– **1.** moo, mu, mew, smeu, smew **2.** *emu*, *immew*, *limu*, *umu*.

NU– **1.** new, knew, nu, Nu, gnu, nous [F.] **2.** anew, *Danu*, canoe, renew, *venue*, *fire-new*, foreknew **3.** ingénue, entre nous [F.], avenue, revenue, parvenu, hoochinoo, detinue, retinue **4.** Tippecanoe.

PU– **1.** pu, pugh, pew, pooh, poo [Scot. & dial. Eng.], spew **2.** *napoo*, shampoo, rompu, pooh-pooh.

RU– **1.** rue, roux [F.], brew, bruh [Malay], drew, grew, grue [dial.], crew, cru [F.], screw, sprew, sprue, true, strew, shrew, through, threw **2.** karroo, imbrue, withdrew, Peru, *froufrou*, accrue, *corkscrew*, *thumbscrew*, unscrew, untrue, bestrew, construe **3.** kangaroo, buckaroo, gillaroo, wallaroo, wanderoo, potoroo, reconstrue, misconstrue, overstrew, overthrew.

SU– **1.** sue, Sue, sou, Sioux, Soo **2.** the Soo, ensue, pursue **3.** aperçu [F.], Daibutsu.

SHU– **1.** shoo, shoe **2.** cachou, cashoo, cashew, *fichu*, *snowshoe*, *horseshoe* **3.** overshoe.

TU– **1.** to, too, two, tu [L.], stew **2.** battue, tattoo, *Bantu*, *Gentoo*, *lean-to*, unto, hereto, thereto, whereto, *set-to*, surtout, virtu **3.** cockatoo, *in situ* [L.]

rumtytoo, Timbuktu, hereunto, thereunto, whereunto, *impromptu*, passe partout, hitherto, thitherto, whitherto **4.** intransitu [L.].

VU– **1.** view, vous [F.] **2.** review, revue, *preview*, *kivu*, *purview* **3.** rendezvous, interview.

WU– **1.** woo, Wu, whoo, whew.

YU– **1.** you, ewe, yew **2.** bayou **3.** I. O. U.

ZU– **1.** zoo, Zu **2.** kazoo, razoo, cousu [F.], zoozoo **4.** Kalamazoo.

UB– **1.** boob [slang], doob, jube, cube, Rube, rube [slang], tube **2.** jujube **3.** inner tube.

UCH– **1.** ooch, hooch, cooch, mooch, mouch, smooch, smouch, pooch [all slang], brooch.

UD– **1.** booed, chewed, dude, food, feud, hued, Jude, cued, queued, lewd, looed, blued, flued, flewed, glued, slued, slewed, mood, mooed, nude, snood, rude, rued, rood, brood, brewed, crude, screwed, prude, trued, shrewd, shood, shooed, stewed, thewed, viewed, wooed **2.** tabooed, imbued, eschewed, miscued, unglued, allude, elude, delude, prelude, illude, collude, postlude, preclude, seclude, include, conclude, occlude, exclude, almud, subnude, denude, renewed, shampooed, abrood, imbrued, accrued, unscrewed, obtrude, subtrude, detrude, retrude, intrude, protrude, construed, extrude, resued, pursued, etude, reviewed, previewed, unwooed, exude, transude **3.** reimbued, unimbued, unsubdued, interlude, unrenewed, misconstrued, unpursued, hebetude, quietude, desuetude, mansuetude, consuetude, habitude, longitude, solitude, amplitude, lenitude, plenitude, magnitude, omnitude, torpitude, turpitude, nigritude, lassitude, crassitude, spissitude, latitude, rectitude, sanctitude, altitude, multitude, lentitude, aptitude, promptitude, certitude, fortitude, pinguitude, servitude, gravitude **4.** inquietude disquietude, solicitude, similitude, definitude, decrepitude, vicissitude, exactitude.

UDZ– **1.** dudes, foods, feuds, Jude's, moods, nudes, snoods, roods, broods, prudes **3.** interludes, solitudes, latitudes, altitudes, multitudes.

UF– **1.** oof, boof, goof [all slang], hoof, loof, poof, pouf, spoof [slang], roof, proof, woof **2.** shadoof, behoof, aloof, reroof, reproof *foolproof*, *fireproof*, disproof, Tartufe **3.** cloven hoof, gable roof, bulletproof, waterproof.

UFT– **1.** hoofed, spoofed [slang], roofed, woofed **3.** cloven-hoofed, bulletproofed, waterproofed.

UG– **1.** boog [slang], fugue, fougue, goog [slang], toug.

UJ– **1.** huge, smoodge, rouge, Scrooge, scrouge, stooge [slang], vouge **3.** subterfuge, vermifuge, febrifuge.

UK– **1.** uke [slang], duke, douc, gook [slang], juke, cuke [slang], Luke, fluke, snook, puke, spook, sook, stook, yeuk, yewk, yuk, yuke **2.** rebuke, chibouk, bambuk, caoutchouc, archduke, beduke, Chinook, charuk, peruke **3.** octateuch, Pentateuch, Heptateuch, Hexateuch **4.** bashi-bazook.

UL– **1.** buhl, fool, ghoul, gool [dial.], cool, school, mewl, mool, mule, pool, pule, spool, rule, drool, tool, tulle, stool, Yule **2.** *jambool*, *jambul*, befool, *whirlpool*, slide rule, misrule, pasul, *toadstool*, *footstool* **3.** vestibule, Istambul, April-fool, molecule, ridicule, vermicule, reticule, Sunday school, swimming pool, wading pool, Liverpool, overrule.

ULZ– fools etc., *see* **UL–** buhl etc. above, plus "s" or "'s"; **1.** gules, Jules.

UM– **1.** boom, doom, doum, fume, ghoom, coom, coomb, loom, bloom, flume, gloom, plume, neume, spume, room, rheum, broom, brume, brougham, groom, grume, soum, tomb, womb, whom, zoom 2. predoom, foredoom, *perfume*, legume, inhume, exhume, illume, *heirloom*, embloom, begloom, engloom, beplume, deplume, displume, simoom, *bedroom*, *tearoom*, *cloakroom*, *ballroom*, *barrom*, *storeroom*, *stateroom*, *courtroom*, *mushroom*, *bridegroom*, assume, subsume, consume, entomb, *costume*, resume, presume 3. anteroom, reading room, dining room, drawing room, dressing room, living room, elbowroom, reassume, hecatomb, disentomb.

UMD– 1. doomed, loomed, bloomed, plumed, spumed, zoomed 2. exhumed 3. unassumed.

UMF– 1. pomph, foomph [both slang].

UMZ– booms etc., *see* **UM**– boom etc. above, plus "s" or "'s."

UN– 1. boon, Boone, doon, dune, foon [slang], goon [slang], hewn, June, coon, loon, lune, moon, noon, spoon, rune, croon, prune, strewn, soon, tune, toon, woon, wun, swoon 2. baboon, bridoon, typhoon, buffoon, lagoon, dragoon, Rangoon, Calhoun, unhewn, jejune, cacoon, lacune, racoon, tycoon, cocoon, balloon, galloon, shalloon, walloon, doubloon, immune, simoon, commune, midnoon, forenoon, lampoon, tampoon, harpoon, impugn, oppugn, expugn, teaspoon, maroon, gambroon, gadroon, spadroon, quadroon, seroon, patroon, poltroon, quintroon, bestrewn, bassoon, monsoon, gossoon, attune, platoon, ratoon, spittoon, altun, entune, pontoon, spontoon, cartoon, festoon, aswoon 3. rigadoon, barracoon, pantaloon, honeymoon, harvest moon, afternoon, tablespoon, macaroon, picaroon, octoroon, overstrewn, oversoon, coquetoon, musketoon, importune, opportune, picayune 4. intercommune, vinegarroon, inopportune.

UND– 1. mooned, spooned, runed, crooned, tuned, wound, swooned 2. Mahound, impugned, attuned, festooned.

UNZ– boons etc., *see* **UN**– boon etc. above, plus "s" or "'s."

UP– 1. boop [slang], dupe, Goop, hoop, jupe, coop, coup, scoop, loop, bloop [slang], cloop, sloop, noop [Scot. & dial. Eng.], snoop, poop, roup, drupe, droop, group, croup, scroop, troop, troupe, soup, supe [slang], stoop, stoep, stupe, stoup, swoop, whoop 2. recoup, saloop, adroop, aggroup 3. cock-a-hoop, Guadalupe, nincompoop, liripoop, loop-the-loop.

UPT– 1. duped, hooped, couped, cooped, scooped, looped, snooped, drooped, grouped, trouped, stooped, swooped, whooped 2. recouped, regrouped.

UR– 1. boor, dour, cure, lure, mure, moor, pure, poor, spoor, sure, tour, your, jour [F.] 2. endure, perdure, coiffure, bahur, nahoor, abjure, adjure, injure, conjure, secure, liqueur, procure, obscure, allure, velure, colure, amour, unmoor, demure, immure, *tenure*, inure, impure, assure, cocksure, ensure, insure, unsure, Ashur, brochure, mature, *detour*, *contour*, gravure, huzoor, causeur 3. perendure, sinecure, insecure, pedicure, manicure, epicure, chevelure, condylure, blackamoor, belamour, Kohinoor, connoisseur, reassure, reinsure, coinsure, cynosure, ligature, tablature, amateur, premature, immature, climature, armature, signature, curvature, comfiture, forfeiture, garniture, furniture, portraiture, sepulture, garmenture, aperture, overture, coverture, voyageur, abat-jour 4. miniature, judicature, temperature, literature, expenditure, discomfiture, divestiture, investiture, autogravure, photogravure, rotogravure.

URD– 1. gourde, cured, moored, toured 2. secured, obscured, endured, insured 3. unsecured, reassured, self-assured, unassured, immatured, uninsured.

URS– 1. bourse.

URZ– boors etc., *see* **UR**– boor etc. above, plus "s" or "'s."

US– 1. use, Duce, deuce, douce, goose, juice, luce, loose, sluice, moose, meuse, mousse, noose, pouce, puce, Bruce, cruse, spruce, truce, trousse, Zeus 2. abuse, caboose, traduce, educe, deduce, reduce, seduce, induce, conduce, produce, diffuse, profuse, *mongoose*, verjuice, excuse, unloose, recluse, occluse, vamoose [slang], burnoose, papoose, abstruse, disuse, misuse, obtuse, retuse, pertuse 3. calaboose, reproduce, introduce, Syracuse, catapuce, charlotte russe 4. superinduce, hypotenuse.

USH– 1. bouche, mouche, smush [dial.], ruche, whoosh 2. bonne bouche [F.], barouche, farouche [F.], cartouche 3. Scaramouch, gobe-mouche [F.].

UST– 1. boost, deuced, joust, loosed, noosed, roost, spruced 2. deduced, unloosed, vamoosed.

UT– 1. Ute, Butte, boot, beaut [slang], hoot, jute, coot, cute, scute, scoot, loot, lute, flute, cloot, plute [slang], sluit, moot, mute, smoot, newt, snoot, route, root, bruit, brute, fruit, soot, suit, chute, shoot, toot, tute 2. refute, confute, argute, cahoot [slang], Paiute, acute, galoot [slang], salute, dilute, pollute, volute, immute, commute, permute, transmute, Canute, minute, cornute, depute, repute, impute, compute, dispute, Rajput, imbrute, cheroot, enroot, en route, *breadfruit*, *grapefruit*, *starfruit*, recruit, nasute, dissuit, *lawsuit*, hirsute, pursuit, *offshoot*, *outshoot*, surtout, astute 3. marabout, attribute, retribute, subacute, persecute, execute, baldicoot, bandicoot, absolute, resolute, dissolute, obvolute, evolute, involute, convolute, Malemute, comminute, disrepute, arrowroot, orrisroot, demisuit, parachute, overshoot, substitute, destitute, institute, constitute 4. electrocute, irresolute.

UTH– 1. booth, couth, sleuth, ruth, Ruth, sooth, tooth, youth 2. uncouth, Duluth, thuluth, vermouth, untruth, forsooth 3. polling booth, voting booth.

UTHE– 1. smooth, soothe 2. besmooth, resoothe.

UTS– boots etc., *see* **UT–** Ute etc. above, plus "s" or "'s."

UV– 1. move, groove, prove, you've 2. behoove, amove, remove, ingroove, approve, reprove, improve, disprove 3. 3. reapprove, disapprove.

UVD– 1. moved, grooved, proved 2. behooved, ungrooved, approved, unproved 3. unremoved, unimproved.

UZ– 1. ooze, use, booze, boos, choose, chews, dues, fuze, fuse, guze, Hughes, Jews, coos, skuse [dial. & coll.], lose, blues, flews, flues, clues, mews, muse, meuse, news, gnus, snooze [coll.] ruse, bruise, brews, Druse, cruise, crews, cruse, trews, strews, sues, twos, stews, shoes, shoos, woos, whose, zoos 2. abuse, taboos, imbues, effuse, refuse, refuze, diffuse, infuse, confuse, perfuse, transfuse, suffuse, accuse, excuse, amuse, bemuse, canoes, shampoos, debruise, peruse, *corkscrews*, chartreuse, masseuse, misuse, danseuse, *horseshoes*, tattoos, Bantus, contuse, enthuse, kazoos 3. disabuse, circumfuse, interfuse, avenues, Vera Cruz, Santa Cruz.

UZD– 1. oozed, used, fused, snoozed, bruised, cruised 2. ill-used, unused, enthused 3. disabused, self-accused.

UZH– 1. rouge 3. Bruges, vouge.

U (you)

2.

DOUBLE (FEMININE) RHYMES IN U (du'al)

Primary or Secondary Accent Falls on Next to Last Syllable; Imperfect Rhymes Are in Italics.

U'a- **2.** skua **3.** ulua, atua **4.** punalua **10.** Apologia pro Vita Sua [L.].

U'al- **2.** dual **3.** eschewal, subdual, renewal, pursual, reviewal.

U'an- **2.** duan, Siouan, Chouan.

U'ans- **2.** nuance **3.** eschewance, renewance, pursuance.

U'ant- **2.** fluent, truant, suant **3.** perfluent, pursuant.

U'ard- **2.** Seward, steward.

UB'a- **2.** juba, Cuba, kuba, Luba, Nuba, subah, tsuba, tuba **3.** Baluba, saxtuba.

UB'al- **2.** Jubal, tubal.

UB'er- **2.** goober, cuber, Khubur, suber, tuber, tubar.

UB'i- **2.** booby, looby, ruby.

UB'ij- **2.** cubage, tubage.

UB'ik- **2.** cubic **3.** cherubic.

UB'ing- **2.** cubing, tubing.

UB'l- **2.** Jubal, ruble, tubal.

UB'let- **2.** cubelet, tubelet.

UB'rik- **2.** lubric, rubric.

UCH'er- **2.** blucher, moocher [slang], smoocher [slang].

UCH'i- **2.** smoochy [slang] **3.** Il Duce [It.], penuchi **4.** hootchy-kootchy [slang].

UD'a- **2.** Buddha, Judah, Nuda **3.** picuda, Bermuda **4.** barracuda.

UD'al- **2.** udal, feudal **3.** paludal.

UD'ed- **2.** snooded, brooded **3.** alluded, eluded, deluded, colluded, precluded, secluded, included, concluded, occluded, excluded, denuded, intruded, protruded, extruded, exuded, transuded **4.** undeluded, unterluded, unprotruded.

UD'ens- **2.** prudence **3.** imprudence **4.** jurisprudence.

UD'ent- **2.** prudent, student **3.** concludent, occludent, imprudent, protrudent **4.** jurisprudent.

UD'er- **2.** lewder, nuder, ruder, brooder, cruder, shrewder, sudor, Tudor **3.** eluder, deluder, includer, concluder, excluder, denuder, intruder, protruder.

UD'est- **2.** lewdest, nudest, rudest, crudest, shrewdest.

UD'i- **2.** boodie, feudy, moody, broody **3.** almude.

UD'ik- **2.** Sudic **3.** paludic.

UD'ing- **2.** brooding **3.** abrooding, alluding, eluding, deluding, precluding, including, concluding, occluding, excluding, denuding, intruding, protruding, exuding.

UD'ish- **2.** dudish, moodish, nudish, prudish, shrewdish.

UD'ist- **2.** Buddhist, feudist, nudist, prudist.

UD'l- **2.** boodle, doodle, [coll., dial & slang], coodle, noodle, nuddle [dial.], poodle, roodle, soodle **3.** caboodle [slang], flapdoodle [coll.]. **4.** Yankee-Doodle.

UD'li- **2.** lewdly, nudely, rudely, crudely, prudely, shrewdly, soodly.

UD'lz– boodles etc., *see* **UD'l–** boodle etc. above, plus "s" or "'s"; **2.** oodles [slang].

UD'ness– **2.** lewdness, nudeness, rudeness, crudeness, shrewdness.

UD'o– **2.** scudo, pseudo **3.** barbudo, picudo, escudo, testudo **4.** consuetudo [L.].

UD'or– **2.** sudor, Tudor.

UD'u– **2.** hoodoo, pudu, to-do, voodoo.

U'e– **2.** gooey [slang], hui, hooey [slang], cooee, blooey, bluey [both slang], fluey [rare], flooey [slang], gluey, tui; *see* also **U'i–** buoy etc. below.

U'el– **2.** duel, fuel, jewel, newel, Reuel, gruel, cruel, crewel, shewel, tewel **3.** bejewel.

U'ent– **2.** fluent **3.** confluent, perfluent.

U'er– **2.** ewer, chewer, doer, fewer, hewer, cooer, skewer, bluer, gluer, newer, ruer, brewer, screwer, truer, sewer, suer, shoer, tewer, stewer, viewer, wooer **3.** eschewer, wrongdoer, subduer, undoer, misdoer, outdoer, canoer, renewer, shampooer, bestrewer, ensuer, pursuer, horseshoer, tattooer, reviewer **4.** evildoer, overdoer, interviewer.

U'erd– **2.** skewered, sewered, steward.

U'est– **2.** fewest, bluest, gluest, newest, truest.

U'et– **2.** chewet, Jewett, bluet, cruet, suet **3.** revuette.

UF'a– **2.** buffa [It.], chufa, gufa, goofa, goofah, luffa, loofah, stufa [It.] **4.** catalufa.

UF'er– **2.** goofer, hoofer, spoofer [all slang], roofer **3.** aloofer.

UF'i– **2.** oofy, goofy, spoofy [all slang], roofy, woofy.

UF'ing– **2.** hoofing, spoofing [both slang], roofing, woofing **4.** bulletproofing, waterproofing, weatherproofing.

UF'less– **2.** roofless, proofless **3.** reproofless.

UF'us– **2.** rufus, Rufus, rufous.

UG'a– **2.** fuga [It.], muga, ruga **3.** beluga, Cayuga **4.** Chattanooga.

UG'al– **2.** bugle, fugle, fugal, jugal, frugal **3.** infrugal, unfrugal **4.** febrifugal, vermifugal.

UG'i– **2.** bugi, boogie, boogey [both slang], luggie, rugae **4.** boogey–woogey [slang].

UG'l– **2.** bugle, fugle.

UG'ler– **2.** bugler, fugler.

UG'li– **2.** bugly.

UG'o– **2.** Hugo **3.** colugo, besugo [Sp.].

UG'us– **2.** rugous.

U'i– **2.** bowie, buoy, chewy, dewy, phooey [slang], gooey, hooey [both slang], cooee, Louis, louey [slang], bluey, blooey [both slang], fluey [rare], flooey [slang], gluey, screwy, tui, stewy, thewy, viewy **3.** *mildewy*, St. Louis, chop suey.

U'id– **2.** fluid, druid.

U'ij– **2.** brewage, sewage **3.** reviewage.

U'ik– **2.** Buick **3.** toluic.

U'in– **2.** ruin, bruin, sewen **3.** aruin.

U'ing– **2.** booing, chewing, doing, hewing, cooing, cuing, blueing, gluing, mooing, ruing, brewing, trueing, strewing, suing, shoeing, stewing, viewing, wooing **3.** eschewing, subduing, wrongdoing, undoing, misdoing, outdoing, boohooing, rescuing, miscuing, canoeing, renewing, shampooing, accruing, construing, ensuing, horseshoeing, tattooing, reviewing, previewing **4.** evil-doing, overdoing, barbecuing, misconstruing, interviewing.

U'is– **2.** Lewis, Louis, brewis **3.** St. Louis.

U'ish– **2.** Jewish, bluish, gluish, newish, truish, shrewish **3.** reviewish.

U'ist– **2.** cueist **3.** canoeist, revuist.

UJ'er– **2.** huger.

UJ'i– **2.** fuji, Fuji **3.** Mt. Fuji.

UK'a– **2.** Uca, nucha, yuca **3.** cambuca, palooka [slang], festuca, fistuca, bazooka.

UK'al– 2. ducal, coucal, nucal, nuchal 3. archducal 4. noctilucal, Pentateuchal.

UK'er– 2. euchre, lucre, fluker, snooker 3. rebuker 4. involucre.

UK'i– 2. fluky, snooky, spooky, rouky, sooky, Sukey.

UK'us– 2. fucus, fucous, leucous, mucus, mucous 3. caducous 4. noctilucous.

UL'a– 2. ula, boola [slang], Beulah, gula, Gula, goolah, hula, Lula, moola [slang], Zula 3. bamboula 4. hula-hula.

UL'er– 2. cooler, mewler, puler, pooler, spooler, ruler, drooler, tooler 4. ridiculer.

UL'ess– 2. dewless, fooless, flueless, clueless, pewless, screwless, viewless 3. reviewless.

UL'est– 2. coolest, foolest.

UL'i– 2. booly, booley, duly, Dooley, coolie, coulee, coolly, bluely, newly, pooly, drooly, tule, Thule, truly 3. patchouli, unduly, unruly, untruly 5. iconoduly.

UL'ij– 2. Coolidge, schoolage.

UL'ing– 2. fooling, cooling, schooling, puling, pooling, spooling, ruling, drooling, tooling, stooling 3. befooling, misruling 4. overruling.

UL'ip– 2. julep, tulip 3. mint julep.

UL'ish– 2. foolish, ghoulish, coolish, schoolish, mulish, pulish 3. pound-foolish, tomfoolish.

UL'u– 2. ulu, hulu, Lulu, Tulu, Zulu 4. Honolulu.

UM'a– 2. duma, pneuma, puma, Yuma 3. mazuma [slang] 4. Montezuma.

UM'al– 2. brumal, tombal.

UM'an– 2. human, Newman, crewman, Truman 3. inhuman, nonhuman, unhuman 4. ultrahuman, superhuman, preterhuman; *see* also **UM'en–** rumen etc. below.

UM'en– 2. rumen 3. albumen, albumin, hegumen, legumen, legumin, acumen, illumine, bitumen 4. catechumen; *see* also **UM'an–** human etc. above.

UM'ent– 3. imbuement, eschewment, subduement, induement, renewment, imbruement, accruement.

UM'er– 2. boomer, doomer, fumer, humor, bloomer, plumer, roomer, rumor, groomer, tumor 3. perfumer, ill-humor, illumer, assumer, consumer, entomber, costumer, resumer, presumer.

UM'erd– 2. humored, rumored 3. good-humored, bad-humored, ill-humored.

UM'i– 2. boomy, fumy, bloomy, gloomy, plumy, spumy, rheumy, roomy, broomy, groomy 3. perfumy.

UM'id– 2. fumid, humid, tumid.

UM'ij– 2. doomage, fumage, plumage, roomage.

UM'ik– 2. humic, cumic, tombic 3. costumic.

UM'in– 3. albumin, legumin, relumine, illumine; *see* also **UM'en–** rumen etc. above.

UM'ing– 2. booming, dooming, fuming, looming, blooming, glooming, pluming, spuming, rooming, brooming, tombing, zooming 3. predooming, perfuming, inhuming, exhuming, illuming, assuming, resuming, presuming, consuming, entombing 4. unassuming, unpresuming, disentombing.

UM'less– 2. doomless, fumeless, bloomless, plumeless, roomless, groomless, tombless.

UM'let– 2. boomlet, plumelet, roomlet, groomlet, tomblet.

UM'or– 2. humor, rumor, tumor; *see* also **UM'er–** boomer etc. above.

UM'us– 2. dumous, fumous, humus, humous, plumous, spumous, brumous, grumous 3. posthumous.

UN'a– 2. Una, luna, puna, Poonah, tuna 3. lacuna, vicuna, Peruna, Fortuna.

UN'al– 2. dunal 3. tribunal, lagoonal, lacunal, communal.

UN'ar– 2. lunar 3. lacunar, sublunar, translunar 4. semilunar, plenilunar, novilunar, interlunar, cassumunar.

UND'ed– 2. wounded 3. unwounded.

UN'er– 2. schooner, mooner, spooner, runer, crooner, pruner, sooner, tuner, swooner 3. ballooner, communer, lampooner, impugner, oppugner, harpooner, marooner, attuner 4. importuner.

U'ness– 2. fewness, blueness, newness, trueness.

UN'est– 2. soonest.

UN'ful– 2. spoonful, tuneful 3. balloonful, teaspoonful, untuneful.

UN'i– 2. duny, luny, loony, Cluny, moony, puny, puisne, spoony, tuny, swoony 3. festoony.

UN'ik– 2. Munich, Punic, runic, tunic.

UN'ing– 2. mooning, nooning, spooning, crooning, pruning, swooning 3. ballooning, communing, lampooning, impugning, oppugning, harpooning, attuning, retuning.

UN'is– 2. Eunice, funis, Tunis.

UN'ish– 2. moonish 3. buffoonish, balloonish, poltroonish.

UN'ism– 3. buffoonism, poltroonism 4. opportunism.

UN'ist– 3. balloonist, lampoonist, harpoonist, bassoonist, cartoonist 4. opportunist.

UN'it– 2. unit 3. Anunit.

UN'less– 2. boonless, moonless, spoonless, runeless, tuneless.

UN'o– 2. uno [Sp.], Juno, Juneau, Bruno.

UN'um– 2. unum [L.] 3. jejunum 6. e pluribus unum [L.].

UN'us– 2. Prunus 3. fortunous, Portunus.

UN'yun– 2. union 3. trade-union, reunion, nonunion, disunion, communion 4. labor-union, excommunion 5. intercommunion.

UP'a– 2. pupa, rupa, supa, stupa 3. macupa [Tag.], arupa, ketupa 4. kamarupa.

UP'e– 2. rupee, whoopee [slang] 4. Guadalupe; *see* also **UP'i–** kewpie etc. below.

UP'er– 2. duper, hooper, cooper, scooper, looper, snooper, grouper, trooper, trouper, super, stooper, stupor, swooper 3. recouper, mosstrooper 4. loop-the-looper.

UP'i– 2. kewpie, loopy, rupee, droopy, croupy, soupy, whoopee [slang].

UP'id– 2. Cupid, Lupid, stupid.

UP'in– 2. lupine.

UP'ing– 2. duping, hooping, cooping, scooping, looping, snooping, drooping, grouping, trooping, stooping, swooping, whooping 3. recouping, regrouping.

UP'l– 2. duple, cupel, pupal, pupil, drupel, scruple 3. subduple, quadruple, octuple, centuple, quintuple, septuple, sextuple.

UP'let– 2. duplet, looplet, drupelet 3. *quadruplet, octuplet, quintuplet, septuplet, sextuplet.*

UP'ment– 2. groupment 3. recoupment, aggroupment, regroupment.

UP'on– 2. coupon, jupon, yupon.

UP'us– 2. lupus, lupous.

UR'a– 2. cura [Sp.], lura, pleura, Mura, sura, surah 3. ahura, asura, caesura, flexura, datura, Keturah, vettura [It.], bravura 4. tambaroora, velatura, angostura 5. appoggiatura, coloratura, fioritura [It.].

UR'al– 2. Ural, dural, jural, lural, mural, neural, pleural, plural, rural, crural, sural 3. subdural, procural, tellural, adneural, hypural, bicrural, caesural 4. sinecural, intramural, extramural, antemural, intermural, interneural, commissural.

UR'ans– 2. durance 2. endurance, perdurance, procurance, allurance, assurance, insurance 4. reassurance, reinsurance.

UR'ant– 2. durant, jurant 3. endurant, obscurant, assurant, insurant.

UR'at– 2. curate, jurat, surat.

UR'er– 2. furor, juror, curer, lurer, moorer, purer, poorer, surer, tourer 3. endurer, adjurer, grand juror, obscurer, securer, procurer, allurer, demurer, inurer, impurer, assurer, ensurer, insurer, maturer 4. reassurer, reinsurer, immaturer.

UR'est– 2. purest, poorest, surest 3. obscurest, securest, demurest, impurest.

UR'i– 2. ewry, fury, Curie, houri, Jewry, jury, fleury, moory, Drury 3. grand jury, Missouri 4. counterfleury.

UR'id– 2. lurid.

UR'ij– 2. moorage, murage.

UR'ik– 2. pleuric, neuric 3. sulphuric, mercuric, telluric, caesuric 4. dolichuric.

UR'im– 2. Urim, Purim.

UR'ing– 2. during, juring, curing, luring, mooring, spooring, touring 3. enduring, adjuring, abjuring, securing, procuring, obscuring, alluring, unmooring, inuring, assuring, ensuring, insuring, maturing 4. reassuring, reinsuring.

UR'ish– 2. boorish, Moorish, poorish 3. maturish 4. amateurish.

UR'ist– 2. jurist, purist, tourist 4. manicurist 5. caricaturist.

UR'li– 2. dourly, poorly, purely, surely 3. securely, obscurely, demurely, impurely, maturely 4. prematurely, immaturely.

UR'ment– 3. abjurement, conjurement, securement, procurement, obscurement, allurement, immurement, inurement 4. reassurement, reinsurement.

UR'ness– 2. poorness, pureness, sureness 3. secureness, obscureness, demureness, impureness, cocksureness, matureness 4. insecureness, immatureness.

UR'o– 2. Uro, bureau 3. maduro 5. chiaroscuro.

UR'or– 2. furor, juror 3. adjuror, grand juror; *see* also **UR'er–** furor etc. above.

UR'us– 2. urus, Eurus 3. anurous, Honduras, macrurous, Arcturus 4. dolichurus.

US'a– 2. Sousa, tuza 3. Medusa, empusa 4. Arethusa, Tuscaloosa, babirusa.

US'al– 3. medusal, occlusal 5. hypotenusal.

US'ens– 2. lucence, nuisance 3. translucence 4. noctilucence.

US'ent– 2. lucent 3. adducent, traducent, abducent, reducent, conducent, producent, translucent 4. noctilucent, interlucent.

US'er– 2. looser, sluicer, nooser, sprucer 3. adducer, traducer, deducer, reducer, seducer, inducer, conducer, producer 4. reproducer, introducer.

US'est– 2. loosest, sprucest 3. profusest, abstrusest.

US'ez– uses etc., *see* **US–** use etc. plus "s" or " 's."

US'ful– 2. useful, juiceful 3. unuseful.

USH'a– 2. fuchsia, Lucia 3. Jerusha.

USH'al– 2. crucial 3. fiducial, minutial.

USH'an– 2. Lucian 3. Confucian, Aleutian 4. Lilliputian, Rosecrucian.

USH'un– 3. locution, ablution, pollution, dilution, solution, volution 4. attribution, retribution, distribution, contribution, execution, prosecution, persecution, elocution, absolution, dissolution, evolution, revolution, involution, convolution, resolution, imminution, diminution, comminution, substitution, destitution, restitution, institution, constitution 5. redistribution, ventrilocution, circumlocution, interlocution, electrocution, irresolution, circumvolution.

USH'us– 2. Lucius 3. astucious.

US'i– 2. goosy, juicy, Lucy, sluicy, moosey 3. Debussy.

US'id– **2.** deuced, lucid, mucid **3.** pellucid, translucid.

US'ij– **2.** usage **3.** disusage, misusage, abusage.

US'ik– **2.** fucic, glucic, mucic **3.** ageusic **4.** anacusic, parageusic.

US'ing– **2.** loosing, sprucing **3.** adducing, traducing, educing, deducing, reducing, seducing, inducing, conducing, producing, unloosing **4.** reproducing, introducing.

US'is– **3.** prosneusis **4.** therapeusis, anacrusis.

US'iv– **3.** abusive, deducive, seducive, inducive, conducive, diffusive, confusive, transfusive, elusive, delusive, illusive, collusive, reclusive, seclusive, inclusive, conclusive, exclusive, obtrusive, intrusive, contusive **4.** inconducive, inconclusive, unobtrusive.

US'less– **2.** useless, juiceless.

US'li– **2.** loosely **3.** diffusely, profusely, abstrusely, obtusely.

US'ment– **3.** traducement, deducement, reducement, seducement, inducement, producement **5.** superinducement.

US'ness– **2.** looseness, spruceness **3.** diffuseness, profuseness, recluseness, abstruseness, obtuseness.

US'o– **2.** trousseau, whoso **3.** Caruso **5.** Robinson Crusoe.

US'om– **2.** gruesome, twosome.

UST'ed– **2.** boosted, roosted.

UST'er– **2.** booster, fooster [Ir.], jouster, rooster, brewster, Brewster.

UT'a– **2.** muta, tutta [It.] **3.** macuta, aluta, battuta [It.], Matuta **4.** barracouta **5.** Mater Matuta.

UT'al– **2.** brutal **3.** refutal, recruital.

UT'ant– **2.** mutant, nutant **3.** commutant, disputant.

UT'at– **2.** mutate, nutate, scutate.

UT'e– **2.** bootee, putti [It.], tutti **4.** tutti-frutti.

UT'ed– **2.** booted, hooted, scooted, luted, looted, fluted, mooted, muted, rooted, bruited, fruited, sooted, suited, chuted, tooted **3.** unbooted, refuted, confuted, saluted, diluted, polluted, immuted, commuted, transmuted, cornuted, deputed, reputed, imputed, computed, disputed, unrooted, uprooted, recruited, unsuited, voluted **4.** executed, prosecuted, persecuted, undiluted, unpolluted, comminuted, undisputed, substituted, restituted, instituted, constituted, obvoluted, evoluted, revoluted, involuted, convoluted **5.** electrocuted.

UT'en– **2.** gluten **4.** highfaluten [coll.].

UT'er– **2.** booter, fouter, hooter, cooter, cuter, luter, looter, fluter, mooter, muter, neuter, pewter, rooter, router, fruiter, suitor, chuter, shooter, tooter, tutor **3.** freebooter, confuter, accoutre, acuter, diluter, commuter, transmuter, minuter, imputer, computer, disputer, uprooter, recruiter, peashooter, beanshooter, sharpshooter, protutor, astuter.

UT'est– **2.** cutest, mutest **3.** acutest, minutest, astutest.

UTH'er– **2.** Luther, smoother, soother **3.** uncouther.

UTH'est– **2.** smoothest.

UTH'ful– **2.** ruthful, truthful, toothful, youthful **3.** untruthful.

UTH'less– **2.** ruthless, truthless, soothless, toothless, youthless.

UTH'ness– **2.** smoothness, soothness **3.** uncouthness.

UTH'som– **2.** toothsome, youthsome.

UT'i– **2.** booty, bootee, beauty, duty, cootie, cutie [both slang], looty, fluty, smooty, snooty, putti [It.], rooty, fruity, sooty, tutti **3.** freebooty, agouti **4.** tutti-frutti.

UT'ij– **2.** mutage, scutage, rootage, fruitage.

UT'ik– 3. scorbutic, toreutic 4. hermeneutic, therapeutic, pharmaceutic, diazeutic.

UT'il– 2. utile, futile, sutile 3. inutile, unfutile; *see* also **UT'l–** utile etc. below.

UT'in– 2. cutin, glutin 3. Rasputin 4. highfalutin [coll.].

UT'ing– 2. booting, hooting, scooting, looting, fluting, mooting, muting, rooting, fruiting, suiting, shooting, tooting 3. freebooting, refuting, confuting, diluting, polluting, saluting, commuting, transmuting, deputing, imputing, computing, disputing, uprooting, recruiting 4. executing, prosecuting, persecuting, highfaluting [coll.], comminuting, substituting, instituting, constituting, convoluting.

UT'ish– 2. brutish, sootish.

UT'ist– 2. lutist, flutist, fruitist 3. computist 4. absolutist, hermeneutist, therapeutist, pharmaceutist, parachutist.

UT'iv– 2. fruitive 4. coadjutive, resolutive, evolutive, persecutive, substitutive, restitutive, constitutive, convolutive.

UT'l– 2. utile, futile, footle, rootle, brutal, sutile, tootle 3. inutle, refutal, recruital.

UT'less– 2. bootless, rootless, fruitless 3. reputeless.

UT'let– 2. rootlet, fruitlet.

UT'li– 2. cutely, mutely, brutely 3. acutely, minutely, astutely 4. absolutely, resolutely, dissolutely, convolutely.

UT'ment– 3. confutement, imbrutement, recruitment.

UT'ness– 2. cuteness, muteness, bruteness 3. acuteness, minuteness, hirsuteness, astuteness 4. absoluteness, dissoluteness.

UT'o– 2. Pluto, scruto, tutto [It.] 3. tenuto [It.] 4. assoluto [It.], risoluto [It.], sostenuto.

UT'or– 2. suitor, sutor, tutor 3. protutor 4. executor, prosecutor, persecutor; *see* also **UT'er–** booter etc. above.

UT'um– 2. scutum, sputum 3. verutum [L.].

UT'ur– 2. future, puture, suture.

UT'us– 2. Plutus, Brutus 3. arbutus, scorbutus, computus.

U'um– 2. tuum.

UV'al– 3. removal, approval, reproval, disproval 4. disapproval.

UV'en– 2. hooven, proven 3. unproven, disproven.

UV'er– 2. Hoover, louver, Louvre, mover, groover, prover 3. Vancouver, remover, maneuver, approver, reprover, improver, disprover 4. disapprover.

UV'erd– 2. louvered 3. maneuvered.

UV'i– 2. movie, groovy.

UV'ing– 2. moving, grooving, proving 3. removing, unmoving, approving, reproving, improving, disproving 4. disapproving.

UV'less– 2. moveless, grooveless.

UV'ment– 2. movement 3. approvement, improvement, disprovement.

U'ya– 2. huia 4. alleluia, hallelujah.

U'yant– 2. buoyant 3. unbuoyant.

UZ'a– 2. Musa, tuza 4. Arethusa 5. lallapalooza [slang].

UZ'al– 2. musal 3. refusal, perusal.

UZ'ans– 2. usance 3. misusance, recusance.

UZ'ant– 3. accusant, recusant.

UZ'er– 2. oozer, user, boozer, chooser, fuser, loser, muser, snoozer, bruiser, cruiser 3. abuser, refuser, diffuser, infuser, confuser, transfuser, suffuser, accuser, excuser, palouser, amuser, peruser.

UZ'ez– 2. uses, oozes, boozes, chooses, fuses, loses, muses, snoozes, bruises, cruses, cruises 3. misuses, abuses, refuses, diffuses, infuses, confuses, transfuses, suffuses, accuses, excuses, amuses, bemuses, peruses, masseuses, danseuses, contuses.

UZH'i– 2. bougie, rougy.

UZH'un– 2. fusion, trusion **3.** effusion, diffusion, infusion, profusion, transfusion, suffusion, allusion, elusion, delusion, illusion, collusion, reclusion, preclusion, seclusion, inclusion, conclusion, occlusion, exclusion, obtrusion, detrusion, retrusion, intrusion, protrusion, extrusion, contusion, Malthusian **4.** circumfusion, interfusion, disillusion.

UZ'i– 2. oozy, boozy [coll.], choosy, choosey [both slang], newsy [coll.], snoozy [coll.], drusy, woozy [slang].

UZ'ik– 2. music.

UZ'ing– 2. oozing, boozing [coll.], choosing, fusing, losing, musing, snoozing [coll.], bruising, cruising **3.** misusing, abusing, refusing, diffusing, infusing, confusing, transfusing, suffusing, accusing, excusing, amusing, bemusing, perusing, contusing **4.** unaccusing, self-accusing, unamusing, interfusing.

UZ'iv– 3. accusive, amusive **4.** unamusive.

UZ'l– 2. ouzel, foozle **3.** bamboozle [coll.], refusal, perusal.

UZ'ler– 2. foozler 3. bamboozler [coll.].

UZ'ment– 3. accusement, amusement.

U (you)

3.

TRIPLE RHYMES IN U (do'a-ble)

Primary or Secondary Accent falls on Second from Last Syllable.

U'a-bl- **3.** doable, suable, stewable, viewable **4.** undoable, subduable, renewable, construable, pursuable, reviewable, unviewable **5.** unrenewable, unreviewable.

U'ant-li- **3.** fluently, truantly **4.** confluently, pursuantly.

UB'er-ans- **4.** protuberance, exuberance.

UB'er-ant- **4.** protuberant, exuberant **5.** unexuberant.

UB'er-us- **3.** suberous, tuberous **4.** protuberous.

UB'i-a- **3.** nubia, Nubia, rubia **5.** rabirubia.

UB'i-al- **4.** connubial.

UB'i-an- **3.** Nubian **4.** Danubian.

UB'ik-l- **3.** cubicle, cubical **4.** cherubical.

UB'it-us- **3.** cubitus **4.** accubitus, decubitus, concubitous, concubitus.

UB'i-us- **3.** dubious, rubious.

UB'ri-kat- **3.** lubricate, rubricate.

UB'ri-us- **4.** lugubrious, salubrious **5.** insalubrious.

UB'ul-us- **3.** tubulous.

UD'a-bl- **4.** alludable, deludable, precludable, includable, concludable, protrudable **5.** unincludable, unconcludable.

UD'er-i- **3.** prudery.

UD'in-al- **4.** paludinal, testudinal **5.** longitudinal, attitudinal, altitudinal, aptitudinal.

UD'i-ness- **3.** moodiness, broodiness.

UD'in-us- **4.** paludinous, testudinous **5.** latitudinous, platitudinous, multitudinous, fortitudinous **6.** solicitudinous, vicissitudinous.

UD'i-o- **3.** studio **4.** preludio.

UD'it-i- **3.** nudity, rudity, crudity.

UD'i-um- **3.** studium **4.** preludium, postludium.

UD'i-us- **3.** studious **4.** preludious, unstudious.

U'el-er- **3.** dueler, fueler, jeweler, grueler, crueler.

U'el-est- **3.** cruelest, crewelist.

U'el-i- **3.** cruelly.

U'el-ing- **3.** dueling, fueling, grueling **4.** refueling, bejeweling.

U'er-i- **3.** ewery, brewery.

U'i-ness- **3.** dewiness, glueyness, screwiness.

U'in-us- **3.** ruinous, bruinous, pruinous.

U'it-i- **3.** cruety, suety **4.** acuity, vacuity, circuity, annuity, strenuity, tenuity, congruity, fatuity, gratuity, fortuity **5.** assiduity, ambiguity, exiguity, contiguity, conspicuity, perspicuity, promiscuity, superfluity, ingenuity, continuity, innocuity, incongruity, perpetuity **6.** incontinuity, discontinuity.

U'it-iv- **3.** fruitive, tuitive **4.** intuitive **5.** unintuitive.

U'it-us- **4.** fatuitous, gratuitous, pituitous, circuitous, fortuitous.

UJ'il-ist- **3.** pugilist.

UJ'it–iv– 3. fugitive.

UK'ar–ist– 3. Eucharist.

UK'er–i– 3. dukery, spookery 4. caducary.

UK'ul–ent– 3. luculent, muculent.

UL'e–an– 3. joulean, Julian 4. Herculean, cerulean.

UL'i–a– 3. Julia, thulia 4. abulia 5. parabulia, hyperbulia.

UL'ish–li– 3. foolishly, ghoulishly, mulishly.

UL'ish–ness– 3. foolishness, ghoulishness, mulishness.

UL'it–i– 4. credulity, sedulity, garrulity 5. incredulity.

UL'i–um– 3. thulium 4. nebulium, peculium.

UM'a–bl– 4. assumable, resumable, presumable, consumable 5. unassumable, unpresumable, inconsumable, unconsumable.

UM'a–bli– 4. presumably 5. inconsumably.

UM'an–li– 3. humanly 4. inhumanly, unhumanly 5. superhumanly.

UM'e–fi– 3. humefy, tumefy.

UM'en–al– 3. noumenal 5. catechumenal; *see* also **UM'in–al–** luminal etc. below.

UM'er–al– 3. humeral, numeral.

UM'er–i– 3. plumery, bloomery 4. perfumery, costumery.

UM'er–us– 3. humerus, humorous, numerous, rumorous 4. innumerous, unhumorous.

UM'in–a– 3. lumina, numina, Rumina 4. alumina.

UM'in–al– 3. luminal, noumenal, ruminal 4. cacuminal, voluminal 5. catechumenal.

UM'in–ant– 3. luminant, ruminant 4. illuminant, nonruminant.

UM'in–at– 3. luminate, ruminate 4. acuminate, cacuminate, illuminate, ferruminate.

UM'i–ness– 3. gloominess, spuminess, roominess.

UM'in–us– 3. luminous, numinous 4. albuminous, leguminous, acuminous, aluminous, voluminous, bituminous.

UM'ul–at– 3. cumulate, tumulate 4. accumulate 5. reaccumulate.

UM'ul–us– 3. cumulus, tumulus.

UN'a–bl– 3. tunable 4. impugnable, expugnable, untunable.

UN'er–i– 3. lunary 4. buffoonery, cocoonery, sublunary, poltroonery 5. pantaloonery.

UN'i–form– 3. uniform, funiform, cuniform, luniform.

UN'ik–ant– 4. communicant 5. excommunicant.

UN'ik–at– 3. tunicate 4. communicate 5. excommunicate 6. intercommunicate.

UN'it–i– 3. unity, munity 4. triunity, jejunity, immunity, community, impunity 5. importunity, opportunity 6. intercommunity, inopportunity.

UN'it–iv– 3. unitive, punitive 4. communitive.

UN'i–us– 4. pecunious 5. impecunious.

UN'yun–ist– 3. unionist 4. Reunionist, nonunionist, communionist.

UP'a–bl– 3. dupable 4. undupable, recoupable.

UP'er–at– 4. recuperate, vituperate.

UP'er–i– 3. dupery, coopery.

UP'er–ij– 3. cooperage.

UP'i–al– 3. rupial, troopial, troupial 4. marsupial.

UP'i–er– 3. loopier, droopier, croupier, soupier.

UP'i–est– 3. loopiest, droopiest, soupiest.

UP'ul–us– 3. lupulus, scrupulous 4. unscrupulous.

UR'a–bl– 3. durable, curable 4. endurable, securable, incurable, procurable, assurable, insurable 5. unsecurable, uninsurable.

UR'a-bli- 3. durably, curably 4. endurably, incurably 5. unendurably.

UR'al-i- 3. plurally, murally, rurally.

UR'al-ist- 3. pluralist, muralist, ruralist.

UR'al-izm- 3. pluralism, ruralism.

UR'at-iv- 3. durative, curative 4. indurative, depurative, maturative.

UR'et-i- 3. surety 4. cocksurety, unsurety.

UR'i-a- 3. curia [L.] 4. Manchuria, decuria, Lemuria, Etruria 5. glycosuria.

UR'i-al- 3. urial, curial, Muriel 4. figurial, augurial, mercurial, purpureal, centurial.

UR'i-an- 3. durian 4. Manchurian, tellurian, lemurian, Etrurian, Missourian, centurian, Arthurian.

UR'i-ant- 4. luxuriant.

UR'i-at- 3. muriate 4. infuriate, luxuriate, centuriate.

UR'i-ent- 3. prurient 4. esurient, luxuriant, scripturient, parturient.

UR'if-i- 3. purify, thurify.

UR'ing-li- 4. enduringly, alluringly, assuringly.

UR'i-o- 3. durio, curio, Thurio.

UR'it-i- 3. purity, surety 4. security, obscurity, demurity, impurity, cocksurety, maturity, futurity 5. insecurity, prematurity, immaturity.

UR'i-us- 3. furious, curious, spurious 4. sulphureous, injurious, perjurious, incurious, uncurious, penurious, luxurious, usurious 5. unpenurious.

US'a-bl- 4. unloosable, produceable 5. unproduceable.

US'ed-li- 3. deucedly, lucidly, mucidly 4. inducedly, pellucidly.

USH'i-a- 3. fuchsia, Lucia 4. minutia.

USH'i-al- 3. crucial 4. fiducial.

USH'i-an- 4. caducean, Confucian.

USH'un-al- 5. elocutional, evolutional, substitutional, institutional, constitutional 6. circumlocutional.

USH'un-er- 5. executioner, resolutioner, revolutioner.

USH'un-ist- 5. executionist, elocutionist, resolutionist, evolutionist, revolutionist, constitutionist.

US'en-si- 3. lucency 4. translucency.

US'i-bl- 3. crucible 4. adducible, traducible, educible, deducible, reducible, seducible, inducible, conducible, producible 5. irreducible, unreducible, unproducible.

US'id-li- 3. deucedly, lucidly, mucidly 4. inducedly, pellucidly.

US'if-er- 3. Lucifer, crucifer.

US'i-form- 3. luciform, nuciform, cruciform.

US'iv-li- 4. abusively, effusively, diffusively, allusively, elusively, delusively, illusively, conclusively, collusively, obtrusively, intrusively, protrusively 5. inconclusively, inobtrusively, unintrusively.

US'iv-ness- 4. abusiveness, effusiveness, diffusiveness, allusiveness, elusiveness, delusiveness, illusiveness, conclusiveness, exclusiveness, obtrusiveness, intrusiveness, protrusiveness 5. inconclusiveness, inobtrusiveness.

US'or-i- 3. lusory 4. elusory, delusory, prelusory, illusory, reclusory, conclusory, exclusory, collusory, prolusory, extrusory.

UT'a-bl- 3. lootable, mootable, mutable, scrutable, suitable 4. refutable, confutable, commutable, permutable, transmutable, computable, disputable, inscrutable, unsuitable 5. irrefutable, unrefutable, unconfutable, executable, prosecutable, incommutable, uncommutable, incomputable, undisputable.

UT'a-bli- 3. mutably, suitably 4. immutably, permutably, transmutably, inscrutably, unsuitably.

UT'at-iv- 3. mutative, putative, sputative 4. refutative, confutative, commutative, transmutative, imputative, reputative, disputative, sternutative **5.** uncommutative.

UT′e–al– **3.** luteal, gluteal, puteal.

UT′ed–li– **3.** mutedly **4.** reputedly.

UT′er–i– **3.** bootery, pewtery, rootery, fruitery **3.** freebootery.

UT′e–us– **3.** beauteous, duteous, luteous, gluteus.

UTH′ful–i– **3.** ruthfully, truthfully, youthfully.

UTH′ful–ness– **3.** ruthfulness, truthfulness, youthfulness.

UTH′les–li– **3.** ruthlessly, truthlessly, youthlessly.

UTH′les–ness– **3.** ruthlessness, truthlessness, youthlessness.

UT′i–fi– **3.** beautify, brutify.

UT′i–ful– **3.** dutiful, beautiful **4.** undutiful, unbeautiful.

UT′ik–al– **3.** cuticle **4.** scorbutical, latreutical **5.** hermeneutical, therapeutical, pharmaceutical.

UT′i–ness– **3.** snootiness, fruitiness, sootiness.

UT′in–i– **3.** mutiny, scrutiny.

UT′in–us– **3.** glutinous, mutinous, scrutinous **4.** velutinous, unmutinous.

UT′iv–li– **5.** substitutively, constitutively.

UT′u–al– **3.** mutual **4.** immutual, commutual, nonmutual, unmutual.

UV′a–bl– **3.** movable, provable **4.** removable, immovable, approvable, improvable, reprovable **5.** irremovable, unapprovable, irreprovable, unimprovable.

UV′i–al– **3.** uveal, fluvial, pluvial **4.** alluvial, effluvial, diluvial, colluvial, exuvial **5.** postdiluvial **6.** antediluvial.

UV′i–an– **4.** alluvian, diluvian, Peruvian, Vesuvian **5.** postdiluvian **6.** antediluvian.

UV′ing–li– **3.** movingly **4.** approvingly, reprovingly **5.** unapprovingly.

UV′i–um– **4.** alluvium, eluvium, effluvium, diluvium, impluvium, compluvium.

UV′i–us– **3.** pluvious, Pluvius **4.** Vesuvius **6.** Jupiter Pluvius.

UZ′a–bl– **3.** usable, choosable, losable **4.** unusable, abusable, confusable, accusable, excusable, amusable, perusable **5.** unaccusable, inexcusable, unamusable.

UZ′a–bli– **4.** excusably **5.** inexcusably, unexcusably.

UZ′at–iv– **4.** accusative, recusative.

UZH′un–al– **3.** fusional **4.** confusional, delusional, illusional, conclusional, intrusional.

UZH′ur–i– **3.** usury.

UZ′i–bl– **3.** fusible **4.** diffusible, infusible, transfusible, protrusible.

UZ′ik–al– **3.** musical **4.** nonmusical, unmusical.

UZ′i–ness– **3.** ooziness, booziness [coll.], chooziness [slang], newsiness [coll.], snooziness [coll.], wooziness [slang].

OO (full)

SEE OO (good), FOLLOWING O (awe).

U (tub)

1.

SINGLE (MASCULINE) RHYMES IN U (tub)

Primary or Secondary Accent Falls on Last Syllable; Imperfect Rhymes Are in Italics.

UB– 1. bub, chub, dub, hub, cub, blub, flub [coll.], club, slub, nub, knub, snub, pub [slang], rub, drub, grub, scrub, shrub, sub, tub, stub 2. *hubbub*, *flubdub* [slang], *subshrub* 3. sillabub, Beelzebub, rub-a-dub.

UBD– 1. dubbed, hubbed, cubbed, clubbed, snubbed, rubbed, drubbed, grubbed, scrubbed, shrubbed, subbed [slang], tubbed, stubbed.

UBZ– dubs etc., *see* **UB–** bub etc. above, plus "s" or " 's"; 3. mulligrubs [slang].

UCH– 1. Dutch, hutch, cutch, scutch, clutch, much, mutch, smutch, rutch, crutch, such, touch 2. *nonesuch*, retouch 3. insomuch, overmuch, inasmuch, forasmuch.

UCHD– 1. clutched, smutched, rutched, crutched, touched 2. retouched, untouched.

UD– 1. bud, dud, cud, scud, Lud, blood, flood, mud, pud [coll.], spud, rud, sud, sudd, shud, stud, thud 2. *rosebud*, bestud.

UDZ– buds etc., *see* **UD–** bud etc. above, plus "s" or " 's."

UF– 1. buff, chuff, chough, duff, fuf [Scot. & N. of Eng.], guff [Scot. & slang], huff, cuff, scuff, luff, bluff, fluff, clough, pluff [dial.], slough, sluff [dial.], muff, nuf, nuff [both slang], snuff, puff, ruff, rough, gruff, scruff, sough, suff [dial.], tough, tuff, stuff, whuff 2. rebuff, Macduff, *handcuff*, enough, cream puff, *dandruff*, *crossruff* 3. counterbuff, fisticuff, powder puff, overstuff.

UFS– buffs etc., *see* **UF–** buff etc. above, plus "s" or " 's."

UFT– 1. buffed, chuffed, cuffed, bluffed, sloughed, snuffed, puffed, tuft, stuffed 2. handcuffed, unstuffed 3. candytuft, overstuffed.

UG– 1. ugh, bug, chug, dug, hug, jug, lug, glug, plug, slug, mug, smug, pug, spug [Scot. & dial. Eng.], rug, drug, shrug, trug, tug, thug, vug 2. *humbug*, *firebug* 3. ladybug, tumblebug, doodlebug, bunnyhug.

UGZ– bugs etc., *see* **UG–** ugh etc. above, plus "s" or " 's."

UJ– 1. budge, fudge, judge, sludge, smudge, nudge, pudge [coll.], drudge grudge, trudge 2. adjudge, prejudge, forejudge, misjudge, begrudge.

UJD– 1. budged, fudged, judged, sludged, smudged, nudged, drudged, grudged, trudged 2. adjudged, self-judged, well-judged, ill-judged, forejudged, misjudged, begrudged.

UK– 1. buck, chuck, duck, cuck [obs.], luck, gluck, cluck, pluck, muck, knuck [coll.], Puck, ruck, truck, struck, suck, shuck, tuck, stuck 2. *springbuck*, *prongbuck*, *roebuck*, *sawbuck*, *woodchuck*, lame duck, *potluck*, dumb cluck [slang], amuck, Canuck, *awestruck*, *moonstruck*, *sun-struck* 3. waterbuck, Donald Duck, chuck-a-luck, panic-struck, thunderstruck, wonder-struck, horror-struck, nip and tuck.

UKS– bucks etc., *see* UK– buck etc. above, plus "s" or " 's"; 1. ducks, dux, lux, flux, mux [dial.], crux, tux [slang].

UKST– 1. fluxed 2. effluxed, refluxed.

UKT– 1. bucked, chucked, duct, ducked, trucked, sucked, shucked, tucked 2. abduct, educt, deduct, induct, conduct, obduct, reluct, unplucked, eruct, instruct, construct 3. viaduct, aqueduct, fumiduct, circumduct, misconduct, usufruct, reconstruct.

UL– 1. dull, gull, hull, cull, scull, skull, lull, mull, trull, sull [dial.], stull, wull [dial.] 2. *seagull*, Mogul, ahull, dehull, école [F.], bricole, *numskull*, [coll.], annul 3. disannul.

ULB– 1. bulb 3. pseudobulb.

ULCH– 1. gulch, cultch, culch, mulch.

ULD– 1. dulled, gulled, hulled, culled, sculled, skulled, lulled, mulled 2. thick-skulled, dehulled, black-hulled, annulled.

ULF– 1. gulf 2. engulf.

ULJ– 1. bulge 2. indulge, effulge, promulge, divulge 3. reindulge 4. overindulge.

ULJD– 1. bulged 2. indulged, promulged, divulged 3. undivulged 4. overindulged.

ULK– 1. bulk, hulk, skulk, mulk, sulk.

ULKT– 1. bulked, hulked, skulked, mulct, sulked.

ULM– 1. culm, stulm.

ULP– 1. gulp, culp [slang], sculp, pulp.

ULPT– 1. gulped, pulped 2. soft-pulped 3. golden-pulped.

ULS– 1. bulse, dulse, dulce, mulse, pulse 2. repulse, impulse, expulse, avulse, revulse, convulse.

ULSD– 1. pulsed 2. repulsed, avulsed, revulsed, convulsed.

ULT– 1. cult 2. adult, incult, occult, penult, insult, consult, result, exult 3. subadult, catapult 4. antepenult.

ULZ– dulls etc., *see* UL– dull etc. above, plus "s" or " 's."

UM– 1. um, homme [F.], bum, chum, dumb, gum, hum, come, scum, Lum, glum, plum, plumb, slum, mum, numb, snum, rum, rhumb, drum, grum, crumb, scrum, strum, thrum, some, sum, tum, stum, thumb, swum, yum 2. *serfdom*, *kingdom*, *dogdom*, *dukedom*, *earldom*, *dumdum*, *begum*, Bonhomme, become, succumb, unplumb, benumb, *humdrum*, *threesome*, *wholesome*, *lonesome*, *awesome*, *toothsome*, *gruesome*, *twosome*, *tum-tum*, *yum-yum*, *Yum-Yum* 3. tweedledum, Christendom, martyrdom, fee-faw-fum, overcome, misbecome, colchicum, unicum, capsicum, solidum, oppidum, orpheum, horreum, labium, stibium, cambium, calcium, stadium, studium, ischium, silphium, lithium, cadmium, hafnium, opium, Arctium, vitium, otium, cingulum, septulum, sertulum, crembalum, sugarplum, symbolum, pabulum, pendulum, minimum, quadrimum, optimum, maximum, labdanum, laudanum, platinum, labarum, cerebrum, kettledrum, panjandrum, conundrum, theorum, drearisome, wearisome, frolicsome, gamblesome, troublesome, meddlesome, quarrelsome, burdensome, cumbersome, bothersome, venturesome, debitum, placitum, cognitum, compitum, vacuum, menstruum, mutuum 4. fee fi fo fum, ceruleum, castoreum, columbium, aerobium, exordium, sporangium, Eryngium, absinthium, agonium, euphonium, polonium, stramonium, ammonium, harmonium, opprobrium, delirium, tellurium, martyrium, gymnasium, potassium, Elysium, sestertium, consortium, nasturtium, caputium, deliquium, viaticum, chrysanthemum, molybdenum, aluminum, ad libitum, accubitum, acquisitum 5. periosteum, equilibrium, polyandrium, hypochondrium, epigastrium, sacerdotium.

UMD– 1. gummed, plumbed, numbed, drummed, crumbed, strummed, thumbed 2. ungummed.

UMF– 1. umph, humph, grumph [Scot.] 2. *triumph.*

UMP– 1. ump [slang], bump, chump, dump, gump, hump, jump, lump, flump, glump [slang], clump, plump, slump, mump, pump, rump, frump, grump, crump, trump, sump, tump, stump, thump, wump [slang]. 2. high jump, bethump, *mugwump* 3. overtrump.

UMPS– bumps etc., *see* **UMP–** bump etc. above, plus "s" or " 's."

UMZ– chums etc. *see* **UM–** um etc. above plus "s" or " 's"; 1. Thrums 2. *breekums, doldrums.*

UN– 1. un [coll. & dial.], bun, done, dun, Dunn, fun, gun, Hun, hon [slang], none, nun, pun, spun, run, sun, son, sunn, shun, tun, ton, stun, one, won 2. well-done, ill-done, undone, foredone, outdone, begun, homespun, forerun, unrun, outrun, grandson, Whitsun, unwon 3. clarendon, overdone, underdone, unbegun, Sally Lunn, overrun, Tennyson, atchison, Atkinson, Sheraton, Wellington, skimmington, Orpington, anyone, everyone, number one.

UNCH– 1. bunch, hunch, lunch, clunch [dial.], munch, nunch [dial.], punch, runch, brunch [coll.], crunch, scrunch, squnch.

UND– 1. Bund, dunned, fund, mund, punned, sunned, shunned, stunned 2. refund, unsunned, rotund 3. moribund, cummerbund, verecund, rubicund, Rosamond, obrotund, orotund.

UNG– 1. bung, hung, lung, flung, clung, slung, pung, rung, wrung, sprung, strung, sung, tongue, stung, swung, young 2. *geebung*, unhung, among, highstrung, hamstrung, unsung, betongue, *shantung*, *oxtongue* 3. underhung, overhung, underslung, hereamong, thereamong, overstrung, mother tongue.

UNGD– 1. bunged, tongued 2. black-tongued, bell-tongued, thick-tongued, sharp-tongued 3. iron-lunged, leather-lunged, honey-tongued, silver-tongued, many-tongued, double-tongued, trumpet-tongued.

UNJ– 1. lunge, longe, blunge, plunge, sponge 2. expunge 3. muskellunge.

UNK– 1. unk, unc [both slang], bunk, chunk, dunk, funk, hunk, junk, skunk, lunk [slang], blunk [slang], clunk [Scot. & dial.], plunk, slunk, monk, nunc, punk, spunk, drunk, trunk, sunk, tunk [dial.], stunk 2. Mauch Chunk, quidnunc, undrunk, tree trunk, unsunk.

UNKST– 1. 'mongst 2. amongst.

UNKT– 1. bunked, junked, skunked, trunked 2. defunct, injunct, conjunct, disjunct.

UNS– 1. once, bunce [slang], dunce.

UNT– 1. bunt, hunt, lunt, blunt, punt, runt, brunt, front, grunt, shunt, stunt, wont, wun't [dial.] 2. *staghunt*, fox hunt, affront, *bifront*, confront, *forefront* 3. exeunt.

UNTH– 1. month 2. *twelvemonth.*

UNZ– buns etc., *see* **UN–** bun etc. above, plus "s" or " 's."

UP– 1. up, dup [dial.], cup, scup, pup, sup, tup, yup [slang] 2. *windup*, hard up, *roundup*, *make-up*, *breakup*, *hiccough*, *hiccup*, *pickup*, *lockup*, *sunup*, *ripup*, *tipup*, *tossup*, *getup*, *letup*, *setup* **3.** up-and-up, loving cup, buttercup, stirrip cup.

UPT– **1.** upped, cupped, supped, tupped 2. abrupt, erupt, corrupt, disrupt 3. interrupt, incorrupt, uncorrupt.

UR– **1.** err, er, 'er, Er, Ur, burr, birr, churr, chirr, fer [dial.], fir, fur, her, cur, coeur, blur, slur, myrrh, smur, knur, per, purr, spur, sir, sur, shirr, stir, were, whir **2.** nightchurr, befur, defer, prefer, infer, confer, chauffeur, furfur, transfer, recur, incur, concur, occur, liqueur, demur, larkspur, hotspur, masseur, farceur [F.], susurr, deter, inter, hauteur, astir, Pasteur, bestir, restir, aver, rever **3.** cocklebur, butterbur, calaber, shillaber, massacre, sepulchre, calendar, calender, islander, lavender, provender, Lucifer, crucifer, Jennifer, conifer, dapifer, rotifer, aquifer, pillager, villager, manager, tanager ,onager, forager, vintager, cottager, ravager, voyager, voyageur [F.], dowager, integer, armiger, claviger, breviger, hardanger, challenger, passenger, messenger, scavenger, harbinger, derringer, porringer, chronopher, publisher, polisher, punisher, cherisher, nourisher, Britisher, vanquisher, rapier, copier, odaler, victualer, chronicler, chiseler, traveler, leveler, hoveler, shoveler, wassailer, labeler, yodeler, quarreler, jeweler, gossamer, dulcimer, lorimer, customer, costumer, parcener, gardener, hardener, lengthener, strengthener, weakener, wakener, quickener, cheapener, deepener, sharpener, loosener, lessener, threatener, sweetener, shortener, fastener, hastener, chastener, listener, moistener, evener, scrivener, cozener, bargainer, almoner, commoner, summoner, coroner, ironer, reasoner, seasoner, poisoner, prisoner, northerner, southerner, easterner, westerner, sojourner, stuccoer, diaper, hanaper, worshiper, caliper, juniper, gossiper, galloper, walloper, jabberer, slumberer, numberer, sorcerer, slanderer, panderer, murderer, pilferer, chamferer, wagerer, staggerer, swaggerer, weatherer, furtherer, cornerer, naperer, scamperer, whimperer, whisperer, caterer, loiterer, shelterer, saunterer, barterer, plasterer, pesterer, roisterer, fosterer, blusterer, answerer, laborer, clamorer, conjurer, murmurer, usurer, venturer, lecturer, capturer, torturer, connoisseur, purchaser, silencer, licenser, trespasser, canvasser, harnesser, accoucheur, amateur, marketer, bucketer, arbiter, forfeiter, surfeiter, scimiter, chapiter, Jupiter, warranter, disinter, frankfurter, winchester, Rochester, harvester, sophister, sinister, presbyter sandiver, caliver, gilliver, Gulliver, Oliver, miniver, Andover, Passover, journeyer **4.** Ambassadeur, ambassador, restaurateur, artificer, admonisher, relinquisher, astronomer, tobogganer, coparcener, enlivener, developer, enveloper, embroiderer, encounterer, upholsterer, deliverer, maneuverer, conjecturer, adventurer, Accipiter.

URB– **1.** herb, gerb, curb, blurb [coll.], Serb, verb **2.** *potherb*, *suburb*, superb, perturb, disturb, *adverb*, reverb.

URBD– **1.** curbed, verbed **2.** uncurbed, disturbed, perturbed **3.** imperturbed, unperturbed, undisturbed.

URCH– **1.** birch, church, lurch, smirch, perch, search **2.** besmirch, research.

URD– **1.** urd, erred, bird, burred, Byrd, furred, gird, heard, herd, curd, Kurd, blurred, slurred, purred, spurred, surd, shirred, turd, stirred, third, word, whirred **2.** *songbird*, *blackbird*, *halberd*, *snowbird*, *bluebird*, *lovebird*, befurred, inferred, conferred, begird, engird, ungird, unheard, *gooseherd*, recurred, occurred, demurred, absurd, interred, averred, Cape Verde, *wayward*, *watchword*, *leeward*, reword, *seaward*, *homeward*, *inward*, *onward*, *downward*, *upward*, *foreword*, *forward* **3.** mockingbird, hummingbird, ladybird, undergird, overheard, reoccurred, disinterred, afterward, sepulchred.

URDZ– birds etc., *see* **URD**– urd etc. above, plus "s" or " 's."

URF– **1.** kerf, scurf, perf [slang], serf, surf, turf **3.** hippocerf.

URG– **1.** erg, berg, burg, bourg **2.** exergue, *Goldberg*, *iceberg*, *Strasbourg*, *Pittsburgh* **3.** Heidelberg, Brandenburg.

URJ– **1.** urge, dirge, scourge, splurge, merge, purge, spurge, serge, surge, verge **2.** submerge, emerge, immerge, asperge, resurge, deterge, absterge, diverge, converge **3.** demiurge, dramaturge, thaumaturge.

URK– **1.** irk, burke, Burke, dirk, girk [slang], jerk, jerque, kirk, lurk, clerk, murk, smirk, perk, cirque, shirk, Turk, stirk, work, quirk, yerk **2.** *hauberk*, Dunkerque, berserk, *patchwork*, *woodwork*, *bridgework*, *clockwork*, *bulwark*, *guesswork*, *network*, *fretwork* **3.** handiwork, fancywork, needlework, openwork, overwork, latticework.

URKS– irks etc., *see* **URK**– irk etc. above, plus "s" or " 's."

URL– **1.** earl, erl [dial.], burl, birl, churl, furl, girl, gurl, herl, hurl, curl, skirl, merle, knurl, pearl, perle, purl, thirl, querl, swirl, twirl, whirl, whorl **2.** unfurl, becurl, uncurl, impearl **4.** mother-of-pearl.

URLD– **1.** burled, furled, hurled, curled, skirled, pearled, purled, world, swirled, twirled, whirled **2.** unfurled, impearled, old-world **3.** underworld.

URM– **1.** berm, derm, firm, germ, sperm, term, therm, worm, squirm **2.** affirm, infirm, confirm, *Landsturm*, *silkworm*, *bookworm*, *glowworm*, *earthworm* **3.** pachyderm, reaffirm, disaffirm, isotherm, angleworm.

URMD– **1.** firmed, germed, termed, wormed, squirmed **2.** confirmed **3.** reaffirmed, unconfirmed.

URN– **1.** earn, urn, erne, burn, Berne, churn, dern [dial.], durn [dial.], fern, herne, kern, learn, pirn, spurn, tern, turn, stern, quern, yearn **2.** inurn, *sunburn*, *heartburn*, *cedarn*, adjourn, sojourn, epergne, discern, concern, lucerne, Lucerne, attorn, *Saturn*, eterne, return, *nocturne*, inturn, interne, sauterne, upturn, *quartern*, astern, *eastern*, *cistern*, extern, *sextern*, *leathern*, *northern* **3.** unconcern, sempitern, taciturn, overturn.

URND– **1.** earned, urned, burned, churned, learned, spurned, turned, sterned, yearned **2.** hard-earned, well-earned, unearned, sunburned, adjourned, sojourned, discerned, concerned, returned, interned, upturned **3.** unconcerned, overturned.

URNZ– earns etc., *see* **URN**– earn etc. above, plus "s" or " 's."

URP– **1.** urp [slang], burp [slang], chirp, lerp, slurp [dial.], purp, turp, terp, twerp, twirp [all slang] **2.** discerp, usurp, *Antwerp*.

URPS– **1.** burps [slang], chirps, slurps [dial.], stirps **2.** discerps, usurps.

URPT– **1.** burped [slang], chirped, slurped [dial.] **2.** excerpt, discerped, usurped.

URS– **1.** Erse, birse, burse, cherce [dial.], hearse, curse, nurse, purse, terce, terse, verse, worse **2.** imburse, disburse, rehearse, accurse, precurse, amerce, submerse, immerse, coerce, asperse, disperse, sesterce, averse, traverse, obverse, subverse, adverse, reverse, diverse, perverse, inverse, converse, transverse **3.** reimburse, intersperse, universe.

URST– **1.** erst, burst, first, Hearst, cursed, nursed, pursed, thirst, versed, verst, worst wurst **2.** *sunburst*, *outburst*, rehearsed, accursed, emersed, immersed, dispersed, athirst, traversed, conversed, unversed **3.** reimbursed, unrehearsed, interspersed, untraversed, liverwurst.

URT– **1.** Bert, dirt, girt, hurt, curt, skirt, blurt, flirt, nert [slang], pert, spurt, cert [slang], syrt, shirt, vert, wort, quirt, squirt 2. begirt, *seagirt*, engirt, ungirt, unhurt, alert, inert, *expert*, assert, concert, exert, exsert, insert, *redshirt*, *Black Shirt*, avert, obvert, subvert, advert, evert, revert, divert, invert, convert, overt, pervert, transvert, dessert, *madwort*, *ragwort*, *figwort*, *steepwort* 3. Adelbert, Ethelbert, Camembert, malapert, inexpert, preconcert, disconcert, intersert, undershirt, ambivert, retrovert, introvert, controvert, extrovert, pennywort, liverwort, motherwort.

URTH– 1. earth, berth, birth, dearth, firth, mirth, Perth, worth 2. inearth, unearth, rebirth, unworth 3. underearth, pennyworth, money's worth.

URV– 1. curve, nerve, serve, verve, swerve 2. recurve, *incurve*, *outcurve*, innerve, unnerve, observe, subserve, deserve, reserve, preserve, disserve, conserve 3. unreserve.

URVD– 1. curved, served, swerved 2. unnerved, reserved, preserved, conserved 3. undeserved, well-deserved, well-preserved, unpreserved, unconserved.

URVZ– curves etc., *see* **URV–** curve etc. above, plus "s" or " 's."

URZ– errs etc., *see* **UR–** err etc. above, plus "s" or " 's"; 1. furze.

US– 1. us, bus, buss, chuss [slang], fuss, guss, cuss [coll.], plus, muss, pus, Russ, Grus, truss, Sus, stuss, thus 2. percuss, discuss, excuss, khuskhus, succuss, nonplus, surplus, untruss 3. harquebus, omnibus, blunderbuss, dubious, tedious, hideous, aqueous, igneous, carneous, corneous, impious, repercuss, overplus, nucleus, copious, nacreous, cupreous, vitreous, gaseous, osseous, nauseous, lacteous, piteous, plenteous, bounteous, courteous, beauteous, luteous, niveous, envious, pluvious, scandalous, libelous, cautelous, scurrilous, marvelous, frivolous, bibulous, flocculous, calculous, calculus, surculous, surculus, nodulous, scrofulous, cellulous, cumulous, cumulus, granulous, querulous, garrulous, infamous, bigamous, blasphemous, venomous, enormous, amanous, bimanous, membranous, larcenous, ravenous, villainous, mountainous, acinous, acinus, hircinous, criminous, resijous, cretinous, sanguinous, ruinous, tyrannous, poisonous, consonous, gluttonous, dipnoous, dichroous, platypus, octopus, barbarous, nectarous, Tartarus, ludicrous, slumberous, tuberous, ulcerous, cancerous, ponderous, thunderous, dangerous, cankerous, humerus, onerous, viperous, Hesperus, prosperous, slaughterous, apterous, dexterous, pulverous, chivalrous, rancorous, nidorous, phosphorous, Phosphorus, valorous, dolorous, timorous, humorous, susurrus, susurrous, sinistrous, verdurous, fulgurous, sulphurous, murmurous, venturous, rapturous, torturous, Pegasus, covetous, halitus, halitous, aditus, fremitus, spiritous, transitus, riotous, vacuous, arduous, sensuous, fatuous, unctuous, fructuous, spiritous, sumptuous, tortuous, mischievous, atavus, flexuous 4. caduceus, polyphagous, analogous, homologous, amphibious, ingenious, calumnious, symphonious, uproarious, opprobrious, Leviticus, noctambulous, monoculous, tuberculous, unscrupulous, edentulous, didynamous, tridynamous, diaphanous, epiphanous, ferruginous, foraminous, contaminous, trigeminous, gelatinous, polygynous, polygenous, ephemerous, polymerous, obstreperous, tetrapterous, preposterous, adventurous, edematous, velocitous, calamitous, precipitous, necessitous, innocuous, promiscuous, circumfluous, superfluous, impetuous, tumultuous, presumptuous, voluptuous, incestuous, tempestuous 5. heterologous, ignominious.

USH– 1. ush [slang], gush, hush, cush, lush, blush, flush, plush, slush, mush, rush, brush, crush, thrush, tush 2. agush, ablush, aflush, reflush, *bulrush*, *onrush*, *outrush*, *tarbrush* 3. underbrush.

USK– **1.** busk, dusk, fusc, husk, cusk, musk, rusk, brusque, tusk **2.** embusk, adusk, subfusc, dehusk, *mollusk*.

USP– **1.** cusp.

UST– **1.** bust, dust, dost, fust, fussed, gust, just, cussed, lust, plussed, mussed, rust, crust, trussed, trust, thrust **2.** combust, robust, adust, *gold-dust*, bedust, *stardust*, *august*, disgust, adjust, unjust, discussed, nonplussed, unmussed, encrust, betrust, entrust, untrussed, distrust, mistrust **3.** unrobust, readjust, coadjust, undiscussed.

UT– **1.** ut, but, butt, phut, gut, hut, jut, cut, scut, glut, slut, mut, mutt, smut, nut, putt, rut, strut, shut, tut, what **2.** abut, rebut, *hagbut*, *catgut*, *woodcut*, recut, uncut, *haircut*, clear-cut, *crosscut*, besmut, *peanut*, *chestnut*, *walnut*, *doughnut*, *burnut*, *beechnut*, astrut, reshut, somewhat **3.** surrebut, scuttle butt, halibut, betel nut, hazelnut, butternut, coconut, occiput, Lilliput.

UTH– **1.** doth **2.** bismuth **3.** azimuth.

UV– **1.** dove, guv, gov [both slang], love, glove, shove **2.** above, truelove, reglove, unglove, *foxglove* **3.** turtledove, ladylove.

UVD– **1.** loved, gloved, shoved **2.** beloved, ungloved **3.** unbeloved.

UZ– **1.** Uz, buzz, does, fuzz, guz, huzz, coz **2.** abuzz, *humbuzz*, chauffeuse [F.], masseuse **3.** dear me suz [slang].

UZD– **1.** buzzed, fuzzed.

U (tub)

2.

DOUBLE (FEMININE) RHYMES IN U (rub'ber)

Primary or Secondary Accent Falls on Next to Last Syllable; Imperfect Rhymes Are in Italics.

UB'er– **2.** dubber, hubber, lubber, blubber, clubber, slubber, snubber, rubber, drubber, grubber, scrubber, tubber, stubber **3.** *landlubber* **4.** moneygrubber **5.** India-rubber.

UB'erd– **2.** Hubbard, blubbered, cupboard, rubbered **4.** Mother Hubbard.

UB'i– **2.** bubby, chubby, fubby [coll. Eng.], hubby, cubby, clubby, slubby, nubby, knubby, rubby, grubby, scrubby, shrubby, tubby, stubby.

UB'ing– **2.** dubbing, hubbing, cubbing, blubbing, clubbing, nubbing, snubbing, rubbing, drubbing, grubbing, scrubbing, subbing [slang], tubbing, stubbing.

UB'ish– **2.** cubbish, clubbish, snubbish, rubbish, grubbish, shrubbish, tubbish.

UB'l– **2.** bubble, double, hubble, nubble, rubble, trouble, stubble **3.** redouble **4.** hubble-bubble.

UB'ld– **2.** bubbled, doubled, troubled, stubbled **3.** redoubled, untroubled.

UB'ler– **2.** bubbler, doubler, troubler.

UB'let– **2.** doublet, knublet, shrublet, tublet.

UB'li– **2.** bubbly, doubly, hubbly, knubbly, nubbly, rubbly, drubbly [dial.], strubbly, stubbly.

UB'lik– **2.** public **3.** republic, nonpublic, unpublic.

UB'ling– **2.** bubbling, doubling, nubbling, troubling **3.** redoubling, untroubling.

UB'lish– **2.** publish **3.** republish.

UCH'er– **2.** Dutcher, scutcher, clutcher, smutcher, toucher **3.** retoucher.

UCH'ess– **2.** duchess, Dutchess **3.** archduchess, grand duchess.

UCH'ez– **2.** hutches, scutches, clutches, smutches, rutches, crutches, touches **3.** retouches.

UCH'i– **2.** duchy, clutchy, smutchy, touchy **3.** archduchy, grand duchy.

UCH'ing– **2.** scutching, clutching, smutching, rutching, crutching, touching **3.** retouching.

UCH'on– **2.** scutcheon **3.** McCutcheon, escutcheon **4.** inescutcheon.

UD'ed– **2.** budded, scudded, blooded, flooded, mudded, spudded, studded, thudded **3.** unbudded, bestudded.

UD'er– **2.** udder, dudder, scudder, flooder, mudder, rudder, sudder, shudder.

UD'i– **2.** buddy, cuddy, scuddy, bloody, muddy, puddee, puddy, ruddy, study **3.** *soapsuddy* **4.** understudy, overstudy.

UD'id– **2.** bloodied, muddied, ruddied, studied **3.** unstudied **4.** overstudied.

UD'ij– **2.** buddage, floodage.

UD'ing– **2.** budding, scudding, flooding, studding, thudding.

UD'l– **2.** buddle, fuddle, huddle, cuddle, scuddle [Scot.], muddle, nuddle [dial.], puddle, ruddle, studdle **3.** befuddle, bemuddle.

UD'ld– **2.** fuddled, huddled, cuddled, scuddled [Scot.], muddled, puddled, studdled [dial.] **3.** befuddled, bemuddled.

UD'ler– 2. huddler, cuddler, muddler, puddler 3. befuddler.

UD'let– 2. budlet, floodlet.

UD'li– 2. Dudley, cuddly, puddly.

UD'ling– 2. fuddling, huddling, cuddling, scuddling [Scot.], muddling, puddling, studdling [dial.] 3. befuddling, bemuddling.

UD'son– 2. Hudson, Judson.

UD'zi– 2. sudsy 3. soapsudsy.

UF'en– 2. roughen, toughen.

UF'er– 2. buffer, chuffer, duffer, guffer [Scot.], huffer, cuffer, scuffer, luffer, bluffer, fluffer, pluffer [Scot. & N. of Eng.], slougher, muffer, snuffer, puffer, ruffer, rougher, gruffer, suffer, tougher, stuffer.

UF'est– 2. bluffest, roughest, gruffest, toughest.

UF'et– 2. buffet, fuffit [Scot.], muffet, tuffet 3. Miss Muffet.

UF'i– 2. buffy, fuffy [dial.], guffy [slang], huffy, cuffy, bluffy, fluffy, pluffy [dial.], sloughy, snuffy, puffy, ruffy, roughie, stuffy 4. ruffy-tuffy.

UF'in– 2. buffin, guffin [dial. & slang], cuffin, muffin, puffin 3. mumruffin 4. ragamuffin.

UF'ing– 2. buffing, chuffing, duffing, huffing, cuffing, luffing, bluffing, fluffing, sloughing, muffing, puffing, roughing, ruffing, soughing, stuffing.

UF'ish– 2. huffish, snuffish, roughish, gruffish, toughish.

UF'l– 2. buffle, duffel, fuffle [Scot.], scuffle, muffle, snuffle, ruffle, truffle, shuffle, whuffle 3. bemuffle, reshuffle 4. double shuffle.

UF'ler– 2. scuffler, muffler, snuffler, ruffler, shuffler.

UF'li– 2. bluffly, scuffly, muffly, snuffly, ruffly, roughly, gruffly, toughly.

UF'ling– 2. scuffling, muffling, snuffling, ruffling, shuffling 3. bemuffling, unruffling.

UF'lz– 2. snuffles, ruffles, truffles.

UF'ness– 2. bluffness, roughness, gruffness, toughness.

UFT'i– 2. mufti, tufty.

UG'ed– 2. rugged.

UG'er– 2. bugger, chugger, hugger, lugger, luggar, plugger, slugger, mugger, smugger, snugger, pugger, rugger, drugger, shrugger, tugger 4. huggermugger.

UG'est– 2. smuggest, snuggest, druggist.

UG'et– 2. mugget, nugget, drugget.

UG'i– 2. buggy, fuggy, luggie, pluggy, sluggy, muggy, puggi, puggy, druggy.

UG'ij– 2. luggage.

UG'ing– 2. chugging, hugging, jugging, lugging, glugging, plugging, slugging, mugging, rugging, drugging, shrugging, tugging.

UG'ish– 2. sluggish, muggish, smuggish, snuggish, puggish.

UG'l– 2. guggle, juggle, smuggle, snuggle, puggle, struggle.

UG'ler– 2. juggler, smuggler, snuggler, struggler.

UG'li– 2. ugly, guggly, juggly, smugly, snugly, struggly 3. plug-ugly [slang]

UG'ling– 2. guggling, juggling, smuggling, snuggling, struggling.

UG'nant– 3. repugnant, oppugnant 4. unrepugnant.

UG'ness– 2. smugness, snugness.

UJ'el– 2. cudgel.

UJ'er– 2. budger, fudger, judger, sludger, smudger, nudger, drudger, grudger, trudger 3. adjudger, rejudger, prejudger, misjudger, forejudger, begrudger.

UJ'et– 2. budget.

UJ'ez– 2. budges, fudges, judges, sludges, smudges, nudges, drudges, grudges, trudges 3. adjudges, prejudges, misjudges, begrudges.

UJ'i– 2. fudgy, sludgy, pudgy, smudgy.

UJ'ing– 2. budging, fudging, judging, sludging, smudging, nudging, drudging, grudging, trudging **3.** adjudging, prejudging, misjudging, begrudging.

UJ'ment– 2. judgment **3.** adjudgment, misjudgment.

UJ'on– 2. dudgeon, gudgeon, bludgeon 3. curmudgeon.

UK'a– 2. bucca, pucka, pukka, yucca **3.** felucca.

UK'er– 2. bucker, chucker, chukker, ducker, clucker, plucker, mucker, pucker, trucker, sucker, succor, shucker, tucker 3. seersucker.

UK'et– 2. bucket, mucket, tucket **3.** Nantucket, Pawtucket.

UK'i– 2. bucky, buckie, ducky, lucky, plucky, mucky, tucky **3.** unlucky, Kentucky.

UK'ij– 2. pluckage, truckage, suckage.

UK'ing– 2. bucking, chucking, ducking, clucking, plucking, mucking, trucking, sucking, shucking, tucking.

UK'ish– 2. buckish, puckish.

UK'l– 2. buckle, chuckle, huckle, muckle, knuckle, truckle, suckle, yukkel **3.** unbuckle, parbuckle **4.** honeysuckle.

UK'ld– 2. buckled, chuckled, cuckold, knuckled, truckled, suckled **3.** unbuckled.

UK'ler– 2. buckler, chuckler, knuckler, truckler, suckler 3. swashbuckler.

UK'less– 2. buckless, duckless, luckless, suckless.

UK'ling– 2. buckling, chuckling, duckling, knuckling, truckling, suckling **4.** ugly duckling.

UK'or– succor; *see* also **UK'er**– bucker etc. above.

UKS'ez– 2. fluxes, cruxes **3.** effluxes, refluxes.

UKSH'un– 2. duction, fluxion, ruction, suction 3. traduction, abduction, obduction, subduction, eduction, deduction, reduction, seduction, induction, conduction, production, affluxion, defluxion, influxion, obstruction, substruction, destruction, instruction, construction **4.** nonconduction, reproduction, introduction, manuduction, self-destruction, reconstruction, misconstruction **5.** superinduction, overproduction.

UKS'i– 2. mucksy, puxy, druxy **3.** Biloxi.

UKS'om– 2. buxom.

UKT'ans– 3. inductance, conductance, reluctance.

UKT'ant– 3. reluctant 4. unreluctant.

UKT'ed– 2. fructed 3. abducted, deducted, inducted, conducted, obstructed, instructed, constructed 4. unobstructed, misconstructed.

UKT'er– 2. ductor 3. abductor, eductor, inductor, conductor, productor, obstructor, destructor, instructor, constructor 4. nonconductor, introductor, manuductor, reconstructor.

UKT'il– 2. ductile 3. inductile, productile.

UKT'ing– 3. abducting, deducting, inducting, conducting, obstructing, instructing, constructing 4. nonconducting, misconducting, reconstructing.

UKT'iv– 3. adductive, traductive, deductive, reductive, seductive, inductive, conductive, productive, obstructive, destructive, instructive, constructive 4. reproductive, introductive, manuductive, self-destructive, reconstructive.

UKT'or– ductor etc., *see* **UKT'er**– ductor etc. above.

UKT'ress– 3. seductress, conductress, instructress 4. introductress.

UKT'ur– 2. structure 3. substructure, constructure 4. superstructure.

UK'us– 2. ruckus, succus.

UL'a– 2. bulla, mullah, nullah, sulla, Sulla, 3. medulla, cuculla, ampulla 4. nullanulla.

UL'en– 2. mullein, mullen, sullen, Sullan.

UL'er– 2. duller, huller, color, culler, sculler, luller, mullar, muller, cruller 3. medullar, recolor, tricolor, discolor, miscolor, annuller, ampullar 4. technicolor, versicolor, multicolor, water-color.

UL'erd– 2. dullard, colored 3. recolored, discolored, rose-colored, flesh-colored, fresh-colored, wine-colored 4. multicolored.

UL'est– 2. dullest.

UL'et– 2. gullet, cullet, mullet 3. surmullet.

ULF'er– 2. sulphur.

ULG'ar– 2. Bulgar, fulgor, vulgar.

ULG'at– 2. vulgate, Vulgate 3. promulgate, divulgate.

UL'i– 2. dully, gully, hully, cully, skully, sully, Tully.

UL'id– 2. gullied, sullied 3. unsullied.

UL'ij– 2. ullage, cullage, sullage.

UL'in– 2. mullein, sullen 3. Cuchullin.

UL'ing– 2. dulling, gulling, hulling, culling, lulling, mulling, sculling 3. dehulling, annuling.

UL'is– 2. dullis 3. portcullis.

UL'ish– 2. dullish, gullish.

ULJ'ens– 3. indulgence, effulgence, refulgence, divulgence 4. self-indulgence.

ULJ'ent– 2. fulgent 3. indulgent, effulgent, refulgent, emulgent 4. self-indulgent, interfulgent.

ULJ'er– 2. bulger 3. indulger, promulger, divulger.

ULJ'ing– 2. bulging 3. indulging, effulging, promulging, divulging.

ULJ'ment– 3. indulgement, divulgement.

ULK'at– 2. sulcate 3. inculcate, trisulcate.

ULK'er– 2. bulker, skulker, sulker.

ULK'i– 2. bulky, hulky, sulky.

ULK'ing– 2. bulking, hulking, skulking, sulking.

UL'ment– 3. annulment.

UL'ness– 2. dullness.

ULP'at– 2. culpate 3. inculpate, disculpate, exculpate.

ULP'er– 2. gulper, pulper.

ULP'i– 2. gulpy, pulpy.

ULP'tor– 2. sculptor.

ULS'er– 2. ulcer 3. repulser, expulser.

ULS'et– 2. dulcet.

ULSH'un– 2. pulsion 3. emulsion, demulsion, appulsion, repulsion, impulsion, compulsion, propulsion, expulsion, evulsion, revulsion, divulsion, convulsion.

ULS'ing– 2. pulsing 3. repulsing, expulsing, convulsing.

ULS'iv– 2. pulsive 3. emulsive, appulsive, repulsive, impulsive, compulsive, propulsive, expulsive, revulsive, divulsive, convulsive.

ULST'er– 2. ulster, hulster.

ULT'an– 2. sultan.

ULT'ant– 3. insultant, consultant, resultant, exultant.

ULT'ed– 3. occulted, insulted, consulted, resulted, exulted.

ULT'er– 3. occulter, insulter, consulter, consultor, exulter.

ULT'ing– 3. occulting, insulting, consulting, resulting, exulting.

ULT'iv– 3. consultive, resultive.

ULT'ness– 3. occultness, adultness.

ULT'ra– 2. ultra.

ULT'ri– 2. sultry.

ULT'ur– 2. culture, multure, vulture 4. vegeculture, apiculture, pomiculture, sericulture, floriculture, agriculture, pisciculture, viticulture, horticulture, aviculture, sylviculture, boviculture.

ULV'er– 2. culver, hulver.

UL'yun– 2. scullion, mullion, rullion 3. slumgullion.

UM'a– 2. summa [L.].

UMB'a- 2. dumba, jumba, rumba [Sp.]. 3. calumba, Columba.

UMB'el- 2. umbel, dumbbell.

UMB'ent- 3. accumbent, decumbent, recumbent, incumbent, procumbent, succumbent 5. superincumbent.

UMB'er- 2. umber, cumber, lumbar, lumber, slumber, number 3. encumber, renumber, outnumber 4. disencumber, unencumber, overnumber.

UMB'l- 2. umbel, bumble, fumble, humble, jumble, scumble, mumble, rumble, drumble, grumble, crumble, tumble, stumble 3. bejumble 4. overtumble.

UMB'ler- 2. bumbler, fumbler, humbler, jumbler, mumbler, rumbler, drumbler, grumbler, crumbler, tumbler, stumbler.

UMB'lest- 2. humblest.

UMB'li- 2. bumbly, fumbly, humbly, jumbly, mumbly, rumbly, grumbly, crumbly, tumbly, stumbly.

UMB'ling- 2. bumbling, fumbling, humbling, jumbling, scumbling, mumbling, rumbling, grumbling, crumbling, tumbling, stumbling 3. bejumbling 4. overtumbling.

UMB'o- 2. umbo, gumbo, Jumbo 3. columbo 4. Mumbo Jumbo, mumbo jumbo.

UMB'ra- 2. umbra 3. penumbra.

UMB'ral- 2. umbral 3. adumbral, penumbral.

UMB'rus- 2. umbrous, cumbrous, slumbrous 3. penumbrous.

UM'el- 2. hummel, pummel, pommel, trummel [loc.] 3. bepummel.

UM'er- 2. dumber, gummer, hummer, comer, cummer, scummer, glummer, plumber, slummer, mummer, number, rummer, drummer, strummer, thrummer, summer, thumber 3. incomer, newcomer, latecomer, succumber, midsummer.

UM'est- 2. dumbest, glummest, mummest, numbest.

UM'et- 2. plummet, grummet, summit.

UM'fant- 3. triumphant 4. untriumphant.

UM'i- 2. chummy [coll.], dummy, gummy, glummy, plummy, slummy, mummy, rummy, crumby, crummie, thrummy, tummy, thumby, yummy [slang] 3. gin rummy.

UM'ij- 2. chummage, plumbage, rummage, scrummage, summage 3. rerummage.

UM'ing- 2. bumming, chumming, gumming, humming, coming, scumming, plumbing, plumming, slumming, numbing, drumming, crumbing, strumming, thrumming, summing, thumbing 3. becoming, *incoming*, *oncoming*, *forthcoming*, succumbing, benumbing 4. unbecoming, overcoming.

UM'is- 2. pumice, pummice, pomace.

UM'it- 2. plummet, grummet, summit 3. consummate.

UM'li- 2. dumbly, comely, glumly, plumbly, mumly, numbly, rumly 3. uncomely 4. troublesomely, cumbersomely.

UM'nal- 3. columnal, autumnal.

UM'ness- 2. dumbness, glumness, plumbness, numbness.

UM'ok- 2. hummock, drummock, stomach.

UM'oks- 2. hummocks, lummox, flommox [slang], glommox [dial.], stomachs.

UMP'er- 2. bumper, dumper, jumper, lumper, plumper, pumper, trumper, stumper, thumper 3. broad jumper, high jumper.

UMP'est- 2. plumpest.

UMP'et- 2. crumpet, trumpet, strumpet.

UMP'i- 2. bumpy, chumpy, dumpy, humpy, jumpy, lumpy, clumpy, plumpy, slumpy, frumpy, grumpy, crumpy, stumpy, thumpy.

UMP'ij- 2. pumpage, stumpage.

UMP′ing– 2. bumping, dumping, humping, jumping, lumping, clumping, plumping, slumping, mumping, pumping, trumping, stumping, thumping 3. high-jumping 4. hurdle-jumping.

UMP′ish– 2. bumpish, chumpish, dumpish, humpish, jumpish, lumpish, plumpish, mumpish, frumpish, grumpish.

UMP′kin– 2. bumpkin, lumpkin, pumpkin 4. Tony Lumpkin.

UMP′l– 2. rumple, crumple.

UMP′ling– 2. dumpling, rumpling, crumpling 3. uncrumpling.

UMP′shun– 2. gumption 3. assumption, subsumption, resumption, presumption, consumption.

UMP′shus– 2. bumptious, gumptious, scrumptious.

UMPT′iv– 3. assumptive, subsumptive, consumptive, resumptive, presumptive.

UMP′us– 2. compass, rumpus 3. encompass 4. gyrocompass.

UM′uks– 2. lummox, flummox [slang], glommox [dial.], stomachs.

UM′zi– 2. clumsy.

UNCH′er– 2. buncher, huncher, luncher, muncher, puncher, bruncher, cruncher, scruncher 3. *cowpuncher*.

UNCH′ez– 2. bunches, hunches, lunches, munches, punches, brunches, crunches, scrunches.

UNCH′i– 2. bunchy, hunchy, punchy, crunchy, scrunchy.

UNCH′ing– 2. bunching, hunching, lunching, munching, punching, crunching, scrunching.

UNCH′on– 2. luncheon, nuncheon, sconcheon, puncheon, bruncheon, truncheon.

UND′a– 3. rotunda.

UND′an– 2. mundane 4. inframundane, intramundane, extramundane, ultramundane, antemundane, supermundane, intermundane.

UND′ans– 3. abundance, redundance 5. superabundance, overabundance.

UND′ant– 3. abundant, redundant 5. superabundant.

UND′ed– 2. funded 3. refunded, retunded, rotunded.

UND′er– 2. under, dunder, funder, plunder, sunder, thunder, wonder 3. down under, hereunder, thereunder, refunder, asunder, dissunder, rotunder, enthunder.

UND′i– 2. undy, bundy, fundi, Fundy, gundy, gundi, Monday, Sunday 3. Whitsunday 4. salmagundi.

UND′ing– 2. funding 3. refunding.

UND′l– 2. bundle, mundle [dial.], rundle, trundle 3. unbundle.

UND′ld– 2. bundled, trundled 3. unbundled.

UND′ler– 2. bundler, trundler.

UND′let– 2. bundlet, rundlet.

UND′ling– 2. bundling, trundling 3. unbundling.

UND′o– 3. secundo [L.]. 5. basso profundo.

UND′rus– 2. thundrous, wondrous.

UND′um– 3. secundum [L.], corundum 4. carborundum.

UND′us– 2. fundus.

UN′el– 2. funnel, gunnel, gunwale, runnel, trunnel, tunnel.

UN′er– 2. dunner, gunner, cunner, punner, runner, shunner, tonner, stunner 3. rumrunner, gunrunner, forerunner 4. thousand-tonner, overrunner.

UNG′er– 2. hunger, monger, younger 3. warmonger, newsmonger, fishmonger, witmonger 4. ironmonger, fashionmonger, scandalmonger, gossipmonger, costermonger.

UNG′l– 2. bungle, jungle.

UNG′li– 2. bungly, jungly.

UNG′us– 2. fungus 3. mundungus.

UN'i– 2. bunny, dunny, funny, gunny, honey, money, punny, runny, sunny, sonny, tunny.

UN'id– 2. honeyed, moneyed.

UN'ij– 2. dunnage, gunnage, punnage, tonnage.

UN'ing– 2. dunning, funning, gunning, cunning, punning, running, sunning, shunning, tunning, stunning 3. rumrunning, gunrunning, outrunning 4. overrunning.

UN'ish– 2. bunnish, Hunnish, nunnish, punish, punnish.

UNJ'ent– 2. pungent.

UNJ'er– 2. lunger, blunger, plunger, sponger 3. expunger.

UNJ'ez– 2. lunges, plunges, sponges 3. expunges.

UNJ'i– 2. plungy, spongy.

UNJ'ing– 2. lunging, plunging, sponging 3. expunging.

UNJ'un– 2. dungeon 3. Melungeon.

UNK'ard– 2. Dunkard, drunkard.

UNK'en– 2. sunken, drunken, shrunken 3. unsunken, unshrunken.

UNK'er– 2. bunker, dunker, funker, hunker, junker, flunker, punker 3. *mossbunker*.

UNK'et– 2. junket, tunket [dial.].

UNK'i– 2. chunky, funky, hunky, junky, skunky, flunky, flunkey, punky, punkie, spunky, monkey.

UNK'ish– 2. monkish, punkish, skunkish.

UNK'l– 2. uncle, truncal 3. *carbuncle, peduncle, homuncle, caruncle*.

UNK'o– 2. bunco, junco.

UNK'shun– 2. unction, function, junction, punction 3. inunction, defunction, adjunction, rejunction, injunction, conjunction, disjunction, compunction, expunction 4. interjunction, interpunction.

UNK'shus– 2. unctious 3. rambunctious, compunctious.

UNKT'iv– 3. abjunctive, adjunctive, subjunctive, conjunctive, disjunctive, compunctive.

UNKT'ur– 2. juncture, puncture 3. conjuncture.

UNK'um– 2. bunkum, Buncombe.

UN'less– 2. punless, runless, sunless, sonless.

UN'let– 2. punlet, runlet, tonlet.

UNSH'al– 2. uncial 3. quinuncial, pronuncial 4. internuncial.

UNST'er– 2. gunster, punster.

UNT'al– 2. puntal, frontal 3. confrontal 4. contrapuntal; *see* also **UNT'l–** gruntle etc. below.

UNT'ed– 2. bunted, hunted, blunted, punted, runted, fronted, grunted, shunted stunted, wonted 3. affronted, bifronted, confronted, unwonted.

UNT'er– 2. bunter, hunter, blunter, punter, fronter, grunter, shunter, stunter 3. head-hunter, affronter, confronter 4. fortune hunter.

UNT'est– 2. bluntest.

UNT'i– 2. punty, runty, stunty.

UNT'ij– 2. frontage.

UNT'ing– 2. bunting, hunting, punting, fronting, grunting, shunting, stunting 3. head-hunting, affronting, confronting 4. fortune-hunting.

UNT'l– 2. gruntle 3. disgruntle; *see* also **UNT'al–** puntal etc. above.

UNT'ness– 2. bluntness, stuntness.

UNT'o– 2. junto, punto.

UNT'ri– 2. country 3. God's country.

UN'yun– 2. onion, bunion, Bunyan, Runyon, trunnion.

UP'er– 2. upper, cupper, kupper, scupper, crupper, supper.

UP'et– 2. scuppet, puppet.

UP'i– 2. guppy, cuppy, puppy 3. *hiccoughy, hiccupy*.

UP'ing– 2. cupping, supping, tupping 3. *hiccoughing, hiccuping.*

UP'ish– 2. uppish, cuppish.

UP'l– 2. couple, supple 3. recouple, uncouple, unsupple.

UP'ler– 2. coupler, suppler 3. uncoupler.

UP'lest– 2. supplest.

UP'let– 2. cuplet, couplet 3. *quadruplet, quintuplet.*

UP'shal– 2. nuptial 3. postnuptial 4. antenuptial, internuptial.

UP'shun– 2. ruption 3. abruption, eruption, irruption, corruption, disruption 4. interruption, incorruption 5. uninterruption.

UPT'ed– 3. irrupted, corrupted, disrupted 4. interrupted, uncorrupted, undisrupted 5. uninterrupted.

UPT'er– 3. abrupter, corrupter, disrupter 4. interrupter.

UPT'est– 3. abruptest, corruptest.

UPT'ing– 3. erupting, corrupting, disrupting 4. interrupting.

UPT'iv– 2. ruptive 3. eruptive, irruptive, corruptive, disruptive 4. interruptive, incorruptive.

UPT'li– 3. abruptly, corruptly 4. incorruptly.

UPT'ness– 3. abruptness, corruptness 4. incorruptness.

UPT'ur– 2. rupture 3. disrupture.

UR'a– 2. gurrah 3. goburra 4. korumburra.

UR'al– 3. deferral, referral, demurral.

UR'ant– 2. currant 3. demurrant, susurrant; *see* also **UR'ent–** current etc. below.

URB'al– 2. herbal, verbal 3. biverbal.

URB'an– 2. urban, Bourbon, turban 3. suburban 4. interruban.

URB'ans– 3. disturbance.

URB'er– 2. Berber, curber, blurber 3. superber, perturber, disturber.

URB'est– 3. superbest.

URB'i– 2. derby, herby, blurby, verby 3. Iturbi.

URB'id– 2. herbid, turbid.

URB'ing– 2. curbing, herbing, blurbing, verbing 3. perturbing, disturbing.

URB'ish– 2. furbish 3. refurbish.

URB'it– 2. turbit, sherbet 3. concurbit.

URB'ot– 2. burbot, turbot.

URCH'ant– 2. merchant.

URCH'en– 2. urchin, birchen.

URCH'er– 2. bircher, lurcher, smircher, nurture, percher, searcher 3. besmircher, researcher.

URCH'ez– 2. birches, churches, lurches, smirches, perches, searches 3. besmirches, researches.

URCH'i– 2. churchy, lurchy, smirchy.

URCH'if– 2. kerchief 3. *neckerchief, handkerchief.*

URCH'in– 2. urchin, birchen.

URCH'ing– 2. birching, churching, lurching, smirching, perching, searching 3. besmirching, researching.

URD'ed– 2. girded, herded, curded, worded 3. begirded, engirded, reworded, misworded.

URD'en– 2. burden, guerdon 3. reburden, disburden 4. overburden.

URD'er– 2. girder, herder, murder 3. absurder, sheepherder.

URD'est– 3. absurdest.

URD'i– 2. birdie, curdy, purdy, sturdy, wordy 4. hurdy-gurdy.

URD'ing– 2. girding, herding, wording 3. begirding, engirding, rewording, miswording.

URD'l– 2. girdle, hurdle, curdle 3. begirdle, engirdle.

URD'li– 2. curdly, thirdly 3. absurdly.

UR'el– 2. burrel, squirrel.

UR'ens– 3. transference, recurrence, incurrence, concurrence, occurrence, deterrence 4. nonconcurrence, intercurrence.

UR'ent– 2. current, currant 3. decurrent, recurrent, concurrent, percurrent, crosscurrent, demurrant, susurrant, deterrent 4. undercurrent, intercurrent.

UR'er– 2. blurrer, purrer, spurrer, stirrer 3. deferrer, preferrer, conferrer, transferrer, transferor, concurrer, demurrer, interrer, bestirrer, averrer.

UR'et– 2. turret.

URF'i– 2. scurfy, murphy, surfy, turfy.

URF'it– 2. surfeit.

URG'al– 2. ergal, tergal, virgal.

URG'er– 2. burgher 3. *hamburger*.

URG'l– 2. ergal, burgle, gurgle, tergal, virgal.

URG'lar– 2. burglar, gurgler.

URG'o– 2. ergo [L.], Virgo 3. a tergo [L.].

URG'us– 2. Fergus 4. demiurgus, thaumaturgus, Thaumaturgus.

UR'i– 2. burry, durrie, firry, furry, gurry, hurry, curry, scurry, lurry, blurry, flurry, slurry, murrey, murry, purry, spurry, surrey, worry, whirry 4. hurry-scurry.

UR'id– 2. hurried, curried, scurried, flurried, worried 3. unhurried, unworried.

UR'ij– 2. courage, stirrage 3. encourage, discourage, demurrage.

UR'ing– 2. erring, burring, churring, furring, blurring, slurring, purring, spurring, shirring, stirring, whirring 3. unerring, deferring, referring, preferring, inferring, conferring, transferring, recurring, incurring, concurring, occurring, demurring, deterring, interring, bestirring, averring 4. disinterring.

UR'ish– 2. burrish, currish, flourish, nourish.

UR'iz– 2. hurries, curries, scurries, flurries, worries 3. snow flurries.

URJ'ens– 2. mergence, vergence 3. submergence, emergence, resurgence, insurgence, detergence, divergence, convergence.

URJ'ent– 2. urgent, surgent, vergent 3. emergent, assurgent, resurgent, insurgent, detergent, abstergent, divergent, convergent.

URJ'er– 2. urger, berger, dirger, scourger, splurger, merger, purger, perjure, verger, verdure.

URJ'ez– 2. urges, dirges, scourges, splurges, merges, purges, verges 3. emerges, asperges, converges.

URJ'i– 2. clergy, surgy 4. metallurgy, dramaturgy, thaumaturgy.

URJ'id– 2. turgid 3. energid, unturgid.

URJ'ik– 3. theurgic, energic, chirurgic, liturgic 4. demiurgic, metallurgic, dramaturgic, thaumaturgic.

URJ'in– 2. virgin.

URJ'ing– 2. urging, dirging, scourging, splurging, merging, purging, surging, verging 3. submerging, emerging, immerging, deterging, diverging, converging.

URJ'ist– 4. metallurgist, dramaturgist, thaumaturgist.

URJ'ment– 3. submergement, divergement, convergement.

URJ'on– 2. burgeon, surgeon, sturgeon.

URK'a– 2. furca, circa 3. amurca, mazurka.

URK'al– 2. furcal, cercal 3. novercal 4. homocercal 5. heterocercal.

URK'er– 2. burker, jerker, jerquer, kirker, lurker, smirker, perker, shirker, worker 3. nonworker, *guessworker* 4. wonder-worker.

URK'i– 2. jerky, lurky, murky, smirky, perky, shirky, turkey, quirky.

URK'in– 2. firkin, gherkin, jerkin, perkin.

URK'ing– 2. irking, jerking, lurking, clerking, smirking, perking, shirking, working, quirking 3. hard-working, non-working 4. wonder-working.

URK'ish– 2. jerkish, clerkish, perkish, Turkish, quirkish.

URK'it– 2. circuit.

URK'l– 2. cercle, circle, turkle 3. encircle, excircle, novercal 4. semicircle, homocercal.

URK'li– 2. Berkeley, clerkly, circly.

URK'ling– 2. circling 3. recircling, encircling 4. semicircling.

URK'som– 2. irksome, murksome, worksome, quirksome.

URK'us– 2. cercus, circus, Quercus.

URL'er– 2. birler, burler, furler, hurler, curler, pearler, purler, twirler, whirler.

URL'et– 2. burlet, pearlet, spurlet.

URL'i– 2. early, burly, churly, girly, girlie, gurly, hurly, curly, murly, knurly, pearly, pirlie [Scot.], surly, Shirley, swirly, twirly, whirly 4. hurly-burly.

URL'in– 2. merlin, murlin, purlin.

URL'ing– 2. birling, furling, herling, hurling, skirling, knurling, pearling, purling, sperling, sterling, thirling, swirling, twirling, whirling.

URL'ish– 2. churlish, girlish, pearlish.

URL'oin– 2. purloin, sirloin.

URL'u– 2. curlew, purlieu.

URM'a– 2. Irma, Burma, derma, syrma, Syrma 4. pachyderma, terra firma.

URM'al– 2. dermal, thermal 3. synthermal 4. pachydermal, epidermal, taxidermal, hypodermal, hydrothermal, isothermal.

URM'an– 2. Burman, firman, Herman, German, germon, merman, Sherman, termen, termon.

URM'ans– 3. affirmance, confirmance 4. disaffirmance.

URM'ent– 2. ferment 3. affirmant, deferment, referment, preferment, determent, interment, averment 4. disinterment.

URM'er– 2. firmer, murmur, termer, termor, wormer, squirmer 3. affirmer, infirmer, confirmer, bemurmur.

URM'est– 2. firmest 3. infirmest.

URM'ez– 2. Hermes, kermes.

URM'i– 2. germy, spermy, wormy 4. taxidermy, diathermy.

URM'ik– 2. dermic, thermic 3. endermic 4. pachydermic, epidermic, taxicermic, diathermic, geothermic.

URM'in– 2. ermine, termin, vermin 3. determine 4. redetermine.

URM'ind– 2. ermined 3. determined 4. redetermined, undetermined.

URM'ing– 2. firming, germing, terming, worming, squirming 3. affirming, confirming.

URM'is– 2. dermis, kermis 4. epidermis, endodermis, exodermis.

URM'ish– 2. skirmish, wormish.

URM'it– 2. hermit, permit.

URM'li– 2. firmly, termly 3. infirmly, unfirmly.

URM'os– 2. hirmos, spermous, thermos.

URM'un– 2. Berman, Herman, German, germen, germon, Sherman, termen, termon.

URN'a– 2. Smyrna, sterna 3. taberna 4. parapherna.

URN'al– 2. urnal, journal, colonel, kernel, sternal, vernal 3. diurnal, hibernal, infernal, supernal, lucernal, maternal, paternal, fraternal, eternal, nocturnal, internal, external, hesternal, cavernal 4. paraphernal, coeternal, diuternal, sempiternal, hodiernal.

URN'ant– 2. vernant 3. alternant, secernent.

URN'at– 2. ternate 3. biternate, quaternate, cothurnate.

URN'ed– 2. learned 3. unlearned.

URN'el– 2. colonel, kernel; *see* also URN'al– urnal etc. above.

URN'er– 2. earner, burner, churner, learner, pirner, spurner, turner, sterner, yearner 3. adjourner, sojourner, returner, discerner.

URN′est– 2. earnest, Ernest, sternest.

URN′i– 2. burny, ferny, journey, pirnie, tourney 3. enurny, attorney.

URN′ing– 2. earning, urning, burning, derning [dial.], churning, learning, spurning, turning, yearning 3. inurning, adjourning, sojourning, *booklearning*, discerning, concerning, returning, interning, upturning 4. undiscerning, overturning,

URN′is– 2. furnace.

URN′ish– 2. burnish, furnish 3. reburnish, refurnish.

URN′ment– 3. adjournment, sojournment, secernment, discernment, concernment, attornment, internment.

URN′ness– 2. ternness, sternness 3. asternness 4. taciturnness.

URN′o– 3. inferno, Salerno.

URN′um– 2. sternum 3. laburnum, Viburnum, alburnum.

URN′us– 3. cothurnus, Avernus.

UR′o– 2. burro, burrow, borough, furrow, thorough 3. unthorough 4. interborough.

URP′er– 2. burper, chirper 3. hyperper, usurper.

URP′ing– 2. burping [slang], chirping, slurping [dial.] 3. usurping.

URP′l– 2. purple 3. empurple.

URS′a– 2. Ursa, bursa, Byrsa, djersa 3. vice versa.

URS′al– 2. ursal, bursal, cursal 3. rehearsal, bicursal, succursal, dispersal, reversal, transversal 4. interspersal, quaquaversal, universal, partiversal; *see* also **URS′l–** birsle etc. below.

URS′ant– 2. versant 3. aversant, conversant.

URS′ed– 2. cursed 3. accursed.

URS′er– 2. bursar, curser, cursor, mercer, nurser, purser, terser, verser, versor, worser 3. coercer, disburser, rehearser, accurser, precursor, amercer, disperser, traverser, reverser, converser 4. reimburser, intersperser.

URS′et– 2. tercet, verset.

URS′ez– 2. hearses, curses, nurses, purses, verses 3. coerces, disburses, rehearses, accurses, precurses, amerces, submerses, immerses, disperses, traverses, reverses, converses 4. reimburses, intersperses, universes.

URSH′al– 2. tertial 3. commercial 4. uncommercial, sesquitertial, controversial.

URSH′an– 2. Persian, tertian 3. Cistercian, lacertian 4. sesquitertian; *see* also **URSH′un–** mersion etc. below.

URSH′un– 2. mersion, tersion, version 3. coercion, recursion, incursion, excursion, submersion, emersion, immersion, aspersion, dispersion, assertion, desertion, exsertion, insertion, concertion, abstersion, aversion, obversion, subversion, eversion, reversion, diversion, inversion, conversion, perversion 4. interspersion, disconcertion, introversion, retroversion 5. animadversion; *see* also **URSH′an–** Persian etc. above; **URZH′un–** version etc. below.

URS′i– 2. mercy, nursy, Percy, pursy, Circe 3. gramercy, Luperci 4. controversy.

URS′ing– 2. cursing, nursing, pursing, versing 3. coercing, disbursing, rehearsing, accursing, immersing, dispersing, traversing, reversing, conversing, transversing 4. reimbursing.

URS′iv– 2. cursive 3. coercive, decursive, recursive, precursive, incursive, discursive, excursive, immersive, aspersive, dispersive, detersive, abstersive, aversive, subversive, eversive, inversive, conversive, perversive, transversive 4. introversive, extroversive.

URS′l– 2. birsle, hirsel, nursle, tercel; *see* also **URS′al–** ursal etc. above.

URS′let– 2. purslet, verselet.

URS'li– 2. tersely 3. aversely, obversely, adversely, reversely, diversely, inversely, conversely, perversely, transversely.

URS'ling– 2. nurseling, verseling.

URS'ment– 3. imbursement, disbursement, amercement 4. reimbursement.

URS'ness– 2. terseness 3. averseness, adverseness, perverseness.

URS'o– 2. verso 3. concurso, reverso.

URS'on– 2. urson, person.

URST'ed– 2. bursted, thirsted, worsted.

URST'er– 2. burster, thirster.

URST'i– 2. thirsty 3. bloodthirsty, unthirsty.

URST'ing– 2. bursting, thirsting, worsting.

URST'ling– 2. firstling, Hearstling.

URS'us– 2. Ursus, cursus, thyrsus, Thyrsis, versus 3. concursus, excursus, Melursus, adversus [L.], conversus, transversus.

URT'a– 2. Berta, Goethe, serta 3. Alberta, Elberta, Lacerta 4. Ethelberta.

URT'al– 2. curtal 3. consertal.

URT'an– 2. curtain, certain 3. encurtain, uncertain 4. overcurtain, overcertain.

URT'ed– 2. skirted, blurted, flirted, spurted, shirted, squirted, verted 3. alerted, asserted, exerted, inserted, concerted, blackshirted, averted, reverted, diverted, inverted, converted, perverted 4. preconcerted, disconcerted, interserted, undiverted, introverted, extroverted, unperverted.

URT'ens– 3. advertence 4. inadvertence.

URT'ent– 3. advertent 4. inadvertent.

URT'er– 2. hurter, skirter, flirter, curter, perter, spurter, squirter 3. *frankfurter*, asserter, inserter, averter, reverter, inverter, converter, perverter 4. preconcerter, disconcerter 5. animadverter.

URT'est– 2. curtest, pertest.

URT'ez– 2. certes, thirties.

URTH'a– 2. bertha, Bertha, Hertha.

URTH'en– 2. earthen, burthen.

URTH'i– 2. earthy, birthy, worthy 3. *seaworthy*, unworthy, *noteworthy*, *trustworthy*, *praiseworthy*.

URTH'less– 2. earthless, birthless, mirthless, worthless.

URTH'li– 2. earthly 3. unearthly.

URT'i– 2. cherty, cherte, dirty, Gertie, flirty, certie, certy [both Scot. & N. of Eng.], thirty.

URT'in– 2. curtain, certain 3. encurtain, uncertain 4. overcurtain, overcertain; *see* also **URT'on–** burton etc. below.

URT'ing– 2. hurting, skirting, blurting, flirting, spurting, shirting, squirting 3. alerting, deserting, exerting, inserting, concerting, averting, subverting, reverting, diverting, inverting, converting, perverting 4. preconcerting, disconcerting, interserting, retroverting, introverting, extroverting.

URT'iv– 2. furtive 3. assertive, exertive, insertive, revertive, divertive, invertive, convertive 4. self-assertive, introvertive, extrovertive.

URT'l– 2. fertile, hurtle, kirtle, myrtle, Myrtle, spurtle, turtle, whortle 3. infertile.

URT'less– 2. hurtless, skirtless, shirtless.

URT'li– 2. curtly, pertly 3. inertly, alertly, *expertly* 4. *inexpertly.*

URT'ness– 2. curtness, pertness 3. inertness, alertness, *expertness.*

URT'on– 2. burton, Burton, Merton 4. Gammer Gurton; *see* also **URT'an–** curtain etc. above.

URT'um– 2. furtum [L.], sertum 3. assertum.

UR'us– 2. byrrus, churrus 3. susurrus, susurrous.

URV'a– 2. urva 3. conferva, Minerva.

URV'al– 2. nerval, serval, vervel 3. acerval, conferval, adnerval, minerval.

URV'ans– 3. observance 4. inobservance, nonobservance, unobservance.

URV'ant– 2. fervent, curvant, servant 3. recurvant, observant, maidservant, conservant 4. inobservant, unobservant.

URV'ate– 2. curvate 3. recurvate, incurvate, tricurvate, acervate, trinervate.

URV'er– 2. fervor, nerver, server, swerver 3. unnerver, observer, deserver, reserver, preserver, observer, conserver 4. life preserver.

URV'i– 2. nervy, curvy, scurvy 4. topsy-turvy.

URV'id– 2. fervid 3. perfervid 4. topsy-turvied.

URV'il– 2. chervil, servile, vervel.

URV'ing– 2. Irving, curving, nerving, serving, swerving 3. unnerving, observing, reserving, preserving, conserving, unswerving 4. unobserving, undeserving, unconserving.

URV'is– 2. service 3. reservice, self-service, disservice, sea service, tea service.

URV'less– 2. curveless, nerveless, serveless, verveless, swerveless 3. deserveless, reserveless, preserveless.

URV'us– 2. curvous, nervous 3. confervous, recurvous, unnervous.

URZH'un– 2. version 3. recursion, incursion, discursion, excursion, submersion, immersion, aspersion, dispersion, aversion, subversion, reversion, diversion, inversion, conversion, perversion 5. animadversion.

URZ'i– 2. furzy, jersey, kersey, Mersey.

USCH'un– 2. fustian 3. combustion, inustion.

US'el– 2. mussel, Russel, trussell; *see* also US'l– bustle etc. below.

US'er– 2. busser, fusser, cusser, musser, trusser 3. discusser, nonplusser.

US'et– 2. gusset, russet.

US'ez– 2. busses, fusses, cusses [coll.], plusses, musses, trusses 3. discusses, nonplusses, untrusses.

USH'a– 2. Russia, Prussia.

USH'er– 2. usher, gusher, husher, lusher, blusher, flusher, plusher, rusher, brusher, crusher, shusher 3. fourflusher.

USH'est– 2. lushest, flushest, plushest.

USH'ez– 2. gushes, hushes, blushes, flushes, plushes, mushes, rushes, brushes, crushes, thrushes, tushes 3. four-flushes.

USH'i– 2. gushy, lushy, blushy, plushy, slushy, rushy, brushy, thrushy.

USH'ing– 2. gushing, hushing, mushing, blushing, flushing, rushing, brushing, crushing 3. unblushing, four-flushing, onrushing.

USH'un– 2. Russian, Prussian 3. recussion, incussion, concussion, percussion, discussion, succussion 4. repercussion.

US'i– 2. fussy, Gussie, hussy, mussy 4. overfussy.

US'ing– 2. bussing, fussing, cussing [coll.], mussing, trussing 3. discussing, nonplussing, untrussing.

US'iv– 2. jussive, tussive 3. concussive, percussive, discussive, succussive 4. repercussive.

USK'an– 2. dusken, Tuscan 3. molluscan, Etruscan.

USK'er– 2. husker, tusker 3. cornhusker.

USK'et– 2. busket, musket.

USK'i– 2. dusky, husky, musky, tusky.

USK'in– 2. buskin, ruskin, Ruskin.

USK'ing– 2. dusking, husking, tusking 3. cornhusking.

USK'ul– 3. majuscule, minuscule, crepuscule, opuscle.

US'l– 2. bustle, duscle, hustle, justle, mussel, muscle, rustle, Russell, trussell, tussal, tussle 3. *arbuscle*, crepuscle, opuscle, *corpuscle*.

US'ler– 2. bustler, hustler, rustler, tussler.

US'li– 2. muscly, rustly, thusly.

US'ling– 2. bustling, hustling, muscling, rustling, tussling.

US'lz– 2. bustles, hustles, muscles, rustles, Brussels, tussles.

UST'a– 2. crusta 3. Augusta.

UST'ard– 2. bustard, custard, mustard; *see* also **UST'erd–** bustard, lustered etc. below.

UST'e– 2. fustee, fustie, mustee.

UST'ed– 2. busted, dusted, lusted, rusted, crusted, trusted 3. combusted, bedusted, disgusted, adjusted, encrusted, entrusted, distrusted, mistrusted 4. maladjusted.

UST'er– 2. buster, duster, juster, Custer, luster, bluster, fluster, cluster, muster, rustre, truster, thruster 3. robuster, trust buster, adjuster, adjustor, lackluster, distruster, mistruster 4. filibuster, readjuster, coadjuster.

UST'erd– 2. bustard, custard, lustered, blustered, flustered, clustered, mustered, mustard, rustred 3. beflustered, unclustered.

UST'est– 2. justest 3. robustest.

UST'ful– 2. gustful, lustful, trustful, thrustful 3. disgustful, untrustful, distrustful, mistrustful 4. overtrustful.

UST'i– 2. busty, dusty, fusty, gusty, lusty, musty, rusty, crusty, trusty.

UST'ik– 2. bustic, fustic, rustic 4. anacrustic.

UST'ing– 2. busting, dusting, husting, lusting, rusting, crusting, trusting, thrusting 3. bedusting, disgusting, adjusting, encrusting, entrusting, distrusting, mistrusting 4. readjusting, maladjusting, coadjusting, self-adjusting.

UST'is– 2. justice, Custis 3. injustice.

UST'iv– 3. combustive, adjustive.

UST'li– 2. justly 3. robustly, augustly, unjustly.

UST'ment– 3. adjustment, encrustment, entrustment 4. readjustment, maladjustment.

UST'ness– 2. justness 3. robustness, augustness, unjustness.

UST'ral– 2. lustral 3. lacustral, palustral.

UST'rat– 2. frustrate 3. illustrate.

UST'rum– 2. lustrum, flustrum.

UST'rus– 2. lustrous, blustrous 3. lacklustrous.

UST'um– 2. custom 3. accustom 4. reaccustom.

UST'us– 2. Justus 3. Augustus.

UT'a– 2. gutta 3. Calcutta.

UT'al– 3. abuttal, rebuttal 4. surrebuttal; *see* also **UT'l–** buttle etc. below.

UT'e– 2. puttee, ruttee, suttee.

UT'ed– 2. butted, gutted, jutted, smutted, nutted, rutted, strutted 3. abutted, rebutted 4. unrebutted.

UT'er– 2. utter, butter, cutter, scutter, flutter, glutter, clutter, splutter, mutter, nutter, putter, sputter, rutter, strutter, shutter, stutter 3. abutter, rebutter, woodcutter, stonecutter, meatcutter 4. bread-and-butter, peanut butter, surrebutter.

UT'erd– 2. uttered, buttered, fluttered, muttered, sputtered, shuttered, stuttered 3. unuttered, well-buttered, unfluttered.

UTH'er– 2. other, mother, smother, brother, tother 3. *grandmother*, another.

UTH'ern– 2. southern.

UT'i– 2. butty, gutty, jutty, cutty, scutty, smutty, nutty, putty, puttee, rutty.

UT'ing– 2. butting, gutting, jutting, cutting, glutting, smutting, nutting, putting, rutting, strutting, shutting 3. abutting, rebutting, woodcutting, stonecutting, crosscutting.

UT'ish– 2. sluttish, nuttish, ruttish.

UT'l– 2. buttle, guttle, cuttle, scuttle, ruttle, subtle, suttle, shuttle 3. abuttal, rebuttal, unsubtle 4. surrebuttal.

UT'ler– 2. butler, cutler, cuttler, scuttler, ruttler, subtler, sutler.

UT'let– 2. cutlet.

UT'li– 2. subtly 3. unsubtly.

UT'ling– 2. buttling, gutling [dial.], guttling, scuttling.

UT'ment– 2. butment 3. abutment, rebutment.

UT'on– 2. button, glutton, mutton 3. *bluebutton* 5. bachelor-button.

UV'ed– 3. beloved.

UV'el– 2. hovel, scovel, shovel.

UV'en– 2. oven, sloven.

UV'er– 2. hover, lover, glover, plover, cover, shover 3. windhover, recover, uncover, discover, self-lover 4. undercover, rediscover.

UV'i– 2. covey, lovey 4. lovey-dovey.

UV'ing– 2. loving, gloving, shoving 3. unloving, ungloving, self-loving.

UV'li– 2. lovely 3. unlovely.

UZ'ard– 2. buzzard, huzzard.

UZ'en– 2. dozen, cozen, cousin.

UZ'er– 2. buzzer, nuzzer.

UZ'ez– 2. buzzes, fuzzes, muzzes.

UZ'i– 2. buzzy, fuzzy, hussy, huzzy, muzzy 4. fuzzy-guzzy, fuzzy-wuzzy.

UZ'ing– 2. buzzing, fuzzing, muzzing.

UZ'l– 2. buzzle, guzzle, muzzle, nuzzle, puzzle 3. bemuzzle, unmuzzle, bepuzzle 4. crossword puzzle, jigsaw puzzle, Chinese puzzle.

UZ'ler– 2. guzzler, muzzler, puzzler.

UZ'lin– 2. muslin,

UZ'ling– 2. guzzling, muzzling, nuzzling, puzzling 3. bemuzzling, unmuzzling, bepuzzling.

UZ'n– 2. dozen, cozen, cousin.

U (tub)

3.

TRIPLE RHYMES IN U (tub′ba-ble)

Primary or Secondary Accent Falls on Second from Last Syllable.

UB′a-bl- **3.** clubbable, scrubbable, tubbable.

UB′er-er- **3.** blubberer, slubberer, rubberer.

UR′er-i- **3.** blubbery, rubbery, scrubbery, shrubbery.

UB′i-er- **3.** chubbier, grubbier, scrubbier, shrubbier, tubbier, stubbier.

UB′il-i- **3.** chubbily, grubbily, scrubbily, tubbily, stubbily.

UB′i-ness- **3.** chubbiness, grubbiness, scrubbiness, shrubbiness, tubbiness, stubbiness.

UB′lik-an- **3.** publican **4.** republican.

UB′lish-er- **3.** publisher **4.** republisher.

UD′er-i- **3.** duddery, shuddery, studdery.

UD′i-er- **3.** bloodier, muddier, ruddier, studier.

UD′i-est- **3.** bloodiest, muddiest, ruddiest.

UD′il-i- **3.** bloodily, muddily, ruddily.

UD′i-ness- **3.** bloodiness, muddiness, ruddiness.

UF′a-bl- **3.** buffable, bluffable, ruffable **4.** rebuffable, unruffable **5.** unrebuffable.

UF′i-er- **3.** huffier, fluffier, snuffier, puffier, stuffier.

UF′il-i- **3.** huffily, fluffily, snuffily, puffily, stuffily.

UF′i-ness- **3.** huffiness, fluffiness, snuffiness, puffiness, stuffiness.

UF′ing-li- **3.** buffingly, huffingly, bluffingly, fluffingly, snuffingly, puffingly, stuffingly **4.** rebuffingly **5.** unrebuffingly.

UG′a-bl- **3.** huggable, pluggable.

UG′er-i- **3.** snuggery, pugaree, druggery, thuggery.

UG′i-ness- **3.** bugginess, slugginess, mugginess, pugginess.

UJ′a-bl- **3.** judgeable **4.** adjudgeable.

UJ′er-i- **3.** drudgery, grudgery.

UJ′i-ness- **3.** smudginess.

UK′er-ing- **3.** puckering, succoring.

UK′i-ness- **3.** luckiness, pluckiness, muckiness **4.** unluckiness.

UK′shun-al- **3.** fluxional, suctional **4.** inductional, reductional, conductional, productional, destructional, instructional, constructional.

UK′shun-ist- **3.** fluxionist **4.** productionist, obstructionist, destructionist, constructionist **5.** reconstructionist.

UKT′i-bl- **4.** deductible, conductible, productible, destructible, instructible, constructible **5.** undeductible, indestructible, uninstructible.

UKT′iv-li- **4.** deductively, seductively, inductively, productively, obstructively, destructively, instructively, constructively **5.** unproductively.

UKT′iv-ness- **4.** seductiveness, productiveness, destructiveness, instructiveness, constructiveness **5.** unproductiveness, reconstructiveness.

UKT′or-i- 4. deductory, inductory, conductory 5. reproductory, introductory, manuductory.

UK′ul-ens- 3. truculence, succulence.

UK′ul-ent- 3. truculent, succulent.

UL′er-i- 3. gullery, colory, skullery, scullery 4. medullary.

ULK′i-ness- 3. bulkiness, sulkiness.

UL′min-ant- 3. fulminant, culminant.

UL′min-at- 3. fulminate, culminate.

ULS′if-i- 3. dulcify 4. emulsify.

ULS′iv-li- 4. repulsively, impulsively, compulsively, revulsively, convulsively.

ULS′iv-ness- 4. repulsiveness, impulsiveness, compulsiveness, revulsiveness, convulsiveness.

ULS′or-i- 4. compulsory, expulsory 5. uncompulsory.

ULT′a-bl- 4. insultable, consultable 5. uninsultable, unconsultable.

ULT′im-it- 3. ultimate 4. penultimate 6. antepenultimate.

ULT′ing-li- 4. insultingly, exultingly.

ULT′ur-al- 3. cultural 5. agricultural, floricultural, horticultural.

ULT′ur-ist- 3. culturist 5. apiculturist, agriculturist, floriculturist, horticulturist.

UM′aj-er- 3. rummager, scrummager.

UM′ar-i- 3. nummary, summary; *see* also **UM′er-i-** chummery etc. below.

UM′ar-ist- 3. summarist.

UMB′ens-i- 3. cumbency 4. decumbency, recumbency, incumbency.

UMB′er-er- 3. cumberer, lumberer, slumberer, numberer 4. encumberer.

UMB′er-i- 3. slumbery.

UMB′er-ing- 3. cumbering, lumbering, slumbering, numbering 4. encumbering, unslumbering, outnumbering.

UMB′er-som- 3. cumbersome, slumbersome, numbersome.

UMB′er-us- 3. slumberous, numberous 4. unslumberous.

UMB′ling-li- 3. rumblingly, tumblingly, stumblingly.

UM′er-i- 3. chummery, flummery, plumbery, nummary, mummery, summary, summery.

UM′er-ing- 3. summering.

UM′ing-li- 3. hummingly, numbingly 4. becomingly, benumbingly 5. unbecomingly.

UMP′i-ness- 3. dumpiness, humpiness, jumpiness, frumpiness, grumpiness, stumpiness.

UMP′ish-ness- 3. dumpishness, lumpishness, mumpishness, frumpishness, grumpishness.

UMP′shus-li- 3. bumptiously, scrumptiously.

UMP′shus-ness- 3. bumptiousness, scrumptiousness 4. assumptiousness.

UMPT′iv-li- 4. assumptively, resumptively, presumptively, consumptively.

UMPT′u-us- 3. sumptuous 4. presumptuous, unsumptuous.

UN′a-bl- 3. punnable, runnable, shunnable.

UNCH′a-bl- 3. punchable, crunchable.

UND′a-bl- 3. fundable 4. refundable.

UND′ant-li- 4. abundantly, redundantly 6. superabundantly.

UND′er-er- 3. blunderer, plunderer, sunderer, thunderer, wonderer.

UND′er-ing- 3. blundering, plundering, sundering, thundering, wondering.

UND′er-us- 3. plunderous, thunderous.

UND′it-i- 4. profundity, fecundity, jocundity, immundity, obtundity, rotundity 5. moribundity, rubicundity, orotundity.

UN′er-i- 3. gunnery, nunnery.

UNG′ar-i- 3. Hungary.

UNG′er-ing- 3. hungering, mongering 4. wordmongering, warmongering, newsmongering 5. scandalmongering, ironmongering.

UN'il-i- 3. funnily, sunnily 4. unfunnily.

UNK'shun-al- 3. unctional, functional, junctional 4. conjunctional.

UNKT'iv-li- 4. adjunctively, subjunctively, conjunctively, disjunctively.

UNK'u-lar- 3. uncular 4. carbuncular, peduncular, caruncular, avuncular.

UNT'ed-li- 3. huntedly, stuntedly, wontedly 4. affrontedly, unwontedly.

UNT'ed-ness- 3. huntedness, bluntedness, stuntedness, wontedness 4. affrontedness, unwontedness.

UNT'i-ness- 3. puntiness, runtiness, stuntiness.

UNT'ing-li- 3. buntingly, huntingly, gruntingly, stuntingly.

UP'le-ment- 3. supplement.

UPT'iv-li- 4. corruptively, disruptively 5. interruptively.

URB'a-bl- 3. curbable 4. uncurbable, perturbable 5. imperturbable, indisturbable, undisturbable.

URB'al-ist- 3. herbalist, verbalist.

URB'i-al- 4. suburbial, adverbial, proverbial.

URD'er-er- 3. murderer, verderer.

URD'il-i- 3. sturdily, wordily.

URD'i-ness- 3. curdiness, sturdiness, wordiness.

URD'it-i- 4. absurdity.

UR'ens-i- 3. currency 4. recurrency, concurrency.

UR'ent-li- 3. currently 4. recurrently, concurrently.

UR'id-li- 3. hurriedly, flurriedly, worriedly.

UR'i-er- 3. burrier, furrier, hurrier, currier, courier, scurrier, purrier, worrier.

UR'i-ing- 3. burying, hurrying, flurrying, currying, scurrying, worrying.

UR'i-ment- 3. flurriment, worriment.

UR'ish-ing- 3. flourishing, nourishing 4. unflourishing, unnourishing.

URJ'en-si- 3. urgency, vergency 4. emergency, assurgency, insurgency, detergency, divergency, convergency.

URJ'er-i- 3. perjury, purgery, surgery, vergery 4. chirurgery.

URJ'ik-al- 3. surgical 4. theurgical, energical, liturgical 5. demiurgical, metallurgical, thaumaturgical.

URK'il-i- 3. jerkily, perkily, murkily.

URK'ul-ar- 3. furcular, circular 4. tubercular, opercular 5. semicircular.

URK'ul-at- 3. circulate 4. tuberculate, operculate, recirculate.

URK'ul-um- 3. furculum 4. tuberculum, operculum.

URK'ul-us- 3. circulus, surculus, surculous 4. tuberculous.

URL'a-bl- 3. furlable 4. unfurlable.

URL'i-er- 3. earlier, burlier, churlier, curlier, pearlier, surlier.

URL'i-est- 3. earliest, burliest, churliest, curliest, pearliest, surliest.

URL'i-ness- 3. earliness, burliness, curliness, pearliness, surliness.

URL'ish-ness- 3. churlishness, girlishness.

URM'an-i- 3. Germany, verminy.

URM'ar-i- 4. infirmary.

URM'at-iv- 4. affirmative, confirmative.

URM'in-al- 3. germinal, terminal 4. adterminal, conterminal.

URM'in-ant- 3. germinant, terminant 4. determinant, interminant, conterminant.

URM'in-at- 3. germinate, terminate 4. determinate, interminate, exterminate 5. predeterminate, indeterminate.

URM'in-us- 3. terminus, verminous 4. coterminous.

URM'it-i- 4. infirmity, confirmity.

URM'it-ij- 3. hermitage.

URN'a-bl- 3. burnable, learnable, turnable 4. unburnable, unlearnable, returnable 5. unreturnable, overturnable; *see* also **URN'i-bl-** discernible etc. below.

URN'al-i- 3. vernally 4. infernally, eternally, externally.

URN'al-ist- 3. journalist 4. eternalist, externalist.

URN'al-iz- 3. journalize 4. infernalize, eternalize, externalize.

URN'al-izm- 3. journalism 4. infernalism, eternalism, externalism.

URN'ed-li- 3. learnedly 4. unlearnedly, concernedly 5. unconcernedly.

URN'er-i- 3. fernery, ternery, turnery.

URN'i-a- 3. hernia 4. Hibernia, Calpurnia, Saturnia, evernia.

URN'i-an- 4. eburnean, Hibernian, Falernian, Saturnian.

URN'i-bl- 4. discernible 5. indiscernible; *see* also **URN'a-bl-** burnable etc. above.

URN'ish-er- 3. burnisher, furnisher 4. refurnisher.

URN'ish-ing- 3. burnishing, furnishing 4. refurnishing.

URN'it-i- 4. modernity, maternity, fraternity, eternity, alternity 5. sempiternity, taciturnity, diuturnity.

URN'it-ur- 3. furniture, cerniture.

UR'o-er- 3. burrower, furrower.

URP'en-tin- 3. serpentine, turpentine.

URP'i-li- 3. burpily [slang], chirpily, slurpily [dial.].

URP'i-ness- 3. burpiness [slang], chirpiness, slurpiness [dial.].

URS'a-bl- 4. amerceable, traversable, reversable, inversable, conversable; *see* also **URS'i-bl-** coercible etc. below.

URS'ar-i- 3. bursary 5. anniversary; *see* also **URS'or-i-** cursory, etc. below.

URS'er-i- 3. cursory, nursery 4. precursory, discursory, aspersory.

URSH'i-a- 3. tertia 4. inertia 5. sesquitertia.

URSH'i-an- 3. Persian, tertian 4. lacertian, Cistercian 5. sesquitertian.

URS'i-bl- 4. coercible, submersible, immersible, reversible, conversible 5. incoercible, introversible; *see* also **URS'a-bl-** amerceable etc. above.

URS'i-form- 3. ursiform, bursiform, furciform, versiform 4. diversiform.

URS'it-i- 4. adversity, diversity, perversity 5. university.

URS'iv-li- 4. decursively, discursively, excursively, aspersively, dispersively, detersively.

URS'iv-ness- 4. coerciveness, discursiveness, excursiveness, detersiveness.

URS'on-al- 3. personal 4. tripersonal, impersonal 5. unipersonal.

URS'or-i- 3. cursory 4. precursory, discursory, aspersory; *see* also **URS'ar-i-** bursary etc. above.

URT'en-si- 4. advertency 5. inadvertency.

URT'es-i- 3. courtesy 4. discourtesy.

URTH'i-li- 3. worthily 4. unworthily.

URTH'less-ness- 3. mirthlessness, worthlessness.

URT'i-bl- 4. insertable, avertible, subvertible, revertible, divertible, invertible, convertible, pervertible 5. inconvertible, controvertible.

URT'in-ent- 3. pertinent 4. impertinent, unpertinent.

URT'is-ment- 4. advertisement, divertisement.

URV'a-bl- 3. servable 4. observable, reservable, preservable, conservable.

URV'at-iv- 3. curvative 4. observative, reservative, preservative, conservative.

URV'ed-li- 3. fervidly 4. observedly, deservedly, reservedly 5. undeservedly, unreservedly.

URV′ens–i– 3. fervency 4. observancy, conservancy.

URV′il–i– 3. nervily, swervily 5. topsy-turvily.

URV′it–i– 3. curvity 4. recurvity, incurvity.

URZH′un–al– 3. versional 4. excursional, reversional, conversional.

URZH′un–ist– 3. versionist 4. excursionist, immersionist, aversionist, reversionist, conversionist.

US′a–bl– 3. mussable 4. discussable 5. undiscussable.

USH′a–bl– 3. hushable, flushable, brushable, crushable 4. unhushable, uncrushable.

USH′il–i– 3. gushily, mushily.

USH′i–ness– 3. gushiness, mushiness.

USH′ing–li– 3. gushingly, blushingly, rushingly, crushingly.

USK′il–i– 3. duskily, huskily, muskily.

USK′i–ness– 3. duskiness, huskiness, muskiness.

USK′ul–ar– 3. muscular 4. majuscular, bimuscular, nonmuscular, unmuscular, minuscular, crepuscular, opuscular, corpuscular.

USK′ul–us– 3. musculus 4. crepusculous, corpusculous.

UST′a–bl– 3. rustable, trustable 4. adjustable 5. readjustable, inadjustable; *see* also **UST′i–bl–** combustible etc. below.

UST′er–er– 3. blusterer, flusterer, musterer.

UST′er–i– 3. blustery, flustery, clustery.

UST′er–ing– 3. blustering, flustering, clustering, mustering.

UST′ful–i– 3. gustfully, lustfully, trustfully 4. disgustfully, distrustfully, mistrustfully.

UST′i–bl– 4. combustible 5. incombustible, noncombustible, uncombustible; *see* also **UST′a–bl–** rustable etc. above.

UST′i–er– 3. dustier, fustier, gustier, lustier, mustier, rustier, crustier, trustier.

UST′i–est– 3. dustiest, fustiest, gustiest, lustiest, mustiest, rustiest, crustiest, trustiest.

UST′il–i– 3. dustily, fustily, gustily, lustily, mustily, rustily, crustily, trustily.

UST′i–ness– 3. dustiness, fustiness, gustiness, lustiness, mustiness, rustiness, crustiness, trustiness.

UST′ri–us– 4. industrious, illustrious.

UT′er–er– 3. utterer, butterer, flutterer, splutterer, mutterer, putterer, sputterer, stutterer.

UT′er–i– 3. buttery, guttery, fluttery, spluttery, muttery, puttery, sputtery, stuttery.

UT′er–ing– 3. uttering, buttering, guttering, fluttering, spluttering, muttering, puttering, sputtering, shuttering, stuttering.

UTH′er–er– 3. motherer, smotherer.

UTH′er–ing– 3. mothering, smothering, brothering, southering.

UTH′er–li– 3. motherly, brotherly, southerly 4. unmotherly, unbrotherly.

UT′ing–li– 3. juttingly, cuttingly, struttingly.

UT′ler–i– 3. butlery, cutlery, sutlery.

UT′on–i– 3. buttony, gluttony, muttony.

UV′a–bl– 3. lovable, shovable 4. unlovable.

UV′el–er– 3. hoveler, shoveler.

UV′er–er– 3. hoverer, coverer 4. recoverer, uncoverer, discoverer.

UV′er–i– 3. plovery 4. recovery, discovery.

UV′er–ing– 3. hovering, covering 4. recovering, uncovering, discovering.

UZ′i–li– 3. fuzzily, muzzily, wuzzily [slang].

UZ′i–ness– 3. fuzziness, hussiness, muzziness, wuzziness [slang].